CRITICAL DICTIONARY OF MEXICAN LITERATURE

(1955-2010)

Originally published in Spanish by Fondo de Cultura Económica as *Diccionario crítico de la literatura Mexicana*

Library of Congress Cataloging-in-Publication Data

Domínguez Michael, Christopher, 1962-
 [Diccionario critico de la literatura Mexicana, English.]
 Critical dictionary of Mexican literature : 1955-2010 / Christopher Domínguez Michael ; translated by Lisa M. Dillman. -- 1st ed.
  p. cm.
 "Originally published in Spanish as Diccionario critico de la literatura Mexicana, 1955-2005 by Fondo de Cultura Económica, 2007."
 ISBN 978-1-56478-606-7 (pbk. : alk. paper)
 1. Mexican literature--20th century--Bio-bibliography--Dictionaries. 2. Authors, Mexican--20th century--Biography--Dictionaries. I. Dillman, Lisa. II. Title.
 PQ7155.D66513 2011
 860.9'972--dc23
                         2011019091

Partially funded by a grant from the Illinois Arts Council, a state agency, and by the University of Illinois at Urbana-Champaign

La presente traducción fue realizada con el estimulo del Programa de Apoyo a la Traducción de Obras Mexicanas a Lenguas Extranjeras (Protrad), dependiente de las instituciones culturales de México convocantes

This translation was carried out with the support of the Program to Support the Translation of Mexican Works into Foreign Languages (ProTrad), with the collective support of Mexico's cultural institutions

www.dalkeyarchive.com

Cover: design and composition by Danielle Dutton, illustration by Nicholas Motte
Printed on permanent/durable acid-free paper and bound in the United States of America

CRITICAL DICTIONARY OF MEXICAN LITERATURE (1955–2010)

TRANSLATED BY
LISA M. DILLMAN

CHRISTOPHER DOMÍNGUEZ MICHAEL

DALKEY ARCHIVE PRESS
CHAMPAIGN • DUBLIN • LONDON

CONTENTS

PROLOGUE

This book brings together two separate projects: an anthology of my work and an author's dictionary. The first is comprised of excerpts, essays, and complete articles published previously in the prologues of *Antología de la narrativa mexicana del siglo XX* (1989, 1991, and 1996) and in *Servidumbre y grandeza de la vida literaria* (1998). There are also some texts, though fewer, from *La utopía de la hospitalidad* (1993), *Tiros en el concierto: Literatura mexicana del siglo V* (1997), and *La sabiduría sin promesa: Vidas y letras del siglo XX* (2001).

On rereading myself, I opted to stand by my previously expressed opinions, and to tolerate any stylistic carelessness, since I would otherwise have been forced to rewrite nearly everything. That would have taken forever and, what's more, it doesn't actually strike me as fair to rewrite without rereading. Unable to reread that many authors, I decided simply to reproduce many passages with only minimal editorial changes, and present them as dictionary entries.

Then, using my personal anthology as a foundation, once I had the idea of a personal dictionary in mind, I wrote entries for most of the authors I had either never written about or not covered at length. This process took place from 2003 to 2007, and most of the entries I wrote appeared in preliminary format as articles in the journal *Letras Libres* and in the *El Ángel* supplement of Mexico's *Reforma* newspaper. For a few authors, I opted for a combination: one already published passage supplemented by a recent column or piece written especially for the occasion.

This *Critical Dictionary of Mexican Literature*, as indicated by the sub-title, begins in 1955, the momentous year that Juan Rulfo's *Pedro Páramo* was published. Choosing this date gave rise to a few problems—as would have been the case with any date—that could only be resolved at the cost of excluding important authors. In the end, I decided to include those born after 1955 as well as authors of any age who died after this year, and those who published books after 1955. I allowed myself only one exception: Jorge Cuesta, who died in 1942 but remained unpublished in book format until *Obras* came out in 1964.

These criteria resulted in the inclusion of many of the more long-lived *Ateneístas* and *Contemporáneos* (José Vasconcelos, Martín Luis Guzmán, Alfonso Reyes, Carlos Pellicer, Salvador Novo, José Gorostiza, Jaime Torres Bodet, etc.), while those who died prior to 1955 (Pedro Henríquez Ureña, Gilberto Owen, and Xavier Villaurrutia, for instance) were excluded despite the enormous influence of their work in the second half of the twentieth century.

As an author's dictionary, this book encourages freedom of choice and interpretative play, as well as the whimsical results and surprise juxtapositions resulting from alphabetical order. To this end, I acknowledge (and appreciate) the precedent (and example) set by Adolfo Castañón, without whose *Arbitrario de literatura mexicana* (1992, 1994, and 2000) this would have been a vastly different project.

With a book of this sort, it's tempting to state that not all of the giants are here, and not all of those here are giants. But the truth is that I took pains to include all of the novelists, poets, and essayists from Mexico (or those who have been writing *in* Mexico for decades) who have impressed me over the course of my twenty-five years as a literary critic. I admire the vast majority of writers included, and there are very few to whom I am indifferent. In some cases, naturally, my high regard is not without discrepancies and differences of opinion. And undoubtedly, among those authors absent, there will be some I didn't have time to read and others whose importance I couldn't assess.

At the end of each entry is a selected bibliography, which is not exhaustive and is intended only as a tool for the reader, highlighting the most common or most comprehensive editions of the author's work. Within entries, asterisks after cross-referenced writers' names are used the first time they are cited in each entry if they have their own entries. As an anthology of my work and an author's dictionary, this *Critical Dictionary of Mexican Literature* has allowed me to organize, at least alphabetically, my writing about Mexican letters. I hope it becomes an increasingly valuable work of reference over the years.

C.D.M.
Coyoacán, Mexico, August 2007

P.S. During the years I spent working on this *Critical Dictionary of Mexican Literature*, I had the support of a National System of Art Creators (SNCA) grant from the Fondo Nacional de la Cultura y las Artes (FONCA), an award I hope to have honored. Finally, in 2006 I received a grant from the John Simon Guggenheim Memorial Foundation that allowed me to finish editing the book.

SELECTED BIBLIOGRAPHY

Antología de la narrativa mexicana del siglo XX, Volume I, FCE, Mexico, 1989.

Antología de la narrativa mexicana del siglo XX, Volume II, FCE, Mexico, 1991.

La utopía de la hospitalidad, Vuelta, Mexico, 1993.

Antología de la narrative mexicana del siglo XX, Volumes I and II, 2nd ed., expanded and reedited, FCE, Mexico, 1996.

Tiros en el concierto. Literatura mexicana del siglo V, ERA, Mexico, 1997.

Servidumbre y grandeza de la vida literaria, Joaquín Mortiz, Mexico, 1998.

La sabiduría sin promesa. Vidas y letras del siglo XX, Joaquín Mortiz, Mexico, 2001.

Prologue to the American Edition

The *Critical Dictionary of Mexican Literature (1955–2010)*, which is now being published in the United States, is a compilation of most of what I've written on Mexican literature over the past quarter of a century. During that time, I've been something of an old-fashioned literary critic, by which I mean that I'm not an academic. I was trained first as a reviewer and then as an essayist at the Mexican literary magazine *Vuelta* (1976–1998), which in turn took its inspiration from the old tradition, so characteristic of the twentieth century, of the *Nouvelle Revue Française* (NRF), *The Criterion, Contemporáneos, Sur, La Revista de Occidente, Horizon*, and a long list of others that will be familiar to all devotees of modernism. At these magazines, literary critics are trained as writers who enter into polemics with other writers and are committed to dialogue with the readers who make up what Spanish poet Juan Ramón Jiménez called the "immense minority." My literary criticism is a product of the times, subject to the way things are done at journals, magazines, and literary supplements. Currently, I write a monthly column at *Letras Libres* and a weekly column in Mexico City's *Reforma* newspaper. This dictionary uses both of those sources as well as numerous texts that appeared in my earlier anthologies and essay collections and are now being made available in English for the first time.

I decided to organize my essays, articles, and reviews in a book that was both a dictionary *d'auteur*—i.e., an "A to Z" of my own criticism—and a personal anthology. To that end, this English edition includes eight new authors who were not covered in the first Mexican edition of 2007. Some are historians that I chose to incorporate in order to honor the idea that literature is not just fiction or poetry but also encompasses well-written historiography. Others are writers who in recent years have significantly enriched Mexican literature in some way. Additionally, this English edition has some "enlarged" entries, to which I have added commentary on new novels, poems, essays, or stories that came out in the last few years. This also turns many of the entries into a journey through my critical opinions and their inevitable transformation over time. Such was also the case in one of the books that inspired me to create this one to begin with: *A Reviewer's ABC* (1961), by Conrad Aiken—whom I've long admired—in which entries for some authors boast two or even three consecutive readings.

The alphabetical layout is quite convenient for the author, allowing for relatively easy periodic updates, but it also poses a few obstacles that readers of the English version should keep in mind: due to its heterogeneous origins, the *Dictionary* places side by side different types of criticism written in different tones and at different times. Some are purely essayistic, others autobiographical, and still others more journalistic. In making the 2007 Mexican edition I made little attempt to homogenize these differences or to give the impression of having always written in one style, trusting that since this is a work of reference and consultation, the reader will likely not be reading from start to finish. And given the personal character of the book, often the amount of space dedicated to specific writers does not correspond to their status in the canon. As critics we often invest more time arguing over contemporary authors than established classics who might not need our support. Nonetheless, this dictionary is also a work of literary history covering literature written in Spanish and in Mexico.

I have updated entries on each author for this edition in the understanding that they serve as orientation for readers as opposed to exhaustive bibliographies. Selected English translations of the authors' works are also noted when they exist. For this and many other things I am grateful to my translator, Lisa M. Dillman, for her generous and monumental work, without whose enthusiasm I would have thought it impossible to carry out this project.

The *Critical Dictionary of Mexican Literature (1955–2010)* is intended to prove useful to university students and professors, and especially to the "immense minority" of curious and voracious readers who indefatigably travel, with no need of passport or degree, through the literature of the world. I hope they find much to consider and to read in the last half-century of Mexican literature.

C.D.M.
COYOACÁN, MEXICO, SPRING 2011

For Judith and Gonzalo

The reviewing of novels is the white man's grave of journalism; it corresponds, in letters, to *building bridges* in some impossible, tropical climate. The work is grueling, unhealthy, and ill-paid, and for each scant clearing made wearily among the springing vegetation the jungle overnight encroaches twice as far. A novel-reviewer is too old at thirty; early retirement is inevitable, "les femmes soignent ces infirmes féroces au retour des pays chauds," and their later books all exhibit a bitter and splenetic brilliance whose secret is only learnt in the ravages on their liver made by their terrible school. What a hard-boiled, what a Congo quality informs their soured Romanticism!

—Cyril Connolly,
"Ninety Years of Novel-Reviewing" (1929)

There is indeed something pitiful, something comic, in any comprehended soul; souls, like other things, are only definable by their limitations. We feel instinctively that it would be insulting to speak of any man to his face as we should speak of him in his absence, even if what we say is in the way of praise: for absent he is a character understood, but present he is a force respected.

—George Santayana,
Interpretations of Poetry and Religion (1900)

Dead is the Sainte-Beuve of our village.
The heirs sold off the *Great Critic*'s books.
I went, out of curiosity, to the auction.
I found my works, dedicated and uncut.
His lampoon of my poetry has become a classic.
For his views have I been excluded always
From surveys, anthologies, histories, revisions.
I open the door, goodbye, and bid farewell:
Rest in peace, *Indefatigable Reader*!

—Julián Hernández,
Legítima defensa (1952)

CRITICAL DICTIONARY OF MEXICAN LITERATURE (1955-2010)

A

ABREU GÓMEZ, ERMILO
(Mérida, Yucatán, 1894 – Mexico City, 1971)

Writers like Ermilo Abreu Gómez are artisans whose work is essential to any attempt at a detailed literary history. Be it colonialist fiction, militant nationalism, *indigenista* writing, or the rediscovery of Sor Juana Inés de la Cruz, Abreu Gómez was central, a man of letters whose perseverance brought beneficial changes to Mexican culture in the first half of the twentieth century. Abreu Gómez would have turned one hundred in 1994, the year that a small rebel group, the Zapatista National Liberation Army (EZLN), took up arms in Chiapas, thereby ending the peace that had reigned during the Partido Revolucionario Institucional's (PRI) control. The neo-Zapatista's demand for a rebel indigenous tradition was proof that *Canek*, Abreu Gómez's most famous novel, was clearly still relevant.

Born in Mérida, Abreu Gómez had already travelled a winding road before coming to *indigenista* narrative. He started off as part of the farcical colonialist literary movement, writing literature that tried to "escape" revolutionary torment via ultra-Spanish, rococo books that idealized a swashbuckling New Spain replete with hot chocolate and nun's cookies. In that vein, he published *El corcovado* (1924) and *La vida milagrosa del venerable siervo de Dios, Gregorio López* (1925). All of the colonialists except the unshakeable Artemio de Valle-Arizpe* soon abandoned a literature whose utter eccentricity became a vanguard joke, as evidenced by Genaro Estrada's *Pero Galín* (1926).

After the colonialist diaspora, Abreu Gómez did the rounds at *Contemporá-neos*, a journal where he published some twenty-five pieces, most of which were on Sor Juana, Carlos de Sigüenza y Góngora, and Juan Ruiz de Alarcón, with a few others on Romantic and modernist writers such as Justo Sierra O'Reilly, Manuel Puga y Acal, and José Peón y Contreras. Abreu Gómez's role at *Contemporáneos* was marginal, indifferent as he was to the cosmopolitan spirit of the poets running the journal. More concerned with vice-regal letters, Abreu Gómez belonged (by age) to the generation of writers in the no-man's-land between the *Ateneístas* and the young *Contemporáneos*. And when the journal went out of publication in 1931 and Jorge Cuesta* decided to strike out on his own with *Examen*, he found in Abreu Gómez an adversary.

Abreu Gómez attacked Cuesta with xenophobic cultural nationalism, and as a result ended up with one of the most resounding slaps in the secular history of Mexican letters. Since then, every time there's a call for "national-ism" in our literature, Cuesta's reply to the Abreu Gómez article published in *El Universal* that fateful April 28, 1932 is invoked. Shortly thereafter, Cuesta wrote, "They are interested in the Mexican, not the man; Mexico, not nature; local anecdote, not history . . . But Mexicans like Señor Ermilo Abreu Gómez will be confused to discover that, as far as understanding what it means to be Mexican, a text by Dostoyevsky or by Conrad is richer than that of any distinctively Mexican novelist . . . ; as far as I'm concerned, no Abreu Gómez can force me to perform the patriotic duty of stultifying myself poring over the representative works of Mexican literature. Let them bore those who find nothing wrong with it; I miss *The Charterhouse of Parma*, and a lot more."

Abreu Gómez was stigmatized by this defeat, which today seems resound-ing, although at the time few found it convincing. It should be noted, in his defense, that he was not the only Mexicanist, nor the most obtuse or acerbic, and that as a victim of Cuesta (whom posterity declared victorious), Abreu Gómez was simply expressing the opinion most representative of belligerent nationalism. Let's not forget that even someone like José Gorostiza* wavered on that polemic.

In 1934, Abreu Gómez published his iconography on Sor Juana Inés de la Cruz and *Sor Juana Inés de la Cruz: Bibliografía y biblioteca*, and both works were essential to the rediscovery of the poet-nun of the Order of San Jerónimo that had been started by Amado Nervo in *Juana de Asbaje* in 1910.

Octavio Paz* says that Abreu Gómez's work was fervent though his scholarship not impeccable. But at the time, Father Alfonso Méndez Plancarte was scandalized at the "desecration" of Sor Juana, and it was thanks to writers such as Abreu Gómez that she came to be seen as part of the literary landscape rather than property of the church cloister.

The young Abreu Gómez's literary incursions into colonialism were not in vain. His New Spain worship, later exchanged for devotion to the Soviet Union, allowed him to undertake an investigation into Sor Juana that became a decisive contribution to our critical tradition. But beyond that, Abreu Gómez was a typical mid-century left-leaning intellectual, a man with one foot in the Communist Party and the other in Mexican Revolution nationalism. The life he shared with Ninfa Santos is a key point of reference if we are to understand the emotional environment and mundane existence of the Latin American left in Mexico.

In the early forties, Abreu Gómez's *indigenista* journey came to an end. *Héroes mayas* (1942) includes three stories, one of which is dedicated to Canek, and tells of the Mayan insurrection of 1861. But the most famous of these tales is not the most intense, as anyone reading later collections such as *Leyendas y consejas del antiguo Yucatán* (1985) or *La conjura de Xinúm* (1958 and 1987) will agree. These texts show how consistent Abreu Gómez's indigenism was. In fact, the popularization of the *Popul Vuh*, the celebrated mythological text of uncertain authorship, was in part due to him.

Abreu Gómez's indigenism, like that of Antonio Mediz Bolio (1884–1957) and Ramón Rubín (1912–2000), nobly resists its own didactic and ideological pretensions. Abreu Gómez is looking for a legend to explain history; he grants himself the use of pedagogical allegory in *Quetzalcoatl* (1947) and has no qualms about idealizing the Mayan uprisings catalogued in our national literature. But Abreu Gómez never broke free of the defensive *costumbrista* mold that mars his writing. It took a Guatemalan, Miguel Ángel Asturias— an admirer and contemporary of Ermilo—to turn Mayan material into a real linguistic achievement, taking risks that Mexican *indigenistas*—already favored by the regime—had no need to take. José Luis Martínez,* at the time, admired the simplicity of *Canek* and wrote that "There is, in this short book, an indigenous emotion, the gentleness of wind, the lightness of a deer, a reflexive melancholy, a generous and essential awareness, filtered perhaps through Western culture but with a flavor that feels autochthonous" (Martínez, *Literatura mexicana siglo XX, 1910–1949,* 1990).

Indeed, there is a cleanness of style in Abreu Gómez that evokes, if we can allow a facile geographical allusion, both the colonial whiteness of Mérida and the flat topography of the Yucatán Peninsula. As both praise and reproach, Abreu Gómez is a narrator who responds to those natural conditions: he's limpid but translucid. We leave him in a place with no rivers or mountains. His indigenism is charitable in the Franciscan sense of the word, a contribution that avoids both racist commiseration and the bloody revenge taken against Fray Diego de Landa, the Bishop of Yucatán. After *Canek,* indigenism became a literature of ethnographic assessment, proven by the fact that writers like Francisco Rojas González (1904–1951) and Ricardo Pozas (1919–1994) were both social scientists. The degradation continued until the publication of *Balún Canán* (1957) and *Oficio de tinieblas* (1962), novels by Rosario Castellanos* that achieved new heights of melodrama and fictional problematizing, and became the swan songs of Mexican indigensim.

Abreu Gómez's work spans several decades of cultural and political journalism, which avoided few of Mexican nationalism's clichés and obsessions. After *Héroes mayas,* he tried to touch a provincial, picaresque nerve and wrote *Tata Lobo* in 1952, one of his truly lamentable books; his childhood and early adult memoirs (*La del alba sería,* 1954, and *Duelos y quebrantos,* 1959) add little to his oeuvre, the most gracious part of which is contained in *Sala de retratos* (1946), where he portrays a hundred of his contemporaries with an ironic affection.

Martín Luis Guzmán (1968), a long monograph and insightful study of the revolutionary novelist, was the last book Abreu Gómez published. Anxious to establish a nationalist canon, Abreu Gómez left the stage with a call to order, making clear that Martín Luis Guzmán was the great classic to whom secular Mexican literature needed to pay homage. From Sor Juana Inés to Mayan rebellions, Abreu Gómez journeyed through Mexican literature with a commitment to collective missteps, and without relinquishing his role as amanuensis, transcribing documents and founding myths. Abreu Gómez, as his wife Ninfa Santos said, was a man "with antennae," whose taciturn head attracted all of the vibrations—good or bad—of his time (*Servidumbre y grandeza de la vida literaria,* 1998).

SELECTED BIBLIOGRAPHY

Leyendas y consejas del antiguo Yucatán, FCE, Mexico, 1985.

Canek: History and Legend of a Maya Hero, trans. and introduction by Mario L. Dávila and Carter Wilson, University of California Press, 1979.

AGUILAR MORA, JORGE

(Mexico City, 1946)

An eccentric figure, Jorge Aguilar Mora is the writer who took the most successful liberties with the avant-garde in the 1960s, as well as the one who most successfully rejected them. A Roland Barthes disciple, the author of two landmark novels (*Cadáver lleno de mundo*, 1971, and *Si muero lejos de ti*, 1979), and a poet (*No hay otro cuerpo*, 1977, *Esta tierra sin razón y poderosa*, 1986, and *Stabat mater*, 1996) ignored by most critics, he is also one of the few Mexican intellectuals to have criticized, for better or for worse, the work of Octavio Paz* (*La divina pareja. Historia y mito. Valoración e interpretación de la obra ensayística de Octavio Paz*, 1978). A university professor residing in Maryland for the past several years, Aguilar Mora is a notable absence in our literary lives, a militant intellectual—for his own peculiar cause—who has acquired more readers, garnered more devotees, and ruffled more feathers than one would imagine given his personality, which is somewhere between surly and somber. I profess an honest admiration for him, albeit one that's still full of unanswered questions and disputed points, since he neither wants nor accepts any correspondence.

In *Un día en la vida del general Obregón* (1983), he began an exploration of Mexican history that he's yet to conclude. As soon as it came out, the book scandalized its editor (the Secretary of Public Education) for its demystification of General Obregón, known as the fierce "manco de Celaya," one-armed man of Celaya, whose decrepitude Aguilar Mora depicted pitilessly. The educational authorities took it out of circulation and then, once they'd removed the State seal, decided to let it back in. After this incident, people began whispering that Aguilar Mora was preparing a "military history of the Mexican Revolution," a project that Martín Luis Guzmán* abandoned in order to write his unfinished and unsuccessful *Memorias de Pancho Villa*. His first step was to compile and prologue the adventures of an Irishman—Ivor Thor-Gray—and a Villa soldier—Juan Bautista Vargas Arreola—in the Revolution.

Una muerte sencilla, justa, eterna: Cultura y guerra durante la Revolución Mexicana (1990) is the work of a war historian researching war from a political perspective. Chuang Tzu, Machiavelli, Guicciardini, Mazarino, Bonaparte, and Clausewitz, as well as Tolstoy and Malraux, hover like ghosts above Aguilar Mora's essays. He's a cultural critic whose passions are stirred by the war of maneuver. He follows both Paz's work and those killed in the Mexican Revolution from the angle of a strategist. His battle plan might be a costly mistake, but there's no denying that his excellent style, attention to formal detail, and personal passion are those of a man intent on winning the war. And since he's not one to admit defeat, he maps an obsessive attempt at destruction, laying it out on the table. But before we get ahead of ourselves with the maneuvers, let's talk for a minute about positions.

This "military history of the Mexican Revolution" is in fact a thanatography, an account of lives—both well known and anonymous—told from the perspective of death, an inventory of bodies buried under the shrapnel of history. It's no less a profession of faith than popular Romanticism, albeit more refined. In *Una muerte sencilla, justa, eterna*, for instance, Julio Torri* is condemned for *De fusilamientos* (1940) in the name of the people's morale, with Aguilar Mora favoring the "shirtless" purity of popular writers over the "ideological equanimity of the bourgeoisie" (sic). He uses the unfortunate Nellie Campobello (1909–1986) to construct a phalanx of primitive (I don't use the term pejoratively) writers whom he feels truly understood the Revolution. Our 1968 radical man of letters returned from Barthes's phalanstery to demand "virility" of our literature. And to call Aguilar Mora a "radical man of letters" is no joke. A representative of the Colegio de México at the National Council of Huelga, Aguilar Mora was in Plaza Tlatelolco during the massacre on October 2 and, like other students outraged by the repression there, went abroad to continue his studies in those heady days of cultural and political radicalism. Somehow he's managed to remain faithful to the model of a politically committed intellectual. His rhetoric has changed; his personal and moral views have not.

So it strikes me as odd that a rhetorician such as himself should forget that his stunning execution scenes present a stylized picture of war, one that serves as much (or as little) purpose as the belletristic style that, in his opinion, Torri employed. A thanatographer obsessed with the memento mori, the Romantic Aguilar Mora worships Death with a capital D. A bit of biography is useful here: his first novel chronicles the journey in search of the body of his brother, who was disappeared by the Praetorian guard in Guatemala for political reasons. *Cadáver lleno de mundo* (1971, literally, "Cadaver full of world"): that beautiful title sums up Aguilar Mora's oeuvre. From intimacy to history, family to country, his writing is at its best when dealing with the *campesino* rebels (victims of the levy) killed by firing squads in 1910.

Aguilar Mora lives history from the club on Rue Saint-Honoré, venerating popular sovereignty as the embodiment of Virtue. To ask a Jacobin of the Terror for charity is to waste your time and risk your neck. If Aguilar Mora doesn't respect his own contemporaries, writers who apply for grants from the Mexican government, it's hard to imagine he'd feel much solidarity for the first so-called contemporaries, *Contemporáneos* like Alfonso Reyes,* Torri, Antonio Caso, and Mariano Silva y Aceves, who lost almost everything in the war and yet wrote magnificently, in political exile or internal exile, in the freezing cold, having auctioned off their libraries. A late-coming Jacobin historian of the Mexican Revolution, Aguilar Mora is a sort of Saint-Just, calling for the ethical guillotine; he's like a Maoist from the horrific proletarian cultural revolution, prescribing manual labor for aristocrats and the petite bourgeoisie, with the virtuous aim of making them pay with their honor for the historical sin of their class. But Torri's execution at Aguilar Mora's wall is just symbolic. What's more shocking is his aestheticizing exaltation of epaulettes and cartridge belts, of the sacred blood of the people, used as hot water to relieve the painful birth of revolutionary violence.

In apparent contradiction to Aguilar Mora's Jacobin dogma lies his distinctive critical talent, seen in salutary paradoxes. He maintains, as few historians have, that the Mexican Revolution was a barbaric chaos, a centrifugal phenomenon where boundaries between *campesinos* and *caudillos*, victims and executioners, were a shadowy blur. In *Una muerte sencilla, justa, eterna,* his detailed reconstruction of the San Diego Plan in which a maverick coalition was to reclaim the southern United States for Mexico, supposedly with the support of Germany . . . explains nothing. That is, history itself here contradicts its chronicler, demonstrating that our civil war was an agrarian revolt indifferent to virtue or the militant proletariat. This book is a resounding—though perhaps unwilling—refutation of the Marxist historiosophy of the Mexican Revolution. Invoking Suetonius, Aguilar Mora's work is a lesson in classicism compared to the pamphleteering manifestations of a romantic lie, like Adolfo Gilly's *La revolución interrumpida* (1971).

Aguilar Mora is in the habit of using Marxist terminology, but he's closer to the Jacobin, Girondin, or Saint-Simonian historians of the French Revolution than he is to Marx. In the good parts of the book, of which there are many, he is reminiscent of the French historians Jules Michelet and Louis Blanc. He depicts, for example, the unforgettable quirks and shady deals of revolutionary figures Lucio Blanco and Ramón Puente, turning *his* Mexican Revolution into a novelty riddled with good stories. His Pancho Villa—who inexplicably later turns up as a Bandit of Providence—and his force of *Dorados* (literally, "Golden Ones")—generously portrayed as an order as strict as the Templars—are transformed into novelistic truth. I accept it as such. But "the great novel of Villist passion" was not to be written.

In the final analysis *Una muerte sencilla, justa, eterna* poses and resolves literary rather than historical questions. The appearance of smokeless gunpowder, for instance, explains how Guzmán, the field marshal, could so clearly see the battlefield. With regard to author Mariano Azuela, Aguilar Mora tells the little known story of the two endings of his foundational novel *Los de abajo* (*The Underdogs*). In 1915, when the novel was first released, Azuela believed in the revolution. A decade later—when the book became canonical—he revised the ending, leaving his hero isolated and hopeless. After it became clear that one million deaths had served only to empower a bunch of kleptocratic, bloodthirsty men of arms, it was only logical for Azuela to become disillusioned. But our virtuous Saint-Just raps Azuela on the knuckles for being a nihilist.

A writer who loves painting, Aguilar Mora pauses reverentially before the executed hero. After his Passion, he wants to know everything about the People's Resurrection. Someone like Torri, who actually lived through the Revolution, had little urge to investigate. For the *Ateneísta*, execution was a callous whim; but for Aguilar Mora in *Una muerte sencilla, justa, eterna*, it's a cosmic drama about the salvation of every *campesino*. How could Aguilar Mora be shocked at Torri's stylizing popular tragedy when he, with this book, becomes the contemporary author who has written the most and the best "literature" of the Revolution of 1910?

If, as Cyril Connolly suggests, it comes to choosing between prosaic realism and good writing, it would be impossible to prove that Aguilar Mora writes like what Connolly calls a Mandarin, in order to exalt the Tough Guys. An extremist both by training and by temperament, he would never accept the lesson of *Enemies of Promise* (1938) about the tolerance a critic owes to warring literary factions. We can't demand liberalism of someone who has dedicated part of his career to condemning the tradition, most notably in Paz's work. But to ignore *Una muerte sencilla, justa, eterna* would be a grave injustice. Let's not repay the critic's arrogance with disdain but with critique. Beautiful, pathetic, a maddening elegy to revolutionary violence, Aguilar Mora's book will remain the work of a great mythographer, the testimony of a writer who is, whether we like it or not, the ultimate Jacobin of Year One of the Mexican Revolution (*Servidumbre y grandeza de la vida literaria*, 1998).

Los secretos de la aurora (2002) is both a meticulous and an odd book, one that undertakes the creation of a wholly fictional universe. That, of course, should be what most novelists do, but, at least nowadays, of those writing in Spanish, few show such stylistic determination, such protean devotion. Aguilar Mora believes, as did José Lezama Lima, that for something to be stimulating, it must be difficult. That belief—passed down through his teacher Sergio Fernández's* baroque style—means that Aguilar Mora's novels offer readers none of the didactic or prosaic simplicity that the genre leans toward today. And that's why Aguilar Mora decided that, more than narrate, he'd write the history of one family, one city, and one revolt from beginning to end, merging these elements in a metahistorical time belonging solely to him. Like Onetti, Carpentier, Mujica Lainez, and García Márquez* before him, Aguilar Mora decided to create a book that started with the map of a city, seen here as an educated polis and as edifice whose ruins are destined to live on in our memories. *Los secretos de la aurora* is divided into four parts, each of which begins with Telémaco, the son who sets off in search of a father missing in battle. Although we know that the father is dead, his death is the device chosen to fill his absence and through whose memory the polis is reconstructed. Through the father, Aguilar Mora presents the city of San Andrés and the Revolt of the Thousand that rocked it.

Family saga, catalogue of erotic encounters, exasperating description of milieu, *Los secretos de la aurora* seems like a traditional novel until we start wracking our brains trying to figure out what tradition it belongs to. It was at that point that I came to terms, not without alarm, with the fact that although it's indirectly related to the great Latin American narrative of the last century, *Los secretos de la aurora* is actually political, in the old sense in which Xenophon would have used the word: the description of a war in which a city-state fights to determine its role in the world, the chronicle of a war taking place in a non-place that is that very city, a tragedy performed by a handful of men and women who are as tired of being heroes as they are resigned to not being gods.

Many novelists, like the dead father in the novel, are competent model makers; few are capable, as Aguilar Mora is, of presenting the exact archaeological miniature of a civilization, reminding us that the novelist must express the imaginary as if it were real. But as I wander through the plazas, bridges, alleyways, and barracks of the city where *Los secretos de la aurora* takes place, I can't help but question the foundations of Aguilar Mora's work, a paradox unique to novelists: that of building a ruins. And I think it's a certain type of Mexican history that he's interpreting here, one born of a bitter need to write the illusory post-classical, personal novel of the Mexican Revolution that Martín Luis Guzmán, Nellie Campobello, or José Vasconcelos* would have written, in an ideal world.

Aguilar Mora has taken care to lay his cards on the table. Although there are echoes of several figures from Latin American history and literature throughout *Los secretos de la aurora*, one historical character, Juan Nepomuceno Adorno (1807–1880), plays a crucial role. A wise nineteenth-century Mexican, he was the curious inventor of a gun that could fire sixty rounds per minute, a machine that recorded documents, and a "superdynamic" railway. The Mexican Adorno published a treatise entitled *Introduction to the Harmony of the Universe; or, Principles of Physico-Harmonic Geometry* (1851) in London, translated into Spanish in 1862. It would be arrogant of me to venture an explanation for a character about whom I know little, but I think I see in him the cave that leads to the volcanic center of *Los secretos de la aurora*. Thanks to this utopist, we undertake an anabasis that moves us away from the sort of phenomenological reflection so prevalent in today's novels.

"The words," Aguilar Mora wrote, "had to be organic, alive, as ancient as the first glimmer, like the first face." With that conviction, these ruins, seen from above, must balance the masculine principle of architecture—the conspirator father, designer of imaginary citadels—with the feminine principle, the mother pianist through whom music speaks, and in particular the piano itself, a sort of demiurge creator whose notes will lead to the city's destruction. That part actually comes from the real Juan Nepomuceno Adorno, who also invented a "melograph" piano, presented at the Paris World Exposition along with a text, *Mélographie ou nouvelle notation musical*, which explained how to use it.

The Revolt of the Thousand is not part of Aguilar Mora's narrative focus. It matters little when it took place, given that, like the Trojan War, it's an event whose inexact date helps keep it always on the horizon. Using this imprecise fictional historiography, superbly evocative when depicting characters' psychology, *Los secretos de la aurora* unveils a second motive: that of conspiracy, which taints the writing of treatises just as it does erotic encounters, and culminates in the election of a traitor who will legitimize the rebellion's failure. Thus unfolds a parallel history—fueled by a missing and perhaps ultimately dispensable sage—which turns the Mexican polis into a farce and moves it to the realm of the imaginary. I am surprised, and encouraged, to see that Aguilar Mora, through the art of the novel, has written a conservative account of history as liberation. The Revolt of the Thousand is condemned to repeat itself endlessly, and to fail again and again. A philosophical novel, one of the few written by Mexicans, *Los secretos de la aurora* is a tribute to tragic pessimism.

SELECTED BIBLIOGRAPHY

Cadáver lleno de mundo, Joaquín Mortiz, Mexico, 1971.
No hay otro cuerpo, Joaquín Mortiz, Mexico, 1977.
La divina pareja. Historia y mito en Octavio Paz, ERA, Mexico, 1978.
Si muero lejos de ti, Joaquín Mortiz, Mexico, 1979.
Un día en la vida del general Obregón, SEP, Mexico, 1983.
Esta tierra sin razón y poderosa, FCE, Mexico, 1986.
Una muerte sencilla, justa, eterna, ERA, Mexico, 1990.
Stabat mater, ERA, Mexico, 1996.
Los secretos de la aurora, ERA, Mexico, 2002.
La sombra del tiempo, Siglo XXI, Mexico, 2010.

AGUINAGA, LUIS VICENTE DE

(Guadalajara, Jalisco, 1971)

In *El agua circular, el fuego* (1995), a prose poem, Aguinaga's verse is often intense, at times inspired, and feels like it's infused with Gaston Bachelard. In Aguinaga's best poems, even when there are a handful of characters or a narrator present, it's actually the absence of man that's notable, an absence that lays bare a topography dominated by the realm of the four elements, with both their harsh catastrophes and their gentle murmurs. In this depopulated world, on this planet of almost frozen landscapes that could be either pre- or post-historic, the poet's experience has come and gone, and the poems are simply a testimony to the fatuous permanence of things: petrified trees or ghostly walls whose presence is seen as symbolic. "La puerta, el eco, el huésped. Sombra interior de un útero / preñado, cargado el tiempo entero de vaticinios, cargado el tiempo entero de postergaciones." ("The door, the echo, the guest. Darkness inside a uterus / pregnant, all of time laden with predictions, all of time laden with delays.")

SELECTED BIBLIOGRAPHY

El agua circular, el fuego, UNAM, Mexico, 1995.
Reducido a polvo, Joaquín Mortiz, Mexico, 2004.
La lámpara de mano. Sobre poemas y poetas, Arlequín, Guadalajara, 2004.
La migración interior. Abecedario de Juan Goytisolo, Vol 299 in "Fondo editorial tierra adentro"/Cona-culta, Mexico, 2005.

AGUSTÍN, JOSÉ

(Guadalajara, Jalisco, 1944)

José Agustín's *Se está haciendo tarde (final en laguna)* is a truly inspired book. I'm taking inspiration here as a reflection of being in tune with the times, holding a fruitful dialogue between everyday vernacular and literary consciousness. In the years since its publication in 1973, the novel has taken on a gravitas that would have been risky to concede it at the time. Vindicating the language of the street made Agustín unique thirty years ago, and my rereading of the book was hardly (if at all) hindered by its colloquialism, perhaps because slang has now become a lingua franca that doesn't mean anything in and of itself. But in *Se está haciendo tarde*, José Agustín had an almost immanent awareness of the lacuna between recreating street talk artistically and merely transcribing it. Few of his imitators and disciples (including himself, unfortunately) have ever surpassed the linguistic genius of *Se está haciendo tarde*.

The book opens with a tarot reader named Rafael arriving at the port of Acapulco and putting himself in the care of Virgilio, the guide who will lead him through the portals of perception. Soon they meet up with Francine, Gladys, and Paulhan, three druggies who, in less than the twenty-four hours over which the novel covers, are inclined to take on a good portion of the existential burden that distressed so much of the West at the time. Strictly speaking, their pilgrimage came after the twentieth century's first wave of counterculture, but thanks to the global village it still broke new geographical and commercial ground. This second spice route, discovered by adventurers and capitalized upon by traffickers, went from Huautla to London to Katmandu, searching for an imaginary Orient in the name of artificial paradise, heterodox spiritualities, new music, and relaxed sexual mores. In Giuseppe Tomasi di Lampedusa's *The Leopard* (*Il Gattopardo*), one of the characters says that everything must change for everything to remain the same. Well, the sixties and seventies gave the impression that everything changed so that everything could remain the same, though really they were decades that—for better and for worse—changed everything. It was the time when Octavio Paz* and José Agustín (and a million or so others) all venerated the *I Ching*.

But on rereading *Se está haciendo tarde*, I was surprised to find that the novel also resonates far beyond the brief but intense period it documents. Like Malcolm Lowry's *Under the Volcano*, a book to which it's indebted, *Se está haciendo tarde* is not just a near-clinical catalog of hard-core intoxication. It's an equally systematic chronicle of a Dantesque journey on which an infernal paradise is gained or lost by dodging the Augustinian obstacles on the path of sin. Free of Judeo-Christian deadweight, the protagonists are unconstrained by the old logic that ties holiness to transgression, and they set off on a pagan odyssey.

This is a drug novel that José Agustín wrote with a finger in two pies: Carlos Castaneda and José Revueltas.* *Se está haciendo tarde* uses marijuana, alcohol, and mushrooms to remind us that the search for ecstasy is not a business (or pleasure) limited to rationalists. A monk wedded to silent prayer can be just as vapid as the most unrefined mushroom-eater around. Years ago, Adolfo Castañón said quite insightfully in his review of the novel that José Agustín's characters, hippies and drug addicts, had something of the mystics about them. In the same vein, Paul Claudel once tried to get Rimbaud to convert to Catholicism and called him a "mystic in primitive state";

he should have added that true mystics only exist in primitive state, unable to provide coherent, artistic articulations of the real or supposed "revelations" that distinguish them from other mortals.

Anyone who's experienced or witnessed the insomniac havoc wreaked by drugs and alcohol will agree that another virtue of *Se está haciendo tarde* is the author's realism, or perhaps verisimilitude: the certainty with which the narrator is overtaken by sensorial fallibility, fleeting self-confidence, the suicidal fate of a man who doesn't know when to stop, can't let the party end. By turns embarrassing, euphoric, nauseating, repetitious, his toxic exultation is not so much lost time as fragmented time. José Agustín conveys a carnival world turned upside down that only makes sense if you ride it like a Möbius strip-cum-rollercoaster.

The book was written in a very symbolic place: the old Lecumberri Prison, which at the time was full of political prisoners and where José Agustín was doing time for possession of marijuana. Like a lot of important fiction, *Se está haciendo tarde* is a novel that couldn't have taken place just anywhere. Agustín situates his infernal paradise in Acapulco, paying it the highest literary tribute, from the Playa de la Condesa to Barra de Coyuca. Acapulco is seen as tragically cosmopolitan, a city sentenced to destitute debauchery right when it was spiffing itself up with a bit of international prestige. It's presented as the Mexican dump whose bewitching reputation comes from the exigencies of the tourist industry and their hospitality.

Equally memorable is the impressionistic sketch of characters, the slow motion camera the narrator uses to render even the most subtle moves and just perceptible changes in consciousness. From the two women whose toxic lifestyle has ravaged them beyond their years to the gay man who shows a remarkable verbal lack of restraint in speaking, to Rafael, the newcomer initiated by Virgilio, a man religiously determined to carry out his mission, all of the characters are portrayed astonishingly well. Even clichés as hackneyed as the setting sun are described beautifully by José Agustín, as though *Se está haciendo tarde* were a novel written in a state of grace. I realize that anyone who can't relate to the childlike sense of wonder felt by watching the world of giants our parents once represented will find my praise excessive.

If what was fleetingly known as the countercultural *Onda* literature (literature "of the Wave") disappeared without a trace, it's probably because José Agustín, the school's leader, exhausted nearly all of the movement's subject matter in this one novel. After *Se está haciendo tarde*, Agustín was spent and barren. Literature nowadays doesn't allow for that kind of exhaustion, instead demanding that writers publish not one book but an entire catalog, optimally timed to coincide with the market's changing seasons. Once upon a time, back in the good and bad old days when literature was associated with romantic rather than material consumption, Agustín and his readers would have been satisfied with just this one real book. But when night began to fall on the sixties and its mythos, Agustín was never forgiven for being the one who turned out the lights and closed the door. It's true he hasn't done himself many favors, putting on public display the least attractive sides of his character (bankrupt ideas, poorly crafted books, superficial motives). But I'm uneasy at the way critics have beaten him up for twenty-five years, with suspect cruelty theoretically aimed at proving that *he* hadn't matured and that *we*, the critics, are his heirs, eternal adults here to disqualify his adolescent outburst. It's as if Agustín himself were being held responsible for extinguishing an infernal paradise, putting a stop to some mythical Golden Age that we've all heard about and are afraid to confess that we longed to belong to.

The novel's full title, *Se está haciendo tarde (final en laguna)* means "It's getting late (end on laguna)," and at its "end" on the "laguna" of Coyuca an intrepid boatman acts as a modern-day Charon, saying "I think we'd better turn back. It's getting late." So we don't find out if those lost souls, caught halfway through a hallucinatory drug trip, ended up crossing the Styx or if they got to stay on the side of the living. I don't know if José Agustín laments having written this novel, which overshadowed the rest of his career; but I can guess that by suggesting the *end* of bliss right from the title, he had an idea about the kind of power he was unleashing.

Selected Bibliography
Se está haciendo tarde (final en laguna), Joaquín Mortiz, Mexico, 1973 and 2001.

ALATORRE, ANTONIO

(Autlán, Jalisco, 1922 – Mexico City, 2010)

Mexican philologist par excellence, Antonio Alatorre practices his love of words like a true *amateur*, in the best sense of the word. Director of the *Nueva Revista de Filología Hispánica* since 1960, he's an eminent academic who favors real conversation over theoretical gobbledygook, and you're more likely to find him with actual readers than with members of the university senate. And he'll be discussing anything from Golden Age literature to the misfortunes of everyday language, from Spanish mystics Sor Juana Inés de la Cruz and Saint John of the Cross to the living memory of Mexican literature, which counts him among its treasures, along with Juan Rulfo* and Juan José Arreola,* with whom it's no accident that he made his first literary forays.

Translator of Marcel Bataillon, Albert Béguin, Ernst Robert Curtius, Antonello Gerbi, and Joaquim Maria Machado de Assis; anthologizer and exegete of the Petrarchan sonnet (*Fiori di sonetti = Flores de sonetos*, 2001); and microhistorian of Autlán who scrutinized both Inquisitorial archives and everyday existence (*Al brujo de Autlán*, 2001), Alatorre can only be criticized for not having published more books. We must forgive him even this sin, however, for having authored *Los 1001 años de la lengua española* (1979). The book is simultaneously a linguistic voyage and the compass needed to navigate any expedition through our letters; and, quite frankly, it's one of the most beautiful (and useful) works of Mexican literature as well.

El sueño erótico en la poesía española de los Siglos de Oro (2003) gives us a perfect example of the way Alatorre reflects, reasons, and expounds. After warning us not to expect too much philosophy from poets (a useful reminder when we consider the excesses of someone like Harold Bloom, who puts Shakespeare above Kant and Hegel), Alatorre takes one topic— erotic dreams—and one period—the Golden Age—and plunges deep into the heart of Spanish poetry, creating a moveable history and making a critical anatomy of one motif, as he stalks it verse by verse. Both obscure poets and poets obscured by philological hermeneutics, like Garcilaso, Boscán, Cetina, Góngora, and Argensola, come to life for the ignorant reader (I am one myself), and thanks to that paradoxical coming-to-life-via-dreams, they become absolutely delectable reads.

Alatorre earns the double merit of having distanced himself, in his youth, from the superficial gravitas of old-school academia, as enamored of holy Roman protocol as it was of garden-variety traditionalism, and again later in life, when he rejected the obscurity of neo-academic criticism, whose murkiness makes students' and professors' heads spin. Though he's never worked regularly as a literary critic, Alatorre deserves our gratitude for his defense of the critic's universality as well as his open disdain for the linguistic police state that Mexican nationalism tried to impose—with no real success—as an attempt to control natural mutations in our language. Paraphrasing his definition of the "brilliant critic" (*Ensayos sobre crítica literaria*, 1993), we could say that he himself is a great philologist for having captured and conveyed the greatest diversity contained in all languages, for being the man who comes closest to expressing the richness and complexity of the poet's creative intuition, exhausting it in so many senses.

SELECTED BIBLIOGRAPHY
Los 1001 años de la lengua española, FCE, Mexico, 1979.
Ensayos sobre crítica literaria, CNCA, Mexico, 1993.
El brujo de Autlán, Aldus, Mexico, 2001.
El sueño erótico en la poesía española de los Siglos de Oro, FCE, Mexico, 2003.

AMARA, LUIGI
(Mexico City, 1971)

I'm sure it's no coincidence that when the poet Luigi Amara has insomnia, he spends his sleepless nights, as he himself confesses in one of his essays in *El peatón inmóvil* (2003), meticulously pouring over Manuel Antonio Carreño's *Manual de urbanidad y buenas maneras*, a classic text on proper etiquette and protocol. In their own way, Amara's poems and essays are themselves a handbook on manners, written by an eccentric *à l'anglaise* who offers polished meditations on the bed as focus of the night, the "promiscuous" exchange of lighters, and the nose, whose appearance and dimension seem to him more a question of free will than one of nature. Born in another time, I dare say Amara would have been a rebel or, worse, a dynamite-wielding anarchist taking direct action against contemporary society, which produces in him "genuina náusea moral," genuine moral nausea, and in whose behavior and customs (drivers' oppression of pedestrians, workaholism), he finds cause for despondency.

But Amara was raised in a prudent age and, like Edmund Burke, one of his Penates, he dislikes big words and Herculean efforts, and thus his poems (and some of his essays) are a strict parceling out of the bare minimum, the miniscule; we could call them nanography. Everyday life, too, must strike Amara as a vast, suspicious continent; it was, after all, his parents' generation that proposed, among other vexingly futile acts, making a "revolution of everyday life." Considering his antecedents, Amara is a pure essayist who refuses to glance down into the abyss of nihilism, preferring instead to follow the urbane customs of the observant *flâneur*, poetizing only those things in the realm of the five senses, while allowing himself to artificially exaggerate some of them, like Thomas de Quincey, another of the authors he read with delight and to whom he is indebted.

For some time now, we've been in the bad habit of calling any intelligent writer a "moralist," using the term in the sententious French "great century" sense, that is, to refer to a misanthrope preoccupied with the waning ethics of his fellow man. But unlike moralists, Amara shows no interest in the solitude of the lone believer, lost in the vastness of the world, or in the "sad travail" of vanity. No, more than a mora*list*, he's a mora*lizer* trying to postulate a limited set of strict rules within the confined dimensions of existence: an elevator, monosyllables, a small library. Of all the essays in *El peatón inmóvil*, "Para una arqueología de los desperdicios" ("For an archeology of scraps") best illuminates this. A quarter of a century ago, someone like Georges Perec would have been content to take detailed inventory of an everyday trash bag. But Amara confesses that he finds the simple practice of logging insufficient as literature, daring instead to find heroism in the moralizer who attempts to make order from the primordial chaos of trash. At the risk of imitating Bachelard's technique, I see the writer concerned with the absolute command of the most trivial objects and things as realizing a childhood fantasy of total omnipotence.

I read a couple of Amara's poetry collections (*Envés* and *Pasmo*, both published in 2003) before I had the pleasure of enjoying *El peatón inmóvil* and I assumed that his essays would sufficiently explain his poetics, even wondering if he might not be the sort of essayist who uses poetry as a means of notetaking or even summarizing his reflections. Amara, a philosopher by profession, makes it a rule to systematically apply the precept that anything can be of interest as long as it's observed carefully and lovingly. As a result of this way of seeing, some of his poems are the most inherently significant of his generation, and his essays show an astute, perceptive intelligence. It could be said that Amara's world is very small—it could even be called banal—but there is no denying that it's an interesting world: in his poems we see the underside of the dining room table, hear the conch made with a hand to an ear, follow the brief evolution of a paper airplane. It's worth noting that on very few occasions does Amara venture out "into the open," and that he does so in an eponymous homage to the miniature city that surrealist Edward James built in a garden in Xilitla, in the Huasteca region of San Luis Potosí.

From Salvador Novo's* defense of used things to Mariano Silva y Aceves's toys and Fabio Morábito* and Luis Ignacio Helguera's* tools, from Margo Glantz's* essays on cosmetics and Hugo Hiriart's* "methodology of paradoxical observation," this microscopic poetics has a more than diminutive history in Mexican literature, one that stands firm in the ranks of Francis Ponge's "voice of things." The world is not as young as Amara sees it, and I see his miniatures as the consummation of the expression Paz used so many years ago to characterize Mexican literature: "the art of dressing fleas." With Amara, we're on the verge of truly mastering that art.

SELECTED BIBLIOGRAPHY

El peatón inmóvil, Ediciones Arlequín, Universidad de Guadalajara, Guadalajara, 2003.
Envés, Filodecaballos Editores/Conaculta, Mexico, 2003.
Pasmo, Trilce Ediciones/Conaculta, Mexico, 2003.
Sombras sueltas, DGE/UNAM, Mexico, 2006.
A pie, Almadía, Oaxaca, 2010.
Los disidentes del universo, Gobierno del Estado de México, 2010.

ARIDJIS, HOMERO
(Contepec, Michoacán, 1940)

In the decisive years following the publication of *Poesía en movimiento* (1965), the anthology most essential to understanding Mexican poetry in the second half of the twentieth century, Homero Aridjis effectively became the "young poet" par excellence. That honor, that distinction, in time became a ball and chain, as when the French poet André Pieyre de Mandiargues asked Aridjis why he didn't write another *Perséfone* (1967), his stunning, beautiful prose poem. Aridjis very judiciously told Mandiargues that no one could be twenty-five again. And then not so judiciously, the Michoacán poet excluded both *Perséfone* and *Mirándola dormir* (1964) from his later anthologies. That inconsequential anecdote might lead us to infer a rather more consequential cause célèbre: that of the child poet who grows up, the adolescent artist who's inevitably killed off by the great poet—or at least the mature writer.

The problem was not that Aridjis moved away from his early works, such as *Ajedrez–Navegaciones* (1969), *Los espacios azules* (1968), and *El poeta niño* (1971), which were marvelous in their own way, but that he became his own work's worst enemy, driven to squander his talents on an apocalyptic hodge-podge that includes eco-sermons and epic novels that are more marketable than historical. In *Los poemas solares* (2005), however, once you get past the mythology and the pre-Hispanic imaginings proposed in neo-Aztec fashion for the umpteenth time, there are compelling and astonishing poems such as those dedicated to dogs, ghosts, domestic devotion, and one's innermost fears. More than a master of image, Aridjis is a master of poetic situations, as when he writes of the "abeja atrapada en una botella" ("bumblebee trapped in a bottle") who "la muerte no la acaba; / escapa su imagen por el vidrio" ("Death does not finish off / its image escaping through the glass").

As a private citizen, Aridjis took up important causes, promoting environmentalism in artistic and intellectual circles. But not even the best causes justify pious poetry and propagandistic literature: the tragic desecration of the planet gets to be as tedious as the misadventures of a virtuous damsel in a trashy novel. Despite it all, however, Aridjis possesses the talent of a true poet, the clairvoyance that Venezuelan critic Guillermo Sucre saw in his faith in the world as "a harmony—a perfection—opposed to the opacity of history" (*La mascara, la transparencia: Ensayo sobre poesía hispanoamericana*, 1985). For José Emilio Pacheco,* who took inspiration in the same sorts of things, poetry serves as a witness to the bloody march of history, but for Aridjis it's an obsession with ecological devastation and the resultant biblical plagues. Contrary to Sucre, however, I don't find him to be mystical. Rather, it makes sense that he's an ecologist: he's interested in nature as moral order.

Aridjis dedicates a few ballads in *Los poemas solares* to friends who have passed on, evoking through them the Mexico of the seventies, the land whose ultimate guardian of the time was María Sabina, she of the hallucinogenic mushrooms. A plethora of Europeans and Americans, San Franciscans and beatniks, ascetics and possessed folks, tourists and pilgrims, got trapped in that infernal paradise, eventually finding—as Malcolm Lowry would have wished—a dark grave. Pilgrimage and mushroom-eating are epochal themes, and we find them in several Mexican writers, including both erudite García Terrés* and Elsa Cross,* who practically levitates. But in Aridjis I find it particularly moving, perhaps because of the line, "Mira, María, las manzanas cayendo del manzano / a las manos del hombre que las está esperando" ("Look, María, at the apples falling from the apple tree / into the hands of the awaiting man").

Son of a Greek immigrant, Aridjis expresses himself in styles both Dionysian and Apollonian, commonly seen as two sides of the Greek coin. Both Sucre and Octavio Paz* have noted that oscillation, and in his prologue to *Poesía en movimiento*, Paz claimed that Aridjis was defined by erotic passion, by the "red and black prints" left by woman, who is both horizon and mirage. *Perséfone* is a fresco offering a glimpse into the everyday minutiae of life in a brothel, a time-honored place that's strangely absent from most literature. But *Perséfone*'s tone is neither Bacchanalian nor romantic: the prostitutes and their lovers file by like naiads, laid bare before the discriminating eye of a demon obsessed with harmony.

SELECTED BIBLIOGRAPHY

Obra poética, 1960–1986, Joaquín Mortiz, Mexico, 1987.

Mirándola dormir. Perséfone, FCE, Mexico, 1992.

Ojos de otro mirar. Poesía 1960–2001, FCE, Mexico, 2002.

Exaltation of Light, ed. and trans. Eliot Weinberger, BOA Editions, 1981.

The Lord of the Last Days: Visions of the Year 1000, trans. Betty Ferber, Morrow, 1995.

Eyes To See Otherwise / Ojos de otro mirar, selected and ed. Betty Ferber and George McWhirter, Carcanet, 2001 and New Directions, 2002.

Solar Poems, trans. George McWhirter, City Lights, 2010.

ARREDONDO, INÉS
(Culiacán, Sinaloa, 1928 – Mexico City, 1989)

Unlike many of my friends, I never got to meet Inés Arredondo. I never even saw her speak in public. But in 1999, I had a dream about her. It was a strictly narrative dream. In it, she appeared before me and bemoaned the fact that no one had commemorated the tenth anniversary of her death. I awoke convinced that I had to write a long piece about Arredondo, the most gifted short story writer of her time, author of *La señal* (1965) of some of the most suggestive, memorable, and terrifying stories of the century. She wrote the only stories that feel like Bible commentary, that could be used to explicate sin. I never did write about her. But at the midnight hour, I hope to be able to repeat a line from "La sunamita" ("The Shunnamite") over and over again like a spell, appealing to "la llama que nos envuelve a todos los que, como hormigas, habitamos este verano cruel que no termina nunca" ("the implacable flame enveloping all of us who, like ants, inhabit this cruel summer that never ends").

Over time, Arredondo has disproved those who thought her writing wouldn't go beyond the *Revista Mexicana de Literatura* and the Mid-Century Generation (also called the Casa del Lago Generation) that included writers like Juan García Ponce* and José de la Colina.* Some thought her reputation would die out right along with the memory of those writers, but instead her texts have become modern classics read by countless newcomers and old hands alike. Among them, of course, are women writers both young and old who go back to reread *La señal* (1965), *Río subterráneo* (1979) and *Los espejos* (1988) almost as a return to origins. You don't have to be au courant on women's writing to realize that for Arredondo, the central issue was not being a woman, but deciding how to invoke the female spirit. A dead newborn in its mother's arms, the revulsion of rape and of consent, chastity as pleasure, lust as a narcotic: these are all things Mexican literature hadn't taken on before Arredondo. Likewise, her female characters, at once domestic and fantastical, enslaved and semi-divine, were new to us.

Her spirit of denial grew out of the books—both modern and Romantic—that she and her generation were reading, especially those of Thomas Mann. But Arredondo really perfected her unorthodoxy by delving into the work of Jorge Cuesta,* as can be clearly seen in *Acercamiento a Jorge Cuesta* (1982), a critical essay that Cuesta's son, Francisco Segovia,* wrote a creative and personal response to in *Jorge Cuesta: la cicatriz en el espejo* (2004).

Paradoxically, that spirit led to a few magnificent, decadent costume balls, some as perfect as that famous Bible-like tale of "La Sunamita" ("The Shunammite"), and other shorter and less dramatic pieces like "Las mariposas negras" and "Sombra entre sombras." Arredondo actually wrote quite little, not so much because she was a perfectionist as because she led an at times unbearable life, plagued by real diseases and imagined ills, deep depression and the devastation wrought by bogus remedies.

Writers have control over their own privacy in their texts, and Arredondo doesn't give much of her personal life away. Fortunately, there's a very well-thought-out book on her, *Luna menguante. Vida y obra de Inés Arredondo* (2000), by Claudia Albarrán. But back in the sixties the author herself, in what was actually a slightly autobiographical talk she gave as part of the 1966 lecture series "New Mexican Writers As Presented by Themselves," was prematurely decisive (or at least she gave that impression) in providing the information she wanted used to condemn or absolve her: Eldorado (an hacienda and sugar refinery), the paradise where she spent her childhood until she was tragically, categorically expelled; memorized literature, she recited aloud, a practice that began with hearing her father recite the epic poem *El Cid* by heart; declaring Kierkegaard the near-exclusive master of truth; phlegmatic eccentricity.

I have no way of knowing what she made of Carson McCullers or Flannery O'Connor, but I can't read the South's best women writers without thinking of Arredondo. And it can't be any other way, because I read her first, discovering first the Sinaloa Gothic: her hellish garden full of Asian trees; the Chinese taking shelter, protected by magnanimous guardians; episodes from the Mexican Revolution that reached Sinaloa like distant, foreign news. She, in turn, was reading Katherine Mansfield and Cesare Pavese.

It doesn't surprise me in the least that when Arredondo and her then-husband Tomás Segovia* went to Montevideo in 1963, her stories grabbed Juan Carlos Onetti's attention. If literature could go back in time, Arredondo's universe would have made Onetti's fictional town of Santa María feel right at home. And Arredondo took pains to contrast her motionless world—a world ruled by a daytime devil, by the solemnity of the sun, the blinding realm of dust and tedium—with the sacred, which could be glimpsed sporadically in signs sent from the spirits.

The sacred in Arredondo, as Fabienne Bradu* wrote in *Señas particulares: escritora* (1987), occurs when two looks are exchanged, creating a pact, as in the fleeting complicity between black man and crying woman in "Año nuevo" or the Faustian understanding between the Shunammite and Don Apolonio, her unexpected old husband. But as other critics have noted, Arredondo's work is less sacred than numinous, imbued with spirits that appear and then disperse. Inventing and catching their signs was what Arredondo set out to do. That's what Huberto Batis, one of her most faithful readers, has said from the start, and we now know that he was the anonymous author of the incisive book flaps on *La señal* and *Río subterraneo* (1979).

Like fellow Sinaloan Gilberto Owen, the poet she'd hoped to finish a book on, Arredondo was a disillusioned Catholic. And like other writers of her generation (Salvador Elizondo,* Juan García Ponce*), she had no interest in deeper religious experiences. For her, the sacred is just a sign, a confirmation that the poet possesses the grace required to interpret the universe.

Her heartless microcosm, cruelly governed by a midday devil—Arredondo's personal demon, one shared with no other writer—became a place worshipped by some readers, a place to wait for a sign. I, for instance, can't think of a single nightfall in any of her stories. My memory must be failing me. But I say this to stress the fact that in all of Mexican literature, there has never been a more melancholy and yet less nocturnal writer.

SELECTED BIBLIOGRAPHY
Obras completas, Siglo XXI, Mexico, 1988.
Albarrán, Claudia, *Luna menguante. Vida y obra de Inés Arredondo*, Ediciones Casa Juan Pablos, Mexico, 2000.
Underground River and Other Stories, trans. Cynthia Steele, University of Nebraska Press, 1996.

ARREOLA, JUAN JOSÉ

(Zapotlán El Grande [Ciudad Guzmán], Jalisco, 1918 – Guadalajara, Jalisco, 2001)

In 1946, in an early and enthusiastic review of the works of Borges and Bioy Casares, Xavier Villaurrutia bemoaned the fact that "while other Spanish American literatures, including our own, trudge monotonously and interminably through the dry, arid deserts of realism and naturalism, Argentine literature lays before us not a mirage but a veritable oasis to quench our thirst for a 'literature of invention.' In the books of Jorge Luis Borges and Adolfo Bioy Casares, as in other contemporary Argentinean books, fiction regains the rights that, in Mexico at least, it has been denied. Because one thing is certain: here, any author who doesn't tackle the themes of realism or concern him or herself with our everyday reality is accused of being dehumanized, purist, or worse." (*Obras*, 1965)

Villaurrutia was making an appeal for what was about to happen: Arreola's arrival on the scene. In 1949 he published *Varia invención*, which took the legacies of Julio Torri* and Efrén Hernández* and expanded them. That "literature of invention" that the *Contemporáneo* poet had been searching for would reach one of its Latin American highpoints in Arreola.

His early stories appeared in the journals *Eos* and *Pan*, in Guadalajara, where Juan Rulfo* also made his first appearance. Arreola had held down a lot of different jobs—including one as an actor in the *Comédie-Française* in Paris—and his debut in Mexican prose was, according to Emmanuel Carballo,* one in which "naïveté became insight, allusion became elusion, the vertical became slanted." Arreola had no prehistory as a writer. From his first book—it was really all one book written slowly over the course of the fifties—he showed himself to be an extraordinary rhetorician, ceaselessly creating self-contained texts on, for instance, provincial life, destiny, and tricks of the mind; undertaking—all with utter originality—invented biographies, imaginary bestiaries, and fantastical short stories . . . Arreola, halfway between Kafka and Borges, an admirer of Marcel Schwob and Giovanni Papini, wrote on an amazing array of all of the literary themes that Mexican literature had either forgotten or discarded. In texts as crystalline as they are poetic, Arreola applies humor as well as erudition to things ranging from the comedy of intrigue to metaphysical speculation. Fully aware of the mid-century intellectual climate, he turned the absence of God into a farce to amuse man and wreak havoc on objects. No wonder Borges said he could have been born in any time and any place. Arreola belongs to that small council of souls who play roulette with words (*Antología de la narrativa mexicana del siglo XX*, I, 1989).

With mischievous affection, Antonio Alatorre* recounts how one day, a fresh-faced young Arreola went to the Guadalajara train station with a bouquet of roses, to await the arrival of French actor and director Louis Jouvet. The incident would have fallen into the annals of small-town forgotten dreams had it not been for the fact that shortly thereafter, thanks to Jouvet, Arreola actually went to Paris. Between 1945 and 1946, he made his debut as a member of the *Comedie Française*, rubbing elbows with Jean-Louis Barrault, gained access to the world of Paul Claudel, Pierre Emmanuel, and Roger Callois, and suffered the formative stress of having been taught—complementarily and contradictorily—by both Octavio Paz* and Rodolfo Usigli.* He returned to Mexico a *comédien*—actor, juggler, mime—who displayed his talent more in writing than he did on the stage, publishing *Varia invención* (1949) and *Confabulario* (1952). Taking the path set out by Julio Torri,* Arreola stripped Mexican prose of any and all ostentation, vulgarity and didacticism. His writing was like a clear day dawning after a night of revolutions and civil wars.

Through his "various inventions," Arreola's work ran a parallel course with the "fictions" of Borges, a metaphorical older brother whose tribute to him must be repeated here. "I haven't seen him often," Borges said. "But I remember one afternoon we discussed the most recent adventures of Arthur Gordon Pym," in reference to Poe's only novel. Arreola's brevity in prose was food for thought for Julio Cortázar—who said so himself in a letter to Arreola in 1954—and many other Latin American writers. Neither Martín Luis Guzmán* nor Alfonso Reyes* had the influence Arreola did on language, an influence wrought by the ease with which he intertwines the ordinary with the extraordinary, the real with the fantastic, achieving such perfection that his works can be read as stories as easily as prose poems. A very curious writer of fantastic literature, one surrounded by fairies and not dragons, Arreola is like a clockmaker who makes daylight stop ticking.

While some writers scare people off, as was the case with Rulfo, others—like Arreola—seem to engender entire movements. Endless pages have been written about the friendship, rivalry, and complicity of the two Jalisco writers. And while it's doubtful that Arreola "sorted out" Rulfo's *Pedro Páramo* manuscript, it is clear that Arreola's choral novel *La feria* (1963), the last official novel he wrote, is a sort of "solar" response to Rulfo's underworld. *La feria* presents a world wide open, and though it can't compete in complexity or dramatic quality with the obscure transcendence of *Pedro Páramo*, in a way it complements Rulfo's novel with another dimension, one which is charmingly poetic, presenting realistic portrayals of village life—rather than death—and customs. "You're as twee and as talented as López Velarde," Arreola claims Paz told him in postwar Paris, and if he did say that, he was right.

Provençal troubadour and cosmopolitan fabulist live side by side in Arreola. His first short story, "Gunther Stapenhorst" (1946) is the now-forgotten cornerstone of the celebrated and polemical Germanophilic exoticism seen in some Mexican writers. In this pilot text, Arreola essentially scripted what would be written half a century later: a German avant-garde architect passionate about Wagner's "total music" and praised by Le Corbusier for a project that's unsuitable as the German pavilion in the World's Fair decides to abandon architecture and take up theater and expressionist cinema. Gunther Stapenhorst breaks with Nazism, engages in submarine warfare, falls prisoner in a concentration camp, and is finally consumed by history. Pablo Soler Frost,* Jorge Volpi,* and Ignacio Padilla* didn't read the story before writing their novels, but they ought to get their hands on "Gunther Stapenhorst," opportunely republished in 2002, in order to find the genotype that precedes them and they might well legitimize them.

Saúl Yurkiévich, in his introduction to Arreola's *Obras* (1995), identifies some essential undercurrents in the master of Zapotlán's work: the humanity of his bestiaries; a hypersexualized awareness falling somewhere between misogyny and the "eternal feminine"; and, finally, faith. According to Yurkiévich, "More than a metaphysical inclination—as seen in his models, Kafka and Borges—Arreola tends to infuse his writing with a certain theological dimension. Arreola is morally and imaginarily penetrated by his Catholic origins, shaped by his doctrinal upbringing."

Arreola is a subtle sort of Catholic writer though, one who, like the convert and martyr Max Jacob, makes each text a prayer in praise of the world, committing angelical peccadilloes that, more than heterodoxy—as Yurkiévich mistakenly assumes—represent a sort of orthodoxy that we might call Chestertonian, but orthodoxy nonetheless. The angels and apostles of the rococo Christianity in which Arreola was steeped—and to whom he dedicated some lovely poems in 1970—are predominant figures in his writing.

In his miniature theology, angels are the "concessionaries and exclusive distributors of human contingencies," a characterization which Arreola upholds in the belief that only repentance can alter the past and enable us to recapture lost time. In *Inventario* (1977) he suggests that no one is *culpable* for Christ's crucifixion, in the sense that each man can ask forgiveness for the sin. This diametrically opposes the Pascalian culpability that José Revueltas* bestowed on the entire human race for its crimes of history. It says a lot about the intellectual insignificance of the Church in post-Cristero War (1926–1929) Mexico that it was two lay writers—Arreola and Revueltas—who took opposing sides in the Augustinian controversy which, centuries earlier, had led to the split between the Jesuits and the Jansenists.

If it's true, as Adolfo Castañón* says, that Arreola invented his own tradition in order to teach himself to read, then we must feel privileged to read through this invention in the taped confessions he dictated, successively, to Jorge Arturo Ojeda (*La palabra educación*, 1974, and *Y ahora la mujer*, 1975), Fernando del Paso* (*Memoria y olvido*, 1994), and his son, Orso Arreola *(El último juglar: Memorias de Juan José Arreola*, 1998). These conversations often reveal the best of Arreola: a pilgrim frolicking in the Scriptures; a knight errant defending his classics—more paperbacks than bedside books—including Marcel Schwob, Giovanni Papini, and Alphonse Allais; a prophet among authors who would only begin to be appreciated by writers of subsequent generations, such as Soviet critic Vyacheslav Ivanov and Gandhi disciple Lanza del Vasto. Reading Arreola is always a much richer experience than one remembered.

A Christian and a sinner, a jester and a phony, an enemy of all forms of solitary life, a man seeking communion with others to the degree of losing himself, Arreola also made his blunders, for instance by appearing on talk shows where he became the butt of sportscasters' jokes. But, truth be told, that's not bad if you consider the moral and intellectual faux pas that we writers often commit. The critic Felipe Vázquez has done a top-notch job exploring the almost tragic ebb and flow we saw in Arreola's later days, when he focused on sound and oral presentation. "At the start of the seventies (when he published his last book), the author of *La feria* regressed, becoming the classic writer caught up in showbiz, an actor on the stage (and sometimes just in the wings) of literature. His writing, however, is removed from and surpasses the media frenzy: it acts on a stage where writing comes to terms with its own absence. Protagonist and agonist are brought together by a fissure that, over time, has become insurmountable: on the one hand, the writer becomes a speaker; on the other, his writing comes to life in silence. This crevice grows deeper when we consider the fact that the public man, the jester, was plagued by metaphysical anguish and often publicly atoned for the contradiction eating away at him. Perhaps because people prefer the jester to the tragic figure, or because conceiving of his literature as mannerist led to mistakenly deeming the author frivolous, or because he felt obliged to wear a jester's mask, his tragic temperament has been side-lined and even ignored as a fundamental component of his creation. When he wrote, Arreola translated that fissure; when he spoke, he made amends for literature."

I met Juan José when I was a child, because my father, José Luis Domínguez Camacho, was his psychiatrist and a man the Zapotlán writer was always generous toward, as Orso Arreola writes in *El último juglar*. Arreola and my father shared a love of chess, wine, and the psychoanalyst Viktor Frankl. I saw Arreola for the last time in Guadalajara in December 1996, when I accompanied him to the launch of *Antiguas primicias*, a short collection of early verse, which served as an excuse for him to invoke, while on a roll, Jean Paul, Schopenhauer, Léautaud, Santa Teresa, Papini, and Saint Paul, a group whose spirits turned that auditorium into the devil's cauldron.

I remember my father and Arreola playing chess for hours and, on occasion, playing tennis in an outfit that made Juan José look part elf and part dandy. Every time he visited our house there arose the possibility that Pandora's box would be opened and from it would fly out not the bad things Prometheus had captured but a stream of quotations, poems, and books. One day, Arreola arrived very shaken up, having fallen asleep reading *Monsieur Proust*, the book Proust's housekeeper Céleste Albaret had written about him. Upon waking he found himself either in a dream within a dream or having a ghostly apparition, for Proust himself was there admonishing him for having neglected his literary obligations, the anguished Arreola recounted. Thanks to client confidentiality, I never found out what my father did to calm him down.

SELECTED BIBLIOGRAPHY

La feria, Joaquín Mortiz, Mexico, 1963.

Obras, ed. and prefaced by Saúl Yurkiévich, FCE, Mexico, 1995.

Arreola, Orso, *El último juglar. Memorias de Juan José Arreola*, Diana, Mexico, 1998.

Vázquez Palacios, Felipe, *Juan José Arreola. La tragedia de lo imposible*, Conaculta/Verdehalago, Mexico, 2003.
Confabulario and Other Inventions, trans. George D. Schade, University of Texas Press, 1964.
The Fair, trans. John Upton, University of Texas Press, 1977.

ASIAIN, AURELIO
(Mexico City, 1960)

Poet, diplomat, translator, professor, Facebook activist, and essayist, Asiain had two stints as editor in chief at *Vuelta* between 1984 and 1998. One day, when someone writes the history of Octavio Paz* and his last literary group, we'll be able to appreciate Asiain's place as one of the best cultural editors in Latin America. And though scant (he's only published *República de viento* in 1990 and a few chapbooks), his poetry is some of the most painstakingly precise of his generation, possessing that "will to perfection" that Paz saw in it. A poem entitled "Amor," for instance: "Esa rama que llevas en la mano tiene el mismo color de hace mil años." ("That branch you hold in your hand has the same color as a thousand years ago.") It's almost manifest destiny (or aesthetic selection) that this perfectionist found his heaven and earth in Japanese poetry, as can be seen in *Luna en la hierba: Medio centenar de poemas japoneses elegidos, traducidos y comentados por Aurelio Asiain* (2007).

Caracteres de imprenta (1996), in turn, is a volume of collected criticism. An authority on Spanish-language poetry, Asiain analyzes with self-assurance and audacity, whether reading his elders (from Josep Pla and Gerardo Diego to Alejandro Rossi* and Gabriel Zaid*) or sifting through those who are most strictly his contemporaries, such as David Huerta,* Orlando González Esteva, and Carmen Boullosa.*

After founding and directing the journal *Paréntesis* (1999–2001), Asiain went to Japan, where, following in the footsteps of José Juan Tablada, Lafcadio Hearn, and Efrén Rebolledo, he held a diplomatic post while also teaching college. Thanks to the internet—which he's availed himself of with true eighteenth-century immoderation—it's easy to find out about Asiain, whose emails contain both delicate *japoneseries* and epitaphs no one would dare publish.

Selected Bibliography
República de viento, Visor, Madrid, 1990.
Caracteres de imprenta, Conaculta/El Equilibrista, Mexico, 1996.
Luna en la hierba. Medio centenar de poemas japoneses elegidos, traducidos y comentados por Aurelio Asiain, Hiperion, Madrid, 2007.

AUB, MAX

(Paris, France, 1903 – Mexico City, 1972)

Long before the centenary festivities, before Spain was celebrating him, Aub was being included in Mexican dictionaries as a Mexican author, not just because of his passport but also because of his profound devotion to us over the course of thirty years. When World War I broke out, Aub's Franco-German family was living in Valencia, which is where young Max lived through Spain's creative Silver Age, emblematized in the year 1929 and destroyed in the Spanish Civil War of 1936–1939. After three years in internment camps, Aub, a socialist of Jewish extraction who had collaborated with Malraux in the making of *L'espoir*, arrived in Mexico as an exile. Here he lived an academic life and wrote prolifically, everything from poetry to novels, and especially plays, which he considered his vocation, though others may not have agreed.

His *Diarios (1939–1972)*, published posthumously in Mexico and Spain, significantly enhanced Aub's literary profile. In them we read of the drama of the Spanish Republic's defeat and the author's firm anti-Stalinism, but we also see a parodic, uncomplicated take on life as a Spanish exile. Added to that is a remarkable will to integrate into Mexican society, seen not only in his incisive, witty literary criticism but also in his stories and anthologies. In his *Diarios*, Aub evaluated the rivalry between Rulfo* and Arreola* with great insight, found in Paz* a poet whose angel's wings weighed him down, and stated that Reyes,* whose friendship lingered in the background, was brought down by the very encyclopedic passion that made him great to begin with.

His *Ensayos mexicanos* (1975), on the other hand, exhibit the critical reserve he felt was required of him as an exile dealing with Mexican literature, and are limited to authors of the Mexican Revolution, with a few interesting pages on Reyes, Xavier Villaurrutia, Rodolfo Usigli,* José Emilio Pacheco,* and José Carlos Becerra.* Aub wisely saved his indignation at Mexican intellectuals' adherence to the autocratic rites of presidentialism for his *Diarios*. His friend Jaime García Terrés* recalls that Aub, an author with a truly vast body of work, "lamented that we didn't read him. The truth is, it was impossible *not* to read him. His work inundated the newspapers."

The author of *Vida y obra de Luis Álvarez Petreña* (1934), *La verdadera historia de la muerte de Francisco Franco* (1960), *La gallina ciega* (1971), and *El laberinto mágico* (1943–1968), one of the greatest series of novels ever written about the Spanish Civil War, Aub, it has been said rather glibly, was a talented writer whose talent never particularly stood out in any one genre. People forget about the disconcerting singularity of *Jusep Torres Campalans* (1958), the fictional biography of a Catalan painter who left Europe in 1914 and became a recluse in Chiapas. Launched internationally along with apocryphal expositions of Campalans's work—this being a painter who would have been friends with Picasso—*Jusep Torres Campalans* is a hilarious, despairing, lucid reflection on the avant-garde; an exploration of Spain's (and Catalunya's) destiny interrupted; a meditation on the search for a paradise lost among the Mexican indigenous; and, finally, an unforgettable way to question (and picture) the notion of authorship.

Jusep Torres Campalans both completes and exceeds Rafael Cansinos-Assens's *La novela de un literato*, an epic that spans Spanish literary society from 1898 to the eve of the Spanish Civil War. By imagining Campalans and Picasso going from Barcelona to Paris, from Montmartre to Montparnasse, from "regenerationist" Barcelona to cubist Paris, from anarchist circles to *ateliers-fortifiés*, Aub portrays the end of bohemia and its tragic transformation into the art world and art market. Campalans is both an ancient and a modern hero. Looking back, he feels let down by Montaigne's and Molière's stances on the great wars, and by the vanities of the court; at the same time, he's disheartened by modern art, which is simply avant-garde. It's no wonder that Aub was proud of being born the same year as Cyril Connolly: like *The Unquiet Grave*, *Jusep Torres Campalans* is a slice of imaginary life whose raison d'être is to upend and disbelieve the age-old artist. Art Critic Jean Cassou, one of Aub's accomplices in the staging of *Jusep Torres Campalans*, wrote in the prologue to the French edition, "It all comes clear the moment we realize that Campalans is as possible as Picasso, and Picasso is as hypothetical as Campalans."

Jusep Torres Campalans is one of the great novels to be written in Mexico. A work overflowing with aphoristic marvels, written in the Spanish of Mexico, the novel is testimony to the towering stature of Aub, a writer Octavio Paz in 1967 called "an example of the Spanish-American Spaniard and for that very reason, one of the few truly European writers of Spain. For the same reason, he's a Mexican writer. Max Aub's range of genres, literary forms and styles must be seen as a pluralistic dialogue within his vast body of work. Not only does this not destroy his unity, but it's that very diversity that constitutes it. Max Aub's dialects are woven into a fabric: a single text. It's not the recovery of Spain—though this is one of his themes—or the preservation of the Spanish language, but its reinsertion into modern language. It sounds so simple, but something so simple is often forgotten in Spain: Spanish is a European, and therefore American, language" (Paz, *Obras completas, IV. Fundación y disidencia*, 1994).

SELECTED BIBLIOGRAPHY

Ensayos mexicanos, UNAM, Mexico, 1974.
Jusep Torres Campalans, Alianza Editorial, Madrid, 1975.
Diarios, 1939–1952, Conaculta, Mexico, 1999.
Diarios, 1953–1966, Conaculta, Mexico, 1999.
Diarios, 1967–1972, Conaculta, Mexico, 1999.

B

BARANDA, MARÍA
(Mexico City, 1962)

María Barranda's narrative poetry, from *El jardín de los encantamientos* (1989) to *Dylan y las ballenas* (2003; *Dylan and the Whales*, 2005), has struggled to avoid the pitfalls of a genre that, as Octavio Paz* said, must combine narrative development and poetic concentration. But Baranda doesn't shrink from the possible feeling of (or temporary frustration) at knowing she's rewriting the same text over and over, understanding as she does that long poems are precisely the terrain needed for a celebratory imagination such as hers. In earlier works such as *Fábula de los perdidos* (1990) and *Los memoriosos* (1995), her tone, somewhere between genetic and cosmogonic, and bolstered by the feminine influence of imagination, doesn't achieve an entirely original sound, which is unsurprising since she was influenced by two of her teachers: Álvaro Mutis* and José Luis Rivas.* One of her best books, *Nadie, los ojos* (1999), is written in a different tone, one we could call anecdotal or incidental. In it, she engraves in stone several harsh epitaphs, bull's-eyes about the funereal customs of our times, reconsidering hospitals, sickness, and death with both bitterness and insight.

"Songs of the world," in the modern age, are no longer celebrations of nature but questions about mankind's role in time. In *Dylan y las ballenas*, Baranda displays her shock at the horrors of our age, of the twentieth century's evil theological backsliding. She more resembles some of the novelists of her generation than she does poets, given the sense of ethical urgency with which she draws a veil over the twentieth century. In poetry, that moral persuasion is as dangerous as it is irrepressible, leading poets to declaim and hurling them onto a stage where Sibyl becomes Cassandra.

Baranda confronts that declamatory tendency in *Dylan y las ballenas*, successfully castigating it by searching for, and then finding, in the poet Dylan Thomas, an accomplice who unburdens her poetic voice of the enormous responsibility for twentieth-century massacres and the wretched aims of progress. Prose poems, particularly those narrating historical events, require at least the shadow of a philosophical argument. Thanks to the invocation of Dylan Thomas, and the echoes of his influence successfully reproduced in this book, Baranda not only reaches some of the greatest heights of her poetic journey thus far but also ends up inscribing her poem in an old Romantic, humanitarian tradition: that of Shelley, who blames God for creating history and exculpates man from original sin. "Es la hora de declinar por los vencidos / de voltear a ver a Dios para pedirle / que tire su basura en otro sitio." ("It is time to decline before the victors / to turn to face God and ask him / to throw his garbage someplace else.") That conviction allows Baranda to close *Dylan y las ballenas*, one of Mexico's most distinctive poems of the turn of the twenty-first century, with a "solar" scene of reconciliation that brings her back to the song of the world, her true literary vocation.

SELECTED BIBLIOGRAPHY

El jardín de los encantamientos, UAM, Mexico, 1989.
Fábula de los perdidos, El equilibrista, Mexico, 1990.
Nadie, los ojos, Conaculta, Mexico, 1999.
Dylan y las ballenas, Joaquín Mortiz, Mexico, 2003.
Ávido mundo, Ediciones Sin Nombre, Mexico, 2006.
Dylan and the Whales, trans. Alicia Knight, *Prometeo* 71–72 (June 2005).
If We Have Lost Our Oldest Tales, trans. Lorna Shaughnessy, Arlen House, 2007.
Ficticia, trans. Joshua Edwards, Shearsman Books, Exeter, 2010.

BARTRA, ROGER
(Mexico City, 1942)

Whether he's seen as an anthropologist of ideas or a historian of myths, Bartra is something of a celebrity in Mexican letters. His inclusion among strictly literary authors, poets, and critics should come as no surprise, for Bartra definitely takes on literature; he tackles the entire array of "civilized" man's uncanny interest in everything in text, everything textual. The son of poet Agustí Bartra and writer Ana Muriá, Catalan intellectuals who came to Mexico as exiles after the Spanish Civil War, Bartra reads in an enlightened and encyclopedic fashion, creating a *vade mecum* of the customs, phobias, and rites that make up the human spirit. He sees these as constituent parts of both the *con*struction and *de*struction of the identity of "the civilized," whom—anthropologist from the start and writer to the end—he views as "savages in the mirror." Bartra is a literary critic—in the way that contemporary essayists René Girard, Hayden White, and Nicola Chiaromonte are—who sees in Rousseau, Lope de Vega, Michelet, Calderón, Daniel Defoe, and Mary Shelley refutation of the so-called social sciences.

In his 1987 book *La jaula de la melancolía* (*The Cage of Melancholy*, 1992), Bartra began to draw a veil over the obsessive discussion of the problem—as grave as it is vulgar—that Mexican culture has struggled with since its earliest vice-regal and *independentista* days: the melancholic concept of "national identity." Bartra ventured away from mythology and into the world of science for metaphors he could employ to dismantle this identity. Using the native *ajolote*, a salamander-like reptile whose neoteny (conservation of larval characteristics in adult forms) confounded eighteenth-century sages, Bartra poses "the Mexican" as a caged creature that cannot develop, or does so only without growing. *La jaula de la melancolía*, a work of anthropological *bricolage*, explains our mythical mutations, from Xolotl—a pre-Hispanic defective deity: a god who doesn't want to die—to the Revolution's short-lived "new man," and including Indians and *pelados*. Bartra concludes that the clinical file on "Mexicanness" is an assemblage created by the political power structure as well as a "burning mirror" in which the culture's political fantasies are played out. In the twenty-first century, Bartra's name can be found among those who—paraphrasing him—made their way through Octavio Paz's* *Labyrinth of Solitude*, challenged the minotaur, and now that the mythical city is buried, spend their time translating its seismic activity, its ominous grumbling.

With *El salvaje en el espejo* (1992) and *El salvaje artificial* (*The Artificial Savage*, 1997), Bartra became one of the most insightful cultural critics of his generation, obsessed with trying to make sense of life in the nether regions of the Western consciousness. That distich also lent Mexican letters some real essayistic heft, all the more valuable for its even balance of academic rigor and imaginative prose. Bartra—both a postmodern and a Marxist traveler—exposes and portrays the lineage of the "savage," presenting him as a figure who is actually native to *Europe*. More than once I've pictured him as the erudite eighteenth-century sage we never had, the one who would counter all the cunning arguments of Euro-centrism without conceding anything to Creole patriotism and its heirs.

A valiant, perceptive observer of contemporary political life, from *Las redes imaginarias del poder político* (1981) to *La sangre y la tinta* (1999; *Blood, Ink, and Culture: Miseries and Splendors of the Post-Mexican Condition*, 2002), Bartra has never stopped speculating on the decline of the intellectual and on his obligation as a critic of every form of tyranny. When the Berlin Wall fell in 1989 and the Institutional Revolutionary Party (PRI) was defeated in 2000, Bartra was there, an ethnographer of the present whose methodological optimism identifies, connects, and then divides the two murky undercurrents of our time: the culture of blood and the culture of ink.

I met Bartra in July 1979. I was an office worker at the Mexican Communist Party's (PCM) center of electoral statistics, and Bartra was one of the main intellectual communists counting the votes that legally constituted the party. But unlike many, Bartra felt that democratizing the country called for a real *aggiornamento* of the Mexican left. He founded *El Machete*, a journal of cultural criticism that, in 1980 and 1981, shed light on the recently opened catacombs of the Mexican left, and it did so with humor, audacity, and depth. Unsurprisingly, the journal scandalized the commissars, who shut it down as soon as they could to appease the Stalinist factions that the PCM allowed finally to destroy it. I had my first job as a cultural journalist, and even political analyst, at *El Machete*. And I was privy not only to the death throes of Marxist heresy but also Bartra's instruction and his demeanor, friendly yet distant and, in his own courteous way, implacable. Later I became his research assistant at UNAM's Instituto de Investigaciones Sociales. Under his tutelage, I learned to conduct research—that is, to trace the flow of those intermingling rivers of blood and ink, guided by a fluvial mariner who stops the boat as often as necessary to collect seemingly trivial samples. Culture—that is, nature sublimated—can only be understood by archeological amalgamation, examining both gold and plastic, both stone and paper, both technique and chance.

In those days I didn't realize that Bartra was teaching me how to tell blood from ink, once I'd grasped the fact that they blend together, and course through the same channels. My turning to cultural and literary criticism is, in large part, due to him. For Bartra, politics was a form of cultural criticism that, moving beyond Marxism, implied being *in* civilization. He expressed his cosmopolitan interests—from agricultural studies of Mexico's heartland to Mexico's own Tarot, with the state as "tower" and revolution as "lightning"— in the realm of literature, seen as prose open to every possible sign. It was a blessing that my first teacher, a friend throughout my metamorphosis, was an anthropologist. Although anthropology may be the "science of man," that doesn't make it humanism, except in cases like Bartra's. The author of *El salvaje artificial* might disbelieve science, but his books are devoted to man's masks, fantasies, and avatars, some mythological and others historical.

As editor of *El Machete* and *La Jornada Semanal* (1989–1994), Bartra advanced the culture of ink, provoking intellectual arguments and reaffirming political pluralism. But the democratizing result never implied abandoning methodological uncertainty, the practice of an anthropologist deconstructing everyday myths. Both as writer and as critic, Bartra has systematically looked beyond our so-called "national culture." Convinced that "man" can only be understood by the whole carnivalesque range of his costumes, rituals, and obsessions, Bartra exposed the "savage" as an invention of European tribes, and the indigenous Mexican—to cite a Bartran stance against *neo-Zapatismo* and its anthropologists—as an academic fantasy.

In *El duelo de los ángeles: Locura sublime, tedio y melancolía en el pensamiento moderno* (2004), Bartra continued the happy evolution of a social scientist engaging in more refined forms of literary essay. The key to Bartra lies in his insistence on seeing himself as an anthropologist, a participatory observer indebted equally to methodological rigor and a search for causality. Through his lens, then, we see an allegorical "spectacle" in which Kant, Weber, and Benjamin are like members of some forgotten Australian or Amazonian tribe that's been decimated by progress and yet is desperately clinging to a discredited mode of self-governance. And Bartra's flawless construction of philosophical tales, crafted with the patience of a silversmith, allows us to see a little bit of ourselves in Kant, Weber, and Benjamin. We identify with their awareness of a modernity that has not fulfilled its civilizing responsibility, yet lacks both the dramatic economy and the stage equipment needed to end the show, lower the curtain, and turn out the lights. That's exactly the type of melancholia that pervades Bartra's work.

In *El siglo de oro de la melancolía* (1999) and *Cultura y melancolía: Las enfermedades del alma en la España del Siglo de Oro* (2001), Bartra began a clinical and anthropological exploration that culminates in *El duelo de los ángeles*. What unites Kant, Weber, and Benjamin is their varying degrees of melancholic temperament, which Bartra has chosen to see as a historically *evolving* illness, in contrast to the fixity of structures. A master of conceptism, of Baltasar Gracián's form of questioning—the "ponderación misteriosa" that makes what we took as suppositions into something mysterious—Bartra turns *El duelo de los ángeles* into a spiritual autobiography, that of an intellectual who, after Marxism was shipwrecked, decided to go it alone on a quest to find himself, far from the commercial routes of the ruinous "invincible" armadas. In the family of Kant, Weber, and Benjamin, Bartra has found angels who conceive of the invisible as a higher plane of reality. All of Bartras's work is a desperate, lucid attempt to resolve Aristotle's Problem XXX.1: "Why is it that all those who have become eminent in philosophy or politics or poetry or the arts are clearly of an atrabilious temperament, and some of them to such an extent as to be affected by diseases caused by black bile, as is said to have happened to Heracles among the heroes?" (trans. Jonathan Barnes)

If Bartra were just an anthropologist, he'd be content with a little erudite demystification. But as a critic studying society via its cultural myths—and artistic sublimations—he reminds us that ruins are actually a "place" in the present, incomplete structures in which humans, savage or civilized, are uncomfortable tenants. Taking on what he sees as the responsibility of twentieth-century intellectuals for the culture of blood and finding evidence of its dogged perseverance in Mexico, Roger Bartra places his bets on the culture of ink. Thanks to his voice, clerics and ideologues fade into the background, leaving an enlightened intellectual in their stead, one who constructs a vision of literature as narrative history equal to nature, an unfolding of parallel lives and maxims written in penetrating ink in the scholarly works of the cloister, yet legible on the plaza's public walls.

SELECTED BIBLIOGRAPHY

Las redes imaginarias del poder político, ERA, Mexico, 1981.

La jaula de la melancolía, Grijalbo, Mexico, 1987.

El salvaje en el espejo, ERA/UNAM, Mexico, 1992.

El salvaje artificial, ERA/UNAM, Mexico, 1997.

La sangre y la tinta. Ensayos sobre la condición postmexicana, Océano, México, 1999.

Cultura y melancolía. Las enfermedades del alma en la España del Siglo de Oro, Anagrama, Barcelona, 2001.

El duelo de los ángeles. Locura sublime, tedio y melancolía en el pensamiento moderno, Pretextos, Valencia, 2004.

Antropología del cerebro. La conciencia y los sistemas simbólicos, Pretextos, Valencia, 2006.

Imaginary Networks of Political Power, trans. Claire Joysmith, Rutgers University Press, 1992.

The Cage of Melancholy, trans. Christopher Hall, Rutgers University Press, 1992.

Wild Men in the Looking Glass, trans. Carl Berrisford, University of Michigan Press, 1994.

The Artificial Savage, trans. Christopher Follett, University of Michigan Press, 1997.

Blood, Ink, and Culture: Miseries and Splendors of the Post-Mexican Condition, trans. Mark Alan Healey, Duke University Press, 2002.

BECERRA, JOSÉ CARLOS

(Villahermosa, Tabasco, 1937 – Brindisi, Italy, 1970)

Frozen in time after the author's early death, Becerra's poetry is like ancient ceramics, akin to Keats's Grecian urn, which has miraculously survived the passage of time and whose cracks and imperfections are inherent parts of its beauty. Part Paul Claudel and part José Lezama Lima, his complete works— posthumously published as *El otoño recorre las islas* (1973)—are a classic in twentieth-century Mexican poetry. In "Relación de los hechos," Becerra rhetorically foreshadowed his own life, using verse as prophets do and speaking to us of what prophets speak: the passage of time, the march of history, the contradiction between city and country, the infinite song of songs, the "carne que se hizo piedra para que la piedra tuviera un espejo de / carne" ("flesh that turned to stone so the stone might have a reflection of / flesh").

Read by both Octavio Paz* and Lezama Lima, Becerra left behind a mature body of work whose influence on Mexican poetry has been so decisive that denying him as a predecessor has become par for the course for each generation of poets. It's shocking to see fifty-year-old poets "killing" a father who died when he was thirty-three. In his day, Becerra managed to skillfully avoid the stifling burden of his teachers like Efraín Huerta* and Carlos Pellicer,* to find his own voice beyond archeology and prosaism, and remove the tropical hues from his palette.

Although it's not one of his best poems and might even be called pompous, "Retorno de Ulises" does portray Becerra's poetic persona. Hearing what people are whispering, and tossed around by the caprice of gods, Ulysses returns disguised as that nobody who must fight off the pretenders to regain his rightful place: almost all of us have been in that place before, the beggar returning for the keys to the kingdom. The legend of the young man dead before his time is as old as cave paintings, and every generation exalts its own, whose sudden disappearance seems like mystical selection. What Ramón López Velarde—often considered Mexico's national poet, a man who also died at thirty-three—was to his time, Becerra was to the seventies. That was when I first read his poetry, fascinated by the paradoxical miracle of his accidental death, which I later discovered took place in the same remote place where Virgil died. Since then, Becerra's silence has been that "música antigua que se oye de lejos" ("ancient music heard in the distance") that "enciende el fuego de la vejez en el brasero de / nuestras casas" ("lights the fire of old age in the stove of / our homes").

SELECTED BIBLIOGRAPHY
El otoño recorre las islas (Obra poética, 1961–1970), prologue by Octavio Paz, ed. José Emilio Pacheco and Gabriel Zaid, ERA, Mexico, 1973 and 2002.

BELLATIN, MARIO

(Mexico City, 1960)

It's not entirely clear how it was that Bellatin, who was raised in Peru, joined the ranks of Mexican literature. But his languorous prose is here to stay, unmistakable in its sinuous precision. His novels, always short, include *Salón de belleza* (1994; *Beauty Salon*, 2009), which deals with the AIDS epidemic; *Poeta ciego* (1998), about Peruvian terrorist organization Sendero Luminoso; and *Flores* (2001), which delves into genetic mutation.

El jardín de la señora Murakami (2000) is a delicate homage to "the beautiful and the sad," the tradition established by Muraski Shikibu, who wrote the first novel in history—*The Tale of Genji*—a thousand years ago. Any writer worth his or her salt has the right and perhaps even the duty to renew beloved traditions. But when *El jardín de la señora Murakami* fell into my hands, I happened to be reading *The Tale of Genji*, so I couldn't quite fall for the chiaroscuro game the author plays, in which a young art critic gets involved with a flawed collector in the late twentieth century. Bellatin barely outlines his story, mingling the faint brushstrokes of calligraphy with typed manuscript, the word with the tone. It doesn't really add up to much, just a small morsel considering where Bellatin could have gone as Ms. Murasaki's exegete. And just as Javier Marías thinks he's the only Hispanic in the world who reads in English, Bellatin seems to feel that having read Murasaki, Tanizaki, and Kawabata authorizes him to blather. It would be hard to claim that *El jardín de la señora Murakami* is an invitation to read Bellatin's Japanese masters.

In *Shiki Nagaoka: una nariz de ficción* (2001), Bellatin takes the game begun in *El jardín de la señora Murakami* one step further, going from homage to Ms. Murasaki—an eleventh-century Japanese intellectual—to recreation of Tanikaki and Akutagawa, albeit incidental. Reading *Shiki Nagaoka: una nariz de ficción* helped me understand Bellatin's *japoneseries* a little better. What we have here is the fictional biography of a writer with a nose so Cyranesque that he's taken for a great writer, "grafted" onto twentieth-century Japanese literature. The book is a bit clumsy. To begin with, the idea that such an odd-looking character could have a "twin brother" whom he could conveniently pretend to be at key moments, in order to avoid unwanted attention, is unworthy of Bellatin: ever since Borges, readers have come to expect a lot more from "imaginary" authors, and supposed incunabula have to do a little better than this to satisfy our hunger. At any rate, I doubt Bellatin would have published this book without Ximena Berecochea's suggestive photographs, which lend the book a nice iconographic framework (these photos serve as "proof" of the author's existence). So, what we have is a sort of wobbly literary installation, supported by the avant-garde's genre-crossing ambitions. But as an installation, it runs the risk of being ephemeral; and as far as novels with photos go, I prefer the genius of W. G. Sebald, to whom no one could remain indifferent.

I must concede, however, that *Shiki Nagaoka: una nariz de ficción* was the work in which I clearly saw Bellatin's master strokes, which are delightful indeed, as long as they're not taken as precepts. For instance, in "Treaty on a Guarded Language," a text within the novel attributed to the imaginary author, Big Nose claims that "it is only through the reading of translated texts that the true essence of what is literary comes clear, for unlike what some scholars claim, in no way is that essence to be found in language."

I see the supremacy of translation over originality that Bellatin's character voices as the key to interpreting his entire oeuvre. In this way, *Salón de belleza* and *Poeta ciego* "translate" terminal illness and secret societies, premeditatively taking their objects out of focus. When his translation decrees infidelity to the original, I like Bellatin; it's when he's pretending to be faithful to *The Tale of Genji* and Akutagawa that he leaves me cold.

The characters in *Flores* (2001) all have one thing in common: severe genetic deformations resulting from highly toxic drugs prescribed to pregnant women. The novel's mutants travel the world, looking for the right way to "translate" their religion or sexuality, given their deformities. Scientist Olaf Zumfelde is the inventor of the medications, and he and his secretary Henriette Wolf are the couple, half Lucifer and half bureaucrat, in charge of either slamming shut or leaving ajar the doors of the mutants seeking compensation. With its thirty-five short chapters, *Flores* is the botanical picture album of a jungle of mutilation and excess, in need of no supplementary photographs to effectively produce its chilling effect. Among its characters, the adopted Kuhn twins stand out, as do Alba the Poet and Amante Otoñal (Autumn Lover), each depicted with Bellatin's astonishing skill for sketching disconcerting characters in a few light brushstrokes.

Regardless of my preference for one type of "translation" over the other, some of Bellatin's characters never cease to amaze me. Beautiful and sad, whether obsessive or innovative they are aware, as we read in *Flores*, of the fact that "you have to wait a few years until, with time, the body naturally transmits its true defects." Bellatin's novels show how translation—taken as the essence of any literary action—rids disease, amputation, and esoteric forms of conspiracy of any moral content. He's fascinated by the symptomatology of our time, eager to monopolize misfortune—as has been done—and obviously finds misfortune to be the way to diagnose the human condition. Bellatin observes with the aseptic morbid curiosity of a nurse: loveless and pitiless, but meticulously efficient as he cleans and dresses the pustules of the sick.

In recent books like *Jacobo el mutante* (2002) and *Perros héroes* (2003), however, Bellatin has given the impression that he's one of those writers for whom literature is not big enough for his talent, one of those who aspire to transcend literature via the multimedia market basket. With installations, "happenings," and generally crazy ideas, if he pulls our leg any more we'll all be double-amputees. And that's a shame for an author who embodies Leclerc's adage, "The style is the man himself."

SELECTED BIBLIOGRAPHY
Obra reunida, Alfaguara, Mexico, 2005.
Lecciones para una liebre muerta, Anagrama, Barcelona, 2005.
La jornada de la mona y el paciente, Almadía, Oaxaca, 2006.
El gran vidrio. Tres autobiografías, Anagrama, Barcelona, 2009.
Chinese Checkers, trans. Cooper Renner, Ravenna, 2007.
Beauty Salon, trans. Kurt Hollander, City Lights, 2009.

BENÍTEZ, FERNANDO
(Mexico City, 1912 – 2000)

Benítez was a new breed of Mexican intellectual, a journalist who avoided the nineteenth-century temptations of bureaucracy, poetry, and bohemia and instead became a rigorous, intuitive "organizer" of culture. Using a format that he turned into a classic—that of the cultural supplement slipped into the pages of a newspaper or magazine with national circulation—Benítez waged impressive battles against the mercantile disinterest and political servitude of the Mexican press. His greatest victory was to decree high culture's inclusion in the paper while simultaneously asserting writers' right to political dissidence. Trained at *El Nacional*, the seat of cultural nationalism in the thirties, Benítez had to wait until the postwar era to undertake his foundational projects: "Mexico in Culture," the cultural supplement in *Novedades* (1949–1961) and even more importantly, "Culture in Mexico," the *Siempre!* supplement (1961–1970).

Benítez revolutionized graphic design (with the invaluable help of painter Vicente Rojo) and turned his supplements into a focal point for new Latin American literature. With the *Siempre!* supplement, he put his weight behind a new intellectual elite barely registering on the public's radar at the time, yet destined to become the critical conscience of the waning Mexican Revolution. In the sixties, while the regime's old intellectuals formed a procession of dark shadows headed for Hades, Benítez lent a hand to young writers eager to transcend political marginality and a moral underground, letting them start working (or picturing themselves) as actors on the national stage. They owe him a lot, as writers like Carlos Fuentes* and Carlos Monsiváis* have acknowledged on innumerable occasions, for without Benítez as a friend and mentor they would likely not have ventured—in the period from the union uprisings in the late fifties to the student movements of '68—to dissent or gained the political credibility that democratic society would eventually bestow upon them for their actions. With his protest for the murder of peasant leader Rubén Jaramillo in 1961 and his confidence in the democratic opening of President Luis Echeverría ten years later, Benítez was a pragmatic liberal who never intended to break with the Mexican Revolution's regime, having experienced both its repressive narrow-mindedness and its magnanimity.

Benítez had a long and happy old age, the patriarch of an intellectual elite who followed in his footsteps and rewarded him with little projects that allowed him to use his splendid talent for organizing events. For instance, *Sábado de unomásuno* (1977–1983) and *La Jornada Semanal* (1984–1989) were supplements where he trained a new generation of writers and journalists who worshipped him as a living relic of cultural nationalism and Latin American cosmopolitanism, a tireless source of anecdotes and, in a uniquely Mexican way, a beacon of the institutional left. Benítez's novels (*El rey viejo*, 1959 and *El agua envenenada*, 1961) make for modest reading, and can't compete with his magnitude as an "organizer" of culture. He'll be remembered best for his wonderful report, *Los indios de México* (1967–1981), the work of an amateur ethnographer whose insights and misconceptions created the image that intellectuals had—at least until the 1994 uprisings—of indigenous life. Comrade and phony, snob and *indigenista*, elitist and popular, Benítez was a master, beyond any shadow of a doubt, eminent among twentieth-century Mexicans.

SELECTED BIBLIOGRAPHY
Los indios de México, vols. I–V, ERA, Mexico, 1967–1981.
Los indios de México. Antología, prologue by Carlos Fuentes, ed. Héctor Manjarrez, ERA, Mexico, 1989.

BERMÚDEZ, MARÍA ELVIRA
(Durango, Durango, 1912 – Mexico City, 1988)

In a city with no mentors, Bermúdez satisfied her need for intellectual nourishment by conversing with aspiring writers. Her hospitality also guaranteed candor, courtesy, and good cheer. A literary woman, she listened raptly to the experimentalist and avant-garde lectures of those preaching the gospels of a new, twentieth-century literature whose rhetoric was foreign to her. This in no way denotes ignorance. A professional critic for decades, Bermúdez was a voracious reader of new literature, particularly Mexican, and wasn't afraid of the likes of Jorge Aguilar Mora* or Humberto Guzmán. She also anthologized Mexican fantastical and crime fiction. [. . .] *Diferentes razones tiene la muerte* (1953) was the only novel she published. But her best stories were published toward the end of her life, in collections such as *Detente, sombra* (1984), *Cuentos herejes* (1984), *Muerte a la zaga* (1985), and *Encono de hormigas (y otros relatos)* (1987). A few of her stories are absolutely delightful, totally faithful to the genre she defended. And her feverishly active later years coincided with a new type of detective fiction that she—as well as Antonio Helu and Rafael Bernal— helped pioneer. When I look back now on her debates with Rafael Ramírez Heredia and Paco Ignacio Taibo II, writers of a retaliatory literature focused on social decay and revolutionary dreams, it's easy for me to say that I prefer Bermúdez's innocence. [. . .] Our fairy godmother dissociated herself from the century and its irritating aesthetics. Happily ensconced in her home, by the fire, she carried on romantic conversations, just as Charles Nodier would have wanted, at a time when old grannies were supposed to be telling children stories about buried treasures and princes. Chesterton's humor and Sir Arthur Conan Doyle's riddles were here daily bread. It was probably Juan José Reyes, her grandson, who gave her Fernando Savater's *La infancia recuperada*, which surely provoked a crafty smile. In it, Savater, a young modern, a Spanish man, an essayist, sides with her, a Mexican old woman feverishly cultivating anachronistic, Anglo-Saxon-style short stories, the woman who wrote the prologue to Emilio Salgari's *Captain Thunder* in the immortal Sepan Cuantos collection. Bermúdez's literary taste favors writers like Reyes,* Bioy Casares, and Borges, whose stories fuse mathematical analysis with fantastical imagination. María Elvira was the spark that jumps from the heat of the hearth, the fire that starts the tale (*Servidumbre y grandeza de la vida literaria*, 1988).

SELECTED BIBLIOGRAPHY
Detente, sombra, UAM, Mexico, 1984.
Muerte a la zaga, SEP, Mexico, 1985.
Encono de hormigas, Universidad Veracruzana, Xalapa, 1987.

BLANCO, ALBERTO
(Mexico City, 1951)

Alberto Blanco's poetry, almost all of which is published in *El corazón del instante* (1998) and *La hora y la neblina* (2005), is more impressive in its tone than its volume. His tone picks up on a multicultural mélange of mysticisms, especially those legitimized by the old California beatniks of yore: Chinese and Japanese poetry, Suzuki-style Zen, and lots of Castaneda dispensing the knowledge of North American Indians. Blanco gives the impression of being a very varied poet who, rather than celebrating nature per se, exalts both painting and landscapes as expressions of *inner* life. *Antes de nacer* (1983), his most ambitious book, is a more graphic than poetic attempt at illustrating DNA, and one flawed more by monotony than radicalism.

Blanco is part of an eclectic school that by 1919 Max Weber had already critically reprimanded in the essay "Science as a Vocation," claiming that "They are ready to play at decorating a private chapel with pictures of the saints that they have picked up in all sorts of places, or to create a surrogate by collecting experiences of all kinds that they endow with the dignity of a mystical sanctity—and which they then hawk around the book markets" (trans. Rodney Livingstone).

This new-age mysticism, more a pantheistic "we're all part of the cosmos" ideology than any complex form of religiosity, is also the source of Blanco's best book, *Cuenta de los guías* (1992). This prose-poetry road trip is in dialogue with Kerouac's *On the Road*, and in it Blanco shows an exceptional and precise command over his own wonder. By traveling the long road to Tijuana, Blanco transforms the city into the center of romantic experience, a vortex of cultural exchanges and semantic translations that reveals the richness of Mexico's western border. Blanco claims that a creator can't be proud, and yet no other Mexican poet is as self-absorbed, a bard turned clairvoyant, speaking truths from which sometimes—not paradoxically—very inspired poems arise. I would be hard put to say whether Blanco—who's had countless disciples and is obsessed with the difference between "bearing fruit" and "leaving a mark"—has left a seed or just a footprint, worn away by a peculiar time that was so intense, so brief.

SELECTED BIBLIOGRAPHY

El corazón del instante, FCE, Mexico, 1998.

La soledad de los optimistas, Cal y arena, Mexico, 2004.

La hora y la neblina, FCE, Mexico, 2005.

Veinte aventuras de la literatura mexicana, Conaculta, Mexico, 2006.

Dawn of the Senses: Selected Poems of Alberto Blanco, preface by Jose Emilio Pacheco, City Lights, 1995.

A Cage of Transparent Words: A Selection of Poems, ed. Paul B. Roth, translated by eight translators, Bitter Oleander Press of New York, 2007.

BLANCO, JOSÉ JOAQUÍN
(Mexico City, 1951)

For about a decade, in the seventies and eighties, José Joaquín Blanco was the most prominent and productive literary critic in Mexico. In *La Cultura en México* and in *Nexos*, he wrote brilliant, unique reviews, and his articles courageously used the first person, making decisive contributions to a democratic acceptance of homosexuality. Both his gracefully fluent journalistic style and his fighting spirit worked in his favor. In every one of my books I've recognized how indebted I am to him, as I am one of his early readers, although I also think that Blanco's cult spirit made him a more marginal character, deaf to almost any sound not coming from the conversations and rumors at his own church.

Of Blanco's extensive bibliography, which includes poetry, novels, and *crónicas*, I'd like to make special note of his munificent and broadminded essays, which lent renewed vigor to Mexican literary criticism, as is notable in *Retratos con paisaje* (1979) and *La paja en el ojo* (1980). In addition, in *Se llamaba Vasconcelos* (1977), Blanco changed Mexicans' perception of the Mexican Revolution's cultural legacy, at least for those of us who could hardly recognize our founding fathers by the streets named after them. And *Crónica de la poesía mexicana* (1981), despite ideological and organizational oversimplifications, offered the first clear perspective on our new poetic horizon in years. I am less convinced by his work as a historian of colonial letters (*Esplendores y miserias de los criollos: La literatura de la Nueva España, I y II*, 1989), in which Blanco's fine sensibilities run up against slightly sloppy scholarship.

I have seen Blanco two or three times in my life, and we've never spoken. But his self-confident ease and sound judgment in essays on Gide, Pellicer,* and Stendhal are inextricably and intimately linked to my training as a critic. In *Pastor y ninfa. Ensayos de literatura moderna* (1996) and *Crónica literaria. Un siglo de escritores mexicanos* (1996), which anthologize most of his essays, it's easy to see that Blanco is one of the few Mexican literary critics to whom we should be grateful, not for a handful of opinions, but for an entire oeuvre.

SELECTED BIBLIOGRAPHY

Se llamaba Vasconcelos: Una evocación crítica, FCE, Mexico, 1977.

Crónica de la poesía mexicana, Katún, Mexico, 1981.

Pastor y ninfa. Ensayos sobre literatura moderna, Cal y Arena, Mexico, 1996.

Crónica literaria. Un siglo de escritores mexicanos, Cal y Arena, Mexico, 1996.

Poemas y elegías, Cal y Arena, Mexico, 2000.

Albúm de pesadillas mexicanas, ERA, Mexico, 2003.

BOLAÑO, ROBERTO

(Santiago de Chile, 1953 – Barcelona, Spain, 2003)

The most influential Mexican novel in recent history was written by a Chilean: Roberto Bolaño. *Los detectives salvajes* (1998; *The Savage Detectives*, 2007) is precisely the Latin American odyssey we'd been waiting for, and as such is also a reflection on literature in general. I'd like to start by saying that Juan García Madero, the aspiring young poet whose diary opens the novel and whose testimony magisterially closes it, represents the universal Immature Being—to use Gombrowicz-style capitalization—that is every literature lover; he is a kid who confronts, in rapid succession, sexual initiation and his vicarious veneration of a literary community. Through his narration of the absurd adventures of the ghost-like, peripatetic fathers of "visceral realism"—a caricature of every avant-garde movement—Bolaño presents a hypothesis on the condition of the contemporary writer.

The Savage Detectives is a literary novel, a detective story, an "exquisite corpse," a roman à clef, and a code to be broken. Between political radicalism and sexual angst, countless Latin American writers have run away, literally or figuratively; countless writers have been Ulises Lima and Arturo Belano: sycophants genuflecting before Rimbaud and Marx, second-rate editors, AWOL poets, occasional traffickers, detectives in search of a Holy Grail that will make sense of the many types of literary failure.

Bolaño lived in Mexico in the seventies, and when he died a friend said, "He was a Mexican writer who never came back to Mexico." *The Savage Detectives* is also a book about Mexico, and quite possibly the most important novel a foreigner has written about this country since Malcolm Lowry's *Under the Volcano* (1949). The ironic assurance of his perspective, his prodigious memory for reconstructing *chilango*—Mexico-City Spanish—and the way he posits Mexico City as one of the cultural capitals of the planet lead me to such an assertion. Or perhaps my faith in his abilities is simply the result of the fact that Bolaño is the only author I know to have noticed that "time when night sinks into night, though never all of a sudden, the white-footed Mexico City night, a night that endlessly announces her arrival, I'm coming, I'm coming, but is a long time coming, as if she too, the devil, had stayed behind to watch the sunset, the incomparable sunsets of Mexico . . ." (trans. Natasha Wimmer).

An annotated edition of *The Savage Detectives* would no doubt make for a particularly delectable stroll through the literary historiography of the past thirty years. But the book's essence resides in Bolaño's oddly Mexican ways, the result of a spirited life that spent exactly the right amount of time with us to avoid falling in love or coming to hate or—worse—getting bored. During the seventies, history and politics deemed Mexico and Chile would develop some close connections. In literature, Bolaño was their most unexpected and everlasting result. (2003)

Bolaño was a true poet, in the oldest and most legendary sense of the word. Not all great novelists turn into poets as Bolaño did, not all of them can become that wise man who gathers the scattered tribe and in so doing reveals to them a new order of things, a foundational tale that modifies both the origin and the purpose—if there is one—of the adventure we call "life," the one that an entire community of scouts—that is, readers—believes in. In just one decade, the decade that turned out to be the last of his life, Bolaño created a whole new literature, in which his modest verse, speculative short stories, and often perfect novellas turned out to be mere mountain huts, little rest stops on the way up to the twin peaks of *Los detectives salvajes* and *2666*, a posthumous book comprised of five novels in one. Having reached the summit, readers, like Verne's Professor Lidenbrock and companions on the volcano Sneffels in Iceland, must descend to the center of the earth.

That Bolaño died in 2003 at age fifty is not insignificant: his oeuvre has ended. Joseph Brodsky, another great writer who died too young and who, unlike Bolaño, had no faith in the possibility of prose containing poetry, once made a claim that I feel bound to quote here: "For some odd reason, the expression 'death of a poet' always sounds somewhat more concrete than 'life of a poet.' Perhaps this is because both 'life' and 'poet,' as words, are almost synonymous in their positive vagueness. Whereas 'death'—even as a word—is about as definite as a poet's own production, i.e., a poem, the main feature of which is its last line. Whatever a work of art consists of, it runs to the finale which makes for its form and denies resurrection. After the last line of a poem nothing follows except literary criticism. So when we read a poet, we participate in his death, or in the death of his works."

On that note, we can introduce the first descending circle of *2666*, *La parte de los críticos* (*The Part About the Critics*): four professors set off in search of Benno von Archimboldi, a German novelist whose international prestige is increased by his decades-old disappearance, a physical absence which deprives his work of the moral, political, or media backing that his presence would confer. *La parte de los críticos* is an elegant lampoon, delivered via breathless narration, of the commercial and academic innards of the "World Republic of Letters," its rites and colloquia, grueling long-haul flights, book market, and those who live either to sustain it or to tear it down. Their hunting trip will take the critical quartet—whose lives are both romantically and professionally entangled—to Santa Teresa, a carbon copy of Mexico's Ciudad Juárez, which Bolaño posits as the blind spot of the universe.

Anyone who's already read Bolaño will find this to be a sophisticated, cosmopolitan version of the plot elements of *The Savage Detectives*: the near-mystical faith placed in the group's Chilean narrator, the young clique, the "on the road" literary community whose road trip is their first real critical education. The professors, however, are not alone. As literary bureaucrats, they must confront, night after night and in hotel after hotel, the constant oneiric presence of that other voice that warns them, in their dreams, of the futility of their enterprise. And Benno von Archimboldi himself, a peregrine falcon about whom we know little at this stage (we find out more in book five), is himself, more than prey to hold up like a trophy, a savage detective to the nth degree. It doesn't really matter if the Mexican "infrarealists" who inspired early Bolaño were not nice guys (or good writers). Neither were the vampires of French Romanticism that Mario Praz ridiculed. What matters is what they left behind: the magnificence of a literary group conceived of as a fugitive band of outlaws and a beginners' academy. In the same way, Benno von Archimboldi represents a figure that the twentieth century had already intuited (think Cocteau, Roger Vailland, or René Daumal) but that only Bolaño has managed to represent in its entirety: the avant-garde writer as classic hero.

La parte de Amalfitano, the second novel, leaves behind the eulogizing to portray a loner, a Chilean professor left in Santa Teresa not so much to the hand of God as to Schopenhauer's voice in his head at night and the brutal murders of women being committed on the US-Mexico border. Amalfitano, in one of the many unforgettable images sprinkled throughout *2666*, hangs a wet copy of Galician writer Rafael Dieste's *El testamento geométrico*, a reflection on space, out on a clothesline, in the wind. That gesture—in the most Chilean of the five novels—tells me a lot. Huidobro's love of cinematic momentum and film noir, Nicanor Parra's antipoems, the "panic fables" written by Alejandro Jodorowsky (that other Chilean Mexican), Enrique Lihn's "instantaneous" poems, and other less prestigious precedents allowed Bolaño to portray the avant-garde as classicist and its practitioners as updated versions of Ulysses, Jason and the Argonauts, and Aeneas.

But the second novel essentially serves for Amalfitano and his daughter to introduce us to the unreal atmosphere and ferocious brutality of Santa Teresa that will make reading *La parte de los crímenes* (*The Part About the Crimes*) almost unbearable. Before that, though, comes *La parte de Fate* (*The Part About Fate)*, Bolaño's homage to US culture and the decisive role that "border" figures such as the black journalist, the preacher, the impossible Communist Party activist in Brooklyn, and the conspiracy theorist—so utterly American—played in his formation. Again he's exceptional: no other Latin American writer (and maybe only Cormac McCarthy as far as US writers go) has come to grips with the symbolic density of the border the way he has. The numinous, bloody depiction of Santa Teresa turns so many other Mexican (and Spanish) border texts into simple journalism at best and a "folklorization" of misery at worst. The same is true of all of the writers who attempted to parody German and Viennese interwar literature. The appearance of a truly great writer compels the rest of us to surrender our pens. That's just merciless natural selection; it's what literature is made of.

Artaud saw Mexico as the mystical center of the world; Bolaño believes Mexico's femicides conceal the horrifying secrets of the earth. Using Sergio González Rodríguez's* *Huesos en el desierto* (2002)—a book-length investigative journalism piece on the Juárez murders—as moral precedent, Bolaño dedicates *La parte de los crímenes* to compulsively deciphering Santa Teresa's horrific crimes. I didn't think it possible to make literature of so much horror while still honoring both the victims and literature. It's one of art's greatest moral impasses. I was wrong. Whether the crimes are to be blamed on waning interest in serial murders or an exponential increase in satanic rites is another matter, one that depends, in *2666*, on Bolaño's narrative strategy.

Either way, the fact is that Benno von Archimboldi ended up in Santa Teresa and, in search of him, so did the quartet of critics. Once we reach the fourth novel, after having heard the testimonies of solitary professor Amalfitano and gregarious journalist Oscar Fate, *La parte de los crímenes* becomes something more than an example of apocalyptic noir. Instead, it's a brutal depiction of Mexico, no longer represented by the garden Paul Valéry saw it as—where Bolaño observes Mexico City writers adrift—but instead by Santa Teresa / Ciudad Juárez, the final frontier of many worlds, the terminus of industrial society, Christianity, the Enlightenment and its aura, and a long, abusive etcetera that only begins to demonstrate the eschatological force of Bolaño, a writer who is sometimes hard to read because it's so unusual to find truth and literature in the same book, as Goethe dreamed.

La parte de Archimboldi (*The Part About Archimboldi*), the last of *2666*'s novels, starts off seeming like a parody of Robert Walser and then turns into what seems like the novel you'd imagine Benno von Archimboldi to have written in Santa Teresa, which ends by solving the mystery of the novelist's identity without invalidating the reader's hunches. In *La parte de Archimboldi* Bolaño leads us by the hand—as if it were necessary, as if other great writers had not already done so—through the abattoirs of the twentieth century. Nevertheless, Bolaño assumes that his readers know a lot (as much as he does) about the crimes of Bolshevism and the Nazi occupation of the Soviet Union, and also knows (this "ideal reader" does) how European artists have depicted the war. But by using expressionism in Ansky's notebooks (another novel within the novel), creating Grosz-like caricatures, and demonic questioning, as if erratically overcome by Gogol's soul, Bolaño's genius comes through, given that our familiarity with the material he's manipulating will always be surprisingly inferior to his own. It's as if the whole novel were aspiring to link two centuries. I think it is. And that its author was Latin American follows a certain Western historical logic.

Postmodern theoreticians can't stand grand literary narratives and they'll find it hard to classify *2666*, a posthumous novel that was most likely unfinished. In the last few pages, when we know who Benno von Archimboldi really is and why he's in Santa Teresa, there are a few tentative paragraphs and brusque temporal jumps—as when we read that the hero is online and using a laptop and then, pages later, read that as he neither read the paper nor listened to the radio, he found out that the Berlin Wall had fallen from his editor's widow, the provocative Mrs. Bubis. But if not for these trivial details, we wouldn't even need Ignacio Echevarría's editorial note about the state of the manuscripts when Bolaño died.

Bolaño thought that all poetry, in any of its multiple disciplines, either was or could be contained in a novel. Only through poetry, as conceived of in

German Romanticism, could Bolaño write *2666*, a novel that takes the entire universe as its setting, which is to say, it takes on the entire era of literature as defined by the twentieth century. And if the setting is the world as universal concentration camp then the major theme is the relationship between literature and evil, the revoltingly hellish drudgery that abounds in truces, renditions, and prisoner exchanges. And if *2666*'s motif is literature and evil, then Benno von Archimboldi, the protagonist, personifies the myth of the writer as anti-hero, nihilist in appearance only, the actor who can recapture the order of pansophy, that secret underground oxygenation that Novalis so craved.

SELECTED BIBLIOGRAPHY

Los detectives salvajes, Anagrama, Barcelona, 1997.

2666, a compilation of five novels: *La parte de los críticos, La parte de Amalfitano, La parte de Fate, La parte de los crímenes,* and *La parte de Archimboldi*, Anagrama, Barcelona, 2004.

By Night in Chile, trans. Chris Andrews, New Directions, New York, 2003.

Distant Star, trans. Chris Andrews, Harvill, London, 2004.

Amulet, trans. Chris Andrews, New Directions, New York, 2006.

The Savage Detectives, trans. Natasha Wimmer, Farrar, Straus and Giroux, New York, 2007.

Last Evenings on Earth, trans. Chris Andrews, New Directions, New York, 2007.

2666, trans. Natasha Wimmer, Farrar, Straus and Giroux, New York, 2008.

The Skating Rink, trans. Chris Andrews, New Directions, New York, 2009.

BONIFAZ NUÑO, RUBÉN

(Córdoba, Veracruz, 1923)

In *Fuego de pobres* (1961), his most important book, Bonifaz Nuño took the old dream of new Hispanic literature and made it come true, creating a poem that fuses the lost grandeur of the Nahuatl with the Greco-Latin world. Despite his frequent (and generally successful) forays into the sphere of popular literature, Bonifaz Nuño is not an easy poet. All of his commentators draw attention to his mastery of meter, perhaps the most challenging in all of modern Mexican poetry. But that expertise often constrains and contains poetic expression, making for dull, boring poems that take on the least attractive characteristics of the baroque. In his early phase, from *La muerte del ángel* (1945) to *El manto y la corona* (1958), Bonifaz Nuño was a doleful bard whose maudlin verses spoke of the academic's descent into the hells of sensuality and heartbreak. But after *Fuego de pobres* he reached great heights, publishing a series of exceptional books including *Siete de espadas* (1966), *El ala del tigre* (1969), and *La flama en el espejo* (1971). These compositions are extraordinary verbal steles, their inscriptions running the gamut from amorous fragments that might have been found on the walls of Pompeii, to the premonitory laments of the pre-Columbian school of Netzahualcóyotl, to contemporary sentimental ballads you might happen to hear in a taxi. In his old age, Bonifaz Nuño has abandoned the baroque in favor of clarity and musicality, in books such as *Albur de amor* (1987) and *El templo de su cuerpo* (1992), which are beautiful cantatas to the suppressed rage of loves lost. Though born in the mountainous Veracruz city of Córdoba, this well-spoken poet has skillfully expressed, like few others, the poor, the compassionate silence and emotional reserve of the *altiplano* Mexican, heir to those ancient classic traditions that Bonifaz Nuño so fervently blended together in his early days. A poet with such an uncanny ear, even in his missteps, demonstrates the rich nuances of twentieth-century Mexican poetry throughout his oeuvre.

SELECTED BIBLIOGRAPHY
De otro modo lo mismo, FCE, Mexico, 1979.
Albur de amor, FCE, Mexico, 1987.
Versos (1978–1994), FCE, Mexico, 1996.

BOULLOSA, CARMEN
(Mexico City, 1954)

On reading Carmen Boullosa's considerable oeuvre once again, I sense a conflict—sometimes fruitful and other times frustrating—between two different temperaments. Starting right with her first two personal, fantastical, slightly crude novels published in the late eighties (*Mejor desaparece* and *Antes*) and working her way through twelve other novels, some plays, a couple of short story collections, and an intensely personal body of poetry, to her most ambitious work, *La otra mano de Lepanto* (2005), Boullosa is not a writer who leaves readers indifferent. She fascinates and irritates: within the same book (and I've read many), whether poetry or prose, I've felt both enthusiasm and vexation.

On the one hand, we have a poet with an incredibly powerful, lyrical voice (many of those who today pass for poets would be thrilled to have it) whose linguistic command is carried out with hyperactive theatricality, creating a veritable cast of characters who in fact are all one, using a thousand different masks: a heroine addicted to erotic confession. In this vein, sometimes lucid and others just exhibitionist, Boullosa fears neither God nor men, and her characters are confessional, whether out of bad taste, childishness, or erratic calculation. It's hard not to find fascinating lines in her poetry, in *La salvaja* (1989), *La delirios* (1998), *La bebida* (2002), *Salto de mantarraya (y otros dos)* (2004), and in some of her novels, particularly in the disquieting way she projects her own voice onto the legend of Cleopatra in *De un salto descabalga la reina* (2002; *Cleopatra Dismounts*, 2003), in which a poetic voice triumphantly sweeps over the prose.

In the other part of her oeuvre, Boullosa has spent her energy repressing or taming that same spirit, giving way to "academic" novels. Interestingly, she writes both styles simultaneously. I take Boullosa's "academic" novels (each very different from the next) to mean those in which she sets out—with varying degrees of success—on a mission: to write a novel that could be considered science fiction (*Cielos de la tierra*, 1997); to trace the reincarnation of woman's body through history (*Duerme*, 1994); to settle scores with reality and nostalgia (*Treinta años*, 1999); to provide a retelling of pirate tales (*Son vacas, somos puercos*, 1991 and *El médico de los piratas*, 1992; *They're Cows, We're Pigs*, 1997); to give in to Mexicanist imaginings (*La milagrosa*, 1993 and *Llanto. Novelas imposibles*, 1992). Boullosa has also written a novel about a woman painter in the Renaissance (*La virgen y el violín*, 2008) and another in which she plays with the idea of fiction, meta-text, and vernacular (*La novela perfecta*, 2006). In *La otra mano de Lepanto*, her most ambitious work to date—the most finely wrought, displaying true baroque spirit—we see the results of her disciplined approach (or her stubbornness): such faithfulness to Cervantes's model makes even the finest adventure novel cumbersome.

As we can see, the savage poet lives side by side with the novelist who has a very professional command of history and fiction, with one eye on academic vernacular (feminism, gender studies, Mexicanness, the New World and its hermeneutic treasures) and the other on the outpourings of her poetry scene. Luckily, the array of themes in her fiction is somewhat deceptive, and in the end the same protean (female) protagonist reigns supreme, whether in the guise of María La Bailadora in the Battle of Lepanto, Claire (her Woolf-esque representation of Orlando), the heroines who loved Montezuma II, or the ventriloquist she uses to speak via Cleopatra.

As a critic who's followed her work from the very beginning, I'm slightly obsessed with the monist need to find synthesis in that which by nature is doubled. Perhaps it's a didactic urge, or a compulsive desire to create order. But I can say that *El complot de los Románticos* (2008) concentrates all of Boullosa's talent; it's the book where her two natures most harmoniously coalesce. There were signs of this maturity in the opening fifty pages of her last novel, *El Velázquez de París* (2007), in which Boullosa co-opts the conversation of a dirty old man in a bistro and has her way with it, until she feels compelled to paint another edifying picture, this time a portrait of the "expulsion of the Moriscos" worthy of Velázquez.

A funny novel with prose that flows like that of her best poems without risking their pathos, *El complot de los Románticos* is entertaining, musical, lively, richly vernacular without being crass, learned, witty, and surprising. Once again everything seems fresh, as in her early works. This all revolves around combining Cervantes's *Journey to Parnassus* and the *Divine Comedy* (and a bit of Michael Ende) with another "descent" into the Mexican inferno. With that comically gargantuan task, Boullosa creates her own sensational Dante, one who travels to Mexico on the back of a rat and doesn't understand Britney Spears or anything else about the contemporary world, but allows himself to be led along by Boullosa's eternal, savage woman, this time a middle-aged Mexican novelist who acts as his guide.

Part remake of Polanski's *Dance of the Vampires*, part rereading of Mexican history in which Boullosa rewinds from the twenty-first to the sixteenth century, *El complot de los Románticos* offers a panorama of muralism (both pictorial and narrative, as in Carlos Fuentes*). And she doesn't shy away from offering harsh political opinions, occasionally giving the novel a pamphleteering tone. The whole thing is Boullosa through and through.

When her "romantics" rise up in rebellion in Madrid's Teatro de la Zarzuela and spoil the meeting of dead-but-resuscitated writers at the literature conference, that's when Boullosa changes the plot of her modern-day *Journey to Parnassus*, a touch that has irked some reviewers. I think she couldn't have made it better, taking up arms against the literature of her times instead, parodying intertextuality and its linguistic Chinese boxes. It's more important that the characters' hilarious adventures are the parody of the novel-within-a-novel, which turns out to be by Dolores Veintimilla, a nineteenth-century Romantic from Quito, glossed in turn by Rosario Castellanos,* the stoic matriarch of Mexican literature, which then takes us—how could it not?—to Sor Juana Inés de la Cruz, and from there back to Boullosa herself. Both diversion and parody of *écriture feminine*, its mythology, high points, and embarrassments, *El complot de los Románticos* is also an act of self-criticism that reinvigorates the significance of Boullosa's entire oeuvre.

SELECTED BIBLIOGRAPHY

Mejor desaparace, Oceáno, Mexico, 1987.

Antes, Vuelta, Mexico, 1989.

La salvaja, FCE, Mexico, 1989.

Son vacas, somos puercos, ERA, Mexico, 1991.

Llanto. Novelas imposibles, ERA, Mexico, 1992.

El médico de los piratas, Siruela, Madrid, 1992.

La milagrosa, ERA, Mexico, 1993.

Duerme, Alfaguara, Madrid, 1994.

Cielos de la tierra, Alfaguara, Madrid, 1997.

Treinta años, Alfaguara, Mexico, 1999.

La bebida, FCE, Mexico, 2002.

De un salto descabalga la reina, Debate, Madrid, 2002.

Salto de mantarraya (y otros dos), FCE, Mexico, 2004.

La otra mano de Lepanto, FCE, Mexico, 2005.

La novela perfecta. Un cuento largo, Alfaguara, Mexico, 2006.

El velázquez de París, Siruela, Madrid, 2007.

La virgen y el violín, Siruela, Madrid, 2008.

El complot de los Románticos, Siruela, Madrid, 2008.

Las paredes hablan, Siruela, Madrid, 2010.

They're Cows, We're Pigs, trans. Leland H. Chambers, Grove, New York, 1997.

Leaving Tabasco, trans. Geoff Hargreaves, Grove, New York, 2001.

Cleopatra Dismounts, trans. Geoff Hargreaves, Grove, New York, 2003.

BRACHO, CORAL
(Mexico City, 1951)

At the risk of employing tautological methodology, I'm going to use a poetic image to describe poetry. Bracho's verse strikes me as a crystal palace through whose windows we gaze out onto a greenhouse. Separated by a steamy pane, we can monitor the marvels and routines of a very particular animal and vegetable world. But this garden wasn't made for strolling or sitting under a tree reading. Both enchanting and enchanted, its plants are poisonous and the creatures living there pretend to be friendly but are not: a merciless "chain of being" governs this world. There to be observed, Bracho's poetry stands guard against any intrusive desire to violate its privacy and mess up a language that is at times too self-conscious of its own preciosity.

In addition to revealing the extreme sensibility of the poet herself, Coral Bracho's first books, *El ser que va a morir* (1982) and *Peces de piel fugaz* (later reissued together as *Bajo el destello líquido*), also reflect a very specific intellectual microclimate. Like her friends Jorge Aguilar Mora* and David Huerta,* Bracho was exceedingly aware of the fact that she was writing in the margins of Foucault, Barthes, and (almost didactically) Deleuze and Guatarri. The essayistic, philosophizing tendency of certain 1980s Mexican poets ran the risk, as Evodio Escalante noted at the time, of aging right along with the influence of the French thinkers. And on rereading *Bajo el destello líquido*, I found myself somehow irked by Bracho's use of theoretical buzzwords like "border," "sediment," "nucleus," "boundary," and, of course, "rhizome." But Bracho, architect and inhabitant of her own unique verbal edifice, was ahead of her time, and twenty years later those words sound mature: talismans that allowed a poet to open her own windows of perception.

After a silence of several years, Barcho published *La voluntad del ámbar* (1998) and *Ese espacio, ese jardín* (2003). While the first book's poetry is more pure and more exacting (and at times insipid, due to its own verbal economy), the second is a return to her earlier poetry, to that garden of old, but it's been weeded now, the ontologies pruned, it's a cleared field where vegetation gives way to transparency, a little world set apart from the "hypothetical observer" of *La voluntad del ámbar*.

Ese espacio, ese jardín is one long poem invoking childhood, a paradise lost that Bracho approaches, spurred on by the presence of death. The

poem is dramatic—although discreetly so like a brief mime or the Schoenberg composition *Pierrot lunaire*. This chamber piece is narrated by several characters, some animals (a fox, a jaguar), and a jester who speaks to
the children in that greenhouse where a normal yet numinous family live;
"su universo es la sal / que refulge un instante, y en otro instante / se dis-
uelve" ("their universe is the salt / that glitters an instant, and in another
instant / dissolves").

Feted for its melodious morphology, Bracho's poetry celebrates the origin
of species, the drama of the "three kingdoms" fatally condemned to complete the chain of being.

SELECTED BIBLIOGRAPHY
Bajo el destello líquido. Poesía 1977–1981, FCE, Mexico, 1988.
Huellas de luz, Conaculta, Mexico, 1994.
La voluntad del ámbar, ERA, Mexico, 1998.
Ese espacio, ese jardín, ERA, Mexico, 2003.
Si ríe el emperador, ERA, Mexico, 2010.

BRADU, FABIENNE

(Athis-Mons, France, 1954)

I don't think it's a coincidence that Bradu, a Frenchwoman, is one of Mexico's best literary critics. From her first book (*Señas particulares, escritora*,
1987) to *Antonieta* (1991) and right through to *Damas de corazón* (1994),
Bradu has been writing a fragmented literary history of Mexican women
that betrays a rigorous, deep-seated, captivating French-style moralism.
She uses a combination of mathematical exactitude and charm in her essayistic portraits of women, a genre that more than a few men (including Choderlos de Laclos, Sainte-Beuve, and Marcel Jouhandeau) have also
honored. Readers of *Damas de corazón* will find cameos of five women
who were the spice of life in twentieth-century Mexican letters: Consuelo
Suncín, María Asúnsolo, Machila Armida, Ninfa Santos, and Lupe Marín.
That they might be considered minor writers is no discredit to Bradu. After
all, who among us can be sure of achieving even secondary stature? Cultural history is built on the ruins of a huge cast of minor or anonymous

heroes without whom we would never have celebrated two or three true protagonists, which is all that any generation really allows itself. The five women Bradu chose for *Damas de corazón* were all important on the literary stage, and over the course of the twentieth century, their contributions have been key. From Suncín—the Salvadoran adventuress loved by José Vasconcelos,* Enrique Gómez Carrillo, and Count Saint-Exupéry—to Ninfa Santos—a magnetic force in the everyday life of the Mexican left—Bradu weaves together several chapters, including in them the vicissitudes of the muralist movement, which would have been very different without the dominating and awe-inspiring presence of Asúnsolo and Marín—Siqueiros's and Rivera's angels (and devils).

In 1983, Octavio Paz* protested against a Museo Nacional de Arte exhibition that drew misleading parallels between Frida Kahlo and Tina Modotti, whose positions in Mexican art cannot be compared. Paz ended his review by stating that the parallels between Kahlo and Modotti could be seen in the unwritten history of their passions, not in their art. In *Damas de corazón*, a sentimental history, Bradu responds to that need. As she did in *Antonieta*, she again sheds light on women's feelings, on the fuzzy boundary between public life and private emotion that these five women inhabited with an autonomy as enviable as it was indiscreet.

I suppose that Bradu, like other women—and men—of her generation, was a feminist. I'm using the term as an honorific, because she was strongly committed to equality of the sexes—in the same way as Roland, Stendhal, and George Sand—but jettisoned sentimentality and *hembrismo*, the Hispanic counterpart to machismo. Unlike many cultural publicists, Bradu shows no signs of exalting Woman simply for her assigned sex, a premise based entirely on women's supposed otherness. *Damas de corazón* is not an epic of the intellectually oppressed woman but a portrait of strong women who lived through marriage and adultery, private life and public commerce, artistic whims and political militancy with exactly the same passion as the men who abused them, idolized them, or were tormented by them. Bradu's women comprise a history of the powerful. While their power no doubt stems from their own lives, it's also portrayed beautifully in Bradu's prose. I have a particularly high regard for the fluency, force, and charm of her Spanish, the language she chose to adopt as her narrative motherland. Bradu portrays Mexican life in the precise ocher tones of the French moralism from which she inherited a love of maxims and incisive brevity [. . .] Her literary portraits of contemporary Mexican women like Antonieta Rivas Mercado and those included in *Damas de corazón* already form part of our most cherished Mexican memoirs, and her critical insight is of the sharpest and liveliest in Mexico (*Servidumbre y grandeza de la vida literaria*, 1998).

If it were possible to sum up the role of the literary portrait in French literature in a couple of words, I'd use Fabienne Bradu's description: it's "the voice of the mirror," an image that appears in place of our faces and tells us not who we are but who we're not, forcing us to look to others for our lost, yearned-for, or hypothetical identity. And the others whom we look to—that Otherness, to use the old, worn-out term—are the world of literature: faces, voices in the mirror. Bradu took this rich memoir style from French literature and melded it with the decision she made years ago to be a Mexican writer, writing (predictably, and fortunately) in elegant, intellectual, self-confident Spanish. Meeting the demands of that Franco-Mexican crossroads, she published *André Breton en México* (1996), *Benjamin Péret y México* (1998), and *Artaud, todavía* (2008), investigations into the surrealist masters' passion for Mexico. In *La voz del espejo* (2008), her latest collection of essays, Bradu adds one more name to her list: Émilie Noulet, the literary critic and Belgian translator who came to Mexico with the Spanish Civil War exiles and tried—though she was unable to complete the project—to publish Alfonso Reyes's* poetry in French.

Since her very first book (*Señas particulares, escritora*), Bradu has painted and drawn an impressive number of portraits with her words. I see (and sense, as someone who worked with her at the journal *Vuelta* for many years) Bradu's work as a twofold space: on the one hand, there's the private, almost intimate studio-workshop; and on the other, the gallery, open to the world, fashionable and yet traditional, noble. In the former she writes literary criticism and biographical psychology, shedding light on how Antonieta Rivas Mercado's mind worked before her tragic suicide in Notre Dame (in *Antonieta*, 1991); picks apart, one syllable at a time, the poetry of Gonzalo Rojas (*Otras sílabas sobre Gonzalo Rojas*, 2002); and documents the failure of a literary investigator trying to shed new light on the life of an artist we'd already stopped being curious about in *Artaud, todavía*.

That's the workshop. In the gallery, I celebrate Bradu's worldliness. She's certainly traveled. She's been to Chile several times, as is clear by her legendary friendship with the poet Rojas (*Las vergüenzas vitalicias: Diario de Chile*, 1999), and her trips to Asia are documented in two travel novels à la Paul Morand: first Japan in *El amante japonés* (2002) and then *El esmalte del mundo* (2006), about India. But Bradu's worldliness goes beyond any sort of touristic "avidity" (a quality the moderns share with no one) and she expresses her passion by capturing the image of other women in the world—including Consuelo Suncín de Saint-Exupéry, Ninfa Santos, and Machila Armida—in *Damas de corazón* (1994) and pricking Vasconcelos's feminine soul in one of her most sensitive portraits in *La voz del espejo*.

Bradu's literary portraits have often been unorthodox. In her 1987 book *Señas particulares*, she looks at seven Mexican writers who at the time were not too famous and had not been the subjects of many studies. She goes well beyond the academic and gives us curious personal insights into Josefina Vicens,* Elena Garro,* and Inés Arredondo.* Rosario Castellanos,* whom she admires for her incessant and at times shocking self-criticism, she also catches in a blatant contradiction in *La voz del espejo*: the Chiapas poet admires Simone de Beauvoir for writing publicly about "contingent love" affairs while simultaneously suffering the predictable turmoil they cause. There are also depictions of photographer Graciela Iturbide writing her unusual memoirs, of poet Manuel Ulacia on his way to Galta in India, and of Rafael Cadenas reading mysticism, which for Bradu—good Bretonian that she is—simply conveys the supernatural (whether reached via magic or esotericism) as the most complicated form of rationality.

Bradu's essays, like Balzac novels, are full of reappearing characters rebelling against the possibility of their destiny coming to a close. Julieta Campos is one, portrayed via her work and her character, both in life and after her death in 2007. In *La voz del espejo,* Antonieta Rivas Mercado reappears too. Bradu, it turns out, was able to catch her on film in the few minutes she appeared on screen. Octavio Paz and Julio Cortázar crop back up, defending themselves from the grave against the Argentines who deny them three times. Marguerite Duras, of all people, is back as the genius loci, and Bradu portrays her with a malice that, as is befitting in good portraiture, walks the line between reconciliation and recognition.

Recalling how Duras's international success ruffled a good portion of her old readers, Bradu says—in a passage I'll quote as an introduction to the style and content of *La voz del espejo*: "Shortly after the publication of *El amante*, when the presses at Minuit publisher were working day and night to meet booksellers' demands, someone stole a black Rolls-Royce on the French Riviera. The owner got his car back a short time later, something not unusual given the make of the car, but he complained bitterly that his copy of *El amante* had disappeared from the glove compartment. I also recall Marguerite Duras's elation on narrating the incident, as if reality had just avenged her of all life's displeasures: one of her novels turning out to be more in demand than a Rolls-Royce. Whether it was true or not, [the episode] became a way for her to go on and on about her Stalinist missteps and blind love of François Mitterrand. Peering out from behind thick spectacles, wrinkled as a Cambodian iguana, puffed up from booze and vests layered on like broken breastplates, ensconced in her haughty silences, Marguerite Duras—whether finally, or unfortunately—was crowned queen of French letters."

SELECTED BIBLIOGRAPHY

Señas particulares, escritora. Ensayos sobre escritoras mexicanas del siglo XX, FCE, Mexico, 1987.

Ecos de Páramo, FCE, Mexico, 1989.

Antonieta, 1900–1931, FCE, Mexico, 1991.

Damas de corazón, FCE, Mexico, 1994.

André Breton en México, Vuelta, Mexico, 1996.

Las vergüenzas vitalicias (Diario de Chile), Vid, Mexico, 1999.

Benjamin Péret y México, Aldus, Mexico, 1998.

El amante japonés, Planeta, Mexico, 2002.

El esmalte del mundo, Joaquín Mortiz, Mexico, 2006.

La voz del espejo, DGE Equilibrista/UNAM, Mexico, 2008.

Artaud, todavía, FCE, Mexico, 2008.

C

CARBALLIDO, EMILIO

(Córdoba, Veracruz, 1925 – Xalapa, Veracruz, 2008)

For some reason, Carballido, renowned as one of the greatest on the short list of twentieth-century Mexican playwrights, has been excluded from our narrative canon, despite the originality and nonconformity of his plays. His first novel (*La veleta oxidada*, 1954) still sounds highly contemporary, its conversations about atonal music setting the scene for a modest yet tragic denouement, and his more recent *Flor de abismo* (1994) still has a lot to offer. After rereading *Las visitaciones del diablo* (1965), I felt utterly perplexed at his exclusion. One of the most beautiful novels in all of modern Mexican literature, *Las visitaciones del diablo* made it to a fourth edition and came out in 1965, a key year in our national letters that also saw the publication of three other important works—*Farabeuf,* by Salvador Elizondo,* *Gazapo,* by Gustavo Sainz, and *La señal,* by Inés Arredondo.* Yet unlike those three, Carballido's novel seems to have been forgotten.

Las visitaciones del diablo is a pastiche of the nineteenth-century romantic melodrama. And at the end of the twentieth century, Carballido's rhetorical talent is still distinctive and inimitable, sensual and delightful. *Las visitaciones del diablo* is a classic, despite being neglected, a book full of the enduring myths of modern literature: the stranger who blows into town, upsetting quiet village life with his courtly chatter; a lackluster existence upended by a giddy love that flies in the face of convention; the crazies in the closet; the lovers eloping on a train to Lorenzo de Medici's "Canzone di Bacco."

The novel's intensity is similar to that of Arredondo's more traditional tales and, like Elizondo's *Farabeuf*, it seems to posit that plotlines are as infinite and varied as the time in which they're written. But more than any similarity to books written in the same period, *Las visitaciones del diablo* possesses the secret style of a playwright; it's a true work of drama, despite appearing on the surface to be "entertainment."

Las visitaciones del diablo is also "regional" literature, used in the noblest sense of a term that's often debased. I think that in mid- to late-twentieth-century Mexican literature, there really only is one "regional" literature, in the sense we mean when we refer, say, to Southern United States fiction or Provençal poetry: the literature of Veracruz, which is its own country in our novel world. Sergio Galindo,* Jorge López Páez,* Juan Vicente Melo,* and Sergio Pitol,* together with Carballido, really are a class unto themselves. And within that class, *Las visitaciones del diablo* must occupy a place of honor, along with Galindo's *Otilia Rauda*, Páez's *El solitario Atlántico*, Melo's *Fin de semana*, and Pitol's *Juegos florales*. Carballido's regionalism is actually a universalism, as is Flaubert's Normandy (*Servidumbre y grandeza de la vida literaria*, 1998).

SELECTED BIBLIOGRAPHY

Las visitaciones del diablo. Folletin romantico en XV partes, Joaquín Mortiz, Mexico, 1965.

Orinoco, Rosa de dos aromas y otras piezas dramáticas, FCE, México, 1994.

Obras narrativas, Instituto Veracruzano de Cultura, Mexico, 2005.

The Norther, trans. Margaret Sayers Peden, University of Texas Press, 1968.

The Golden Thread and Other Plays, trans. Margaret Sayers Peden, University of Texas Press, 1971.

CARBALLO, EMMANUEL
(Guadalajara, Jalisco, 1929)

Carballo has a distinguished curriculum: he promoted up-and-coming writers in the sixties, his bibliographies of nineteenth-century authors have multiple editions, and the contribution he made via his interviews was recognized in the collection *Protagonistas de la literatura mexicana* (1965 and 1986). Now that *Diario público 1966–1968* (2005) has been released, it's time we finally recognize Carballo's legacy and give him his due credit.

As a literary journalist, his influence was decisive in promoting and recognizing the *Ateneístas* and *Contemporáneos* as our modern classics. *Diario público 1966–1968* is both a chronicle of cultural life and a collection of his most important reviews. In many of them, Carballo's commentaries and analyses were spot-on—for example, his lack of faith in Fernando del Paso's* *José Trigo* (1966), which he deemed well conceived and ill achieved. He may have been overly impressed by José Agustín* and quite harsh (though not without reason) in his verdict on Juan García Ponce's early novels. He also covered poets and wrote of what he saw as the false promise of poet Marco Antonio Montes de Oca* and the ill-fated Raúl Navarrete (1942–1981). His friendship with Carlos Fuentes,* with whom he published *Revista Mexicana de Literatura* from 1955 to 1958, ended somewhat poorly, once each had finished taking advantage of the other. And he erred, in one way or another, in his appraisals of Juan Rulfo,* Juan José Arreola,* and Jorge Ibargüengoitia;* but all self-respecting critics—and Carballo commanded respect—venture a few opinions for which they're later mercilessly reproached. That's just the price you pay for being there at the time.

Carballo was both fair and generous with the authors whose early autobiographies he edited and wrote prologues for (in the series "Nuevos escritores mexicanos del siglo XX presentados por sí mismos")—Salvador Elizondo,* Gustavo Sainz, José Emilio Pacheco,* Homero Aridjis,* Tomás Mojarro, Sergio Pitol,* Juan Vicente Melo,* Carlos Monsiváis,* and a few others—confirming his place as *the* literary critic during a tremendous period in Mexican letters, one that he endorsed in all its splendor.

After an incident in which Cuban writer Reinaldo Arenas accused Carballo, his editor at the time, of having denounced him as a dissident and pocketed his royalties for *El mundo alucinante* (1968), his lucky star turned into a falling star. His downward trajectory, sprinkled with occasional tantrums in which he'd claim that other researchers were plagiarizing his bibliography cards, was tied to his infatuation with Castro and Che Guevara, which left him, like so many other Latin American intellectuals, a changed man. When Carballo finally distanced himself from the Cuban Revolution and the ideological deception upholding it, it was already too late and he'd missed his opportunity to become one of the key critics of the Latin American Boom he had watched unfold. Those unfulfilled dreams come through in books such as *Protagonistas de la literatura hispanoamericana del siglo XX* (1986) and *Ya nada es igual. Memorias, 1929–1953* (1994).

Reading through the pieces in *Diario público 1966–1968*, which Carballo recorded over the course of those two years and which were originally published in *Excelsior*, is actually a bit depressing. He had a critic's intuition, that sense of the situation Kierkegaard talked about, but he lacked an essayist's skill. Carballo wanted to be at the top but his writing wasn't literary enough to merit that; and despite the generosity and bravery he displayed during his best years, he spent his later days mostly concerned with his reputation.

SELECTED BIBLIOGRAPHY
Protagonistas de la literatura mexicana, SEP, Mexico, 1986.
Diario público 1966–1968, Conaculta, Mexico, 2005.

CARDOZA Y ARAGÓN, LUIS
(Antigua, Guatemala, 1901 – Mexico City, 1992)

In March 1983, Mexico City's Palacio de Bellas Artes was packed to the gills for ceremonies honoring the centenary of Marx's death. From a box seat on the verge of collapse, I saw the legendary Cardoza y Aragón for the first time in my life, a diminutive old man who sounded like a prophet of Israel resurrected, preaching the Promethean nature of Marxist thought, convinced that "materialist eschatology"—as he called it in a speech he gave on behalf of exiled Latin American poets—would continue to unleash magnetic powers into the present and future. Many of us there thought that after the suppression of the Polish solidarity movement the crisis of Marxism would enter a long, dark, frustrating limbo. But Cardoza y Aragón took a teleological view of Marx and perhaps, thus, saw it as natural that Marxism, which he saw as a mode of critical thought, should be in crisis. From the 1930s on, this Guatemalan poet chose to inhabit the dangerous Marxist universe, which, despite believing itself to be rule-governed, is actually a place where chaos, luck, terror, hope, and necessity all play a hand in toying with man. Still, no one at the centenary that night could have guessed that by the end of the eighties, the USSR—which Cardoza y Aragón defended, calling it a superior civilization despite all evidence to the contrary—would collapse under its own weight, leaving Marxism (in all its polymorphous forms) in purgatory.

In his prologue to *Iconografía de Luis Cardoza y Aragón* (2004), David Huerta* suggests that a twentieth-century leftist such as Cardoza y Aragón had no choice but to live in a world of tragedy, torn between the liberating impulse of Marx's thought and the wretched reality with which the communists besmirched his name. As the founding father of our vanguard and a heterodox surrealist (as only a great Latin-American poet could be), Cardoza was one of those who dared to defend Marxism from Stalinism, the saturnine son that devoured its father. And he waged war in the realm of aesthetics, lashing out at the Revolutionary Writers' and Artists' League (LEAR) in the thirties and contesting their reigning puritan dictatorship, a socialist realism that quashed the creative freedom that made Cardoza's *Pequeña sinfonía del Nuevo Mundo* (1948) possible.

The young André Breton once famously tried to blend Marx and Rimbaud in an attempt to both "transform the world" and "change life." Like very few interwar intellectuals, the leader of the surrealist movement renounced an illusion that dishonored so many artists. Cardoza on the other hand, like Louis Aragon and Paul Éluard, undertook the unworkable task of trying to keep avant-garde aesthetics and world revolution united under the aegis of the Russian Revolution, which had become a totalitarian regime. In *André Breton: Atisbado sin la mesa parlante* (1982), Cardoza brings a 50-year-long discussion to a close, unsuccessfully in my opinion. He claims that Éluard and Dadaist Tristan Tzara (and not Louis Aragon) died without knowing the horrors of Stalinism and concludes that Breton, a petit-bourgeois intellectual, eventually gave in to capitalism. But Cardoza (dissident intelligentsia) knows this applies to himself as much as Breton, and at the end of the day he'd rather be a saint than a heretic. Thus he claims that materialism, as a metaphysics, is a "giver of some certainty." Cardoza y Aragón was seduced by the saintly desire to be a "giver" and pursued it as if persecuted from the oft-burned and plundered church that was Guatemala, serving as a diplomat and a representative during the country's democratic decade (1944–1955), and writing a book honoring his homeland: *Guatemala: Las líneas de su mano* (1955).

The critic who explained the radical originality of Mexican muralism, Cardoza y Aragón never—as far as I'm aware—censured any work of art in the name of dogma. But neither did he tame the commissar within, an alter ego who plagued the poet with exhaustive defenses of the USSR and upheld the idea of sacrificing freedom in the name of faith. After a call to order, the commissar heads off to oversee the political discipline of other militants, and the poet is set free, walking a tightrope that his readers (from poet José D. Frías to David Huerta*) admired, penning *greguerías* (similar to aphorisms) that the great linguistic acrobat Ramón Gómez de la Serna taught him: they were "humor plus metaphor," bull's-eyes, poetry in prose, and prose in poetry. At times, it's true, he gives way to pleonasm, syllogism, amphibology, and tautology (or "nonsense," a term I use in the praiseworthy sense José Bergamín gave it). But the commissar returns, oh, he always returns.

Cardoza y Aragón was a Spinozan pantheist bedazzled by the "matter" of the world. In *Lázaro* (1994), his testamentary poem, he returns to the subject of resurrection, placing his confidence in the regenerative power of matter, through which he and Lya Kostakowsky (his wife) will be reunited not in heaven (deemed tedious) but in "infinity," which we all know about but don't think about. Surrealism for Cardoza, like the baroque for Eugenio d'Ors, is an "intrahistorical" state of mind, one that can never be contained by any one time. The appeal of eternity—hardly historical, but dialectical nonetheless—is palpable in *Lázaro*, as it is in all of Cardoza's poetry.

If I wanted to give a budding Latin American writer some sort of foundational gift, I'd choose *El río: Novelas de caballería* (1986), Cardoza y Aragón's extensive autobiography. It serves as a compass that a writer might use to find his way on a map of the twentieth century. Unfolding Cardoza's atlas, we find Paris and New York to the North: from modernism to the avant-garde (via Enrique Gómez Carrillo and Vicente Huidobro) to the newly married poet's journey to García Lorca's estate. To the East, there's the Generation of

'27 writers and the Spanish Civil War, the ivory tower overlooking the sea and the *chanson de geste*. To the South, the Chile of Neruda, whose center spreads far and wide. And the axis would be the old New Spain, the one discovered by Bernal Díaz, the one Antonin Artaud traveled by mule on his way to the Tarahumara Sierra. For Cardoza, the literary history of that period would conclude with Jorge Cuesta's insanity. *El río* lets us become spectators in time, astonished critics of Diego Rivera on his scaffolding, neighbors living in Coyoacán, the only Trotskyist neighborhood on the face of the planet, and the one where Cardoza died.

Cardoza y Aragón lived most of his life in Mexico, first between 1922 and 1944—when he nurtured the Mexican avant-garde—and then from 1953 until his death. But he never felt Mexican. That was hard to understand for those of us who loved him, but completely understandable for a Guatemalan who inhabited what Kafka called a "minor literature." It's odd that Cardoza, a close friend of García Lorca, Neruda, and Artaud, found favor with only one compatriot—Miguel Ángel Asturias—who was almost his polar opposite in every respect and about whom he wrote the book *Miguel Ángel Asturias: Casi novela* (1991). In it, he faces off with Asturias, a Nobel Prize winner who, Cardoza claimed, became more bitter with each prize he won, eventually turning into a bottle of vinegar. An admirably honest work, this "almost novel" attempts to explain the life of a man who was almost totally foreign and often repulsive to Cardoza. He was a friend for over fifty years and an occasional servant to Guatemalan tyranny, one of those inconsistent Latin American larger-than-life figures. Cardoza finds Asturias's invention of a Guatemalan tongue fascinating, but he also repudiates the didacticism and reverse folklore of indigenist literature.

I envy those friends of mine who visited Cardoza y Aragón regularly at his home on Callejón de las Flores. There was only one other occasion when I managed to see him in person. It was in 1986, at the Museo Rufino Tamayo, at the book launch for *El río: Novelas de caballería*. I stood beside him, reading nervously from my notes and expressing my wonder at and admiration for this omniscient, spectral elderly man. Cardoza was a Marxist when the world began, as many of us managed to be when that world (with all its grand methodology and gratuitous cruelty) came to an end. His centenary was celebrated erroneously, since we now know that he was born in 1901 and not 1904. But I (along with others before me: Villaurrutia, Cuesta, Paz,* Pacheco*) still see Cardoza y Aragón as the inventor of the literary cosmology in which I live and dream.

SELECTED BIBLIOGRAPHY
Poesías completas y algunas prosas, FCE, Mexico, 1977.
Malevich. Apuntes sobre su aventura Icárica, UNAM, Mexico, 1983.
Guatemala. Las líneas de su mano, FCE, Mexico, 1986.
El río. Novelas de caballería, FCE, Mexico, 1986.
Miguel Ángel Asturias. Casi novela, ERA, Mexico, 1991.
André Breton. Atisbado sin la mesa parlante, FCE, Mexico, 1992.
Pequeña sinfonía del Nuevo Mundo, FCE, Mexico, 1992.
Lázaro, ERA, Mexico, 1994.

CASTAÑÓN, ADOLFO
(Mexico City, 1952)

Castañón is critic, translator, poet, and editor in one, a writer-librarian who sees in the preservation and cataloging of the (universal) forest of books a guarantee, a safeguarding of the domain of literature. His work can be classified in many ways, provided you respect the coordinates laid out by Michel de Montaigne and Alfonso Reyes,* the lares and penates reigning over his efforts. "Criticism might be the only coherent expression of high culture," Castañón has written, and he has dedicated at least three collections of reviews and essays to Mexican, Latin American, and European letters: *Arbitrario de literatura mexicana* (1993), *América sintaxis* (2000), and *La gruta tiene dos entradas* (1994). His analyses range from Reyes (*Alfonso Reyes: El caballero de la voz errante*, 1988 and 2007), Paz,* and Cuesta* to Jean Paulhan, Ramon Fernandez, and Roger Caillois, three French masters who are required reading in order to make sense of his most appealing ground: exploring the Spanish-American "known world," which he's traveled joyously and tenaciously, an eternal pilgrim in this vast homeland. *América sintaxis* includes essential reading on Argentines José Bianco and Silvina Ocampo; Brazil's Nélida Piñón and José Sarney; Colombian writers Nicolás Gómez Dávila, Álvaro Mutis,* and Fernando Charry Lara; Cuba's José Kozer and Eliseo Diego; Chilean poets Nicanor Parra and Gonzalo Rojas; Spain's Fernando Savater; Nicaragua's Ernesto Mejía Sánchez; Peruvians Luis Loayza and Julio Ramón Ribeyro; Dominican writer Pedro Henríquez Ureña; and Venezuelans José Antonio Ramos Sucre, Mariano Picón Salas, Alejandro Rossi,* and José Balza.

It's a bountiful harvest indeed, a rich and unusual collection of writers spread throughout an America that Castañón has traveled both literally and as a reader. It should come as no surprise that it's in his travel writing where Castañón's personality shines through the most, as in his journey through the old continent (*Por el país de Montaigne*, 2000) and in *Lugares que pasan* (1998), where we read the adventures of a literary pilgrim for whom literature is synonymous with civilization, and with all types of orality. Thus Castañón writes of Céline in the delta of the Orinoco River, examines Latin Americans' tendency to hole up in the mountains and repudiate historic city centers, travels to Madrid to clutter up Ramón Gómez de la Serna's "back room," turns the Canary Islands into a terra firma and Lisbon into an island, dissects titular etiquette as Octavio Paz receives his Nobel in 1990, and chronicles his pilgrimage to the Holy Land, which no Mexican writer since José Vasconcelos* had done.

Castañón is also a publisher, reflecting on his decades at the Fondo de Cultura Económica in *El mito del editor y otros ensayos sobre libros y libreros* (1993) and *El jardín de los eunucos* (1998). In the spirit of other publishers such as Daniel Cosío Villegas, José Luis Martínez,* and Jaime García Terrés,* Castañón too has defended the Mexican state's enlightenment tradition which, via autonomous cultural institutions, sees bolstering the canon as the most enduring form of public education. Honor and sacrifice have been Castañón's currency in working as a state publisher, and by combining those qualities with his erudition and good taste, he became a very young patriarch.

In addition to his work as publisher, Castañón was also a literary editor at *La Gaceta del Fondo de Cultura Económica*, which he galvanized in the eighties, its most fruitful period. And although most of his criticism was published in literary magazines, he also found the time to write poetry (*La campana y el tiempo: Poemas 1973–2003*, 2004) and imaginative prose (*Batalla perdurable: A veces prosa*, 2003), the least interesting genres in his oeuvre, which is essentially exegetic and celebratory. In *Cheque y carnaval* (1983), *El reyezu-*

elo (1984)—a caustic collection of satires—and *Lectura y catarsis* (2000), his brief papers on George Steiner, Castañón's criticism has begun to lean more toward conversation and classicism, leaving behind the bitter, philosophical cynicism of his early books. In his recent collection of aphorisms, *La belleza es lo esencial* (2005), he writes, "A critic is like a dog: if he's got a master, there's little chance that he'll bite anyone in the house. If he doesn't, he's too busy to think about getting into fights. And after that he's too old to bite."

Castañón has been both a teacher and a brother to me. In 1987 I had the immense good fortune to formalize my literary education by working with him at FCE and, years later, together with Aurelio Asiain,* Fabienne Bradu,* Eduardo Milán,* and Guillermo Sheridan,* we were all on the editorial staff at the journal *Vuelta*. I owe the existence of entire chunks of my library to the desire to emulate his, and though I might now own some of the books he recommended, I'm sure I'll never be able to read them as well as he has.

In charge of a library (and, since 2004, a member of the Mexican Academy of Letters), Castañón might also be seen as the lighthouse watchman, always on the lookout, over time witnessing the evolution of the hardworking hordes on their way to the port of Mexican literature. Thus he guarantees the free circulation of new literature, collates manuscripts, and evaluates drafts, determined to show newcomers and outsiders hospitality, to give them passports so that they might (at their own risk) make their way into our imagination. At night, he sleeps with one eye open, leafing through the instructions left behind by his classics and scanning the horizon so he can welcome new ships ashore at dawn.

Selected Bibliography

Arbitrario de la literatura mexicana. Paseos I, Vuelta, Mexico, 1993 and 1995; Lectorum, Mexico, 2000.

La gruta tiene dos entradas. Paseos II, Vuelta, Mexico, 1994; Aldus, Mexico, 2002.

América sintaxis, Aldus, Mexico, 2000.

Viaje a México. Ensayos, crónicas y retratos, Panamericana, Madrid, 2008.

Algunas letras de Francia, preface by José de la Colina, Veintisiete letras, Madrid, 2009.

CASTELLANOS, ROSARIO
(Mexico City, 1925 – Tel Aviv, Israel, 1974)

Castellanos's accidental death was appalling and premature, and her intellectual life and literary posterity are equally truncated and accident-ridden. She was the first decidedly professional woman writer in Mexico, and she still serves as an effective antidote to the mercenaries who have turned new forms of "women's writing" into good business and spiritual prostitution. Unlike so many of our contemporaries, Castellanos wrote poetry, fiction, and criticism out of a love for literature itself, bolstered by her own tenacity and self-criticism.

José Joaquín Blanco* wrote, in *Crónica de la poesía mexicana* (1977), "Rosario Castellanos is a story of loneliness and a steadfast, open-hearted literary ambition, that unfortunately demanded greater talent and rigor than she was able to offer in a environment hostile towards her. She wrote a lot, and her texts are perhaps more valuable for the obstacles she attempted to overcome than for her results. Her narrative and poetic challenges were great and she took them on admirably, criticizing both life in Chiapas and Mexican women's oppression— from which she herself suffered, blindsided in the cultural milieu by people who were generally quite inferior to her. Resentful of the Mexican intelligentsia, she spent her later years elsewhere, seeking the respect and recognition that the cultural media denied her, and fell into traps such as ostentatiously playing the role of a Mexican Simone de Beauvoir, adulated and decorated by women's magazines, and pretending to be anti-intellectual—which proved very detrimental to her writing, since she was essentially a woman of letters, and a writer with limitations who needed rhetorical support . . ."

Thirty years after her death, rereading her work confirms—and I say this with a heavy heart—the standard trajectory of an author who announces the promised land and dies before setting foot on it. As a writer she worked through tensions that were resolved not in her own works but in those of her heirs. *Poesía no eres tú* (1972), a collection of nearly all of her poetry, is a bittersweet read. Her moral inclination to declaim (and complain) is held in check by a rigorous intellect, one that often hits the mark when reflecting on the finer points of poetic meditations usually reserved for certain types of philosophy. "Lamentación de Dido" is a poem as well wrought as it is antiquated; but Castellanos's best poems—such as those in *De la vigilia estéril* (1950) and *En la tierra de en medio* (1972)—are the ones in which she paints a sardonic, humorous portrait of herself, trapped by the conventions of domesticity (ironic, given that her death by electrocution occurred in a domestic mishap while she was serving as the Mexican ambassador to Israel). A generation would have to pass before her insights really yielded a good crop of women writers, writers who might have read her as girls but then forgot her influence in the face of more prestigious names. It's no surprise that there are echoes of Castellanos's female or feminized rhetorical figures in poets like Carmen Boullosa* and María Baranda.* Women, in their texts, wear more audacious masks and are no longer "mother" or "spinster," but the way Castellanos used the female voices of Cassandra and the sorceress in her neo-classic Dido is still so utterly relevant that it's become academic.

Her fiction is less influential in contemporary narrative, essentially confined to two novels, *Balún Canán* (1957) and *Oficio de tinieblas* (1962). The latter is the first-rate historical tale of a nineteenth-century indigenous uprising in Chiapas that ends with the crucifixion of the Indian leader, but it's ill served by a problematic narrative structure and overly theatrical dramatization. Castellanos longed to write great, dramatic poems, and when she tried (*Salomé y Judith*, 1959), there too, she failed. But we are indebted to her for writing about indigenous issues with subtlety and human contradictions, as well as recognizing the concrete place of the indigenous in Mexican history. Castellanos, along with Peruvians José María Arguedas and Manuel Scorza, was part of a generation of Latin American writers determined to leave behind the one-dimensional primitivism of *indigenista* writing, exploring the linguistic richness of indigenous books of knowledge and language. But the merciful objectivity with which she portrayed the Indians of Chiapas did not have the desired effect: half a century later, indigenism—in fiction—is still bogged down in folklore and didacticism, although it has begun to value oral tradition as a source, the indigenous themselves as authors, and the ideological appeal of reverse racism.

Everything that can be said about (and against) Castellanos must take one honorably decisive mitigating circumstance into consideration: no other Mexican writer has been so immediately and resolutely self-critical. In confessions and interviews, Castellanos was the first to recognize bad influences, hollow pretensions, and aesthetic failures, from her early and inevitable deference to Gabriela Mistral to her inexperience in drama and short stories, and including an unwarranted writing-off of nearly all of her poetry. Insecurity, modesty, maybe even a type of audacity? I really don't know. But that self-critical demeanor leads us to read her literary criticism—perhaps her most enduring legacy—in a new light. In *Juicios sumarios* (1966) and especially in *Mujer que sabe latín . . .* (1973), she found fitting and much loved interlocutors: Simone Weil, Violette Leduc, Lillian Hellman, Isak Dinesen, Flannery O'Connor, Mary McCarthy. When writing about these women—some of whom were still unknown in Spanish when she reviewed them—Castellanos was finally able to speak confidently and to find people who truly agreed with her about topics of great concern—from the way Catholicism branded a young woman's soul to the wan, impenetrable essence of misogyny. Had she lived longer, Castellanos would have been able to examine the philosophical problem she found in Weil, the one that turned out to be at the core of her work: the way victims become complicit in their own subjection.

SELECTED BIBLIOGRAPHY
Obras reunidas, I. Novelas, FCE, Mexico, 2005.
Obras reunidas, II. Cuentos, FCE, Mexico, 2005.
The Nine Guardians: A Novel, trans. Irene Nicholson, Readers International, Columbia, LA, 1993.
The Book of Lamentation, trans. Esther Allen, Penguin Books, New York, 1999.

CASTRO LEAL, ANTONIO
(San Luis Potosí, 1896 – Mexico City, 1981)

The most blatant and representative example of "critic as failure," Castro Leal lived through the periods of the *Ateneístas* and the *Contemporáneos*. Though he was a good publisher, and for decades was considered *the* critic, his legacy is mediocre. There's not a single idea in *Repasos y defensas* (1987)—which Salvador Elizondo* prefaced quite mercifully—that merits the title "critic." With the decorum—but not the elegance or influence—of Alfonso Reyes* and the timidity—but not the valor—of the *Contemporáneos*, his greatest feat was canonizing *La novela de la Revolución Mexicana* (1960). [. . .] He loved literature; that's not in question. Given how many poets and novelists find success despite an utter lack of talent, we shouldn't be surprised that criticism isn't always a feast of geniuses. How this came about was that between 1930 and 1960, the Mexican intelligentsia's mission was essentially to legitimize a sort of despotism—the result of an Enlightenment that was never fully realized—that began in the fine arts and made its way through the other sectors of public life. That's why they kicked Vasconcelos* out of the club. Castro Leal's story is not unique; it can also be seen in literary critics like Antonio Acevedo Escobedo, Francisco Zendejas, José Luis Martínez,* and Emmanuel Carballo.* Each of them left criticism to make a career out of the cultural welfare state: diplomacy, politics, or journalism. Or they sought other ways to guarantee their legitimacy, like founding literary prizes. (*Servidumbre y grandeza de la vida literaria*, 1998)

SELECTED BIBLIOGRAPHY
Repasos y defensas. Antología, prologue by Salvador Elizondo, notes by Víctor Díaz Arciniega, FCE, Mexico, 1987.

CERNUDA, LUIS
(Sevilla, Spain, 1902 – Mexico City, 1963)

In the now-famous autobiographical piece published in the Mexican edition of *La realidad y el deseo* (1958), Cernuda told of how he came to Mexico already enamored of the country. It was only after he decided to leave his professorship in the US and put down roots here that he became disillusioned, after having paid Mexico such lucid, reticent homage in *Variaciones sobre tema mexicano* (1952). And although he ended up disenchanted with Mexico, Mexican literature—in a rather unequal exchange—appropriated *him* entirely, consecrating a tomb for the poet in the national pantheon, seeing Cernuda as a body that germinated in foreign soil.

Immediately after Cernuda's death, Octavio Paz,* Tomás Segovia,* Juan García Ponce,* and José Emilio Pacheco* paid him tribute, and as James Valender has stated in *Luis Cernuda en México* (2003), many others later followed suit. But of all the descriptions I've read of the hyper-sensitive poet, the best one is a snapshot taken by José de la Colina,* both for its brevity and its tenderness. "Thin, dark, short, with a high forehead, pencil mustache, hard little eyes, and well packaged with discreet English elegance, Luis Cernuda would walk out, utterly alone, into the Mexico City streets; and we, the kids of Spanish refugees, took him for what we'd been told he was: a *señorito*, a dandy; that was why we played the same trick on him who knows how many times. He'd be walking down the street, maybe smoking his pipe, and suddenly there would be a shout behind him. 'Hey! Cernuda!' hurled treacherously like a stone out of somewhere, or nowhere, and he'd turn quickly, and look around, searching the east and the west, the north and the south, searching the street like a jackal on the plain, he'd frown and you could tell he was disconcerted, disoriented, losing his bearings, suddenly submerged in a hostile abyss . . . There was no way for him to know we were just a gang of exile kids shouting at him and then hiding in a doorway, or a hallway, or behind a tree, or a car, just as there was no way for us to know what a great poet the man we were virtually knocking off his feet was."

Redundancy aside, Cernuda was an exile in exile, and he wrote many indispensable pages about Mexico. In *Variaciones sobre tema mexicano* (1952), as José María Espinasa* has pointed out, at first glance the poet's observations seem shaky, but upon deeper examination reveal an Azorín-like tone and quite a profound understanding of and intuition about Mexico. The poet was born again here, and his last two works, *Ocnos* and *Desolación de la quimera*, came out the year of his death. Mexico, for Cernuda, was a strange and charming nation, as old as Castile and Andalusia and with a civilization that, rather than negating Spain, complemented and, in a way, explained it.

In Mexico, too, Cernuda wrote literary criticism on the Generation of '27 and English poetry, included in *Estudios de poesía española contemporánea* (1957) and *Pensamiento poético de la lírica inglesa* (1958). In his book *Leer poesía*, Gabriel Zaid* finds that "systematic writing does not suit" Cernuda, and that the most valuable aspect of his criticism is the commentary he offers as a colleague, as a fellow poet. I'd qualify that statement, adding that Cernuda chose to go against the grain, to be an Anglophile rather than a Francophile hanger-on, embracing heterodoxy as had José María Blanco White a century before him.

Although criticizing Cernuda is now considered in bad taste, it should also be remembered that plenty of people—such as Tomás Segovia—admired the poet but were irked by the man: a moralizing romantic hero; an eternally rebelling adolescent; the king of self-proclaimed freedoms; a man full of redeeming virtues, turmoil, and heroics.

There's a page of his that I've turned back to several times, a fragment that exemplifies the venerable critic's simultaneous passion and aloofness. He's explaining that Edison once gave his friend Lord Tennyson a phonograph and some records, including one on which Tennyson read some of his own verses. Back then, Cernuda writes, each listener had to hold a rubber tube to his ear in order to listen; otherwise the sound was too high-pitched to be understood. So Tennyson was the first poet to hear his recorded voice and, commenting on the experience, said that the insufferable static was the posterity of words, while what you heard through the tubes was just the ephemeral glory of the moment. In that ambiguity—the space between the strident sounds of time and the faith in one's vocation—resides Cernuda's destiny as perhaps the most enduring Spanish poet of the twentieth century.

Selected Bibliography

Desolación de la chimera, 1956-1962, Joaquin Mortiz, Mexico, 1962.

La realidad y el deseo, 1924–1962, FCE, Mexico, 1964 and 1966.

Variaciones sobre tema mexicano, introduction by José María Espinasa, FCE, Madrid, 2002.

James Valender, *Luis Cernuda en México*, FCE, Mexico, 2003.

Selected Poems, ed. and trans. Reginald Gibbons, Sheep Meadow, New York, 1999.

Written in Water: The Prose Poems of Luis Cernuda, trans. Stephen Kessler, City Lights, San Francisco, 2004.

Desolation of the Chimera: Last Poems, trans. Stephen Kessler, White Pine Press, Buffalo, New York, 2009.

CERVANTES, FRANCISCO

(Querétaro, Querétaro, 1938 – 2004)

Cervantes, like Luis de Camões and Rosalía de Castro, has written both in Spanish and in Galician-Portuguese. And although we might think of his verses in the latter as some sort of amorous flirtation, *Heridas que se alternan* (1985) is a world unto itself in Hispano-American poetry. In the mid-sixties,

Cervantes took what at the time was the road untraveled, one that led him to discover Portuguese literature almost single-handedly. In "Cantado para nadie" (literally, "Sung for Nobody"), we read: "La cólera, el silencio / su alta arboladura / Te dieron este invierno. / Mas óyete en tu lengua: / Acaso el castellano / No es seguro." ("Anger, silence / their towering spars / Gave you this winter. / But hear yourself in your tongue: / Perhaps Spanish / Is not certain"). It would be redundant for him to have switched back and forth between Spanish and Portuguese: instead what Cervantes did was accept his ghosts and inhabit that final frontier. In one of his essays, Gabriel Zaid* ventures, "Galician and Portuguese can be lived as if they were a sensual, melancholic means of speaking Spanish. And it's there in the convex mirror of a familiar language—where each word can be caressed, explored, and recognized as if it were *not* familiar—that Cervantes creates poetry in such a singular way."

Cervantes's "Lusitanian delirium," as Álvaro Mutis* calls it, is filtered through poems and fragments of *chansons de geste* that come from somewhere between the Middle Ages and the Renaissance. It's a world of lances and trophies, damsels and barons, buried weapons and maritime routes. Cervantes compiled *Odisea de la poesía portuguesa moderna* (1985), created the pseudonym Leopoldo Stahl, and translated both Pessoa and Pessoa's distinguished biographer João Gaspar Simões. He released the early part of his oeuvre in the beautiful *Heridas que se alternan* and later published *Los huesos peregrinos* (1986), *El canto del abismo* (1987), *El libro de Nicole* (1992), and two anthologies, *Materia de distintos lais* (1993) and *Ni oído ni hablado* (2001).

In *Heridas que se alternan*, the poet explains, "Once, in the early days when the Portuguese language was absolutely vital to my survival, I heard a word I wasn't sure how to spell but was something like 'estalinhas.' It referred to the noise you make when you crack your knuckles, or rather, that was what the act of doing it was called. And it seemed the perfect term to express the voices coming through in my poems. But those same voices hinted that, whether asleep or awake, they were rising up from the throat of that protean being who lives inside us all and who can only be realized in death [. . .] Futile sounds, wickedness. Senseless pain. They were the obsessions of beings that once existed, that refuse to depart the face of the earth. And all of this was in my bosom, troubling me; I had no choice but to lend them my voice and feelings as their battleground, which doesn't mean they were triumphant."

By choosing to pay tribute to the Portuguese cause, the "Christ child of nations" as it was called in the sixteenth and seventeenth centuries, Cervantes was doing more than writing literature about literature. Ida Vitale explained it well: the central figure in Cervantes's poetry is uprootedness, and that absolute uprootedness could only be expressed through the people whose time, as Jorge de Sena (one of the poets Cervantes translated) said, "dissolved in space and whose space didn't have enough time to dissolve in time." The oldest of our contemporary poets also turned out to be the most modern, for it was Cervantes (as well as Octavio Paz* in *Cuadrivio* in 1965) who first brought us Fernando Pessoa.

It seems forever ago, but the Fondo de Cultura Económica, under the direction of José Luis Martínez* and Jaime García Terrés,* was once a publishing house staffed by writers; we kept long, odd hours so we'd be able to publish the house catalog and work on our own writing, too. The old building that stood on Avenida de la Universidad deteriorated as the century drew to a close, and managerial stupidity allowed it to be mercilessly torn down. But it used to have a central hallway, with our cubicles coming off it. The layout respected our need for privacy, expressing a monastic deference to the solitary practices of reading, writing, translating, and editing. I still dream about those corridors, the labyrinth where I finally knew I'd found my literary vocation. Many of us who so often wandered those halls are still around; others are gone forever. In my time there I got to see Wenceslao Roces dictating his translations of Marx; the wonderful publisher Alba Rojo; wise Nahuatl experts bent over their treaties like Fray Bernardino de Sahagún had in his day; and editors poring over galley proofs, people who, having survived several wars, were still able to spot a typo a mile away. Among the *La Gaceta del FCE* editors wandering those halls in 1988, I remember Adolfo Castañón* with a different edition of Chamfort in each jacket pocket, the Spinozan Hinojosa,* the poet and Eliot translator López Mills,* Daniel Goldin searching for Hebrew source texts for a predictably neverending Scholem translation, *Tel Quel* writer Moreno Villarreal,* poet César Arístides—practically a child at the time—searching for sympathy with the devil, editor Rafael Vargas, who was such a good friend of Peruvian poets César Moro and Martín Adán that he went to Perú to pick them up, and José Luis Rivas,* laughing uproariously as he wrote pagan "gospels."

But of that whole spectral battalion, Cervantes was the most representative of the quick-wittedness and the quick tempers. We called him "the
vampire," as he pounded on his Remington (we still used those outdated
contraptions), searching for the best way to translate Machado de Assis. The
great poet Cervantes, guest at the Hotel Cosmos on the old Avenida de San
Juan de Letrán, seemed to be warning us even then that "el hombre fue, el
hombre ha sido / el que pasó, el que vino, el que se va / el hombre fue, que ha
sido, / oh tiempo que duele de sus horas; / el costado del tiempo, tocado por
el fuego / arde con igual velocidad; / las llamas lo envuelven transparente /
y el hombre no sabe de sí mismo, / tiene una boca a la moda y sentimientos
adecuados a los tiempos" ("the man was, the man has been / he who passed,
he who came, he who goes / the man was, who has been, / oh time that pains
of its hours; / the side of time, touched by fire / burns just as quickly; / the
flames engulf it, transparent / and the man does not know of himself / his
tongue is in vogue and his sentiments suit the times").

SELECTED BIBLIOGRAPHY
Cantado para nadie, Poesía completa, FCE, Mexico, 1997.

CHUMACERO, ALÍ
(Acaponeta, Nayarit, 1918 – Mexico City, 2010)

During the nineties, Mexican culture became somewhat obsessed with collections and compilations. We had a proliferation of annotated editions
and rediscovered materials presumed to have been lost in a general bibliographic renaissance; it was as though time's corrosive effects were being felt
more quickly, compelling us to regirder our foundations. And though Chumacero's place in contemporary Spanish-language poetry is already well
established, the publication of his body of critical work now allows us to
examine the little-known history of literary criticism in Mexico in greater
depth and perspective.

Los momentos críticos (1987) is a book of reviews and essays originally
published in the national press, from 1940 (just before the founding of *Tierra
Nueva*) to the start of the seventies. Miguel Ángel Flores did exemplary work

in creating a clear, manageable tome of criticism we didn't know existed. This not only enhances the prominence of one of our best poets but also takes us on a trip through the bull's-eyes, near misses, and failures of literary tastes.

It takes time to appreciate the historical importance of the ephemeral world of prologues and bibliographic texts. For example, Chumacero's brief reflections on the modernists illustrate how a moderately popular generation of poets only began to be critically vindicated by later generations. It's important to remember that Salvador Díaz Mirón was the only modernist to earn acceptance by *Contemporáneos* like Jorge Cuesta* and Xavier Villaurrutia,* who were initially quite reluctant to read him. So when Chumacero brushes the dust off of Manuel Gutiérrez Nájera, Luis G. Urbina, and Amado Nervo, what we're reading is actually a restructuring of our literary past—a project born of a poet's curiosity and sensibilities. [. . .]

The lesson we learn from a spellbinding book like *Los momentos críticos* is that by gathering scattered materials, they take on historicity and critical intelligibility: the layout Flores gives the book makes for comprehensive reading and allows us to follow a twenty-year journey through Mexican letters. Some of Chumacero's best essays are those on Villaurrutia and Ramón López Velarde, the latter rigorously scrutinized shortly before universal renown replaced his provincial fame. In this and other cases, Chumacero expressed his own individual opinions, which later became taken for granted. Commenting lucidly on Villaurrutia, he writes, "his nocturnes . . . are the culmination of his finely tuned sensibilities; they represent the decision to penetrate the soul of things with fury, all the way to the crux of a world not made for us, and shrouded in a brilliant mysterious aura that only the poet can capture."

His poetry criticism was seen as marginal to that of others in his generation. But without saying so, via Urbina, López Velarde, and Villaurrutia, Chumacero is engaging with the contemporary works of Octavio Paz,* Efraín Huerta,* and Rubén Bonifaz Nuño,* as well as with his own poetry, teasing out nuances and striking chords that echo into the past and (now that we can read it) the future.

Even more illuminating are the aesthetics of his "mistakes." Included in *Los momentos críticos* is an often cited and rarely read piece in which Chumacero reproaches Juan Rulfo* for his use of time in *Pedro Páramo*, claiming that Rulfo's stories are superior to his only novel. This is 1955 we're talking about here. It would be at least five years before Rulfo became world-renowned. Chumacero's objection—shot down by public opinion—is still more valuable than many people's recognition, for we see in it that literature, like *Pedro Páramo*, has a sort of "eternal present," that crucial moment when a work confronts time and traditions that are paralyzed by the emergence of something entirely new. Reading Chumacero's review of Rulfo thirty years after the fact is like an invitation to bow down before the mysteries—of chance, of taste—that determine what makes an enduring classic. Can we ever really understand the undisclosed methods that led Chumacero astray in his Rulfo critique? What alchemy determines literary success or failure?

Los momentos críticos—"critical moments"—lives up to its title. This is a book of many "present" tenses, of critical moments when personal readings tackle literary tradition, with mixed results: admiration, bull's eyes, mistakes. The logbook of a poet who truly *lives* criticism, it's also a position piece on Mexican culture: Chumacero places López Velarde and the *Contemporáneos* at the heart of poetic tradition; he discusses writers' moral obligations; he searches for the meaning of Mexicanness.

Mexico is not the only country whose poets and writers are discussed, however. Chumacero also paves the way for the critical reception of Borges and the Spanish exiles (Enrique Díez-Canedo, Pedro Garfias, Emilio Prados), well before others were doing so. That's because for Chumacero, "the aim of artistic output is not to try to erect posthumous statues, nor is it to superimpose prestige on the work created. Neither the seductiveness of the future nor fame in the present count—or at least they shouldn't—when it comes to poetic effect."

Chumacero's prose—crisp, precise, elegant—is in and of itself a vindication of the idea of reading as criticism. It's a shame that he stopped practicing, though comprehensible that he would at some point in his literary career. Still, regretting his absence, we now have to undertake imaginary critiques of contemporary writers we'd have liked to see him review. Now that criticism has essentially become a business of flattery and people bristle when a reviewer actually criticizes a book, it would be wise to close by quoting the poet who said, in an interview with Marco Antonio Campos: "A critic not only helps books coming out get read but also helps make the chaos of the imagination—or worse, the imaginations—begin to look like a continuum that, at the end of the day, will lead to what we call 'literary tradition.' Tradition is not what's died, what's left when an activity is gone. The critic should be one who orders and orients, and the more critics there are, the better" (1987; *Servidumbre y grandeza de la vida literaria*, 1998).

Chumacero's silence since *Páramo de sueños* (1944), *Imágenes desterradas* (1948), and *Palabras en reposo* (1956) has been heard more loudly than many of the verses he published in those years. And despite the near-proverbial prestige of the great writer who no longer writes, there have been few such as him who've been so present in both the publishing world and the private life of our national literature. He has a very mixed group of disciples, protégés, and friends; and few are the Mexican writers who have never heard his idiosyncratic laughter ring out by the rosy fire of a cantina or cascade like a waterfall flooding the desert beauty of his poetry as he bent over a stack of proofs. Chumacero started off writing poems about Heidegger treatises (they were being translated by Spanish exiles in Mexico in the forties) and ended up combining refined form with the storminess of a sometimes contemplative and often furious bard in poems such as "Monólogo del viudo" and "La noche del suicida."

An outstanding student, he got the rhetorical gods that the *Contemporáneos* had erected to step down from their pedestals and surrender to women, liturgy, and drunkenness in impassioned dialogues. Octavio Paz saw Chumacero as a modern obsessed with the Christian embodiment of images, and Ramón Xirau* deems him a "sensualist," a poet of pleasure and enjoying the instant. Recently, Eduardo Hurtado asked, "What if time allied with chance, as it did for the ancient Greeks, and published Chumacero's verse? What if in two thousand years from now a reader found these fragments, translated into a different language but with the same rhythm?" (Hurtado, *Este decir y no decir*, 2003). That's the question we're left to mull over, faced with a very brief oeuvre and a far greater posterity, the posterity of a man who wrote fragmented poems whose incompleteness hints at totality. "Yo pecador, a orillas de tus ojos / miro nacer la tempestad" ("I, sinner, in the shores of your eyes / watch as the storm is born"), Chumacero says, and reading his sculpted verse, engraved half a century ago in the stone of tradition, I suspect that this poet is one of those unusual men who remain silent out of joy.

SELECTED BIBLIOGRAPHY
Palabras en reposo, FCE, Mexico, 1956 and 1965.
Los momentos críticos, ed. Miguel Ángel Flores, FCE, Mexico, 1987.
Poesía reunida, Mónica Mansour, Conaculta, Mexico, 1991.

COLINA, JOSÉ DE LA

(Santander, Spain, 1934)

Some time ago, I wrote that I couldn't offer de la Colina any excessive praise, since he's a writer who disregards flattery by instinct; I'm going to attempt, therefore, to articulate my enthusiasm rationally. In *Libertades imaginarias* (2001) he demonstrates that reading is an art form, analyzing not only essays, novels, and poetry, but also the murky borderlands of incipits, aphorisms, riddles, pop songs, anagrams, stuttering, and palindromes. After all this, de la Colina then returns to Plato, to the name as attribute of the named, and wonders why writers have the names they do: if Quevedo is, as his name suggests, really "que-ve-do-(ble)," or "he who sees double," why Poe is lacking the "t" that would make him a "poet."

Without trying to suggest a taxonomy, we can infer certain precepts in de la Colina's work, and though they're playful and irreverent, they're also categorical: reading well means not just rereading but also knowing that one bad poem or infelicitous expression is a threat to all of literature. And if *Libertades imaginarias* is Colina's grammar, we can add to it his rhetoric: the beautiful *ZigZag* (2005) and the moving *Personerío: del siglo XX mexicano* (2005), two books that guarantee his place as one of a handful of Mexican writers who seem to write even more beautifully the older they get. There was a time, twenty-five years ago, when de la Colina's literary output was limited to a few good collections of short stories (*Ven, caballo gris*, 1959, and *La lucha con la pantera*, 1962), and he seemed destined to become yet another *oiseau triste*, like his friend Carlos Valdés, one of those writers who seem to have it all until circumstances take it away. But de la Colina stopped inscribing his work with what sounded like beggar's remorse passing for self-criticism, as we see in *Traer a cuento: Narrativa, 1959–2003* (2004), a collection of his short stories, some of which will be anthologized long after we're dead. I'm thinking, for instance, of "La tumba india" and "Muertes ejemplares," which recount the deaths of Hemingway, Pedro Garfias, and Poe ("tekeli li, tekeli li!"), and "La última música del Titanic," with its flawless prose.

Son of a militant anarcho-syndicalist typesetter who was also captain in the Republican infantry in Spain, de la Colina and his family came to Mexico as exiles in 1941. Since that time, in Alejandro Rossi's* well-chosen words, he's lived a paradox, being "such a Spanish writer" and yet having "such a thoroughly Mexican biography." Honor and umbrage are the two overriding sentiments in de la Colina, a gentle tyrant capable of carrying out obvious injustices but also the unofficial teacher of one or two generations of writers who did their time in literary journalism at *Revista Mexicana de Literatura, Vuelta, Plural, La Letra y la Imagen, Sábado*, and *El Semanario Cultural de Novedades*. Forty years of literature have passed beneath his gaze.

A self-defined "liberal atheist for whom some things are sacred," de la Colina is the sort of heterodox that Menéndez Pelayo would gladly have called a bête noir. Disillusioned with the Cuban Revolution in 1964, de la Colina became a tireless polemicist, railing against what he called "the church of the left." But once the Berlin Wall had fallen, the anarchist bug bit him again, and one afternoon in 2004 he had no qualms about interrupting a disingenuous reading of *Don Quixote* given by a high and mighty, condescending senator.

The pieces in *ZigZag*—an apt and witty title—comprise a sort of literary self-portrait that contains everything from an homage to Polvorilla (the family cat) to a memoir about "going to the movies" that does much to explain how de la Colina ended up a good friend of Luis Buñuel as well as one of the most incisive film critics of the Spanish language. The book also expresses both nostalgia and esteem for the *tertulias* that educated (and warped—exile is hell) the Republican writers led by Simón Otaola. It even includes an homage to XELA, the classical music station that disappeared with the twentieth century, and in whose memory de la Colina hums Chausson's symphonic "Poeme for violin" along with poet Gerardo Deniz,* another Spanish exile born the same year as de la Colina. *ZigZag* concludes with a condemnation of bullfighting, "that bloody binge," an execration I must fervently applaud, for it's a "comedy of the shallowness and affectation of man versus the enormous truth and true aristocracy of the beast to be sacrificed."

Rossi says that what distinguishes de la Colina is that he's a "professor without a dais, better suited to a café or a long walk." *Personerío* is perhaps the book that best justifies that description. The book is also quite novel, because although most of the individual "portraits" had been previously published in the national press, there was no way to imagine the new phantasmagorias that would result from placing conventional characters side by side in one tome: Reyes* becomes seductively flirty; we get new perspective on Revueltas;* we see the image of Arreola* in his bookbinder's workshop. de la Colina knows the rules of the game: portraits are neither caricatures nor funeral masks. After all, he's a very wise reader of writer Ramón Gómez de la Serna, he of the one-liners, as evidenced by the almost-realist almost-monologue he coaxes out of Juan Rulfo* and the tender portrayal of Juan Vicente Melo,* whom the gods blessed not only with literature, music, and parties but with exemplary friends who rescued him time and again, in life and death. *Personerío* also includes an entry on the wonderful novelist Sergio Galindo* and another on the pathetic Guadalupe Amor, appraised with an evenhandedness alien to the enduring affectation of her clan. *Personerío* is the family album of the latter half of twentieth-century Mexican literature, with de la Colina as photographer.

de la Colina's oeuvre brings me the same joy I felt in my late teens when I read Reyes's *La experiencia literaria.* In both cases, it was as though I'd discovered a warehouse of all the ingredients of literature, and with them I could create not one but many jigsaw puzzles, any of which might be the vocation of writer, whether just yearned for or carried out.

No less vital are de la Colina's incursions into the near-barren (due to poor crops) field of popular literature. In *Libertades imaginarias* he discusses Carlo Collodi's *Pinocchio* (1873) and the songs of Francisco Gabilondo's singing cricket, Cri-Cri. de la Colina elevates both to the height of art, likening them to Robert Louis Stevenson and Blaise Cendrars, two of his favorites. All epics, he reminds us, are a series of rites of passage: passing a test, taking an exam. I was fascinated to learn in *Libertades imaginarias* that during the Spanish Civil War (1936–39), children in Spain, like me, also believed that "Pinocho," as he was called in Spanish, was part of the Pin Dynasty: since "ocho" is Spanish for "eight," it seemed clear that there must have been Pin One, Pin Two, Pin Three, etc, before finally it came to "Pin-Ocho," Pin Eight. de la Colina finds in Collodi's work, as did Elena Croce before him, a transition from the pure fable to pedagogical novel. From invention to pedagogy, it seems I belonged to the last generation educated by Francisco Gabilondo Soler (Cri-Cri) . . . and de la Colina.

SELECTED BIBLIOGRAPHY
Libertades imaginarias. De la literatura como juego, prologue by Alejandro Rossi, Aldus, Mexico, 2001.
Traer a cuento. Narrativa (1959–2001), introduction by Adolfo Castañón, FCE, Mexico, 2004.
Personería: del siglo XX mexicano, Universidad Veracruzana, Xalapa, 2005.
ZigZag, Aldus, Mexico, 2005.

CROSS, ELSA
(Mexico City, 1946)

Both profound and delicate, Cross became a recognizable force with her very first verses, inspired by Cavalcanti and Provençal poetry. But it was in India, where for decades she has gone on spiritual retreats, that she became one of Mexico's few genuinely religious poets. *Canto malabar* (1987) is an outstanding theological prose poem that exudes true religiosity, which is essentially the numinous perception of the supernatural. Cross's generation was rife with pilgrims as inclined to find—in the East or the West—the Holy Grail as they were to be disenchanted and whine about it. But Cross left that chorus behind, her voice ringing out clearly as that of a survivor, a woman whose poetry makes it clear that the journey is never-ending: "Defiendo mi huida / Finco de madrugada mi distierro. / Historia borrosa, vista de través" ("I defend my flight / Inhabit my exile at dawn. / Hazy story, seen through"). In her treatment of Krishna and Radha's love, and of the medieval Hindu poet saints, Cross's readings go well beyond that of spiritual tourism. In fact, from an irreligious perspective—which may go against her intentions— she can be read as a great explorer. Her itinerary extends beyond India and the "dithyrambs" of *El vino de las cosas* (2004), as she treks through Greece (both ancient and everyday), a destination previously visited by Mexican poets such as Jaime García Terrés* and Hugo Gutiérrez Vega.

In *Los dos jardines: Mística y erotismo en algunos poetas mexicanos* (2003), Cross offers a critical perspective on both her poetics and her spiritual genealogy. In that overlap where religious ecstasy meets physical rapture, she identifies with Catholics López Velarde, Alfredo R. Placencia, and Concha Urquiza; in displays of sensuality, she recalls Guadalupe Amor's sonnets; and clearly she feels an affinity with Paz's Indian phase. But perhaps it's Concha Urquiza (1910–1945)—our Simone Weil—in whom Cross discovers alarming, paradoxical sources of her identity. Her voyages to India could be described in the same terms she uses to define Urquiza's poetry, in which "a devastating image of God is perhaps what confronts anyone on an extreme mystical journey that severs all else, destroys what had previously made up the safe, conventional world, banishes [one] into the darkness of the spiritual night, or the desert."

Faith, in literature, guarantees nothing; religiosity must be convincing, as it is in Cross's poems, in which thousands of Indian gods whisper and the sacredness of Buddhist avatars is felt through the senses, a conviction. In *El diván de Antar* (1990), Cross writes that "Los dioses habitaron esta carne / y sus huellas ardieron. / Los ojos estallaban, / por dentro, un fuego lo devoraba todo. / El mundo era una grieta / una rajadura en la noche / tan vasta / como la conciencia abierta / hacia sí mismo. / Y de allí detenida / la carne frágil" ("The gods inhabited this flesh / and their footprints burned. / Their eyes burst, / fire, within, devoured all. / The world was a crevice / a crack in the night / as vast / as consciousness open / unto itself. / And there it stopped / fragile flesh"). Cross has been reproached (by Alberto Paredes, to be fair) for never having achieved great poetic heights. But those heights can't be reached by someone who practices the Middle Way, shunning extremes. And it's there that I find the awe implicit in a recurrent communion that, paradoxically, rejects all sacraments—which in fact is paradoxical only in the West.

"I had the unsettling impression I was returning home after years, perhaps centuries away," said Manuel Mujica Lainez when he visited the Bomarzo Monster Park in Viterbo, Northern Lazio, for the first time. Enormous sculptures, the "monsters" of Bomarzo create a delirious depiction of the Roman gods, created by Pirro Ligorio in 1552 and commissioned by Count Pier Francesco Orsini as an act of revenge on his fate when his wife Giulia Farnese died. The spot obsessed Argentine novelist Mujica Lainez (1910–1984), who dedicated a book to the park. The eponymous *Bomarzo* (1962) is one of the most persuasive, well-wrought historical novels ever to be written in Spanish. Later, in 1967, Alberto Ginasterra adapted the book first into a cantata and then into an opera, which led to *Bomarzo*—scheduled to open at the Teatro Colón in Buenos Aires—being censured by the Argentine government for immorality and pornography. But the censorship, which some critics saw as an enigmatic symptom of the military repression to follow a decade later, served only to attract more readers to Mujica Lainez and garner greater fame for composer Ginasterra.

Elsa Cross, too, returned home to Bomarzo, that lion's den. Her most recent book is also entitled *Bomarzo* (2009), this one a remarkable long poem. It's tempting to use a seven-hundred-page *Bomarzo* and a sixty-six-page one to illustrate the insurmountable rivalry between literature and poetry. It might prove easier, however, to simply be astonished at the *déjà vu* felt by both Mujica Lainez and Cross at the traumatic, seductive horror of Bomarzo. And yet, nothing—except the perfect ruins of the monster park—unites the Mexican poet and Argentine novelist. No one could be less ascetic than Mujica Lainez, one of the most Gothic spirits in Latin American literature; and Cross's poetry is certainly ascetic. The novelist (perhaps the most painterly of Spanish-language novelists) uses *Bomarzo* to paint the terrified face of one of the Renaissance's accursed cities, a hodgepodge of civilization.

Cross, on the other hand, sees the monstrous garden as a fragment of ancient times representing the philosophical world. Nietzsche—whom Cross here reads beautifully—writes that after Socrates, philosophy was ruined; *Bomarzo* shows the resolve with which Cross decided to write a Heraclitian, pre-Socratic poem, and to find within it a vestige of the past. "Tanto de nosotros quedó también atrás. / Cosas olvidadas antes que ocurrieran. Y aquello que causaba insomnios y furores, por lo que hubiéramos vendido el alma, / aparece ahora como un drama vulgar, / y todo se reduce / a una pulsera con el broche roto—o a un pedazo de vasija: / hileras de hiplitas desnudos con sus lanzas, el pene curvo como réplica de la barba" ("So much of us also left behind. / Things forgotten before they occurred. And that which caused insomnia and fury, for which we would have sold our soul, / now seems a vulgar drama, / and everything is reduced / to a bracelet with a broken clasp—or a piece of crockery: rows of naked hoplites with their lances, the curved penis a retort to the beard").

Reading *Bomarzo* I was surprised by the anticlimactic change Cross's poetry has undergone since the publication of her dithyrambs in *El vino de las cosas* (2004), which was the last book of hers I had read. In a reverse of the standard trajectory (or at least the biographical convention that passes for such), her recent poetry abandons transparency, leaves behind the simplified means of conveying Buddhism that a good number of her books exude—those written under the reign of India, an empire where at times nothing is mysterious or occult. It is, in fact, obsessive explanation that makes it indigestible, as Octavio Paz said. Put simply, Cross was a classicist first and now, with *Bomarzo*, seems to have become a Romanticist. Strictly speaking, she has always been and continues to be a mystic poet. After all in an interview with Daniel Saldaña París (*Ingrima*, August, 2008), she admitted—with a convenient dose of false modesty—that her intellectual training, religious dogma, and philosophy all dissolve, when she needs them to, in mysticism.

Written in mid-2005, *Bomarzo*, like all poems of this type, has something foreboding about it. It's not that Cross had never before seen the terrible, Nietzschean face of God, no. What's new in *Bomarzo* is the steadfastness with which she fixes her gaze on Greek scapegoat rituals of sacrifice. Cross sees Bomarzo as a repository for living creatures decaying in the face of "la brutalidad de la visión" ("the brutality of the vision"), a world in time where "la vida nuestra se prolongaba como una impunidad" ("our life was prolonged like an indemnity").

The gods in this Dionysian book, "ebrios, locos, posesos" ("inebriated, crazy, possessed"), are less than magnanimous. Bomarzo's allegories, written in stone—as presented by Mujica Lainez in his novel—turned their backs on the enlightened paganism of the Renaissance. Cross, too, wades into those cathartic waters, asking at the end if, rather than seek a cure, we might not do better with "una herida que no cerrara / una punzada constante" ("a wound that never heals / a constant twinge"). I don't know if those conversing in *Bomarzo* are dreaming or not, if Cross herself is awake or asleep. Nor do I know how she would respond to the academic question of whether her Greece is that of the "unitary logos" or the world of dreams. But that matters little in *Bomarzo*, her most narrative and most dramatic poem, as well as her most impressive: the one in which Heraclitus appears—as per a certain tradition—as the first Romantic.

SELECTED BIBLIOGRAPHY

Espirales. Poesía reunida, 1966–1999, UNAM, Mexico, 2002.

Los dos jardines. Mística y erotismo en algunos poetas mexicanos, Ediciones Sin Nombre/Conaculta, Mexico, 2003.

El vino de las cosas. Ditirambos, ERA, Mexico, 2004.

Cuaderno de Amorgós, Aldus, Mexico, 2007.

Bomarzo, ERA, Mexico, 2009.

Paredes, Alberto. *Una temporada de poesía. Nueve poetas mexicanos recientes (1966–2000)*, Conaculta, Mexico, 2004.

Visible y no visible / Seen and Unseen, bilingual edition, trans. John Olivier-Simon, Ediciones Sin Nombre, Mexico, 2009.

Selected Poems, ed. Tony Frazer, trans. Anamaria Crowe Serrano, Shearsman Books, 2009.

CUESTA, JORGE

(Córdoba, Veracruz, 1903 – Mexico City, 1942)

No Mexican writer has died such a terrible death as Cuesta did on August 13, 1942, nor has anyone received such well-deserved posthumous reparations. Twenty years after his self-castration and suicide in a Tlalpan insane asylum, scholars began to collect the papers of the poet and critic who had never published a single book in his life. But 1964 was a critical year for Mexican literature, because that's when UNAM published the first four tomes of Cuesta's *Poemas y ensayos*. That first edition, compiled by Miguel Capistrán and Luis Mario Schneider, was followed by three others, restoring Cuesta's name and position as the posthumous prince of Mexican criticism. And since the time when Juan García Ponce* and Octavio Paz* shied away from association with him, few other writers have done so. Writing about Cuesta has turned into an indispensable rite of passage for three generations of burgeoning critics. That's the destiny of a man who, having lived in the shadows, in 2004 had had his centenary in broad daylight, a secret writer who became the conscience of an entire literary tradition. (2004)

Cuesta was Mexico's first modern intellectual, and his reputation still stands firm at the end of the twentieth century. There might be disagreement about his poetic prowess, but no one doubts the significance of his intentions. We accept the limitations of his thinking but grant him extenuating circumstances. Cuesta's point of departure was his profound sense of certainty.

Friends and enemies, successors and the man himself agreed that "rootlessness" was the term that best defined his life and work. Ironically, Cuesta's presence is now deeply rooted in Mexican culture, as if over the years his texts have sent out shoots into the garden of the future. It would be unjustified to try to deny his accomplishments on the basis of his rhetorical skills. After all, his is one of very few moral victories posterity has ever conceded a Mexican writer. When Cuesta was writing in the thirties, the search for an "authentic" Mexican identity was in full swing. At the time, his privileging of intellectuals and European tradition flew in the face of a burgeoning, post-revolutionary cultural nationalism. But since the seventies there has been a general consensus about Cuesta's visionary literary and political criticism. And to declare that his work has achieved political consensus essentially means that he has a vital place in the cultural *polis*. Cuesta has become a point of reference because he was right, or because we take his points to be our own. He was practicing modern criticism in inhospitable conditions, and at the time his assessment wasn't taken as criticism but attack. In retrospect it makes sense that he was misunderstood; likewise, it would be wrong, now, not to acknowledge our indebtedness to him.

More than anything, he was a literary critic, although he delved insightfully into other art forms and politics as well, implicitly criticizing Mexican culture at large. It's obvious that he paid no attention to either seminal ethics or aesthetics, but one of his strong suits was that he set his own limits. Cuesta saw criticism as both intellectual exercise and moral positioning. And his oeuvre is comprised of a well-achieved balance between the two.

Cuesta's modernity necessitated taking a stance, viewing "tradition" as something to be created, a process of selection. Unlike T. S. Eliot, the Mexican poet didn't have a methodical critical memory on which to base his decisions. Instead, he saw the critic as a *creator* of tradition and set out to draw a map with which to read it. At the time, Mexican literature didn't even have a hallowed academic history to be contested. After the Mexican Revolution, we clung to academic bedrock (neo-classicism, modernism), halfheartedly admired poet Sor Juana, argued over whether playwright Ruiz de Alarcón was Mexican, or worshipped the heroes of political romanticism. None of that met Cuesta's criteria. For him to find his place as critic, he had to invent chunks of literary history [. . .]

Cuesta is Mexico's twentieth-century Faust. And as our first modern critic, when he died, he left behind a critical body of work that I see as a series of Faustian contracts that set forth three principal tenets: first, that any intellectual who delves into ideological politics is dealing with the devil; second, that literary criticism obeys its own autonomous, aesthetic laws not subject to external reality; and third, that literary critics must accept a priori their status as outcasts, diabolical figures, fallen angels, society's black sheep. Cuesta made no moral judgments about the political stances taken by the intellectuals of the day, but he did highlight the enormous responsibility that declaring ideological positions entailed.

He invented a genealogy, giving critics a new self-sufficient role and granting them autonomous functions. By disassociating himself from "Mexican" tradition, he created the conditions required to reinvent a non-nationalistic canon, the establishment of which was his aim. This is why he launched an attack against Romanticism, preached constitutional liberalism, and elevated muralist José Clemente Orozco—whom he saw as authentic—to the heights of Olympus, in his own personal classicism. In each of these maneuvers, Cuesta is the exhausted negotiator who can't give up until he knows that he's sold his soul to the devil at the right price.

In the long run, his crusade benefited us. His works are canonized: his ideas are now taken for granted in high culture and low, in the Ivory Tower and the public plaza. That doesn't mean that the money he coined was never counterfeited—or misappropriated—by those of divergent academic tendencies. Faust was a businessman, too, an unwise architect who dreamed of rerouting Nature's river through human industry.

Cuesta's essays are like carefully taken minutes, detailing the relationship between artistic creation and its diabolic possibilities, its relationship to power. A moralist and guarantor of the ethics of responsibility, he criticizes ideologists eager to use "national spirit" as a way to hide their views. Two of the things that mattered most to him were twentieth-century intellectuals' betrayal of the universal values they should have upheld (i.e. their becoming communists or fascists) and limiting State interference in civil matters. Cuesta's spirit is watching over us today, in our current nationalistic fervor.

Although Cuesta was the architect of many safeguards, he also brought on his own downfall. After having pacted intellectually with the devil in his essays, his diabolical maneuvers turned physical and he attacked his own body. In this battle, tragically, he was not victorious, and he lost both the fight and his life (*Tiros en el concierto: Literatura mexicana del siglo V*, 1997).

SELECTED BIBLIOGRAPHY

Obras reunidas, tomo I. Poesía, prologue by Francisco Segovia, ed. J. Martínez Malo and V. Peláez Cuesta, FCE, Mexico, 2003.

Obras reunidas, tomo II. Ensayos y prosas varias, prologue by Christopher Domínguez Michael and ed. J. Martínez Malo and V. Peláez Cuesta, FCE, Mexico, 2004.

Obras reunidas, tomo III. Primeros escritos. Miscelánea. Iconografía. Epistolario, ed. J. Martínez Malo and V. Peláez Cuesta, FCE, Mexico, 2007.

D

D'AQUINO, ALFONSO
(Mexico City, 1959)

Books written by eccentrics have a way of aging: authors who beguile (or repel) are hypersensitive and, if exposed to light, their eccentricity becomes just another convention. I can't predict what destiny awaits the poet D'Aquino, but I can say that since his first book, *Prosfisia* (1981), he's written a bold, incorruptible body of work. D'Aquino's publishers say that his poetry is "rigorous and insidious to the point of obsession" or "transparent to the point of incandescence," which isn't saying much when what most stands out—radical experimentation of poetic form—has been withering away in academia for some time now. A man who rubs words together like stones until they ignite (to astonishing effect), D'Aquino's poems range from the trivial to the fantastic. His is a luxuriant world that flourishes like the jungle after a rain, an infinite expanse of land inhabited by insects, stones, lusty fruit, wet dogs: in short, the stuff of dreams when you have blood poisoning and are delirious or hallucinating.

"During Antiquity and the Middle Ages," wrote José María González de Mondoza*—an oft-overlooked critic who studied both eccentric and very eccentric writers—"it was commonly believed that there existed a monster called a basilisk who could kill with his glance; some said his breath could kill. But he lost his powers if man saw him before he saw man, and since logic prevailed, an easy way to kill him was hit upon: by holding up a mirror to him, he'd see his own image and die."

At any rate, basilisks are all over the place, from Isaiah (11:18 "and the weaned child shall thrust his hand into the den of the basilisk") to Sor Juana Inés de la Cruz, so it's no surprise that D'Aquino, a bestial poet, would dedicate a book to the fabled creatures (*Basilisco*, 2001). Almost a poetic "reptile park," the work delves into the world of that serpent first discussed by Pliny the Elder, seen in the Middle Ages as a strange chicken-snake hybrid hatched from a yolkless egg. Maybe D'Aquino is trying to tell us that when held up to a mirror, his poetry sees itself as monstrous, and by perishing it takes part in the great chain of metamorphosis.

SELECTED BIBLIOGRAPHY
Piedra no piedra, UAM, Mexico, 1992.
Naranja verde, Vuelta, Meixco, 1996.
Tanagra, Conaculta, Mexico, 1996.
Basilisco, Ediciones Sin Nombre, Mexico, 2001.
Astro Labio, Magenta, Mexico, 2010.

DÁVILA, AMPARO
(Pinos, Zacatecas, 1928)

Modern masters' critique of society is different from that of old realists, due to two subsequent tendencies. The first transcends phenomenological barriers. Writers such as Elena Garro,* Rosario Castellanos,* Eraclio Zepeda, Sergio Galindo,* and Jorge López Páez,* if read carefully, often invoke rites of passage, transvaluing things once taken to be static into fluid, interior representations of reality. This occurs when a population is depicted representing itself: Chamulas unable to take the enemy city, Indians discovering another plane of reality during some roadside incident, a child perceiving events via a literarily modified perspective. These narrative inventions are ultimately intended to provide some sort of three-dimensionality to setting, characters, or overall vision. Thus, realism stops being an *imitation* (or sublimation) of reality and becomes an *interpretation* of it. It stops being an obligatory technique—the indispensable mediator—and becomes a narrative choice based on research, which eventually gets old and disappears. Then the second tendency develops, dissolving the traditional boundary between text and the world as seen by realists.

Dávila's prose is quite useful in attempting to explain the second tendency. The first one made realism real. The second, by taking it to the extreme, denies it altogether. Dávila's stories go from critiques of provincial asphyxiation to utterly fantastic tales in one fell swoop, without making a stopover at magical realism. Hers are primitive texts that leap from everyday existence to magical occurrence and avoid the realm of community or society. This method yields fantastic literature, although that's nothing new: its origins predate written text and are to be found in legends and minstrelsy. There had, of course, been fantastic tales in Mexican literature already. Alfonso Reyes,* in 1910, wrote "La cena," a so-called "invention," an intellectual intrigue that consisted of constructing a textual artifact only to dismantle it. Like a magic trick, it created an illusion and then delighted in seeing it go up in smoke. But Dávila's books—*Tiempo destrozado* and *Música concreta* (both from 1959)—can't be explained without the prior existence of realism and the attempt to dissolve it. Proportionally speaking, Dávila is like Welsh supernaturalist Arthur Machen. She starts with the illusion of realism, the generally atmospheric rhythm of her narration slowly annulling the precepts of reality until the fantastic springs forth. Her characters are a—somewhat facile—distortion of conventional reality (stockholders, bureaucrats, children, widows), and the invisible, unclassifiable, unspeakable element that inhabits her texts seems diluted and antiquated compared to more recent, more radical texts. But if Dávila's world itself is not entirely original, her choice of that world at that time certainly was. She rejects the utopian view of the natural world by perforating it. Hers is an otherworldly departure from realism and an entry into a panicked world of terror, which her stories portray discretely, almost timidly, and always intriguingly. (*Antología de la narrativa mexicana del siglo XX*, I, 1989)

See also RIVERA GARZA, CRISTINA.

SELECTED BIBLIOGRAPHY
Cuentos reunidos, FCE, Mexico, 2009.

DELTORO, ANTONIO
(Mexico City, 1947)

Deltoro once said in an interview, "Light is my Madeleine. When I was a boy I'd go into the bathroom while my father was taking a shower, and I was fascinated by his skin and his body and I dreamed—without closing my eyes—that just like him, time would one day give me the same skin and hairy body. Now, when I bathe in the morning, in the same *altiplano*, that has the same tone of light, sometimes I see not my own body, but his. And that vision is the result of affection, and wonder, and time."

You have to tread carefully when it comes to poets and their assertions. Between the poetics and the poems lies an abyss called vanity. But it's true that the father's presence is there like a guardian in Deltoro's poetry (*Hasta donde es aquí*, 1984; *Los días descalzos*, 1984; *Balanza de sombras*, 1997). His is not a thundering, awesome father but a kindly parent, a protector freed from the guillotine of parricide and free of blame. A man on whom the poet casts his glance, whether in his library or in his skin. And all of the creatures and objects in Deltoro's poetry—from a portrait of Melville to pillows to beetles—are nuanced, like the father, and eternally reside on a never-ending Thursday, the day Deltoro (as well as poet Pedro Salinas) deems the most enigmatic of all, both auspicious and foreboding. While other poets seek out otherness and enigmas, Deltoro opts for all that's overlooked in the visible world.

SELECTED BIBLIOGRAPHY
Poesía reunida (1979–1997), UNAM, Mexico, 1999.
El quieto, Biblioteca Sibila, Sevilla, 2008.

DENIZ, GERARDO
(Madrid, Spain, 1934)

Deniz's poems are the most bizarre fusion of worlds in all of Spanish-language poetry. His work is seen as hermetic without being unintelligible, an adventure rife with hidden dangers and riddles that turns us, the readers, into addicts ambling through a universe that is, as Aurelio Asiain* said, spectrally romantic, falsely essayistic, and dubiously poetic—if by "poetry" we mean the hackneyed conventions that the twentieth century has tried its best to do away with. I doubt Deniz qualifies as an "antipoet," but if he does it would be wise to stick T. S. Eliot in that category, too. And if Deniz's poetry isn't accepted as "poetry," we would do well to recall that Ezra Pound said that the first writer to determine what comprises poetry has a clear advantage over all those who follow and share his opinion.

Asiain has said that Deniz's formal passion is "ruled by the pleasure of a sensuality that appeals, more than anything, to sensory perception. It's not unusual in a poet such as Deniz, for whom words are just as material as things, to hear the most unusual voices; to hear lexicons of geometry, anatomy, chemistry, philology, music, and the many languages of man, all mixed together in a completely natural way. Nor does it seem odd that, along with alliteration, neologism, and creative syntax, each page of Deniz's poetry cites other poets, and contains secret allusions and many other things, all of which benefit the poem" (Asiain, *Caracteres de imprenta*, 1996).

When *Adrede* came out in 1970, Octavio Paz* was the work's first defender, praising it enthusiastically while also admitting to some reticence. Paz said, for instance, that Deniz's words jumped out like "obese women, weighted down with talismans," and sometimes seemed like "sandbanks" of all that had been read. But he also took note of the fact that Deniz took a lone stance against the by-then observable tendency to confuse literature (and sometimes even poetry) with the publishing business. By my generation, decades later, Deniz had become the most admired and studied poet around. Poets, critics, and translators like Asiain, José María Espinasa,* Fernando Fernández, Josué Ramírez, Mónica de la Torre, and Luis Ignacio Helguera* saw Deniz as a radical break from the prevailing poetic routine.

At the launch for *Amor y oxidente* (1991), Asiain asked, "How can we explain the enthusiastic reception Gerardo Deniz's poetry has received in the past few years? We might have expected a somewhat lonely fate for this difficult, hermetic work [. . .]. I suspect that Deniz's public good fortune is attributable to more traditional and less prestigious grounds: his felicitous phrasing, precise tone, masterful meter, and the confident prosody with which fertile and often extravagant imagination come through."

Deniz himself is the one who opened his work to interpretation, in *Mansalva* (1986), an anthology of his first three books—*Adrede, Gatuperio* (1978), and *Enroque* (1986)—that alternates poems from each book, creating a new order. This juxtaposition, as Espinasa said, brings certain things out into the open, making it easier to interpret Deniz's verse, in great part thanks to his own commentary. It's unusual indeed for a poet known for being hermetic to open up this way, offering concrete explanations for some of his "mysteries." In his *Diccionario de autores latinoamericanos* (2001), César Aira, an incisive critic of Mexican letters, examines Deniz's didactics: "Little by little, he's published exegeses of some of his poems. These are most interesting, as they shed light on the otherwise mysterious historical and encyclopedic allusions the author is partial to, and what had seemed purely verbal orchestrated effect is shown in fact to be a perfectly logical tale; it goes without saying that without the author's collaboration, the reader could never do this. That these publications exist and have been published at all, regardless of how few there are, is enough to fill the rest of his oeuvre with promise and make it even more intriguing. In fact, these texts suggest a method to his poetry writing, one that could allow for a mechanical reconstruction of all Deniz's poems [. . .], little philosophical novels filled with adventures that can be reread ad infinitum (because they're never fully understood), and always with pleasure."

After *Enroque* and *Grosso modo* (1988), Deniz seemed to become more of a sensual, anti-romantic poet with a paradoxically narrative, moral bent. At the aforementioned *Amor y oxidente* launch, Asiain said, "Many of his poems are renderings of a time in hell (resembling Quevedo more than Rimbaud, both in verbal dexterity and in their distinctive spirit): the vain conceit of poets, erudite stupidity, the delusions of doctrinaire thought, the bad faith of a good conscience, lack of love [. . .]. Just enunciating those hells is enough to prove that this poet's labyrinths are all of our labyrinths, and that his poetry—unlike most—truly deserves to be called civic. His setting is much less likely to be a desk than it is a city street, and his is a very concrete city [. . .]. He's as likely to pen an epigram as a song, as likely to tell a fantastic tale as to 'listen' to *musica universalis*, and then head down into the metro tunnels or wander the outskirts of the city or get lost in the rooms of his soul. With a writer like Deniz our poetry comes out the winner, not because he's one of us, but precisely because he's not. The density of his inner world and the outer intimacy of his adventurous spirit, which lead him to delve into the unexplored territory of morals, make him irreplaceable."

His Quevedo-like spirit allowed Deniz to go from being a poet condemned to the limbo of "pure poetry" to an author of sui generis political poems where the polis's agonists and protagonists are mocked venomously. Sor Juana and José Vasconcelos,* Freudian and Marxist coteries, José Emilio Pacheco* and post-civil-war Spanish exiles are everyday victims of a poet who has no qualms about deriding them in articles like those in *Anticuerpos* (1998).

Then there's his eroticism, that ironic appeal to the joy of romantic flings and the mortal remains of the flesh, which prompted Espinasa to note of *Enroque* that "some of the strangest love poems of our tradition are found in this book. It has neither Jaime Sabines's* rhetoric disguised as candor, nor Tomás Segovia's* soaring lyricism, nor the tone of Bonifaz Nuño's* pounding love. Its intensity is—precisely—unpoetic" (*Hacia el otro*, 1990).

Both of Deniz's realms, the bedroom (the personal) and the public plaza (his profuse outer world), are contained in his prose poems, where his talent reaches its greatest heights: *Picos pardos* (1987) and *Amor y oxidente* (1991), followed by *Mundonuevos* (1991), *Op. cit.* (1992), *Alebrijes* (prose, 1992), *Ton y son* (1996), *Letritus* (1996), *Cubiertos de una piel* (2002), and the English translations of some of his poetry in *Poemas / Poems* (2000). His entire oeuvre can now be found in the collection *Erdera* (2005).

Picos pardos is like a Flaubert tale reenacted: in the commotion of an important political night in the city, a prince and a vizier battle their way to a passionate denouement involving Rúnika, the damsel who acts as partner in crime. *Amor y oxidente*, in turn, could be seen as satirizing the search for knowledge. Maybe. And like *Gatuperio*, this poem comes from what for Deniz is a fabulous magma: the novels of Jules Verne (*20,000 Leagues Under the Sea* and *Five Weeks in a Balloon*) and of astronomer Camille Flammarion (*The Plurality of Inhabited Worlds*).

Like the nineteenth-century sages who inspired him, Deniz—who initially wanted to be a chemist—was bitten by the science bug in his youth, and then drifted away from positivism as an intellectual discipline. He decided to write a periodic saga featuring characters who (like Captain Nemo, Professor Aronnax, and Captain Spero) set off on marvelous, speculative Denizian journeys. This spirit of speculation, whether in science or poetry, is what reigns supreme in Deniz, as in Verne, so we could say that the Mexican poet's response to an illustration of the inside of the *Nautilus* is akin to a landscape of his soul. "The whole submarine looks as though it's made of huge, open, half closed, and closed books. There are enormous books on the tables, on the chairs, on the floor. There are drapes, tassels, frames, whole panoplies that exceed even Verne's evocative loquacity."

There are a couple of things one should know about the life of Gerardo Deniz—pen name of Juan Almela—in order to understand the man who tried (unsuccessfully) to place literature fourth or fifth on his list of vocations. The son of Spanish exiles who came to Mexico via Geneva in 1942, Deniz proved himself in *Paños menores* (2002), his fragmentary autobiographical work, to be one of the most diabolically literary (and learned) people on the Mexican cultural scene, and one of its guardians. Deniz is not just, as David Huerta* called him, "an incredibly erudite man with an expert knowledge of music," as was Quevedo; he's also a grammarian, expert in several different languages, and grammarians, despite their unsociability, exercise their arrogant pride on the people.

In "Exilio y literatura," the central text in *Paños menores*, we find the crux of Denizian experience. Called to talk about a topic (exile) that has moved (and bored) the twentieth century, a never-ending spout of heroism and chicanery, repository of so much bad prose, Deniz goes off on a tangent. A beautiful, despotic tangent only conceivable in a writer like him, not so immune to the nightmares of history, as we see in *Picos pardos*. Not even the Gnostics, feeling exiled from the light of the earthly world, manage to move Deniz, for whom one can "feel exiled from places that in fact do exist, but where one never lived."

The creative suffering brought on by inhabiting so many worlds, that feeling of exile that's multiplied in his poems, proves that Deniz is not—as was once suspected—the umpteenth person to gloss Joyce, tirelessly excreting the contents of the unconscious to hurl it onto the typed page. "Posible," the most didactic poem in *Gatuperio*, spurs a gloss from which one could infer that Deniz is a materialist poet with vaguely Lucretian roots, a man who sees ash as the quintessence, the ruins, the destiny of so many philosophies that have been consumed, fuel for transcendence.

As per his own confession, Deniz sometimes chooses the ever-changing material world over the fraudulent empire of absolutism. That leaves us with an index of the paradoxical relationships between science and poetry as they arise in Deniz's soul, "harto de poetas y de pluralidad de los mundos, el ilustre / Leverrier ensartó un gato en el sable y cesó al ujier de modo / fulminante / según consta en la historia," ("sick of poets and of plurality of worlds, the illustrious / Leverrier skewered a cat on his cutlass and stopped the doorman / devastating / as the story goes").

Music, and more precisely "melomania," the almost boundless listening freedom offered by the twentieth century, is one of Deniz's passions. He knows that only half-deaf poets claim an arguable association between music and poetry. For Deniz, "poetry creates, at most, tiny debatable worlds. Music, on the other hand, attracts whole swathes of life, places, and times, with all their colors, smells, and flavors—and all that without losing the main thing, the music . . ." Although I share his belief that "the overlap between the two genres (is) not too promising," it's hard not to feel that Deniz has indeed created poetry overflowing with those huge swathes of life, places, and times that are music.

SELECTED BIBLIOGRAPHY
Erdera, FCE, Mexico, 2005.
Poems, trans. Monica de la Torre, Lost Roads/Taller Ditoria, Mexico, 2000.

E

ELIZONDO, SALVADOR
(Mexico City, 1932 – 2006)

For the past several years, rereading Elizondo has become one of my least reprehensible habits. At this stage in my life, I often do what Elizondo himself proposed in his *Autobiografía precoz* (1966 and 2000), which is to alternate between talking to the dead and babbling with the living, so I'm predisposed to enjoy his work more. I believe I've now read *Farabeuf o la crónica de un instante* (1965; *Farabeuf*, 1972) four times, and I feel better after each visit to Doctor Farabeuf, who now appears before me willing to chat when he once seemed to command silence. He's a French surgeon, a literary precept, the first know-it-all, and because the narration is so disembodied, it's his ghost who fills the room. Only on the surface is his conversation monothematic, and I've learned quite a lot from his obsessions.

People often forget that Elizondo was a literature professor at the Universidad Nacional and an advisor at the now-defunct Mexican Center for Writers. Though I never went to his house in the Santa Catarina area of Coyoacán where he lived in Mexico City, I mention his profession in light of the pedagogical side of his work. His books are a gradual learning process, one that's allowed me to modify my opinions and qualify my judgments to the extent that, for instance, I no longer think—as I did—that *Farabeuf* and *El hipogeo secreto* (1968) are Elizondo's most stimulating works. The latter is like an unfairly relegated collection of Russian dolls, and I tend to agree with

César Aira, who said, "Comprised entirely of self-reference, his . . . novel, *El hipogeo secreto*, is about writing a novel called 'El hipogeo secreto,' and so on, and includes pictorial references (to Chardin, and maybe Piranesi), and of course, a love interest. Although critics have agreed that this novel is extraordinarily inferior to his last, it might actually be superior, and even extraordinarily superior" (*Diccionario de autores latinoamericanos*, 2001).

After *El hipogeo secreto*, Elizondo played around (convincingly) with a self-destructive urge, as can be read in the renowned litany from *El grafógrafo* (1972). "I'm writing. I'm writing that I'm writing. Mentally I can see myself writing that I'm writing and I can also see myself writing . . ." But, as we can see in his *Narrativa completa* (1998), Elizondo's writing was awaiting a finale grander than that of the literary innovations of the sixties. Adolfo Castañón,* one of his most thought-provoking critics, says that Elizondo is the most talented Mexican writer there is when it comes to expert experimentation with the entire range of narrative possibilities, using motifs entrenched in classic twentieth-century literature, from writing as an intellectual pursuit to the orgasm-as-death analogy.

After *El grafógrafo*, Elizondo entered an increasingly complex and extensive phase of his oeuvre, which can be seen in *Cuaderno el escritura* (1969), *Camera lucida* (1983), *Elsinore* (1987), and *Teoría del infierno y otros ensayos* (1992). This is "pure" literature, essay and narrative, made even more perfect by his flawless prose, the best of his generation. What Elizondo said of Paul Valéry's *Monsieur Teste*, I could just as easily say of Elizondo himself: "On rereading him now, the ideas in play somehow seem clearer, more radiant, less complicated and much more dramatic than they did then, when everything was tinged with that melancholy brought on by the failure of spiritual endeavors, particularly those that, at one point in our lives, we'd set ourselves as challenges" (*Estanquillo*, 1993).

Elizondo's literary universe, which he himself says contains Quevedo and Gracián, Blake and Joyce, is narrow, succinct, sparse, ruled by a monomaniacal voice. Even over the years, Elizondo added only a few names to his canon: Conrad, Pound, Junger, and—of course—Dostoyevsky. In essence, he's the heir of Mallarmé and Valéry. And those who share his lineage are like harbingers of infertility, metaphysical believers in the Impossible Book, methodological skeptics awaiting the death of the author as they sit by the open tomb of literature.

Although Elizondo founded a journal called *S.nob*—a contraction of "sans noblesse"—in the sixties, he does indeed belong to a certain nobility, one that assumes the privilege of disdaining the masses and their bourgeois novels and their busy schedules, convinced that "going in search of lost time is a great way to waste time" and a long etcetera well suited to aristocratic obsessions. But while there might be such a thing as "noble" literature, it's not free from the virus of fiction. Perhaps the "mal de Teste" Elizondo diagnosed himself with was just a way for him to keep the romantic fiction bug in check.

Knowing that almost everything seen as Satanic would eventually become passé, that transgression would become the contemporary art norm, Elizondo abandoned his decadence and rid himself of his erotic obsessions of yore. His loyalty to Mallarmé and Valéry—his own Don Quixote and Sancho Panza—meant denouncing novels of Decadentism, black masses, or perverse esthetes. The Puritanism, geometric obsession, and "pure" technical prose of Mallarmé and Valéry are a familiar reaction against the byzantine, romantic works of the likes of Poe and Baudelaire. The wicked side of Elizondo, he of Chinese torture, de Sade, and Bataille, he of *Farabeuf* and *El hipogeo secreto*, became subtler, more luminous in works like *Camera lucida* and *Elsinore*.

It was by embracing the notion of a "project" that Elizondo found a way to keep writing, although it might have seemed that he wasn't. He did it by following that pontifical maxim that opens Cyril Connolly's *The Unquiet Grave*: "the true function of a writer is to produce a masterpiece . . ." The project is that space where the genie appears on stage, just when his existence is denied. *Camera lucida* contains Elizondo's canonical texts: projects that become masterpieces. It's a collection of essays and stories disorderly in appearance only, and as Dermot F. Curley says, it *projects* several issues that explain Elizondo's ideas about writing: "Log" suggests that the "desert isle" of a blank page is enough to merit *not* writing another *Robinson Crusoe*; "La veranda" explains the gimlet-laden role of the veranda on tropical evenings; "La legión extranjera" considers, reviews, and then discards the French colonial novel's raison d'être; and "Anapoyesis" is the tale of a machine Professor Émile Aubanel invented to process the latent energy of Mallarmé poems.

Following his most difficult approach ("I'm dreaming that I'm writing this book . . .") Elizondo wrote *Elsinore*, which is both an extraordinary memoir and—like *Farabeuf*—a "chronicle of an instant," one of the most effective coming-of-age tales in all of Mexican literature in which two boys run away from a military academy in California (which Elizondo actually did attend) and end up in a little boat on a lake. Using his meticulously spatial mind to evoke visual images, Elizondo proves himself a great artist, seemingly a born portraitist.

The author of many still-unpublished works—including the nocturnal diaries or "nightly dailies" that are stirring up startling curiosity—Elizondo was ironically apolitical and yet managed to be an insightful historical witness of the times, as anyone who reads collections such as *Contextos* (1973) or *Estanquillo* (1993) will see. An admirer of Russian formalism and other twentieth-century art of the masses, he had no qualms about saying that the Third Reich's best painter was Hitler himself. He was the type of writer who looked beyond the gathering storm clouds of journalism and the cobwebs of historiography, nonchalantly making affirmations like this: "The dissolution of the Soviet Union the other day has enormous significance for me, both philosophical and, in a sense, sentimental and nostalgic. To think that the supreme scientific doctrine that enjoyed a brief moment of irrefutability with Michurin's giant pears, Pavlov's two-headed dogs, Makarenko's kids, etc.; to think that an aesthetic that bore early but stunning fruit like *The Battleship Potemkin*; to think that so many things we admired or were impressed by in our youth were, in essence, nothing but quackery, just Hegel's ideas manipulated by two bourgeois jokers followed by millions and millions of men the world over for five generations, and all of it lost its meaning and its significance from one day to the next. Now that the Soviet Union of our childhood and youth—that of close-shaven commissars, muddled Madrid brigades, and the charming domesticated Muscovite *Ninotchka*—no longer exists, we'll surely feel some ill-placed nostalgia for a time we thought of as heroic but that, as of yesterday, will be lost time."

His morbid and seemingly disdainful powers of historical observation are already apparent in his *Autobiografía precoz* when he unflinchingly evokes Nazism in a way few others had before, recalling the long-lost days of his childhood in Germany with an anti-Semitic nanny named Anne Marie. In the same memoir, Elizondo portrays himself drinking with William Burroughs at the Chelsea; pages later he's awed at the birth of his daughter, whose very existence negates his cynicism. After love affairs with both cinema and painting, once he'd done his time in both heaven and hell, Elizondo left New York and Paris behind and found that being a Latin American writer was not entirely deplorable after all. Once noting that the problem with Rome is that Romans are dull, this cosmopolitan writer lived the life of a retired Mexican gentleman, admiring Emperors Maximilian and Charlotte, listening excitedly to the fireworks in his neighborhood, and being the proud grandnephew of Enrique González Martínez, the poet whose academic precision he shared and in whose verse he found a connection with Paul Valéry.

In thick, fat handwriting as expressive as a series of ideograms, Elizondo wrote his own destiny when he recalled in *Autobiografía precoz* that "The Venerable Bede compares human life to a lost skylark that flies into an enclosure, swiftly glides through it, and then flies back out into the night. An autobiography is to life what that moment is to the skylark's flight."

Julien Gracq said that Valéry had minimized the pleasure of reading in order to maximize the care he took in verifying the professionalism of the writing. Though he meant it as a compliment, the same cannot be said of Elizondo, since the pleasure of reading him increases in tandem with the "professionalism" of his writing. That achievement is what makes him a classic, in at least two senses. First, the meaning of his work evolves without losing any of its mystery over time (during a period in which his generation epitomized Mexican classicism by rigidly adhering to the form and expressing the anxiety of the modern condition). And second, Elizondo is a classic in the sense described by Spanish critic Juan Malpartida, who said that his work is essentially an attempt to unravel man's poetic ability, unearthing and explicating the devices that enable it to capture beauty photographically. Every time I decide to reread Elizondo, it's as if I see that skylark flying and dream of daring to catch it in my hand.

SELECTED BIBLIOGRAPHY

Neocosmos. Antología de escritos, ed. Gabriel Bernal Granados, Aldus, Mexico, 1966.

Salvador Elizondo, Empresas Editoriales, Mexico, 1966; rev. ed.: *Autobiografía precoz*, Aldus, Mexico, 2000.

Obras, Vuelta, Mexico, 1993.

Obras, I-III, prologue by Adolfo Castañón, El Colegio Nacional, Mexico, 1994.

Narrativa completa, prologue by Juan Malparida, Alfaguara, Mexico, 1999.

Pasado anterior, FCE, Mexico, 2007.

La escritura obsesiva, RM, Madrid, 2009.

El mar de iguanas, Atalanta, Madrid, 2010.

Curley, Dermot F., *La isla desierta. Una lectura de la obra de Salvador Elizondo*, FCE, Mexico, 1990.

Farabeuf, trans. John Incledon, Garland Publishing, New York, 1992.

ENRIGUE, ÁLVARO

(Guadalajara, Jalisco, 1969)

"The road would be long. All roads are long that lead toward one's heart's desire." That line, from Conrad's *The Shadow Line*, struck me when I read it, and years ago I jotted it down on a now-faded index card. I classify certain travel books, whether fiction or nonfiction, under that tag. Enrigue's novel, *El cementerio de sillas*, is one of them. It's a book, in the author's own words, faithful to the "art of navigation that—if there's no battle or storm—consists of staying awake as you fight tedium; that's what it comes down to and, strangely, that's also what the sort of enduring, moderate happiness that can be achieved on the high seas is all about."

Enrigue the Navigator tells the story of a family going back to the times of the Cyclopes; treks through North African deserts ruled by Emperor Tiberius; crosses the sixteenth century from Flanders to Puebla; adds to the never-ending stories about Jesuit conspiracies; and finally hones in on a contemporary Mexican family who seem unworthy of their ancient roots. But *El cementerio de las sillas* is not a "historical novel," if by that we mean the kind of marketable fiction published by any academic with a degree or two who decides to dramatize some era or other in order to shed light on the hackneyed conventions of our time. Ever since the five-hundredth anniversary of Columbus's voyage, Spain and Latin America have been plagued by inept historical reenactments: the "discovery" and conquest of America lend themselves beautifully to the art of pulling the wool over readers' eyes.

While it's true that *El cementerio de las sillas* takes place in history, the novel's historiography serves as an indicator of the voyage's inverted (or lost) time. On a deeper level lies a fictional reality that Enrigue makes credible by presenting us with a poor soul who lives on pizza and desperately wants to escape this century and the hovel where he lives in Mexico City's Colonia Mixcoac. The man, whose surname is Garamántez, is a chip off the old Herodotus—specifically, *Histories*, book IV, chapters 183–184, in which the historian tells of the fabled Garamantes, an extinct tribe of hunters and farmers who occasionally crop up in mythologists' conversations.

In that vein, Enrigue decided to write a weighty enough adventure story to function also as a meditation on our origins. In *El cementerio de las sillas*, similar to Melquíades's last stand in *One Hundred Years of Solitude*, the beginning is at the end of time. And since the end of this novel pays homage to the grandeur of the American continent, you might be inclined to think it's a roundabout way of talking about the origins of Mexican identity. I don't think it is. If Enrigue's soteriology demonstrates anything, it's his indifference to origins, a sort of inverse manifest destiny. If any old Puebla family can be descendents of the Garamantes, then origins are just a beautiful but useless subterfuge. Enrigue believes in values and, loyal to the rhetoric of adventure stories, he exalts courage, friendship, and *mestizaje*; but none of these attributes implies any sort of overarching quintessence.

When he began his voyage, Enrigue was less concerned with foreign lands than he was with making sure his ship never sailed off course, and he put all of his narrative talent into the endeavor, using a confident, calculated language that sets him apart from other contemporary writers. *El cementerio de las sillas* is a book in which a single voice speaks through its many narrators and protagonists, a voice discernible by its sense of humor and present-day Mexican Spanish. In its conversations, which span centuries, it's always Enrigue speaking in an ironic falsetto, with crafty suspicion and mestizo pride. Using this language, the novel introduces a powerful cast of characters including Carib Indians, the Flemish Christophorus Gaaramanjik, and his final avatar, the Garamántez who travels to Puebla to solve the mysteries of his ancestry, fending off death with a stack of chronicles, the sort of "suit of armor" only a literature student could conceive of.

Critics seem to have formed a certain, often cranky, consensus that there are essentially only two convincing ways to write contemporary short stories.

One dates back to Borges and condemns authors to be never-ending commentators; the other prides itself on following Chekhov's method (or Raymond Carver's, in its more up-to-date manifestation). After reading *Hipotermia*, I think I can say that Enrigue is one of the few Mexican writers not writing either Borgesian or Chekhovian short stories.

In *Hipotermia*, both publisher and reader—and Enrigue himself—feel the urge to seek some sort of "hybridity" and turn the collection into a novel. Despite the fact that the literary times in which we live celebrate cross-fertilization and tearing down genre boundaries, I think Enrigue is an exemplary short story writer, so good in fact that by unexpectedly leading us into this genre of old, he presents it as if made anew, a species awaiting baptism. He knows it too, and with the self-confidence good writers are prone to, Enrigue has no qualms about confessing the secret of his poetics. "It's something I've done since I was a boy: pretend I have a secret life, one that nobody can see. It's like I'm a blind man in the Bible. Although he regained his sight, he has to pretend he didn't, because Jesus Christ himself ordered it that way."

All of Enrigue's fictional talent stems from that statement, and there's often only one type of narrator in his stories: a man who's a failed writer and yet pulls all the strings in the comedy of his own life, his alter ego. The creator or hack (or cook in one of the stories) reflects and analyzes so much throughout *Hipotermia* that I'm tempted to say Enrigue's only weakness is that he becomes a commentator on his own work, laughing at his own jokes almost as a form of therapy. But it couldn't have been any other way in this implicitly existential book that traverses a dense emotional jungle; in fact, that's what was lacking in his first book of short stories, *Virtudes capitales* (1998).

Hipotermia could also be read as travel fiction of a sort, the logbook of an explorer voyaging to the mysterious source of the river. Like Somerset Maugham in the Far East, Enrigue went to Washington, DC to corroborate and refine his preconceptions about the human condition. These days, on a planet characterized by air traffic, few people have soul-searching experiences when they travel. But the details Enrigue found in Washingtonians (and Dalmatians, in another story) could only appear (in the ghostly sense of the word) to a writer profoundly concerned with issues of moral theology, with unjustified acts that lead us to distinguish good from evil.

In the "Grandes finales" section of *Hipotermia*, Enrigue satisfies his urge (both loving and concerned) to explore lost civilizations and languages. These, too, were the stuff of *El cementerio de las sillas*. *Hipotermia* tells one story about the extinction of the last Dalmatian and another traces the museographic history of Ishi, the last Yahi Indian. These archeological hidden treasures turn Enrigue into a sort of sublimated Egyptologist, making his first novel, *La muerte de un instalador* (1996), reminiscent of Gautier's *The Mummy's Foot*, where the ruins of postmodernism are symbolic of Antiquity. The notion of fictional character as survivor and repository of a family, a clan, a dynasty, permeates Enrigue's books. In *Hipotermia*, failures with happy endings make possible sentences like this one, about the people who lived through the Mexican earthquake of 1985: "Though it might be hard for earlier generations to accept, what we had was a Hemingway-style revolution, (with us) as stretcher-bearers."

Months ago I read a statement by French poet and essayist Charles Péguy that now seems written expressly to describe Enrigue's world: "Fathers are the great adventurers of the modern world." Enrigue's stories often have father and son as lone heroes, accomplices on an odyssey whose routine ending in Ithaca is one of the great achievements of an author who rejects Carver-style mini-tragedies and instead reduces myths and legends to their most concise, as in "Escenas de la vida familiar" and "Ultraje," the latter being one of the best Mexican short stories in recent years and worthy of a Terry Gilliam production. By explaining the transformation of a trash truck into a pirate ship, Enrigue presents his own style of metamorphosis, the kind that occurs when a piece of literature turns a literal reading into an Olympic curse.

Enrigue's new novel *Vidas perpendiculares* (2008) is, in a sense, like a second version of *El cementerio de sillas* (2002), one that perfects that novel's journey through the centuries in search of a family's lineage. By establishing the circular nature of his obsessions and then mastering them, Enrigue has set himself apart as a mature writer who has come of age. In the school of contemporary Latin American novelists he belongs to—and is one of the best of—it's uncommon for a writer to turn down a sure bet, to refuse cliché formulas that attract readers not looking to be challenged.

Vida perpendiculares is a historical novel. But not because it traverses the three ages (the divine, the heroic, and the human) that early modern prophets divided history into, nor because it invokes the imperial legion who killed Christ in Palestine, nor because it recounts the adventures of a seventeenth-century monk-hunter (and friar), nor for the Francisco de Quevedo-esque tone that ebbs and flows in verses and harangues, nor because it dares to record pre-linguistic humanity and risks describing prehistoric milieus that less ambitious writers would avoid. Nor is it a historical novel because Enrigue's sources of inspiration include Georges Duby, Mel Gibson, prehistorians, Tacitus, Saint Paul, Jesuit metapsychologist Carlos M. de Heredia's *Las memorias de un repórter en los tiempos de Cristo*, and Mark Twain, who used his own time machine to plumb the lives of King Arthur and Joan of Arc.

Vida perpendiculares is a historical novel because its fictional substance is grounded, if I'm not too far off base, in some of the ideas of Neopolitan philosopher Giambattista Vico (1668–1745). With delightful eloquence, clever imagination, and fantasy, Enrigue toys with phases of world history that come and go through recurring cycles—Vico's *corsi* and *recorsi*. And Enrigue's talent stands out: this is some of the most polished prose in Spanish, notable not only in its felicitous phrasing but also in the final flourish with which Enrigue ends each chapter, without exception. These are signs of a true storyteller.

What Vico was aspiring to was a form of psychological empathy, an anti-Cartesian method based on the conviction that the mind can only understand what it has made, and to paraphrase what he writes in *Scienza Nuova* (1725), although the mind clearly perceives itself, it does not *make* itself. The focus of that knowledge, the protagonist who embodies it, is Jerónimo, a boy who's been reincarnated multiple times, and recalls each of his lives throughout the course of history—and his past lives have certainly lived a lot.

A novel so noble as to be grounded in the history of philosophy, *Vidas perpendiculares* is not by any means boring, but it does ask a lot of its readers. Once again, they'll find Enrigue's phlegmatic, sardonic prose, which almost banks on being reread, in order to fully appreciate and understand the problems it poses and then solves. Such is the case with his tale of two cities, which posits a Babylonian Mexico City against a sad and empty Guadalajara; with his tale of Jesuit education, a unique purgatory that becomes art in Enrigue's prose; and with the eternal battle between pagans and Christians, which takes permanent hold.

Vico, in his autobiography, explains how when he was seven years old, he fell down a staircase, and spent five hours "unmoving and deprived of all feeling," which made his family fear that, his skull fractured and numb, he'd be left retarded. "Thank God," he says, using third person, "that fate did not come to pass . . . but healed from the accident, he was affected from then on with a gruff, melancholic nature . . ."

Like Vico, the protagonist Jerónimo, born in Lagos de Moreno, Jalisco, in 1936, is taught by Jesuits and, rather than becoming a halfwit like Juan Rulfo's* character Macario, turns into a Borges-style, "memorious" Funes, a character who forgets nothing, as the first critics of *Vidas perpendiculares* have already noted. Jerónimo, throughout the course of his lives, is always dying. But while other novelists (Carlos Fuentes* in *La muerte de Artemio Cruz*, Broch in *The Death of Virgil*) decided to stuff their moribund men with every memory they could think of on their deathbeds, Enrigue did the opposite, allowing memories to substitute for death.

Vidas perpendiculares might have ended with any of the lives that overtake Jerónimo, who lives simultaneously through many ages. But instead Enrigue decided to be faithful to the new religion and subjects Jerónimo to a higher law, that of love, a decision that would have satisfied the Neapolitan philosopher but might displease some contemporary readers. It's as if the author is unwilling to carry the art of memory that his novel summons through to its logical conclusion. Enrigue decided to put an end to the errant Jerónimo by freeing his avatars and having him find peace through sex, climax, and serenity. Which is almost like killing Melmoth the Wanderer or the Wandering Jew.

SELECTED BIBLIOGRAPHY

La muerte de un instalador, Joaquín Mortiz, Mexico, 1996.
Virtudes capitales, Joaquín Mortiz, Mexico, 1998.
El cementerio de las sillas, Lengua de Trapo, Madrid, 2002.
Hipotermia, Anagrama, Barcelona, 2005.
Vidas paralelas, Anagrama, Barcelona, 2008.
Vidas perpendiculares, Anagrama, Barcelona, 2008.
Hypothermia, trans. Brendan Riley, Dalkey Archive Press, Forthcoming, 2013.

ESPINASA, JOSÉ MARÍA

(Mexico City, 1957)

Poet, translator, literary critic, and cinematographer, Espinasa is also one of the most steadfast Mexican independent publishers around. And among the writers I've met, he's one of the best readers, too: much of the poetry and fiction I read is based on his recommendations, many of which he freely lent out from his own personal collection, from Léon Bloy to Luis Cernuda,* Henri Bosco, some of Elena Garro,* Paul Gadenne, and Juan Ramón Jiménez. My only complaint about Espinasa is that he hasn't written enough criticism, which is completely understandable for someone committed to publishing a few of the best Spanish-language authors around. But in addition to his publishing enterprises he does have some indispensable books of criticism, which prove him to be a reader who moves with the same ease through mid-century Mexican fiction as he does through contemporary Argentinean poetry: *Cartografías* (1989), *Hacia el otro* (1990), *El tiempo escrito* (1995), and *Temor de Borges* (2003). He possesses a unique ability to unearth the secret qualities of a text, often buried beneath the dust of hackneyed conventions. This he's proved repeatedly in essays on Inés Arredondo,* Sergio Galindo,* Tomás Segovia,* Jesús Gardea,* Héctor Manjarrez,* and others in which he seems to have said all there is to say. Subtle tones, understatement, silence, and marginal notes characterize the writers Espinasa is most passionate about.

SELECTED BIBLIOGRAPHY

Cartografías, Juan Pablos Editor, Mexico, 1989.
Hacia el otro, UNAM, Mexio, 1990.
El tiempo escrito, Ediciones Sin Nombre, Mexico, 1995.
Temor de Borges, Ediciones Sin Nombre, Mexico, 2003.
Actualidad de Contemporáneos, Ediciones Sin Nombre, Mexico, 2009.

F

FADANELLI, GUILLERMO

(Mexico City, 1963)

A few weeks after reading Guillermo Fadanelli's *Lodo* (2002), I went to see Liliana Cavani's *Ripley's Game*, based on the Patricia Highsmith novel of the same name. Both film and novel (and every Patricia Highsmith book) serve to show us that man is always closer than he thinks to committing murder. It's an undeniably modern premise that invokes an amateur Nietzscheanism (thankfully there is no other kind), although the notion really harkens back to Dostoyevsky.

"Killing a man is the greatest desire we keep tucked in our pockets," says philosophy professor Benito Torrentera, the antihero of *Lodo*. The novel tells the story of a poor soul who becomes involved—out of boredom or a longing for the spotlight—in a series of perfect crimes, seduced by Eduarda, an ordinary woman who he thought personified the grandeur and cruelty of all women. The erotic impulses of Professor Torrentera, who feels compelled to live dangerously, land him in jail, though first he's able to visit Tiripitío, the Michoacan town where Augustine Brother Alonso de la Vera Cruz founded the Estudio General, or Gimnasio Mayor, the first school of philosophy on the American continent.

Fadanelli started off as a Manichaean writer and might have ended up simply an underground writer. But he was talented enough to stop his counterculture moralizing, and through rigorous moral philosophy evolved into the adept author of *Lodo*. Fadanelli has insightful, intelligent opinions about almost every subject his narration takes on, and he's one of those writers who analyzes things from every possible angle. To give just one of many examples, Professor Torrentera and Eduarda's journey becomes a voyage through the anatomy of professions and feelings, from the mysteries of city life to the cruelty of Mexico. In addition to being philosophy disguised as a novel, *Lodo* just might be a meditation on man's "victimizable" condition, the state he's in once tamed and broken. In the novel, Professor Torrentera confesses, "I harbor no special hostility toward women. I simply fear them because I know the damage they can do me." The book is full of aphorisms, too, which Fadanelli sprinkles ably throughout. Here's one I underlined: "The bigger a person's suitcase, the bigger the imbecile." I once had the occasion to travel with him, and I can testify to the fact that his suitcase was the smallest. But baggage is another thing, and Fadanelli takes the whole world with him when he travels.

SELECTED BIBLIOGRAPHY
Lodo, Debate, Mexico, 2002.
Compraré un rifle, Anagrama, Barcelona, 2004.
La otra cara de Rock Hudson, Anagrama, Barcelona, 2004.
Dios siempre se equivoca. Aforismos, Joaquín Mortiz, Mexico, 2004.
Educar a los topos, Anagrama, Barcelona, 2006.
Malacara, Anagrama, Barcelona, 2007.

FELIPE, LEÓN

(Tábara, Spain, 1884 – Mexico City, 1968)

During his lengthy exile in Mexico, León Felipe (pseudonym of Felipe Camino García) came to epitomize the "poet as patriarch" for a public slightly larger than a tiny minority. Even in his worst poems—which are truly dreadful—there is something moving and resonant about his voice. The most Spanish-sounding of all the Spanish poets, he manages to be both an anarchist and a Catholic without being hypocritical, a blasphemous Christian for whom hell is not an end but a means. Trained as a pharmacist, León Felipe escaped the miseries of village life and ran off to the city, where he found a whole new world of stars and signs.

In 1942, Borges criticized León Felipe's "prosopopeiac" translation of Whitman's "Song of Myself," claiming he'd made the American bard sound like Spanish poet and statesman Núñez de Arce. In his defense, León Felipe wrote, "I renounce no one. All the world is mine and valid for a poem, everything, even the theatrical and stately tone of Núñez de Arce. Whitman is theatrical and stately as well. And so am I. What I do with the Book of Jonas, I do with Whitman as well, if that's the way the wind blows." Something unique at the time in Latin America, he was a poet convinced that his own voice emanated from the Old Testament. But his prophetic status didn't exempt him from the self-effacing humor and un-poetic sarcasm so characteristic of the tensions of modern poetry.

Octavio Paz,* an admirer of León Felipe since the pair met at an antifascist convention in Valencia in 1937, said that poems like his had never come out of Spain before. And though he preferred to call León Felipe a moral dissident, in "Nocturno de San Ildefonso" and some of Paz's autobiographical poems it's impossible not to hear echoes of León Felipe the poet, in particular *Español del éxodo y del llanto* (1939). That's unsurprising, given that they both saw the same "revolutionary Pharisees" sacrifice honorable poets during the Spanish Civil War.

León Felipe married Mexican Bertha Gamboa and lived in Mexico briefly on several occasions—the first in 1923—before settling there permanently after the fall of the Spanish Republic. The founder, together with Juan Larrea and Jesús Silva Herzog, of *Cuadernos Americanos* in 1941, he also published *El pescador de caña* (1938), *El hacha* (1939), *Español del éxodo y del llanto*, *El gran responsable* (1940), *Llamadme publicano* (1950), *El ciervo y otros poemas* (1958), and *¡Oh, este viejo y roto violín!* (1968), which sounds angelic even at its worst, according to Gabriel Zaid.*

"Now he's famous on earth, in heaven, and in hell," wrote Ermilo Abreu Gómez* in 1946, by which time the Spanish poet was a usual suspect on the Mexican cultural scene, as close to *Contemporáneo* poet Salvador Novo* as he was to the Spanish Republican exile community, in which he had both friends and enemies. Even Luis Cernuda,* who evinced the shortcomings of his poetry, paid him tribute, as did Vicente Aleixandre, Luis Cardoza y Aragón,* and Max Aub.*

Like a few other Spanish exiles, later in life León Felipe mistook heartfelt gratitude to the Mexican state with servile complacency, and he ended up writing and publishing an ode to President Gustavo Díaz Ordaz in 1967, which garnered him the antipathy of a younger generation that saw him (not without reason) as an unprincipled pawn sometimes called to the stage by the authoritarian regime. At his worst León Felipe was a facile poet whom philistines of every ilk found easily digestible. When he died, Aub commented sarcastically that the poet's ties to powerful Mexican politicians earned him a "national funeral" presided over by Novo and Agustín Yáñez*—the government's official literati—which was not such a paradoxical send-off for an anarchist, since they tended to become conservative by the time they died. In fact, it was at his funeral that Novo made that infamous statement about how happy he was that the military occupied the Ciudad Universitaria in the fall of 1968.

But times change, and now at the start of the twenty-first century when a veil of anarchy blankets the young generation protesting the cruel world, León Felipe has once again become a legitimate, approachable poet. Even the communiqués of *subcomandante* Marcos are peppered with tender metaphors and rhetorical devices from León Felipe's *Antología rota* (1947). Of all the demagogic poetry the Spanish Civil War bequeathed, very little conserves the moral and literary dignity of *Español del éxodo y del llanto*. It's libertarian poetry, directed against clerics and commissars alike, hostile to the Church and the Party, brimming with prophetic imagination and, deep down, paradoxically skeptical about the poet's possible role as oracle. "¡Yo también! Yo no fui más que una mueca, / una máscara / hecha de retórica y de miedo" ("And I! I was no more than a face, / a mask / made of rhetoric and of fear"). This is the mark of a prophet: his capacity for anger transcended the drama of the times, and thus the Christian anarchist's best verses have not grown stale.

SELECTED BIBLIOGRAPHY

Antología rota, Losada, Buenos Aires, 1997.
I Haven't Come to Sing, trans. Stephen Kessler, Green Horse Press, 1976.
León Felipe: The Last Troubadour, trans. Criss Cannady, Blue Moon Press, 1979.

FERNÁNDEZ, SERGIO
(Mexico City, 1926)

Seen as a figure caught between his own generation—who have "lost" their provincial paradise—and the sixties' experimentalists, Fernández is an au-

125

thor who deserves to be read more generously. He's a contemporary of Carlos Fuentes,* Salvador Elizondo,* and Juan García Ponce,* but he faded into the background beside the more combative and determined intellectuals on stage. For a time, I thought that his richly ornamental style had taken hold more in his contemporaries' and disciples' work than in his own work. But I was unfair, and fifteen years later, when literary fame is often a degrading commercialization that prizes banality and castigates rigor, I can no longer afford not to recommend novels like *Los signos perdidos* (1958), *En tela de juicio* (1964), and especially *Los peces* (1968) and *Segundo sueño* (1976).

Los peces is one of those portraits of an instant in which the near lack of plot revolves around an erotic encounter involving a priest and a woman reminiscent of the Spanish philosopher María Zambrano. But while *Los peces* might be one of those minor gems more representative of the literary climate of its time than of the author's talent, *Segundo sueño* deserves to be seen as a sylvan isle in the archipelago that includes Carlos Fuentes's *Terra Nostra* (1975; *Terra Nostra*, 2003), Fernando del Paso's *Palinuro de Mexico* (1976; *Palinuro of Mexico*, 1996), Juan García Ponce's *Crónica de la intervención* (1982), and Jorge Aguilar Mora's* *Si muero lejos de ti* (1979), forming a microcosm in which the radical, romantic student disobeys his conservative, neoclassic teacher.

A diary of the writing of the biography of a Renaissance painter, *Segundo sueño* is a novel full of insider nods and abstruse embellishment. It's a long book full of unwavering beauty, one of those novels that pays off on the magnificently wrought last page, making the effort required on the reader's part absolutely worth it. Fuentes, in *Terra Nostra*, invites readers to join hands with Malraux and Philip II for a tour of the Escorial and the best museums—both real and invented—in the world; but Fernández, in *Segundo sueño*, constructs a baroque, museum-like miniature habitable only by those who prefer writing to fiction. Although solipsism, long-windedness, and a rococo tone conspire against Fernández here, it must be said that *Segundo sueño*, both a treatise and a catalogue, is one of the few truly pictorial novels in all of Mexican literature.

A long-standing university professor and author of the autobiography *Los desfiguros de mi corazón* (1983), Fernández is also a skilled portrait artist who specializes in women from around the world. His *Retratos del fuego y la ceniza* (1968), written in the antiquated style—both doctoral and journalistic—of Sainte-Beuve, paints meticulously detailed pictures of the heroines of Durrell, Choderlos de Laclos, Azuela, Cervantes, Stendhal, and Flaubert. But perhaps his notion of determination, taken originally from Sor Juana Inés de la Cruz, condemns Fernández's literary scope, since what he said began as "serious, heartrending, and hopeful" turned into a production-line devoid of any novelistic truth. Cloistered away in academia, Fernández ended up cheapening his research, engaging in quack practices like palm reading and astrology and getting a few of his more gullible students involved. But there are always important chapters of literary history to be written. And I wouldn't be surprised if a baroque novel like *Segundo sueño* and an eccentric like Fernández were at some point able to find the devoted readers that we were unable or unwilling to be.

SELECTED BIBLIOGRAPHY
Los signos perdidos, Compañía General de Ediciones, Mexico, 1958.
En tela de juicio, Joaquín Mortiz, Mexico, 1964.
Los peces, Joaquín Mortiz, Mexico, 1976.
Los desfiguros de mi corazón: Un anecdotario, Nueva Imagen, Mexico, 1983.
Retratos del fuego y la ceniza, FCE, Mexico, 1983.

FERNÁNDEZ GRANADOS, JORGE
(Mexico City, 1965)

In the year 2000—which, forty years ago, was the year kids like me imagined ourselves as old men living on Mars—poet Fernández Granados published two books: *Los hábitos de la ceniza* and *El cristal*. It should come as no surprise that they're incredibly different from each other: we're talking about a highly educated poet whose well-trained spirit can toy deftly with multiple registers. He can be solemn or witty, though he does strive to keep his melancholic nature in check. His is a Renaissance melancholia rather than a Romantic one, busy detecting the bilious humors of nature and not the soul: more Richard Burton and Giordano Bruno than Gerard de Nerval.

But he's by no means outdated, and in *Los hábitos de la ceniza* we find many pages illustrating the central obsession of poets (and more than a few fiction writers) born in the sixties: minimalism (or, as it was once called, the school of *Monsieur Teste,* based on Valéry's intellectual "Mr. Head"). Minimalism tends to reduce experience to a superficial testimony, as if the flesh, the devil, and the world had all shrunk dramatically and the writer's only option was to become a centipede and navigate a few short centimeters, taking inventory of the objects and sensations closest to the mind. That dusty repudiation, the expedition through a few random domestic objects, is all it takes to get lost in what Octavio Paz called "the art of dressing fleas." We see it, for example, in "Mínimos Ulises," where Fernández Granados hopes "que la vida alguna vez cambie de tema" ("that life will at some point change the subject") so we can inhabit "lugares hechos a la medida de nuestras debilidades / donde alguna vez fuimos lo mismo / pero de otra manera, acaso más modesta" ("places made to fit our failings / where at some point we were the same / but in a different way, perhaps more modest").

The best two or three poems in *Los hábitos de la ceniza* harken back to Ecclesiastes: "Para qué más libros / teatro vacío donde actúa el alma / y deja su millar de soliloquoios, / vanidad del papel contra el olvido" ("What point more books / empty theater where the soul acts / and leaves its thousand soliloquies, / vanity of paper against oblivion"). The heartache caused by the vanity of knowledge and knowing is even better manifested in "Las cosas," where the poet alludes to blindness, and in "Non Serviam," a magnificent lamentation for the children who'll never be born. In other poems, such as "Laúd de Villaurrutia" and "Cama de Onetti," the writers in the poems' titles are the ones who must accept responsibility for the "cansancio (natal) del descreído" ("(innate) weariness of the unbeliever").

While in *Los hábitos de la ceniza* Fernández Granados reads Ecclesiastes as an early condemnation of all things Faustian, in *El cristal* we see the other side of the coin. Here he presents the poet as the last genuine repository for intellectual curiosity. *El cristal* is a veritable photo album whose visual force, beyond a shadow of a doubt, harkens back to Max Ernst's collages and (Fernández Granados himself says so) to Athanasius Kircher, the top Renaissance polymath.

Like Kircher himself, whom both Sor Juana and Fray Servando read assiduously, *El cristal* posits poetry as the meticulous recording of both terrestrial wonders and celestial marvels: a taxonomy of the universe in which zoology, botany, and astrology are their own world, not part of the now-blurry border between scientific classification and fantastic mythology. Fernández Granados's prose poems are rife with creatures like the "alima," a cat who "drinks milk to nourish her stealthy force," "pyraustas"—"white butterflies that live in the fire"—and a lizard that "detests this chilly planet as two silent old enemies detest one another." Some might say there are enough encyclopedias of fantastic zoology already; I'd say there could never be enough. It's worth noting that Fernández Granados, like many readers of his generation and the one prior (myself included), take Bachelard's poetics as a sort of skeleton key that can be used to open all doors. The French theorist's concept of "material imagination" has gone from innovation to noble but worn out topic, immediately recognizable on any poet's résumé.

If forty years ago someone had shown me the family, genus, and species of the creatures in the pages of Fernández Granados's poetry, I don't know what I'd have thought. But now I can say that those immortal, fantastic, ever-present (though sometimes forgotten) figures are visible—and belong to this world—thanks to Fernández Granados himself, who names, invokes, and classifies them.

SELECTED BIBLIOGRAPHY
El cristal, ERA, Mexico, 2000.
Los hábitos de la ceniza, Joaquín Mortiz, Mexico, 2000.
Principio de incertidumbre, ERA, 2009.

FUENTES, CARLOS
(Panama City, Panama, 1928)

Fuentes's body of work is the most complex and varied in all of Mexican fiction. It's because of his novels that Mexicans can no longer talk about "progress" in literature. His books take on every conquest and tendency in contemporary fiction. A compendium and critique of the "modern novel," a means of destroying myths and of deifying new idols, Fuentes's oeuvre both establishes and suspends the limits of modernity. The thirty-five years between *Los días enmascarados* (1954) and *Cristóbal Nonato* (1987; *Christopher Unborn*, 1989) form a trajectory that conceals a mystery extending beyond the limits of his literature, with Mexico as its obsessive center point. Fuentes wanted to do it all: from recreating a Mexican cosmogony to refounding the history of the language, while keeping both feet on the shores of the Atlantic. How well he managed and what the limits are of a project so ambitious that it outstrips most of the fictional adventures of our time are questions to be examined here.

Despite its simplicity, "Chac Mool," the first story in *Los días enmascarados*, contains within it all of Fuentes's universal potential. The story is touchingly transparent, as has been noted repeatedly. In it, a bureaucrat—who could have been the protagonist in Josefina Vicens's* *El libro vacío*—buys a statuette of Chac Mool in La Lagunilla. The Mayan rain god figurine comes to life, eventually causing the protagonist to run away and then die. Fuentes began his career infusing an indigenous statuette with life, using it as a fictional alibi and cosmological cultural angle. The plot development is based on the golem's visceral and mechanical transformation. The Chac Mool appears to have devoured not only its anodyne owner in the story, but also Fuentes himself: the hateful mestizo that the divinity morphs into after consuming its creator's body eventually becomes the grotesque nation we read about in *Christopher Unborn*.

Los días enmascarados is unlike any other work of literature of its time. There is, no doubt, something of Arreola's* versatile mastery in it. And one thing it does have in common with other works of the period is its ontological fixation, the search for Mexicanness that still obsesses Fuentes. But the solution to the Mexican genetic puzzle proposed all the way back in that first book had no fictional antecedents at the time, and no one could have foreseen the Herculean dimensions of Fuentes's "modernist" resurrection of old gods.

Los días enmascarados covers every theme in Fuentes's very deliberate "modernism": the fictional plundering of myths, semantic digression, historical deconstruction, a critique of "traditional" modernism, and futuristic conjecturing.

Emmanuel Carballo,* with whom Fuentes founded *Revista Mexicana de Literatura* in 1955, interviewed the author in 1962. In the interview, Fuentes talks about his early days and outlines his development since that time. "'Chac Mool' came about, like many fictional pieces, after reading a local news section in the paper. A Mexican art exhibition traveled to Europe in

1952. It included Chac Mool, the rain god. And he produced storms and cataclysms. People would put coins in his belly, and immediately a terrible storm would be unleashed. That news brief brings up something obvious to all Mexicans: how alive are the cosmological forces of a Mexico that's been lost forever, and yet refuses to die and still crops up from time to time in some sort of mystery, or apparition, or reflection? The story revolves around the persistence of old forms of life" (Carballo, *Protagonistas de la literatura mexicana*, 1986).

Uprootedness is a permanent point of departure for both Fuentes and his critics, but his cosmogony lacks the chthonic depth of someone like Juan Rulfo.* It's not hard to see that it derives from a banal amalgamation of things: a blend of touristic gaze, folklore, and ontological anxiety. And he uses the same trick in all of his prose. But what he was able to do very successfully with his immense talent was sell it to the world and present it as an often genius act of fictional magic.

Let's go back to the Carballo interview with the author. "Is it true, Carlos, that part of your literary exertion includes sparring with your words like a boxer?" "It is. I don't like to just offer my hand to a word, ask it to take a seat and strike up a conversation with it. I like to grab it at the door and slap it around and see how the sassy word responds. We need to set up a sort of artistic customs office for words, not just let them in with their commonly accepted meanings. Words contain much more than what their everyday usage confers [. . .] I grew up in an English-speaking country, in a culture that thought and lived in English. My constant struggle to preserve my Spanish was one that spanned my entire childhood. I was a kid on the verge of losing my native language every twenty-four hours. For me, language meant nationality: it was an oppressive set of meanings always subject to struggle, to reconquest [. . .]. After *Los días enmascarados*, I felt the need to fight both Castilian words and the terrible feudal literature we inherited, so proud of its immaculate character, its purity, its heraldry, its seniority."

Fuentes's great advantage was that he wasn't at all steeped in the Mexican prose tradition and only slightly in the Spanish one. That freedom allowed him to explicitly establish the modernist novel in Mexico. But like all conquistadors, he ignored his predecessors. Calling twentieth-century Hispanic literature "feudal"—not just the Generation of '27, but Valle-Inclán, Reyes,*

Guzmán,* Gómez de la Serna, and Julio Torri*—is downright pedantic. There's no doubt that his arrogance yielded a windfall that those bogged down in tradition couldn't access. That's why he never tried to find himself in Mexican fiction. He had no need to. After all, it's no wonder he openly identifies D. H. Lawrence and Aldous Huxley—British literati who wrote about Mexico—as two of his maestros. But unlike them, Fuentes came to stay: one of the brightest critics of official nationalism became the most complex and radical of Mexicanists. José Revueltas,* Juan Rulfo, and Agustín Yáñez* were raised on the novels of the Mexican Revolution. Fuentes was younger and turned up with a purpose and a yearning: he wanted to name Mexico. The touristic innocence of "Chac Mool" became a promise to keep. And that's what sets Fuentes apart from his strict contemporaries. When modern masters like Rosario Castellanos,* Jorge López Páez,* Sergio Galindo,* and Elena Garro* were literarily set free by Juan Rulfo and got busy exploring their childhoods, Fuentes—a metaphorical orphan—was deciding to create the whole world in one mellifluous, fell swoop.

Fuentes's story really begins in 1958 with the publication of *La región más transparente* (*Where the Air is Clear*, 1960). This is when author and work, character and reputation, like Siamese twins, were born. And ever since then, the Mexican intelligentsia has struggled either to disassociate them, or to understand them as a whole. In her *¡Ay, vida, no me mereces!* (1982), for example, Elena Poniatowska* recalls raptly: "Along with the book comes a sophisticated, cosmopolitan young man, all set to prove that the world is his. In the same way Pita Amor turned up at clubs like the Sans Souci and the Leda, naked beneath her mink coat, shouting, "I'm queen of the night!" Fuentes stamps, chomps at the bit, and waits for the starting gun, the door that will swing open automatically, the starting gun, the shot fired into the air. At thirty (he was born November 11, 1928, a Scorpio), Fuentes is a tall guy, with no inhibitions, handsome, thin, well dressed—often in white linen—as impeccable as Alec Guinness in *The Man in the White Suit* . . ."

The criticisms that the novel unleashed at the time now seem trifling. The collapse of nationalist rhetoric that Rulfo triggered was so deep that it could somehow be ignored. It was silently mythical. Fuentes, on the other hand, fought with a never-before-seen tenacity, taking center stage in the well-lit arena of cultural nationalism. His victory is unforgettable. Using every artistic resource he could, audacious as could be, and blindingly brilliant, Fuentes founded the novel as *profession*. And ever since then, alas, Mexico has had its very own novelist. (*Antología de la narrativa mexicana del siglo XX*, II, 1991)

Fuentes's collected works chronicle the decline and fall of a writer who, having started out as the founder of the modern Mexican novel, ends up as the recorder of the collapse of the very concept of "Mexicanness." In the fifty years between *Los días enmascarados* (1954) and *La silla del águila* (2003; *The Eagle's Throne*, 2006), Fuentes founded and then exhausted the notion of a fertile Mexico, trapped in a time that goes back to the creeping chaos of those pre-Hispanic idols that can be glimpsed behind the altars of the Black Legend, idols that continue to manipulate a nation whose genetic inability to modernize is Fuentes's terrible, unrelenting obsession. Obsessed with the philosophizing ontology of Mexico begun by local academics in the mid-twentieth century, Fuentes has managed to turn his own work into proof of the "underdevelopment" he himself denounces endlessly: fiction that's not interested in the human condition but in the fossilization of the Mexican character, prose less interested in the history of Mexico than in the deterministic confirmation of a set of mythological laws drawn upon to explain the nation's destiny.

That same young ("Joycean and Cardenist," as José Joaquín Blanco* called him) writer who bedazzled Mexicans in the fifties with his cosmopolitanism became, sooner rather than later, a provincial writer, given that his readers grew up and became citizens of the world, while he insisted (and still does) on explicating the mysteries of the Mexican soul to an ever-shrinking international readership. We get the most cutting example of Fuentes's premature aging by simply comparing him to Octavio Paz,* his teacher and friend. Their intellectual evolution makes an interesting comparison, since Paz, who in his 1969 book *Posdata* explained the October 2, 1968 Tlatelolco massacre metaphorically, using the symbolism of the pyramid of sacrifices, had a young enough spirit to jettison the categories he himself had established in *El laberinto de la soledad* (1951; *The Labyrinth of Solitude*, 1961) and then reinterpreted contemporary Mexico profanely. The most obvious heir of *El laberinto de la soledad*, Fuentes, on the other hand, never found his way out of the labyrinth, nor did he really even try.

After *La región más transparente* and *La muerte de Artemio Cruz* (1962; *The Death of Artemio Cruz*, 1964), Fuentes became the young grandfather of Mexican literature, the recorder of mythologies, and the holder of the keys to the apocalypse that both pre- and post-Tenochtitlán massacre were condemned to.

With each passing decade, more and more pieces have broken off of Fuentes's monumental undertaking, and few are those who've managed to stand by idly watching its deafening collapse. For critics who were in their twenties in 1968 (notably Blanco,* Adolfo Castañón,* Enrique Krauze,* and Evodio Escalante), the idea of standing by idly while Fuentes engaged in his obsessive examination of the labyrinth of all things Mexican—a labyrinth in which he now resides alone—was unthinkable. Since *Cristóbal Nonato,* his last substantial fictional endeavor, Fuentes has displayed surprising intellectual penury in each of his novels, so misguided that not even his best friends dare to defend *Diana o la cazadora solitaria* (1994), *Los años con Laura Díaz* (1998; *The Years with Laura Díaz*, 2000), *Instinto de Inez* (2001; *Inez*, 2002), and *La silla del águila* in public. But if we're disappointed by Fuentes, it's only because we stupidly (and even sympathetically) keep hoping that he'll go back to being who he once was. Like it or not, many of the dreams and nightmares that late-twentieth-century Mexican intellectuals had are expressed in Fuentes's moralizing inferno.

We have to ask: Was there ever really a great Fuentes? Or was his whole oeuvre and the determination of his critics just some inbred paroxysm of the Mexican nationalist dispute? Well, there was a great Fuentes, the one who wrote *Terra Nostra* (1975; *Terra Nostra*, 1977), the only one of his books that can be read beyond the borders of Mexico, the novel that will outlive him. Everything he wrote seems planned as part of the course that would lead him to *Terra Nostra*—a relative of Cortázar's *Rayuela*, García Márquez's* *One Hundred Years of Solitude*, and Vargas Llosa's *Conversation in the Cathedral*— in the same way that all of his subsequent novels seem like a furtive expedition through the treasures of *Terra Nostra*, so much so that thirty years later it resembles a pillaged fortress, burned down by its own architect.

A royal chronicle of both the grandeur and the misery of the House of Austria, a world theater with Cervantes, Tirso de Molina, and Quevedo on stage, *Terra Nostra* is a great novel of the Black Legend and a fantastic comeback to Marcelino Menéndez Pelayo's ultra-Catholic *Historia de los heterodoxos españoles (History of Spanish Heretics)*. At a time when Spanish literature was settling some very old scores with the Spanish Civil War and Francoism, Latin America was forging ahead with a polysemic fictional reconciliation with Spain and its ghosts. The novel's stylistic complexities, which might discourage wimps (and would absolutely terrify the sort of reader Fuentes now courts), are more than compensated for by the sonorous beauty of his prose. Similarly, the intermittent and ingenious apparition of characters such as the dwarf Barbarica, Ludovico, and the blind mouse string together a set of stories that seem more like the original invention of baroque than a takeoff on it. In *Terra Nostra*, Fuentes offers us (as in *Cervantes, o la crítica de la lectura*) a Spanish and Latin American collection that created a new breed of reader determined to reinterpret the destiny and the decline of the great European empire without which it is impossible to understand New World culture.

The novel has had an enormous (and insufficiently recognized) impact on Latin American writers, particularly those determined to continue chronicling the Indies. They all look to *Terra Nostra*, a sort of imperial encyclopedia that generously opens its doors and allows them to trawl through everything from Quevedo, Golden Age theater, chronicles of the Indies, and crypto-Judaism to the criticism of French Hispanist Marcel Bataillon and Spanish cultural historian Américo Castro.

Few writers have shown Fuentes's talent for extracting and expressing the secrets of painting, as can be seen in *Viendo visiones*, his collected writings on art. Like Argentine Manuel Mujica Lainez, Fuentes really knows how to look at a canvas and find its hidden creatures, bringing them to life in a new and exceptional way. And that method makes *Terra Nostra* a sometimes ingenious commentary on Velázquez, Luca Signorelli, and Goya; in the same way that the paintings analyzed are subject to magical, incessant metamorphoses, the heroes of *Terra Nostra* start from their fixed historical or literary reference points (Carlos V, Felipe II, the Count-Duke of Olivares, Hernán Cortés, *La Celestina*, *Don Quixote*, *El Burlador de Sevilla*), and are then reproduced throughout the book, turning into autonomous creations with lives of their own.

The New World section of *Terra Nostra*, halfway through the book, avoids Fuentes's typical *mexiqueneries*, instead presenting Latin America as an inkling of the sixteenth-century European spirit, which he sees as perhaps less medieval than it really was. And his self-awareness, his desire to use the novel as a sort of defense, is right on track, as *Terra Nostra's* scope allows, for example, for the novel to successfully defend the idea that Spanish America should have been the home of Erasmianism.

Paradoxically, the most outdated thing about *Terra Nostra* is the very drive that made it possible, the slightly antiquated—though at the time feasible—idea of interpreting the end of the millennium via a 1968 Paris lens, which opens and closes the novel. Like so many intellectuals, Fuentes was excited by the youth rebellion, seeing it as a prophetic and playfully creative moment whose influence would wipe out the nuclear threat of the Cold War. But the old fox Max Aub* noted in *Paris: La revolución de mayo* (1968)—one of *Terra Nostra's* sources—that Fuentes had written an "excellent essay-report . . . on the events of May in Paris, but so naïve at times! It's not the first time they've discovered the Mediterranean from the Sorbonne" (*Diario, 1966–1972*, 2003).

Turning the circus of the barricades on Boulevard Saint-Michel into a propitiously fictional means of explaining the whole baroque whirlwind that began with the Comuneros Revolt in Castile in 1521 was to Fuentes's great credit; what's less so is the apocalyptic air that flourishes in *Terra Nostra* and spreads like a virus throughout all of his subsequent books. Armed with a copy of Norman Cohn's *In Pursuit of the Millennium*, Fuentes saw the year 2000 as the predictable date for an apocalypse in which Latin America, having a monopoly on all of the Boom generation's misfortunes, would play a starring role. But although those commercial prophesies slightly mar the book's majesty, they in no way invalidate it as one of the greatest Mexican novels that, in the Platonic world of criticism, ought to have been his first and last.

Now at the start of the twenty-first century Fuentes seems almost millennial, a Methuselah who turned each of his years into eons and each of his novels into prolonged agony. No Mexican writer has aged as poorly as Fuentes, a constant caricature of himself, a self-promoting machine who, in between cocktail parties and good causes, insists on hunting down archetypes as old as himself, ones that exist only as characters in his fictional reality. What in another writer would have been a virtue—creating an entire universe—in Fuentes is a tragedy, given the didactic effort he puts into forcing worn-out symbols to fit a historical and political reality that he refuses to explain. Time has served only to ossify his stylistic defects and pedagogical spirit, misfortunes that became (not solely thanks to him) the communal blemishes of an entire generation of the Mexican intelligentsia: a love-hate relationship with the PRI (Partido Revolucionario Institucional), the courtly vocation of the scholar, cosmopolitanism as a product of ontological taunts, and especially, the offended superiority of the civilizer who finds no homage to his motherland adequate, since no one can be a prophet in his own land. The novelist lives on as a veteran of eloquence, a man from another time for whom literature is an extension of public life, a pre-historic writer who invokes a series of ghosts who account for that "Mexican time" that Fuentes knew and that he sees— maybe rightly so—as an eternity from which we'll never awaken.

SELECTED BIBLIOGRAPHY

La región más transparente, FCE, Mexico, 1958.

La muerte de Artemio Cruz, FCE, Mexico, 1962.

Terra Nostra, Joaquín Mortiz, Mexico, 1975.

Cervantes o la crítica de la lectura, Joaquín Mortiz, Mexico, 1976.

Los días enmascarados, ERA, Mexico, 1982.

Cristóbal Nonato, FCE, Mexico, 1987.

La silla del águila, Alfaguara, Mexico, 2003.

Las buenas conciencias, UNAM, Mexico, 2003.

Viendo visiones, FCE, Mexico, 2006.

Where the Air is Clear, trans. Sam Hileman, Farrar, Straus and Giroux, New York, 1960.

Terra Nostra, trans. Margaret Sayers Peden, Farrar, Straus and Giroux, New York, 1977.

The Good Conscience, trans. Sam Hileman, Farrar, Straus and Giroux, New York, 1987.

Christopher Unborn, trans. Alfred MacAdam, Farrar, Straus and Giroux, New York, 1989.

The Death of Artemio Cruz, trans. Sam Hileman, Atlantic Books, 1991.

The Eagle's Throne, trans. Kristina Cordero, Random House, New York, 2006.

G

GALINDO, SERGIO

(Xalapa, Veracruz, 1926 – 1993)

Like Jorge López Páez,* Sergio Galindo is a writer who created a whole new way of conceiving of the provinces, seeing them as both constraining and liberating, both a judgmental place and a locus of freedom. Prior to these two writers (and Agustín Yáñez*), rural Mexico wasn't so much a fictional setting as a collection of preconceived ideas or tics, and occasionally a made-up village that almost always attempted to give some sort of storybook portrayal of local customs. But these writers (together with Elena Garro*) took their childhood memories as a point of departure. They had to stop thinking about "society" in order to present us with the shattered communities that can only be explained via individual experience.

Galindo is the most insistent of these novelists. He's written somewhat extensively, with limited variety and an unchanging style, but he's also quite profound. When *Polvos de arroz* (1958) came out, it essentially paved the way for his future work, for his avowal to write about the voiceless, the outcasts, and the cast-outs, those whom fiction had previously ignored. The superfluous are a central obsession for him, in each and every book. Even in his weakest work, Galindo's unlucky men and women lay bare the writer's double will: on the one hand, he has a traditional commitment to the art of storytelling; on the other, he wants to push the bounds of realism, forging into unexplored territory.

Galindo has no qualms about delving into the social and private life of his native Veracruz. No doubt that's the *modernista* in him. After all, let's not forget that the subtitle of *Madame Bovary* is "Life in the Provinces" (also translated as "Scenes from Provincial Life"). But Galindo's human parade is different. What he does is attempt to draw the curtain, to hide the scene from what Octavio Paz* calls the "judging eyes" seen in fictional representations of rural life. Galindo's work betrays an anxiety he makes no attempt to hide: fear that the common man's stories are disappearing. *El bordo* (1960; *The Precipice*, 1969), for many, was his best attempt at preserving them.

Galindo's texts do have a certain amount in common with other nouveau roman literature of the times; but what's most notable is the way he makes use of material discarded by realists (at least those prior to the mid-century). His take on village life includes the marginalized (elderly, children, women) and the way they're treated. He showcases stories involving the power of those who have no power, vestiges of "minor magic" in a population disregarded by literary tradition. Few writers have constructed entire casts of minor characters the way Galindo has. And his "discovery" of the province as laboratory relies on them. His research was carried out over thirty years, not always successfully and sometimes fortuitously sidetracked by books like *El hombre de los hongos* (1976), in which he fearlessly strays from his comfort zone. At other times, Galindo shows a certain sentimentality, seen in novels like *Los dos ángeles* (1984) in which Mexico City—not his home ground—is used as a pretext to display a humanitarianism that, though moving, is also passé and insipid.

It's not until *Otilia Rauda* (1986; *Otilia's Body*, 1994) that Galindo reaches the pinnacle of his writing career. He isn't a man of ideas but a storyteller, and in *Otilia Rauda* he creates one of the most finely wrought Mexican novels of all time. The book's got it all: life in Veracruz in the thirties, the village-cum-prison, bandit worship, the ups and downs of politics, and Otilia Rauda—the eponymous heroine—rising up from among superfluous men to achieve unforgettable status. Otilia escapes the monotony of the typical Mexican fictional portrait: she's not a depiction of local customs or part of the scenery, but determination personified. *Otilia Rauda*, in its own way, is a "total" novel, a new approach to realism free from grand cosmogonist ambitions.

SELECTED BIBLIOGRAPHY

El bordo, FCE, Mexico, 1960.

Otilia Rauda, Grijalbo, Mexico, 1986.

Espinasa, José María, *El tiempo escrito*, Ediciones Sin Nombre, Mexico, 1995.

The Precipice, trans. John and Carolyn Brushwood, University of Texas, 1969.

Otilia's Body, trans. John and Carolyn Brushwood, University of Texas, 1994.

GAOS, JOSÉ

(Gijón, Spain, 1900 – Mexico City, 1969)

Gaos is a truly exceptional figure in Mexican culture, as both his students and a fair few distant observers have repeatedly pointed out. Every tribute to him notes, and rightly so, that this disciple of José Ortega y Gasset came to Mexico in 1939 as an exile, and invented both the term and the concept of *transterrado* ("translanded"). More than defining a situation, it in fact describes his life's work and intellectual endeavors.

Although some exiles saw the term as twee or felt it expressed excessive zeal for their hosts, I find it disturbing that the term has still not been included in the *Diccionario de la Real Academia Española*, as it should be. At least on this side of the Atlantic, *transterrado* captures a moment in history and an intellectual temperament perhaps unlike any other. Its exact meaning—at least as far as Gaos is concerned—can be gleaned by anyone who reads volume eight of his *Obras completas* (1996), comprised of mid-century articles, reviews, and essays dedicated to Mexican philosophy, which express the author's constant, fervent, militant gratitude for his Mexican "empatriation." A preliminary example can be seen in Gaos's defense of Mexican writer Alfonso Reyes,* whose friendship he chose over that of Ortega (their bond having already been broken when the latter accepted Franco's victory) when the Spaniard made pejorative comments about Reyes.

That was in 1947. But prior to that, Gaos had already given Samuel Ramos, Antonio Caso, and José Vasconcelos* more respect as philosophers than any

Mexican had had the guts, conviction, or affection to do. Shortly thereafter, Ramos would find himself in the uncomfortable position of being invariably cited as a precursor of Paz's* major work, *El laberinto de la soledad*, which pays him his due only to leave him behind. But Gaos portrays him as a sort of intuitive, concurrent Ortegan scholar. With regards to Caso, whom no one of my generation knows anything about anymore, Gaos says that his *La existencia como desinterés, como economía y como caridad* (1919) deserves a spot beside the works of Bergson and Boutroux. In Caso's blending of Christianity and liberalism, which he expressed in journalistic articles for philosophical purposes, Gaos found a loyal, anti-totalitarian thinker—there weren't many around at the time—and an example of what was then being advertised as innovative Christian existentialism. Finally, with reference to Vasconcelos, Gaos very eloquently expressed the political and moral revulsion he sometimes felt, citing the same pages of *Todología* that so many readers have been amused and scandalized by. Vasconcelos, who was the first to downplay himself as philosopher, must have been quietly grateful for Gaos's methodical conviction, which recognized his creation of a philosophical system.

Emilio Uranga, one of his students and member of the Hiperión Group, a philosophical circle, said Gaos was "a Spaniard without Spanish" and that his writing prolonged his teaching in a "tedious and inept" way. Anyone who's dived headfirst into *Obras completas*, as I once did, might share that opinion. But anyone wishing to avoid that punishment and find a less grueling Gaos will enjoy *Filosofía de la filosofía* (2008), a perfect anthology compiled by Alejandro Rossi* for those unfamiliar with his more literary side. It showcases a good writer taking a break from philosophical philology (his specialized field), from translations (of Husserl, of Heidegger), and from the academic texts that were his daily bread.

Also outstanding are the excerpts from *Confesiones profesionales* (1958), which explain how and why Gaos came to his philosophical vocation after his mentors Xavier Zubiri, Manuel García Morente, and Ortega allowed him to experience three phases of "the thinking of the thinker." *Confesiones profesionales* is one of a handful of great memoirs published in Mexico, along with José Moreno Villa's* *Vida en claro* (1944) and Octavio Paz's *Itinerario* (1993): short books, syntheses written in a light style, like carry-on luggage, which is how Gaos talked about his decision to come to Mexico, by thinking that the provisional is always definitive.

Also significant in *Filosofía de la filosofía* are the essays written when Ortega died, in which Gaos resolves to judge the more political Ortega and his liberalism, and does so in a balanced but solemn way, making note of how much patience his mentor had for the monarchy and how little he showed the Spanish Republic. Those articles, Rossi says, make for "a fascinating case of affect and intellectual distancing between master and disciple: neither mimesis nor facile, fatuous critique."

I was surprised by "La caricia," an unexpected text that Rossi calls a "very fine example of existential phenomenology." The essay derives from Greek mythology, specifically King Priam embracing the knees of Achilles when he asks for the body of his son Hector to be returned; Gaos manages to change our perception of that act. An embrace ("caricia"), concludes Gaos, is the least animal of all human gestures.

By way of prologue, I suggest reading "Imagen de José Gaos," one of the superb essays in Rossi's *Manual del distraído* (1978), along with the short foreword he wrote for the 1989 Spanish edition of *Filosofía de la filosofía*. The two texts provide a "harsh and irreverent" analysis of what had died and what lived on in Gaos's legacy. Rossi describes him as one of the main players in philosophy—which he called the "frustrated discipline par excellence"—in general, and metaphysics—"an errant adventure"—in particular, a wayward soul whose life was devoted to contemplating the philosophical ruins of the West.

Selected Bibliography
Filosofía de la filosofía, ed. and prologue by Alejandro Rossi, FCE, Mexico, 2008.

GARCÍA BERGUA, ANA
(Mexico City, 1960)

El umbral: Travels and adventures (1993) is one of those novels published after a lengthy period of contemplation, a book that matures as the heart's wounds heal. That's what makes García Bergua's readings of nineteenth-century Romanticism come through so clearly. Julius, the novel's fantastical hero, is an unusual character in Mexican literature, a man with so little Romantic imagination that he seems to have saved himself for the end of the twentieth century. In him, García Bergua presents a man who traffics in human souls, one whose adventures are reminiscent of Raphael in *The Magic Skin*. As in Balzac's novel, Julius is a man who makes a deal with destiny, a contract that materializes when the angels wield a pen at their will, a talisman that will decide his fate. The fantastical-Romantic element here makes no pretentious attempt at criticism or periphrasis. Instead, García Bergua delves into the tradition as if she were a nineteenth-century writer herself. What in another author would have been taken as naïveté or calculated pastiche, in her is a virtue, the enviable virtue of a writer saved from the horrors of analogy by a sense of humor. And her knowing smile guides the reader through *El umbral*'s every room (the book's title means "threshold" or "door"). The book is both a portrayal of Spanish republican exile and a "fantasy" novel, in the most generous sense of the term.

The link between the author's readings and romantic experience make *El umbral* an innocent novel without being naïve. I dare to venture that García Bergua will have a hard time writing her next book, since this one is the sort that wrenches everything from writers, paralyzing them with the fear and grandeur of creating another. She writes with the apparent ease of someone tinkling on piano keys, unaware of how haunting the melody created is until the sound is gone and what's left is just a memory. And having dedicated the book to her brother Jordi, who died in 1979, it's fair to assume that García Bergua would support that comparison. How are Jordi García Bergua's *Karpus Minthej* and Ana García Bergua's *El umbral* similar? Both are fantastical, both are Romantic, and both demonstrate Thomas Hardy's belief that the *genius diaboli* migrates from soul to soul. The García Bergua siblings have given Mexican literature a rare and unsettling sinecure we might call family resemblance. (*Antología de la narrativa mexicana del siglo XX, II, segunda edición corregida y aumentada*, 1996)

Literary history is rife with authors who lost their creative powers after an exhausting, intimate, epic first novel. But rather than lose her battle after the Romanticist catharsis of *El umbral: Travels and adventures*, Ana García Bergua evolved into one of the few Mexican writers who really know how to use history (and historiography) to build true fictional castles in the sky. Her second novel, *Púrpura* (2000), is a farce that recounts the path taken by a young, rural student who goes to the big city to break into the film industry. And in *Rosas negras* (2004), she invites readers along for an understated spiritual novel full of the sort of quiet devotion that's one of the signs of a mature writer.

García Bergua shows increasing mastery over the art of parody, which we could already see in *Púrpura*, a melodrama that pays homage to Mexican cinema and the schmaltzy props that projected the private lives of a nation on the silver screen. The daughter of film historian Emilio García Riera and a tongue-in-cheek reader of the most flippant Salvador Novo,* García Bergua devoted *Púrpura* to the diehards who hung around Xavier Villaurrutia's experimental theater. This is a book for those who were indifferent to the claim Octavio Paz* made in an attempt to explain Villaurrutia's inexplicable unpopularity: today's good taste is tomorrow's schmaltz. García Bergua delves deep, taking us behind the scenes, and *Púrpura* is a rock-solid novel about male homosexuality in which the protagonist is a hopeless romantic like some of Stanislaw Jerzy Lec's *Unkempt Thoughts*, a man who "moved from Sodom to Gomorrah" and lived to tell the tale.

Rosas negras takes place in the early 1900s in a provincial Mexican city, where the soul of a bourgeois man is trapped in a lamp at his favorite restaurant, stuck there due to the poor electricity flow. The plot revolves around the sensitive light flickering on and off, a novel technique that García Bergua explores fully. With its curiously modern plot, *Rosas negras* turns the man's inconsolable widow into a heroine who one way or another manages to find both love and self-esteem, in beautiful prose full of *mots justes*. Unlike Minerva, the widow won't put down her arms: instead she takes up prurient, pornographic instruments that her abducted husband used to use in the bedroom, and which she rescues from his bequest.

A Chestertonian at heart, García Bergua even manages to work in stink bombs hurled by local anarchists attempting to disturb the peace and other Belle Époque and "turn-of-the-sextury" (as Guillermo Sheridan* called it) touches. *Rosas negras* is a comedy of intrigue with just enough metaphysics to forge a style steeped in the affectations of romance novels, feuilletons, and nineteenth-century domestic melodramas. A student of Juan José Gurrola and Ludwik Margules, García Bergua's theatrical training has made her one of the few Mexican novelists with a sense of dramatis personae: her secondary characters are as well-developed as her protagonists, and there's never any dead weight in her tightly constructed plots.

Her grace—that apparent ease with which she writes—reveals a writer for whom historical documentation is both vital and painstaking, which also means that it's invisible, as it should be. Like a Merchant Ivory set, there are no insignificant details, nothing that hasn't been historically or literarily researched or corroborated.

Her strength as prop master and library rat serves her less well in short stories. *El imaginador* (1996) and *La confianza en los extraños* (2002) don't quite work and come off as top-heavy compared to the meditated craftsmanship of her novels. Her stories are curiosities, sketches, and often simply anecdotes too lightly sprinkled with humor and imagination well within the constraints of the newspaper format for which they were originally intended. Improvisation just isn't her thing. To write, García Bergua needs the wide-open space of a set designer, which she can only have in the scope of a novel.

Oftentimes novelists fall back on "history" out of laziness, believing the past to be an inexhaustible resource full of free material, plotlines, sets, and extraordinary characters. Patted on the back by the public and fattened up by publishers, they churn out at best insipid reproductions of the past, disposable photocopies, baubles instead of treasures. Then they emerge from the cave convinced that their saddlebags are full of gold, and it's only when they get to market that they realize in fact they were full of the proverbial glass beads. Not so García Bergua. What *El umbral* did for Spanish republican exile, what *Púrpura* did for the Golden Age of Mexican cinematography, *Rosas negras* does for fin-de-siècle decadence: it's a "true" fictional reinvention.

García Bergua is also one of our few contemporary humorists, which leads her to be seen as a descendent of Jorge Ibargüengoitia.* And although both are from the theater (farce) world, I think it's an unfair comparison, one that does neither of them justice. Ibargüengoitia was a sarcastic writer and his corrosive mocking of Mexican legends and rural life was like a settling of scores with the country of his youth, a place that pained him. In

García Bergua I don't find that sublimated hatred of Mexico—a place where the only self-criticism you could read came from police blotters—so characteristic of Ibargüengoitia.

García Bergua's work, on the other hand, is fashioned in libraries and newspaper archives; her relationship to Mexican history is more archeological. Her painstaking historical reconstructions flow not towards the satirical moralizing of Ibargüengoitia but toward the old romantic notion of dreaming while awake. García Bergua is faithful to the magical realm of European Romanticism (Nodier, Hoffmann, Von Chamisso) whose final flourishes left their mark on Mexican modernism. Like the spiritualist Amado Nervo and like Manuel Gutiérrez Najera, whose urbane impressions bordered on fantasy, García Bergua is a writer who gathers all of the domestic details of daily life and then presents us with a reality that's symmetrical in appearance only; on stepping through to the other side of the mirror, she subverts all convention. And although it's a discredited term, hers really is "escapist" literature, to such a degree that when the incubi and succubae of sexual identity crop up—as they do in *El umbral* and *Púrpura*—they take on angelic qualities that make them even more unsettling to readers accustomed to the subtleties of Romanticism.

The word "ouija" was invented around 1860 by a Maryland coffin manufacturer. He coined the term to refer to the signs sent from "beyond" to mediums, who received them on touching the alphabetical spirit board. Though it's a combination of the French "oui" and German "ja," he insisted it was a term sent to him by ancient Egyptian spirits. And although you won't find it in most Spanish dictionaries, the word is easy enough to find in English and online. That's how it is with *Rosas negras*, too. For a writer like García Bergua, the past is made of miniscule, parallel universes, and though they've been expunged from history, if you obey a few odd but intelligible laws, you can live there pretty comfortably. And humor is one of the spirits' weapons of choice: they use it to keep evil at bay.

SELECTED BIBLIOGRAPHY
El umbral. Travels and adventures, ERA, Mexico, 1993.
Púrpura, Alianza Editorial, Madrid, 2000.
Rosas negras, Plaza y Janés, Mexico, 2004.

Pie de página, Ediciones Sin Nombre/Conaculta, Mexico, 2007.
Isla de bobos, Seix Barral, Mexico, 2008.
Edificio, Páginas de Espuma, Madrid, 2009.

GARCÍA BERGUA, JORDI
(Mexico City, 1955 – 1979)

Jordi García Bergua died in 1979, and luckily for those of us who never got to meet him, he left behind the novel *Karpus Minthej* (1981). Often, it seems impossible to avoid making morbid connections between a deceased artist and his posthumous publications, and in this case the novel is actually *about* death, which can be felt in almost every word in the book. So in this case there's absolutely no way to separate the two. Literary history is sprinkled with enough paradoxes of this sort to almost form a tradition: *Karpus Minthej* is an extraordinary novel largely due to its testamentary nature. In it, a certain Mexican writer, bitter at the oblivion he's fallen into and his blocked old age, mocks a certain poet who died young, and thus in the eyes of his generation had the perfect excuse for not writing more. Written a century ago, *Karpus Minthej* would have been just as valid, I think.

It's not easy to take on the most formidable characteristics of a generation whose most basic trait is decadence. Ronald Firbank, Marcel Schwob, Oscar Wilde, Aubrey Beardsley, and Félicien Rops, the saga of Venice and its putrid decay, and the Byronic re-conquest of Greece are all integral to this novel. More than the story of the author's untimely death, the book seems to successfully represent everything the decadent "black modernists" set out to do but didn't fully achieve, a century earlier: symbolist gardens full of Novalis's "blue flower" of destiny and Herder's "yellow flower" of the Orient; the persistence of the Romanticist idea of eternal love, the loss of all that unites art and heroism. If *Karpus Minthej* gives us a timeless, masterly portrayal of that lyricism, it's not because we have any unfailing belief in progress. The author isn't our contemporary; he belongs back with Jean Moréas, José Asunción Silva, Jean Lorrain, and the first José Juan Tablada. What García Bergua gave the hundred years between him and his generation was the cunning ability to transform the artificial into artifice.

That sort of balance—displays of lyrical intoxication and symbolic tuber-culosis—is not easy to sustain in this day and age. Nowadays, any worship of *Decadentismo* is pretty much a stale, commercial cop-out, and there's no shortage of writers willing to pretend they're "accursed" as a means of con-cealing garden-variety bitterness. García Bergua's genius lay in his shame-lessness, his brilliant (and perhaps unintentional) insolence in writing a morbid, "exhausted" novel and doing it well, maybe even very well, as if the anguish brought on by his influences had somehow produced the singular purity of his work. *Karpus Minthej* shines for its crystal-clear prose, for the authenticity of its dandyism, and for its exceptional distillation of literature. We can forgive—and secretly even appreciate—the innocent digressions about life and destiny that reek of Nietzsche and yet leave a delicate fra-grance of early Ruskin, Mathew Arnold, and the best of Wilde lingering in the air. Perfumes whose scents have volatilized through overuse, adulterated scents, in *Karpus Minthej* recapture something of their unsettling essence.

The book is unlike Rodenbach's *Bruges-la-Morte*; nor is it similar to Huys-mans' *Against the Grain*. García Bergua's unforeseeable resolution doesn't involve his character plucking the petals off flowers, overlooking a "dead" city, or attempting to choose God over a gun. Instead, after a series of illogi-cal crimes in the Balkans that lead him to Greece, his protagonist gets lost without a trace in a dream. In the appendices, Karpus wakes up after World War II, frozen in a place that might be the morgue, time, or a hospital. After his protagonist's clearly Byronic voyage, the author bequeaths us an open locket in which we see no portrait at all, but instead the disconcerting void of an open end.

The novel captures pedantic erudition, aristocratic child's play in a Ve-netian palace, a dandy recanting in putrid ports, and the ambiguous loss of destiny. In it, García Bergua delves deep into the jungles of literature to write a book that could have been written a century ago in any language. But it wasn't. Instead, it's the late masterpiece of Mexican *Decadentismo*. (*La utopía de la hospitalidad*, 1993)

Selected Bibliography
Karpus Minthej, FCE, Mexico, 1981.

GARCÍA MÁRQUEZ, GABRIEL
(Aracataca, Colombia, 1928)

Last night I finished rereading *One Hundred Years of Solitude*, something I'd been putting off for ages for fear of being disappointed. Now that I've done it, I'll just dive headfirst into clichés and say that thanks to García Márquez I got to be the thirteen-year-old kid reading it for the first time again. Macondo was still there. And there were a few pages, entire paragraphs, and things like Colonel Aureliano Buendía's "armpits studded with sores" that took me right back—with Melquíades's magic talisman—to the bedroom where I first read the book a quarter century ago. And I made sure to find an edition with the Vicente Rojo cover like the one I read.

If reading is a job, rereading is an art regulated by both memory and forgetting. For this job, I refrained from consulting any critical works on García Márquez before plunging in. I heroically resisted the morbid temptation to read the critical study Vargas Llosa wrote about his then-friend, *Historia de un deicidio* (1971), now a rare book worthy of Macondo's Catalan bookseller. With *One Hundred Years of Solitude* I gave in to the selfish conceit of being alone with my memories. Could it be? It could. The novel managed to rid me of my historical obsession. While I read, I forgot about the genealogy of Macondo, about Faulkner, Onetti, Carpentier, and Rulfo,* about Colombian and other Latin American novels of violence with their savagery and their excessive cruelty; I even forgot about the Boom, magical realism, and García Márquez himself.

Given that the first person is the only one who counts in literary criticism, with *One Hundred Years of Solitude* the dispute over whether rereading forms part of literary history or part of each reader's autobiography becomes a moot point. To reread is to pull taut the thread that links literary myths to one's personal mythology. Julio Cortázar's *Rayuela*, for example, was a book I couldn't stand on rereading. Maybe it was a reflection of the turbulent, melancholy waters of adolescence, the period we look back on as the roughest storm we weathered. But the second time around, neither love nor Paris were the way Cortázar had told me the first time. Not even La Maga. His sentimental realism expired quickly for me. *One Hundred Years of Solitude*, on the other hand, throws realism out the window, as Borges does. Instead, myths or fragments of mythology appeal directly to our emotions and our intellect. Any relation to the phenomenological world is strictly coincidental.

So let me say again that *One Hundred Years of Solitude* is a foundational novel, in the way that *The Iliad* and *The Odyssey* are, indifferent to attributions of authorship, impervious to the dogged excavations of Heinrich Schliemann and his successors. That Homeric flavor authorizes new generations of writers to see García Márquez with either healthy ignorance or sincere disdain. But those of us who came of literary age with *One Hundred Years of Solitude* are in enormous debt to his prose. García Márquez has outlived a legion of imitators, some contrite, others shameless. He pioneered a trend. But boy, what a trend.

I was overwhelmed, too, by how sonorous the prose is. There's a distant yet omnipresent musicality to it. Those who said that not since the Siglo de Oro had there been such linguistic debauchery were right. On the other hand, I found myself indifferent to the fastidious heraldry of Aurelianos, Amarantas, and José Arcadios. I feel like I reread García Márquez the way people reread poets for centuries, whether Ovid or Virgil. No literary theory seems as satisfactory as the grave coincidence of the umpteenth Aureliano's curiosity and the execution of Melquíades's prophecy. Every reader has his or her own time. In that sense, for me—and for a few other generations—García Márquez is a Homer. (*La sabiduría sin promesa: Vidas y letras del siglo XX*, 2001)

SELECTED BIBLIOGRAPHY
Cien años de soledad, Editorial Sudamericana, Buenos Aires, 1967.
One Hundred Years of Solitude, trans. Gregory Rabassa, Harper and Row, 1970.

GARCÍA PONCE, JUAN
(Mérida, Yucatán, 1932 – Mexico City, 2003)

Because Juan García Ponce suffered from multiple sclerosis, writing eventually became his life. Or at least it was his only form of "active life," as Albert Béguin said of poet Joë Bosquet, another writer who relied on fiction to keep his poetic voice from splintering in pain. Over the decades, the man who had been the insolent young leader of his generation became a smiling spiritual master who wrote by night, practicing his profane religion to combat anathema and oblivion. Anyone who ever went to visit Juan knows I'm not exaggerating when I say that the energy emanating from his paralyzed body was contagious: it suffused his friends with mysticism, making us want to emulate him, to be worthy not only of his strength and determination but of the books and artists he taught us to love, read, and study. Those interested only in seeing the saintly halo of a sick man quickly learned that García Ponce didn't suffer fools gladly. He didn't brook vanity or superficiality. But Juan aroused amazing devotion among writers and painters, Tyrians and Trojans, scholars and artists of all political and aesthetic leanings. When we went to see Juan, we set aside our small-town pettiness and pointless squabbles.

Our impression of García Ponce has been created by his fifty books. By comparison, we critics fail as critics since he said nearly everything there was to be said about himself in his novels, short stories, and essays. The artist as hero, the seer. Both pornographer and educator, he taught us to read Robert Musil, Pierre Klossowski, and Georges Bataille, so that we'd have the keys to his ancient kingdom. Or was it the other way around? For Juan, reading was the offspring of literature, prose the depraved mother of thought.

It's hard to talk about García Ponce without falling back on the same tired old clichés we've all used to describe his work for so long that it's become the stuff of legend. He's become almost sainted, provided we take sainthood to be the kind of demonology he doggedly recreated. Whenever I try to write about him I become flustered, because his first impression was so hypnotic. In the end, I suppose García Ponce readers sign a pact with his work, a pact of love that also allows for outrage and tolerance. I understand those who reject his work. But I was a teenager when I first read him, and I signed that pact. He himself sets forth the idea in "Tajimara," one of his early stories: "to watch is to accept." But even poor Faust complained when Mephistopheles came to collect. So much so that Goethe heard his prayers and granted him a salvation so implausible that Thomas Mann and García Ponce were the only ones who understood it. What I mean is, I've never ignored the pernicious clauses in that contract, but I'd still renew it again and again.

Like so many people, I owe García Ponce many debts of gratitude. Proud of the books he'd read and the women he'd loved, Juan was the kind of man you could turn to not just for professional, academic, or artistic help but also with personal problems, existential anguish, and romantic debacles. But I'd like to recall here just one of the many professional reasons I'm grateful for his munificence in regard to literary criticism. In 1995 Juan asked me to preface his *Cuentos completos*, and along with my praise I had no qualms about including reservations. I still believe what I wrote at the time: "I'm irked by García Ponce's compulsive repetition, by a certain messiness of form, by multiple plotlines and images that mushroom, and especially by his insensitivity to the historical nature of taste. Even if sexuality is essentially the same across generations and civilizations, the interpretation of eroticism varies greatly. What thirty years ago was scandalous, today is seen as quaint local custom." Juan accepted my preface as it stood, enthusiastically even, proving himself to be one of the very few writers who escaped the resentful, fanatical tyranny of wounded pride. When he invited us to read him, he understood that it was also to criticize him, as he knew that without criticism there is no literature. And he both demanded and celebrated it.

García Ponce was at the heart of the cohort who cut their teeth at the dynamic Casa del Lago, a performing-arts center of unrivalled importance in Mexican life in the sixties, built in the early twentieth century under Porfirio Díaz. García Ponce's life is the story of a generation; his is a hallowed family that includes Juan Vicente Melo* and Vicente Rojo, Inés Arredondo* and Tomás Segovia,* Mercedes de Oteyza and Michèlle Alban, Huberto Batis and even Juan's beloved enemy, Salvador Elizondo,* with whom he actually had a friendly conversation not long ago (a fact that must have gladdened the souls in purgatory). His clan also includes painters like Juan's brother Fernando García Ponce, Lilia Carrillo, Roger Von Gunten, and Manuel Felguérez, as well as the people hanging around Octavio Paz* at the literary journals *Plural* and *Vuelta*.

García Ponce's friends, born around 1932, were artists to the core: meticulous, outspoken critics; courageous citizens (as was Juan during two historic political moments: the student movement of 1968 and the massive electoral protests of 1988); tormented or happy souls; marvelous, vulgar people who fully realized the modern, critical nature of Mexican culture. Their emergence was posthumous recompense for the *Contemporáneos* poets—their real forefathers—and their publishing enterprises were the culmination of the cosmopolitan tradition of Alfonso Reyes* and Paz at the center of modern Mexican literature. In almost unheard-of fashion, García Ponce's circle also evolved in an entirely natural, selective way: new generations of painters, some new writers, got to experience that heady sort of time that stood still at his house, a time I can't define.

García Ponce's oeuvre may be the most extensive in all of Mexican literature. Many of his books will become timeless, and I'd like to highlight two of them: *Encuentros* (1972), which is a trio of perfect stories, and *Crónica de la intervención* (1982), the compendium of all his obsessions. How many people have actually read *Crónica de la intervención,* that "book of the future" à la Blanchot? Not many. Dictated to Michelle Alban in the seventies, the novel clocks in at over fifteen hundred pages and is reputed to be of poor quality, due to the unconventional way it was "written." I won't deny that it's full of endless sentences in which the subject gets lost along the way and grammatically deplorable paragraphs. But it's also full of García Ponce's most moving fictional lyricism, and this alone makes it a little-known episode in the adventures of twentieth-century Latin American literature, an example that easily equals the greatest creations of world literature in both scope and aspiration.

The story of two identical women, Mariana and María Inés, and their circle of lovers, *Crónica de la intervención* is a novel written from multiple perspectives, all of which are visibly manipulated by the ultra-omniscient narrator who simultaneously *tells* the story and reflects on story-telling as an art. Inspired by Robert Musil's *The Man Without Qualities* and Heimito von Doderer's *The Demons*, García Ponce didn't quite possess the systematic clarity of the Austrian novelists. On the other hand, *Crónica de la intervención* is so extraordinarily evocative that at times it rivals Proust. It's also a great example of Thomas Mann's ideas about art versus will. Like Mann, García Ponce is deeply nostalgic for the nineteenth-century novel and by writing about its decline turns *Crónica de la intervención* into a novel of highs and lows, of the sublime and the pathetic, with a cast of lords and servants, kooks and sages, recluses and those constantly in the public eye.

García Ponce's take on eroticism was essentially shaped by reading Georges Bataille and Pierre Klossowski, though it's important to note that he also translated Marcuse's *Eros and Civilization* in 1965. In its own way,

Crónica de la intervención is like the erotic invention of an imaginary civilization: sexuality is the driving force behind the novel, which is aspiring to act as a substitute for history. And although the "spitting image" games played between Mariana and María Inés, twins and demiurges, virgins and succubae, seem to escape the narrator's grasp and become tiresome for the reader (they're more talking statues than characters), *Crónica de la intervención* has a remarkable supporting cast. There's Brother Alberto, the dissolute cleric who caricatures several 1960s "reform" monks; the revolutionary Diego Rodríguez, who's based on José Revueltas;* and Evodio, the chauffeur who ends up murdering his boss, modeled on Musil's Moosbrugger. Also astonishingly well developed is Francisca, a character based on Inés Arredondo,* whose descent into insanity is distressingly intense, as is her lover's unsuccessful attempt to save her.

Crónica de la intervención is not the roman à clef of a generation (as *Pasado presente* was in 1993), and only very idiosyncratically is it even a novel about Mexico, a country named only once in the entire book (oversight or intention?). Like Robert Musil's Kakania, García Ponce's "Parallel Action" is based around the organizing of the Festival of Youth at the Mexico City 1968 Olympics. His distant, skewed perspective presents us with an imaginary country whose relationship to the real country ends up producing one of the most suggestive and least feted *Mexican* novels of our literary history. The genital rites of a secret community are interrupted by a gruesome nightmare that leads to the dramatic dénouement. The 1968 student movement gave rise to a lot of hot air, and it really says something about the power of fiction that García Ponce, on the surface apolitical, was the writer who best distilled the essence of civil disturbance. Mariana dies on October 2, 1968 in the Tlatelolco massacre, and the scene he describes is so poignant and poetic that it must be quoted: "The meeting's third speaker had already begun when some fireworks were set off, lighting up the still neutral, late-afternoon sky. Fireworks like the kind at a fair or the celebration of a national holiday, though unexpected, anachronistic. An almost tender display. Fireworks soaring slowly up into the sky, and then dissipating on their way back down. Some of those present must, at some point, have thought back nostalgically to their past. The end of the day; the tenuous start of darkness. Many looked, their eyes following those lights as they silently extinguished in space. And then the sound of bullets, imposing an order that was not human."

Crónica de la intervención ends with the aesthete's paradoxical fascination with the life-giving potential of rebellion and the historical extermination of an idyllic, erotic civilization. It's a paradise inhabited by ethereal women and analytical minds, characters who are utterly innocent in their perversion, immune to disease and to the crimes of our times. We could say that this novel, which ends by appealing to the possibility of its own endless rewriting, could do with some editing. But for García Ponce, in a wheelchair from 1967 on, the will to survive was like a physiological refusal. He refused to cut anything, as if doing so would spur his foretold death. Like an inverse "magic skin," García Ponce's life got longer in tandem with his literary output. And that erotic drive, that determination to beat death, is what lies behind *Crónica de la intervención*.

In the end, the García Ponce of *Imagen primera* was also the last look we got, as he died on December 27, 2003. Paradoxically one of the most active lives in Mexican culture, he was a theologian of pornography, a libertine fortune teller, a reader of Hermann Broch and Jorge Luis Borges, a collector of both charming ladies and femmes fatales, a sadist and proponent of the "eternal feminine," an art critic who stepped through the looking glass, a compulsive writer, a sick man who beat death through his own sickness, an artist and hero who indulged us with his books.

SELECTED BIBLIOGRAPHY

Crónica de la intervención I and II, FCE, Mexico, 2001.
Obras reunidas, I. Cuentos, FCE, Mexico, 2003.
Obras reunidas, II. Novelas cortas, FCE, Mexico, 2003.
Obras reunidas, III. Novelas cortas II, FCE, Mexico, 2004.
Obras reunidas, Novelas.
    I. *La invitación. La casa en la playa. La cabaña.*
    II. *Inmaculada o las placeres de la inocencia.*
Pasado presente, FCE, Mexico, 2005–2007.
Encounters, trans. Helen Lane, Marsilio, 1989.

GARCÍA TERRÉS, JAIME
(Mexico City, 1924 – 1996)

According to José Emilio Pacheco,* one of García Terrés's most loyal disciples, the author was respectfully but inaccurately characterized as aristocratic. This is no doubt due to his lineage; he was the grandson of eminent Porfirio Díaz supporters. In *Lo snobismo liberale* (1964), a short book Elena Croce wrote about the world of her father, Italian philosopher Benedetto Croce, a different definition better describes Mexican high culture, which was intimately linked to the power and the downfall of the Revolution's regime, which García Terrés was representative of.

For Elena Croce, "liberal snobbery" goes hand in hand with being civilized, a quality typical of the chosen few that included her father, Thomas Mann, Hugo von Hofmannsthal, and Bernard Berenson, artists and men of letters who decided to renounce the industrial, utilitarian "nobility" of their class. Instead, they opted for another type of bourgeois—in the noblest sense of the term—lifestyle, one signified by courtesy and good manners, one that saw finesse as the landscape of the soul and the love of work as the wise man's dedication to the public good. That elite, Elena Croce recalls, dressed in English fashions and imposed their Anglophile ways by exhibiting a liberalism that (barely) held on to the effusiveness of the romantic soul, which harbored a "private, reactionary sadness," as poet López Velarde said.

First at the *Revista de la Universidad de México* (1953–1965), then as advisor, assistant director, and director general of the Fondo de Cultura Económica (1971–1988), and finally in charge of the *Biblioteca de México* (the journal and library), García Terrés was a public figure who doubled as a poet, a patrician whose convictions were grounded in the beliefs of "liberal snobbery": artistic refinement drives education (and not the reverse); great prose is the gauge of civilization; and the superior lifestyle (and travel) of a poet demands that he honorably serve the State by accepting posts in universities, museums, and publishing.

Alejandro Rossi* said that García Terrés had "liberal tendencies," and he was right. As both adjective and noun, "liberal" defines his personality, even literarily. His was a politically grounded, practical faith in the civilizing authority of the Mexican State—a faith not without its risks. Logically, that

State should have repaid the faith that the "republic of letters" placed in it by guaranteeing conditions favorable to its reproduction, given that the elite were an independent spiritual force whose goals were in line with the Revolution's old liberal dream. And though post-revolutionary governments paid attention to the intellectuals and granted their most prominent members (Jaime Torres Bodet,* Agustín Yáñez*) ministerial or diplomatic posts, the firmly held belief that the government *always* protected writers, providing grants and other stimuli, is false. In fact, that policy wasn't instituted until decades later, between the Luis Echeverría and Carlos Salinas de Gortari administrations, a fact that worried García Terrés as late as 1959. "In Mexico there is no institution, either official or decentralized, that systematically protects writers in their capacity as writers. The budget line dedicated to the promotion of culture is risible. Education is almost exclusively taken to mean literacy campaigns, which would be fine if they were effective and if we simultaneously recognized that training and maintaining a cultural elite is as—if not more—important than the vague attempt to teach the alphabet to a population burdened with all forms of destitution" ("El ambiente literario en México" in García Terrés, *Obras, III,* 2000).

It was at the Universidad Nacional Autónoma de México (UNAM), where in 1968 intellectual "autonomy" became critical, that García Terrés took it upon himself to train and maintain that cultural elite, in the rather grand way that his standing allowed for. The *Revista de la Universidad de México* turned criticism into the most efficient means of getting the fine arts accepted by the public at large. The journal was a veritable roll call of the biggest names in Mexican letters: Reyes,* Pacheco,* Octavio Paz,* Juan José Arreola,* Juan Rulfo,* Carlos Fuentes,* Juan García Ponce,* Juan Vicente Melo,* and Carlos Monsiváis;* Luis Cernuda's* poems, Gabriel García Márquez's* first short stories, and the then-new Latin American literature (Gonzalo Rojas, Nicanor Parra, Sebastián Salazar Bondy, Ernesto Sábato), all sharing pages with Erich Fromm.

La feria de los días (1961) is a collection of early García Terrés political and cultural articles, which appeared regularly in *Revista de la Universidad de México, El Observador, Cuadernos Americanos,* and even the *Excélsior* newspaper. Like all books of its ilk, it expresses some opinions that are outdated, but it also displays the timelessness of the author's moral character. In writing about a troubled France going from the Fourth to the Fifth Republic, and the trio composed of Minister Pierre Mendès-France, President Charles de Gaulle and his bad moral conscience, and novelist François Mauriac, García Terrés was in fact yearning for that sort of "high politics" for Mexico.

García Terrés was at times prophetic, to his regret. He once said, for example, that with the death of José Vasconcelos*—whom his generation detested, for valid reasons—the man's legend would be born. More important, however, is a seemingly insignificant opinion expressed several times throughout *La feria de los días* and that was exceedingly rare among Mexican poets and novelists at the time: in 1959, García Terrés located the central problem with Mexican public life squarely in political freedom, and said that "the ideal solution, the ultimate goal, resides in the untrameled right to vote."

It's not easy (nor is it always expedient) to move from liberal temperament to democratic conviction. But García Terrés did it in *La feria de los días*, a thinly disguised testimony to how stifling it was even for a patrician like himself to be living in the glory days of the "institutionalized" Revolution, characterized by routine corporate and police repression promoted by the press's vociferous anti-communism. From its cautious attack on a regime allergic to anything that wasn't remorseful self-censure to an enthusiasm for the Cuban Revolution reminiscent of President Cárdenas, *La feria de los días* at times seems limited to the sort of good-conscience enthusiasm characterizing the *gauche caviar* that the PRI tried so hard to cultivate. But more often, it's the expression of liberal eloquence, as when García Terrés undertakes a combined defense of Boris Pasternak refusing his Nobel prize to appease the Russians while simultaneously standing up for freedom of expression in Mexico.

Reloj de Atenas (1977), the result of the author's years as Ambassador to Greece (1965–68), is one of the best travel books in Mexican literature. If García Terrés aspired to live on the world stage and the twentieth century was Mexico's Great Century, there could have been no better setting than the diplomatic world, and no better place than Greece for the poet to confirm his unruffled gravitas. Under the aegis of Giorgos Seferis, who became his friend and translator, García Terrés was on his Hellenic mission when the 1967 military coup occurred, an event that proved to be a pivotal moment in his humanist development. Trained in a school whose very essence was the "politics of spirit" put forth by Valéry, the Mexican Ambassador maintained the dignity of the post despite diplomatic impotence at the persecution of his Greek friends. King Constantine's court had been turned into a barracks.

The private journals that later became *Reloj de Atenas* must have been bitter company for García Terrés when he left Greece in 1968 and returned to Mexico, where President Díaz Ordaz's authoritarian "solution" to the student uprisings resulted in a situation painfully similar to that of the Greek military coup: loss of civil liberties and xenophobic hysteria. However, of all literary public servants (García Terrés came back in order to head the library and archives of the Ministry of Foreign Affairs), only Octavio Paz really took a stand, renouncing his post at the Mexican Embassy in India. Years later, writing the epitaph for Antonio Carrillo Flores (Minister of Foreign Affairs in 1968), he deemed that inaction "Mexican pragmatism," essentially a cop-out to justify the contradiction between a theoretical defense of citizens' rights and an always-opportune loyalty to the government in power. Like so many of his generation, García Terrés was not immune to that weakness, also characteristic of the world of "liberal snobbery" according to Elena Croce. She saw in the liberal elite an "informal, mystical, and slightly sacrilegious faith in men like themselves, rather than in the religion of freedom, which presupposed the duty to prove oneself by carrying out the vulgar, everyday tasks of reality so lacking in seductive qualities."

"Cosmopolitanism" was a pejorative term in early García Terrés texts, as it was initially for Octavio Paz, too. But ironically, benefitting so much from their geographical and literary travels, the pair of them also restored lost honor to "being cosmopolitan." There might be no more appropriate a universal figure than the poet-translator, and we can see García Terrés's real itinerary in the writers he translated: John Donne, W. B. Yeats, Tristan Corbière, Jules Laforgue, and Hölderlin. In *El teatro de los acontecimientos* (1988) and the posthumous texts included in volume II of *Obras* (1993–2000), we get to be part of his most worldly society journeys: from his meeting with Ezra Pound in Athens to his visits with the best poets in Greece; from his portraits of Lionel Trilling, Graham Greene, and Lillian Hellman to his open speculation about the slippery souls who fascinated him (Julio Torri,* José Gorostiza,* Juan Rulfo,* and Luis Buñuel) and about whom he wrote many incisive, eloquent pages.

"Liberal snobbery" strikes me as a kind of modern-day stoicism, a characteristic typical of the sort of stock García Terrés came from. I find, on considering his poems, that the ones I like best are those in which the man of letters seems to be taking a stroll through private life, like a patrician in his garden, joking rather seriously about the frivolous, privileged concerns of citizens and the brilliant joys of literary life, but also penning lamentations on death's call at the family aquarium and rodents running on their wheels. Of his collected poetry, published in *Las manchas del sol*, 1956–1987, I prefer the last two volumes (*Corre la voz*, 1980, and *Parte de vida*, 1988) for their subtle tone, which Zaid* finds located "in the welcome dodging of obvious musicality, Romanticism, and haughty discourse. Instead, we have the pleasingly distant poetic voice, leaving veiled signs of intelligence between the lines." (Zaid, *Obras, 2. Ensayos sobre poesía*, Mexico, 1993)

It's curious that García Terrés, who didn't like Borges back in the fifties (for rhetorical as well as political reasons), should end up writing similar sorts of poems, displaying a metaphysical offhandedness, emotional reserve at the fatuous flames of posterity, the "infinite library," and the rambling prose of literary biography. Among the most felicitous poems are "Envío" (from *Todo lo más por decir*, 1971), which recounts the intimate drama of someone who finds getting up a source of nerve-wracking problems; "Perseverancia," epitaph of epitaphs in which the poet "lo recuerdan / puntuales sus catorce descendientes / y las bibliografías" ("is remembered / as punctual by his fourteen descendents / and bibliographies"); "Limpieza general," which Zaid likes so much for its mythological exaggeration of a domestic mishap; and "Sazón del alba," the wait for "cuantas calladas horas faltan aún para reconocer / el fruto verdadero" ("the many quiet hours still to go to recognize / the true fruit"), which can be justly read as the poet's testimony. Given that García Terrés is a poet who struck out against all those who find literary life dry or not very dynamic, it should come as no surprise that several of his poems are like brief, imagined biographies: "La vocación" about Kavafis; "Ezra Pound en Atenas"; and "El duque y la duquesa," a marvellous evocation of Gutiérrez Nájera; and "Lowell," a tortuous depiction of a poet's downfall, "un libro que se acaba en el alba / la última lección de su verdad esquiva" ("a book that ends at dawn / the final lesson of his elusive truth").

In García Terrés we see evidence of what Zaid characterized as "social" poetry's "descent to the plain sincerity of colloquial poetry, to the simple song of human poetry," a move that became more perceptible after Gorostiza's masterpiece *Muerte sin fin*. On that move, García Terrés, like Zaid himself, was a poet who managed to venture into the prosaic without becoming trivial (as some of his disciples did), humorously rejecting transcendental poet-as-creator-of-the-world hoopla and concentrating on the cantos of great poetic tradition, as we can see from the first pages of *Los reinos combatientes* (1961).

In addition to the liberal man of letters and the stoic poet, there's a third side to García Terrés: the prudent surveyor of all things hidden, of the psychological infernos he found in Freud, in Gilberto Owen, and in the Eleusinian Mysteries. That a stoic like García Terrés should decide to take hallucinogenic mushrooms and turn his trip into poetry in "Carne de de Dios" (1964) says a lot about how sophisticated that elite was; it also says a lot about the limits of "liberal snobbery." He may have glimpsed those limitations himself when, years later, he wrote a hesitant review of mycologist R. Gordon Wasson's *The Road to Eleusis*, making clear that his own experience had been a one-time event undergone out of curiosity. Like the parlor esotericism (is there any other sort?) of Yeats, García Terrés's (solo, domestic) hallucinatory trip was, if anything, a sign of the spirit of the times. Surprisingly, his account of it is very similar to those written by hippies and indigenous *jipitecas* during the same period, folks making a pilgrimage to Huautla hoping to trip with legendary, indigenous *curandera* María Sabina. A newcomer himself, he unjustifiably disdained the others as ignorant.

Poesía y alquimia: Los tres mundos de Gilberto Owen (1980) is—as both Aurelio Asiain* and Octavio Paz said at the time—an overinterpretation. It really is going too far to maintain that the author of *Perseo vencido* (1948), who'd never been part of hermetic circles and had no readers of that ilk, would have written his greatest poem in some alchemistic code. Nevertheless, García Terrés's pursuit of corroboration is the stuff great books of criticism are made of. *Poesía y alquimia* is a beautiful chapter in the history of Mexican poetry: it's because of García Terrés that Owen is the second-most studied poet of the *Contemporáneos* (after Gorostiza). And all you have to do is compare *Poesía y alquimia* to others' supposedly alchemist readings of Jorge Cuesta* poetry to see the difference between literary criticism and academic waffle.

Unlike Reyes, the teacher he distanced himself from, García Terrés moved to Greece and introduced us to modern Greek poets: Cavafy, Elytis, Sikelianos, Embirikos, and Seferis. Reyes gives us ancient Helade and Athenian rhetoric; in *Reloj de Atenas*, García Terrés gave us the third-world ruins of a modern Greece that resembles authoritarian Mexico. In that difference is a mark of Mexican letters' progress towards modernity, to a time when great archeology is confused, as it should be, with the unprestigious, contemporary ruins we inhabit here. That's what civilization is, and that's how García Terrés saw it and wrote it.

It was his protection of both criticism and the canon that allowed García Terrés's cultural endeavors to be so brilliant and so impartial. His efforts were manifest not only in the *Revista de la Universidad de México* but in the FCE catalog and at the extraordinary Hispano-American literary journal *La Gaceta del FCE*. He had a formidable (and subtle) talent for taking a group of individuals and deciding exactly which editorial or intellectual task was best suited to whom. Only a liberal temperament can turn a collection of individuals into a community of talent that way.

When I was a kid, García Terrés was the first writer I ever saw in his library, and years later he was coincidentally the one who commissioned me to write my first book, as he did many other writers over the course of not one but two generations. And although he'd have hated the grandiose assessment, García Terrés is comparable (maybe even superior) to Vasconcelos in terms of arts and culture promotion and administration.

In the second half of the twentieth century García Terrés held the posts of principal and teacher at a school, because he was convinced—like Hofmannsthal and other members of the liberal elite depicted by Elena Croce—that the secret of artistic personality could and must be passed down like a Holy Grail. It was a new school, a public school, and in time it deteriorated; it's been closed down now for years. But scattered here and there, those of us who were educated as readers and writers there still carry García Terrés's legacy around with us, like a pocket edition of the *Odyssey*.

SELECTED BIBLIOGRAPHY
Obras I. Las manchas del sol, poesía, 1953–1994, FCE, Mexico, 1995.
Obras II. El teatro de los acontecimientos, FCE, Mexico, 1997.
Obras III. La feria de los días, 1953–1994, FCE, Mexico, 2000.

GARDEA, JESÚS

(Delicias, Chihuahua, 1939 – Mexico City, 2000)

This strange and often misread writer got a late start and died fairly young, leaving behind an unusually monochromatic and impressive body of work: thirteen novels and his collected stories, *Reunión de cuentos* (1999), which are some of the best of the genre. With novels like *El sol que estás mirando* (1981), *La canción de las mulas muertas* (1981), and *El tornavoz* (1983), some of his early readers (myself included) thought Gardea was something of a third-generation Faulkner with his fictional town of Placeres. But we were wrong. Nor is he like García Márquez. Instead, Gardea falls more in line with writers like Juan Rulfo* and Juan Carlos Onetti, and as José María Espinasa* points out, unlike other epigones he never tried his hand at waving the wand of magic realism. No, Gardea eventually—and completely—gave up on fiction, and at the time of his death was seen as an author verging on the unintelligible.

Espinasa, the critic who wrote most loyally and perceptively about Gardea, noted that he tended to "privilege creating atmosphere over all else: the baked dirt, the zenith where the 'sun that you're seeing' leaves all exposed skin with no shadow . . . The legends and turns of phrase of northern Mexico are used like construction materials in building that tone, that atmosphere . . . At the heart of Gardea's narrative is what's glimpsed behind the curtain at the hairdresser's, what's seen through the shutters or a half open door, splitting reality into not a *moral* black-and-white but a plastic one" (Espinasa, *Hacia el otro*, 1990).

It is in his stories, though, where Gardea achieves a mastery grounded in the almost maniacal refinement of his expressive abilities. In anthologies like *Los viernes de Lautaro* (1979), *Septiembre y los otros días* (1981), *Las luces del mundo* (1986), *De alba sombría* (1987), *Difícil de atrapar* (1995), and *Donde el gimnasta* (1998), Espinasa saw "an atypical short story writer: his stories tend to be sparse, lean, so spare they become imprecise. But it's not that simplifying the story makes it transparent. Quite the contrary: they have a vibratory, impressionistic tone to them. His stories' literary origins are with [Rulfo's] *El llano en llamas*, but they're also rooted in other Mexican narratives such as those of Revueltas,* [Mauricio] Magdaleno, and Ramón Rubín, and they follow anthropological trends like microhistory. Nevertheless, the extreme formalism of his later books distances him from those writers. Lining up all of his books, we see his evolution towards a voluntarily dry, formalized style that contains the words, feelings and even rhythms of spoken language, and yet is totally unlike it . . . It's clear that his prose is not extravagant, that his stories have a limited number of themes (he's been reproached for this, told that all of his stories are one), but those limited themes are particularly well constructed. It's not the stories themselves that are similar, it's the texture."

Gardea's last novels—*Soñar la guerra* (1984), *Los músicos y el fuego* (1985), *Sóbol* (1985), *El diablo en el ojo* (1991), *La ventana hundida* (1992), and *Juegan los comensales* (1999)—paved the way for his posthumous book, *Tropa de sombras* (2003). I've read it twice and still don't know what it's about. Is it a nightmare that takes place in an abandoned hovel in the middle of the desert in the middle of the night? Is it the story of four armed men who escape from prison aided only by a flashlight? Or is it some kind of dramatization akin to the theater of the absurd, a means of punishing language? *Tropa de sombras* is one of the few Mexican books of our time with a writer thoroughly unwilling to make even the most minimal concession to traditional realism, which is so often recycled into some publishing trend. I find this notable—even a bit heroic—in an author like Gardea, a born storyteller whose rhetorical expertise would have enabled him to renounce solitude and attract the world's stage.

That "narrator of the desert" who I initially saw as an accomplished artisan happy to populate northern Mexico's desolate desert plains with literary output turned out to be a lone wolf who took geographical barrenness and nature's emptiness and created a poetics of desolation. Gardea's stories are just about the most melancholic there are in contemporary Mexican literature, located in a place where man gets lost in his shadow.

A dental surgeon in Ciudad Juárez, Gardea relished his reputation as the first provincial novelist to achieve a certain degree of renown without ever relocating to Mexico City. I spoke with him in person once, on behalf of a friend who wanted to translate him into German. The conversation lasted three or four hours and I can recall almost nothing about it; it was as if he had a mask he put on to attend to inevitable, tedious professional matters. Gardea's biography also includes a years-long, deliberate absence from the literary world, which makes me think he's like those writers Faulkner praised who, like vultures, were not hated, or envied, or needed by anyone. No one messes with them, they're never endangered, and they can live on anything.

SELECTED BIBLIOGRAPHY

Reunión de cuentos, FCE, Mexico, 1999.

Tropa de sombras, FCE, Mexico, 2003.

GARIBAY, RICARDO

(Tulancingo, Hidalgo, 1923 – Cuernavaca, Morelos, 1999)

Garibay is the writer who successfully portrayed the city via its language. For him, the city constantly and compulsively emits verbal signs. Right from the start—*Mazamitla*, 1955—back when he was still caught up with rural clichés, Garibay learned how to turn language into a driving force behind his narratives. When his stories change scenes, they're spurred on by a dizzying torrent of words. Garibay, author of *Beber un cáliz* (1965) and *Bellísima bahía* (1968), also has no qualms about introducing extra-literary materials into his texts: radio and television scripts, cinematic progression. And this paraphernalia is not wasted. It's a calculated strategy that offers an endless array of uses for the colloquial language that Garibay learned to hear and that he taught contemporary urban writers to listen to.

His bitter words also turn the city (and not just Mexico City, but anyplace overwhelmingly urban) into a place where societal decay impregnates everything. Garibay's poetic imagery condemns.

He published a very decent novel quite late in life: *La casa que arde de noche* (1971). In it, it's clear that his almost academic expertise in colloquial language is not just a catalog of expressions. It's a stylistic calculation that makes him choose the most intense words in his repertoire, demonstrating throughout the novel that he's a cruel and precise realist, a prose writer instilled with deeply poetic sadness [. . .]. It's no coincidence that his work appeared at the same time that the poetry of Rubén Bonifaz Nuño* and Efraín Huerta* began to embrace popular themes, including dance halls and bus trips. Garibay's pathos proved to us that colloquial language could be exaggerated in a *literary* way, rather than as a means of moral atonement. (*Antología de la narrativa mexicana del siglo XX*, I, 1989)

SELECTED BIBLIOGRAPHY

Obras reunidas, I–VI, introduction by Vicente Leñero, Océano/Consejo Estatal para la Cultura y las Artes del Gobierno del Estado de Hidalgo, Mexico, 2001.

GARIBAY KINTANA, ÁNGEL MARÍA
(Toluca, Mexico State, 1892 – Mexico City, 1967)

Encyclopedia compiler, Bible scholar, and expert on Nahuatl and Ancient Greece, Father Garibay was one of Mexico's few real twentieth-century sages, in the fullest sense of the word. The man whose ecclesiastical career took him all the way to the rank of lay canon of the Basilica of Guadalupe in 1941 had previously been a parish priest in towns like Hilotepec, San Martín de las Pirámides, Huizquilucan, Tenancingo, and Otumba, places where he learned the Otomi language. This man had never set foot outside of Mexico—and may never even have seen the sea—and yet he singlehandedly advanced the Mexican Church's philological tradition. He continued both the ethno-linguistic endeavors of Franciscan friar Bernardino de Sahagún—whose *Historia general de las cosas de la Nueva España* he published in 1956—and the enlightenment project of Fracisco Javier Clavijero. Father Garibay also published the canonical works of Friar Diego Durán, Friar Diego de Landa, and Manuel Orozco y Berra.

Although he's often ignored in twentieth-century classical literary studies, Father Garibay possessed the Greek expertise that Alfonso Reyes* lacked and had the Christian charity that José Vasconcelos* was so proud of lacking. He respectfully waited until Reyes died before publishing his own *Mitología griega* (1962), a reference book whose usefulness and elegance are somewhat overshadowed by anachronistic, apologetic, and pompous prose. But we'd do well to remember that his *Historia de la literatura nahuatl* (1954) opens by making the comparison that Vasconcelos refused to consider, between Hindustani literatures and West Indian literatures. An isolated scholar working in both ancient Greek and the modern languages of the high plains, the founder of UNAM's Seminario de Cultura Náhuatl, Father Garibay was also the only Spanish speaker to translate the Greek comedies and tragedies in their entirety. And while his versions of Aristophanes's eleven comedies published in 1967 might not be the most strictly faithful of Spanish translations, I find them the most beautiful and flavorful.

As a Catholic, Garibay was concerned with all things universal; and like Reyes and Vasconcelos, his work was intended to be part of a classicist project that would serve as a model for modern culture. What he did was reconstruct the Mexican tradition's weakest link: Nahuatl literature. From *La poesía lírica azteca* (1937) and *Llave del náhuatl. Colección de trozos clásicos con gramática y vocabulario para utilidad de los principiantes* (1949 and 1961) to *Poesía náhuatl* (1964–68), Father Garibay posited philology as the only means of weeding a field overgrown with Hispanism and indigenism. The former—sanctioned by racist rigmarole—denied the literary existence of what Vasconcelos actually referred to as "that civilization without a soul," and as for the latter, the Mexican Revolution *indigenistas* were happy just to print educational and legendary picture cards depicting indigenous heroism.

As is always the case in philology, over the course of time Nahuatl studies have disproved many of the hypotheses and attributions put forth by Garibay and his disciple Miguel León-Portilla.* After John Bierhorst's polemical interpretation of the *Cantares mexicanos*, it seems clear that the transcribing of Nahuatl poetry was unrelated to any notion of authorship. Nor does it represent some Apollonian means of counteracting the undeniably militaristic and sacrificial nature of Mesoamerican city-states. Instead the *cantos* would seem to be ceremonial songs, hermetic invocations of the gods, kings, and dead warriors, a dramatic consequence of the Conquest. And although Father Garibay had no qualms about conceding that *some* of his sources came after 1521, it's more likely that the entire corpus postdates Cortés.

Garibay's recension has been criticized for its "extreme pre-Columbianization" of manuscripts because he arbitrarily omitted any annotations he found problematic, out of a desire to turn the *Cantares* into a sort of Greek anthology in accordance with the great tragics. Paradoxically, he—a Catholic priest—excised all Christian influence on Nahuatl poetry that was probably written after the Conquest. Trained in the nineteenth-century Romantic school, Father Garibay tried to invest the Aztecs with a national literature of the stature of his civilizing ambitions. That was the impetus behind *Historia de la literatura náhuatl*, and that's the caveat we should keep in mind on reading it. Thus, as Gertrudis Payàs says, it should come as no surprise that Garibay was awarded the Premio Nacional, along with architect Pedro Ramírez Vázquez, designer of the National Museum of Anthropology, the monumental project that the Mexican Revolution's regime used to honor the archetypal Aztec that it wanted to project itself as.

For anyone who studies literature as an expression of the history of ideas and is blind to the charms of falsified identities, Garibay's classicist impulse is as interesting and as fruitful as comparable projects carried out in the sixteenth and seventeenth centuries by Fernando de Alva Ixtilxóchitl and Carlos de Sigüenza y Góngora. While they translated Latin culture into a Christian, neo-Aztec code, Father Garibay offered a noteworthy synthesis, as useful for introducing one to Nahuatl poetry as it is for understanding modern Mexican literature. In *La literatura náhuatl* (1990), Amos Segala summarizes the great scholar's aims and limitations thus: "Father Garibay, in whom we sometimes ignore the routine reliance on not just Nahuatl texts but also on Greco-Latin ones as well as the Old Testament, often tried to establish meaningful links between Indo-European, pre-Hellenic, or Biblical texts and Nahuatl ones. These connections and relationships are not only a convenient means of ennobling the literary production of a people who have already been manipulated in myriad ways as an attempt to ennoble their true nature; they also serve to locate that literature in a realm that is principally his own and turns this into an eminently religious phenomenon: the expression of a collective that recognizes itself, reflects on itself, begs, doubts, suffers, and celebrates all within a specific, ineluctable, omnipresent cosmovision. The *canto* and the literature for him have no other role, no function other than serving as beautiful proof of this Weltanschauung, of which they are both the essence and an example."

There's no doubt that Garibay Hellenized the world of Nahuatl letters, turning what León-Portilla called "toltecáyotl" into a classical register acceptable to both the Catholic Church and the "institutional" Revolution's *indigenistas*. But he had to walk a tightrope between the two of them in order to pull it off. Not even if we accept this politically motivated reading of the situation can we disdain Garibay's talent for rediscovering (and inventing, to some degree) post-Cortés Nahuatl literature. It was a tremendously beautiful and unexpected flowering that enriched the Spanish language until it was tragically cut off in 1556, when the Santa Cruz de Tlatelolco indigenous school was closed down. So it's no surprise that Garibay concluded his *Historia de la literatura náhuatl* solemnly, looking at the case of Bartolomé de Alva Ixtlilxóchitl (third son of Fernando), who in the mid-1600s translated and adapted Lope de Vega and Calderón de la Barca plays into Nahuatl, planning a new type of religious play, an auspicious cultural fusion that, as Garibay lamented, was cut off "mid-flight."

His classicism also sparked a predictable Romantic reaction. Though Garibay continued with the Pre-Tridentine ecclesiastic tradition that posited and accepted the convergence between paganism and Christianity, between the Nahuatl legacy and the spiritual conquest, for publicists of the "new indigenous literature" (anthropologists, academics taken with the Neo-Zapatista cause, left-wing post-Council priests) Spanish could only be the "language of the conquistador," isolating the indigenous from the very context that allowed their survival: the Catholic, Hispanic civilization that claims Republican Mexico as heir. If we take modernity to mean our collective ability ("we" being the barbarians) to speak and make sense of the languages of the city, then Garibay's legacy is huge. Notwithstanding the inevitable liberties taken by an archeologist at his first dig, he restored an entire literature, allowing indigenous languages to assume a past—fifty years later—likely to yield new artistic expression. Books like León-Portilla's *Visión de los vencidos* (1961), which used Garibay translations, not only changed the way we read the Conquest but also filled contemporary Mexican Indians with eschatological hope for cultural politics. When someone like Carlos Montemayor,* academic and classicist, decides to strike out on a new path in indigenous literatures, it's impossible not to read his eagerness as the culmination, as well as the negation, of Garibay's legacy.

Both celebrated and belittled as the late-blooming flower of Mexican humanism, Father Garibay was also a modern priest. He was the first to suggest women be inducted into the Mexican Academy of the Language and one of the few early voices warning the Germanophilic public opinion against the extermination of European Jews. Writing in *Excelsior, El Universal,* and the journal *Ábside,* mouthpiece of the Catholic literati, Garibay was taken seriously. His knowledge of Greek and Aramaic guaranteed his acceptance as a pro-Semitic intellectual, translator of the *Proverbs of Solomon*, the *Wisdom of Ben Sira*, and the *Wisdom of Israel*.

Editor of the *Diccionario Porrúa de historia, biografía y geografía de México*, Garibay also offered mid-century bigwigs a bit of rococo Aztec glory to display at academic meetings and on society pages, by coyly translating into Nahuatl the menu at Salvador Novo's* restaurant, La Capilla. But as regent of good taste and chronicler of Mexico City, Novo's respect for Garibay went well beyond that authoritarian paradise that allowed the institutional elite to make peace with the remote Axayácatl and Montezuma monarchies. The priest and scholar was, for him, the unexpected fulfillment of the classicist dream that had gone unrealized in his generation.

Flipping through the pages of *Letras de México* (the March 1943 edition), I found a photo of Father Garibay looking astonishingly young, leaning with staged carelessness against the wall of a pyramid. In the picture he's got a long beard, tousled hair, and he's wearing a jacket and straw hat. He could be a 1970s hippie in search of magic mushrooms. Or a Marxist anthropologist doing fieldwork. Or a nineteenth-century archeologist, sage and adventurer, satisfied to have cleared the jungle and discovered the Mayan treasure. Thinking about the disarming, agreeable ubiquity of this man, who controlled several fields over an extended time, I closed my eyes for a minute and then opened them again. Now it looked like Father Garibay. But who knows, it could have been Indiana Jones.

SELECTED BIBLIOGRAPHY
Historia de la literatura náhuatl, Porrúa, Mexico, 1954.
Poesía náhuatl, UNAM, Mexico, 1964–1968.

GARRO, ELENA
(Puebla, Puebla, 1920 – Cuernavaca, Morelos, 1998)

Garro's life and work exemplify the most shocking and controversial story in all of Mexican literature. She married Octavio Paz* in 1937, and the couple lived a turbulent life together until they were legally divorced in 1959.

Garro had a paradoxical relationship with Paz's light and shadow. On the one hand, he represented all that was ominous in the world to her, and her stories and novels hinge on an imaginary persecution led by her ex-husband; on the other, without his lifelong economic support, Garro's troubled life (and that of their daughter, Helena Paz) would have been even more ill-fated. In an interview with Gabriela Mora in the last years of her life, Garro said, "I want you to know, categorically: first, that I live *against* him, I was born against him, I had a daughter against him, I loved my family against him, I studied against him, I danced against him, I had lovers against him, I wrote against him, and I defended the Indians against him, I wrote about politics against him; in short, everything, everything, everything I am is against him . . . You only have one enemy in life and that's enough. And my enemy is Paz."

In June 2006, declassified documents proved that Garro was a Federal Security Directorate (DFS) informant under President Gustavo Díaz Ordaz before and during the 1968 student movement. Given that she had supposedly gone into exile because of her role in the movement, this discovery shed a lot of light on an entire chapter of the political history of Mexican literature. Contrary to what she and those who later facilitated her return to Mexico claimed, it had already come out that the reason for Garro's unpopularity had nothing to do with any persecution by Paz. In fact, her discredit stemmed from her actions during the summer of 1968, which now seem laughable—the sort of thing you'd find in a spy novel that only Garro herself could have written. But the weeks following the October 2 Tlatelolco massacre were no laughing matter for those she denounced as the intellectual authors of the student uprising.

On August 17, Garro published an article in *Revista de América* entitled "The Cowards' Conspiracy," in which after blaming intellectuals for inciting students she then spun off into a panic of truly apocalyptic proportions. "Rumor has it that thousands were killed during the uprisings and secretly cremated by the government. Those arrested, injured, and jailed also supposedly number in the thousands. So why don't the intellectuals seek out the families of those murdered or wounded and offer them up to public opinion? Why don't they demand punishment for the intellectual authors of these massacres?"

Then five days after the Tlatelolco massacre, on October 7, Garro came out in the national press accusing National Autonomous University (UNAM) rector Javier Barros Sierra and a group of "extreme left-wing" artists and intellectuals (including Carlos Monsiváis,* José Luis Cuevas, Rosario Castellanos,* Leonora Carrington, and many others) of leading the students to "promote agitation and blood-spilling." The declassified files have revealed other peculiarities as well. For instance, a telegram of support was sent by Argentine writers Jorge Luis Borges, Adolfo Bioy Casares, and Manuel Mújica Lainez to President Díaz Ordaz after October 2, surely the result of a desperate call from Garro, who was a close friend of Bioy Casares.

Then in *El Universal* on October 23, in concert with her mother's denunciations, Helena Paz published an open letter to Octavio Paz, who had just resigned from his post as Ambassador to India out of protest. In that pathetic letter to her father, Helena said, "Your condemnation should have been directed at the bums who sent the dispossessed youth to their death and destruction . . . You must know that those responsible for the disaster have no scruples. First: because they let them fall and then turned their backs on the fallen. Second: because they turned them in to the police, in whose hands I'm sorry to inform you they're much safer than they are with those dried-up brains hungering for power. Third: because they hurled insults ranging from cowards and murderers to spies, traitors, informers, provocateurs, swindlers etc, just because they lost the bloody battle of Tlatelolco, which the intellectuals organized but—of course—did not attend . . . Those young people weren't peaceful, and what made them violent—you don't know them—was an unjust cause and devious leaders who orchestrated their loss."

What happened to Garro in 1968? Where and how did the outrageous adventure of this terrible yet beguiling woman begin? The details released by the Federal Institute for Access to Public Information (IFAI) help solve many of the riddles. They published (and I'll discuss later) her personal diaries (*Testimonios sobre Elena Garro*, 2002) and political articles (*El asesinato de Elena Garro*, 2006), both edited by Patricia Rosas Lopátegui.

Based on a carefully established chronology, we know that during the sixties Garro was navigating the rough waters of official agrarianism and that in her desire to redeem the *campesinos*, she befriended Carlos Madrazo, national president of the Institutional Revolutionary Party (PRI) between 1964 and 1965. Garro idolized the politician from Tabasco and, given her frustrated reformist bent, she saw him as the savior Mexico had been await-ing. From the articles in *El asesinato de Elena Garro*, we can see that she truly believed in the ideals (always at risk of being betrayed) of the Mexican Rev-olution-turned-government and their "revolutionary nationalism." Mexico's intellectual life is full of this sort of messianic infatuation.

After accidentally crossing paths with the student movement, Carlos Madrazo died in a suspicious plane crash in 1969. But even before then, by Au-gust of 1968, given the momentum of the student movement, Garro had begun to fear (or be forewarned) that repression would befall the youth and end up claiming victims within the official party's (more or less) tolerated dissidents.

Prone to wild, runaway fantasies, Garro tried to buy protection for herself and her daughter in exchange for continuing to inform political police of go-ings-on in the intellectual circles involved in the movement. Playing double agent, Garro ended up getting played, being a spied-on spy who thought she was using the DFS when in fact they were using her. Really, it was Paz's resig-nation that triggered events. Terrified at the dangerous challenge to author-ity her ex-husband had made by resigning from his post at the embassy, and afraid she'd be dragged further into a dubious situation, Garro plunged into paranoia that immediately resulted in her alleged denunciations. It's likely that the information she'd already provided the DFS was of little use, and doubtless that her public accusations were taken as preposterous, even by the punctilious government intelligence. But the tendency to justify Garro's conduct in 1968 with all sorts of shrewd arguments makes it necessary to come right out and say that she made a grave mistake: she endangered many friends and colleagues, and she contributed decisively and excessively to the lynch-mob climate in which Mexican intellectuals lived, post-Tlatelolco.

The rest of the story is even more lamentable. When Garro decided to end her self-imposed exile in Paris and Madrid, Paz's literary and political enemies welcomed her back to Mexico almost like a saint. But they soon dis-appeared when they saw her unrestrained, compulsive spending. Nothing was enough to cover Elena's expenses, and she could burn through vast sums of money in days or sometimes hours. Not since Léon Bloy's *The Ungrateful Beggar* has literature seen such a diseased relationship to money as Garro's.

Recuerdos del porvenir (1963; *Recollections of Things to Come*, 1986), her first novel, was both a farewell to Mexican Revolution literature and one of Latin America's classic novels of magical realism. And although in my opinion, her later novels were like rough drafts flung mercilessly to the public, they've aroused much admiration in impartial readers such as César Aira. In his *Diccionario de autores latinoamericanos* (2001) he writes, "*Y Matarazo no llamó* (1991), datelined 'Paris, 1960,' is a gloomy novel of condemnation, and one of the writer's best. *Inés* (1995), probably her best novel, once again foregrounds mother and daughter persecuted by an ex-husband so brutal, so diabolical, that Augusto in her earlier *Testimonios sobre Mariana* seems almost benevolent by comparison. In 1996 she published multiple works: *Un corazón en un bote de basura*, a short and relatively light novel; *Busca mi esquela* and *Primer amor*, two novellas, the second of which is set in postwar France where the fates of a mother and her daughter, Natalia and Irene, (two Saint Barbaras) . . . fleeing from various threats, are tied up with those of young German prisoners; and *Un traje rojo para un duelo*, a very dense novel set in Mexico, with a mother and daughter—Natalia and Irene—persecuted by a sadistic ex-husband and his family. Finally, *El accidente y otros cuentos inéditos* (1997) is a collection of three remarkable stories that allude to earlier works by the author . . . *La vida empieza a las tres* (1997) is another collection of three novellas. And another novel was published posthumously, *Mi hermana Magdalena* (1998), set in Mexico, Paris, and Ascona and featuring the by-now customary monstrous husband, this time shored up by an equally malevolent mother-in-law. In recent years, two nonfiction books have also been published. [One is] *Memorias de España 1937* (1992), the delightful account of a trip to war-torn Spain to support the Republic, taken by a group of Mexican intellectuals that included the very young Elena Garro and Octavio Paz, newlyweds at the time."

Some biographical background is crucial to understanding Garro's character, because of the transubstantiation between her suffering and literature. No madness is as full of method as Garro's. She is able, for instance, to distance herself from herself in a cruelly sardonic way in *Andamos huyendo Lola* (1980), *Testimonios sobre Mariana* (1981), and *Reencuentro de personajes* (1982). Artistically, she's at her best in *Testimonios sobre Mariana*, a novel set in a fantastical, post-World War II Paris where there can be no peace for Mariana, surrounded as she is by gods and monsters. Subjected to the oppression of Augusto (her husband Octavio Paz), and Vicente (Adolfo Bioy Casares), Mariana is a de Sade-like heroine. But her subjugation is relative: the character is both victim and executioner, nymph and vampire. And her destiny (and that of her daughter) is ambivalent, given that both live on after death, spectrally, surrounded by surrealist sycophants and White Russians. As César Aira states, after *Testimonios sobre Mariana*, Garro's novels became an obsessive variation on a theme: the noxious power of a man persecuting a mother and daughter, protagonists of a *folie a deux* that feeds off of catastrophe.

As it turns out, the very public exhibition of Garro's misfortune didn't end with her death. Her diaries and private papers fell into the hands of University of New Mexico professor Patricia Rosas Lopátegui, who came up with *Testimonios sobre Elena Garro*—Garro's diaries with Rosas Lopátegui's commentary—which she calls an "exclusive, authorized biography." The book is a shocking example of inept manipulation of a writer's legacy, not only because of its utter disrespect for even the most basic rules of academic publishing, but for the way the author flaunts her bad faith and unqualified resentment page after page. In the name of some misinterpreted feminism, Rosas Lopátegui obsessively charges Paz, the whole of literary society, and the Mexican state with a permanent conspiracy against Garro, and she takes it all to utterly absurd extremes. While for Garro, this alleged persecution was the stuff of life, for Rosas Lopátegui it's simply ridiculous. Her commentary not only gets in the way of Garro's texts but is full of psychoanalytic inferences, soundbites of purportedly literary theory, proof of her ignorance of Mexican Spanish, a lack of knowledge of Mexican national history, and unfounded bile. The whole of it makes searching for Garro amid all the gibberish a nauseating ordeal.

Rosas Lopátegui's presentation is so outrageous that Elena Poniatowska,* who wrote the book's prologue, actually felt obliged to discredit much of it. She writes that "the information Elena [Garro] gives [Rosas Lopátegui] is a hodgepodge of contradictions if not falsehoods" and that Rosas Lopátegui idolizes Garro without questioning anything she says, treating her like a saint and martyr. And, defending Paz, Poniatowska—who was a friend of the couple and thus knew firsthand—refutes Rosas Lopátegui, recalling that in the late fifties the poet was wildly enthusiastic about Garro's work and that he admired his wife, who never ceased to "amaze him, or perhaps worry and concern him, sending him to the pits of hell."

Contrary to the ravings Rosas Lopátegui tries to pass off as biographical truth, Poniatowska clarifies that in the sixties, Garro's political and journalistic career was protected by several politicians in the Díaz Ordaz regime and that there was never—in 1968 or at any point during her self-imposed exile—any "intrigue, conspiracy or plot against her. Elena's novels and stories were read and reviewed . . . and the only assassination [a reference to the title] of Elena was a result of her own life, cut off from reality and even from herself."

El asesinato de Elena Garro, along with the IFAI revelations, pulls the rug out from under the slander with which the author tried to turn her ravings into a character assassination of Paz and other writers. In any event, that was a fairly useless undertaking since Garro (and this is part of her genius) can't be spun into political correctness. Despite the exploitation of her private papers and political articles, reading Garro's file gives a chilling picture of the hell she inhabited. And in spite of her insanity, she has to be admired for her impressive oeuvre. In the seventies, while she was living in Madrid, her diaries reveal her to be frequently delirious, living off the unsuspecting victims she extorted while simultaneously falling victim to the abuses of a real "court of miracles." Thus, while she was comparing Paz's work to that of Charles Manson, she was also claiming Hitler was a communist agent and fervently reading the Falangist press, trying to figure out how to "escape" from a Spain transitioning to democracy and fearing she'd fall victim to a communist conspiracy.

Garro's greatness lay in the successful sublimation of her suffering. While her private diaries make clear that she suffered from a tremendous and pathological persecution complex, a heightened sense of artistic awareness in her novels imposes the truth, postulating a critical complicity between the persecuted and their torturers, as in *Reencuentro de personajes* (1982). In this crime novel, the drama would be almost unbearable if not for the noble stratagem chosen by Garro to measure her heroine's misfortune: characters from F. Scott Fitzgerald and Evelyn Waugh novels pop up in the text, indicating that only literature can console the stormy landscapes of the soul. Only on the surface is Garro a temperamental, unsystematic writer. Her prose is immediate, candid, and forceful, free of metaphor and utterly penetrating, presenting a reality comprised of the most systematic and reiterative loneliness, melancholy, and horror. In her novels, stories, and plays, Garro is the twentieth century's great Mexican writer, the only one whose work could possibly make up for the chaos and bitterness of her errant intellect.

Selected Bibliography

Un hogar sólido, Universidad Veracruzana, Xalapa, 1958.

Los recuerdos del porvenir, Joaquín Mortiz, Mexico, 1963.

La semana de colores, Universidad Veracruzana, Xalapa, 1964.

Felipe Ángeles, Cóatl, Guadalajara, 1967.

Testimonios sobre Mariana, Grijalbo, Mexico, 1980.

Andamos huyendo Lola, Joaquín Mortiz, Mexico, 1980.

Reencuentro de personajes, Grijalbo, Mexico, 1982.

La casa junto al río, Grijalbo, Mexico, 1983.

Y Matarazo no llamó, Grijalbo, Mexico, 1991.

Memorias de España 1937, Siglo XXI, Mexico, 1992.

Inés, Grijalbo, Mexico, 1995.

Un corazón en el bote de basura, Joaquín Mortiz, Mexico, 1996.

Un traje rojo para un duelo, Ediciones Castillo, Monterrey, 1996.

Busca mi esquela y Primer amor, Ediciones Castillo, Monterrey, 1996.

Revolucionarios mexicanos, Joaquín Mortiz, Mexico, 1997.

Mi hermana Magdalena, Ediciones Castillo, Monterrey, 1998.

Teatro de Elena Garro, ed. P Rosas Lopátegui, New Mexico, 2000.

Obras reunidas I. Cuentos, introduction by Lucía Melgar, FCE, Mexico, 2006.

Obras reunidas, FCE, Mexico, 2006–2009.
  I. *Cuentos.*
  II. *Teatro.*

Rosas Lopátegui, Patricia, *Testimonios sobre Elena Garro*, Ediciones Castillo, Monterrey, 2002.

—, *El asesinato de Elena Garro*, Porrúa, Mexico, 2005.

Recollections of Things to Come, trans. Ruth L. C. Simms, University of Texas, 1986.

First Love and Look for My Obituary, trans. David Unger, Curbstone Press, 1999.

GLANTZ, MARGO

(Mexico City, 1930)

There are those writers—Nabakov and V. S. Naipaul, for instance—who brag about hating music, and writers who use novels and short stories as a means of expressing their utter melomania. Margo Glantz and her novel *El rastro* (2002), however, fit into neither category. It's not only one of the most finely wrought Mexican novels in recent years, it's also the only one I can think of in which classical music and its performers don't *adorn* the text but are in fact the spirit of the entire book. Inspired by Glenn Gould's interpretation of the *Goldberg Variations*, *El rastro* is very different from Thomas Bernhard's book *The Loser*, which also features the Canadian pianist. The latter is an elegy on artistic failure, while Glantz's novel is a "variation" on the theme of the heart.

Glantz's previous fiction doesn't quite manage to strike the right balance between essay and novel. It seems to be missing the dramatic tension that is ever-present in *El rastro*. Like a good musical composition, this novel lasts exactly as long as it takes to develop its theme and then concludes. In it the narrator, in a flash that alludes to the text's brevity, attends the wake of her ex-husband, a musician. With prose that reproduces the beats of the king of organs, *El rastro* hits notes that evoke pianists Richter, Gould, and Barenboim as much as they do the castrati, Bach as much as Schubert: all of these are the themes Juan (the dead man) carried in his heart while he was alive. Glantz takes the medical cause of Juan's death (a coronary) and devises a little treaty on the heart, symbol and vessel of passion since the beginning of time. And she does it by assuming not only philosophical but anatomical discourses, as often as the protagonist's interior monologues allow her.

Feelings are "ghostly" manifestations of a body's life (and death); but at the wake, Nora (the mysterious heroine) has to confront all of the physiological vulgarities and contingencies surrounding death, a situation that's simultaneously comical, embarrassing, and solemn. It takes a long life in literature to be able to write a book like *El rastro*.

Selected Bibliography
El rastro, Anagrama, Barcelona, 2002.
Saña, ERA, Mexico, 2008.

Obras reunidas, FCE, Mexico, 2006–2010.

    I. Escritos sobre literatura colonial.

    II. Narrativa.

    III. Escritos sobre literatuira popular mexicana del siglo XIX.

The Wake, trans. Andrew Hurley, Curbstone Press, 2005.

GONZÁLEZ DE LEÓN, ULALUME

(Montevideo, Uruguay, 1932 – Querétaro, Querétaro, 2009)

Daughter of the Uruguayan poets Roberto and Sara de Ibáñez and Mexican by choice for the last fifty years, González de León first came to be known via the journals *Plural* and *Vuelta*, where she was an active contributor. A faultless translator unfazed by syntactical enigmas and metric nightmares, she has published well-known Spanish translations of Lewis Carroll, e. e. cummings, and Valery Larbaud.

Octavio Paz* once famously said that for some poets "language is matter in perpetual motion, like color: a vibration, a wave, a rhythmic tide that encircles us with its millions of arms, in which we rock and we drown, we're reborn and we die. For others language is a geometry, a configuration of lines, which are signs that engender other signs, other shades, other lights: a drawing. Ulalume González de León belongs to this second family; for her, language is not an ocean but an architecture of lines and transparencies."

In another vein, Ramón Xirau* pointed out the "games, riddles and nonsense rhymes from the English tradition" present in her poetry. But more than that, in her choreographed twirls and beautifully wrought acrobatics, we can see a personal drama evolving, one that is hers alone. González de León seemed to doubt Xirau's belief that hers is a "verbally complex universe" and thus titled her collected works *Plagios* (2001). The gesture stresses—coquettishly—the ancillary nature of her own poetry, as if it were nothing but the painstaking notes of a good student written in the margins of true poetry. This is where I see unfolding the story of an educated woman who, having handily earned the "room of her own" that Virginia Woolf fought for, finds herself imprisoned in a golden cage. And despite accolades from demigods like Jorge Guillén and René Char, González de León saw herself (and this makes her poems more ambiguous) as something of a parlor writer, a wordsmith tucked away in a privileged realm of refinement that doesn't care if it's seen as frivolous. The beauty of the form was enough.

But love often wreaks havoc in the world, and so it is that another style of González de León's poetry comes out via her encounter with poet Jorge Hernández Campos,* her poetic accomplice. Like Lewis Carroll, González de León moves through the looking glass, leaving behind that room of her own to inhabit a time of two lovers, a faintly fairy-tale turn in which Sleeping Beauty—a character from the earlier first phase—has woken up and dares to recognize something of herself in the portrait of Dorian Gray. In González de León's later poems, the revulsion of aging and a belief in the immortality of souls (conceived as a fusion of bodies) sit side by side in apparent harmony.

According to Irving Singer—philosophical writer and historian of eroticism—the notion of love as a kind of magical fusion may have first cropped up in Plato's discourse on love to Aristophanes, in the *Symposium*. After explaining that men and women were once whole but are now split apart, Aristophanes goes on to say that love is the pursuit of that original whole, that we're in search of what's been severed. That appears to be the road González de León has taken of late: like François Villon, the French poet who wrote "Ballad of Dead Ladies," she can't imagine the "belles" after death and, like Aristophanes, she puts her faith in the power of love to restore the lost whole.

Selected Bibliography
Plagios, FCE, Mexico, 2001.

GONZÁLEZ DE MENDOZA, JOSÉ MARÍA
(Sevilla, Spain, 1893 – Mexico City, 1967)

A descendent of Admiral Diego Hernández de Mendoza and the Marquis of Santillana, González de Mendoza came from a noble Spanish family who lost their fortune and were forced to immigrate to Mexico in 1910, when he was just an adolescent. Though a gracious literary critic, he was unable to swim against the tide of general oblivion. In fact, Ramón Xirau* and Luis Cardoza y Aragón* are of the very few people who've written about the man who signed his articles "Abate de Mendoza" ("Abbé," or "Father Mendoza"). Xirau published his *Ensayos selectos* (1970), and Cardoza y Aragón made known that it was Abbé Mendoza and not Miguel Ángel Asturias who translated the *Popul Vuh* and other Mayan texts, using Georges Raynaud's 1927 and 1928 French versions. In Paris, as a student at the Ecole des Hautes Études during the twenties, Abbé Mendoza formed part of the literary "reconquest" that took the pre-Cortés world and used it to create a new Latin American literature, amid a climate of languishing European exoticism.

That in itself would merit respect for the footnote González de Mendoza receives in Mexican literary history, but I think he deserves greater regard than that. More than a literary academic and diplomat (under the aegis of Alfonso Reyes* and Jaime Torres Bodet*), Abbé Mendoza—among many other things—was the exegete of José Juan Tablada and the first to plan his complete works; a devotee of Apollinaire (whose brother Albert he had dealings with in Mexico); author of numerous notable pieces on Sor Juana Inés de la Cruz, Mariano Azuela, Camile Flammarion, and Balzac; and an outstanding Cervantes scholar who researched tirelessly to confirm the mistakes and deceits recounted in *Supercherías y errores cervantinos* (1917), written by Francisco A. de Icaza, a Mexican turned Spaniard (the inverse of Mendoza himself).

"Abbé" Mendoza began his career at a time when modernism was turning avant-garde, and thus he published both chronicles and "synthetic stories" in the *El Universal Ilustrado* fiction series. Of the former, *Color de Francia* came at the tail end of the fin-de-siècle school of Latin American *crónicas*; while of the latter, his *La luna en el agua* (1925) and *El hombre que andaba y otros cuentos inverosímiles* (1925) were like a cross between Reyes's style and lyrical fiction. Together with Reyes he crisscrossed Paris, following Fray Servando Teresa de Mier's footsteps, and the travelogue that recounts this and myriad other adventures is also a tale of the fading nineteenth century.

González de Mendoza's critical sympathies were ruled by friendship and the sort of conformity that agrees to take one thing as another. Like André Billy (another forgotten critic, squire of Apollinaire and spreader of the doctrines of Sanislas de Guaita), Abbé Mendoza both commented on the high points of the literary world and stuck his nose into its nether regions. He wrote so much more, for instance, about the life and work of tragic poet José Dolores Frías (1891–1936) than either the *Ateneístas* or the *Contemporáneos,* that unsuspecting readers would be forgiven for thinking he'd made the man up. Known as "Vate Frías" (Bard Frías), he was the last of the bohemian modernists, and if he was famed for anything it was for not having written a single word of his "complete works." But as he said in a piece left for posterity, he was the culmination of modernism, which Juan Ramón Jiménez considered a time as varied and marvelous as the Renaissance. During his lifetime, however, Vate Frías published little more than some *Versos escogidos* (1933), to which Peruvian scholar Ventura García Calderón wrote the prologue.

Abbé Mendoza, a virtuous man, saw "Bard" Frías as both his equal and his opposite. "At that time, Frías and I were both in Paris. We were supremely antithetical. He was a Dionysian devotee, and I a taster of herbal teas and mineral waters; he, such a lazybones that he'd take a taxi the three hundred meters from the Plaza de Rennes to the Café La Rotonde, and I, partial to long walks; although we were, in a word, opposites, in numerous fundamental respects we had in common a love of literature and music, and a fondness for watching day break. Except that he being a night owl and I an early bird, we got there from opposite sides."

Vate Frías took his first trip to Paris as a war correspondent in 1917, and he sent numerous articles to *El Universal* and *Revista de Revistas.* He returned between 1921 and 1925, which is when he wrote the prologue to Cardoza y Aragón's first book (*Luna Park*); enunciated his French; wrote calligrams à la Apollinaire and terrible derivative poetry in the style of Rubén Darío; and planned several books (*Vidas inejemplares, El nómade alucinado,* and *Nativitatis prosa*) that Mendoza saved from "the rhythm of the vine," which was both the title of his collected poems and the measure of his ill-fated drunken life. In 1934–1935 he cropped back up in Paris, an unlikely tour guide for the Mexican Legation. The sort of man it was better to have met than to know, Frías also studied sacral music in his hometown, at the Querétaro Conservatory; then in Paris, his adopted home, he religiously attended mass in winter, when churches were warmed to the sounds of Beethoven's "Mass in C," Charles Gounod's "Saint Cecilia," and Palestrina's "Pope Marcelus."

Abbé Mendoza's six articles on Vate Frías included in *Ensayos selectos* are somewhat enigmatic. On the one hand they show affection for an unlucky friend and pity for a drunkard and bad poet, and they form part of the picaresque history of literary lowlifes written by people like Rafael Cansinos-Assens in Spain. But there's also a sort of cryptic temptation to present Frías—via commentary and correspondence—almost as an early version of Valéry's invented "Monsieur Teste," for whom misspellings and intellectual improvisation are more reminiscent of Apollinaire and César Vallejo than they are of decadent modernism. In one of his letters, for instance, Vate Frías says to Mendoza, "Mexico is an absurd problem: MXCOIE. Who could possibly establish any balance between three consonants and three vowels when one of the consonants is the absurd letter X?" In another, Frías signs off with "Atelier Da Vinci, Viva la de Guadalupe. Paris 12 + 12 = 34 + 10 - 20. Euclid overwhelms me."

Naturally, Abbé Mendoza lacked the rhetorical panache and flight of fancy to posit Vate Frías as the Mexican vanguard's missing link, the Martín Adán we never had, the loutish poet that some radicals yearned for. But it's not hard to see the projection of a common destiny in the calculated empathy that the irreproachable academic tried to establish for the ill-fated bohemian. They both sublimated their suffering, turning it into honor. Both were overshadowed by great authors (Mendoza in real life, by Reyes; Frías in his dreams, by Darío). And both were minor players doomed gradually to be dropped from encyclopedias.

After a drunken binge that had begun in Amecameca, Mexico, a year earlier, Vate Frías was detained one night in Mexico City on his way out of a dive bar. He was charged with immoral behavior and taken to the police station, where he died on June 5, 1936, with his head cracked open. In his book *La bohemia de la muerte* (1929 and 1958), Julio Sesta catalogues the victims of the bottle and other drugs, creating a literary catafalque of overdoses. His epitaph for Vate Frías is, of course, deplorable, and ends with the double-entendre of Frías's last name ("frías" also meaning "cold" in Spanish): "Y—¡yo acuso!—un empujón / de dos o tres policías / dio con tu cráneo de fuego / contra unas piedras frías . . ." ("And—j'accuse!—a shove / from two or three policemen / crushed your skull of fire / against the cold stones . . .")

Abbé Mendoza's end was less dramatic but still heartbreaking in its own way. A petty dignitary, his funeral honors were presided over by Torres Bodet. Shortly thereafter, however, his archives were plundered, and his desperate widow Concepción Andrade y Escandón went to both the police and the press about it. It seems that the larcenist was forced by the attorney general's office to return part of the booty, which included portraits and letters that Tablada had left to Mendoza. Well known for this and other capers, the thief to this day makes the rounds at conferences, memorials, and round tables.

Since that time Mendoza has been making his way slowly but steadily towards oblivion. Rather than letting him carry on that path, let's take a moment to recall what he said about old books. "We don't really understand old books. Is it laziness that makes them suddenly collapse on top of each other on the shelf? When we've answered that question, our enemy the Enigma will be weaker. Old age makes the obscure psychology of books more explicit. New ones are gregarious and anonymous, like soldiers. Old ones acquire personality, through what we intuit must have been a painful history. When the book came off the press it was immaculate, dominical. But the knife trimmer turned what was an enjoyable deflowering into a mechanical operation, or maybe an impatient finger damaged the pages; then understanding went by the way; and now there it is, excessively sullied, null and void, piled up with others like Armenians after a razzia . . . But they'll always retain a hint of whiteness in the depths of their pages, the same way a courtesan holds onto the faded scent of perfume of her first embrace."

SELECTED BIBLIOGRAPHY
Ensayos selectos, ed. and prologue by Ramón Xirau, FCE, Mexico, 1970.

GONZÁLEZ RODRÍGUEZ, SERGIO
(Mexico City, 1950)

Of the writers working with Carlos Monsiváis* during the final stages of the journal *La Cultura en México*, González Rodríguez is one of the most profound and insightful. Within that group it was often difficult to distinguish individual writers' prose, since they were all interested in using historical chronicles as the "common card" of national identity, portraying literary history as low-brow academic production, and advancing new myths as a means of revitalizing cultural nationalism [. . .]

El Centauro en el paisaje (1992) is like a "deck" of texts that the author spreads out on the table. González Rodríguez's readings are very generational, and it's nice to play a round with an author whose cards are marked in our favor. He opens his first hand by discarding the queen of spades (Walter Benjamin) and then slowly laying down his face cards: Roland Barthes and his "mythologies," Breton, Paz,* Cioran, and culturalists like Paul Ricœur and Fredric Jameson. Finally, he closes by playing the aces of postmodernity: Jean Beaudrillard and Paul Virilo.

González Rodríguez easily adopts the lingua franca of a certain type of trendy, contemporary essay (Reyes* calls it the "centaur" genre, and given the book's title, that's apt indeed), but he does so without any pretense of exclusivity. The Italians Roberto Calasso and Claudio Magris are two of the style's most brilliant exemplars, as indebted to Borges as to Benjamin. Call it "narrative essay" or call it "essay-fiction," the genre in question favors fragments, gives in to the allure of aphorisms, and promotes the idea that culture—be it classic or modern, popular or elitist—is a labyrinth with no center, a site where any thread is a valid jumping-off point.

Not everyone can carry off this kind of writing, which appears on the surface to be so open to possibilities. The line between eclectic sage and well-informed dilettante is blurry indeed, and the risks González Rodríguez runs in taking it on go beyond sounding opaque or pretentious. But he navigates them well. *El Centauro en el paisaje* is structured around dualities (the city and writing; the sacred and the technical; memory and desire; the normative and the monstrous), which turn out to be an insightful way to signpost the book's readings. González Rodríguez is like a diligent student glossing and assessing the obsessions of Benjamin, Steiner, Paz, Bataille, and Jünger. His clear, straightforward style and lack of rhetorical excess work in his favor; and he's undoubtedly an astute reader—something not altogether common in Mexican essayists. But these virtues add little to the experience of a reader already familiar with the source texts.

The book's strong suit is the section on Mexican images, making it quite distinct from other essay collections. González Rodríguez successfully inserts details and passages from the Mexican tradition without using them like Archimedes's lever to foreground ostentatious works of "national culture." It's such a relief to read a book published in Spain (and a finalist for

the Anagrama Essay Prize) that talks about Rafael López, Eduardo Lizalde,*
and Alfonso Reyes* without clamoring on about nationality, and a book that
alludes to a city that could be none other than Mexico City, and doesn't try
to disguise it.

El Centauro en el paisaje creates coherence by implicitly rejecting the ontological obsession with "national culture." There's nothing novel about in-
sisting on the universality of Mexican culture, but there *is* something novel
about "minimizing" it as naturally as González Rodríguez does, locating it
on the horizon as one more detail. The essayist discards the nationalist tradition as a unifying axis and instead fragments episodes in an effort to develop
them in the context of so-called postmodernity.

Los bajos fondos (1988) is a book that doesn't achieve its potential. But
some of its themes—fin-de-siècle spiritualism, the role of brothels—are reexamined in *El Centauro en el paisaje*. Others offer new takes on Gabriel
Ferry, Breton and Mexico, Luis G. Urbina's cinema, Juan García Ponce,*
Gnosticism, and the adventures of inventor Juan Nepomuceno Adorno.
And all of them are written in somber, elegant prose and with intellectual
insight. *El Centauro en el paisaje* is a book that both asks for and offers generosity, a clear, precise synthesis of certain contemporary mythologies, and
a collage in which Mexico breaks free of the nationalist "ontosphere" as one
more sign of critical imagination. (1993; *Servidumbre y grandeza de la vida
literaria*, 1998)

La noche oculta (1990), González Rodríguez's desolate novel, is a book that
can't be disassociated from its author's intellectual preoccupations. An essay-
novel, *La noche oculta* uses a Ouija board to invoke D. H. Lawrence; delves
into the unlikely scheme of Nazi miracle workers who dreamed of setting up
some sort of Xanadu in Mexico; reveals that Borges got the idea for *The Book
of Sand* in Mexico; and delves into the clandestine geography of a city that
jealously guards the hermetic secrets of a nonexistent book. To this list (offered by Adolfo Castañón*) we can also add Jesús Vizcaya, the unusual protagonist. He's quite a rarity in Mexican literature, an amateur intellectual and
follower of the occult whose life's quest results in a novel that openly declares
itself "literary." Along with José María Pérez Gay's character Consul Arvide
(from *La difícil costumbre de estar lejos*, 1984) and Pedro Ángel Palou's fic-

tionalized Xavier Villaurrutia (from *En la alcoba de un mundo*, 1992), Jesús Vizcaya is one more to add to the list of characters whose way of life forms a large part of the novel's narrative crux. Before them, Mexican literature avoided its own heroes, and characters tended to be either part of a tragic chorus taking a step toward claiming national ontology (I'm thinking here of Fuentes's Artemio Cruz and Ixca Cienfuegos) or else would-be mythological figures ranging from Pedro Páramo to the varied cast of caudillos, thugs, bums, and castaways—male and female—holding forth from a room that was just barely their own. The imaginary cast of Mexican literature was made up essentially of talking statues and moving figures who were allowed to live and suffer, but not really think [...]

La noche oculta also explores the place where popular theosophy meets political millenarianism, a place that produced books like Pacheco's* *Morirás lejos*, Gay's *La difícil costumbre de estar lejos*, and Luis Arturo Ramos's *La casa del ahorcado* (1993). In all three cases, Mexico appears as a country that neither was nor is immune to the delirium of national socialism. Like Pacheco and Ramos, González Rodríguez is an author who refuses to conceive of Mexico as a place untouched by the shadows/ignorance of the West that we've often believed ourselves to be either fortuitously or naïvely free from. [...] Castañón does a good job of summing up González Rodríguez's place: "I don't know if *La noche oculta* is an excellent novel. I do, however, feel that it's an authentic book, one that is unwavering in its loyalty to the idea that originally generated it." (*Arbitrario de literatura mexicana, Paseos, I*, 1993)

I recently spent a day (and I can't call it a pleasant one) reading González Rodríguez's *Huesos en el desierto* (2002). The book, part journalism and part cultural commentary, chronicles an intellectual's journey into a geography of danger that's all too real: Ciudad Juárez, which for over a decade has become a mass grave for hundreds of women. By way of conclusion, González Rodríguez states, "It's plain to see that the existence of (well over) a hundred serial killings of women in Ciudad Juárez, Chihuahua—and civil organizations place the numbers far higher—seems to imply, as Robert K. Ressler states, the involvement of one or two serial killers as well as common murderers. We're talking about the product of a sacrificial orgy, misogynist in nature, whose victims are systematically sought out and selected (from the streets, factories, shops, and schools), amid a web of protection and inaction on the part of Mexican authorities over the past decade—in particular, the police and judicial authorities who in turn rely on the support of a wealthy group of entrepreneurs." There are numerous hypotheses as to who is responsible, both for masterminding the crimes and actually committing them, and González Rodríguez examines every one, considering each as part of a whole, pieces of the puzzle.

It all adds up to "a place halfway between something and nothing," a true "ecosystem of evil" sanctioned by complicities that include the entire political system and implicate an almost magical cover-up of judicial responsibility, police ineptitude so colossal that it can only be complicity, and a sickening breeding ground of frenzied activity on the part of politicians of every ilk and party, narco-traffickers, devil worshippers, paid henchmen, serial killer investigators, scapegoats of Arabic extraction, journalists, coroners, in short, a cast of demons so varied that they'd make any fictional portrayal seem obscene and farfetched. But Ciudad Juárez is real, too real, and it's marked by sacrifice and impunity. More than an obviously much-needed (though impotent) denunciation, what was required was a thorough intellectual investigation, and that is what González Rodríguez has given us. The book is so unseemly that it might only be able to be read by future generations, those to whom the idea of femicide as a domestic industry is utterly unknown, those who haven't lived through a time when the most sickeningly savage, misogynist violence is seen as a blood flag.

Essayist and novelist in the same way as Roberto Bolaño* or Spain's Javier Marías, González Rodríguez revamps one of the finest traditions of Mexican civil literature, the one requiring writers to stick to the facts and risk their integrity in the name of the outraged, the offended, the humiliated. José Revueltas* did it in novels, Elena Poniatowska* did it in chronicles. In the face of crime, the artist resolves to solve the riddle of a reality that requires order, common sense, and practical justice. Sticking to the facts, in *Huesos en el desierto* González Rodríguez successfully depicts the tortuous path that is the search for truth (which is the victims' honor), without resorting to a prose style that's like a pornography of violence, so often used in texts expressing moral outrage.

Huesos en el desierto needed to be not only a brave book but also an extraordinarily well-conceived and even better written one in order to carefully and valiantly tread through the burial ground of Ciudad Juárez. González Rodríguez is a civilizing writer, immune to abstractions and doctrines, who is committed to the lives of the hundreds of women who need to be paid the highest, most intelligent tribute. Reading the fifteenth-century epigraph of *Huesos en el desierto* makes me want to close my eyes in secular prayer: *Lege rubrum si vis intelligere nigram* ("Read what's written in red if you want to understand what's written in black").

SELECTED BIBLIOGRAPHY

La noche oculta, Cal y Arena, Mexico, 1990.
El Centauro en el paisaje, Anagrama, Barcelona, 1992.
Huesos en el desierto, Anagrama, Barcelona, 2002.
El triángulo perfecto, ERA, Mexico, 2003.
La pandilla cósmica, Plaza y Janés, Mexico, 2005.
De sangre y de sol, Sexto Piso, Mexico, 2006.
El vuelo, Mondadori, Mexico, 2008.
El hombre sin cabeza, Anagrama, Barcelona, 2009.
Infecciosa, Mondadori, Mexico, 2010.

GONZÁLEZ SUÁREZ, MARIO
(Mexico City, 1964)

From *Nostalgia de la luz* (1996) to *Marcianos leninistas* (2003), González Suárez's books have often intrigued me, even though I find some of them erratic and dissatisfying. But with *De la infancia* (1998), his impeccable prose alone is enough to successfully pull off what we might call a "going-of-age" novel, or a novel of "miseducation," to paraphrase Thomas Bernhard. The book fits in with those of (and I'm including only Mexicans here) José Martínez Sotomayor, Jorge López Páez,* and Carmen Boullosa.* Like them, González Suárez sees childhood as the writer's most fertile ground.

The book's plot is not complicated. It's the story of the literal and spiritual moves made by a family terrified of the father. Giving readers no break, no room to breathe (the air is heavy, the atmosphere gloomy), and no sentimentality, *De la infancia* transports us to a time of primeval cruelty, plunging us deep into somber depths for the hour and a half it takes to read the book. It's actually not a "fantastical" tale, as the publishers claim. Rather, as with Bergman sometimes, it's just that there's no need to do anything unnatural in order to imbue the air with a supernatural mist. And that paranormal feeling isn't a result of the author's imagination, which is far from extraordinary; instead it stems from the painstaking care he takes with his prose, conceived of as (pardon the cliché) the only way to regain lost time. His obsession with ludic, erotic, and domestic details creates a jittery, childlike vernacular that comes across with remarkable authenticity.

Recently it seems that contemporary Latin American fiction, as if making up for so many years of being at home, stuck like Nervo's "La amada inmóvil" ("The immobile lover"), has taken a shine to outrageous, madcap voyages. Those who opt for it know that the greatest odyssey has already been written by Roberto Bolaño in *The Savage Detectives*. But in *Marcianos leninistas*, González Suárez plots a trip around the world in eighty days, where the days are the childhood and adolescence of kids like me, the last generation in the twentieth century to feel so attracted to science and the chimera of communism. Michel Houllebecq, a writer I detest, said something that I readily admit to agreeing with: that he missed the fantastic, fraternal feeling he had for old communists when he was growing up. González Suárez's characters (like those of Salvador Elizondo* and Mauricio Molina,* two more Sputnik enthusiasts) live in a Soviet universe, a place populated by avenging heroes and space dogs. It's an alluring world, a separate order, a nice alternative to Disneyland. Unlike the amusement park, the Soviet world enjoyed a certain prestige; there was a secret air of exclusivity and prohibition about it in the Latin American periphery. In *Marcianos leninistas*, that mystery is explored via a trip to the old USSR, a land full of atomic bomb shelters aimed at preserving hell for all eternity. The first sixty pages of *Marcianos leninistas* are dedicated to introducing Uncle Arturo, a crusader in the cause happy to lose himself in vast ideological plots that unfold not so much in utopia as in the entire galaxy. González Suárez is one of very few writers who have managed to capture the atmosphere and illusion that kids like us lived in, turning the end of a dream into a fictional reality I'd call "childhood's end," after the Arthur C. Clarke novel.

Selected Bibliography

De la infancia, Tusquets Editores, Mexico, 1998.

El libro de las pasiones, Tusquets Editores, Mexico, 1999.

Marcianos leninistas. Ludibrium, Tusquets Editores, Mexico, 2002.

GONZÁLEZ Y GONZÁLEZ, LUIS

(San José de Gracia, Michoacán, 1925 – 2003)

González y González was a phenomenal writer, his style all the more persuasive for being so unexpected. His remarkable bibliographic contribution, *Pueblo en vilo. Microhistoria de San José de Gracia,* a classic in provincial historiography, came out in 1968, the "axis year"—as Octavio Paz* called it—full of dramatic, photogenic events. Translated into French, and later prefaced by Nobel Prize winner and Michoacán resident J.M.G. Le Clézio, this is one of Mexico's great books.

From the beginning, González y González conceived of his work as literary, and said as much in the prologue to *Pueblo en vilo*: "Local historiography, like biography, seems closer to literature than other historical genres, perhaps because individual lives demand a literary treatment, perhaps because the historian's clientele is allergic to the customary dryness of contemporary historians. A writer of local history should be a man of letters."

Pueblo en vilo was revolutionary even for the revolutionary times in which it was published. Free of dogmas and statistics, González y González's sonorous, utilitarian, warm, friendly Spanish prose in this book epitomized what became one of the most peculiar styles in Mexican literature—which counts him as one of its premier historians. His language is so felicitous that it would be absurd to describe it without quoting him. Only a man like González y González could call historians "Clionauts," talk about "literature and viviture" and call Maximilian "Emperor Goldbeard" without sounding condescending or boorish.

González y González was a historian who went back to write the "world history" of San José de Gracia, his hometown, after mastering the great world of modern historiography. By contrast, it would be impossible to write a *less* provincial book than *El oficio de historiador* (1988), a guided tour of the history of history, from Thucydides to Paul Valéry by way of Macaulay, Nietzsche, Collingwood, and a plethora of contemporary Marxists and structuralists. Didactic without being professorial, magisterial without taking any of the "pedantic license" genuine masters are so often granted, scholarly without being stuffy, González y González is a joy to read. Strictly speaking, he's a historian's historian, a treatise writer: his is a world of files, notebooks, footnotes, and schedules, and he has the ability both to rely on and to ignore the filing cabinet. González y González was not only an eminent historian and unwitting revolutionary—if only for his tolerant, liberal temperament, as his most influential and prolific disciples (Jean Meyer,* Enrique Krauze*) have noted—but a true officiate: someone who mastered, transmitted, and celebrated his subject. He lamented the fact that "the obsession with turning Clio into a scientific deity has made us forget her essential quality—that of muse" and wrote accordingly.

González y González also segued gracefully from microhistory to national history, studying almost every period and writing *La ronda de las generaciones* (1984), another exemplary book. In fewer than two hundred pages, as if toying with the ruling elite described by Ortega y Gasset, he compiles a superlative, very convincing brief history of Mexican culture from the mid-nineteenth-century Reforma to the mid-twentieth century, with no digressions and no lacunae. What seems like a list turns out to be a genealogy. I'll limit myself to citing a few of his definitions—almost aphorisms—to make my point. The Reforma "intellectuals" (a word González y González dislikes and tends not to use) "were not irreligious, they were 'priest-haters.' Romanticism and irreligiosity didn't get along." Scientists were "men of aloof, phlegmatic make-up, little frock-coated, mushroom-hatted figurines," and as for the "blues," i.e. the modernists, "prep school positivism goes in one ear and out the other" as they were a *"nepantli* generation, caught between two ages, in the waning days of the nationalism, liberalism, and Romanticism." "For as long as the revolutionary generation ruled, there was no peace," González y González said, while recognizing that the generation of 1915 "managed to go from a fierce, cruel, antireligious campaign to a tolerance of credos worthy of Nordic countries."

The enormous influence González y González had is deceptive; seen now, at the dawn of the twenty-first century, it seems unremarkable. But at the time, *Pueblo en vilo* swam against the tide, and it won. Microhistory, with its slow-moving diligence, didn't recount the great history of ideologies in conflict, or the hysteria for the (abstract) revolution expressed by Trojans and Tyrians alike, but instead documented the lives of what he called the "revolutionized." So González y González, a man proud to be a Catholic, a rancher, and a provincial, wrote a book that set itself apart from cookie-cutter works of "historical materialism." Like Bertrand Russell, González y González thought it neither advisable nor desirable to be an impartial historian. But by avoiding both resentment and pathos in glossing the displeasure with which victims and witnesses—interviewed by the Museum of Popular Culture—recall wartime in their hometowns in his celebrated essay, "La Revolución Mexicana desde el punto de vista de los revolucionados" (1986), González y González touches a nerve many of us had forgotten we had.

My father's mother, for example, was born at the end of the Porfiriato, and the "fuss"—as she called it—kicked up left her an orphan. After 1915—that fateful year—she ended up in an orphanage and by the time she left, she was half dead from Spanish flu. Her memories of the Mexican Revolution are of fires, hunger, and rapes, and for years she dreamed of the return of her prodigal brother, who'd been snatched away from home, and forcibly drafted. But perhaps more shocking than my grandmother's stories was the inability of my university progenitors to see any relation between *that* revolution and those we celebrated at the dinner table—Russian, Chinese, Cuban—as well as their obliviousness to the fact that my uneducated grandmother was the historical consciousness of the century. I'm sure my case is not unique. I had to read González y González in order to give my "revolutionized" grandmother her posthumous due.

Selected Bibliography
Obras, 1–6, El Colegio Nacional, Mexico, 2002–2006.
San José de Gracia: Mexican Village in Transition, University of Texas Press, 1974.

GOROSTIZA, JOSÉ
(Villahermosa, Tabasco, 1901 – Mexico City, 1973)

Writing an unconditional masterpiece might in some ways be terrifying, but it also gave Gorostiza a kind of brazen peace of mind, a certainty beyond a shadow of a doubt that he'd be posthumously celebrated. *Muerte sin fin* (1939; *Death Without End*, 1969) is still the Mexican poem most read by authorities, most discussed by academics, and most inspirational for new poets who—generation after generation—use it to renew their familiarity with the supreme demands of the poetic form. Later in life Gorostiza became a diplomat and worked his way up to being Mexico's éminence grise during the apex of the Cold War—the 1962 Cuban missile crisis. But as far as literary output is concerned, after *Muerte sin fin* there are only a handful of poems, some unrealized projects, and a novel that Octavio Paz* says he destroyed after it was unfavorably compared to Pierre Klossowski's *La bain de Diane* (1956). One thing that stands out in the meager *Prosa* (1969) is his "Notes on poetry," written in 1955, which doesn't shed much light on the mysteries of *Muerte sin fin*, but does give us a better picture of the man whose precision made him the biggest Mexican poet. "I like to think of poetry not as something that happens within man and is inherent to him, to human nature, but as something that exists in its own right, in the outside world. That way, I am free to see it as outside myself, in the same way that you can best see the sky from the false but admirable hypothesis that the earth is suspended from it, in the middle of the dark night. For the eyes, the truth lies in the world that turns around it. For the poet, poetry exists by its own virtue and is there, everywhere, within the grasp of all the eyes that might want to see it."

SELECTED BIBLIOGRAPHY

Prosa, ed. Miguel Capistrán and epilogue by Alfonso Reyes, Universidad de Guanajuato, Guanajuato, 1969.

Poesía y poética, ed. Edelmira Ramírez, ALLCA XX/FCE/UNESCO/Conaculta, Madrid, 1988 (Archivos Collection).

Death Without End, trans. Laura Villaseñor, University of Texas, 1969.

GUZMÁN, MARTÍN LUIS

(Chihuahua, Chihuahua, 1887 – Mexico City, 1976)

Guzmán's reputation was founded on his flawless prose and intensely moral depictions. Octavio Paz* says that Guzmán writes like an historian of Antiquity. Plutarch, Thucydides, and Tacitus are regularly invoked by both Guzmán and his readers, and he takes after them in many ways. A classical education, fine Spanish prose, and an Anglo-Saxon sense of dramatic tension are all part of it. But Jaime Torres Bodet* compared him to seventeenth-century writer La Rochefoucauld, and it's an unsettling analogy. Both gentlemen set off to war and then came back from it to write about human character. Guzmán and La Rochefoucauld were of the same ilk. Both wrote moral portraits and viewed them as a product of the tension between a fatalistic destiny and the principle of selfishness. Guzmán didn't have time to become Duke of Saint Simon: his "court" was more like railroad tracks and abandoned campfires. But the issue at hand in both *El águila y la serpiente* and La Rochefoucauld's maxims is freedom and its ethical limits. Guzmán's biographical sketches are unforgettable: Carranza, a dying Porfirio Díaz, Madero, Eufemio Zapata have become fixtures in a memoir of tragedy that is unique in its individualism, utterly subjective and undeniably literary. The sketches' moral insights can either destroy or restore a man's position among men [. . .]

In theater, "staging" politics means paying attention to the stage: positioning and scene changes define the characters. As in Pierre Corneille's "Orthon," there's a game of musical chairs in which each empty seat is occupied by a different form of power. For Guzmán, power is by definition always being split—not like matter, but refracted like light. Guzmán joined the war in 1910, spurred on by a suspicion shared by many revolutionaries. "Morally impossible not to side with the Revolution and materially and psychologically impossible for the Revolution to achieve the regenerative aims that justify it": Guzmán is a politically committed writer, a moral portrait artist. Like José Vasconcelos,* he was essentially a political virgin in 1910, ignorant of war. But a desire for adventure and civil indignation sent them both to battle. Vasconcelos fell in love with it, coming back a political Casanova, but for Guzmán politics were never spiritual and the fires of ideological passion never burned within him. In fact, they gave him the chills, turning him into the chronicler of disputed virtue.

El águila y la serpiente presents an anti-Romantic interpretation of politics as autonomous passion, an exercise in speculation. Guzmán never really *believed* in the Mexican Revolution. His youthful enthusiasm dissipated, and what was left was a sharp eye scrutinizing the spectacle of man. Think of

Stendhal, who, before joining the Napoleonic campaign in Russia, wrote to his sister in his Russian diary, "I'll join the army if I can. What attracts me to it is the desire to get a close view of those barnyard dogs called men." (trans. Robert Sage) (*Tiros en el concierto: Literatura mexicana del siglo V*, 1997)

Guzmán's great novels—*El águila y la serpiente* (1928), *La sombra del caudi-llo* (1929), and *Memorias de Pancho Villa* (1938–1951)—illustrate the great, classic Mexican style of the first half of the twentieth century. But even over the course of fifty years, his oeuvre never turned into some preserved "ar-cheological villa"; his novels stopped belonging to the political (and ideo-logical and propagandistic) phase of the Mexican Revolution and became Spanish-language world classics, timeless portrayals of political passion. In 1958 he published *Muertes históricas,* and his chronicles of the decline of Porfirio Díaz and Venstiano Carranza prove that before Juan Rulfo* stepped onto the scene, Guzmán was Mexico's greatest writer.

SELECTED BIBLIOGRAPHY
Obras completas, vols I and II, FCE, Mexico, 1985.
Obras completas, FCE, Mexico, 2010.
    I. *El águila y la serpiente y otros libros.*
    II. *La sombra del caudillo y otros libros.*
    III. *Memorias de Pancho Villa.*
Memoirs of Pancho Villa, trans. Virginia H. Taylor, University of Texas, 1965.
The Eagle and the Serpent, trans. Harriet de Onis, Dolphin Books, 1965.

H

HELGUERA, LUIS IGNACIO
(Mexico City, 1962 – 2003)

When French writer Alfred de Musset died, Sainte-Beuve said, "As with an army, so with a nation; it is the bounden duty of every generation to bury their dead." (trans. Forsyth Edeveain) Helguera was the first of the writers who started with me at the journal *Vuelta* in the eighties to die. He was both a music critic and a man of letters, something very uncommon in any language and exceedingly rare in Spanish-language literature, which has a well-earned reputation for turning a deaf ear to music and is often seen as more visual than musical. But Helguera, unlike other music lovers, dared to use the hypersensitivity, arrogance, and love of conversation so characteristic of his breed to write criticism. Together with Jomi García Ascott's *Con la música por dentro* (1982) and Juan Vicente Melo's* *Notas sin música* (1988), Helguera's book *El atril del melómano* will become a vital reference work, taking its place on that exclusive shelf where music and Mexican literature sit side by side.

Critics tend to be systematic. Shortly after I published a narrative anthology, he published his *Antología del poema en prosa* (1993). We both took delight in literary squabbles and the two of us quarreled more than once. But we were critics and that's just the way it is. Our last argument was byzantine and, like all good arguments, dragged on for years. It was about chess, which he loved and I disparaged as a foolish pastime, probably to annoy him. But we were both raised by chess players. And it seemed to me that his gentlemanliness, like his anger, stemmed from a charming decorum and a misunderstood sense of honor. As a music critic, and sometimes as a poet, Helguera could be irresistibly charming. "Tachycardia," he wrote, "is the stenography of the heart" (In Spanish, "stenography" is "taquigrafía").

With his death, it's impossible not to think of Carlos Díaz Dufoo the second (1888–1932), whose *Epigramas* (1927) seems to sum up Helguera's fate: "He never understood that his life was two lives." More than a poet, Luis Ignacio was a prose writer enamored of aphorisms and maxims, the author of a handful of books of grace, joy, and music's underlying seed of destruction. With his shocking death, I lost a contemporary, a fellow critic, and a willfully awkward interlocutor.

Luigi Amara* recently gave me a copy of *Zugzwang*, one of Helguera's posthumous books. I sliced it open with my letter opener (the pages are uncut) and began to leaf through it (and then read it) angrily, bitterly. It was as though the book's mere existence were a sign of death's victory, one more irrefutable proof of its author's demise, five years ago now. But once I got past that, I began to like the poems in *Zugzwang*, some of which Helguera had already lined up for publication. The more I let myself dwell in that place where an "enchanted kiss" turns a poet's premature (and tragic) death into the symbol of his defects—now seen as virtues of a prophetic order—the more I liked the poems. What can I say? The dead do with us what they will.

The publishers decided to include—as stated in Víctor Manuel Mendiola's introduction—not only the poems Helguera had given them but also some that he'd deliberately excluded, as well as others that were "unfinished." This is a short, dense collection, and perhaps it ought to be readers not personally affected by Helguera's life and death who decide if Antonio Deltoro* is right when he says in the prologue that "a considerable part of our best poetry in recent years" is to be found in *Zugzwang*.

Though known as a music critic, aphorist, editor of an anthology of prose poems (*Antología del poema en prosa en México*), and essayist who loved the lofty heights of philosophical thought, Helguera left behind a handful of captivating poems, some of which I only discovered in *Zugzwang*. Back when I read *Murciélago al mediodía* (1997), I tended to see his poems either as fragmented units of a work to come or as judicious aphorisms. That's probably his best book, the one in which it's easiest to discern what he saw as the boundaries of his world, the terrain of this short-lived writer: the fluid border between poetry and prose; aphorisms and *greguerías;* essays and short stories. Thinking in musical terms—which is how Helguera thought—*Murciélago al mediodía* is a collection of bagatelles. Thinking in terms of chess—which was the subject of another of his posthumous books, *Peón aislado: Ensayos sobre ajedrez* (2006)—one could say that Helguera practiced openings, defenses, and gambits, but never played full games. In the only game he finished, death beat him, and *Zugzwang* is an expression of the fatal energy Helguera had at a time when he was knocking insistently at death's door. By the time he tried to fend it off, it was too late.

In chess, "Zugzwang" refers to a fatal move a player is forced to make. It's perhaps too easy of an association, but in the last poems in the collection, every move Helguera makes is perilous. Some oscillate between sarcastic confession and a tenor—distant but faithful—that sounds like nineteenth-century Romanticist poet Manuel José Othón. I don't know whether Helguera realized that provincial, bucolic inspiration—which there's stacks of—were the real grounds of his poetry, the silt of his verses, as can be seen in "Recuerdo y olvido," "Visión," "Globo," "Nido," and "El campo." It's no coincidence that composer Silvestre Revueltas—more small-town, errant bard than dandy or *poète maudit*—was his hero. The same association can be seen in his homage to the Russian Borodin: Helguera, the exigent music critic, chose to honor a composer who was distinctly un-modern, a creator of "noble and humble" music, a sentimentalist unconcerned about being seen as outdated.

Zugzwang includes a few poems that strike me as absolutely magnificent, including "Sonámbula" and "Afinador de pianos," the latter being one that Deltoro discusses in his prologue. Although he felt obliged—by mandate of convention—to talk of sadness and rage, the author of these poems is a happy Helguera, the devotee of Brazilian composer Heitor Villa-Lobos and his eight cellos. They're almost humming, although melomaniacs aren't supposed to do that. This Helguera had yet to forsake himself to helplessness, had yet to sink into an abyss where he had not even the "Satanic pride" of Byronic poets. *Zugzwang* is a logbook of agony expressed through pages I find memorable as calls for help and sometimes as silliness. "Fiesta," "Coral," "Blues en AA," and "Hospital I" are marked by sordidness and desperation, alcoholism and alcohol idolatry, to an almost unparalleled degree in contemporary Mexican literature. These poems are paradoxically sincere, written at a time when it made no difference if good intentions paved the way to hell.

SELECTED BIBLIOGRAPHY

Antología del poema en prosa en Mexico, FCE, Mexico, 1993.

El atril del melómano, Conaculta, Mexico, 1997.

Murciélago al mediodía, Vuelta, Meico, 1997.

Peón aislado. Ensayos sobre ajedrez, prólogo de Eliseo Alberto, DGE/El Equilibrista/UNAM, Mexico, 2006.

Zugzwang, El tucán de Virginia, Mexico, 2007.

De cómo no fuí el hombre de la década y otras decepciones, Tumbona, Mexico, 2010.

HERBERT, JULIÁN
(Acapulco, Guerrero, 1971)

Is there such a thing as "twenty-first-century Mexican poetry," a new poetry that differs from (to use an antiquated term) "postmodern" twentieth-century poetry? If so, then Herbert's is it. *La resistencia* (2004) is a rereading of Ovid, a book of poems notable for the way Herbert errs, both in the sense of wandering and in being off the mark, as compared to Cavafy or Czeslaw Milosz. And in *Kubla Khan* (2005), his mimetic tendency is even more pronounced, colluding, as the title suggests, not only with Samuel Taylor Coleridge but also with Borges, one of the most insightful commentators on Coleridge.

Right from his first book, *El nombre de esta casa* (1999), Herbert garnered a certain level of fame in young poets' circles, with easily recognizable poems like "Autorretrato a los 27" and "Los que cumplieron más de cuarenta" ("Those who are over forty"). "Los que cumplieron más de cuarenta / se enojan si les hablas de tú / se enojan si les hablas de usted" ("Those who are over forty / get mad if you call them *tú* / get mad if you call them *usted*"). But at the time that lighthearted tone seemed too reminiscent of the sort of invented autobiographical "double" that's only memorable in poets like Jaime Gil de Biedma, whom Herbert admired. In *El nombre de esta casa* Herbert was still "unschooled," following Tomás Segovia's observation that young poets can have no school but their own youth. But it is clear that Herbert was conversant with history, five thousand years of which was revealed to him through his reading (and conveyed to us via his obsessive relationship with the information society), like José Emilio Pacheco* in his early days, up until *No me preguntes cómo pasa el tiempo* (1973).

But being of a generation that's removed from humanitarian pathos and ecological transcendence, Herbert invokes altered voices that speak in glosses, fragments and aphorisms: "Cosa, cosa / por qué me has abandonado?" ("Thing, thing / why have you abandoned me?"). That verse from *La resistencia*, somewhere between nostalgic and beholden, is reminiscent of Jorge Cuesta's *Canto a un dios mineral*, Gorostiza's* *Muerte sin fin*, and Eduardo Lizalde's *Cada cosa es Babel*, Mexico's greatest and most distinctive metaphysical poems. Yet it seems that Herbert has forbidden himself to write this sort of poetry and instead knocks on other doors and hits the panic button when contemplating the ruins of the twentieth century as recorded by W. H. Auden, Joseph Brodsky, and Milosz. And like Walter Benjamin's Berlin chronicles and the most resolutely cartographic facet of Romanticism, Herbert's imitations posit the poet as magician of the city, happy to travel the circumference of the civilized.

In the end, Herbert's poetic voice in *La resistencia* is sort of an anthology, in which he uses Ovid and to a lesser degree Job to find his own voice. "Cada pie un rasgo de estilo, / un oráculo impreso / geometría fulminada. / Joyas que pule y desgasta la rivera mientras el río murmura su desesperación" ("Each foot a scrap of style, / an oracle in print / geometry declaimed. / Jewels that polish and wear away the shore while the river murmurs its desperation"). Herbert is a poet who believes, like Brodsky, that "a footnote is where civilization survives" (from "Footnote to a Poem").

In *Kubla Khan*, Herbert makes use of an everyday form of visual (and perhaps existential and phenomenological) dissemination: channel surfing. He uses television to "splice" poetry, giving us Xanadu as both the kingdom Coleridge spied and the Olivia Newton-John song. Good poets almost always aspire to be not just readers but inventors. But what's even better is to invent *and* offer another *Kubla Khan* where—fleetingly, as convention requires—we glimpse a pleasure dome and an Abyssinian maid and are offered the milk of Paradise. For me, it proved incredibly helpful while reading Herbert's *Kubla Khan* to read Mexican poet Nelly Keoseyán's Spanish version of Coleridge in *Una visión en dos sueños: La balada del viejo marinero / Kubla Khan* (2005) at the same time.

Modestly. That's the only way to follow Borges, when in "The Dream of Coleridge" he assures us that Coleridge's poem "give(s) rise to the conjecture that the series of dreams and labors has not yet ended" (*Other Inquisitions, 1937–52*, trans. Ruth Simms) and that perhaps the secret resides in the very last illusion. Herbert's *Kubla Khan* is part of that series. It's a poem that informs us that Xanadu is also the name of one of the first hypertext systems that eventually led to the creation of the World Wide Web, and then says "Cuando digo Occidente digo / parque de accidentes / cual si la faz del sol a punto de ponerse / fuera un álbum de ventanas: estampitas" ("When I say the Occident I say / park of accidents / as if the surface of the sun about to set / were an album of windows: little sketches").

From Gil de Biedma to Ovid and from Pacheco to Coleridge, Herbert's poetry has followed the slow and catastrophic course that takes what was once a collection of readings and turns it into a poet's universe. But the dangers that lie in wait for Herbert come from within, from his having cultivated a second self, both literal and predictable, one who writes novels and short stories about those artificial paradises that are better suited to poetry than hyperrealism. All you have to do is read his own poetry to see that. Mexican literature, in my opinion, doesn't need another "underground" counterculture poet like Parménides García Saldaña, and it concerns me that a poet as pure as Herbert would run for the post.

As the publishers of *Kubla Khan* said, his fluency with Mexico's patrician forefathers gives us the opportunity to read back to another "fragment," this one from just a generation and a half ago when in 1971—the year Herbert was born—Jaime García Terrés* wrote "Ezra Pound en Atenas." But we also have Herbert's "Ezra," the poem he dedicated to Pound. While García Terrés harkens back to a world of heroes and demigods at a time when you could still actually go to Athens and find Pound there, Herbert writes of faded pottery on which you can still make out a skirmish from the Battle of Agincourt, the face of a goddess, a bureaucratic inscription to a scholar, the name of a lost tragedy.

SELECTED BIBLIOGRAPHY
El nombre de esta casa, Fondo Editorial Tierra Adentro, Mexico, 1999.
La resistencia, Filodecaballos, Mexico, 2003.
Kubla Khan, ERA, Mexico, 2005.
Canibal. Apuntes sobre la poesía mexicana reciente, Bonobos, Mexico, 2010.

HERNÁNDEZ, EFRÉN

(León, Guanajuato, 1903 – Mexico City, 1958)

Hernández brings us back to writers like Alfonso Reyes,* Julio Torri,* and Mariano Silva y Aceves. But what in Reyes was clockwork unrelated to any theory, and in Torri was an awareness of prose's critical function, and in Silva y Aceves was built-in obsolescence, in Hernández is simply a narrative reality. A man who secretly synthesized their qualities, he soaked up both the *Ateneístas'* intellectual ideas and the *Contemporáneos'* lyrical prose, and the result was the first definitive work of the mid-century.

Cerrazón sobre Nicómaco (1946) is brilliant fiction. Reading it, it's impossible not to think of Kafka. Or maybe of Kafka's century. Hernández's anguish—"awfully mournful fiction" is the story's subtitle—casts a pallor that intensifies human acts. Every time clouds pass overhead we get a different character: the impertinent humanist, the pained jokester, the absurd situationist. Efrén's Nicómaco is a victim of bureaucracy's systematic chaos, which he rebuffs via rambling digressions. If Hernández's poetics are prosaic, as Octavio Paz* said, it's only because he successfully uses all things poetic—many of which are not strictly lyrical—in his texts.

Very discretely, Hernández forwent the history worship of realism and rejected the Romanticist notions of lyricism. His idea of the text was that of a programmable machine, à la Queneau. A contemporary of Borges and of Felisberto, Hernández shares with them the idea of fiction as the primal reality. (*Antología de la narrativa mexicana del siglo XX*, I, 1989)

SELECTED BIBLIOGRAPHY
Obras. Poesía. Novela. Cuentos, introduced by Alí Chumacero, bibliography by Luis Mario Schneier, FCE, Mexico, 1965 and 1987.
Obras completas, vol. I and II, ed. Alejandro Toledo, FCE, Mexico, 2006.

HERNÁNDEZ, FRANCISCO
(San Andrés Tuxtla, Veracruz, 1946)

When the poet Hernández got writer Juan Rulfo's* autograph, he was so dazzled that the maestro had to rouse him from his daze, assuring him that it really was his name. I think that tells us something. Admiration is one of the hardest feelings to tackle in text, and it gives us insight into Hernández's inner self. In his early books, such as *Mar de fondo* (1982), Hernández was a bit nostalgic for the locales of his childhood and adolescence, and also tried briefly to be a "sleepwalking" poet reminiscent of Xavier Villaurrutia— or at least allowed himself a certain surrealist playfulness. But later he felt the need to pay his respects to the saints of Romanticism—Hölderlin, Schumann, Trakl, and a few others. And since then he's continued to show his admiration, as is seen in *Imán para fantasmas* (2004), where he pays homage to Octavio Paz,* Aimé Césaire, and Salvador Díaz Mirón. Luckily, this has resulted not in bookish poetry but in the creation of a Silenus mask behind which the chosen poets speak.

A man who sees literature as a way of expressing suffering, Hernández has written two notable books: *De cómo Robert Schumann fue perseguido por los demonios* (1988) and *Habla Scardanelli* (1992). His is an anguished poetry that's more hermetic than Romantic, an expression of renunciation always reminiscent of Hölderlin and radical sacrifice. "Escribo con mano firme, sin vino / un trago de tinta no es un / mal substituto" ("I write with steady hand, no wine / a swig of ink is not a / bad substitute"). Implicit within Hernández's poetry is the question of how to tackle romantic angst a capella, sans the warmth and comfort of dramatic plotlines. Wavering between brilliant madness and cold analytical calculation, Hernández adopts the alter ego of jovial troubadour Mardonio Sinta, a pen name that harkens back to the *coplas* of Veracruz and its history. For he knows that, as Carlyle said, only by seeing a man laugh can you ever really know him. Hernández's poetry shows an abstaining Silenus educating Dionysius in the lost epics of intoxication, a man who cries and shouts with the same intensity with which he sinks into the most tranquil contemplation.

SELECTED BIBLIOGRAPHY
Poesía reunida (1974–1994), UNAM, Mexico, 1996.
Mascarón de prosa, Conaculta, Mexico, 1997.
Segunda antología personal, FCE, Mexico, 1999.
Mardonio Sinta (Francisco Hernández), *¿Quién me quita lo cantado?*, Oro de la Noche, Mexico, 1999.
Soledad al cubo, Secretaría de Cultura de Puebla, Mexico, 2001.
Imán para fantasmas, ERA, Mexico, 2004.
Mi vida con la perra, Calamus, Mexico, 2007.
La isla de las breves ausencias, Almadía, Oaxaca, 2009.
Población de la máscara, Almadía, Oaxaca, 2010.

HERNÁNDEZ CAMPOS, JORGE

(Guadalajara, Jalisco, 1921 – Mexico City, 2004)

The few texts that Hernández Campos has left behind are like scant yet vital fragments of some classic Latin writer, author of a handful of heartrending elegiac verses and a few tribunal poems. *La experiencia* (1986) and *Sin título* (2001) are the only books available by an author whose poems Aurelio Asiain* says are "never pastiches or parodies, but instead carry echoes— in their syntax, their lexicon, their rhetorical devices—of ancient Greek poetry and Old Testament verses, medieval Spanish poetry and Golden age poets, Pablo Neruda and Federico García Lorca, Eugenio Montale and T. S. Eliot . . . His quotations and allusions, not used as witty remarks or knowing winks, are simply the most outwardly obvious signs of a creative enterprise that sees poetry as an interplay of languages, and thus its multiple forms are not just some experimental whim. The twenty-two poems—both many and few—in *La experiencia* include an orthodox sonnet, nine-syllable ten-line stanzas in blank verse, traditional couplets, 'broken-foot' verse, refrains, medieval poetic forms, free verse, lines taken from detective stories, dramatic monologues given in a theater in ruins, poems that use prose with no disharmony . . . All of that speaks of a poet who, it's time we recognize, is as tuned in to life on the streets as he is to the richness of libraries and whose spirit is as attentive to terms buried in the dictionary as it is to insults in everyday language. His poems are some of the most authentically *colloquial* in Mexico, not just because they really do use language just 'as it's spoken' in our country but because on reading them we witness a real dialogue with language." (Asiain, *Caracteres de imprenta*, 1996)

In the fifteen years between *La experiencia*—whose love poems hark back to the passions of a man who with each new woman ironically devoured *himself*—and *Sin título*, the book dedicated to poet Ulalume González de León,* we see an old man squeezing every drop out of love, enjoying the most blissful moments, and appealing to a virility that abandons the sallow bitterness of the tally in favor of the grateful jubilation of a man who has finally found a love potion to cauterize life's scars, purge elegiac discourse, and take us to its logical conclusion: "La poesía, manto de armiño / nos cubre los hombros / un instante; / luego resbala y cae sobre el fango / sin que podamos impedirlo" ("Poetry, that ermine cloak / covers our shoulders / an instant; / then slips off and falls into the mud / and we can't stop it").

Love is a contingency stripped of any illusion of eternity; woman is seen through an instant: "desde la atalaya destemplada del insomnio, / entre tus pies desnudos / pájaros picotean / segundos endurecidos" ("from the feverish watchtower of insomnia, / between your bare feet / birds peck / hardened seconds"). Few Mexican poets make it to old age in any state fit to settle scores with eroticism the way Hernández Campos did, his voice cracking in those final verses when masculinity gives way to serenity and surrender.

That Hernández Campos's work ends with such mournful verses makes sense if you know that he was also the author of one of the most extraordinary short stories in Mexican literature. Begun in 1957, completed in 1985, and included in *La experiencia*, "El samaritano" tells the story of a boy who follows the railroad tracks from Guadalajara to Mexico City in search of his mother. On the way, he runs into a couple of drunks who feed him and then rape him, etching into him a brutal life lesson that confirms Dostoyevsky's views: destroying love in the body and soul of a child is the most unspeakable of all crimes.

An excellent translator (most notably of T. S. Eliot), a spiritual citizen of Catullus's and Juvenal's Rome, an actual resident in contemporary Rome from 1951 to 1964, Hernández Campos was not just a great reader of the elegiac Latins but also a court bard, the author of "El presidente" (1954), a theatrical monologue in which Asiain says that the poet's voice functions as an ear tuned in to raucous polyphony. And the shouting voices impart a Catiline oration on Mexican presidential absolutism, turning it into colloquial and vernacular poetry, a lyrical version of what Martín Luis Guzmán* mythologized in *La sombra del caudillo* (1929).

Later, impassioned by the despotic, fawning, shameless, insidious ways power was established in Mexico, Hernández Campos expressed his distress through journalism, sometimes as a critic of the government and other times as its fervent apologist. In 1994 he felt it his duty to defend the state against the neo-Zapatista rebellion and did so with an insightful vehemence (and a touch of irascible machismo), that solidified his reputation as one of the most virulent critics of the Mexican left.

The Ancien Regime bred two or three generations of scholars like Hernández Campos, refined courtiers who never held high public office but turned their dangerous, sadomasochistic relationship with the Mexican government into a way of life. But few of them left a record of it the way Hernández Campos did. In some of his poetry, he registers the ambiguity, horror, and fascination provoked by Mr. President in a court as big as the republic. More than the civil condemnation it was seen as when it first came out, "El presidente" is a true imprecation (with a touch of morbid fascination) of presidentialism. "Discurso que se estaba formando en la cabeza cortada de Cicerón," another of his political poems, is a leisurely tour of the ruins that remain of history's powerful.

By identifying power with the father, Hernández Campos trapped himself in that labyrinth. "Porque el poder es ese pétreo mascarón / que resurge / cada seis años / siempre igual a sí mismo, siempre / reiterativo, ambiguo, obtuso, laberíntico, / siempre equivocado / e incapaz, que para eso es el poder, de enmendar / y aprender, / y nada es posible perdonarle, como tampoco / hay nada por qué odiarle" ("Because power is that big stone mask / that reappears / every six years / always identifcal to itself, always / reiterative, ambiguous, obtuse, labyrinthine / always wrong / and unable, that's why it's power, to amend / and to learn, / and you can't forgive it for anything, just as / you can't detest it for anything"). In "Padre, poder" and earlier poems, the poet forgives his father and hopes that "un día me perdonen / mis hijos / cuando ellos descubran, / a su vez, que / no soy / no he sido / el poder" ("that one day they forgive me / my children / when they discover, / in turn, that / I am not / I was not / power").

Given this interest in power, it's not surprising that Pier Paolo Pasolini, that alleged victim of power, seemed an exciting figure to Hernández Campos, who examined his official death certificate, confessed before his dead body, and dedicated a poem to him in *La experiencia*: "¿Cómo es que ahora Pasolini aparece exhibido fuera del tiempo, como en una Pietá, sobre las rodillas de la historia? ¿Cómo hubiéramos descrito el cuerpo muerto de García Lorca, el cadáver de Miguel Hernández, cifras en que se convirtieron, también ellos, de la pasión por la *polis*, de la pasión de la poesía trabada en lucha con la política? Monstruosa epifanía: muere el poeta y ya la justicia habla con un verso casi pasoliniano. La justicia, megáfono de la poesía" ("How is it that now Pasolini appears out of time, like a Pietá, on history's lap? How would we have described the dead body of García Lorca, the cadaver of Miguel Hernández, symbols, them too, of the passion for the polis, of the passion for poetry wedged in with the struggle of politics? Horrific epiphany: the poet dies and now justice speaks in almost Pasoliniesque verse. Justice, megaphone of poetry"). By buying into the idiotic, farfetched idea—one of the worst that the left has had—that Pier Paolo Pasolini, an incredibly complex figure, aristocrat and populist, scholar and agitator, had indirectly been murdered by the State (Evil incarnate), Hernández Campos doesn't betray himself; he explains himself: what he loved about the State was its sacrificial mystification. And in poetry and prose, he dedicates many pages both magnificent and repulsive to its crimes and subtleties. Hernández Campos is one of the few twentieth-century Mexican writers to speak of love and of power and he has something profound to say about both. Not bad.

SELECTED BIBLIOGRAPHY
La experiencia, FCE, Mexico, 1986.
Sin título, Joaquín Mortiz, Mexico, 2001.

HERRASTI, VICENTE F.

(Mexico City, 1967)

La muerte del filósofo (Acarnia en lontonanza), Herrasti's third novel, attempts to imitate the almost-lost rhetorical style of fifth-century Greek writer Gorgias, the author of *Encomium of Helen* and *The Defense of Palamedes*, who Plato used in one of his dialogues. Now, every swindler knows you can pawn off any old bauble to the masses as long as it's ancient. The remote past is seen—de facto—as prestigious and fairy-tale-like: Edward Bulwer-Lytton began marketing it in 1834, with *The Last Days of Pompeii*, and to this day the wire racks of airport bookstores attest to the fact that the tradition is alive and well. But Herrasti decided to swim against the current, proposing not a plot but a style.

I don't know Greek and I don't know whether or not the author (who at the end of the novel claims not to be the author) is insinuating that he does when he writes in the novel's appendix that he tried to recreated Gorgias's "very peculiar syntax" using "the expansive qualities of Spanish." But regardless of any feigned erudition, so common in contemporary fiction that no one questions it anymore, *La muerte del filósofo* (2004) is a book with some truly spectacular pages, such as those depicting the gallows where suspects do time for the murder of the tyrant Jason, and others in which some solid research into Hippocratic treatises creates a convincing Doctor Jantias engaged in the art of diagnosis.

In his first novels I was delighted by the way Herrasti genuinely exhibited his apprenticeship as a writer, almost haughty in the odyssey he'd begun as an adolescent artist à la Rimbaud in *Taxidermie* (1995), and insolent in his search for the impenetrable Aleister Crowley in *Diorama* (1998). And on finishing *La muerte de un filósofo* I felt truly grateful for such a tightly constructed, well-wrought novel. But as soon as I read the appendix, I was filled with doubts. In a bibliographical note, Herrasti succinctly explains his motives and boasts of a predictably confirmed obsession with the novel's millennial backdrop (Ancient Greece). Suddenly, rather than having read a good novel—which it is—I felt as if I'd witnessed an academic experiment in historical fiction that actually ended where it should have begun, without delving into the soul of the potentially extraordinary character of the slave Akorna. It was the feat of a geometric creator who scaled the summit and, on staring down into the crater of fictional truth, was either too scared or too timid to jump into the fire. We get just a glimpse of the grand, overarching vision the author seemed to have. But then rereading my review of Herrasti's previous novel *Diorama*, I detected the haphazard logic of a critic trying to make sense of a writer. First, I'd accused him of rash intemperance. Now I was claiming he was too calculated and calling him stingy. I can only come up with one explanation: readers only get riled up by writers who share their emotional obsessions with them.

Rather than for commercial (and I use the term the way Edmund Wilson did, as the opposite of classic) purposes, Herrasti uses political, historical, and linguistic motifs to create a memorable style. He's the only Crack generation writer who seems to see writing less as the inevitable or fateful consequence of literary thought and more as a mental framework, a structure that the artist has an opportunity to lay his stakes on creating.

The tyrant Jason, the philosopher Gorgias, and the slave Akorna in *La muerte de un filósofo* are acting out a charade, the essence of which can be seen in their triangulation of power, knowledge, and servitude. And Herrasti's painstaking rhetoric actually allows us to hear the echoes of an early drama performed in the polis far better than we can in the amusement park of contemporary fiction set in the twentieth century. In the kingdom of Kronos the tyrants actually tried to preserve history before philosophers came to burn it down.

SELECTED BIBLIOGRAPHY
Diorama, Joaquín Mortiz, Mexico, 1998.
La muerte del filósofo, Joaquín Mortiz, Mexico, 2004.

HINOJOSA, FRANCISCO
(Mexico City, 1954)

Hinojosa is a writer I could see as a seventeenth-century master of optics in Amsterdam or The Hague, grumbling about the hackwork Spinoza was doing, distracted as he was by philosophy. Hinojosa's stockpile includes every known type of lens and microscope, plus a whole host of nefarious, mechanical devices. The shortsighted and astigmatic come to his clinic in the hopes of seeing better and leave with the wrong prescriptions, happily and obliviously deceived. Those who wanted to see red come out convinced everything is blue, and cross-eyed folks see triple. That kind of talent for distortion is a trait of a true short story writer, the kind there are so few of in so many literatures: a master of caricature, of the artistic exaggeration of characteristics and circumstances. The habits of incompetent men, bureaucratic ineptitude, lost ambitions, and police blotters are enough for an illusionist whose rhetoric sets off with the aim of eliminating almost all of the "literature" from literature. So it should come as no surprise that Hinojosa is such a successful children's author, since kids don't confuse repetition with tedium or exaggeration with pointillism. When he writes for adults—whatever that means—Hinojosa uses his wit for moralistic purposes, since caricature tends to be more moralizing than other genres. He exaggerates to expose, and exposes to impose sanctions.

But unlike other moralists, Hinojosa is a doctor who doesn't care about what happens as a result of his diagnoses. Whether elaborate jokes or straightforward black humor, Hinojosa's stories are crafted with extreme formal economy and every apparently pointless element is utterly indispensable to the tale's dramatic development. You read his stories and witness multiple murders, hyperbolic academic careers, work-place betrayal, a kidney transplant, a political scandal that ends up closing down the university. Whether hilarious or macabre, Hinojosa is the only one who could spin these yarns; they're all controlled by the lenses prescribed by the alchemist of light obsessed with disordering the world or creating order out of chaos.

Negros, hueros, héticos (1999), Hinojosa's collected short stories, is significantly weightier than much of the ephemeral garbage infesting bookstores today. Perhaps inadvertently, Hinojosa has written a new *Gulliver's Travels*.

His academic Gullivers are Professor Aldecoa and graduate Tapia fleeing from their own Lilliput, Brobdingnag, Laputa, Balnibarbi, Glubbdubdrib, convinced that it's normal and even inevitable that everyone be surrounded by midgets and giants, victims of the grandeur or pettiness of civilizations and their savages. Hinojosan characters swan through cities and continents, crimes and punishments and degradations using the lenses their creator gives them for their trips. Unlike Swift, though, Hinojosa doesn't seem to believe that satire serves a pedagogical function or is a clandestine form of condemnation. In his long poem *Robinson perseguido* (1981), Hinojosa first embarked on visually deforming literary and cinematographic legends and came out with some very disquieting caricatures. And between *Informe negro* (1987) and *Un tipo de cuidado* (2000), he's been writing not so much a human comedy as an ogre's.

"It's hard to define a true eccentric in this day and age, when narrative originality has been discredited, making concessions to all manner of passions and sentiments," said Guillermo Sheridan,* long ago, with reference to the Hinojosas and their stories. He went on, then, to enumerate the characteristics of their eccentricity—ferocious, drunken, quick, trivial—that set them apart. Sheridan's description—found in *Paralelos y meridianos* (2007)—also makes clear that Hinojosa is no Rubén Darío-style eccentric—not religious, decadent, or morbid. Instead, his eccentricity stems from the noble branch of pataphysics—a kind of philosophy dealing with the imaginary—along with its corollary of parody, self-parody, and pastiche. One day, someone will create an anthology of pataphysics and black humor, and whether it's Mexican or universal, Hinojosa—already renowned for a significant body of literature in addition to his children's literature—will figure prominently.

Only from an author like Hinojosa could we expect a "novel in verse" such as *Poesía eras tú* (2009). The title, which means, "Poetry you were," is an allusion to Rosario Castellanos's* *Poesía no eres tú* (Poetry you're not), a fine, solemn work. Some have seen Hinojosa's book as an inconsequential, unorthodox tale of Mexican versification. I'd be more inclined to say that this "epic" is a fluid, tragicomic narration that—over the course of fifty verses written in different meter—chronicles the dying days of a love story between two swineherds: he, a poetaster; she, a businesswoman and deputy elect.

Her political appointment sends Zaharí away from her lover, who is the only voice we hear speak. Unlike the bygone precedent set by the *Song of Solomon*, *Poesía eras tú* is not a dialogue between the two, which would, perhaps, have resulted in a nicer, more successful book. But Hinojosa sets out to do quite a lot in his great theater of the world. *Poesía eras tú* is a long, amatory epic, told via the lover's nightmares, jealous rages, binges, hangovers, professional blunders, cuddles, family misfortunes, and bouts of domestic violence.

The couple's affair comes to a climax during a trip to New York after which their love begins to fade. And since ballads, boleros, *rancheras*, and naïve poetry have all been butchered, Hinojosa discards the possibility of courtly—sublime—love and fleeting affairs; in *Poesía eras tú*, he decides instead to examine long-term relationships, using the categorization set out by Cordoban poet Ibn Hazm: "Some men there are whose love only becomes true after long converse, much contemplation, and extended familiarity. Such a one is likely to persist and to be steadfast in his affection, untouched by the passage of time, what enters with difficulty goes not out easily" (*The Ring of the Dove*, trans. A. J. Arberry)

As with all true humorists, it's hard to know whether or not to take Hinojosa seriously. Some will see *Poesía eras tú* as frippery. Others will find that this poem-novel catalogs Mexico's sentimental opprobrium, the source of all our ills. The latter strikes me as feasible as far as premise, since Hinojosa's stories often derive from profound indignation at the moral bankruptcy and hilarity of conventionalism. Hinojosa says the novel occurred to him while reading a letter of power of attorney, which he decided to rewrite in poetic form. His technique involves singling out overstatements, and then creating something grotesque by watering down the reality that made them bearable. According to Sheridan, his exegete: "You never know why he hurtles through these lives, nor who he evokes them for, but you do know why: to emphasize the hilarious reality of nonsense as moral foundation, like a raging infection that thrives against all odds."

Since *Robinson perseguido* (1981), his first book—also poetry, Hinojosa has been toying with classic heroes, whether universal or Mexican, and dropping them into awkward situations via a time machine that preserves only the archetype, seeing everything else as trickery. The poet drafting his verses in *Poesía eras tú* is a swineherd like Eumaeus, the man who received Odysseus dressed as a beggar, treated him kindly and offered him food and shelter. But Hinojosa's swineherd is a less faithful, criollo Eumaeus: a lyrical, fickle creature who looks on falling out of love with resignation, fate, and guile.

SELECTED BIBLIOGRAPHY

Negros, hueros, héticos, Ediciones Sin Nombre, Mexico, 1999.
Un tipo de cuidado, Tusquets Editores, Mexico, 2000.
La verdadera historia de Nelson Ives, Tusquets Editores, Mexico, 2002.
La nota negra, Tusquets Editores, Mexico, 2003.
El tiempo apremia. ¡México, cuántos cuentos se cometen en tu nombre!, Almadía, Oaxaca, 2009.
Poesía eras tú, Almadía, Oaxaca, 2009.
Hectic Ethics, trans. Kurt Hollander, City Lights, 1998.

HIRIART, HUGO

(Mexico City, 1942)

If someone one day decides to write a history of Mexican literary unorthodoxy, Hiriart's name will have a special, beloved place in it. A man who chronicles imaginary civilizations, critiques taste, and stages vulgar fantasies, Hiriart is a writer any modern literature would be proud to claim as its own. And if his fame and fortune never exceed the borders of the country he happened to be born in, we'll know that there is no longer grace, intelligence, or hospitality in the world's prose and theater.

His book *Sobre la naturaleza de los sueños*, however, is a philosophical treatise, in the most ancient and sophisticated sense. I can't think of anything like it in contemporary Spanish-language literature. It's a strange book, written by a modern as if he were an ancient, a work dedicated to good common people by a writer who doesn't confuse erudition with pomposity or exquisiteness with impenetrability. Hiriart communicates in the manner of ancient philosophers. Anyone reading *Sobre la naturaleza de los sueños* is in for something extraordinary indeed in this day and age: an author thinking aloud, pontificating about dreams in the public plaza, the place where the human and the divine have settled their disputes since the beginning of time. Hiriart is the kind of guy you'd like to meet at the Banquet or the Garden of Epicurus, or see defending the Academy of Athens from Emperor Justinian—or even dismembering a corpse with Descartes after having gotten the gravediggers drunk. But on top of all that, he's a playwright. Of course only a man of the theater could boast so beautifully that he'd written a hypnogogic (and hypnotic) work without having read "any books on the topic, so as not to deviate from my reflections or warp my mental processes," as if there wasn't already an enormous body of knowledge on the collective unconscious, as if countless scholars hadn't already written about it. It's no dishonor to Hiriart to say that *Sobre la naturaleza de los sueños* masterfully expands on the Artistotelian interpretation of dreams. It would be most unusual for a book like this to be anything but, given how few writers have such a close, working, and imaginative relationship with the classics as Hiriart does. When Alfonso Reyes* wrote of Athenian rhetoric, he did so with the modesty of a lover of Greco-Latin philology. But Reyes's didactic erudition seems amateur next to Hiriart's philosophizing imagination. It's easy to honor Isocrates as a matter of course. In fact, it's pretty much required. But it's astonishing to read a modern who takes on Aristotle as if the intervening twenty centuries were the blink of an eye. The difference between Reyes and Hiriart is that of classicist aspirations versus classical dissertation.

Following a scholastic (in the original sense of the word) order of presentation, Hiriart develops a delightful treatise on the nature of dreams. I'm paraphrasing some of his hypotheses rather loosely here:

• Dreams are an ever-shifting present. Dreams are only ever present. It's impossible to "summarize" a Scarlatti sonata. Dreams are not like stories but like music.

• A dream is an activity in which the lateral imagination (perceivable in a state of wakefulness) stops being latent and takes over the mind entirely.

• In dreams things don't happen; implications develop. A dream is a conjecture of the imagination that doesn't take place anywhere. There are no superfluous details in dreams. In a dream nothing is anomalous; everything is meaningful.

• Dreams are movement, a struggle between configuration and evaporation. It matters not what they mean but what they are. Divination and interpretation are irrelevant.

So Hiriart sits squarely among those who reject dreams as a prophetic vision or an obscuring of reason. The view disputed by shamans and philosophers is as old as dreams themselves. And although the word "oneirocritica" (the interpretation of dreams) was popularized by the second-century diviner Artemidorus, it was initially used to keep wise men safe from the influence of the art of divining ("mantikos") used primarily in dreams. It was materialists like Anaxagoras and Democritus who claimed dreams were a function of the body and not the soul. Atoms, according to Democritus, emit images that penetrate our senses. Both gods and demons were seen as idols, "imagoes" of men. Hippocrates and company talked about dreams as being divine in origin, but then as doctors viewed them as related to the body's humors. Thus the road to psychophysiology was paved by Aristotle.

But the other side of the coin—the one admired by Homer, the one that saw dreams as prophetic—was more attractive to a public eager for supernatural explanations of existence. Those who crossed the "gates of horn" (from the *Odyssey*) of "true" dreams were legion; those who preferred the "gates of ivory" few. Antiphon the Sophist wrote the first interpretation of dreams, along with a therapeutics of the soul. Up until Freud, "oneiromancy" was considered therapeutic gnosis if it was considered at all. Even Plato's death was taken as some sort of mantic mystery.

Aristotle's rejection of oneiromancy was as convincing as it was modest. In his *Parva naturalia* there are three treatises on the topic: "On Sleep," "On Dreams," and "On Divination in Sleep." These tracts were compiled towards the end of his life and after the death of Plato, when the Stagirite went back to Athens to found the Lyceum. *Parva naturalia* is an ancillary work, one that shows Aristotle leaning heavily towards the natural sciences. Still, the Aristotelian study and interpretation of dreams could easily have come from the first paragraph of his *Metaphysics,* a book I'm sure Hiriart had in mind when he wrote *Sobre la naturaleza de los sueños.* "All men, by nature, crave perception. One sign of that is their love of sensations. Indeed, sensations are loved for their own sake, regardless of utility, and the visual are loved above all others."

Explained in the three sleep-related treatises in *Parva Naturalia*, Aristotle's dream interpretation was in turn the product of an earlier text, "On Memory and Recollection," which was considered the groundwork for Western gnosiology until Descartes came along. There, Aristotle developed the notion of selective memory without which it's impossible to uphold the idea of dreams as an immanent—rather than divine—manifestation. So what did the Stagirite say about dreams in *Parva naturalia*? In principle, that dreams—that is, what we see while we're asleep—are, like all things, act and potency, a faculty of the soul and a function of the body, such that:

1. Bodily function determines the soul's ability to dream.

2. Oneiric sensitivity resides, as does everyday activity, in "common sense" (in the Aristotelian usage, clearly), as it's as easy to forget something while awake as it is to remember a dream and vice versa.

3. A dream is an activity of the imagination.

4. Dreams not only represent images but also generate opinions and judgments.

5. Bodily desires form part of a dream. A person who is thirsty will dream of water. But those dreams do not determine the totality of the phenomenon. They are "excretionary" dreams.

6. Dreams are only as real as the imagination. Oneiric divination is just something sanctioned by the masses' considerable credulity.

Hiriart only quotes Aristotle twice in *Sobre la naturaleza de los sueños*. Clearly, given that his unusual treatise is not an academic review piece but a speculative, empirical essay, he's not obliged to acknowledge his influences. But I dare say that his interpretation of dreams is an advancement of *Parva naturalia* as meticulous as it is magisterial. Averroës, the great Arab commentator of Aristotle, summed up his teacher's doctrine in a way that would resonate with Hiriart: "Of all the faculties of the soul, dreams are principally related to the imagination, whether they be true dreams or false dreams."

The Mexican scholiast's central thesis—that dreams are an activity of the imagination, which is a result of "common sense"—is strictly Aristotelian. In fact, what Hiriart calls "oneiric conjecture" was foreseen by the Stagirite in the fourth treatise of *Parva naturalia*, where he states that just as thinking of a person in dream does not signal or cause his presence, neither are dreams signs or causes of what occurs but simply conjecture. This, he says, is why many dreams go unrealized: conjecture, in effect, is neither permanent nor general.

Hiriart may have taken from Aristotle the notion of conjecture as what unites the senses, but Aristotle would have been fascinated by Hiriart's explanation of the supposedly "oracular" nature of dreams. The illusion of dreams as oracular, Hiriart says, stems from the fact that they possess no synoptic structure. And anything that can't be conventionally narrated becomes a hotbed of symbols, whether ill-fated or auspicious. On this point, Hiriart applauds Aristotle's ambiguity with regard to dream divination. And he himself equivocates, forgiving Freud just when he had him over a barrel. Killing off the great shaman of the moderns is no easy feat.

The irresistible lack of psychoanalysis in *Sobre la naturaleza de los sueños* is not just an affectionate homage to Aristotle; it also serves Hiriart's purposes. Naturalist philosophers know that they'll pay dearly for even the slightest concession to transcendental doctrines. Better to show some Aristotelian skepticism than hurl abuse at those crossing the "gate of horn." Freudian dream interpretation is archetypical and anecdotal. A comparison of Freud's 1909 *The Interpretation of Dreams* and Artemidorus's book of the same title, written during the time of Marcus Aurelius, leaves those who claim psychoanalysis is epistemological without a leg to stand on. Aristotle and Hiriart would agree that Freudian dream divination—like Artemidorus's—is utterly lacking in scientific validity. Their symbolic interpretations reflect the hopes and fears of the second- and nineteenth-century men. They're essentially personal inventories of Viennese bourgeois psychology and pagan decadence, though they do share certain archetypal similarities (those established by Jung, though he clearly had a deeper, more nuanced understanding of cultural anthropology).

And the similarities between Freud and Artemidorus don't end there. Both were therapists either loved or detested by their contemporaries; both wrote manuals that popularized the private realm of dreams. Cicero went as far as to lament the disappearance of the Aristotelian spirit and the profusion of shamans of every ilk. But still, enlightened as he was, he didn't hesitate to consult dream interpreters when times were tough enough to cloud his thought processes. He acted as many modern rationalists do. But like Aristotle, Hiriart leaves raving about divination to the Platonics, Romantics, and psychoanalysts' patients. Hiriart (like Aristotle) is concerned with how things work, not what they are. And in these times of metaphysical angst and mass esoteric pomposity, his call to common sense and meticulous, creative writing is a welcome relief.

Aristotelian psychophysiology was discredited during the Renaissance, when Harvey and Vesalius proved classic notions about blood circulation and respiration to be false. Contemporary neurophysiology, which uses the electroencephalogram, proposes a biochemical etiology of dreams. Interestingly, we moderns tend to discard the most rational aspect of Aristotelian dream interpretation, the part that grants "common sense" sovereignty over the five capricious senses, whose odd number meant they were out of harmony with the four elements. This is where Hiriart leaves Aristotle behind and follows Descartes, whose *Treatise on Man, Passions of the Soul,* and *Meditations on First Philosophy* guide his precepts, which are based on the rejection of any of the "inherent attributes" of scholasticism. Instead, he lavishes examples, doubts, and games. The philosopher here becomes a performer with the perfect props and stage apparatuses at his disposal, and the audience sits awed by the acrobatics of a genius who never falls from the trapeze.

I can't predict whether or not *Sobre la naturaleza de los sueños* will have a place in contemporary dream interpretation. And out of ignorance, I can't comment on Hiriart's secular analytical philosophy influences. But originality is a modern superstition only overcome by those who carry on a spirited, brilliant dialogue with the classics, as he does. The ancients are brought back to life, transformed by this puppeteer-like writer who delights in playing spiritual pranks. *Sobre la naturaleza de los sueños* exalts the essay as genre; it's a masterpiece of critical imagination. In fairness, I ought to say that it wasn't much trouble for me to track down some of the author's sources. I was an informal student of Hiriart's for a few intense months. During that time he never bothered to read any of the nonsense his students wrote. He said it was more important to learn to think than to learn to write. And he insisted we read Aristotle, Descartes, and Robert Burton's *The Anatomy of Melancholy.* Sometimes, words will come back to haunt your dreams. (*Servidumbre y grandeza de la vida literaria,* 1998)

Theater and philosophy, two incompatible genres, turned Hiriart into one of the few truly sparkling wits of the Spanish language. I've always been perplexed by the fact that he doesn't seem to get the worldwide recognition he deserves. No Mexican writer is as well equipped to host just about any banquet, be it in a Golden Age open-air theater or the tavern where Doctor Johnson entertained the gonorrheal Boswell before a roaring fire.

Hiriart's oeuvre can be divided into four genres: novel, treatise, short essay, and theater. And despite the fact that he's an eternal philosopher who proposes (and stages) problems, axioms, and paradoxes, his first loves were sculpture and painting, which he's never stopped practicing and sees as well-matched with his writing. So the puppeteer and master of props is also a philosopher; the philosopher is a novelist; the novelist, a playwright and theater director; the stage man, a columnist who in turn paints and sculpts.

His first novels, *Galaor* (1972) and *Cuadernos de Gofa* (1981), were published several years before the trend of what pundits call postmodern literature, which turned pastiches, historical parodies, and imitations of imitations into everyday affairs. People forget that *Galaor*, an acclaimed (and anti-Cervantes) rewriting of a novel of chivalry came out at a time when Mexican literature was split between novels obsessed with self-referentiality and those that were *engagé*, youth-oriented, and colloquial. *Galaor* set the precedent for a good part of the best novels to come out of Mexico around the turn of the twenty-first century, whether byzantine tales of the high seas or the lives of Greek philosophers. He was the knight errant who sanctioned all the sorcery.

I reread *Galaor* and still find it a relevant and meaningful work, and I go back to *Cuadernos de Gofa* from time to time as well. I never tire of Professor Gaspar Dódolo and the natural history and spiritual geography of the inhabitants of the imaginary kingdom of Gofa, where the flora and fauna of resentment, the cowardice of the tropics, the ports of inebriation, and the cavern of avarice comprise an entire civilization. I'm a reader who tempers enthusiasm with comparisons, and years ago I drew parallels between Hiriart and Henri Michaux and Jonathan Swift; today those similarities seem insignificant and I see *Cuadernos de Gofa* as simply unique.

Of Hiriart's later novels, I was never convinced by *La destrucción de todas las cosas* (1992). Despite enjoyable dramatics, it seemed overwhelmed by its weighty premise: positing the Conquest of Mexico in the future. Apocalyptic literature is so commonplace in Mexico that it's developed its own conventions, and Hiriart seemed to take no pains to stray from them. Nor did I particularly like *El actor se prepara* (2004), a short treatise on moral theology disguised as a detective novel in which the plot doesn't quite work; the book adds nothing to Hiriart's legacy. *El agua grande* (2002), on the other hand, strikes me as the acme of his already polished prose. It's a philosophical account of the narrative form that simultaneously tells the story of a blind singer who sees the light in a Mexico City cantina and—after an odyssey of sorts—becomes a guru. That's how Magistrodomos tells it to his disciple, weaving a tale as he analyzes it, dissecting the art of narration as he enacts it, and creating a very agreeable brand of philosophy along the way.

Hiriart's writing stems from skilled dissertation, from using rhetorical arts to theatrically and magisterially astound the reader (or spectator), imitating the philosopher-mathematicians he studied and who, thankfully, led him away from Heidegger and Hegel, existentialism and historiosophy. Some people don't take Hiriart seriously as a treatise writer, deeming his sense of humor and etiquette inappropriate. That's their loss—and mistake. Not many treatises per se have been written in Mexico, and *Sobre la naturaleza de los sueños* (1995) should be added to the list of those considered classics: Alfonso Reyes's *El deslinde* (1944), Octavio Paz's* *El arco y la lira* (1955), and Tomás Segovia's *Poética y profética* (1982). Hiriart's treatise is an eminent inquiry into dream interpretation that dances around Aristotle and adds to his ideas. A Catholic and a non-drinker, Hiriart is also the author of a therapeutic treatise called *Vivir y beber* (1987).

In *Los dientes eran el piano: Un estudio sobre arte e imaginación* (1999) and *Cómo leer y escribir poesía* (2003), Hiriart repeats the method used in *Sobre la naturaleza de los sueños* to less felicitous results. Once the reader is familiar with his rhetoric, the repetition gets old. Meticulous observation doesn't always necessarily turn a cat into a Chinese vase, as the illusionist would hope.

More than for his treatises—which helped me to at least *conceive* of things I can't articulate—I assume Hiriart will be remembered as a pure essayist, a columnist who turned short pieces in literary publications into an art form. Collections like *Disertación sobre las telarañas y otros escritos* (1980) and *Discutibles fantasmas* (2001) are magnificent additions to his bibliography. In the latter, which I just finished, he weaves a narrative around children's education in general, and piano for kids in particular (Bartók, Tchaikovsky, Schumann), subtly stitching in high math, fine autobiographical observations, and a clever micro-metaphysics of fear. *Discutibles fantasmas* includes a description of lunch with the poet Gonzalo Rojas eating octopus in its own ink, which (thanks to Brecht's quip about paying as much attention to what one says as to what one eats) leads to a characterization of the poet himself as an octopus (of words, poems) in his own ink. His portrayal of Gonzalo Rojas applies equally to himself: baroque but strict, intense without being lachrymose, an artist who's neither trivial nor grandiloquent.

I've seen most of Hiriart's plays, whether directed by him or others. On stage, his miniscule world is laid bare, warts and all. Bright lights illuminate both his brilliance and his carelessness, the result of arrogant improvisation and the belief that everything can be resolved by the author's autocratic magic wand. But from *Hécuba, la perra* (1982) all the way to *El caso de Caligari y el ostión chino* (2000), I have always—at least for a few minutes, which in the theater is an eternity—been enraptured by his theatrical creatures, which overflow with charm.

Reading some of the pieces (quatrains, sketches, staged fantasies) collected in books like *Minotastas y su familia* (1999) and *La repugnante historia de Clotario Demoniax y otras piezas y ensayos sobre teatro* (2005), I discovered that—contrary to what I would have assumed—Hiriart's theater isn't literary. By that I mean, once distanced from their exhilarating performances, the plays don't hold up well on paper alone. Nor is his a theater of ideas— and it can't be since we're still suffering the havoc wrought by the existentialists fifty years ago when they used theater as a vehicle for philosophy.

Minotastas y su familia, for example, harkens back to the memorable miniature theaters and miraculous props that made the book possible. *Ámbar* (1990), in turn, is more a spoken novel or libretto than it is a real play, and *El tablero de las pasiones de juguete* is a didactic play set around the legend of Faust (mixed with Greek mythology), which seems characteristic of the "original" moderns. *Camille o historia de la escultura de Rodin a nuestros días* (1987) is the most "commercial" of his plays. And *La repugnante historia de Clotario Demoniax* is a collection of theater pieces, including one beautiful play—*La caja*—that stands out as the most representative of Hiriart's theater.

Without the stage, Hiriart would lose his axis of gravitation; his work would be chaotic and without form. His plays demand the order of the stage: backdrops, curtains, and all the props (and toys) typical of what is essentially dramatic literature. He presents the story as mimesis, staged by means of a conflict between characters that's played out in their dialogue.

Many of his disciples—I was one, and include myself here—have tried to explain his "mechanical" genius, to discover the secret. Some, including David Olguín in the prologue of *Minotastas y su familia*, believe what Hiriart says about himself: that he's obsolescent, a man who never lost his boyish wonder and simply replaced toy soldiers with actors and characters. I've studied the writers who influenced him and learned a lot along the way: reading Artemidorus and confirming that Hiriart gorged himself on *Les deux masques* (1883), that fabulous history of theater written by Paul de Saint-Victor, the *Moniteur Universel* critic and son of the Count of Saint-Victor, who in turn was author of a treatise on the imagination. But taken separately, the pieces don't do much to explain the whole: his magnificent, mechanized imagination, the creation of his robotic characters, puppets, marvels, and wonders.

I recently spent a few delusional nights imagining I could save a few Mexican books from "the destruction of all things" (the title of one of Hiriart's books), and tried to decide which they'd be. A fair few of those that merited the honor were written by Hiriart himself. May the powers that be concede a long and healthy life to the engaging, edgy Hugo Hiriart.

SELECTED BIBLIOGRAPHY
Galaor, Joaquín Mortiz, Mexico, 1972; Tusquets Editores, Mexico, 2000.
Disertación sobre las telarañas, Martín Casillas, Mexico, 1980; FCE, Mexico, 1987.
Ámbar, Cal y Arena, Mexico, 1990.
Cuadernos de Gofa, Joaquín Mortiz, Mexico, 1981; ERA, Mexico, 1998.
La destrucción de todas las cosas, ERA, Mexico, 1992.
Sobre la naturaleza de los sueños, ERA, Mexico, 1995.
Los dientes eran el piano. Un estudio sobre arte e imaginación, Tusquets Editores, Mexico, 1999.
Galaor, Minotastas y su familia, prologue by David Olguín, El Milagro, Mexico, 1999.

Discutibles fantasmas, ERA, Mexico, 2001.

El agua grande, Tusquets Editores, Mexico, 2002.

Cómo leer y escribir poesía, Tusquets Editores, Mexico, 2003.

El actor se prepara, Tusquets Editores, Mexico, 2004.

La repugnante historia de Clotario Demoniax y otras piezas y ensayos para teatro, Tusquets Editores, Mexico, 2005.

El arte de perdurar, Almadía, Oaxaca, 2010.

Learning Spanish, Writing Poetry, trans. Christopher Winks, FCE, 2005.

HUERTA, DAVID
(Mexico City, 1949)

Incurable (1987) came out over twenty years ago and I think I've reread it three times (not counting additional, multiple consultations). It's hard to decide if this is the kind of book you always open up to just the right page, as W. H. Auden said, or if it's always "the *unjust* page," as Huerta says. Both oracle and prophecy, divination and fate, it's hard to pin down a work like *Incurable*; but in the time since its publication, it's become decisive in the history of late twentieth-century Mexican literature.

Incurable is a 389-page poem in nine parts. It's been considered—hypothetically—a free-verse novel, and it can be interpreted in a thousand different ways. But perhaps there are three substantive approaches: reading it as a long narration; listening to it as if it were Joycean chatter; or consulting it as a private dictionary of modernism (or postmodernism).

Twenty years ago, I wrote an enthusiastic review of *Incurable*, a misguided offering made out of admiration. At the time I said it was—or could be—a novel. And in response I received (and accepted as valid and sound) harsh criticism accusing me, as the reviewer of novels that I was in 1987, of thinking that a poem turns into a novel simply by virtue of its length and apparent narrativity, of making a crude assertion that betrayed my ignorance and inexperience. To my surprise, a similar line of reasoning has been advanced by persevering readers like Ronald Haladyna, Gilberto Prado Galán, and Carlos Oliva Mendoza. Even Huerta himself says that in *Incurable* lies "a novel with a very diluted, very tenuous thread, but a novel all the same."

The poem opens: "El mundo es una mancha en el espejo" ("The world is a speck on the mirror"), and we could trace the genealogy of that verse throughout Huerta's oeuvre. He has a sort of youthful angst and is eager to explain the mysteries of the light and shadows, to know what's going on through the neighbor's windows. The imagery is like that of modernist Baudelaire—Walter Benjamin's Baudelaire, to be precise—and it's also more characteristic of a novelist than a poet. Huerta the storyteller—whose longest story is *Incurable*—was already saying in *El jardín de la luz* in 1972, that "En el espejo del baño / se guarda la imagen del principio" ("In the bathroom mirror / lies the image of the beginning") as well as "Y nada ocurre / al fondo de un minuto" ("And nothing happens / at the bottom of a minute").

Huerta is one of those poets for whom "the image is the secret cause of history," as Lezama Lima says. And all of history can be condensed into one exasperated minute, as seen in *Cuaderno de noviembre* (1976). Jaime Moreno Villarreal,* one of the few to resist the temptation to interpret to death, to plunder the treasure trove that is Huerta's poetry, gets to the point when he says that the versicle, so characteristic of Huerta (yet bequeathed by José Carlos Becerra*), should be read as a fragment used as exegesis. Its purpose: explication, doctrine or interpretation, and recollection. It all comes back to versicles, and that's what *versare* means—to meditate and reflect—according to Quintilian. Though it seems particularly well suited to being read all at once, you have to keep coming back to versicular poetry.

At the dawn of the twenty-first century, Huerta is the Mexican poet most read by young poets, many of whom prefer the more Spinoza-like propositions of *Cuaderno de noviembre* to the finely wrought affirmations of *Incurable*. But whether opting for the shorter path or meandering down the long one, we find a miniscule civilization only decipherable with the help of more poetry, written to describe it: "Destrucción de un texto o corrección de estilo, autocrítica" ("Destroying a text or editing the style, self-criticism"), Huerta says.

After *Cuaderno de noviembre*, Huerta had to choose between the theoretically sententious, slightly radical Catiline tone of *Huellas del civilizado* (1977) and the lusty exuberance of *Versión* (1978), the product of an extravagant and talented poet. Either way, he's immortal, undying, a ravaged romantic hero. In *Versión* Huerta says that Artaud was right, "siempre es

mejor / abrazarse a uno mismo y roer estos huesos en un / rincón aparte"
("it is always better / to hold oneself and gnaw these bones / off in a corner").
The Romanticism of the bones, a trace of Artaud trying to rear his head, became more pronounced in time and gives us the consumed poet of *Incurable*
on the verge of a nervous breakdown, awaiting truth, awaiting illness.

There is surprisingly little criticism on *Incurable,* and what there is tends
to betray a crude and often triumphal disdain. Some misguided critics opted
to remain silent; others insulted the book's extravagance or manipulated
the poet's words, decontextualizing them so that his ambiguous statements
turned into commentary on his own work. You can see how easy it is to
misrepresent a line like this, for instance: "The book started off aspiring to
be a masterpiece, in Cyril Connolly's terms, and ended up being simply a
very big book."

Even defenders of Huerta or of *Incurable* (the two are not necessarily the
same) tend to think that the book isn't really saying much worth bothering
to try to understand, that it's "not philosophy," as if its hundreds of versicles
(and corresponding meters) were just mildly enjoyable fireworks, like a wild,
intense, postmodern Mexican night (which of course it is), erudite verbiage
that turns out to be pretty meaningless.

Aurelio Asiain,* who in *Carácteres de imprenta* (1996) was one of the few
to read the book in good faith and not simply bite off chunks of it with the
green teeth of envy, was reserved, seeing it as "only rhetorically philosophical." But after Lucretius, really, has there ever been a philosophical poem that
wasn't only *rhetorically* philosophical? Can poetry (whether Dante, Goethe,
or Victor Hugo) relate to philosophy in any way other than rhetorically? I'm
fairly sure that Santayana, an authority on Lucretius, would agree with me
on this one. Asiain is right, though (and this is his larger point) to note how
heavily *Incurable* relies on mundane academic philosophy and to wonder to
what degree it actually creates its own music.

Thirty-some years after the 1970 heyday of postmodernity, we can now
answer that question. Foucault, Deleuze and Guatarri, Barthes, and Kristeva
hover in the background of *Incurable* like ambient noise, the way Heidegger
does in José Gorostiza's* *Muerte sin fin*, the way Plotinus does in José Vasconcelos.* This sort of "epochal orchestra" can also be detected in Alí Chu-
maceró* and other mid-century poets steeped in existentialism (translated

by Spanish exiles in Mexico), in the same way that a philosophical background (from materialism to empirio-criticism) shines through in Eduardo Lizalde's* *Cada cosa es Babel*.

You don't have to have loved (or hated) French postmodern jargon or structuralist theory to accept the fact that those *maitres à penser* thrived in the poems published in *La Mesa Llena*, the short-lived journal that brought Huerta and company together in the late seventies. Though it's not exactly "hermetic poetry," the poems in *Cuaderno de noviembre* and *Peces de piel fugaz* (Coral Bracho*) are perfectly à la page, as is the episodic poetry of Paloma Villegas,* Jorge Aguilar Mora,* and Héctor Manjarrez* (though it was responding to other influences). Regardless, Huerta is not as "philosophical" as someone like Enrique González Martínez was in his day. Instead he relies more on his early, formative readings than other Mexican poets, which we can see in his almost militant praise of the gods of Marxism, psychoanalysis, and feminism whose words, echoes, and resonances are sprinkled throughout *Incurable*. Despite having made no pretense of writing a "philosophical poem," Huerta is pretty daring, a poet who, as Brodsky might have said, was searching for flesh and instead found words, an immanent world of citations. In *Incurable*, he says, "Yo me creí la segunda persona, pero seguí escribiendo" ("I felt I was the second person, but I kept writing").

As "pure poetry" (the sort that Henri Bremond saw residing between the demon of the verse and the demon of silence), *Incurable* has a few faults. Perhaps the most important (and he picked up on this) is that many of his verses are "archaeological," in the sense Eliot intended when talking about Pound. Poetry can be overwhelmed by a profusion of scholarly references and epistemological concerns. Of course, readers can participate in their own readings, intervening when and where they wish, skipping verses that distract or bore them. That's any reader's prerogative, and I've never seen why it should be any more acceptable in reading Claude Simon than Balzac. *Incurable* is a "wreath of modernist horrors," as Huerta himself said, whose aporias, paradoxes, oxymorons, recantations, and digressions question the primacy of the *logos*. This is true whether you see it as postmodern (as Haladyna does) or as a late, spectacular, modernist poem (as I do).

A not-love poem, *Incurable* is both a testimonial and the auspicious narration of new forms of battle between men and women. In Octavio Paz,* man celebrates woman as a sacred symbol; in Rubén Bonifaz Nuño,* man's defeat turns him into a dumbstruck, jittery adolescent; and in Tomás Segovia,* woman is the only measure of the world. But in Huerta, the monstrous male is not content to escort muses or bemoan his abandonment. Instead, in poetry overpopulated with muses, courtesans, ballerinas, and Amazons, with women who are philosophers, theosophists, and painters, man attempts to solve the mysteries of his *own* character, while woman is seen as the scandalous, castrating, equal-rights-demanding feminist (feminism being a social barometer for the generation of 1968 that Huerta belonged to). *Incurable* is what you'd get if you strained Casanova's *Histoire de ma vie* through a structuralist sieve. It's what happens, according to Huerta, when "I hide the letter that I am in the text of the world."

"The world is a speck in the mirror" is the verse that lets us into that world, reduced to scale, shrunk down by the poet. This is what Raymond Queneau called "the evangelical world," a stage filled with the ghosts and replicas of poets and ideologues, musicians and warlords. Alberto Paredes, in *Una temporada de poesía* (2004), describes *Incurable* as the "museum of an era." Huerta captures that evangelical era via a procedure like the one Jean-Pierre Richard used in his Victor Hugo essay: he highlights certain poets' genius in order to show the heterogeneity of the period by separately identifying its constituent parts: objects, events, laws, people, questions. They might not sit well together, might even be hostile to one another, but they're the poem's "juice": the fragment seen as snapshot of the world. And through this procedure, "The world is a speck on the mirror" that slowly fades away as that which is "incurable" spreads.

Both representative and prophetic, *Incurable* is one of those books that, as Brodsky said in "Child of Civilization," combines "pure linguistic necessity" with "perishable flesh" out of an "urge to spare things of one's world, of one's personal civilization, one's own non-semantic continuum." It's a poem about civilized man ambling through the end of modernity, a circular journey, sometimes just a lunatic in his cell, a "trip around my room" where the mind is overcome by religious (but not mystic) trances. The book ends with a philosopher's propaedeutic ("serving as preliminary instruction") silence. It's a semantic boundary, one required by the agonist's actions and maladies: failed adolescent suicide, alcoholism. But it's not until "El fumador," a decidedly autobiographical poem included in *Hacia la superficie* (2002) that we get that glimpse of the poet's difficult life that some have tried in vain to find in *Incurable*.

Some of the book's chapters have a familial, genealogical—and even theatrical—dimension. This is true in the poetic dialogue with the father that requires the intervention of Becerra, imago of the older brother. And it runs from "El Tajín" to "La Venta" and from there to the "archeology" of the future's ruins, which in *Incurable* are connected to the poetic image of the father. "A las fórmulas de mi amor y de mi odio—la primitiva sal de mis vocabularios" ("To the expressions of my love and of my hate—the rock salt of my words"). It's inexplicable to me how some miscontrued sense of modesty keeps Mexican critics from analyzing or at least mentioning the relationship between poet son (David Huerta) and poet father (Efraín Huerta*) as if kinship in some way discredited one or the other of them (or both).

Those who see poetry as a path to asceticism or a search for silence, those who tear their hair out at *Incurable*, are the ones who will most benefit from reading to the end, since Huerta's Wittgensteinian demand for silence is filtered through a reading of Maurice Blanchot's *The Unavowable Community*, which justifies the entire enterprise. It's the story of a gestation, a novel that—like in an old novel—stumbles at times, drags at times, takes a few missteps; it's a poem that can be as boring as life itself or as oppressive as the times we live in; it's the torment of not-love that stands up to books like Lowry's *Under the Volcano*, which is what it should be measured against.

After *Incurable*, Huerta must have feared more than most either being paralyzed or pigeonholed by his masterpiece. Well, for those who found *Incurable* too hard to decipher, too Poundian, too epic, next came *Historia* (1990), whose poems—despite being written at the same time as *Incurable*—can almost be read as a form of therapy after a long illness. They're like a reduction of themes, a sort of diet. Clearly the poet wanted nothing more than not to be deemed so ill that he was "incurable." Since then Huerta's poetry has continued to evolve in new directions. *Lápices de antes* (1993) can be read like calligraphy, a book written to showcase the beauty of the act of writing; *La sombra de los perros* (1996) proves his skill in short verse. *La música de lo que pasa* (1997) takes another tack. The most "literary" of his poetry collections, this book faces up to the anguish of one's influences, including Walcott and Heaney as well as Char and Beckett (who's portrayed memorably).

Finally, in *El azul en la flama* (2002), Huerta emulates Gorostiza, employing a totally different rhetoric unlike anything he used from *Cuaderno de noviembre* to *Incurable*. The lexicon—which was almost lexicography—of *Incurable* is nowhere to be found. That loquacity is gone, and the poet's verse is free of the Lezama Lima-like "cosas egipcias de encierro y furia" ("Egyptian things of lockup and fury").

The time the civilized poet of *Incurable* takes to reach shore after his journey is a lifetime, an experience readable in emotional erring and mental disorder: "Me acerqué a la puerta de vidrio como si yo mismo fuera una ficción" ("I approached the glass door as if I myself were a fiction"). The poem's hero is probably a lyric poet but, as Paredes notes, he's a character with no specific, verifiable identity. Someone speaks in the poem, or maybe (like Ulysses) Nobody does. But that character has got a finger on the pulse of his nervous sensitivity, and he ends up recording the mood of the times, registering a psychological (Huerta wouldn't call it spiritual) landscape that's made of the texts and the ghosts of a small coterie of radicals who spanned the globe, here finally holding hands. *Incurable* is a civilized odyssey that takes maniacal, obsessive, compulsive possession of tomorrow, a book to be left out in the room, "cierto libro abierto en cierta página" ("a certain book left open to a certain page"), a manifestation of knowledge.

SELECTED BIBLIOGRAPHY
El jardín de la luz, UNAM, Mexico, 1972.
Cuaderno de noviembre, ERA, Mexico, 1976.
Huellas del civilizado, La Máquina de Escribir, Mexico, 1977.
Versión, FCE, Mexico, 1978 and 2005.
Incurable, ERA, Mexico, 1987.
Historia, Ediciones Toledo, Mexico, 1990.
Lápices de antes, Toque de Poesía, Mexico, 1993.
La sombra de los perros, Aldus, Mexico, 1996.
La música de lo que pasa, Conaculta, Mexico, 1997.
Calcinaciones y vestigios, ISSSTE, Mexico, 2000.
Hacia la superficie, Filodecaballos, Mexico, 2002.

El azul en la flama, ERA, Mexico, 2002.

La calle blanca, ERA, Mexico, 2006.

Before Saying Any of the Great Words, trans. Mark Schafer, Copper Canyon, 2009.

HUERTA, EFRAÍN

(Silao, Guanajuato, 1914 – Mexico City, 1982)

As Huerta's reputation as political poet par excellence fades, his work remains. And this has led to the inverse of what tends to happen, as his poetry is now freed of a burden. It's poetry you return to fondly, regardless of which of his three distinct poetic voices you want to hear: the blasphemous bard condemning a Mexico City that's disappeared; the tender, elegiac writer; or the eavesdropper whose "poeminimals" are like fireworks in the verbal sky, still lighting new flames today.

According to José Homero, in *La construcción del amor. Efraín Huerta, sus primeros años* (1991), Huerta laid out his poetics right from his first books, now collected in *Los hombres del alba* (1944). In this book, we see an everyday surrealist sans esoteric or subconscious pretensions who hits upon memorable elegiac images such as those seen in "La muchacha ebria." Huerta's poems, quite atypically for a Mexican poet, aren't tied to juvenile exploits and don't get bogged down in routine demagoguery or proselytizing. To wit, Octavio Paz,* honoring his childhood friendship with Huerta, said that even at his most propagandistic, one could appreciate the truth of his poetic voice.

The idea that Huerta was uncultured, as some of his most naïve readers claimed (at times to Huerta's delight), is absurd. On the contrary, he was a writer always concerned with his own learning and enlightenment, with enriching himself; he studied the Spanish lyric tradition and mastered it with grace and elegance. It's interesting, too, that a popular poet, a man who wrote about the soul and used common verse forms, was also the author of *El Tajín* (1963), a poem many Mexican poets—and many different *types* of Mexican poets—see as canonical, one of those foundational texts that calls poetry to take the stand as witness to the destruction of history, its ruinous destiny a motif. Huerta's work has spawned many offspring. And as his son, the poet David Huerta, asserted (with reference to a comment made by José Emilia Pacheco*), Huerta's descendents comprise "a whole school in Mexican poetry. Not the only one, of course, and at times not the most admirable—in large part because it can get bogged down in a visceral, alarmist rhetoric that hasn't polished its rough edges on the diamond dust of many of the poems of, say, Efraín Huerta."

In that vein, he wrote many of his best poems later in life. More than his declarations of love and hate for Mexico City, readers prefer works like "Praga, mi novia," "Sílabas por el maxilar de Franz Kafka," "Juárez Loreto," and "Barbas para desatar la lujuria," whose rhetoric *seems* easy to imitate but definitely is not. What he does is express a bohemian, libertarian, and, yes, chauvinist spirit, but only Huerta is able to do so in such a way that it sounds—at least to me—somehow surprising and refreshing. Jorge Portilla claimed in *Fenomenología del relajo* (1966) that Mexicans' rowdy, wild character would disappear with the arrival of the classless society, but Huerta's raucous linguistic freedoms can be read as analogous: both a public and private display of Mexican culture.

It would be unfair to ignore what Huerta's son—one of his most thoughtful critics—called in the prologue to *Poesía completa* (1988) his "political obstinacy." Despite having been thrown out of the Mexican Communist Party (PCM) in 1943, Huerta was still considered the official poet of Mexican Stalinism, so much so that he was one of the last western writers to dare to write a prayer for the dead for Stalin ten years after the 1956 Twentieth Congress of the Communist Party of the Soviet Union.

Amor patria mía (1980) is an outstanding addition to Huerta's oeuvre, a uniquely patriotic poem in the world of Latin American verse. Without abandoning the requisite solemn devotion, Huerta manages to combine the story of a tragic event—the excommunication of Father Miguel Hidalgo, leader of the Mexican War of Independence—with a lyrical resolution—a humorous speech on national history that a man delivers to his lover in bed. Huerta's playful poetic voice married well with the opening-up of Mexico in the 1980s. When opposition parties of both the left and right finally presented serious challenges to fifty years of Institutional Revolutionary Party (PRI) hegemony, the left had to abandon its crudest Stalinist customs, and began resurrecting popular mythology in more heterodox ways. The Mexican left, whose identity is so wrapped up in 1968, had in Huerta its national poet, with all the advantages and disadvantages that brought. He himself expressed it better than I ever could, in one of his "poeminimals": "Ahora me cumplen o me dejan como estatua" ("Now they respect me or they neglect me like a statue").

There's no doubt that his "poeminimals," published in several collections during the latter years of his life, will live on as the most memorizable part of his oeuvre, harkening back to the popular speech they're born of, as David Huerta notes. His is one of the most good-humored poetic universes in Mexican literature, his deeply gratifying "poeminimals" often comparable to aphorisms. I see his work as one of the few verbal treasures that—idiosyncratically, uncritically—I wouldn't hesitate to call national.

SELECTED BIBLIOGRAPHY

Poesía completa, ed. Martí Soler, prologue by David Huerta, FCE, Mexico, 1988.

José Homero, *La construcción del amor. Efraín Huerta, sus primeros años*, Concaulta, Mexico, 1991.

500,000 Azaleas: The Selected Poems of Efraín Huerta, trans. Jim Normington, Curbstone Press, 2000.

I

IBARGÜENGOITIA, JORGE
(Guanajuato, Guanajuato, 1928 – Madrid, Spain, 1983)

The key event in Ibargüengoitia's literary biography occurred just a few months after his birth on July 17, 1928: President Elect General Álvaro Obregón was murdered. The writer felt the circumstances surrounding the assassination to be so fascinating that before writing the novels *El atentado* (1962), *Los relámpagos de agosto* (1964; *The Lightning of August*, 1986), and *Maten al león* (1970; *Kill the Lion!*, 2008), he read countless memoirs—some vicious, some crude, some absurd, some important—of the Mexican Revolution's generals. The crime, committed by a deranged Catholic pretending to be a caricaturist, had many unforeseen consequences, not least of which was Ibargüengoitia's work, most notably *Los relámpagos de agosto*, which writer Francisco Liguori called the *Don Quixote* of Mexican literature.

That qualification, later amended by Gabriel Zaid's* comment that Ibargüengoitia hadn't exactly written a *Don Quixote* but *had* penned several "novelas ejemplares" worthy of Cervantes, is only a slight exaggeration. If we take the novel of the Mexican Revolution to be, at least for a time, the equivalent of our novel of chivalry, then there's no doubt that Ibargüengoitia was the first critic to parody and satirize the revolution's institutional administration, hanging it out to dry. Of course, he often disavowed the humorous nature of his work, saying he wasn't being funny, just telling it like it was.

If I were attempting (albeit unwisely) to decide who the most idiosyncratic Mexican writer was in 1932, I'd put my money on Ibargüengoitia, and here's why: while the obsession with writing a "modern" novel can be traced back to the *Contemporáneos* (ultra-modern *à la française*, readers if not of Proust then at least of Giraudoux), Ibargüengoitia's work—which seems like a natural outgrowth—had far less prestigious antecedents and less accepted premises. Essentially, Ibargüengoitia's work might never have come to exist, while novels like Salvador Elizondo's* *Farabeuf*, Juan Vicente Melo's* *La obediencia nocturna*, and Sergio Pitol's* *El desfile del amor* could have been foretold. The time was ripe for them to be written.

Ibargüengoitia was an outstanding student of Rodolfo Usigli* who refused to follow his teacher's tortuous path in Mexican theater. What he did imitate, however, was Usigli's stupendous crafting, in every piece he wrote, regardless of how trivial (considering what a prolific columnist he was, that verges on the amazing). But back to theater: if we heed what critics like Luis de Tavira and David Olguín said, and believe what playwrights obsessed with Mexican history (Vicente Leñero,* Ignacio Solares, Flavio González Mello) wrote, then it seems Ibargüengoitia's polemical theater career went from tale of woe to almost the road to perfection. Ibargüengoitia, if I understand correctly, brought us everything from Bernard Shaw to Bertold Brecht.

Usigli's *El gesticulador* (1937; *The Impostor*, 2006) is the story of an impostor who makes up lies and betrays the morally destitute—or mentally unstable—Revolution-cum-Government. But Ibargüengoitia's *El atentado* goes much further, telling a scandalous, revisionist tale. In this work, the glorified armed uprising of 1910 and its aftermath are portrayed as a pathetic, farcical bloodbath. Emmanuel Carballo,* acting as commissar, was right in 1964 when he lamented the fact that the Cubans had not perceived the ideological reach of the novel they'd awarded the Casa de las Américas. Unsurprisingly, the book went on to be censured successively by materialist, dialectical, and structuralist scholars. And as recently as 1982, critic José Joaquín Blanco* lavished well-deserved and enthusiastic praise on Ibargüengoitia, but also noted an "anarchizing fatalism" that he saw as likely motivated by ignorance of the "economic and social" factors that had made the Mexican Revolution possible. Nevertheless, reading Juan Villoro* and Víctor Díaz Arcinie-ga's excellent critical edition of *El atentado. Los relámpagos de agosto* (2002) confirms that numerous Mexican writers—from Sergio Pitol* to Fabrizio Mejía Madrid*—have read Ibargüengoitia profitably, and many have written pieces to honor him (myself included).

Ibargüengoitia's greatest achievement in Mexican journalism was to de-scribe everyday life as absolute adventure. There have been seven collec-tions of articles published since his death (*Autposias rápidas, Instrucciones para vivir en México, La casa de usted y otros viajes, Misterios de la vida di-aria, ¿Olvida usted su equipaje?*, and *Ideas en venta*), and all of them delight, showcasing Ibargüengoitia's unique voice. He's a writer who on the surface seems to speak only of himself, and joining him on "a trip around (his) neu-rosis" that goes from Coyoacán to Paris and from Cairo to Buenos Aires, is a sublime privilege. Although it seems as though he discusses a wide variety of topics, in fact everything boils down to two: the infinite idiocy of patriotism and the irreversible degradation of human geography, a subverted Eden he stoically resigned himself to inhabiting.

I still immensely enjoy reading Ibargüengoitia and treasure many of his articles. Even more than his sense of humor, I love the way he cap-tures the slow death of liberal thinking that has become—who would have guessed?—one of the most distressing trademarks of contemporary de-mocracy. Unfortunately, I don't know if his broad parody of Mexican life published in the old *Excelsior*—the sad but true history of Mexico during Luis Echeverría's presidency (1970–76)—would appeal to the paper's new readers. Back then the country was duped by cronyism; it might just be too remote a past. In light of things like the ongoing femicides in Ciu-dad Juárez, it's likely that Ibargüengoitia's *The Dead Girls* harkens back to a Mexico that's a bit too rustic, a place governed by simplistic, brutal laws and crass, ridiculous heroes.

Although cut short by an early death, Ibargüengoitia's oeuvre can be com-pared to the vast collection of articles by Carlos Monsiváis, probably the most representative figure of the rival school of thought. The 1964 tiff that put them at odds (Monsiváis defended Alfonso Reyes,* a victim of Ibargüen-goitia's caustic disdain) was symbolic of two opposing ways of reading the waning years of the Institutional Revolutionary Party (PRI)—all twenty-five of them. Despite the contrast between Monsiváis's polysemic reading and the almost Spartan simplicity of Ibargüengoitia's irony, both writers fed off of the same institutional "agelastia" (a term Guillermo Sheridan coined to describe the party's idiosyncratic solemnity, derived from the neologism "agelos" that Rabelais used to designate an inability to laugh). But while the Protestant Monsiváis saw the PRI's mythologizing of popular figures as a sign of democratic promise, Ibargüengoitia showed the reserved decorum of a provincial Catholic dandy horrified at the idea of the masses coming to level the playing field and destroy progress. By writing about himself, Ibargüengoitia expressed what the country felt; Monsiváis by contrast wrote all about Mexico, which was in fact a self-portrait.

Sheridan, who in many ways was Ibargüengoitia's understudy and heir, said that the success of both *Los relámpagos de agosto* and *Los pasos de López* (1982)—a hilarious revisionist history of Hidalgo's 1810 revolutionary plot—came not only from the author's use of the "superfluous" man as antihero but also his rejection of the metaphysical tyrants so typical of Latin American literature. Ibargüengoitia returned the genre to its rightful place, that of Valle-Inclán's *Tirano Banderas* (1926), opposing the nationalist archetypes that were already cropping up impassively in Carlos Fuentes's* books.

Ibargüengoitia wrote a fair few articles on the idea of fulfilling what he called "Quetzalcóatl's second prophecy." The Spaniards' arrival was the first; the second was the "disembarking" of newly mythologized Indians: neo-Aztec glorification. A bogus enterprise that horrified muralist José Clemente Orozco, this deification nevertheless spurred many solemn reflections and has continued to feed the fantasies of anthropologists, radicals, and posers. Unsurprisingly, it struck Ibargüengoitia, a man who suffered no identity crises, as risible. And although when he died he was still a distinguished contributor to the journal *Vuelta*, he never hid his discomfort at Octavio Paz's* "mystagogical" side, and he found the image of Susan Sontag with a copy of *The Labyrinth of Solitude* under one arm, agog at the mysteries of Mexico, quite hilarious.

By contrast, Evelyn Waugh, wrote a woefully critical book about Mexico (*Robbery Under Law*) that inspired writers as dissimilar as Elena Garro,* Ibargüengoitia, and Sergio Pitol. In it, he laments the wasteland he was horrified to discover during his begrudging and ill-timed visit in 1938, during the Catholic persecution. He finds absolutely nothing poetic about the lunar landscape; this he makes perfectly clear, calling Mexico dry and cracked and asking readers in the prologue: "Is civilization, like a leper, beginning to rot at its extremities?"

Given the soulless prostitute murders portrayed in *The Dead Girls* (1977), I wonder if Ibargüengoitia-the-misanthrope's view of Mexico was not quite similar to Waugh's. It's no wonder that he saw humor as the opposite of affectation, which he said was typical of the middle classes and which, in another century, was more appropriately called philistinism. We call Ibargüengoitia's humor "black" only for lack of a better term; Zaid called it Nietzschean in its revelatory dimension. Regardless, it's what he used to populate what Waugh saw mercilessly as a wasteland.

SELECTED BIBLIOGRAPHY

Los relámpagos de agosto, Casa de las Américas, La Habana, 1964; Joaquín Mortiz, Mexico, 1965.

La ley de Herodes, Joaquín Mortiz, Mexico, 1967.

Maten al león, Joaquín Mortiz, Mexico, 1969.

Viajes por la América ignota, Joaquín Mortiz, Mexico, 1972.

Esas ruinas que ves, Novaro, Mexico, 1975; Joaquín Mortiz, Mexico, 1981.

Las muertas, Joaquín Mortiz, Mexico, 1977.

Dos crímenes, Joaquín Mortiz, Mexico, 1979.

Los pasos de López, Oceáno, Mexico, 1982; Joaquín Mortiz, Mexico, 1987.

Autopsias rápidas, ed. Guillermo Sheridan, Vuelta, Mexico, 1988.

Teatro completo, vols I, II and III. Joaquín Mortiz, Mexico, 1989–90.

Instrucciones para vivir en México, ed. Guillermo Sheridan, Joaquín Mortiz, Mexico, 1990.

La casa de usted y otros viajes, ed. Guillermo Sheridan, Joaquín Mortiz, Mexico, 1991.

Misterios de la vida diaria, ed. Aline Davidoff, Joaquín Mortiz, Mexico, 1997.

¿Olvida usted su equipaje?, ed. Aline Davidoff, Joaquín Mortiz, Mexico, 1997.

Ideas en venta, ed. Aline Davidoff, Joaquín Mortiz, Mexico, 1997.

El atentado. Los relámpagos de agosto, ed. Juan Villoro and Víctor Díaz Arciniega, ALLCA XX/FCE/UNESCO/Conaculta, Madrid, 2002 (Archivos Collection).

The Dead Girls, trans. Asa Zatz, Avon Books, 1983.

Two Crimes, trans. Asa Zatz, Chatto and Windus, 1984.

The Lightning of August, trans. Irene del Corral, Bard/Avon, 1986.

The Impostor, trans. Ramón Layera, Latin American Literary Review, 2006.

Kill the Lion, trans. Helen Lane, FCE, 2008.

J

JANDRA, LEONARDO DA

(Pichucalco, Chiapas, 1951)

Those of us who were around when da Jandra appeared on the Mexican literary scene look back on those years warmly, even gratefully. After his early
novels, which some of us read in a state of absolute wonder, in the early '90s
da Jandra himself became protagonist of quite a tale. He and his wife—painter
Agar García—carved out and lived a fantasy that lent some much-needed
color to the decade. Since 1979 the couple have lived an isolated life on near-
deserted Cacaluta Beach in Oaxaca, ascetic Robinson Crusoes with no running water or electricity. But unlike many garden-variety utopians who took
the road to transgression or otherness after 1968, da Jandra did not return to
the city empty-handed after a stint on mushrooms, his revolutionary ideas
cauterized. Instead, he turned out a fictional creation—the *Entrecruzamientos*
trilogy, published between 1986 and 1990. Its originality lies not in its themes
(civilized man going "back to nature," the search for alternative spirituality
in the face of bankrupt Western logic) but in the almost "solar" spirit and
refreshing brazenness with which he pours the new wine of his "lost years"
of post-Marxist philosophy into the old wineskins of education, of the chasm
between Western Athens and Jerusalem, and the "toltecáyotl" (the supposed
corpus of Mesoamerican philosophical tradition), that substratum of "Mexicanness" that da Jandra the Hispanophile began searching for back then.

One result of da Jandra's secluded life in Cacaluta was that it brought on, as is natural with those who leave the world behind without disconnecting entirely from the current century, a desire to commune with others. And that desire turned the "savage" into a noble, the deserter into a gentleman. For five years, da Jandra and Agar—by then public guardians of Huatulco National Park—became the unique hosts of their own Oaxaca-style "Decades of Pontigny." They'd invite a group of rash and eccentric writers and artists to come and eat, drink, and debate on the beach, to do nothing but spend their days talking under the sun about all things human and divine. I was lucky enough to attend once, and I doubt we reached any earth-shattering conclusions or came up with any ideas worthy of going down in the annals. In fact, I'd give two-to-one odds that if any of our discussions had been recorded, they wouldn't be worth listening to; it was just a bunch of overexcited scholarly chatter, enlivened further by the fact that it took place at a time when literary chatter was not so rampant as it is now. I have no idea if those gatherings helped da Jandra in his ecological cause, as they were theoretically intended to do. What I can say for certain is that da Jandra, a sort of Mexican B. Traven (pen name of the anonymous author of *The Treasure of the Sierra Madre*), was inspired to organize these get-togethers by noble, selfless, childish glee and the genuine desire to see his "city friends" swim on his almost private beach on the Mexican Pacific.

In time, novels—some as finely crafted as *Arousiada* (1995), written in half Spanish, half Galician—weren't enough to satisfy da Jandra, who longed to expound and to teach. He was spurred on by his failed attempts at writing German-style philosophical treatises, *Totalidad, Seudototalidad y parte*, and *Tanatomicón*, both written under the pen name of S. C. Chuco. After that, he turned to a form of expression more befitting his roving mind: the pure essay. For this, he adopted a more characteristically Hispanic personality, that of the philosophizing prognosticator. Which leads us to *La hispanidad, fiesta y rito. Una defensa de nuestra identidad* (2004), a book that often falls short of but sometimes surpasses its intimidating title (*Hispanicity, Celebration and Rite: A Defense of Our Identity*).

Before delving into an analysis of the book I should state that, despite dusting off his copies of Marx's *Grundrisse* and Engels's *Anti-Düring* (virtually obligatory for those of his generation) in search of the sacred beetles of wisdom, da Jandra was never a Marxist. He was immune to the German's charms after a diet rich in Unamuno and Ortega. And yet you'd be hard-pressed to find anyone less open to liberalism in any of its various forms. The predictable and perhaps lamentable result of all this is that da Jandra ended up taking the path of traditionalism. Anyone on the Mexican intellectual scene nostalgic for Ramiro de Maeztu or José Vasconcelos (Sr. and/or Jr.) can breathe a sigh of relief, for in *La hispanidad, fiesta y rito*, they've been brought back to life.

If we ignore the insurmountable contradictions that at times render the book almost unreadable, the argument is actually rather straightforward. Given that "Spain is no longer the problem, and Europe is no longer the solution," as da Jandra says, the spiritual reserves of Hispanic identity have moved to Mexico. And since Mexico is virtually collapsing as a result of de-Mexicanization, folks have decided to cross the ole Rio Grande to set up shop in the US. The Cosmic Race is currently comprised of Mexicans (and other Hispanics) who victoriously invade the empire, and anyone fearing the loss of our collective identity should have faith in these new settlers. Chicanos, da Jandra concludes, will set us free.

If the *Diccionario de escritores mexicanos* is correct in stating that da Jandra got his PhD in philosophy in Galicia (Franco's homeland) during the waning years of Francoism, then it seems quite a Freudian slip for him to have neglected to explain to his readers (who, given the pedagogical nature of the book, I assume are young) the origins of the contemporary notion of Hispanicity. da Jandra's inspiration does not stem so much from Unamuno (who managed to give it a pluralistic slant) as it does from Maeztu. And Maeztu, as Ambassador to Argentina during the 1930s, took his cues from Father Zacarías de Vizcarra (who in turn was inspired by the prophecies of Saint Bridget), who saw Hispanicity—the beacon of the apostle Santiago (James)—as the way to free Catholics from the liberal, democratic plague of the French Revolution. Maeztu died at the start of the Spanish Civil War and became a patron martyr of Spanish fascism, which after the defeat of the Axis Powers in 1945 took root in Spain via a slightly more benevolent brand of national Catholicism, thanks to Franco's prudence.

Now, I'm not here to find fault with da Jandra for searching out new ideas in old books, turning to Menéndez Pelayo, Juan Valera, and that implacable theocrat Juan Donoso Cortés—grandfather of the Nazi right—to resolve the conflicts of Mexican identity ("mexicanidad"). Nor do I censure him for having found inspiration in the "politically incorrect" ideology of Maeztu's Hispanism. My point is simply that the whole identity minefield almost always stirs up fanaticism and moral condemnation; and that's critical because *La hispanidad, fiesta y rito* is full of "good vibes" and "positive energy" that could easily throw unwary readers off. That's why da Jandra pays his respects to Américo Castro and the Spain of three cultures (Jewish, Muslim, Christian), when it's clear that this new Mexican traditionalist agrees with Ángel Ganivet (although mistakenly attributing the idea to Unamuno) that "the most important philosophy of any nation is its own, albeit far inferior to the imitation of foreign philosophies," such as that of Ortega, who would have "turned his back on the purest manifestation of empathy, the utterly Hispanic linking of the aesthetic and the ritual." This brings us to those who believe that "the concept of Hispanicity both predates the national reality of Spain (as a nation) and extends far beyond it." Let me make clear that it's not Maeztu I'm quoting here, but da Jandra.

Each time he gets trapped in the dead end of the most antiquated Hispanism, da Jandra manages to back out, making multicultural concessions to and professions of democratic faith that essentially invalidate many of his initial arguments. All of which adds up to *La hispanidad, fiesta y rito* containing a series of platitudes and a lot of drivel, occasionally interspersed with penetrating observations. Although his take on *El laberinto de la soledad* is a comic error (taking literally Paz's metaphor of Mexicans as "sons of bitches"), da Jandra's mestizo-philia is as plausible as the Institutional Revolutionary Party (PRI) mestizo speeches that helped erode the racism of Mexican society.

But indigenism is what's really a Hispanist's bag and—after forgiving ideological racist Guillermo Bonfil Batalla—that's what gets da Jandra into hot water. Once he's made the analogy between Nazism and Aztec human sacrifice, da Jandra comes out with a page of prose worthy of Vasconcelos himself. I can't resist the temptation to quote here. "Indigenism is rich in authentic Mexicanness. There is the headstrong will to exist, there is art and talent and more than anything, there is the sacred. Nevertheless, the indigenous soul was denied some of the most important evolutionary values and violently deprived of the expressions of civility that push men beyond the horde and lead them to share and respect the same God, the same Constitution and the same human and divine laws. To date, there has been no point in searching for revolutionary morality, fair and representative political consciousness or any new science in the hatred and misery eating away at indigenism. What's worse, despite all the rites and all the celebrations, the indigenous soul had none of the love and forgiveness that consecrate the everlasting devotion to the Holy Mother and the Son of God. Oppressed and discriminated against, the indigenous inverted the morals of the Son of God incarnate: where there should have been love and goodness, instead there continued to be resentment and hatred."

Now, I'm no indigenist. I'm not a fan of any of its variants, and I'm skeptical of any and all of the ethical, political, and religious sanctity attributed as some sort of birthright to Mexican indigenous groups. And that's precisely why reading such a blatantly racist paragraph—a veritable excommunication of the indigenous, condemning them to a life as an erring horde—I'm even more convinced of the pernicious conglomeration of interests that lie behind any and all "identity" fanaticism, whether proclaimed by subcomandante Marcos or sustained by da Jandra. On some points, you'd be forgiven for thinking that EZLN spokesman and the Hispanist philosopher were one and the same. After reading *La hispanidad, fiesta y rito* it strikes me as critical that the liberal concept of the individual and citizen not be forgotten; that's the only way out of the dark cave of the sometimes traditional, sometimes revolutionary, always abominable identity claptrap.

The biggest weakness of this anti-liberal manifesto, however, lies not in its re-positing of Maeztu's doctrine nor in its Neo-Vasconcelos stance but in its very conception of identity. Drunk on Hispanism, da Jandra is not overly concerned about Mexicanness itself, given that he sees Mexicans as (to use Roger Bartra's* terms) a mutant species somewhere between non-beings and cosmic achievements, an entomological accident that will abandon its defective corporal prison and return to the cosmos. da Jandra offers not a single example of any gastronomical, linguistic, poetic, or athletic particularity that might distinguish Mexicans from Spaniards or Salvadorans, as did Samuel Ramos and Octavio Paz* before him (for better or for worse). And if he doesn't go into details, it's because he knows—as do most identity ideologues—that there is no identity; it doesn't exist. It's just a political weapon disguised as a metaphysical concept, and as such identity is just a word, as hard to grasp and easy to espouse as "dialectics," "pseudo-totality," and "absoluteness," concepts that once flummoxed the young da Jandra.

If you interrogate moderately educated people about national identity, their answers tend to be vague, melodramatic exaggerations that are, when it comes right down to it, correct: the concept inevitably harkens back to folklore and patriotic traditions encouraged by the State. The fact that da Jandra's philosophical readings haven't gotten him any further than popular opinion is proof of both how phony the supposed intellectual complexity of the concept of identity is, and the political ease with which it appears when a liberal society is new, or weak, or threatened. da Jandra feebly associates identity with rites and celebrations, taking an idea in *The Labyrinth of Solitude* that Paz had taken from French culturalism. Without going into the role of the sacred in modern culture (as did Romanian scholar Mircea Eliade, Italian writer Roberto Calasso, and Argentine poet H. A. Murena), da Jandra is content to talk about ritual, which leaves him drowning in trite folklore. He goes to the US in search of celebrations and rites practiced by Mexicans living there and finds the Cosmic Race, which will take the baton of Hispanicity by way of Broadway and Cinco de Mayo celebrations. Maybe it's going overboard to tell da Jandra that what he, as a tourist, takes as "Mexicanness" is in fact US ethnic pluralism, and that few things are in fact more profoundly "American" (read: of the US) than César Chavez's labor movement, the "Spiritual Plan of Aztlán," or a "national Chicano consciousness," as gringo as the Black Power movement or affirmative action. Erudite ignorance and making the sign of the cross appear to be the preferred stances of the prophets of Hispanicity when confronted by the Protestant demon of the US. da Jandra carts out all the clichés about the Evil Empire, brought back to life by anti-liberal ideologues. For him, the United States is a vast empty continent where everyone worships the God of money, the land that the Cosmic Race has been tasked with redeeming.

da Jandra does get one up on Vasconcelos, who didn't envision a Mexamerica to be populated with red-skinned Atlases who, as migrating "wetbacks" are chided for having left their Hispanic side back in old Mexico.

Instead they turn up in LA as bloodthirsty worshippers of the Aztec god of war, Huitzilopochtli. Like all identity ideologues, da Jandra projects his own zealous, privileged, ethnicist fantasies (in this case, the Chicano neo-Aztec) onto society—comprised in fact of Mexican workers searching not for a lost identity but for a living wage.

Despite his treatise-writing inclination, da Jandra has never been a systematic soul, either in person or in his texts. In fact he's more the opposite. When I first met him, it was hard to find a more vibrantly contradictory character in all of Mexico, intemperate in the aggressively Iberian manner of José Bergamín, a guy who could be utterly charming when he let up with the theory. Eclectic and kinetic, he'd have been unbearable as a professor or guru. But by the same token, his defects turned him into a novelist who delighted in telling tales of dialectics and maieutics. That all seems so long ago now. In dialogues between Eugenio and Don Ramón in *Entrecruzamientos*, Hispanicity was one of the topics under discussion. Today it seems clear that, like Vasconcelos, da Jandra will one day lament having wasted so much time wandering the desert of Reason when what he really should have been doing was reciting the rosary. It won't be the first time a rebel searches his soul and then returns meekly to the flock professing his good faith, hurling anathemas in the name of saving souls, whether they be of godless Indians or of Mexicans who've sold *their* souls to the demon of liberalism.

SELECTED BIBLIOGRAPHY
Entrecruzamientos, Almadía/Conaculta, Oaxaca, 2004.
La hispanidad, fiesta y rito, Plaza y Janés, Mexico, 2004.

K

KRAUZE, ENRIQUE
(Mexico City, 1947)

"Yes—writing lives is the devil," said Virginia Woolf, and this quotation in turn opens *Writing Lives. Principia Biographica*, by Leon Edel, the most brilliant contemporary biographer. It's an affirmation relevant to the eight biographies Enrique Krauze wrote of the Mexican Revolution's caudillos, which kick up a "devil" of a storm of literature, biography, history, and politics. Krauze's books have been well received by the public, but not so much by critics, for reasons ranging from a generalized scorn (from both literary and historical circles) for mass-market books to the backlash from those who reject Krauze's liberal politics.

Krauze writes biography and not history, and it's important to make a Plutarchan distinction between the two fields; he follows the rich Anglo-Saxon biographical tradition. So my comments begin by fully accepting the biographical nature of his books, as well as their essentially literary style. His decision to write about the icons of the Mexican Revolution— Porfirio Díaz (*Místico de la autoridad*), Francisco I. Madero (*Místico de la libertad*), Emiliano Zapata (*El amor a la tierra*), Francisco Villa (*Entre el ángel y el fierro*), Venustiano Carranza (*Puente entre siglos*), Plutarco Elías Calles (*Reformar desde el origen*), Álvaro Obregón (*El vértigo de la victoria*), and Lázaro Cárdenas (*El general misionero*)—could have been seen as an exercise in redundancy. After all, with the exception of Díaz, isn't this the twentieth-century pantheon? There have been thousands of pages written on each of them, covering their ideological and rebellious views, from the most academic and scholarly to the most trivially anecdotal. Krauze was swimming against the tide. But biography, as Italian historian Arnaldo Momigliano said, is the art of selection; it's paradoxically a genre founded on impossibility: really, the lives of men cannot be *told*. And although the idea of writing the biography of B. Traven or some obscure Latin scholar seems complicated—searching for details of the life of a man who wanted to be anonymous or one who had fallen into oblivion—it's even harder when you consider the plethora of information, a veritable library of Babel—out there about history's heroes. But Krauze did what he set out to do: write biography. It's a genre that hasn't fared as well as it should have in Spanish. Maybe our reservations about biography stem from the Counter-Reformation, from the indignant feeling that judging a man's life is not the task of man but of God. And contemporary Mexican scholars have now put history (and its collective, universal laws) in the place of God. Even on a rhetorical level, biography leaves people uneasy when compared to intellectual certainties.

But biography is a *literary* genre. People forget that "literature" is not synonymous with "invention." And Krauze's *Biografía del poder* (1987; *Biography of Power*, 1997) is a literary, rather than historical or political, work. It's blessed with masterful rhetoric and makes no attempt to be anything other than a book about politicians' passions. Eight *historical* lives, mediated by a biographer who also successfully arouses his readers' morbid curiosity. It matters not that the lives of these heroes are already in the public domain. For those who meddle in others' lives, there's no such thing as too much information. It's important to point out that Krauze isn't attempting to shift our historical perspective on the Mexican Revolution or provide any complete and definitive version of events. What he wants to do is shine the light of biography onto *individual lives*—and thanks to historicism, placing those two words side by side is no longer considered as redundant as it should be. The light of biography, as I said, is based on selection, on taking into account the shadows, backgrounds, and lines on the faces of those who have disappeared. As literature, *Biografía del poder* gets to determine its own aims. With each biography, the historical figure is brought back to life; each man breaks free from the "universality" of spirit that Benedetto Croce believed in. *Biografía del poder* has many outstanding formal qualities: it's classically concise, expressively restrained, and treats its readers intelligently. And I want to highlight this since no one has commented on it, as if historiography, too, did not require talented writing.

Krauze describes an almost planetary system orbiting the star of power, with each of the eight "planets" traveling its course of light or darkness. It's been said that he didn't uncover any new information. But he *does* include some quite notable findings (such as that of Madero's spiritualist diary), so the only thing that snub does is to show scorn for the importance of good style, and the ability of graceful, elegant writing to make sense of history. *Biografía del poder* is not the first and won't be the last contribution to Mexican Revolution history. But it is one of its more lucid moments, and its lucidity stems from examining the gravitational pull guiding each of the planets' movements. Krauze is not always on the mark, but he's not aiming to be definitive. To produce skillful sketches, he searches every face for signs of existential contradiction and then contemplates historical variants. And what is biography, if not an attempt to uncover the role of determination versus fate?

If power is the magnetic star in *Biografía del poder*, the most novel aspect of its planetary system is the one concerning the light and darkness of religious faith. The eight revolutionaries (for they were all revolutionaries, just as they were all martyrs, dictators, liberators, and often murderers) swing like pendulums between "motherland or death," with religiosity as an essential presence in their lives. And frankly, it's about time someone rejected the Jacobin underpinnings of our historical tradition and delved into more sacred and liturgical sources. Krauze, along with Max Weber, takes the view of the spirit connecting man with time, the hero with the dominant society that eventually sacrifices him. But this isn't any Thomas Carlyle-style concept of hero worship; Krauze forges his own way, searching out historical missions that lend his writing an intimate tone. His biographies weave together strong foundations with multiple instances of chance and coincidence. They examine the symptoms: Díaz's authoritarian mysticism, Zapata's love of the primitive, and Calles's fanatical anti-fanaticism are all parts of a sentimental education that affected the course of our history. Madero is the most clear-cut example. Krauze unveils his belief in "spirits" (and the need to consult them) as the secret decision-maker behind Madero's whole democratic ideology. Almost as surprising is some of the information in Carranza's biography: his heartfelt devotion to the legacy of the nineteenth-century War of Reform reveals a side of him that's been effaced by both his official mummification and aggrieved victims. And with writers Martín Luis Guzmán* and Fernando Benítez,* Krauze here continues to tell the tale of one of the most tragic, absurd, and intoxicating chapters in Mexican history: Carranza's assassination at Tlaxcalantongo.

Rooting through the hypocritically secular official story in which archetypes lose all complexity and have all the depth of cardboard props, Krauze searches for the origins of their political myths. He doesn't simply deny the myths; rather, he takes them on and tries to unravel them. There can be no one "true" Villa or Carranza, because like it or not, certain lives simply belong to the rough (and irrational) seas of history. Suetonius thought Caesar might be lying; the truth is fickle stuff.

Biografía del poder is partly about the adventures of Mexico and partly about the political legacy of those caudillos. And now things are going to get complicated, since it's time to talk politics. The wealth of recent historiography on the Mexican Revolution is encouraging. The official folklore has been dead for twenty years, exposed as a farce with no stage and no actors, just props. But critical versions that challenged the state, especially post-1968, tended to be ideologically messianic and lacking in empiricism. The sheer plurality of phenomena—the multiple revolutions that occurred between 1910 and 1940—couldn't be explained by the theory of permanent revolution, nor did they fit in with the concept of the "cycle of bourgeois revolutions." But we've moved on, and since that time, Ramón Eduardo Ruiz has questioned the revolutionary nature of the insurrection; Arnaldo Córdova has differentiated political transformations from social ones; and François-Xavier Guerra has examined the decisive role of the Porfirian elite. Also remarkable are: Friedrich Katz's enthralling investigation into the importance of foreign policy and foreign countries in regard to the Mexican Revolution; F. J. Schryer's findings on the social structure of the revolution's armies; Antonio García de León's work on rebellion in Chiapas; and Jorge Aguilar Mora's depiction of a different side of Obregón. These are just some of the contributions that mark the end of the long romanticized historiography of the Mexican Revolution.

So how does *Biografía del poder* fit into this new, revisionist intellectual climate? If we take Adolfo Gilly's *La revolución interrumpida* to be the last romanticized study of the revolution, a book that was unforgettable for its epic tone but brought down by its dogmatic legality, we can see *Biografía del poder* as a classicist work. Krauze goes back to a view of history based on the idea of actions speaking for themselves. As a biographer, Krauze makes no attempt to pawn off ideology as history. And therein might lie the book's weakness. For it seems that its title contradicts its spirit, if what we're expecting is for *Biografía del poder* to be an anatomy of power. In Díaz and Cárdenas (the builders of the State), Villa and Zapata (the people's rebels), Madero and Carranza (martyrs to legitimacy), and Obregón and Calles (caudillos) we see a craving for that brand of glorious, erratic power that only a revolution can induce. But beyond that obvious historical commonality, each biography reveals an inscrutable *individual* passion, one that's utterly unique despite the author's attempt to collectively baptize them all in the font of power.

Krauze said recently that his generation was more enthralled by power than by culture. If that's the case, *Biografía del poder* is a book by a writer sucked in by the disgraceful magnetic attraction of that star, about those who died in its flames. But each of the eight paths to immolation, whether quick or slow, is willfully diverse. If power is everything, then nothing is powerful. So Krauze's biographies turn out to be the adventures of a biographer among the human and political passions consumed during an age that was both historical and apocalyptic, a time when everything had just died and nothing was yet born.

Biografía del poder depicts the Mexican Revolution's state-endorsed pantheon of heroes (Díaz being earlier). It's important to note that in Mexico, until recently, the "state" was inextricably linked to the social, the civil, and the collective unconscious of a generation. Krauze doesn't try to demystify any of this—that would be an impossible task. He accepts the myth with scientific shrewdness and takes it apart with beautiful prose that's both historically and stylistically outstanding. But he runs a political risk. Krauze is an intellectual who thinks solely in terms of the political world, and politics is unforgiving. So *Biografía del poder* will likely be taken as a revision of the pantheon, given that he recognized its existence and perhaps even its validity when he took on the project.

By way of antidote, then, it's interesting to reflect on one of his inclusions and one of his exclusions. The former, Porfirio Díaz, president and dictator from 1884–1911, makes it impossible to sustain the idea that Mexico was in some sort of Dark Ages prior to the revolution, given the advances made during Porfirian rule. The latter concerns a ninth biography that was not included because the man resolutely refused to exercise any power: social reform activist and anarchist Ricardo Flores Magón.

We'll never resolve the dispute between Droysen and Burkhardt about the nature of biography. For the former it would be impossible to write a biography of power, since men like Caesar and Frederick the Great belong to history, not to men. Droysen felt that biographies could only be written about failed men or adventurers—those who belonged solely to themselves, and by extension, to us. But Burkhardt felt that without the biographies of great men the Renaissance would have been impossible and the divine would never be seen as a human quality. And therein lies the creative nucleus of Krauze's interpretations, the enthralling territory where the political animal sounds out the limits of his own existence.

Krauze reconquers biography for Mexican culture. Writing for a large audience while upholding high literary standards is rare indeed; it brings back to life that humanistic passion that is the art of written conversation. "Yes—writing lives is the devil," and Krauze wrote them while avoiding all the traps lain by the devils of power and their signatories. (1988; *Servidumbre y grandeza de la vida literaria*, 1998)

In the time between *Caudillos culturales de la Revolución mexicana* (1977) and *Siglo de caudillos* (1994), Krauze went from meeting his academic publication quota to passionately exceeding the obligations of a historian read by thousands of Mexicans. And it should be noted that he became popular by voicing opinions that were, if not blasphemous, at least vexing to a political and intellectual class numbed by either Marxist dogmas or by the bureaucratic formulas prescribed by the Institutional Revolutionary Party (PRI) regime.

In 1982 Krauze questioned how wise it was to nationalize the private banking system, thereby sealing his intellectual fate. But by choosing to be unpopular with the party faithful, he gained the considerable audience of ordinary citizens he now enjoys. And along with his moral courage came stylistic evolution: since then his writing has improved consistently, perhaps because he knows his readers appreciate his clarity and rhetorical skill. Of course, Krauze is not exempt from the dangers inherent in the didactic fervor that inspires him, but *Siglo de caudillos* demonstrates that by courting the public he's chosen to hone his prose rather than dumb it down or use it to pontificate.

Biografía del poder was a work full of historiographic findings presented by a spirited historian who took the profiles of heroes and turned them into humans, rather than gods. With *Siglo de caudillos*, Krauze embarked on a perhaps more grandiose undertaking: it's the work of a historian seeking his peers' understanding. That's a double-edged sword, and that's how the book will be judged by academics and future critics.

Daniel Cosío Villegas was a historian who exploded onto the twentieth century intent on transgressing, determined to pillage graves and clear away cobwebs of history, indifferent to the cries of lost souls, wanting to wake the vampire from his millennial slumber. His books on the Porfiriato (the Porfirio Díaz period, 1876–1910) and the Restored Republic of 1867 finally and fully discredited the old nonsense about Mexico being in the dark ages until the Revolution. Cosío Villegas opened the doors and windows of the house of horrors that was the nineteenth century, but after correcting the public's misconception, he simply cataloged what he'd found. And while we were airing out the nineteenth century, his soul flew out the open windows. In *Siglo de caudillos*, Krauze—one of his disciples—managed to trap it.

The nineteenth century is incredibly hard to pin down, vacillating as it does between high tragedy and low farce. In that ebb and flow it's hard to distinguish between figures who have been presented as cardboard cutouts. Even well-educated Mexicans see men like Hidalgo, Morelos, Iturbide, Santa Anna, Juárez, Maximiliano, and Porfirio Díaz as symbols rather than historical realities: bravery, martyrdom, revelry, outrage, intransigence, reverie, authority. Many Mexicans are unaware of how astonishingly rich the cast of nineteenth-century players really was: names like Abad y Quepo,

Guerrero, Mier y Terán, Victoria, Bravo, Gómez Farías, the Lerdo de Tejada brothers, Santos Degollado, and Ocampo mean little or nothing to most of us. So *Siglo de caudillos* will fascinate the curious, surprise the ignorant and order the partial or confused memory of readers with a panorama that allows anyone to reconstruct the century, following Krauze's detailed, straightforward instructions.

So what path does Krauze take, after initially following the road set out by Cosío Villegas? First he delves deep into the history of ideas—which Cosío Villegas wasn't ready to do—starting with the motives behind our War of Independence, which has fascinated an increasing number of scholars over the past 25 years. Then, he sets things straight in regard to the vast and questionable bibliography on General Santa Anna. And when he gets to Juárez, Krauze rolls up his sleeves, offering a succinct biography of the first Indian president that is reminiscent of Lytton Strachey's expressionistic sketches, though his Victorians compare unfavorably to the complex historical arrogance of the Oaxacan autocrats of the best chapters of *Siglo de caudillos*.

Krauze couldn't resist the temptation to locate a sort of republican Arcadia prior to our secular history, idealizing the Restored Republic (1867–76) as a democratic space that Mexicans lost and forgot. *Siglo de caudillos* explains this decade prior to Díaz's "Porfiriato" as a productive, fertile time not exempt from authoritarian tensions. And his examination of the Porfiriato is a careful call to reconciliation. Fully aware of symbolic importance, Krauze knows that as long as Díaz's remains continue to be "exiled" in Paris, Mexico's historical memory will not rest easy.

But the main players in *Siglo de caudillos* are the conservative Lucas Alamán and liberal José María Luis Mora, more like brothers than enemies. In the ideological conflict that unites and divides them, Krauze finds the key to unlocking the nineteenth century, weaving an imaginary thread through other pairs, such as Juárez and Díaz, who resolved their tensions successfully, and Iturbide and Santa Anna, who didn't.

Krauze is a scholar interested in his subjects' roots, and he bases *Siglo de caudillos* on race, a historiographic choice in line with the century he's covering. Not long ago, when there was more Marxist history around, that choice would have been considered scandalous. But for Krauze the nineteenth century is a time of criollo failure, indigenous courage, and mestizo achievement. In this way, too, he's a popular historian for whom biography is the nexus that explains the caudillos he finds so fascinating. (1994; *Servidumbre y grandeza de la vida literaria*, 1998)

SELECTED BIBLIOGRAPHY

Siglo de caudillos, Tusquets Editores, Mexico, 1994.
Biografiía del poder, Tusquets Editores, Mexico, 1997.
La presencia del pasado, Tusquets, Mexico, 2006.
Retratos personales, Tusquets, Mexico, 2007.
De héroes y mitos, Tusquets, Mexico, 2010.
Mexico: Biography of Power, trans. Hank Heifetz, Harper Perennial, 1997.
Redeemers: Ideas and Powers in Latin America, trans. Hank Heifetz, Harper, 2011.

L

LEDUC, RENATO
(Mexico City, 1897 – 1986)

An uninhibited bohemian who drank anything in sight, Leduc was a journalist and poet who brought street life to Mexican literature, introducing that seedy side of things that modernism saw as unwholesome and that writer Salvador Novo* began celebrating with outrageous extravagance. Leduc's prose was unlike any at the time, as all encompassing as the city itself. Rough, it was a place with no ideological redemption or moral culpability. Unrefined, it vindicated the beauty, richness, and wit of slang. Ironic, it let a bunch of venereal riffraff into high society's dapper literary salons. But the reputation of this popular poet, columnist, bullfighting critic, and epicurean of the world eclipses his truly imaginative prose.

Leduc's writing is gold in a plunderer's sack. *Los banquetes* (1932 and 1944) is a just sample of his wide-ranging and yet-to-be collected oeuvre, in which attempting to distinguish between genres often proves quixotic. Tempestuous reflections written from the bar of a cantina, *Los banquetes* is a philosophy of life, an example of a clinical eye and the love of words, regardless of origin [. . .]. Story, treaty, digression, it's a critic's protest against the aesthetic, spiritual and political conventions of the time. Gide-like sensuality and political millenarianism are mocked by this carefree cynic and admirer of Henry Miller and Charlie Chaplin (to whom he dedicates his third and final dialogue, in the name of heroism) who saw style as the best map to guide one through the binge of life. (*Antología de la narrativa mexicana del siglo XX*, I, 1989)

SELECTED BIBLIOGRAPHY
Obra literaria, prologue by Carlos Monsiváis, FCE, Mexico, 2000.

LEÑERO, VICENTE
(Guadalajara, Jalisco, 1933)

A loner, Leñero was never part of his generation's cliques or their obsessions. While those who were strictly his contemporaries opted to go off on metaphysical and sensorial quests, he stuck to a meticulous brand of realism favorably influenced by the *nouveau roman*, new journalism, and the Catholic novel. With *Asesinato* (1985), he attained a degree of hyperrealism I have no qualms about qualifying as perfect. It's a painstakingly documented reconstruction of the murders of ex-governor of Nayarit Flores Muñoz and his wife in Mexico City in 1978, a "novel sans fiction" that has nothing to envy in Truman Capote's *In Cold Blood*.

Leñero had already begun to show signs of stylistic perfection in *La gota de agua* (1983), the story of a humdrum event (the lack of water at the writer's home) told with such narratological intensity that it reads like a nail-biting, intricately woven detective novel. *La gota de agua* is an accomplished mocking of the old "new" French novel.

There's no doubt that Leñero is the consummate stylistic craftsman of Mexican fiction. He possesses a mathematical mind, a wealth of knowledge about realism, and a plethora of rules—many taken from theater. These qualities make his novels exciting, movable constructions. But Leñero's narrow intellectual horizons keep him from being the greatest Mexican novelist.

A practicing Catholic, a cautious yet persistent follower of Latin American liberation theology, he shows his limitations when it comes to confronting political and religious ideas, as is the case in *Pueblo rechazado* (play, 1969), *El evangelio de Lucas Gavilán* (novel, 1979; *The Gospel of Lucas Gavi-*

lán, 1990), and *Jesucristo Gómez* (play, 1986). That's when he becomes as simplistic and dogmatic a writer as the political theology he adheres to. He seems to have been spared the crises of consciousness undergone by other illustrious Catholic writers such as Léon Bloy, Georges Bernanos, and Graham Greene. Instead, he seems too sure of his convictions, which are few and firm. His mind, so adept at dismantling the factual contradictions of realism, dithers when it finds them in the realm of consciousness. Maybe it's too late for Leñero to suffer the sort of crisis of consciousness that would confer to his writing the contradiction it needs and lacks; but if it did, his writing would take on immeasurable, astonishing force.

But that doesn't mean he's not a Catholic writer in terms of Christian modernism. It's impossible not to think of Pascal on gleaning his concerns. Strict as a Jansenist, Leñero hits the mark admirably when he sets out in search of truth—a search he knows is never-ending. His realism is a methodical demonstration of the farce of history, which for Leñero is played out more in events than ideologies. His plays *El juicio* (1971), about the motives of León Toral, the man who killed Obregón, and *El martirio de Morelos* (1981), about the trial of the insurgent priest, national hero, and suspected treasonist, were slaps in the face of the outdated official history (and had censors frothing at the mouth).

It's only natural that Leñero should criticize judicial power. That's where a moral realist (think Leonardo Sciascia or Federico Campbell) finds the indelible traces left behind by both victims and executioners. In novels like *Los periodistas* (1978) and *Asesinato*, his magnifying glass grotesquely distorts the corruption and dishonesty of Mexican society. His narrators tend to hold back, rarely intervening in those books, despite the fact that Leñero himself is a character in *Los periodistas*, a victim of the Echeverria takeover of the *Excelsior* newspaper. But the novelist simply registers the facts and lets them speak for themselves—forcefully. (*Antología de la narrativa mexicana del siglo XX*, II, 1991)

Comprised of stories and chronicles both real and invented, *Gente así. Verdades y mentiras* (2008) offers generous insights into Leñero's preoccupations and his faith in literary realism as a means of cross-examining and documenting life. In the past Leñero has successfully investigated the psychology of the powerful and their killers: he's a moralist whose religious and political beliefs don't have to be spelled out in order to compete with publicly accepted truth. Whether he's talking about León Toral—the priest who killed General Obregón and the antihero of *El juicio* (1971)—or writing a "novel sans fiction" (*Asesinato*, 1985) that reconstructs the death of wealthy grandparents at the hands of their grandson, or telling the story of a pro-independence hero broken by the Inquisition (*Martirio de Morelos* [1981]), Leñero documentarily reconstructs events as a narrative art form. But because he's a journalist who generally has no need to judge, he uses the methodological reserve of an aphorism by Italo-Argentine poet Antonio Porchia as ominous epigraph in *Gente así*: "He who tells the truth says almost nothing."

The best of *Gente así* follows that methodical rule, applying it to the murky waters of literary vanity, chess, and most notably the realm of Catholicism and its heterodox observers who are essentially the protagonists of the book. One good example can be seen in Father Tomás Gerardo Allaz, a Dominican publicist of Swiss origin who practiced what he preached in regard to evangelical poverty, displaying it with what Leñero saw as a self-satisfied "pride of humility" and told the priest as much.

Leñero was more than a simple observer of the tribulations that Catholic Mexico underwent after the Second Vatican Council, and in *Gente así*—a collection of anecdotes and of inventions—he tells of Bishop Sergio Méndez Arceo being "obliged" to carry out an act of Christian charity he hadn't planned on after a meeting at the journal *Proceso*, whose board he sat on as either a fly on the wall or a silent partner. In addition to the bishop there are several other characters identified by various narrative voices: Gerardo Medina, the Partido de Acción Nacional member who spoke out against the Corpus Christi Massacre of June 10, 1971; Antonio Estrada, the novelist who wrote about the last *Cristeros*; Iván Illich, the Yugoslav reform theologian who Leñero sees as parallel to Tolstoy's character with the near-identical name (Ivan Ilyich), taking refuge from the wracking pain of illness in opium.

Leñero situates Iván Illich—along with Méndez Arceo and Gregorio Lemercier, the Benedictine who introduced psychoanalysis to monks—in the land of heretics: late seventies Cuernavaca. With all his strengths and weaknesses, in his agony he's accompanied by poet Javier Sicilia, who serves as intellectual executor. *Gente así* is an assertion of the frank opinions of Leñero, a prudent man surrounded by crazy monks and warrior bishops. We can only hope that he doesn't take to heart the George Bernanos line he quotes to Father Allaz, in which "the trick is to forget oneself," so that his recollections may one day become the sort of disinterested, coherent memoirs we see so rarely in Mexico. Leñero would excel at such a book, which might also tie up some loose threads: literary life as seen by an outsider; enthusiasm for liberation theology and its clerics; his time at the journal *Proceso*. All of this adds to *Los periodistas* (1978), which recounts the coup against the Excelsior newspaper, and *Vivir del teatro* (1982 and 1990), his memoirs as a playwright.

But *Gente así* is also more than a fascinating inquiry into the land of heretics. In it, too, Leñero cannot help but offer his take on Mexico's greatest, most hallowed literary mystery, giving readers his narrative version of Juan Rulfo's* silence. He also chronicles the Mexican sojourn of Chilean writer José Donoso, which ended abruptly in 1964 and serves to allow Leñero to reflect on the vanity of old writers. He also shows an inclination for literary plagiarism as one of the allures of picaresque literature and in that vein writes a story in memory of Rafael Ramírez Heredia, the detective writer. *Gente así* even offers a different version of the life (and death) of a young Dostoyevsky and mini-biographies of others, including deceased filmmaker Jaime Casillas Rábago, whose life Leñero adapts for a remake.

I'm not surprised that chess plays such a central role in the book, given that the pompously dubbed "game of science" is comparable to Leñero's literary mind: both exhibit simultaneously a finite predetermined structure with infinite possibilities for exploration, harmonious movements with fatalistic results, incontrovertible rules of faith and a certain Pascalian futility. The search for truth is like winning at chess: moral victory sans the eschatological milieu, which is how I—pompously—define Leñero's Catholicism. "Ajedrecistas," the story I'm talking about, is a variation on chess which has either two or three protagonists, depending on how you look at it: the great Mexican master Carlos Torre Repetto, who stopped playing when he lost his mind; the journalist Luis Ignacio Helguera, who interviewed him before he died in a plane crash in 1953; and his homonym, poet and chess player Luis Ignacio Helguera,* who also died prematurely, fifty years later. Like so many of the tales in *Gente así*, this one showcases Leñero's virtues: a captivating style combined with expertly manipulated suspense, something Leñero shines at whenever he's passionate about the subject.

SELECTED BIBLIOGRAPHY

El juicio, Joaquín Mortiz, Mexico, 1971.
Los periodistas, Joaquín Mortiz, Mexico, 1978.
El evangelio de Lucas Gavilán, Seix Barral, Barcelona, 1979.
Teatro completo, UNAM, Mexico, 1985.
Asesinato, Plaza y Janés, Mexico, 1985.
Tres de teatro, Cal y Arena, Mexico, 1988.
Vivir del teatro, I, Joaquín Mortiz, Mexico, 1982.
Vivir del teatro, II, Joaquín Mortiz, Mexico, 1990.
Gente así, Alfaguara, Mexico, 2008.
Teatro completo, I, FCE, Mexico, 2008.
The Gospel of Lucas Gavilán, trans. Robert G Mowry, University Press of America, 1990.
No One Knows Anything, trans. Myra S. Gann, Danzón Press, 1995.

LEÓN-PORTILLA, MIGUEL

(Mexico City, 1926)

When he speaks, León-Portilla seems to take on the rhythm, cadence, and conversational and anecdotal phrasing of the Nahuatl literature that he's spent more than half a century devoted to and which he in fact—not so paradoxically—founded. His conversation is colorful, chatty, entertaining. It could almost be part of the *icniuhcuicatl*, or friendship songs, comprising one section of *La tint negra y roja* (2009), his magnum anthology of Nahuatl poetry illustrated with Vicente Rojo's artwork.

A disciple of Father Ángel María Garibay Kintana* (1892–1967), León-Portilla has been considered an international authority ever since his publication of *La visión de los vencidos* (1959). This was not only one of the most influential books in Mexican history but also material evidence, a work that lent a voice to the silenced world of Mexico-Tenochtitlán, perhaps the most thoroughly destroyed city—militarily and metaphysically—in the history of the world, after Cortés's success in 1521.

World history, always, is León-Portilla's point of departure. He takes up where Bartolomé de Las Casas and Bernardino de Sahagún—the monks who established ethnography as a valid science and developed the modern concept of "law of nations"—left off. I wouldn't call León-Portilla a multiculturalist or relativist; rather, he's an old-school humanist, a scholar determined to reopen the old indigenous Santa Cruz de Tlatelolco school, a utopia of peace and harmony. His life and work have been devoted to that, from *La filosofía náhuatl estudiada en sus fuentes* (1956) and *Los antiguos mexicanos a través de sus crónicas y cantares* (1961) to *Quince poetas del mundo náhuatl* (1993) and *Para entender a Bernardino de Sahagún* (2009).

An authority through and through, León-Portilla is one of Mexico's most venerated citizens. But he's also been questioned. Critics note that while Garibay Hellenized Nahuatl literature, León-Portilla "Aztecized" a world that had already been irremediably altered by European Catholicism. They also argue over how appropriate it is to apply any notion of authorship to the pre-Cortésian corpus of literature. But Garibay and León-Portilla didn't just recover the writing of an entire culture; they gave Mexican Romanticism— whether fairly, artificially, or belatedly—a "national," autochthonous literature that the nineteenth century had been unable to found or establish.

The author of *Toltecáyotl. Aspectos de la cultura náhuatl* (1981), an erudite, didactic book published midway through his career, is, I want to stress, a Renaissance scholar. He sees the world with the eyes of Campanella and Sir Thomas More and Vasco de Quiroga. And while his condemnation of the "destroyers" of the Indies has something of Erasmus to it, his real heroes are not so much the Nahuatl artists and wise men but the *tlamatimine*—Franciscan and Dominican missionaries, monks and pious ethnographers who, in the sixteenth century, helped the vanquished survive in body and soul. If he had to pick between Herodotus—the first historian—and Thucydides—father of "scientific history"—I'm fairly certain that León-Portilla would choose Herodotus without a second thought. Herodotus was a magnanimous observer, a collector of curiosities, and a spokesman for the peoples, nations and wonders of the world. León-Portilla doesn't think human sacrifice and war should be seen as the center of the Aztec world. I imagine that, for him, it's equivalent to seeing the Inquisition as the heart and soul of Spain. Some think it is, and they have their reasons. León-Portilla isn't one of them. A man who knows his Mexican history so well that even in casual conversation he regularly quotes and cites verbatim, he's more interested in the current cultural and political situation of the indigenous. And their future. Despite the skepticism that scornfully sees indigenous literature as incipient—simultaneously naïve and antiquated—León-Portilla promotes and exalts the twenty-first-century indigenous literature being written in Nahuatl, in Mayan Yucatec, in Mextec, in Zapotec. Twice now he's helped bring indigenous literature into the world, and he's proud of his roles—historian, philologist, and philosopher. His world is a utopia in which the gaping wound of 1521 has finally formed a scar.

SELECTED BIBLIOGRAPHY
La filosofía náhuatl estudiada en sus fuentes, UNAM, Mexico, 1956.
La visión de los vencidos, UNAM, Mexico, 1959.
Los antiguos mexicanos a través de sus crónicas y cantares, UNAM, Mexico, 1961.
Toltecayótl. Aspectos de la cultura náhuatl, FCE, Mexico, 1981.
Quince poetas del mundo náhuatl, UNAM, Mexico, 1993.
La tinta negra y roja, ERA/El Colegio Nacional, Mexico, 2009.
Para entender a fray Bernardino de Sahagún, Nostra, Mexico, 2009.
The Broken Spears, trans. Lysander Camp, Beacon Press, 2007.

LIZALDE, EDUARDO
(Mexico City, 1929)

Lizalde is one of the Mexican poets I'm most attached to, not only because of his bountiful elegies, epigrams, and malicious gossip but also for his political transformations over the course of the "delinquent" century, as he calls the twentieth century. The pivotal year for him was 1956, though only in part because that's when his book *La malahora*, one of his sins of youth, was published. It was also the year of the twentieth Congress of the Communist Party of the Soviet Union, when Nikita Khrushchev denounced Stalin's crimes, disillusioning Lizalde and thousands of other communists the world over.

In 1960, Lizalde was expelled from the Mexican Communist Party (PCM), along with José Revueltas,* and together they formed the Spartacus Leninist League, with the aim of providing the Mexican proletariat with true theoretical leadership. Educated during the Khrushchev thaw, Lizalde is a poet representative of that condition: unable to keep being a communist, unable to stop being one. Lizalde believed, as the disenchanted writer Italian Ignazio Silone said, that the last battle would be between communists and ex-communists.

"Poeticism," in Mexico, was a tiny movement that Lizalde, Enrique González Rojo, and Marco Antonio Montes de Oca* began as an attempt to revolutionize poetry. The disastrous result of subordinating avant-garde aesthetics to avant-garde politics, it harked back to the early Soviet years. As Lizalde himself later confessed, the poeticists' "scientific" creation of poetic images simply resulted in bad engagé literature. *Odesa* and *Cananea* (1958), for example, are redundant poetic versions of what Sergei Eisenstein did a superb job of creating on film.

Having been a communist in the twentieth century is an experience that leaves an indelible mark, something that shapes one's framework and reflections; it's a rhetoric as persuasive as that of the Dominicans or the Jesuits, something you carry with you the rest of your life. A book like *Autobiografía de un fracaso: El poeticismo* (literally, "Autobiography of a Failure: Poeticism"), for example, which Lizalde published in 1981, could only be the work of an anguished, analytical ex-communist.

My rereading of Lizalde's *Nueva memoria del tigre* (1993 and 2000) took me through several states of mind, and finally left me convinced that he's a much more complex, stimulating poet than I'd remembered. Much of his political poetry, whether Catilinian invectives against President Díaz Ordaz or poems that demonstrate the trajectory of his anti-Stalinism, is inevitably dated. Lizalde's voice, a booming baritone, is always the same and eventually grows tiresome. A fan of the opera, he knows the risks of declaiming rather than singing an aria, but he can't quite hit the high notes.

In Lizalde's *Cada cosa es Babel* (1966), the first book he thinks of as legitimate, his need to subject himself to a professorial examination of his own philosophy—so characteristic of Marxist intellectuals—yields magnificent results. By returning to Hegel, *Cada cosa es Babel* becomes a hylozoist work, not just a dialogue with José Gorostiza's* *Muerte sin fin* (*Death Without End*) and Jorge Cuesta's* *Canto a un dios mineral* but a philosophical poem only a modern could write, because in it the poet usurps the role Antiquity had reserved for philosophers of addressing the end of the world or calculating the limits of language. Rather than the first book of the "new" Lizalde who appeared after the purges of his extended adolescence, as Evodio Escalante claimed in *La vanguardia extraviada* (2003), this is the culmination of poeticism, a poem finally free of triviality, poor taste, and theoretical waffle, which had made the experimental writing of his youth so bad.

Gabriel Zaid* once reproached Lizalde for his "great-poem-world-vision" (*Leer poesía*, 1972). But *Cada cosa es Babel* has been read more as a philosophy, the poet either channeling the sublime or acting as Adam naming the animals in paradise. Years later, falling back on his parodic talent, Lizalde wrote *Al margen de un tratado* (1982–83), where instead of Hume, Kant, and Hegel (all unassumingly present in *Cada cosa es Babel*), he takes on Wittgenstein's *Tractatus logico-philosophicus*. And that wasn't the final stage of Lizalde's evolution. In 2004 he wrote *Algaida*, a terrestrial poem in which things return to a neo-classical order, as if the task of naming begun in *Cada cosa es Babel* had finally resigned itself to nature.

In *El tigre en la casa* (1970), *La zorra enferma (malignidades, epigramas, incluso poemas)* (1974), and *Caza mayor* (1979), Lizalde shines, revealing a great poetic voice that rarely falters, a dry martini to contrast with the cloying sweetness of Jaime Sabines,* who was more suited to the so-called "bohemians" who praised, recited, and memorized his poetry. But that doesn't mean Lizalde is an enemy of *tertualias*; in fact, few poets are more social, expressive, and conversational than he is, directly addressing Sabines, Rubén Bonifaz Nuño,* and Rosario Castellanos* in *Caza mayor*. It's as if he were making up for the lost time of communism and poeticism, by applying for membership in the club of his contemporaries, happy at being the last to arrive and not looking like a hermit.

Like Propertius, Catullus, and Juvenal, Lizalde takes on both epigrams and erotic elegy. After steeping himself in Latin poets, he concentrates on carnal love, the all-consuming type, from Paolo and Francesca to Casanova. Falling back on the timeworn contrast between stoics and epicureans, we might say that Lizalde stands out from the typical stoic laments of mid-century poets, taking on an epicurean re-writing of the great Romantic themes of Salvador Díaz Mirón and the postmodernist themes of Ramón López Velarde in particular. In "Para una reescritura de Manuel Acuña" (from *Al margen de un tratado*), he sums up—in a few parodic verses—excesses of the flesh, being weary of women, and the frippery of feelings ill-spent on the whole romantic experience. Salvador Elizondo,* who'd read Lizalde right from his early poeticist days, was amazed at the precision of his language, at his tremendously penetrating insights "into the most abominable states of life" (*Museo poético*, 1974). That's pretty resounding praise, which could be seen as a dart in the portrait of many of our great modernist poets.

Lizalde's approach, the modern man piggybacking on the ancients, could be seen clearly years later, when he explained *Rosas* (1994) as a book that grew like a weed out of the translation of Rainer Maria Rilke's *The Roses*. The poems "were first conceived as playful Rilkean apocrypha or lighthearted parodies with a certain romantic whiff reminiscent of *art nouveau* paintings and divans. The exercise, which consisted of plucking the same string over and over again in order to squeeze every possible nuance out of the exact same weary melody, naturally failed. And what I ended up with were frequently disrespectful epigrams and pastiches, and poems, or glosses of other texts that were more like my own obsessions."

Communist and ex-communist poet, philosophical commentator, reader of Wittgenstein and López Velarde, epigrammatist: Lizalde had many sides. But there's at least one more we need to look at to get a complete picture of who he was: his lament to Mexico City, *Tercera Tenochti-*

tlán. Published in two parts (1982 and 2000), this poem gives Octavio Paz's* "Hablo de la ciudad" ("I speak of the city") from *Árbol adentro*, 1987 (*A Tree Within*, 1988) a run for its money in terms of being the last great Mexican urban poem of the twentieth century. Paz's poem is resolutely didactic, and though inspired by Mexico City it ends by condemning the capital, giving a Baudelairean description of the modern metropolis. But *Tercera Tenochtitlán* wiped the slate clean. After this, there wasn't a single poet left with enough spirit to take on the final vision of the Aztec capital, a full-frontal nude, a take that turned conquistador Bernal Díaz del Castillo's primitive image on its head.

The solemn, brutal tone of Lizalde's lament is at times so magnificent as he describes the urban underworld that all I can do is paraphrase it: the city is a desiccated ossuary and a terrestrial paradox, a giant sewer worse than any prophesy, a fiendish place full of cops and other sundry nocturnal spirits, serpents surprised to find that they're made of stone. After the declarations of love and hate made by Efraín Huerta* (to whom the poem is dedicated), poetry about the city had pretty much become a broken record full of run-of-the-mill jeremiads and lacking in anything poetic; Lizalde, with *Tercera Tenochtitlán*, put an end to all that.

Tercera Tenochtitlán ends with the city as a dilapidated bookcase, a library turned on its head, an omen bringing to an end the enduring theme of the vengeance of the gods, which must take place in the city of the Aztecs. It's a concept that tormented not just Lizalde but Octavio Paz, Carlos Fuentes,* José Emilio Pacheco,* and younger writers like Homero Aridjis* and Hugo Hiriart.* Several of them have written novels which imagine an apocalypse (like Lizalde) that stokes its fires on the idea of eternal return, the second coming of the fall of México-Tenochtitlán to Hernán Cortés on August 13, 1521, one of the few dates in world history that we can call the day an entire civilization died with no fear of exaggeration.

Interestingly, Lizalde is also author of a novel called *Siglo de un día* (1993) that few people read, most likely because it's essentially a novel in verse, something modern fiction readers find both tedious and offputting. But tellingly, the novel's storyline is constructed around another day: June 23, 1914, when Pancho Villa's troops took Zacatecas.

The novel has its charm, and it speaks to the vital importance Lizalde sees in the confluence (illustrated by both Paz and Revueltas) of the poet and history. *Siglo de un día* places the Mexican Revolution center stage and describes it via the pathetic failure of the man assigned to narrate it. At the end of *Tercera Tenochtitlán*, Lizalde says, "No escribo yo estos versos . . . / Me son dictados, hablados al oído, por los dioses abolidos y por los modernos, por nuestros siempre quejumbrosos fantasmas familiares" ("I do not write these verses . . . / They're dictated to me, spoken into my ear, by quashed gods and by moderns, by our ever plaintive family phantoms").

By the time I came to share Lizalde's views it was already too late, so it's impossible for me to be indifferent to his work. Anyone like me whose first political article, in 1981, was a call for Revueltas be reinstated into the Mexican Communist Party (PCM) can only feel a sort of familial intimacy with Lizalde. And that's not even getting into other ways in which I unintentionally emulated him, such as being one of the few Mexican writers who actually carried out the illustrious task of reading all of Marx's *Das Kapital*. At least Lizalde was able to use the book for a smattering of adolescent poems. But once the battle between Guelfs and Ghibellines is left behind, Lizalde's poetic persona still stands, an unlikely Byronic hero who refuses to give his life for a just cause and instead, alone and exhausted, thinks back over his duels with tigers and tigresses. A Sandokan who's thrown in the towel, a veteran pirate resigned to being one of those atheists who have lost even their last hope, as he says in *Caza mayor*.

SELECTED BIBLIOGRAPHY
Nueva memoria del tigre, FCE, Mexico, 2005.
Almanaque de cuentos y ficciones (1955–2005), ERA, Mexico, 2010.

LÓPEZ MILLS, TEDI
(Mexico City, 1959)

The vast majority of Mexican poets, if asked about their religious beliefs, would declare themselves agnostic. Interrogated further, they might accept the term "gnostic," used in Harold Bloom's sense to describe contemporary, individual religiosity. More indifferent than atheistic, poets' religion tends to alleviate the anguish brought on by the absence of God by calling on household deities, Lares and Penates, "poderes invisibles o meras abstracciones, divinidades protectoras de dispensas, de estancias, de mansiones" ("invisible powers or mere abstractions, divinities protecting pantries, rooms, mansions"), as López Mills defines them in *Luz por aire y agua* (2002). It matters not whether there are "uno o muchos dioses" ("one or many gods"), or if they're inside or out, as long as they make themselves known *hic et nunc*, here and now.

The deities watching over the world are palpable (if not always visible) in poets like López Mills who seek to control a world of domestic spirits, happy inhabitants of a neighborhood that only needs a few streets to contain an entire universe. But López Mills doesn't dally in "the art of dressing fleas," as Octavio Paz* called the trivial poetry so characteristic of certain Mexican poets. In *Luz por aire y agua*, for instance, her verses progress, moving assuredly toward the kind of philosophical questions that make poetry meaningful to begin with. It goes far beyond the sort of academic paganism that we nonbelievers often fall victim to. When she's not parading certain characters through her poetic court, López Mills fuses Montaigne with Freud (to take another of Bloom's standpoints), as when she has a daughter writing her mother's epitaph wonder, "¿Si me conozco te conozco?" ("If I know me, do I know you?"). With rarely seen tenderness, that one line combines the classics and modern self-analysis.

Adolfo Castañón* found López Mills's first book, *Cinco estaciones* (1989), to be full of "limpid, metallic verse"; in the time since then, her poetry has become even more refined, culminating in *Un jardín, cinco noches (y otros poemas)* (2005).

López Mills is a descendent of the modernism that takes on, as she says in *Segunda persona* (1994), "el lastre—pecio y rodio—de algunos actos y de algunos hechos / las huellas de un estilo enorme" ("the deadweight—wreckage and rhodium—of some acts and some facts / the traces of an enormous style"). But her poetry is much more than devotion to the old nineteenth- and twentieth-century masters she has translated and recreated; hers is saying something else. López Mills's verses remind me (and I'm not entirely sure why) of the yellow prairies painted by early North American artists to describe the desolation of the soul; and I find a certain air of Mallarmé about her: her words say just what they mean.

SELECTED BIBLIOGRAPHY
Un lugar ajeno, Ediciones del Equilibrista, Mexico, 1993.
Segunda persona, UAM, Mexico, 1994.
Luz por aire y agua, Conacula, Mexico, 2002.
Un jardín, cinco noches, Taller Ditoria, Mexico, 2005.
Contracorriente, ERA, Mexico, 2006.
La noche en blanco de Mallarmé, FCE, Mexico, 2006.
Parafrasear, Bonobos, Mexico, 2008.
Muerte en la rua Augusta, Almadía, Oaxaca, 2008.

LÓPEZ PÁEZ, JORGE
(Huatusco, Veracruz, 1922)

The journey back to childhood is one that can really only be undertaken—as Proust proved—once a writer's prose has matured. Elena Garro* and Rosario Castellanos* pulled it off, and so does López Páez, with decanted purity. In its traditionalism, *El solitario Atlántico* (1958) is the result of a new inquiry, an inner journey embarked upon from a place of stoic apathy that's hostile to the great metaphysical concepts of being and stakes its claim on the transcendent triviality of existence. In *El solitario Atlántico*, we read, "My imagination perfected the splotches, turning them into confident strokes: the huge ship lulled by breezes: blue canoe and yellow transatlantic." López Páez's child is a liberator, a father to the man. His prose in this novella is almost silent, chromatic, full of a luminosity reminiscent of Katherine Mansfield, and with a veiled presence of evil that harks back to Henri Bosco. (*Antología de la narrativa mexicana del siglo XX*, I, 1989)

SELECTED BIBLIOGRAPHY
Mi hermano Carlos, FCE, Mexico, 1965.
La costa, Joaquín Mortiz, Mexico, 1980.

El solitario Atlántico, SEP, Mexico, 1985.
Silenciosa sirena, Joaquín Mortiz, Mexico, 1988.
Los cerros azules, Joaquín Mortiz, Mexico, 1993.

M

MAGAÑA, SERGIO

(Tepalcatepec, Michoacán, 1924 – Mexico City, 1990)

The last Bohemian, playwright Sergio Magaña lived in a lively part of Mexico City, on Calle Santa Cruz behind the Alameda, amid both revelry and squalor. In 1982 I went to one of his infamous gatherings (theater students really lived it up) with Julio Ramírez and Jaime Casillas. Someone's guitar and the music from *Santísima*—one of Magaña's recent plays, which had not a single woman in the cast—were playing in the background. Knowing it was going to be mostly gay, I was uneasy when I got there. When you're twenty, the idea of sexual "otherness" is distressing. But I ended up sitting chastely on Magaña's lap (he'd known me since I was a kid).

Magaña was both sweet and gruff. Born in Michoacán, he had the festive personality of a man from Veracruz and a lover from Oaxaca. It was from him that I heard, perhaps for the first time, of playwrights like O'Neil, Seki Sano, Salvador Novo,* and Tennessee Williams. And his description of how hideous actress Tamara Garina was is something I'll never forget. I saw Magaña for the last time at a revival of *Moctezuma II*, perhaps his most memorable play.

I have no right to judge his theater. Magaña made his name during the years when Mexican existential angst was front and center. And his particular quest didn't quite transcend *costumbrismo*, a somewhat folkloric portrayal of customs, which sometimes happens when nationality and the search for identity collide. In the forties he wrote his first novel (*Los supli-cantes*) and a book of short stories, *El ángel roto*. These early ventures didn't achieve posterity, and there's a reason for that.

Praising a work because its author died is a form of immorality. But anyone who hasn't written a generous obituary, please raise your hand. *El molino de aire*, a novel written in 1954 and published in 1981, is not an extraordinary novel. But it is an honest if unspectacular example of a different type of narrative, one that broke away from "provinces as memoir" trend. Magaña's book is akin to some of those written by Sergio Galindo,* Emilio Carballido,* and Jorge López Páez.* It's a *Bildungsroman* written by the young artist when he had conquered the city and decided to settle scores with his childhood. *El molino de aire* is both a biting testimony and a watercolor, sweet but not sickly. A book about sensual awakening, it has the Mexican Revolution of 1910 and its Catholic ramifications as its overwhelmingly theatrical backdrop. Magaña simply insinuates, as violence takes the stage. *El molino de aire* concludes with a promise to return that the author never kept. Sergio never went back to the provinces or to writing novels. Instead he stayed on to witness the turmoil of the city whose dramas he then staged.

Sartre thought that a generation with no grandparents would be happier, since they could invent traditions as they saw fit. I wonder. Old people, like children, are easily idealized. That party back in 1982 ended before dawn with a communal desecration of the flagpole in Mexico City's Zocalo, after which Magaña—the playwright moved by Aztec Emperor Montezuma's fateful naïveté—left without saying goodbye, sauntering happily among dumpsters full of rotten fruit and skipping over sleeping drunks like a kid playing hopscotch, faintly backlit by the first lights of dawn. (*Servidumbre y grandeza de la vida literaria*)

Selected Bibliography

El molino de aire, Universidad Veracruzana, Xalapa, 1981.

Los signos del zodíaco, FCE/SEP, Mexico, 1984.

Moctezuma II. Cortés y la Malinche (Los argonautas), Edimusa, Mexico, 1985.

MANJARREZ, HÉCTOR
(Mexico City, 1945)

Rebellion, grace, and revolution are the three ports where Manjarrez docks in his first book of essays. *El camino de los sentimientos* (1990) is a collection of sixteen texts written between 1971 and 1989, though we know he wrote a lot more during those almost twenty years. But Manjarrez avoided the temptation to write the kind of criticism that would have made him a Mexican demigod, a status he doesn't want and one that's a goal for many of our younger essayists. He's written quite a consistent oeuvre, and this book confirms it. It's one of the most brilliant intellectual portraits of the eighties.

Manjarrez's two decades as a writer culminate, for now, in *El camino de los sentimientos*. There's a certain distance between the precocious, cocky storyteller of *Acto propiciatorio* and the insolent avant-garde artist of *Lapsus*, between the aphoristic poet of *El golpe avisa* and that of *Canciones para los que se han separado*, and finally, between the evidently sentimental novelist of *No todos los hombres son románticos* and that of *Pasaban en silencio nuestros dioses*. And that's precisely the distance I'm about to explain.

How can we trace his sentimental journey? Manjarrez chose the immediate past as a way to navigate writing. While *Acto propiciatorio* teems with childhood and teenage recollections, *Lapsus* is a novel whose very ambition condemns it to premature if not instantaneous aging, as I'll explain shortly. He attempted to sum up the radical culture of the 1960s just as they were coming to an end. As a poet, Manjarrez glosses the emotional experiences of his generation, which is why he's been excluded from their cliques and their anthologies. It's an exile he accepts, though I don't know whether he's happy about it. *No todos los hombres son románticos* contains several of the best stories of the decade, plainly illustrating the battle over the body that was raging at the time. His most recent novel, *Pasaban en silencio nuestros dioses*, brings the cycle to an end, though I can't yet predict how it will go down in our collective memory.

Alfonso Reyes* said that the immediate past was the most thankless of all. I realize that quoting Reyes in a text about Manjarrez might seem disconcerting or simply absurd since the two had endless differences so obvious that I won't bother to go into them. But they also have some seductive similarities. Both are refined cosmopolitan men who find the steadfast perseverance of Virgil for Reyes, or The Rolling Stones for Manjarrez, as topics worthy of a long literary conversation. Both write among the best and most suggestive literary "portraits" in Mexican literature. Reyes never met Isocrates. Manjarrez, to my knowledge, never made the acquaintance of Kerouac. But when they portray them, you feel as if they're speaking directly to the men, as though they were eyewitnesses to what was going on at the time. And their greatest similarity resides in the fact that both the wise Hellenist and the young scribe who lived the avant-garde knowing it was destined to fail are pagan authors. I'll grant that malevolence causes pain in their books, but the religion of crime and punishment is alien to their literature. Manjarrez says as much in *El camino de los sentimientos* when he searches his library for an author who will lead him away from the only form of redemption he sees as true: laughter. Like all moderns, Manjarrez finds religious spirits seductive, but since "not all men are Romantics" as per the title of his earlier novel, we know that being seduced might hurt but it won't kill you.

Manjarrez is a sentimental writer by choice. When I say "sentimental," I'm thinking of authors like Laurence Sterne, Italo Svevo, Ford Maddox Ford: those unafraid to go on a quest to be touched, or to lay themselves bare in order to convince. Their joy can be as profound as their melancholy. And that's why Manjarrez meddles (yes, meddles) with his favorite authors in this book, which is organized into three parts: rebellion, grace, and revolution. He adores the rebels (particularly those without a cause and those who lose), he's moved by grace, and he respects revolutionaries.

The essays on Cleaver, Kerouac, Gombrowicz, and Lowry are among the most lucid literary sketches ever written by a Mexican. In the past Reyes identified with Goethe; Octavio Paz portrayed Sor Juana Inés de la Cruz; Juan García Ponce sanctified Klossowski; Federico Campbell probed Sciascia; Sergio Pitol* searched for affinities with slaves. That's not a very long list. Manjarrez tries to make sense of *his* kind using all sorts of rhetoric: first-person, dialogue, digression. It's an investigation as open as it is erudite. His culture is cosmopolitan, avant-garde, Mexican. Each text abounds with meticulously chosen French, English, and *chilango* (Mexico City) expressions, and often Italian and German ones, too.

Writing about the militant black writer Eldridge Cleaver, Manjarrez refers to "his short, intense time." Well, that time is the same one that dates Manjarrez himself, and it's no accident that *El camino de los sentimientos* culminates with a reflection on 1968. He's not ashamed to live and to relive what he calls "the radical movie" that was the sixties, seeing it—I think—not as an educational experience but as a sort of genesis.

Manjarrez loves the lunacy of his rebels, as seen in the first set of essays, although one of them is portrayed in a negative light: Albert Camus. But while he might see Camus as a "*prof de philo,*" he respects his differentiation between rebellion and revolution. Paradoxically, although that distinction was popularized by the lambasted Camus around mid-century, it was put forth much earlier by Ortega y Gasset in *La rebelión de las masas* (*The Rebellion of the Masses*) and then later by Paz in *Corriente alterna*. But that's not what concerns him. Manjarrez is taken with Cleaver and his fall, from the Black Panthers to Reagan's reelection; with Kerouac, whose trajectory he covers affectionately but not complacently, freeing him of the sanctimonious hogwash with which imported Californians regale him; with his mentor Gombrowicz, whom he's incensed to discover admired the bourgeois Thomas Mann, though he manages, very shrewdly, to explain why. These are inviting, sky's-the-limit pieces written in the best essayistic tradition. His subjects are not just original but intimate, sometimes almost secret, the choices of a man of letters who knows his bookshelves with the precision of a navigator and the obsession of a stamp collector. That's why it's such a pleasure to stroll through texts with "Madame Teste," whom he invents and invokes to critique *Monsieur Teste* and pique Paul Valéry, whom he actually likes.

But the problem begins with Artaud, the oldest essay in the book. Artaud: more than an artist, but not a revolutionary. This concept divides the book. Who to support, the lunatics or the revolutionaries? And how can we reconcile the two? That's the great twentieth-century question of those who thought Marx and Rimbaud went hand in glove. The solution, for Manjarrez, starts with Cortázar.

His essay on revolution and the writer, from 1984, is the longest and most serious in the book. In it, he doesn't joke, criticize, ridicule, try to understand, get to the root, or explain away any unusual transformations. He quite skillfully compares Argentine writer José Bianco to Julio Cortázar through the latter's collaboration with the journal *Sur* and his commitment to the Cuban and Nicaraguan revolutions. It's an honest and honorable piece that eschews extremism and offers readers information and explanations that shed light on the times and context. But in the final analysis, despite its merits, it's a limited probe of Manjarrez's own consciousness, so cautious that it's a bit spineless. He ends up being overly indulgent of both Cortázar and the Cuban Revolution, attributing the writer's political blunders—as Paz did when Cortázar died—to the naïveté of his political vocation. And even as late as 1984, Manjarrez doesn't dare call the Cuban regime by its name: totalitarian dictatorship.

That sort of inhibition clashes with Manjarrez's critically playful spirit, and what's worse is that I think he's lying to himself. For as we'll see, he shares Cortázar's weakness—his naïve shortsighted candor—when it comes to revolutions. It's interesting to compare the two. Manjarrez draws attention—and rightly so—to the lack of evil in Cortázar's work; but when *Pasaban en silencio nuestros dioses* came out, Fernando Solana—also rightly—complained that Manjarrez was an author obsessed with the "feasibility of good." So what we find is a sentimental "cronopio" (Cortázar's fictional beings) in love with the lunatics and taken with the rebels but not very demanding of his revolutionaries (which Kundera—another of Manjarrez's subjects—saw as a geometric combination of the two).

José María Espinasa* was wrong when he said Manjarrez lived on a diet of "demented, steadfast hope." If he has hope, it's cautious, deliberate, rationalist, perhaps naïve but certainly not demented and much less steadfast. That's why his essay on Cortázar, despite being instructive, lacks the passion he reserves for the death of José Revueltas. Cortázar, you see, wasn't a lunatic. But Revueltas was "a lunatic monk in the most Trappist period of militant communism." And this text is flawless: in addition to being a critical consideration of the writer's moral stance in 1976—the year Revueltas died, the year the Dirty War began, a time even I recall as sordid and ominous—it is a magnificent description of Revueltas's fate in Mexico. After exhuming Dostoyevsky and Sartre, Manjarrez takes on Mexicans José Vasconcelos,* Martín Luis Guzmán,* Jaime Torres Bodet,* Salvador Novo,* and then Octavio Paz, whom—along with Revueltas—he sees as the only twentieth-century Mexican writer not to have been blinded by the light of his fame. And although

Paz doesn't get his own essay in *El camino de los sentimientos*, his presence is a constant, lucid, uneasy point of reference throughout.

Manjarrez spent many years living in Europe, and in 1971 the idea of returning to Mexico filled him with panic. But return he did, and the distance he gained abroad translated into a distinctive critical methodology that enabled him to understand both Graham Greene's Mexico-phobia and the euphoria with which Mexicans welcomed the presence of Malcolm Lowry.

A skilled radiographer of the contradictions that unite and divide literature and politics, Manjarrez does capitulate on a few occasions. His review of Elena Poniatowska's* books, for instance, is long and tedious. There's nothing wrong with continuing to insist that she was an astonishingly opportune writer, or praising her courage and her promotion of figures, like activist Rosario Ibarrez de Piedra, who so desperately need and deserve that promotion. But between 1981 and 1990, what Manjarrez calls her "felicitous prose" went so far downhill as to become an advertisement for the sins of the left. It's a shame that Manjarrez was so polite that he didn't bring up the role Poniatowska's own literature played in that commercialization. He claims quite confidently that neither Poniatowska nor Cortázar belong to that god-given organism he calls "the culture of the left." Does Manjarrez himself belong to it? No, not if it's taken in the old sense of the partisan left. Yes, if we mean a moral and intellectual stance that renounces injustices while analytically tolerating the blunders—tragedies, even—of a left that has at times found in him a fellow traveler.

El camino de los sentimientos ends with a paper from 1989 that he presented in Germany a few days before the fall of the Berlin Wall. Despite Manjarrez's amazing intuition when it comes to "sentimental journeys," this is one of his most rambling, incoherent texts. This disciple of Gombrowicz, a formalist so meticulous that he refuses to publish hundreds of pages he's written because he's not satisfied with them, here tries to sum up 1968 as it draws to a historic close in 1989. And it's too early to reconcile form to history.

Nevertheless, this flawed essay articulated an intuition that a few days later the Czechs, Hungarians, Germans, and even the victims of Ceausescu would corroborate. According to Manjarrez, revolution was not only still a valid concept but actually more relevant than ever, as it had been divested of its bloody utopias. He would agree with French philosopher Edgar Morin's idea that the revolutionary mindset won't disappear from Western tradition but will, sooner or later, radically change shape. And that seems to be the case, now that many of the ideals that first led to the modern idea of revolution have not been achieved. That's the crisis of the left that Manjarrez now inhabits.

El camino de los sentimientos confirms something that both old and new Manjarrez readers had suspected: the novelist, short story writer, and poet was also a closet essayist, with one of the sharpest, freest, and wittiest minds of our time. His "sentimental journey" has been long but by no means is it close to over. He'll keep rummaging through his bookshelves, in search of utterly personal yet universal conversation with rebellion, grace, and revolution. (*Servidumbre y grandeza de la vida literaria*, 1998)

The young Héctor Manjarrez was a pagan writer enraptured by foul language, revolution as a Dionysian cult, counterculture as a new school for women (and men); he was a modern eager for constant change, the total metamorphosis of all things, constellations, and bodies. But the gawky vanguard novelist of *Lapsus* turned into the joyful nostalgic of *No todos los hombres son románticos* and then the serene bard of *Canciones para los que se han separado,* who finally shut the gate to his Epicurean garden with the novel *Pasaban en silencio nuestros dioses.*

Unlike other writers of his generation, Manjarrez has not squandered his talents on vain or intranscendental books. He writes a lot and publishes little, though his eight books in twenty-six years have an unusual position in Mexican libraries. He's a presence and yet he's not. His books, like those of García Ponce,* demand the reader's fervent, a priori devotion. He's the kind of writer who's made a lifelong pact with his own demons.

Maybe Manjarrez's childhood was longer than most of his peers', depriving him of certain types of "literary" experience. His work, from the boisterous experimentalism of *Lapsus* to the soothing concision of his latest poems, suffers from an exemplary but at times frivolous playfulness. His characters, like Cortázar's "cronopios," are happy and immature, but always fairy-like. And that saves them, gracefully, from the infernal paradises created by Revueltas and Rulfo* that became the Mexican canon. Not even his zealous revolutionaries were imbued with any reliable notion of transcendence.

Ya casi no tengo rostro (1996) reveals right from the title (literally, "Now I almost have no face") the anxiety (and indiscreet revelry) of a man discovering the long shadows of ontological collapse. I don't think Manjarrez has left the pagan camp (in which I'd place writers like Fernando del Paso,* Leonardo da Jandra,* and Julián Meza, among others). As it happens, he's a somber skeptic when it comes to the triumph of cruelty and of religion. A man with no religious anxieties, a self-confessed and convinced materialist, in these eight magnificent stories Manjarrez tells of his fear of death, his doubts about the afterlife, and his uncertainty about the idea of transcendence.

"Dos mujeres," the first story in the collection, desecrates the sanctity of sexual first rites with a malicious, meddling Serbian cook. In "La ouija" three Latin American revolutionaries find themselves in a fix brought on not by history but by a séance. "Bolero," perhaps the best story in the book, is an homage to the femme fatale, who in this case is a guerrilla who melds clandestine love with conspiracy theory and ends up disappearing without a trace, like a goddess who doesn't get a second chance on earth. "El lago y el mecate" is a brief account of insanity reminiscent of Thomas Bernhard that betrays a dislike of fellow man that also crops up in "Fin de mundo," the book's last story. Here, eroticism ends up becoming a fatal adventure of sexual desperation.

To be clichéd, we could say that the themes in *Ya casi no tengo rostro* are Romantic, while their handling is classical. And true mastery over the short story form in Spanish is rare indeed today. Spanish novelist Javier Marías is an anglophile who makes fun of the ease with which we accept any type of writing as a short story. Jorge Luis Borges, another anglophile, may be responsible for that, since it's one thing to be an unequalled commentator on the genre (as he was), and quite another to imitate it. A third anglophile, Manjarrez writes stories so rhetorically faithful to the genre that he successfully juggles several registers, from strict realism to magisterial horror, as in "Misa de difuntos."

Manjarrez's prose has lost some of its rhetorical wit in favor of a more concise, agile, at times coarse style, one meticulously planned to avoid all exuberance. Maybe that's what's required for him to talk about a universe that is no longer the best of all possible worlds, a place that has gone back to being evil, almost phantasmagorical, a place where lunatics and insects, empty men, impossible women, and broken revolutionaries play Ouija, unable to choose between transcendence and superstition.

"Música," the second story, might be the one that best portrays the author's farewell to his garden of delights, a place where men and gods unmade the world and traveled through time, reckless in the face of evil. But the music plays on. Few Mexican narrators merit the praise Manjarrez does: whether immature or pig-headed, sensible or insolent, he's grown along with his readers. That's why, thanks to the diagnostic powers of his provocative prose, I have faith in his wisdom. *Ya casi no tengo rostro* delves into that region where "... what's once been / can never be destroyed, there sure must be / Original elements which live for aye, / And into which all things can be resolved, / At their last hour, that there may still remain, / Matter from which the world may be renewed." (Lucretius, trans. Sir Robert Allison) (1996; *Servidumbre y grandeza de la vida literaria*, 1998)

Sex (with or without love), for Manjarrez, is the experience whereby one person is taken prisoner by another—by his or her beauty, attributes, misery, cruelty, or talent. For that and other reasons *La maldita pintura* (2004)—in particular the last 20 pages—is one of the finest and most impressive books to come out of Mexico in recent years. In it, a painter imprisons two women in the top room of his house in Primrose Hill, London. There, they're endlessly condemned to pose nude, reduced to the status of permanent, living installations.

None of Manjarrez's strict contemporaries have progressed the way he has, so substantively, anxious to challenge "form" in new ways, book after book. It makes sense, of course, given that he's a writer who was raised on characters as divergent as Gombrowicz (the Young) and Artaud (the Cruel). And of course his influences extend far beyond literature, to painting and music: Lucien Freud, Francis Bacon, Mick Jagger, and Keith Richards.

But despite his constant evolution, when I read back over his work I find similarities between the stories in *Acto propiciatorio*, from 1970—written when he was just twenty-three and had been in London and Paris almost ten years—and *La maldita pintura*, the culmination of his "art." Manjarrez is a very painterly writer, his texts extremely visual, and we get a glimpse of this right from "Johnny," the first story in *Acto propiciatorio*, in which the cowboy steps out of the TV to escape his world and sets up camp in the home of a middle-class Mexican family. *La maldita pintura*, too, is the story—and history—of an image, as its title (literally, "Damn painting") suggests. Here it's the image that "Dos" ("Two"—the characters are all numbered rather than named) composes by locking up two women. In both cases, the ease with which Manjarrez steps through the looking glass, lays himself on the line, and challenges the concept of verisimilitude is remarkable.

His early stories are the work of a "primitive" (as José María Espinasa said years ago), and in them the influence (both good and bad) of Carlos Fuentes* is readily discernible. It's almost as easy to make out (and share) Fuentes's vision of the new Mexican middle class in his own *La región más transparente* (*Where the Air is Clear*) as it is in Manjarrez's *Acto propiciatorio*. The image merits taunting and jibes, no doubt, but occasionally it's also quite moving. Nevertheless, the resulting caricature of the bourgeoisie (and their heroes) comes off a bit coarse and the technique seems somewhat rudimentary, so we end up with the caricaturist as the one caricatured.

But *Lapsus*, his first novel, presents a writer in control, a man of his generation in exactly the way André Gide warned against: without being *ahead* of the times, he's simply constrained by their conventions. Manjarrez himself confirmed that limitation when he declared himself to be part of the "wave" of the sixties. But when the tide went out, *Lapsus* was left on the shore, outdated almost by definition. To be fair, on rereading it, I found the novel less dull and more coherent than when I first picked it up a quarter of a century ago.

Regardless of datedness, the book is an exotic trip through the late sixties with protagonists Haltter and Heggo (pronounced, in Spanish, "Alter" and "Ego"), the transmutations of a writer engaging in a bit of phlegmatic self-parody. Rummaging around in the Joycean fragments that make up *Lapsus*, we find entire chapters of good prose, notably "Lucy in the Sky with Diamonds." Mercifully, Manjarrez didn't confuse "experimental" with "anything goes," and thus *Lapsus*—counterculture novel par excellence—is paradoxically written not only in English and French but also in a spectacular Spanish. This alone proves that the author trained, refined, and mastered his linguistic ear, a virtue that became a constant in his writing, saving him in his darkest hours through an ability to play with political idioms, take street language and make it bilingual and trilingual, hone in on dialectical peculiarities and intellectual inferences, and showcase his passion for "young" writing. Utterly in tune to the sounds of language, he ably invents and preserves vernacular cultural heritage, almost always aware of the thin line between cultured and colloquial, immortal and fleeting.

Lapsus is like a little museum in London or Paris, a memorial to the sixties in those cities. Manjarrez put a patina on his times and knew that's what would happen if we read the book's appendices and political, literary, and musical annotations: Lenin and John Lennon, Jacques Brel and Leo Ferré, Carlos Fuentes and Frantz Fanon, Mao Zedong and LSD, the Vietnam War and Allen Ginsburg, his anti-prophet, The Doors and Octavio Paz.

"There they were, the sixties: impotent and delightful, sappy and sincere, just like they had been," he wrote some time later. From the Weimar Republic to Woodstock, the last days of the old regime epitomize the "pleasure of living," as Talleyrand said, and even Raymond Aron—a man with no sympathy for the zeitgeist of 1968—admitted that only the twenties could rival the sixties in terms of that pleasure.

After the diptych that was *Acto propiciatorio* and *Lapsus*, Manjarrez didn't publish another book until 1978, when *El golpe avisa* came out. Reminiscent of Rodolfo Usigli,* it's a straightforward collection of poems, unique in a decade of a poetic innovation for its meditative simplicity, the lament of reason in the face of cruelties of the heart and a (proverbially) British stiff upper lip.

Much ado has been made—not for nothing—about *No todos los hombres son románticos* (1983), the collection of stories that confirmed Manjarrez as a great nostalgic, a sentimental, a photographer of days gone by. Some of the stories—predictably, the more political ones—are not quite short stories per se: they're lyrical testimonies of a man who believed for too long that the sexual revolution and the political revolution went hand in hand. Despite all the non-conformist, radical, and "new left" verbiage of *Lapsus*, it wasn't until the fall of the Berlin Wall that Manjarrez really took stock, as becomes clear in *El camino de los sentimientos*.

Manjarrez begins *No todos los hombres son románticos* with a reference to the Beatles ("Can't Buy Me Love") and another to Paul Nizan's *Aden Arabie*'s opening lines ("I was twenty years old. I won't let anyone say that's the most beautiful time of life"). But Nizan's presence just lends a flavor of the times; the book's heroes tend to be young men who are about twenty (some even younger), coming of age in London or Belgrade. At the novel's core lies Manjarrez's obsessive, striking, central motif, which we might call the "abducted lover"—men and women sequestered by sex. (And this begins in *Actos propiciatorios*, where in "The Queen," a Mexican bellhop tries to rob an English starlet staying at the hotel and ends up her slave, *à la* Rachilde: stylized, masochist fantasy). In "Cuerpos" an Englishwoman does away with a helpless young lover who reappears in "Pudor," this time victim of a Slovenian prostitute in Belgrade. More sadistic than romantic, really, the theme also crops back up in "Fin de mundo," the last story in *Ya casi no tengo rostro* (1996), in which a troubled couple find themselves on a beach in Nayarit surround by tarantulas. It's the last of the curses that had plagued them, biblically, from the start.

Pasaban en silencio nuestros dioses (1987) is written with a lightness of touch that allows Manjarrez to flaunt his command over the setting. The plot revolves around the practical and ideological implications of the slogan "The personal is political" in a small town. The result could only be hilarious, and that's how Manjarrez sees it, in this "radikalski photonoveliski" that's essentially a meditation on masculinity. Like D. H. Lawrence in *Women in Love*, Manjarrez is a writer who feels obliged to lay out the premises of a new morality. I don't think there's ever been another book in Mexico that manages to describe with such hyperrealist rawness the sexual initiation fantasy of a man at a gathering that today we'd call a "self-help" meeting.

Manjarrez's ear is like a sixth sense, a *moral* sense. What I mean is, his spy-like ability to ably infiltrate, comprehend, decipher, and translate allows him to manipulate his characters and thus précis his own epoch. So *Pasaban en silencio nuestros dioses* quite credibly portrays the "petit bourgeois" life of the Mexican left—at the time comprised solely of bohemians and college kids who feared the State for its selective repression and its ability to co-opt. *Pasaban en silencio nuestros dioses* has two endings: first, when servant Doña Reme accidentally eats some marijuana cake; second, the death of José Revueltas. And between that middle-class idiosyncrasy that allows Mexicans to have "hired help" with no qualms, and the communist heretic par excellence breathing his last, the seventies fade away.

Female orgasm, open homosexuality, prevention and punishment of domestic violence, women's difficulty finding self-esteem at work: these are just a few aspects of the new world order Manjarrez so skillfully portrays, by turns with pathos, humor, and solidarity. And those obsessions are the stuff of his subsequent novel *El otro amor de su vida* (1999), one of the few comic novels of Mexican literature worthy of Capra, Cukor, or Woody Allen. Taking place one Sunday in Tlapan, it tells the story of a college woman in the process of changing boyfriends, while her best friend, mother, a local cop, and a Mexican-Polish cellist who just happened to be passing by all enter and exit the stage in a perfect comedy of errors. Again, we have the sequestered lovers motif: the new couple gets locked in her house, and in their attempts to get out the author avails himself of the characters' props, steps, and dialogues. In this novel and *Rainey el asesino* (2002), Manjarrez fully achieves what he set out to do.

An homage to R. L. Stevenson, Sir Arthur Conan Doyle, and Joseph Conrad—the authors of London's own thousand and one nights—*Rainey el asesino* (along with *La maldita pintura*) is the author's return to the scene of the crime, the streets of his youth. And as in dreams, here the return to the past takes place in the present. This short novel takes a scathing look at the horror of Latin American dictatorships in the seventies and eighties, which in Mexico were experienced as the arrival of hundreds of Argentinian, Uruguayan, and Chilean political exiles. Manjarrez's worldly wisdom turns them into a fictional cohort of heroes and opportunists, femmes fatales and unforgettable friends, a spreading wave of historical reality that upset Mexico's political and intellectual elites, at the time still provincial, placid, isolated.

Set in Argentina and England, *Rainey el asesino* chronicles the temptation of carrying out "private," individual justice to offset the impunity granted to murderers and torturers. It took a few years for Manjarrez to create his account of those times, from the perspective of observer-participant, and he did it in the best of all possible ways: by avoiding the easy way out (straightforward testimony) and setting forth what's at the core of an issue he knows much more about.

The novel tells the story of a wealthy Argentinean doctor who decides to avenge the death of a distant relative, an Argentine recruit executed at close range by a British officer in the Falklands-Malvinas War in 1982. Thus in order to carry out his revenge against what turns out to be a mysterious aristocrat, he relies on the help of an ex-lover, victim, and survivor of the military dictatorship. In fewer than ninety pages, Manjarrez not only pays homage to the masters of British fiction but formulates a reflection on morality, on collective guilt, and private justice. Héctor Manjarrez is one of the few Mexican writers we can still call, in the fullest sense of the term, a man of the world.

SELECTED BIBLIOGRAPHY
Acto propiciatorio, Joaquín Mortiz, Mexico, 1970.
Lapsus, Joaquín Mortiz, Mexico, 1971.
El golpe avisa, ERA, Mexico, 1978.
No todos los hombres son románticos, ERA, Mexico, 1983.
Canciones para los que se han separado, ERA, Mexico, 1985.
Pasaban en silencio nuetros dioses, ERA, Mexico, 1987.
El camino de los sentimientos, ERA, Mexico, 1990.
Ya casi no tengo rostro, ERA, Mexico, 1996.
El otro amor de su vida, ERA, Mexico, 1999.
Rainey el asesino, ERA, Mexico, 2002.
La maldita pintura, ERA, Mexico, 2004.
El bosque en la ciudad seguido de *El cuerpo en el DF*, ERA, Mexico, 2006.
Yo te conozco, ERA, Mexico, 2008.

MARTÍNEZ, JOSÉ LUIS

(Atoyac, Jalisco, 1918 – Mexico City, 2007)

Hernán Cortés stands out as the best book Martínez has written over the course of his more than fifty-year career. Literary history and historical literature are his calling, and "calling" is precisely the word needed. We're talking about not just a man of letters who decided to bestow upon Mexico one of the best libraries in the country but a researcher whose modesty is rivaled only by his breadth of knowledge and the appeal of his projects. Martínez comes from a longstanding tradition, one reflected in earlier scholars working at the end of the colonial period and the beginning of Mexican independence, such as Juan José Eguiara y Eguren, Francisco Xavier Clavijero, and Joaquín García-Icazbalceta. And although the climate of the times kept Enlightened debate from soaring to any particularly great heights, the cloistered atmosphere did encourage bibliophiles and bibliographers, men dedicated to preserving knowledge, who quietly weathered the storm and saved scholarship from the fire or—worse—from neglect and oblivion.

Although not all of Martínez's critical work, begun in the early forties, has been published, he was the first man who sensed that the duplicitous postrevolutionary narrative was drawing to a close, and the one who enthusiastically—and sensibly—welcomed a new generation of writers in the sixties. And then the critic known for his good manners and restraint faded away, happily replaced by the public servant and historiographer.

Martínez's most recent works are more historiographical than they are historical. Rather than opinions and ideology, he opted for events and their documentation. And his anthologies and collections are self-consciously didactic, in the noblest sense of the term. Martínez never morphed his scholarship into hermeneutics, nor did he use it as a seal of intellectual prestige. His dedication to enriching the tradition is reminiscent of the sort of humanism Spaniard Antonio Machado and Alfonso Reyes* exhibited earlier in the century. And if his work sometimes seems too neutral or superficial, that all comes to an end with *Hernán Cortés* (1990). With great tact, Martínez lays the responsibility for an event—the conquest—that has divided our historic conscience since 1521 on the reader's shoulders.

Hernán Cortés is a biographical accompaniment to the four volumes comprising *Documentos cortesianos*, documents that Martínez himself tracked down and elucidated. And if that book's style is not brilliant, its perspectives certainly are; after all, Martínez is not aiming to be a poet but to paint a picture. It's pointless to attempt to enumerate his virtues as a researcher as he's got so many. Suffice it to say he offers a plethora of information and an economy of prose. When a scholarly book dependent on such a vast bibliography is engrossing right down to the footnotes, you know the author has achieved an enviable balance.

After narrating "the encounter," Martínez delves into Cortés's murky past, his earlier voyage to the Indies and expedition to Mexico. Then he moves on to the conquistador's political genius, his ability to sail against the current, and the conscious creation of his own heroism in his letters to the throne, *Cartas de relación*.

As with Bernal Díaz de Castillo (a chronicler Martínez prefers, for his humanism), the pages dedicated to the meeting between Cortés and Montezuma are the most fascinating. We read of an epic in which Cortés's sheer force of will trammeled what should have been assured victory for Montezuma. Martínez condemns the massacres at the Temple, at Tepeaca and Cholula, whether committed by Cortés or his captains. Of course, wars of conquest have always been bloody. So is it pointless to condemn as immoral something that, by definition, is immoral? Cortés violated the warrior's code of honor, just like Alexander the Great and Napoleon before and after him, not to mention twentieth-century conquerors. If the Aztecs had been victorious, they'd have shown no more clemency.

After the narration of the fall of México-Tenochtitlán, the book's historical and biographical qualities truly shine through. We witness the founding of a new culture, built on the remains of a civilization that was exterminated and yet lives on in the *mestizaje* encouraged by Cortés himself, both out of Catholic zealotry and feudal avarice.

It's impossible to ever really know a hero. Even Droysen, the biographer of Alexander the Great, asked if legendary lives could be pulled from history to come to life in biographies. Well, in the failed 1525 expedition to Hibueras, the tedious bureaucratic procedures (known as "judgments of residence") evaluating Cortés's performance, and his failed vice-regal pretensions, we glimpse a fragmented face whose expressions range from Rivera's caricature to gray Hispanist hagiography. Martínez depicts multiple images of Cortés, many of which are unexpected. Another aspect of the biography meriting special mention is the cast of secondary characters that Martínez presents three-dimensionally, giving *Hernán Cortés* the stunning density of a novel: servants, friars, soldiers of fortune, converted indigenous, a wife who was presumably strangled, and the inscrutable Doña Marina, "la Malinche."

Hernán Cortés came out around the time of the five hundredth anniversary of what Álvaro Mutis rightly called "an astonishing nautical feat." And the material Martínez puts at our disposal, despite his reserve, charts an unequivocal course. The Cortés of 1521 goes from legendary conquistador to "marquis of the Valle de Oaxaca," a State builder capitalizing on unprecedented historical conditions; and finally, the "Don Hernando" of the fall, a noble begging for funds and recognition, a pitiful portrait of the results of patrimonialism in Hispanic culture.

Hernán Cortés himself is still on trial, as it were, and it's ridiculous to expect there to be any historical verdict that might satisfy both the defense and the prosecution. Like all things (including history), justice is relative, especially when people are looking for absolute rulings a posteriori. On one side we have the phony, shallow, messianic Aztec worship that tries to negate Mexico's role in the Spanish-speaking Western world. For that camp, post-1521 Mexico is just a cheap imitation of Europe. But just as shocking is the "candor"—to put it politely—with which some foreign scholars (J.M.G. Le Clézio being the most recent) accuse the Spanish of having destroyed the dubious Garden of Eden that Europe's dirty conscience conjures up in order to delude itself with folksy nonsense. By comparison, the image of historian Lucas Alamán in 1836, hiding Cortés's body in a crypt so no one could find and desecrate it, is moving, although José Vasconcelos* went too far by demanding the conquistador be honored by the erection of monuments to his memory in every town in Mexico.

Few actually know where Cortés's remains are today. But Martínez takes us to the Iglesia del Hospital de Jesús, the poor, abandoned church that houses his body. Through fate, or perhaps providence, the grandeur and the misery of the conquistador's life now reside in near oblivion. But *Hernán Cortés* is memorable for scholar and layperson alike. Historians may argue over its relevance; meanwhile, readers will put down the book and be led to the conclusion that Martínez didn't dare write openly: Hernán Cortés is the founder of Mexico. (1990; *Servidumbre y grandeza de la vida literaria*, 1998)

For many years, José Luis Martínez's house on Calle Rousseau was—for countless writers, researchers, and historians—the best library in Mexico, and its doors were always open. Martínez himself not only collected a wealth of books of inestimable value over the course of his life but also gave freely of his time until his death on March 20, 2007. Acting as cicerone, he'd lead guests through his labyrinth in person, and via telephone respond to bibliographical queries, linguistic riddles, and bookish quandaries. Martínez felt equally obliged to safeguard every source on Hernán Cortés as he did the most modest monograph on a poor Mexican municipality.

His interests included ancient civilizations and a good part of modern literature, but Martínez's great passion was Mexican literature, from the lost "poet king" Nezahualcóyotl to the *Contemporáneos* poets of the twenties and thirties. Two works stand out from his vast bibliography: *El ensayo mexicano moderno* (1958 and 1993), an anthology that sheds light on a great many things, and *Pasajeros de Indias* (1983), a scholarly and highly enjoyable read.

Martínez preserved—perhaps with excessive zeal—the posthumous work of Alfonso Reyes, and studied Paz with the punctilious modesty and loving devotion of an expert. Paz's insights struck him as the most decisive to have been made during his long life as a reader. Martínez discussed several works in progress at the time of his death in a review in *Letras Libres*, at least two of which should be completed out of loyalty to his memory: the editing of correspondence between Reyes and Dominican writer Pedro Henríquez Ureña, and the editing of Reyes's diary, which he was to undertake with a group of colleagues.

Martínez was an "institutional" man in the public sense in which the word was used until fifty or so years ago. He viewed "organizing" culture as the highest honor a writer could aspire to and, like his mentor Torres Bodet,* he served the State exemplarily, in Paris and Athens as a diplomat and government official, and at home at the National Institute of Fine Arts and National Print Works. The last twenty-five years of his life were dedicated to modernizing the Mexican Academy of Language, where he served as honorary director until his death. But of all the public works on his extensive résumé, the one that stands out most is his directorship of the most important publisher in Latin America, the Fondo de Cultura Económica (1976–1982). In his time there he firmly established their ecumenical reputation for publishing texts designed to safeguard Mexican culture from second-rate books in circulation for purely profit-driven motives. Perhaps no other collection proves this better than the Revistas Literarias Mexicanas Modernas (Modern Mexican Literary Journals), which included *Tierra Nueva*, a journal he founded with Jorge González Durán and Alí Chumacero,* poet and close friend.

Those of us in Mexican literary history owe a lot to Martínez. I myself was tremendously honored when chosen—me, who never knew whether to use the informal *tú* or the formal *usted* with him—to write the volume covering the last fifty years for the twentieth-century Mexican literary anthology *Literatura mexicana del siglo XX*. Coauthored by the two of us, the book was published by Conaculta in 1995. Neither of us was satisfied with the result, and at the time I openly, and frankly, expressed my differences of opinion with his view of literary history, which is that it can possibly exclude literary criticism. But in no way did he change the way he treated me as a result, remaining both affectionate and profoundly tolerant. Prudence and equanimity were no doubt his most laudable qualities. His biography (and those of Enrique Krauze* a few years earlier) served as an incentive to other writers: we measured ourselves against his writing.

Many good things will be said about Martínez. I think back with great nostalgia to the last time I visited him: he was keen to boast about one of the "jewels" in his library, a very odd medical text called *El himen en México* (yes, literally, "the hymen in Mexico"), which he was tickled to have in his possession. With his death, a long line of scholars dating back to colonial times comes to an end. Martínez was bibliophile (and bibliographer and bibliomaniac) of the Almighty.

SELECTED BIBLIOGRAPHY

Literatura mexicana. Siglo XX, 1910–1949, Robredo, Mexico, 1949; Conaculta, Mexico, 1990.

El ensayo mexicano moderno, FCE, Mexico, 1968, 1971, and 2001.

Nezahualcóyotl, vida y obra, FCE, Mexico, 1972 and 2003.

Pasajeros de Indias. Viajes trasatlánticos en el siglo XVI, Alianza, Madrid, 1983.

Hernán Cortés, FCE, Mexico, 1990.

Martínez, José Luis, and Christopher Domínguez Michael, *La literatura mexicana del siglo XX*, Conaculta, Mexico, 1995.

Primicias. Antología, ed. Adolfo Castañón, El Colegio de Mexico, 2008.

MEJÍA MADRID, FABRIZIO
(Mexico City, 1968)

Mejía Madrid is a writer who sees Woody Allen not—solely—as creator of madcap, comic fantasies but as chronicler of the hearts and minds of the

Mexican intelligentsia—or at least a certain sector of the Mexican intellectual elite, a tiny yet influential nation that resides (or used to) in certain university faculties. At one point, before the Institutional Revolutionary Party (PRI) lost power, said elite was seen as analogous to "civil society"; *La Jornada* newspaper was its coat of arms and Carlos Monsiváis* its lay patrician. But then the Democratic Revolutionary Party (PRD) began gaining power in the Valley of Mexico, and what had been an exclusive *gauche divine* lost much of its pedigree, victim of its own victorious democratization.

Rather than trumpet its heroes, the urbane left chooses to proclaim its defeats. Or perhaps they simply dissect them with the dour, psychoanalytic fervor of a man trawling through his past—failed—relationships: the 1986–87 student movement, the Cuauhtémoc Cárdenas candidacy, the strange path of Subcomandante Marcos, the electoral campaign and political mobilization that so nearly gave Andrés Manuel López Obrador the chance to lead a democratic dictatorship. That sort of mindset, born of the half truth that sees civics as forged of a reaction to the abuses of power, can be seen in Monsiváis, in Elena Poniatowska,* and in Juan Villoro.* And the baton has been passed to the idiosyncratic Mejía Madrid, raised in the "red belt" of Mexico City's Copilco neighborhood, beside UNAM's Faculty of Philosophy and Literature.

In *Tequila, DF* (2008), Mejía Madrid's most recent novel, the protagonist is a *poète maudit* adrift in the groundswell of countercultural resentment and esoteric ingenuity, a man who would be memorable were he not anachronistic and inopportune. But it's impossible not to consider the precedents set by Bolaño's* *Los detectives salvajes* (1997; *The Savage Detectives,* 2007) and Juan Villoro's *El testigo.* Who would have guessed that "infrarealism" was the comic barometer of Mexican literature? It's the avant-garde stamp we were awaiting. Mejía Madrid is an epigone. That's not the worst fate one could hope for, to be sure; we all emulate our masters to some degree, and only strikingly original writers ever manage to break free and produce exceptional books that we very occasionally get to read and admire. Such is the very apropos case of Roberto Bolaño.

But Mejía Madrid has one up on the average epigone, as he's been aware of his status from the start, and his resignation has turned the anguish of influences into creative fervor. From Monsiváis's 1987 book *Entrada libre* to Mejía Madrid's own *Salida de emergencia* (2007), the latter has followed the former with filial loyalty, and since his mentor opened up a whole wide world to him, Mejía Madrid has also discovered other latitudes: the life and death of twenty-first-century anarchist Brad Will, the local porn industry, citizen anti-crime movements. *Salida de emergencia* does, however, reiterate certain clichés and uphold certain historical myths: whether it's the Oaxacan teachers' strike or the Atenco civil unrest, the radical left is always the victim. And in *El rencor* (2006), another Mejía Madrid novel, a caricatured—often hilariously so—PRI monster is always the cold-blooded killer.

I can't help but identify with many elements of Mejía Madrid's literature; he's a talented satirist and commentator on the generation born in the sixties. There's the Woody Allen-esque panic at receiving AIDS test results, the volunteer rescuer brigades who went out after the 1985 earthquake, the old Gandhi bookstore and its confined immensity. But I can't relate to the litany that ends *Hombre al agua* (2004), his best-known novel. It's the umpteenth declaration of love and hate to Mexico City, in this case taking inspiration from an old New Spain map that shows the city under the apocalyptic sign of the beast. In what are probably some of the author's most derivative pages, he falls back on the desolate spectacle of a military quartermaster roaming the scorched earth in search of provisions that the merciless trackers have already taken to the generals.

Tequila, DF is a well-structured novel that narrates the same thing from four different angles, the method Lawrence Durrell used in *The Alexandria Quartet*. Mejía Madrid probes the life of a misanthrope (the experimental poet) as seen by himself, his friend, his ex-wife, and "Mejía," a writer researching his life. And he does it with his habitual sarcasm, and without confusing fiction and literary-historical journalism, as he did in *Hombre al agua*.

More than the unswerving skeptic or *costumbrista* writer, the Mejía Madrid I most prefer is the author of *Viaje alrededor de mi padre* (2004), a novel far more "exotic" than others more successfully and less honestly marketed as such. The book's premise, at first sight, seems the worst of all possible concepts: it's narrated by God, who not only turns out *not* to be the best narrator but also insists on paraphrasing the Old Testament, something not even Thomas Mann did well. "And yet it moves," because that's where Mejía Madrid really exploits his mastery of pastiche, satire, and grotesque exaggeration. There are two truly phenomenal passages: the one written in a Shakespearean tone chronicles the "rise and fall" of the House of Cawdor, and the other, about the fate of "comrade Beria," is half Dostoyevsky and half Bulgakov, a strangely lyric (and oneiric) admonition that turns *Viaje alrededor de mi padre* into both a surprise addition to Russian nihilism and essential reading. Though at times he walks away empty-handed, Mejía Madrid is a tenacious writer, and over time, by the laws of literary inheritance, he's become a legitimate heir, taking what once belonged to his masters and making it his own.

SELECTED BIBLIOGRAPHY
Hombre al agua, Joaquín Mortiz, Mexico, 2004.
Viaje alrededor de mi padre, Aldux, Mexico, 2004.
El rencor, Joaquín Mortiz, Mexico, 2006.
Tequila, DF, Mondadori, Mexico, 2008.

MELO, JUAN VICENTE
(Veracruz, Veracruz, 1932 – 1996)

Afflicted by multiple diseases, near death more than once, Melo seemed to defy his ailing body and survive on spirit alone, erring between the foggy capital and sunny port of Veracruz, a man who'd outlived himself, immune to the tragedies of the flesh thanks to the joy of his soul. Born in 1932 (as were Salvador Elizondo* and Juan García Ponce*), Melo wrote the most expressive novel of his generation, *La obediencia nocturna* (1969), a book that on rereading I can happily claim as a modern classic for Mexico. Protégé of León Felipe,* author of two collections of short stories (*Los muros enemigos*, 1962, and *Fin de semana*, 1964), Melo fell silent after *La obediencia nocturna*, perhaps struck by "second-novel syndrome." When Juan Vicente died on February 9, 1996, I found out that *La rueca de Onfalia*, that purported second novel he'd been working on for twenty-five years whose very existence some of us thought was a fiction, indeed existed.

A dermatologist in Paris at the Hospital Saint-Louis—where he talked literature with another famous doctor, the evil Louis-Ferdinand Céline—Melo was almost impossible to understand without some medical perspective. His stories, like his novel, view life as a sort of leprosy that ravages the skin while inducing metaphysical truths. But though medicine was his profession, music was his passion. Composer Mario Lavista's musical scores illustrate *La obediencia nocturna*, and Melo effectively founded contemporary music criticism in Mexico in the 1960s. Today, José Antonio Alcaraz, Juan Arturo Brenan, Luis Ignacio Helguera,* and Gerardo Kleinburg are among his disciples. Leafing through the pieces in *Notas sin música* (1969), I find myself wondering which "melo"-dies Melo loved best. As a critic he was very fair to Mexican musicians, from Manuel M. Ponce to his beloved Mario Lavista. His criticism was like a desert sermon on modernism, preached to a prudish crowd listening hesitantly to his tributes to Alexander Scriabin, Albert Roussel, Eric Satie, Darius Milhaud, Francis Poulenc, the Vienna school, and Olivier Messiaen. But he also mocked the humanitarian nonsense of some writers—"Sunday musicians" he called them—such as Georges Duhamel in France and Jaime Torres Bodet* here in Mexico, philanthropists who believed Beethoven's Ninth was "about" freedom and decided to elucidate the deaf public.

Melo died dearly loved by his friends and honored by the establishment: generosity triumphed over oblivion. When I first met him as a boy, I saw him as overweight, strolling through the cafés of the recently inaugurated Zona Rosa in Mexico City, smiling diabolically. As an intern in March 1984, I saw him again at his first national tribute in Xalapa, and though he looked as skinny as the Holy Ghost, he was a dancing fool, going strong all night long. At the ceremony, he gave thanks for what he called a "preposthumous homage." And in the middle of the dance, when I was trying to convince a young lady of the virtues of love at first sight, he recognized me and blew me a kiss, as if urging me to take the bull by the horns. (*Servidumbre y grandeza de la vida literaria*, 1998)

Posthumous editions dwell on the dark side of the literary institution. Discarded notes, half reworked drafts, and carefully prepared wills redacted to be read after an author's death lead to moral dilemmas, legal proceedings, and philological quarrels. Sometimes an executor breaks a promise and publishes a text instead of burning it. Other times unscrupulous relatives plunder the writer's archives. And more than once writers have prepared their own posthumous publications in an attempt to insure posterity.

A year after Melo's death, we finally get to read *La rueca de Onfalia*, the legendary novel whose very existence was questioned and whose contents many feared would be a shambles. Why risk a reputation like Melo's, which ended brilliantly in 1969 with *La obediencia nocturna*? Similar speculation had come up around Juan Rulfo,* who was said to have written another novel called *La cordillera*. But if that book ever did exist, wasn't Rulfo right to have destroyed it, hence running no risk of publishing a book inferior to his two lone masterpieces?

Melo, on the other hand, arranged for the publication of *La rueca de Onfalia* a few days before he died, which is why before discussing the novel itself, I need to draw attention to a few things. Ana María Jaramillo—who rescued and transcribed the manuscript—maintains that the 121-page volume was written by Melo in the late sixties. The author would make what were only superficial changes over the course of the following twenty-five years, she says. I see no reason to doubt her testimony (which, regrettably, is not included in the book), especially since stylistically the novel seems contemporaneous—if not previous—to *La obediencia nocturna*. *La rueca de Onfalia* just might be the missing link between *Los muros enemigos* (1962), *Fin de semana* (1964), and *La obediencia nocturna*, a book that remains the magisterial culmination a great decade in Mexican fiction. And now for the good news: contrary to concerns and more than a few reasonable predictions, *La rueca de Onfalia* is a beautiful book.

So first, what does "la rueca de Onfalia" mean? I've been told that José Emilio Pacheco* has already done the legwork on this. At risk of reiterating what he's already found, I consulted some mythological sources and discovered that Omfale, queen of Lydia, bought Heracles (or Hercules) once he'd performed his twelve labors. While Omfale's slave, Heracles amuses his mistress by dressing as a woman, holding the wool while she knits and using his own needle to serve her in more ways than one. Omphale, she of the perfumed hair, and Heracles, strong and hard, end up making love and having several children. Apparently on one occasion, Pan, who was in love with Omphale, snuck into the queen's rooms and chose the wrong bed, fooled by Heracles's silken clothes, and ended up with a god-awful slap from the hero. Since that time, mythographers assure us, to avoid confusion Pan demanded that his visitors be nude.

Ovid, Lucian, and Plutarch tell the story of Omphale and Heracles, of the hero's labors, of the disingenuous servitude that inverts the roles of master and slave, the "mytheme" that warns of the dangers of vague boundaries between masculinity and femininity. Symbolically, Omphale's distaff—the "rueca" of the book's title—represents the woman's realm as well as passing time: like sand in an hourglass, wool can no longer be woven once the staff is empty. It's the inexorable passing of time and the pulled thread of generations that undoes the cloth of the world.

Perhaps before reading the myth, Melo listened to Saint-Saëns's brief symphonic poem (*Le Rouet d'Omphale*, op. 31, 1872), which the French musician interpreted thus: "The theme of the score is female seduction, the triumph of weakness over strength. The staff is just a pretext, chosen because of the rhythm and the overall pace of the piece. Those who might be interested in the details will find Hercules moaning over one of the knots that he can't untie and Omphale mocking the hero's efforts expended in vain."

La rueca de Onfalia transposes their tale to a Veracruz family whose saga Melo felt compelled to tell. And no author has undertaken such a natural adaptation since the lyrical novels of Gilberto Owen, Xavier Villaurrutia, and Jaime Torres Bodet* (who adapted the myths of Ixion, Narcissus, and Proserpine). Melo does a better job than the poets who published in the journal *Contemporáneos* of achieving fragmented classicist images—one of the great adventures of modern literature—that hark back to Joyce's *Ulysses*.

I said that *La rueca de Onfalia* is a beautiful book. But it's not a great novel. Many of its pages are memorable for the musicality of their prose and evocative visuals. When Florelia and Doctor Rosique replicate the affair between Omphale and Heracles and he refuses to put on her dress, Melo chalks one up for the moderns, a small but decisive victory. He tried to write a provincial novel that would incorporate tropes including the spinster, the monstrous child born of sin, vigils, and vendettas . . . But Melo's posthumous book gets stuck once the author begins playing piano, toying around with a series of charming but elusive variations on a theme. *La rueca de Onfalia* is better than a draft but not quite a well-wrought novel. It's a decent first version, like a Veracruz *Buddenbrooks*, an unfulfilled promise of excellence.

It's a shame that Melo, whose life was full of disease and accidents but also music and festivities, lacked the temperance of less-inspired writers such as

Sergio Galindo.* He was destined to be a writer who feared the completed work, who disdained literature at the expense of life. He wasn't our last Romantic, because there's always another Romantic. But the book leaves the nagging doubt as to why he postponed its publication until his death, and when and why he decided—if in fact he did—to leave it as a work in progress. The rebel son of an aristocratic family, he may well have feared some private scandal would be disclosed. It's the surprising naïveté of the Romantic who loses his rebellious side the moment he's handed the keys to the city. So what does *La rueca de Onfalia* represent? Not Hercules himself, but his costume as the marvelous Omphale, the beautiful silk he was wearing when Pan came upon him (1997; *Servidumbre y grandeza de la vida literaria*, 1998).

Selected Bibliography
Juan Vicente Melo, Empresas Editoriales, Mexico, 1966.
El agua cae en otra fuente, Universidad Veracruzana, Xalapa, 1985.
Notas sin música, FCE, Mexico, 1988.
La obediencia nocturna, ERA, Mexico, 1993.
La rueca de Onfalia, Universidad Veracruzana, Xalapa, 1996.

MENDOZA, ÉLMER

(Culiacán, Sinaloa, 1949)

Few contemporary Mexican writers embody Cyril Connolly's "tough guy" (or Philip Rahv's "redskin writers") better than Mendoza—authors who see the streets, the market, and the morgue as the places where the battle over the soul—and literary form—is waged. At least two of Mendoza's novels (*El amante de Janis Joplin* and *Efecto tequila*) are fast-paced, hard-boiled page-turners, books you read with growing horror at the culture of violence he depicts with remarkable aptitude. Narco-trafficking and police brutality—a two-headed monster—and Argentina's Dirty War are topics that seem to lend themselves to fictional truth rather than a miserabilist overworking of reality.

Normal folks fall victim to indignation on a regular basis, but good writers can't let themselves yield to that temptation: outrage gets in the way of reflection and turns into a moralizing artifice. Of course, I'm aware that that's precisely what Mendoza was accused of, by no less a critic than Rafael Lemus, who wrote: "I said Élmer Mendoza but I could have named others. In any other country, he'd be an author; in ours, he's a symptom. His realism is that of many, the most representative. There's no point listing the authors who share his *costumbrismo*—it's not so much a style as it is a certain air, an obsession in Mexican narrative. We know we've read many novels like his, but we can't remember the titles or authors. What is it that's so familiar? The way of observing and representing what's "real." It's a narrow realism. Only what I observe is real: the real world matters; objects don't. (Nothing reminiscent of the nouveau roman's still-lifes here). The world is more real than life: action more than tedium, events more than emotions, the social more than the personal. It's no surprise that this realism can't recreate the fullness and emptiness of existence. Nor are the formal results a shock: it produces conventional works because its way of contemplating the world is conventional. Welcome to Mexican realism."

But contrary to what Lemus says, *El amante de Janis Joplin* (2001) introduces one of the most credible characters in contemporary Mexican fiction. David Venezuela, the poor devil Mendoza condemned to live and die in 1970s Sinaloa, is an idiot savant worthy of Gogol and Dostoyevsky. Over the course of a few months during which he kills a drug lord in self-defense and finds himself initiated into the world of organized crime, this wastrel—whose actions are dictated by an unidentified voice that could just as easily be his conscience as full-blown schizophrenia—tries and fails to be a pitcher in L.A., has a sexual encounter with a debilitated Janis Joplin (or a shadow of her), and gets tangled up in a plot hatched by the forces of repressive brutality—narcs and guerrillas. Any other writer, lacking Mendoza's astonishing ear for slang and literary language both, would have taken this material and churned out hollow, fraudulent trash, a commercial fabrication destined to fade into oblivion. But Mendoza, with incisive humor, paints a memorable picture of his hometown of Culiacán at a time when opium traffickers—*gomeros*—didn't even dream of becoming international kingpins and radicalized students were just beginning their catastrophic adventure in urban terrorism. In Mendoza's world a police chief manages to find a guerrilla training-manual by interpreting a book of Octavio Paz poetry he finds in a copy of *Libertad bajo palabra* left in a safe house. The book narrates the subsequent qualitative increase in violence, as noted by Federico Campbell and Sergio González Rodríguez,* writers more than conversant with the topic. Mendoza chronicles how what used to be almost "rural" criminality was transformed into a disturbing TV spectacle that—unlike thirty years ago—transpires amid the anarchic, raucous state of democracy.

I was less convinced by *Efecto tequila* (2004), even though I assume this book required Mendoza to take greater linguistic and literary risks. By having the plot unfold in Spain, Brazil, and Argentina, he ditched the "Culiacán writer" label and legitimately aspired to join the ranks of contemporary novelists whose mandate is to write international novels and who need boarding passes as much as Stendhal needed the Napoleonic Code. *Efecto tequila* satirizes and recreates the forays of an Argentine torturer detained in Mexico while working as an automotive executive. There's not a lot that Mendoza can add, as a novelist, to the horror of the Argentine dictatorship: absolute evil is aesthetically insurmountable.

Befittingly, Mendoza uses humor to tail and snare the torturer, this time in the guise of Elvis Alezcano—alias Hendrix's Guitar—described by Argentine authorities as "a Mexican in the service of the British in '82." More than a character per se, this Mexican spy is a conduit that allows Mendoza to hone his linguistic ear once more, this time tuning into the Spanish of Madrid and Buenos Aires. The righteous hero, confident and full of self-esteem, acts as a sort of nod to Mexico: the brave man sallies forth, restoring justice and moral cohesion and setting the world to rights. Mendoza's not the first to propose such a redeemer and it might be a comfort to him to know that Mexican writers very different from him have also yielded slightly disappointing results, unfocused characters. His hyperrealism seems to spring from authors who taught him the difficult art of writing about violence without resorting to that base style of literature that doesn't so much denounce the world's depravity as assault the reader's morals.

SELECTED BIBLIOGRAPHY

El amante de Janis Joplin, Tusquets Editores, Mexico, 2001.
Efecto tequila, Tusquets Editores, Mexico, 2004.

MEYER, JEAN
(Nice, France, 1942)

Mexico—like France—is a country that takes people in, and of all the French writers who have made Mexico their adoptive home, few are as beloved as Meyer. Perhaps none is dearer to the hearts of those who see him not just as a voice but an eminent authority who was able to make sense of history itself. If Meyer, whose family is Alsatian, had decided not to stay on in Mexico after arriving in 1965 to research the Cristeros, if he'd lost all interest in us after publishing *La Cristiada* (1973–1975), we'd still be immensely indebted to him.

La Cristiada is a historiographical work, the kind that appears once in a blue moon and becomes an almost miraculous act of redress. In it, Meyer traces and tracks the origins, conflicts, and consequences of the civil war that lasted from 1926 to 1933, with a three-year truce that served only to disarm those who had surrendered, since not doing so would have been heresy. The war cost the lives of 250,000 Mexicans, only 90,000 of whom were soldiers (on either side). And unlike the victims of the Mexican Revolution, who officially stopped piling up with the Constitution of 1917, the Cristeros were not only stigmatized by defeat but also wore the scarlet letter of civilian casualties, as Meyer learned from his mentor Luis González y González.* The sulphurous stench of the Catholics suffocated the regime—more Jacobin than liberal—that made its peace with the Mexican Catholic hierarchy and the Vatican in exchange for their betrayal of the *campesino* rebellion. All of that is documented in *La Cristiada*, a twentieth-century historiographical masterpiece. I can't stress enough: this is one of those books that alters our moral compass, changes the sequence of events, and forces us to reread and rewrite our history. Meyer is the Mexican historian of religious freedom par excellence.

In attaining that stature, he didn't (as González y González writes in his prologue to the 1991 edition of *La revolución mexicana*) simply apply sixties university Marxism; nor did he hole himself up in Mexico City; nor did he accept the post-revolutionary regime's whitewashed version of their will to uproot rural Catholicism (finally halted by the combination of compassion and common sense that made Lázaro Cárdenas great). Thus, before the duty of memory had a chance to become journalistic "truth," Meyer came out with *La Cristiada.* In *La gran controversia: Las iglesias católica y ortodoxa desde los orígenes a nuestros días* (2005), he asserts that historians should not emulate Chateaubriand, who—overshadowed by Napoleon—set out to avenge history. Meyer doubts the benefit of judging the past, which is all that public scrutiny often leads to.

I make note of the fact that Meyer is a French writer who became Mexican not solely because he has written and published in Spanish since the mid-sixties (including historical fiction: *A la voz del rey* in 1989 and *Los tambores de Calderón* in 1993, which was reissued in 2010 as *Camino a Baján*) but because historiography is and always has been a branch of literature, and ought to be seen as such. Anyone reading the apologia in *La revolución mexicana* will discern Meyer's literary virtues: without resorting to romanticizing sermons, without propagandizing, relying solely on the moral force of the evidence, he disproves the whole of the revolution's mythology.

I don't know if the past is provable, but Meyer's work convinces me that it forms part of a national imagination—a vivid spoken and written imagination that readers will attest to in *Yo, el francés: La intervención en primera persona* (2002). This "autobiography" recreates the testimony of the nineteenth-century French officials who came to Mexico—and then left—with Emperor Maximilian. Meanwhile, *Samuel Ruiz en San Cristóbal* (2000) shows Meyer as a skillful historian of the present as well, testifying to the controversial actions of indigenous catechumens and their bishop before, during, and after the neo-Zapatista uprisings of 1994.

But Meyer wasn't content just to be a Mexicanist. National histories—and literatures—eventually asphyxiate universal spirits. And Meyer's strange case of political exile—a Frenchman expelled from Mexico in 1969, he then went to Paris—he decided to learn Russian, the language of the people he was studying. He wanted to be on the front line of the Soviet Union's disintegration in order to compare the seemingly incomparable: the Cristeros' role in Mexico, and the communists' obliteration of the Russian peasantry. And if that weren't enough, he also undertook a comparative spiritual study of Mexican Catholicism and the Orthodox Church.

If we take ecumenism to be the substitution of religion for ethics, then Meyer is probably Catholic without being ecumenicist. Thus he "found" the lost sanctuaries of the Bajío in the parish of Saint-Irenée, a schism of the Russian Orthodox Church in France. And like the Polish poet Czeslaw

Milosz, Meyer says he feels lost in a world in which Heaven and Hell have no place, where people no longer believe in the afterlife, which is why he thinks religious history should be the first one to be recounted. In that sense, Meyer joins the ranks of Juan Rulfo* and Tarkovsky, the author of *The Passion According to Andrei*. He's been faithful, over the course of many books, to his mentors: the indefatigable Pierre Chaunu, historian of the crusades Steven Runciman, and the great microhistorian González y González. With his Clint Eastwood air, Meyer has all the allure of what his first teacher Fernand Braudel saw as the power of the historian: the ability to bring everything he touches back to life, to surround himself with extraordinary men and women, and, thus, to defy death.

SELECTED BIBLIOGRAPHY

A la voz del rey, Cal y Arena, Mexico, 1989.

Los tambores de Calderón, Diana, Mexico, 1993.

Samuel Ruiz en San Cristóbal, Tusquets, Mexico, 2000.

Yo, el francés. La intervención en primera persona, Tusquets, Mexico, 2002.

La revolución mexicana, Tusquets, Mexico, 2004.

La gran controversia. Las iglesias católica y ortodoxa desde los orígenes hasta nuestros días, Tusquets, Mexico, 2005.

La Cristiada, FCE/Clío, Mexico, 2007.

Camino a Baján, Tusquets, Barcelona, 2010.

The Cristero Rebellion, trans. Richard Southern, Cambridge University Press, 2008.

MILÁN, EDUARDO

(Rivera, Uruguay, 1952)

Mexico became a refuge for thousands of political exiles in the 1970s, as it had during the Spanish Civil War. Some were survivors of prisons and internment camps. Most were professors or university students, militants or sympathizers of the outlawed left in Chile, Uruguay, and Argentina. At universities, in political circles, and at literary cafés, you heard accents from Buenos Aires, Córdoba, Santiago, Concepción, Montevideo. But compared to the nearly forty years of the Franco regime—a period long enough that the Spaniards became Mexican—South American dictatorships were relatively brief, and after a decade of rabble the military returned to the barracks. Once democracy was reestablished, most of the exiles returned home.

Only a few of the writers stayed on, and one of them was Uruguayan poet and critic Eduardo Milán. His case is not at all representative. The son of a militant urban guerrilla sentenced to 24 years in prison, Milán came to Mexico in 1979 but apparently decided not to take part in the activism with which the exile community recreated—to scale—the rocky political geography of the continental left. Like other Uruguayan writers, Milán became involved with the journal *Vuelta*, where he served on the editorial board and became one of their most loyal poetry critics. But anyone reading his poems—especially those of the splendid period of *Errar* (1991), *La vida mantis* (1993), *Nivel medio verdadero de las aguas que se besan* (1994), and *Circa 1994* (1996)—will find that his poetry bears no relation to the Mexican poetry of his generation. I say that with relief. Milán not only kept his own style but also kept to his own world, a place ruled by music—from Vinicius de Moraes to Charlie Watts—thanks to his sensitive ear.

Since that time, Milán has been indispensable to Spanish-language poetry on both sides of the Atlantic. He co-authored the anthologies *Pristina y última piedra: Antología de poesía hispanoamericana presente* and *Las ínsulas extrañas: Antología de poesía en lengua española (1950–2000)*. And prior to that, with Jacobo Sefamí, Roberto Echavarren, and José Kozer, he edited *Medusario* (1996), a sampler of Latin American poetry that revered a "neo-baroque" spirit that the editors located somewhere between the old vanguard (from Huidobro and Girondo to Octavio Paz*) and colloquialism (Parra, Cardenal, some Neruda), designating a "third way" that included poets as divergent (and these are only the Mexicans) as David Huerta,* Coral Bracho,* José Carlos Becerra,* and Milán himself. As Felipe Vázquez notes in *Archipiélago de signos: Ensayos de literatura mexicana* (1999), Milán was determined to reflect upon the "postmodern" evolution of Mexican poetry. He's not, of course, the only one to have done so. He is perhaps, though, the one who took the most risks.

Milán's literary criticism has been faulted for its reliance—which has waned over the years—on a type of jargon more River Plate than post-structuralist, a tone discernible in books like *Una cierta mirada: Crónicas de poesía* (1989) and *Resistir: Insistencias sobre el instante poético* (1994). But in Milán's defense, it's important to admit that as critics we all rely on our own particular jargon, which eventually becomes entrenched. So over the years, we end up developing certain aversions, other propensities, and using stock phrases and outdated coquetries. Milán's critical vocabulary comes from a particular era. Had he lived in another time, he'd have been seen as Lukácsian or Sartrean, but regardless, his good taste and anti-conformist stance would have risen above any theory or label.

Milán's informal schooling in "concrete poetry"—which thinks itself austere, meticulous, and Loyolan—reminds me of Julien Gracq's joke about Mallarmé, who he said packed his bags every time he heard the clarion call of "metalinguistic modernity," prepared to head out in the service of the vanguard. The path of spirituality and levitation eventually led Milán to more sophisticated poetry, that of a reader of Saint John of the Cross and Miguel de Molinos. He's fond of sound-play and assonance, devices that helped him find a home after detours suggestive of Nicanor Parra, Gonzalo Rojas, and Haroldo de Campos and other Brazilian concrete poets. Then, in Argentine exiled poet Juan Gelman (1931), he finally found the mentor he'd been searching for.

Epiphany, in the Joycean sense, is a concept central to Milán, as it is to so many contemporary poets. But for very few does it work as well as it does for him: sudden visions, gestures and words, memorable representations of pure thought. *Nivel medio verdadero de las aguas que se besan* presents the ego as troublemaker, talking to itself, creating an ill-fated opposition: "Si usted no fuera humano y no cayera del caballo por amor, / ¿sería ardilla? Sería / pero caería del árbol por amor. No hay forma / que por amor no caiga / hasta las muy enfermas . . ." ("If you were not human and did not fall from the horse for love, / would you be a squirrel? You would / but you'd fall from the tree for love. There is no form / that does not fall for love / even the very sick ones . . .")

Personal and confidential without being entirely autobiographical, Milán's poetry plays with the limits of language yet remains undeniably grounded in the realm of family, safe from hermeticism. As Nicanor Vélez says in the prologue to his Milán anthology (*Querencia, gracias y otros poemas*, 2003), few poets so shamelessly allow their children, wife, prematurely deceased mother, and imprisoned (and freed) Tupamaro father to grace the pages of their poetry, turning what might have been withering sentimentalism into sensitivity. But after *Son de mi padre* (1996), Milán returned to the ideological values of his younger days. By my calculations that was when—victim of a political epiphany—he decided to leave *Vuelta*, using Paz's ailing health as an excuse to slam the door behind him.

In addition to postmodern domestic, Milán can also be a "little devil" more characteristic of turn-of-the-century modernism. This other poet distrusts man, conceived of as a curse by the pregnant woman, by the child. Man, here, is controlled by his demons. For this voice, gratitude is inconceivable and paying debts to society is heretical; this man only breathes easy when he knows that "el monstruo ya no está / y solo a veces hay ruido en el techo / para que sepamos que puede aparecer cuando quiera—cuando quiera, querer: ése es su poder" ("the monster is gone / and only sometimes are there noises on the roof / to let us know he can appear whenever he wants—whenever he wants, to want: that's his power").

The poet of *Querencia, gracias y otros poemas* passes himself off as a sage, a wearying Eastern guru, a Buddhist fellow traveler who consults astrologers and spiritual advisers. Not only does he "engage" in *engagé* poetry but he dispenses wisdom and blessings. Naïvely, I never saw this coming, this extravaganza in which Milán simultaneously presents us with poetic art and a roll call of his most intimate, personal beliefs. Having started off obsessed with form and literary theory and old post-structuralist rhetoric, he ended up with twee affectation. But it's the sort of affectation—*cursilería*—defined by Ramón Gómez de la Serna as the only thing that would be saved from each historical moment. And Milán, as a poet, was always safe. As he said in *Alegrial* (1997), "Podemos ser sagrados pero preferimos ser perfectos / o sea trágicos" ("We could be sacred but we prefer to be perfect / that is tragic"). It seems to me that Milán's epiphanies are what's left of Barthes's *Fragments*, which we loved so much at the time even though now it seems gauche to admit it.

SELECTED BIBLIOGRAPHY
Una cierta mirada. Crónicas de poesía, Juan Pablos Editor/UAM, Mexico, 1989.

Manto, FCE, Mexico, 1999.

Querencia, gracias y otros poemas, ed. and prologue by Nicanor Vélez, Galaxia Gutenberg/Círculo de Lectores, Barcelona, 2003.

Resistir. Insistencias sobre el presente poético, FCE, Mexico, 2004.

MIRET, PEDRO F.

(Barcelona, Spain, 1932 – Mexico City, 1988)

The years go by, but when they do a roll call of Rubén Darío-style "eccentrics" in Mexican literature, Miret keeps making the list. His teacher, friend, and defender Luis Buñuel died; so did Luis Ignacio Helguera*—so young—the last and most enthusiastic of the Miret devotees, the one whose prose poems and short stories were going to carry on his name. But during the last decade, Gerardo Deniz* prefaced the reedition of *Esta noche . . . vienen rojos y azules* (1964, 1972, and 1997), Mario González Suárez* included him in his twentieth-century Mexican fiction anthology *Paisajes del limbo* (2001), and José de la Colina* proclaimed his loyalty by publishing his Miret essay in *Libertades imaginarias* (2000). So Miret is gone but definitely not forgotten, and perhaps it's befitting his strictly literary nature to remain in that state of latency. Miret is Céline without the bile, an author without a subject, a man who belongs to no one and yet, at times, invents history, mocks it without a second thought and with a certain indifference.

I reread *Insomnes en Tahití* (1989), Miret's posthumous novel, and it struck me—even more so the second time around—as both singular and important. I believe it's the only Mexican novel to date comprised entirely of dialogue, which takes place over the course of 141 pages. Miret, like Ivy Compton-Burnett—the English writer and darling of nouveau roman officiants—writes conversation unlike any other. His are written in Spanish and French, and despite being implausible and pedantic, they never seem stilted or gratuitous. It's no coincidence that Miret excels at dialogue (as he does at superficial, opaque description): he was once a prestigious scriptwriter. As Buñuel noted, his world is not exactly magical or entirely fantastical. It's pure reality, filmed in black and white, a model reproduced to scale by the author, who before working in film had studied architecture.

Insomnes en Tahití recounts the conversations taking place over the course of a tourist's sleepless night on Tahiti. And in the same way that in Rulfo's* town of Comala, everyone is a child of Pedro Páramo, here every islander appears to be a descendent of Paul Gauguin. And all of them want to sell the protagonist—at any cost, but not any price—Gauguin "originals," paintings and lithographs signed by the painter. Their banter and barter produce an enigmatic and highly original storyline. *Insomnes en Tahití* might be read as a meditation on authenticity and authentication in the art world—from Leonardo da Vinci to the avant-garde, from the museum to the market, something another Spanish-born Mexican, Max Aub,* also dealt with in the brilliant novel *Jusep Torres Campalans* (1958).

Although it's a technical study of the possibilities of fictionalized dialogue, *Insomnes en Tahití* also deals with history. World War II and its heroes and villains and consequences are speculated on here—as well as in *Rompecabezas antiguo* (1981), Miret's most interesting book of stories. And finally, *Insomnes en Tahití* is a book that—only partially tongue-in-cheek—deals with the subject of "Orientalism," the term now used reproachfully to describe Western curiosity about the mindset of "savage" Others. The world, as Miret represents it, is filtered through the blinds of the tourist's hotel room.

It seems likely that Buñuel recommended Miret read Raymond Roussel (1877–1933), who had a profound influence on the surrealists. *Insomnes en Tahití* is like a homage to the French millionaire poet and his *Impressions of Africa* (1910), a move that secures him a place on the world list of eccentrics. Roussel was an admirer of Verne (so much so that he wouldn't stand for certain people pronouncing his name) and of Pierre Loti, a French writer and naval officer who'd done training in the South Seas and written about Tahiti. Roussel traveled to the island in search of the natives he'd read about in Loti's work and managed to get his picture taken with them. Paradoxically, Roussel reveled in the fact that none of his own books were in the slightest influenced by his travels. At any rate, Roussel leads to André Breton, to Salvador Dalí, and to Buñuel, and then we have a direct line to Miret, who was born in Barcelona in 1932—a year many great Mexican writers were born—and died in 1988 in Cuernavaca, Morelos, where he arrived as a seven-year-old exile from the Spanish Civil War.

I'll close with the de rigueur personal anecdote. In 1987, Adolfo Castañón* and I went to an exiled writers' conference in Veracruz. I have no idea why they invited me, particularly as I'm a homebody who rarely ventures out of the neighborhood. At any rate, one day Adolfo and I played hooky, rented a car, and went to visit some nearby beaches. In Chachalacas we horsed around in the dunes wearing turbans, pretending to be Buzzati characters. Later that evening we met back up with the real exiles in the historic town of Antigua. And there was Miret, in a forest of Antigua's petrified trees and surrounded by fellow exiles, looking happy and at home.

SELECTED BIBLIOGRAPHY

La zapatería del terror, Grijalbo, Mexico, 1978.

Rompecabezas antiguo, FCE, Mexico, 1981.

Prostíbulos, Pangea, Mexico, 1987.

Insomnes en Tahití, FCE, Mexico, 1989.

Esta noche . . . vienen rojos y azules, prologue by Gerardo Deniz, introduction by Luis Buñuel, Conaculta, Mexico, 1997.

MOLINA, MAURICIO
(Mexico City, 1959)

Molina's first novel belongs to that influential apocalyptic tradition we've seen develop recently in Mexican literature. The trend began with the arrogant excesses of Carlos Fuentes's* *Cristóbal Nonato* (1987; *Christopher Unborn*, 1989) and can be traced through the works of José Agustín,* Homero Aridjis,* and Hugo Hiriart,* all of whom are convinced that the destruction of Mexico City—and thus by extension the spirit of the nation—is an ineluctable literary fact, whether by ecological disaster, US invasion, political collapse, or cyclical repetition of the fall of 1521. For Molina, however, there's a difference: his apocalypse already occurred, in the form of lunar eclipse [. . .]

Eclipse is the metaphor Molina chooses in order to fictionalize his firm belief in the decisive influence of the stars on the lives of men. *Tiempo lunar* (1993) takes for granted the control exerted by lunar phases (star-crossed and otherwise) over modern culture. More than a postmodern sentimental almanac or a novel about the 1969 moon landing—like Auster's extraordinary *Moon Palace*—Molina's book owes a lot to the current futuristic and apocalyptic aesthetics in film. *Tiempo lunar* is more *Blade Runner* than it is "Pepsicóatl" (a term coined by Carlos Fuentes* that combines Pepsi and Aztec god Quetzalcóatl, melding a consumerist world and hollow nativist worship). The devastated metropolis in question might be Mexico City, but it looks suspiciously like the post-Soviet Moscow of Vladimir Makanin's *Escape Hatch*.

I don't bring up Paul Auster and Russian novelist Makanin out of some "comp-lit" compulsion to find parallels. What matters is the *universalization* of the apocalyptic setting, the emergence of that world literature Goethe dreamed of—although now it's a nightmare that's hardly eased by the proliferation of Babel. In few new Mexican writers do we find "trafficking" with contemporary narrative so present as in Molina, eager as he is to harmonize with the postmodern aesthetic.

It's fair, therefore, to admonish his adherence to futuristic thriller clichés. Yes, it's true that they allowed him to write a well-structured novel, but his insistence on the visual also makes for some shortcomings. The hero of *Tiempo lunar* repeats all the hackneyed moves of a part-time investigator trying to solve the mysterious disappearance of his best friend; drinking, smoking, and fooling around with the heroine without realizing her body contains the key to the novel. The sex scenes are more stylized retro aesthetic than intimate, detailed sensuality. *Tiempo lunar* is a novel written by a director who asked his characters to overact, and whose actors didn't get the parody. But Molina did what he set out to do. Superimposing a lunar map over Mexico City has a powerful distancing effect, and the thriller takes a backseat thanks to the closing scene, when photographer Ismael disappears surrounded by poltergeists in a sort of Eternal Return. (*Antología de la narrativa mexicana del siglo XX*, vol II, second revised edition, 1996)

For about a decade now, Molina has been publishing collections of short stories including *Mantis religiosa* (1997), *Fabula rasa* (2001), and *La geometría del caos* (2002) in which he follows the same type of character: the vagabond, the *flâneur*, the wanderer, the figure who is consciously and voluntarily dissociated from the "community," that place located on a street so familiar it's mysterious. But it just might be that Samuel Beckett and Lucia Joyce—disturbed, ill-fated daughter of James—are Molina's most finely depicted characters. *La ballerina y el clochard* (2005) is a play that abridges—to exactly the degree required by the theater—the family drama that was Lucia's obsession with Beckett, who at the time was working as her father's assistant.

One of the least studied phenomena in contemporary Mexican literature is the growing—and tragic—distance between writers and the theater, or between dramaturgy and literature. Authors who work in both realms—such as Hugo Hiriart*—have become anomalies. Perhaps after *La ballerina y el clochard*, given the visual nature of his imagination (and the oddity he's taken to be by "moderns"), Molina will be one of the writers best poised to raise the curtain of Mexican literature once again.

SELECTED BIBLIOGRAPHY
Tiempo lunar, Osa Mayor, Mexico, 1993.
La ballerina y el clochard, prologue by José Ramón Enríquez, UNAM, Mexico, 2005.

MONSIVÁIS, CARLOS
(Mexico City, 1938 – 2010)

A mainstay in Mexican cultural, political, and literary life over the best part of the past fifty years, Carlos Monsiváis was also a great mystery—extraordinarily original, influential, private. His Mexican readers, and the writers—myself included—taught by him in one way or another tended to think of him as mythic (or mythological), a legend founded at the beginning of time. It was tempting to think he'd always been around, and that the era that began in 1968 was—at least rhetorically—not so much a national historical episode as it was the work of Monsiváis—whose greatness, of course, resided precisely in his ability to create that illusion.

The routine back and forth that was Monsiváis's everyday public life became tiring, led to sacrilegious desires of parricide, and made us wonder: would Mexico survive without his vigilance? But regardless of ideological disputes or passing irritations, there's one thing I have no doubts about: liberal, democratic Mexican culture would have been inconceivable without him. I can't think of higher praise for an intellectual.

Monsiváis was the one who actually defined himself—not without bitterness—as a member of the first generation of Americans to be born in

Mexico. So it's no coincidence that the first serious study of his work came out of US academia (Linda Egan's *Carlos Monsiváis: Culture and Chronicle in Contemporary Mexico*, 2000). I'd go so far as to add that Monsiváis would actually have been incomprehensible without US culture. I dare say he's as voracious as Walt Whitman before the Civil War, feverishly collecting the language and imagery of the street to compose *Leaves of Grass*, that hymn to high and low culture both. Monsiváis showed a similar poetic passion, all the more admirable in him because—entirely lacking the soul of an artist— he tried to see every man as poet-cum-critic.

A reader of the Bible, Monsiváis remained faithful to his Protestant upbringing, searching for the truth with evangelical passion and attempting to heal the oppressed via the word. Time and again, this puritan prophet expelled the merchants from the temple. And on the way to Adrianople this pilgrim became the cornerstone of the Church of Civil Society, whose rites started off chaotic and ended up becoming a secular service over which Monsiváis often presided, almost always in order to lash his flock.

"Sin was the central theme of my childhood and in some way the idea . . . has continued to govern over me to this day," the young Monsiváis wrote in his early autobiography *Carlos Monsiváis* (1966). That declaration revealed the paradoxical continuity between his Christian upbringing and his becoming one of the great "secularizing" intellectuals of Mexican society, a writer who practically unleashed a crusade against the idea of sin being used as a moral bludgeon wielded in the service of power. But few were more openly agnostic than Monsiváis, and I say this not because of his depiction of faith healer Niño Fidencio in *Los rituales del caos* (The Rituals of Chaos) or his regular dredging up of barbarities committed by the hierarchs of the Church. Monsiváis was not just anticlerical: he was the harshest, most heartfelt Mexican anti-Catholic around. Even novelist Martín Luis Guzmán,* famous for his tirades against superstitions and Catholic "miracles," looks like a Jacobin despot by comparison. And although he never said so openly, I think Monsiváis saw the Church as not just superstitious and fanatical but intrinsic to the Mexican exaltation of the culture of poverty.

The "godfather" of the generation of '68, as Enrique Krauze* called him, Monsiváis has to be seen, in his role as public intellectual, as one of the nation's great *mafiosi*, an astute and unrelenting political animal. And although he took a mid-century trip to the catacombs of the Mexican Communist Party (PCM) and paid heartfelt homage to their dead in *Amor perdido*, Monsiváis was a leftist with no ties to any Marxist-Leninist groups. Thanks to his Protestant upbringing and the revulsion he felt for all forms of impunity, he was a liberal in both the individualist US sense of the term and the State-centered, anti-clerical Juarist Mexican one. He lacked the slightly naïve, Thoreau-inspired love of equality and civil disobedience and was a militant defender of the State as guarantor of secularism. That double liberalism allowed Monsiváis to pass democratic tests that others failed, such as his staunch loathing of the Castro regime. It also enabled him to bring feminist and gay rights agendas into the public forum.

Monsiváis was one of few on the Mexican left to try to achieve strict equivalence between political and social freedoms. But it wasn't always an easy balance, as seen by his ambivalent stance vis-à-vis the EZLN (Ejército Zapatista de Liberación Nacional), the guerrilla group that found so much sympathy among Mexican university students and the international left in 1994. Monsiváis dissociated himself from the sacrificial mysticism of Subcomandante Marcos because it sounded like repetitive Christian martyrdom, but he accepted the neo-Zapatista movement's rejection of republican order.

The "love of the oppressed" so characteristic of Monsiváis at times deprived him of reason. The rebel, in his view, was always theologically right; the moral imperative was always on his side, particularly if he was young, and thus forgiven for choosing misguided methods of battle. The students who brought the Universidad Nacional Autónoma de México (UNAM) to a standstill for nearly a year were, for Monsiváis, "kids" committed to fighting an unfair battle against the political powers that were, by definition, malevolent. True to the masochism exhibited by most evangelists, he continued to offer his ill-humored, reticent, paternal protection to General Strike Council activists even after they mistreated him in 1999–2000. Also shocking was his lamentable—and perhaps fleeting—blindness to the phony Juarism of López Obrador, something Monsiváis should have been the first to see through. When it came to the oppressed—real or fake—Monsiváis was blind, and he used his dialectical skills in the service of causes that I can only imagine must have led to some painful soul-searching and crises of conscience. It's a romantic image, but it couldn't have been easy to be a "soldier of peace, brotherhood, and justice" as well as the self-appointed "ombudsman" of society, as Linda Egan ironically calls him.

The group that Monsiváis and his collaborators founded in 1968 in *La Cultura en México* was simultaneously a feat of democratic courage and their source of legitimacy during the seventies. And when the 1988 election fraud and subsequent uprisings divided the complex alliance of professors, politicians, and writers at the magazine *Nexos*, Monsiváis, riding a wave of public acclaim, entered the next phase of his career: moral leadership rooted in his public visibility and moral probity. Since that time, as Adolfo Castañón* notes, Monsiváis has been the only Mexican writer the general public recognizes. Applauded by audiences the moment he stepped into an auditorium and stopped on the street by citizens wanting a picture with him, he was not so much a politician on the campaign trail as he was a wildly successful preacher, the hierarch of an invisible church that congregated whenever the faithful heard his voice.

Monsiváis's work introduced us to a mythographer and ethnographer whose profession destined him to substitute his own icons for fallen idols. Plenty of the pop icons that the intellectual elite respects—or at least tolerates—owe their worship to the literary beatification of Monsiváis, who found paradigms of Mexicanness (some insufferable, some touching) in figures as varied as Mexico's golden age film starlets, composer Agustín Lara, *ranchera* singers Juan Gabriel and José Alfredo Jiménez, rocker *sic transit* Gloria Trevi, and union leader Fidel Velázquez. And, an unwilling *costumbrista*, he also lent his analytical insights to a few luminaries who'd lost their alleged sociological significance, such as singer-songwriters Raphael and Emmanuel and TV presenter Raúl Velasco. The overnight arbiter was destined to pass judgment on fifteen-minute stars.

A cultural analyst who nearly always found universal solutions to Mexican problems, Monsiváis, over the course of time and countless articles, slowly undermined the canon of Mexican identity. In its stead, he heaped Whitmanesque praise onto ordinary folks who—thanks to his mediation—became myths and archetypes. Nevertheless, Monsiváis was a true pluralist for whom the exploration of "difference" culminated in universal values, which can easily be seen in his stance on the EZLN's indigenist agenda. He sympathized with the right to rebel against a shameful reality without appealing to skin "the color of the earth" and blood rights. A key moment in his evolution occurred when (breaking with the views Octavio Paz* expressed in *The Labyrinth of Solitude*, his least intelligible book) Monsiváis said that the October 2 massacre at Tlatelolco had effectively annihilated "the supposedly close link between the Mexican and death." But contrary to what one might think, his texts were not paeans to multiculturalism and had no truck with the reverse racism of books like *Mexico profundo* (1987) by Guillermo Bonfil Batalla. For Monsiváis, to paraphrase Marshall Berman, identity melts into air.

At the start of the twenty-first century, Monsiváis seems more part of Mexico's political memory than its literary tradition, which makes it necessary to reinstate him as a man of letters, the author of works like *Días de guardar* (1970) (*Days of Waiting*), *Amor perdido* (1976) (*Lost Love*), *Escenas de pudor y liviandad* (1988) (*Scenes of Modesty and Frivolity*), *Entrada libre* (1987) (*Free Entry*), *Los rituales del caos* (1995), *Aires de familia: Cultura y sociedad en América Latina* (2000) (*Family Resemblance: Culture and Society in Latin America*), and *Salvador Novo: Lo marginal en el centro* (2000) (*Salvador Novo: The Marginal in the Center*), the most personal and genuine of his books, in which he named Novo as the crucial link in the great Mexican tradition. Monsiváis's popularity with the general public has meant that his newspaper articles, which would fill many volumes, eclipsed his relatively few books. Still, it's worth noting that he often didn't seem to care about overwrought prose lacking in expository clarity, and his writing could be a tiresome organizational mess that substituted phrases for paragraphs. At his worst, he assumed that we ever-faithful readers spent decades studying his syntax and jargon and had infinite patience.

Monsiváis was a man of the margins who made it to the center, a spectator who became spectacle, a liberal who saw utopia as the equal distribution of hope. He was not the lone savior adored by his flock, but a pessimist who knew, sadly, that he could only save himself and that good works redeemed no one. He traveled to the nether regions terrified of the trumpets of the apocalypse, a sage who prophesied by acting as collector of the words, gestures, and actions of this country. If Mexico were to disappear—I mean, hypothetically—Monsiváis would have a pair of each species on his ark.

Selected Bibliography

Días de guardar, ERA, Mexico, 1970.

Amor perdido, ERA, Mexico, 1978.

A ustedes les consta. Antología de la crónica en México, ERA, Mexico, 1980.

Entrada libre. Crónicas de la sociedad que se organiza, ERA, Mexico, 1987.

Escenas de pudor y liviandad, Grijalbo, Mexico, 1988.

Los rituales del caos, ERA, Mexico, 1995.

Aires de familia. Cultura y sociedad en América Latina, Anagrama, Barcelona, 2000.

Salvador Novo. Lo marginal en el centro, ERA, Mexico, 2000.

Las herencias ocultas del pensamiento liberal del siglo XIX, IESA/CEA, Mexico, 2000.

Imágenes de la tradición viva, FCE, Mexico, 2007.

Escribir, por ejemplo (de los inventores de tradición), FCE, Mexico, 2008.

La cultura mexicana del siglo XX, ed. Eugenia Huerta, El Colegio de Mexico, 2010.

Moraña, Mabel and Ignacio Sánchez Prado, eds., *El arte de la ironía. Carlos Monsiváis ante la crítica*, ERA, Mexico, 2007.

Egan, Linda, *Carlos Monsiváis: Culture and Chronicle in Contemporary Mexico*, University of Arizona Press, 2001.

Mexican Postcards, trans. John Kraniauskas, Verso, 2000.

MONTEMAYOR, CARLOS

(Parral, Chihuahua, 1947 – Mexico City, 2010)

The way Carlos Montemayor metamorphosed into a champion of indigenous cultures is one of the most interesting phenomena of Mexican literary life. Here was a member of the Mexican Academy of the Language, an academic, historian, exquisite poet, and translator of both ancient and modern languages. In short, he had all the credentials of a mainstream man of letters, a full member of the cultural establishment. But *Guerra en el paraíso* (1991), his novel about the guerrilla movement in Guerrero in the seventies, announced his transformation from erudite scholar into zealous intellectual consumed by the struggle. How was it that he climbed down from the Ivory

Tower and ended up not in the streets but the jungle? *Encuentros en Oaxaca* (1995) chronicles the encounters between Montemayor and contemporary indigenous literatures. The book, part confession and part essay, is nothing out of this world. But on reading it, we realize that only a man like Montemayor could become the scribe of the Indians and their mouthpiece for us non-indigenous Mexicans. People's initial shock at this was slightly unjustified. After all, humanists—from Fray Bernardino de Sahagún to Ángel María Garibay Kintana*—were the ones who essentially invented and reconstructed ancient indigenous literature. A radical Protestant catechumen in his youth, Montemayor had an epiphany—the kind that's a private revelation to a single individual, conferring upon him a higher understanding of reality. It's odd that it's Protestant theology that sees epiphany as an individual phenomenon, while Catholics see it as a sudden, miraculous manifestation of God to *all* men. At any rate, be that as it may, Montemayor's epiphany is exciting because it's a *linguistic* spiritual event rather than a political or religious conversion.

In the early eighties, Montemayor served as an adviser at a series of indigenous literature workshops put on in Oaxaca for the promotion of popular culture. There, he had a rare opportunity for a classically trained humanist: to be present at the "birth" of a literary language and to help foster its construction. As soon as he asked—between sips of mezcal—the indigenous writers to recite for him in Chatino, Mixtec, and Zapotec, the epiphany occurred. The gob-smacked humanist began—euphorically—to draw comparisons between indigenous languages and Ancient Greek. Apparently, the scene unfolded in a cantina called La Farola, located beside the Oaxaca city market, a place known by tourists as the site where the consul in Malcolm Lowry's *Under the Volcano* meets his tragic fate. Somewhere between the sawdust and the urinal, Montemayor underwent the rites of initiation that introduced him to a whole new, pre-Homeric world, one that he was immediately determined to translate. The indigenous poets could rest easy: for the first time, they were not Sahagún's informants, nor US academics' informants. Instead, Montemayor would act as informant *for* them.

The respectable initiate immediately spelled out the main issues with contemporary indigenous literature, things that both the Indian scholars and National Indigenous Institute linguists alike revealed to him. First, the writers couldn't decide whether to translate their oral traditions into Spanish or phonetically transcribe them. Second, the linguists tended to defend (and desire) the writers' political naïveté, as if it were something sacred. So, paradoxically, they rejected transliteration—which obviously required vast lexicographical, grammatical, and linguistic expertise—since it would destroy the natural state of those literatures (i.e., orality), corrupting them via a Westernization that would turn the Indians into equals rather than Others. So presumably the linguists felt guilty for being intellectuals. The idea of their stepchildren becoming beneficiaries of the oppressor's knowledge was unacceptable, a nightmare. Third, the most straightforward solution—writing in Spanish—was rejected by the majority of the indigenous writers themselves, who saw that as a radical denial of their own cultures. The language/nation association was simply taken for granted.

Montemayor, spellbound by his linguistic epiphany, ardently supported the idea of writing in indigenous languages and left the linguists to deal with their tortuous pedagogical and rhetorical arguments. In a matter of hours, this respected Virgil commentator was offering workshops, teaching the writers the basics of Spanish meter, and discovering the difficulties of transliteration right along with them. His generosity overcame the political reticence of his newfound friends, and Montemayor in turn guaranteed the good faith of his intentions. He got to know the writers—some well established, others in the making—listened to the well-founded objections of those who preferred to write in Spanish, and rejected them with missionary zeal. If kids no longer wanted to speak Zapotec, they'd have to be convinced with Franciscan patience. The elders' words had to be gathered with Augustinian perseverance. It was accepted, with the best Jesuit casuistry, that some would write in Spanish, provided that it was the most direct route to the indigenous language. And thus a sandal-clad Montemayor set out into the desert, beginning a sort of reverse evangelization whereby he didn't *save* indigenous literature, he invented it. Attempting to give the Indians their own classicism, he promoted an experiment in *culteranismo*.

The chronicle of an epiphany, *Encuentros en Oaxaca* is the story of an urban intellectual who didn't want to idealize the Nahuatls but ended up kneeling down before them. Again, what's unique is that Montemayor didn't take the path of Christian mercy, Eleusinian fascination, or revolutionary blame—the three most common routes to indigenism. No, it was linguistics that felled him. The indigenous, he said, "write and think and speak Spanish, which is not their language, better than I speak or write Modern Greek or French." And with that, he turned his disciples into Homeridae, masters of Minoan truth . . . But Montemayor neglected to consider that Modern Greek was of no practical use for his day-to-day living. Indigenous writers' bilingualism is more a necessity than an intellectual choice. By extrapolating from his naïve postulation, he developed a stance unfit for a man of his education. Like any radical college kid, he accepted that our language is essentially "the language of the conquerors," a linguistic reality imposed by genocide, an attachment to be cast off in the next couple of generations. But just a few pages prior he transcribed his Zapotec friends' testimony, and they were complaining about not understanding one another, about how dialectical variety divided them as an ethnicity to such a degree that—beyond their own families, or very specific rituals such as asking for a girl's hand—they were forced to use Spanish as lingua franca of Oaxaca.

Now, I'm no philologist, but common sense seems to indicate that so-called lingua francas are linguistic systems whose rhetoric and historicity are pretty important. The view of language as an instrument of the dominant class, part of the superstructure, is something that even Stalin—supreme linguist of the people when he died—refuted in 1950, disavowing Soviet linguist Nikolai Y. Marr's ideas. Montemayor's hot air on this topic reminds me of a few Argentine teachers in high school who told us, twenty years ago, that English was the "language of the Empire" and learning it equated to colluding with the enemy. Did our humanist forget about bipolar linguistic systems, in which one language is written and another spoken? Couldn't these "possessing" languages have developed, over the course of centuries, one demotic variant and another scholarly one? If Mexican Spanish is full of indigenous expressions, couldn't Montemayor—in his pre-crusade days— have offered us a comparative study of the five hundred years of Hispanicization and its linguistic influence on the indigenous universe? If *Encuentros en Oaxaca* is the chronicle of an epiphany, Montemayor himself is responsible for having produced an anthology of indigenous literature that proves how hard it is to turn that individual revelation into collective redemption.

Who are today's indigenous writers? The intellectual Indian elite. Now, I've got nothing against urbane intellectual associations, even less so with the idea of indigenous communities forming their own. In fact, I see it as terrific news. To think that the Colegio de Santa Cruz de Tlatelolco—founded by Bernardino de Sahagún in 1535 to produce an indigenous clergy and dissolved twenty years later—is alive at the end of the twentieth century is fabulous. The indigenous today, like it or not, are part of modern Mexico. And just like their colleagues at the journals *Nexos* and *Vuelta*, they speak multiple languages, get government grants, started off reading Pablo Nerudo and Amado Nervo, and are now fed up with Roland Barthes and US linguists I've never read. Few are self-taught; most went to public school, and some went abroad for graduate school. And unlike the novitiates at the Tlatelolco school, they don't have to pledge loyalty to the Archbishop of Mexico or the King of Spain. They're regular Mexican citizens: some are Catholic, others Protestant or Pentecostal; their political preferences, I'm sure, range from the Institutional Revolutionary Party (PRI) to the Zapatista National Liberation Army (EZLN). Some are apolitical; others are green. And like all twentieth-century intellectuals, they have a battle to fight. Theirs uses the internet to demand indigenous representation in ten Mexican languages.

The thing is, though, that these indigenous intellectuals have something else in common with us, too. Something bleak and uncomfortable. They lack readers. In Mexico, an officially literate country, people don't read. In Mexico, very few read literature, be it good or bad. In indigenous regions— and this is not news—the rates of illiteracy are astonishing. And if they don't read in Spanish, there's certainly nothing to suggest that they're going to read complex transliterations into Mayan, Nahuatl, Otomi, Chinantec, Tzeltal, and Tzotzil that Montemayor (and the Summer Institute of Linguistics, that maligned US institution that has saved so many indigenous languages on the verge of extinction) is so passionate about. The Hispanicization of Indians that José Vasconcelos* dreamed of might have failed, but so did the bilingualism promoted by Manuel Gamio. People will only read in indigenous languages—and this is the cruel paradox that Montemayor sidesteps— when the Indian nations are politically and educationally integrated into a democratic society. Whether the road to that integration is via the EZLN or the government is another matter. Meanwhile, indigenous scholars—like all writers—will have to keep fighting for readership, whether in Mayan or Spanish. The indigenous literatures project is a saga delightful for its noble, utopian grandeur.

In the prologue to *Los escritores indígenas actuales* (1995), Montemayor—a man who anthologizes poetry, fiction, and theater—entirely avoids the issue of a literature with no readership. Of course it's not the first time a scholar has dodged the question of the public. A cloistered literature is still literature. After all, until the invention of the printing press and the Lutheran schism, Europe was a society with no readers, and that doesn't diminish the importance of the *Summa Theologica* or the *Divine Comedy*.

Having profiled the indigenous intellectual elite, we can talk about what they publish. But first—unbidden—Montemayor himself asks whether the texts anthologized in eight languages are even literature at all, in the Western sense of the word. Given that I'd include in that category anything that can be read phonetically, regardless of whether it comes from the Chinese or Tzeltal, I won't go into Montemayor's differentiation between oral communication and the art of language. It's a precaution he took to appease those who claim oral traditions are not literature. In fact it was an illiterate society that created the conditions for Homer.

Montemayor recognizes that the indigenous oral tradition—with the Zapotecs as a very notable exception—tends to be unwritten, but he is quick to clarify that all of Mexico's indigenous languages are linguistic systems as complex as French, English, Spanish, and German. Well, that's half true. It's one thing to reject a racist distinction between "dialects" and "civilized languages" (which is rare in modern linguistics), and another to ignore the historicity of language. Nahuatl might *theoretically* be as complex as German, but in *fact* it's not. Why? Because for 500 years the indigenous language was displaced and made subservient to a more powerful lingua franca in the same way that Greek and Latin—languages of the Eastern and Western church—overshadowed the Aramaic that Jesus Christ spoke.

Indigenous languages are not dead languages. Not only are they spoken by thousands of Mexicans but they're also—as we've seen—now being phonetically transcribed. A language can be wounded by military or religious conquest. But it can't be preserved by decree. Government campaigns to "defend" any language are ridiculous. If Imperial Rome had been able to do it, today there would be no Spanish, French, or Portuguese—happily corrupted forms of Latin. These are truisms for linguists and esoteric mysteries for political propagandists, whether Hispanist or indigenist. Indian writers, like their non-indigenous counterparts, have bought into the Western, European, Romantic notion that ties Indian nations to their native languages, a concept in line with Herder's *Volkstum*.

Developing an alphabet for an ideographic language is unrelated to the good or bad intentions of the dominant class. Nahuatl, the hegemonic language of central Mexico in 1521, was transliterated and preserved thanks to the missionaries' zeal and their illustrious Indian pupils. The Spanish conquest was no linguistic extermination. In 1627, King Philip IV ordered there be schooling in native Mexican languages, just as the Mexican Ecclesiastic Council had decreed in 1585. The viceroyalty needed indigenous languages not just for evangelical purposes but also to smooth their mediation between the crown and autochthonous caciques. Use of the vernacular was not persecuted by the Inquisition's Holy Office, which was so attentive to Spain and Portugal's converted Jews. In fact, after prelates Juan de Zumárraga and Diego de Landa burned most of the codices, Spaniards forgot all about the problem, to such a degree that historian Serge Gruzinski talks of a "repaganization" during the seventeenth century, and David Brading recalls New Spain Creole patriotism as an exaltation of the Aztec past.

The Spanish Empire—heir to the Roman model—used Spanish as the lingua franca, Latin as the liturgical language, and decided not to worry about the demotic languages, including the one Carlos V and the Bourbons originally spoke. The government of the Mexican Revolution, by contrast, was ideologically indigenist. Their greatest failure—making the material progress of the nation benefit all ethnicities—is viewed with uncertainty by contemporary Indians, which is why the 1994 Chiapas uprising was such a muddled phenomenon. It was, on the one hand, a vociferous condemnation of how "Western" Mexico had become; by the same token, the indigenous community was demanding that the government fulfill their responsibilities to the people [...]

This has all been a roundabout way of saying that Montemayor—a Creole—attempted to create a classicist identity for a slew of languages that are not only not dead but have just been born. The future of indigenous literature is the responsibility of indigenous writers; classicists won't be the ones to "save" Mexico's indigenous languages.

The poetry, prose, and theater in Montemayor's anthology *Los escritores indígenas actuales* are the work of very young writers, some even teenagers.

Their output, therefore, is as green, antiquated, and unconfident as that of 95% of Spanish-speaking writers' workshop attendees. Montemayor goes on about Zapotec syllabification and accentuation, but he doesn't have anything to say about the quality of the work itself. Whether in prose or in verse, readers will find moralizing parables, righteous allegations, and poorly transcribed oral legends.

Syrian and Aramaic only developed alphabets when Christianity came onto the scene, and it took 200 years to develop their literature [. . .] I don't accept the objection I am sure to hear from well-intentioned folks who will demand we take into account the living conditions of these writers when evaluating their artistic production. Reverse racism is a perverse form of solidarity. I prefer to take Montemayor at his word: if the indigenous are not Others, then let's treat them as equals. Bad literature is not a sociological or political problem; it's a literary one. And we're talking about a literary tradition that's in its very early days. It's a sad irony that the best indigenous writer I know, Jesús Morales Bermúdez (1956), wasn't included in the anthology because he writes in Spanish.

In volume II of *Los escritores indígenas actuales* the writers speak for themselves. Domingo Meneses Méndez, a Chol Indian, writes an essay about the linguists' fear. He says that writing in Spanish might make Indian writers "a danger to their own culture." His authoritarian words reflect the customs of the indigenous community, which might be Arcadian but are certainly not democratic. He sees men of letters as priests responsible for their folklore but indifferent to the reader. Zapotec Indian Javier Castellano Martínez is bolder. He satirizes—it was about time someone did—Francisco Rojas González (1904–1951), the godfather of mid-century indigenous literature, for his paternalism and his fuzzy toponomy. But he also makes fun of fellow Indians who adapt Grimm's tales or *Arabian Nights* to peddle to revolutionary or mushroom-eating tourists. This Zapotec critic is the only one to assume the foundational nature of his enterprise [. . .] Ubaldo López García, a Mixtec Indian, shares with readers the process of his convoluted, regressive journey: 1) He studied the Selden Codex in a specialist workshop. 2) He interpreted the pictograms and explained each one in Spanish. 3) He gave a version in Mixtec, the language spoken during the time the Codex dates from. 4) He then translated them back into Nahuatl, the language spoken (but not read) by the residents of Jaltepec, his addressees. To be sure, this elaborate project has more in common with Borges than with Nezahualcóy-otl, the poet prince.

Montemayor's endeavor sees the indigenous nation as a product of Herder's equation: language + land + religion, with one important change: the creation of a literature in the ethnic language. He conveniently jettisons religion from the equation, which is logical, because his Indian theology ignores the Christian side of indigenous culture. Anyone who stresses how "syncretic" Mexican Christianity is has clearly never read a good history of the Catholic church, which was much more spectacularly syncretic in China and the Southeast, as far as risky dogma goes, than it was among Chamula or Tarahumara Indians. It's fair to reject the idea of the Spanish language as the epitome of nationality, but it's not fair to forget that Christianity triumphed in the New World—as in the Roman Empire—because it was more powerful and convincing than paganism [. . .]

All religions spring from the ashes of others; the history of monotheism is the chronicle of violence legitimized through conversion. Out of humanistic or multicultural beliefs, Montemayor might deny that there was a spiritual conquest in the New World, as there was in Rome or Damascus. But indigenous societies are spectacularly Christian. In fact, the worst of the violence in Chiapas was between Catholic and Protestant Indians. The EZLN, to a large degree, was the work of catechists radicalized by liberation theology. Subcomandante Marcos's prose is as evangelizing as the *Popul Vuh* . . . Mexican Spanish owes part of its splendor to the indigenous, just as baroque architecture owes part of its splendor to the anonymous Indian workers who built it. People have never chosen their language. The Church of Jerusalem had to preach in Greek, just as Alva Ixtlilxóchitl, Alvarado Tezozómoc, and the Inda Guaman Poma created the Spanish of America. And Mexico's indigenous culture is a complex, Christian civilization that can't be negated by a linguistic epiphany. (*Servidumbre y grandeza de la vida literaria*, 1998)

SELECTED BIBLIOGRAPHY
Minas del retorno, Argos Vergara, Barcelona, 1982.
Los escritores indígenas actuales, I and II, Conaculta, Mexico, 1991.
Encuentros en Oaxaca, Aldus, Mexico, 1996.
Obras reunidas, I. Novelas. Guerra en El paraíso. Las armas del alba, FCE, Mexico, 2007.

Blood Relations, trans. Dale Carter, Plover Press, 1995.

Words of the True Peoples: Anthology of Contemporary Mexican Indigenous-Language Writers, ed. Montemayor, Carlos and Donald H. Frischmann, University of Texas Press, 2004.

MONTERROSO, AUGUSTO

(Tegucigalpa, Honduras, 1921 – Mexico City, 2003)

Augusto Monterroso is one of the most original figures in the already rich body of twentieth-century Latin American literature. He was raised in Guatemala and came to Mexico in 1944, the victim of political persecution, and his writing eliminated the artificial boundary between Mexico and Central America. In fact, it transcended all borders and turned us—his readers—into contemporaries of an absolute time called literature, where Aesop and Kafka, Cervantes and Cortázar, Virgil and Pessoa live side by side.

Already a classic before he died, he reinvented the fable and taught countless others how to write. Everyone agrees that his unclassifiable prose meets none of the expectations of world literature. Books like *Obras completas (y otros cuentos)* (1959; *Complete Works and Other Stories*, 1995), *La oveja negra y demás fábulas* (1969; *The Black Sheep and Other Fables*, 1971), *Movimiento perpetuo* (1972; included in *Complete Works and Other Stories*), *Lo demás es silencio* (1978; *The Rest is Silence*, 1981), *La letra e* (1983), *Los buscadores de oro* (1993), and *Pájaros de Hispanoamérica* (2002) are, more than a list of his works, a tradition in itself and a school of literary taste. We could talk about his perfect Spanish, his infallible inventiveness, or the amazing ease with which he condensed entire libraries into astonishing brevity. We could heap on him the same praises we would on Isaac Asimov, Italo Calvino, or Gabriel García Márquez;* rivers of ink will flow, but the mystery will remain intact. We just can't articulate exactly what type of writer he was or know what long and winding road led him to personify that perennially discreet form of genius. They say you can't improve upon perfection, and his texts—from the celebrated fables to his "simple" literary notes—are perfect. For Monterroso, "classic" was the opposite of laurels and solemnity, of tedium and inaccessibility, of academia and pomposity. His literature was like the result of the most sparkling, lively conversation.

It's been said that Monterroso was a Roman, and maybe that's true. But his Rome bore no relation to Cicero; it was, instead, the place where those immortal spirits frolicked, a hotbed of theologies, the place where superstitions and spells and enchantment began, not ended. He was our Apuleius, his books a marvelous evolution of *The Golden Ass*. He ditched the tedious Latin American jungle stories for fabulous fables and dazzling tales.

Monterroso declined to write obituaries when writers died, refusing to debase the noble art of the epitaph with the triviality that speed required on the occasion. In that sense, these notes could be taken as indecorous, a senseless contest to add yet more adjectives and praise to a writer who could easily do without them. But Monterroso has many friends. And I think I'm right in saying that his best friend was Bárbara Jacobs, his wife of many years. In 1995 she published *Vida con mi amigo*, a strange confession, more dialogue than autobiography, about her years with the writer. Monterroso and Bárbara Jacobs had one of the most beautiful literary relationships in the annals of history, one that many readers find tremendously moving.

On the morning of February 8, 2002, I, like the rest of the world, awoke to the news of Monterroso's death. My first thought was of a book. I remembered, as a boy, staring at a bookshelf at home and noticing a thin volume whose spine read: Monterroso. *Complete Works*. Of course at the time I didn't know it was the title of a book rather than his collected works. But then, as now, I wondered how so much literature could fit in such a tiny book. It was like magic, the work of a writer who knows the magic word.

SELECTED BIBLIOGRAPHY
Cuentos, fábulas y lo demás es silencio, Alfaguara, Mexico, 1996.
Pájaros de Hispanoamérica, Alfaguara, Mexico, 2002.
Corral, Wilfrido H., ed., *Refracción. Augusto Monterroso ante la crítica*, ERA, Mexico, 1995.
The Black Sheep and Other Fables, trans. Walter Bradbury, Doubleday, 1971.
Complete Works and Other Stories, trans. Edith Grossman, University of Texas Press, 1996.

MONTES DE OCA, MARCO ANTONIO
(Mexico City, 1932 – 2009)

The son of a Mexican Revolutionary general, Montes de Oca has always claimed that poets should stick to poetry and do so as zealously as mendicant friars collecting alms, their fate in the hands of devout women, usurers, and the all-powerful. He's the most "poetic" of Mexican poets, a man whose extraordinary lyric production over the course of fifty years began with *Ruina de la infame Babilonia* (1953; *On the Ruins of Babylon*, 1964) and continued through the four unpublished books that make up *Delante de la luz cantan los pájaros, 1953–2000* (2000), an intimidating 1182-page opus that virtually defies the limits of bookbinding. No other Mexican poet (and likely no other Spanish-language poet) exhibits such a wealth of images; his readers could compile their own personal anthologies with no risk of overlapping poems. But critiques of Montes de Oca tell a tale that can only be compared to that of Juan Ramón Jiménez or Pablo Neruda—poets whose *poetry*, by the way, is alike in appearance only. Few poets' work has raised such objections; it's as if the more Montes de Oca publishes, the less his work is valued.

Octavio Paz*—a critical figure in Montes de Oca's evolution and his most faithful defender—was the first to lash out against the criticism, though in the process of rejecting others' analyses he added some unfalteringly harsh words of his own. In 1959, when the poet had already published *Contrapunto de la fe, Pliego de testimonios, Razón de ser*, and *Delante de la luz cantan los pájaros*, Paz said: "Some critics reproach him for his wealth of images, an objection as absurd as criticizing the slenderness of the poplar or the whiteness of the snow. I'm not surprised by their unfavorable reactions. After years of Parnassian anemia, it's only natural that Montes de Oca's verbal explosion—with its slips and lack of taste, I admit, but also with fresh, impressive energy—seems scandalous. Health is scandalous in a sanatorium . . . No, poetry is never excessive. I never tire of Montes de Oca's triumphs; I get tired when he loses heart, when he repeats himself, and particularly when he substitutes philosophical or religious commonplaces that strike me as conformist for original expression. In short, when he preaches ("the old peace of God and the new one of men"); when he philosophizes ("the outside and my self are waters of the same river"); when he insists on using picturesque, abstract expressions ("to expose the truths of my realm, the divine forceps, the smallpox of rain peck the face of the puddle," etc). It's not poor taste (what is taste, after all?) but systematic rigidity that hinders the vision. A cement structure—what they call depth or content—overgrown with wild vegetation." (Paz, *Obras completas, 3. Dominio hispánico*, 1994)

The comment about Parnassian anemia referred to the world of Enrique González Martínez and Jaime Torres Bodet* and the overall lack of rebellion that, until Montes de Oca came along, was almost singlehandedly represented by Paz. Other more conservative poets like Alí Chumacero* looked on Montes de Oca with a mixture of wonder and condescension. "Vigor and excess, plasticity and violence, immodesty and cruelty, all poured into a catalog of imagery, defend these imperfect poems that suddenly emerge 'like a tree in the middle of the sea.' Overflowing, we could say; explosive, bursting; the enemy of repose, alien to meditation, Montes de Oca confronts poetry with the incorruptible inexperience of youth." (Chumacero, *Los momentos críticos*, 1987)

More than a decade later, Montes de Oca—the last Mexican poet to still use the "vosotros" form—published several more impressive books, including *Cantos al sol que no se alcanza* (1961), *Fundación del entusiasmo* (1963), *La parcela del Edén* (1964), *Vendimia del juglar* (1965), and *Pedir el fuego* (1968). Given this now extended bibliography, Gabriel Zaid* wondered about the kind of wordplay that confused even de Oca's most avid readers. "His poetry has mystery, seduction, brio. It's a luxurious antechamber for something that never quite appears and thereby, as in some of Pirandello's work, takes on all due splendor. This is not to say that splendid things don't suddenly emerge: *Árboles milenarios desde el primero segundo*. But the things that emerge never unfold; they don't let us follow them anywhere. Reading a Montes de Oca poem—not to mention a book—all the way through is a frustrating experience. That's not the way to do it. You must take it like a book of hours or a series of 'greguerías' [humorous aphorisms]." (Zaid, *Obras*, 2, 1999, originally from *Leer poesía*, 1972)

In a 1994 piece added to his *Diario público, 1966–1968* (2005), Emmanuel Carballo* is harsh and bitter in his assessment of the young poet he'd once been enthusiastic about. "After 1966, Montes de Oca published numerous anthologies teeming with his own work (more than he ought). Nevertheless, he never exceeded what I said in 1967. He never wrote the definitive book, the dazzling poem. He systematically began a rudimentary, monotonous project: the plagiarizing of his own work, repeating structures and poetic discourses with slight variations. He didn't achieve the heights of great poetry, and figures in the past, as one of the most representative of our young poets of the fifties and sixties . . ."

Carballo's affront is all the more inappropriate because it's paradoxically unfair. Montes de Oca tried, time and again, to reinvent himself but was unable to go against his own nature. He tried prose poetry (in *Las fuentes legendarias,* 1966 and *Sistemas de buceo,* 1974), visual poetry (*Lugares donde el espacio cicatriza,* 1974), and a return to "concrete" poems (as in *Vaivén,* 1986). And it's that erratic search for metamorphosis that led Zaid to compare his poetry to Ramón de la Serna's "greguerías" (humorous aphorisms), though the comparison seems inaccurate since the "humor" part is entirely lacking in Montes de Oca, a rather solemn poet.

"You can't read *greguerías* one after the other," José Moreno Villa* admitted, but nor can you simply break apart Montes de Oca's images, which is why I was driven to read almost all of his poems in search of that mystery Zaid mentioned, the thing that keeps getting away although we don't want it to. And in the end, the majesty, the quantity, and the totality prevail.

Not much has been written about Montes de Oca himself, the Vulcan poet who pounds out his words with a hammer. And though much of his work has yet to be explored, there are a few fair critiques, including that of Evodio Escalante. He was fascinated by the young poet who preached against usury and chose to educate himself by attending workers' colloquia, a messiah who makes an appeal for a "new man" poetics and a verbal restitution of the golden age. Some see in Montes de Oca a Heraclitus-like "flow," a ceaseless river that drags everything with it; and Ramón Xirau* notes the Romantic nature of his poetry, which he feels conquers new realms. Finally Adolfo Castañón* sees him as a rank and file surrealist (surrealism being one of the twentieth century's versions of Romanticism). Often, however, his surrealist imagery is purely academic, like singing scales before a concert.

Almost all Romantics share Wordsworth's view of the child as father of the man. And multiple childhoods, for Montes de Oca, are like Hindu avatars. He suggests that himself in *Marco Antonio Montes de Oca* (1967), his early autobiography, on recalling Juan José Arreola's* hospitality: "We threw ourselves keenly into games of table soccer, dominoes, pillow fights, and playing with matches. Then came ping-pong or that game with paper boats where we'd lie down and squint at the horizon, on the lookout for Italian or Madagascan battleships. That was my fourth consecutive childhood!"

For Montes de Oca the poet is a demiurge who eternally delights in childhood, which is a place out of a fantastical Rubén Darío story or a José Antonio Ramos Sucre modernist fable. Despite having grown up reading Dostoyevsky and Kierkegaard, Montes de Oca sees adolescence and infancy in ways very divergent from them, as is evidenced in *Las fuentes legendarias* (1966) and *El corazón de la flauta* (1968), which carry vestiges of *Twenty Thousand Leagues Under the Sea*, *The Golden Legend*, *One Thousand and One Nights*, and Greek mythology. His is a universe regulated by the harmonic relationship of elements and populated by thousands of boundless, gregarious words that bring to life a knightly saga complete with princess and dragon, rites of passage and magic tricks. Here's a passage chosen almost at random from *Las fuentes legendarias*: "Mummies awaken, only unconscious. They move toward the esplanade dragging bandages of half-peeled fruit skins. Their long hibernation abandoned, they walk beneath the full moon covered in a haggard air followed by plots, whole neighborhoods, strands of tinsel and worldliness. They come to witness, both curious and cursory, the new order the magician brings to life."

Overall, Montes de Oca is well served by his celebratory, joyous, almost pagan Christianity. But, impervious to the dark side of modern poetry, it's an unreal world, sometimes too beautiful to be poetically believable. Many of his verses, for example, are dedicated to carnal love, but after examining his collections (I prefer *Pedir el fuego: Poesía, 1953–1987*, the most manageable), you're not left with the impression that he's an erotic poet. And other feelings like hatred, vanity, and envy seem irrelevant to his poetry, which is odd given that he's written thirty books. Closer to Bécquer than to the Romantic prophets, Montes de Oca shows no evil for long periods of time. Deep down, like Gómez de la Serna, the human aspect is alien to him. It's just poetry. But without his vast repository of seemingly infinite images, Mexican literature would be a cross to bear.

SELECTED BIBLIOGRAPHY

Pedir el fuego. Poesía, 1953-1987, Joaquín Mortiz, Mexico, 1987.

Delante de la luz cantan los pájaros. Poesía, 1953-2000, FCE, Mexico, 2000.

Las alas de la palabra, prólogo de Víctor Manuel Mendiola, FCE, Mexico, 2010.

On the Ruins of Babylon, trans. Rolf Hennequel, Wattle Grove, 1964.

MORÁBITO, FABIO

(Alexandria, Egypt, 1955)

Morábito's entire oeuvre, whether prose or poetry, is staunch in its dedication to Roman household gods, the Penates, and records the private ceremonies through which father acts as author. In a world that's grown weary of talking about everyday existence and its upheavals, Morábito is a new sort of household poet, unafraid of both the mediocre and the melodramatic, aware of the fact that almost all of his literary experience lies somewhere between "hambre de poesía" ("hunger for poetry") and "falta de prosa" ("lack of prose"). No other contemporary Mexican writer—and Morábito is one of the greats—has proved to be such an incisive reader of certain Latin classics, managing to exhibit an art of living akin to Stoicism: temperance in one's dealings with others, prudence (but not coldness) in showing emotion, and most notably an enduring belief in humans and their objects as the essential tools required for any science of man (including literature). "No soy un religioso / en busca de visiones" ("I'm not a religious man / in search of visions"), said Morábito in *Lotes baldíos* (1985), and then went on to present a drunken "recolector de escombros, / pepenador de absurdo, / el único que sabe / discernir materiales, / el último humanista / especialista en todo, el único filósofo / con quien se dignarían / a hablar Platón y Sócrates" ("collector of rubbish, / scavenger of the absurd, / the only one able to / discern materials, / the last humanist / specialist in it all, the only philosopher / with whom Plato and Socrates / would deign to speak").

That knowledge—the foundation of Morábito's poetry—has yielded poems fascinating in their simplicity and so penetrating as to be almost numinous. In Schoenberg's "Transfigured Night," the mystery is solved when a woman confesses that she's pregnant; in *Alguien de lava* (2002), Morábito manages to stop time at the inverse instant, exhibiting a man's desire not to have a child. It was impossible for someone who wrote "almost stories" not to become a short story writer, and his are both fantastic (*La lenta furia*, 1989) and realist (*La vida ordenada*, 2000), because Morábito is also an academic writer searching for the essence of each literary form. And although his stories tend to disappear in a ragbag of fragments, poetic prose, and fiction that passes for a story without actually being one, in at least four of the tales in *La vida ordenada*, Morábito teaches us masterful lessons about the internal structure of a short story.

"Ventanas encendidas, mi tormento. / Gente sólo visible en esta hora. / De día los edificios son triviales, / de noche la fragilidad de su interior me hechiza. / Se espía buscando desnudeces, / pero también por hambre de poesía, / hambre no de la piel de otro, / sino de una manera de gastar latidos, / de ver cómo transcurre un corazón ajeno. / Por eso morbo y poesía andan juntos. / Falta de prosa, mi tormento" ("Illuminated windows, my torment. / People visible only at this hour. / By day the buildings are trivial, / by night the fragility within them bewitches me. / One spies searching for nakedness, / but also from hunger for poetry, / hunger not for the skin of another, / but for a way to wear out heartbeats, / to seeing how the heart of another slips past. / Thus illness and poetry go together. / Lack of prose, my torment"), says Morábito in *Alguien de lava*. And it's that same curiosity that in *La vida ordenada* turns everyday domesticity into an investigation into the nature of humanity, whether through the odd behavior of a mute maid, a family space undergoing a Cortázar-like invasion, or a property rental that turns into an orgy, either real or dreamed (does it matter?).

In *También Berlín se olvida*, Morábito chooses another foreign city (like Mexico City, where he has lived since 1969) as his setting, employing that combination of affectionate curiosity and methodical distance that are his signature. In magnificent prose (surely subjected to obsessive rewrites), in texts resembling stories, memoirs, and essays, Morábito turns Berlin into a transitory home subject to the same laws as the rest of his oeuvre.

It's not the traveler's gaze that prevails in this book but that of a sedentary figure in motion, a figure that in small spaces and short time frames manages to reproduce the obsessions of home. Morábito, for instance, is fascinated by *Kleingarten*, those tiny urban gardens used by city dwellers to grow fruits and vegetables in a parody of rural retreats. Morábito says these little homes are "related spiritually to the country homes of patrician Romans and to Italian Renaissance villas, sharing with them the curious feeling of being the 'perfect nest' that tends to provoke the most outlandish fantasies." There's something confessional about this statement: fantasizing about the "perfect nest," "the desire to reproduce in a miniscule space the universe of a complete abode" is the central motif of his writing.

Domesticity reigns over Morábito's abodes and gardens, whether urban, as in *También Berlín se olvida* (2004) or bucolic, as in *Los pastores sin ovejas* (1995). In several of the episodes taking place in Berlin, he both invents and christens "nests," lyrical living spaces like train compartments that, when the train passes, turn the rails into "una suerte de mar para los pobres o los sedentarios" ("a sort of sea for the poor or the sedentary"). A car accident glimpsed by the nosy narrator becomes the painting of a trestle, bucolic and hyperrealist at the same time.

Morábito, who has penned unforgettable verses about domestic tiffs and the loneliness of an adult standing in a playground, sometimes errs on the side of sentimentality, seeming convinced that every aspect of existence is a malleable tool in the hands of a gifted writer. Assuming that mine is a mind poisoned by history and that what I'm about to say stinks of moralistic reproach, I'll add that "El muro," variations on the theme of the Berlin Wall, first struck me as ingenious and in the end seemed trivial. There's no such thing as a sanctified place that can't be demystified by a writer, but I see in Morábito a certain professorial propensity to reduce the world to the poetic dimensions of a dollhouse, making everything banal. To posit Hitler's concentration camps, as he did in *Los pastores sin ovejas*, as a negative of bucolic fields, or turn the Berlin Wall into a trapdoor, as he does in *También Berlín se olvida*, is a mistake.

Having situated himself between Kudamm and Kantstrasse, the avenues where his Berlin stories take place, Morábito gives us "Mi lucha con el alemán," the tale of his failed attempt to learn the language, a lucid and persuasive profession of faith and one notable among writers of his type. In it he manages to portray a writer's daily travails, superstitions, and superficiality as the same time as he justifies our vocation.

Morábito's books have strange effects on me. It's as if they make sense of the age-old family rituals. When my neighbors brought me my copy of *También Berlín se olvida*, I was reading a book that could be a literary twin: Léon-Paul Fargue's *The Pedestrian of Paris*. It had taken me years to get the book and I was finding it unsatisfactory, as it struck me as a collection of almost touristic Parisian vignettes. I put down Fargue in order to read Morábito, and just as Morábito found that his failure to learn German opened a new narrative door, I found that his book helped me understand Fargue: I'd been looking for maps when in fact there were homes, illuminated in the distance.

But the best way to define Morábito's art is one I quoted long ago; it comes from *Volupté*, the only novel written by French literary critic Charles Augustin Sainte-Beuve, in which the critic explains the theories of Lamarck: "His conception of the universe was simple, naked and sad. He built the world with the least possible number of elements, crises and time periods. The way he saw it, things created themselves out of continuity and with no instantaneous transformations or movements. His genius of creation was long, blind patience."

Novels about childhood form an archipelago in Mexican literature. I recall visits to many of its isles: *El solitario Atlántico* (1958) by Jorge López Páez, *Las batallas en el desierto* (1981) by José Emilio Pacheco,* *Elsinore* (1987) by Salvador Elizondo,* two of Carmen Boullosa's* novels (*Mejor desaparece* and *Antes*, 1989 and 1991), and my own *William Pescador* (1997). And I can't, I repeat, help but imagine these books as islands, isolated by their circular geography, autarchic, chunks of land far from their chronological continental counterparts, unconcerned with synchronic fiction.

Recently, three other novels have cropped up to form a complementary atoll: *Edén* (2006) by the much-missed Alejandro Rossi,* *Yo te conozco* (2009) by Héctor Manjarrez,* and *Emilio, los chistes y la muerte* (2009) by Morábito, his first novel. In all three, the world of children is governed by its own laws and adults are only allowed in as temporary—and incomprehensible— visitors, forced into a certain Freudian, episodic servitude.

I think it's probably fair to say there's no Mexican writer as good as Morábito, if by goodness we mean mastery over form, the ability to execute intention, to materialize dreams. He's not aspiring to conquer new territory, to expand the discipline. Morábito is master of the contained world, of simplicity. At times, it seems—as I said in a text on his 2004 *También Berlín se olvida*—that his world, his characters, are nude, exposed, living in a state of elective poverty.

The plot of *Emilio, los chistes y la muerte*, as others have noted, seems nonsensical and in the hands of a less talented writer would be utterly puerile. It's about a twelve-year-old boy who, armed with a "joke detector," visits a cemetery near his house where he meets (and ends up getting to "know," in a foretaste of the Biblical sense) a grieving woman who has recently lost a son Emilio's age. Eurídice (Eurydice) is her name, which is conspicuous, but what's less so is the manner in which she meets Emilio's mother. The plot also centers on the boy's father, and takes in a handful of characters who hang around at the cemetery, engaged in acts more metaphysical than practical, despite seeming the opposite: secret love affairs, casual flings, keeping watch over the necropolis, altering the dates on tombstones in an effort to keep the living from being too far from the dead.

In general, I don't tend to imagine the scenes in the novels I read. It doesn't come naturally to me, and I stick Judaically to the literalness of the text and its iconoclasm. But the visual power of *Emilio, los chistes y la muerte* actually forced me to imagine almost everything, scene by scene, a product of Morábito's talent for reducing everything to scale.

Emilio, los chistes y la muerte is an adventure story condensed down to its very essence. There's nothing missing. The hero goes through the decisive rites of passage vital to any myth: risky excursion into unknown territory, sexual awakening, encounter with a witch or enchantress (any woman who's lost a child turns into the weeping ghost, *La Llorona*), the battle for succession between father and son that concludes with an injury that leads to the progenitor's loss of power, after Emilio makes him fall down a staircase. There's even an element of exoticism, since in big cities today it's odd to imagine a kid playing in a cemetery to begin with. Our funeral customs are "postconciliar": we don't bury our dead, we cremate them. The novel is Mexican in its Spanish and its "cempasúchil," the orange marigolds used in Day of the Dead celebrations; but there is one memorable scene that could only, I think, have occurred to a true Roman Catholic like Morábito, born in Alexandria, Egypt to Italian parents: when the acolyte lifts his cassock to urinate. In Mexico City—simultaneously Jacobin and Guadalupan—even the idea is almost blasphemous, and it's one that will be etched into my memory as if I'd seen it in a neo-realist film.

Once the world of sleeping beauty is abandoned, when the living end up dead, Emilio's adventures—which include both Oedipal and homoerotic pleasures—end with a death trance in which the hero must prove his mettle, using his ingenuity to free himself from the darkness he's been plunged into. Maybe I'm reading too much into it, but I think it's no coincidence that the boy's name is Emilio, like that of Rousseau's eighteenth-century treatise. It's clear that this Emilio—Morábito doesn't hide things from his readers—undergoes a natural education. Both instinctive and mythical, he's interested in the origin of language. That's why the most original thing about the book is the boy's joke detector, which he carries with him like a talisman. The device captures the primordial and the experience of language, the profane and the sacred, laughter and prayer. *Emilio, los chistes y la muerte* is one of Mexican literature's perfect novels.

SELECTED BIBLIOGRAPHY
Pedir el fuego. Poesía, 1953–1987, Joaquín Mortiz, Mexico, 1987.
Los pastores sin ovejas, Ediciones El Equilibrista, Mexico, 1995.
La vida ordenada, Tusquest Editores, Mexico, 2000.
Delante de la luz cantan los pájaros. Poesía, 1953–2000, FCE, Mexico, 2000.
La lenta furia, Tusquets Editores, Mexico, 2002.
También Berlín se olvida, FCE, Mexico, 2004.
Grieta de fatiga, Tusquets Editores, Mexico, 2006.
La ola que regresa. Poesía reunida, FCE, Mexico, 2006.
Emilio, los chistes y la muerte, Anagrama, Barcelona, 2009.

MORENO VILLA, JOSÉ

(Malaga, Spain, 1887 – Mexico City, 1955)

Rarely has Mexico received a foreign writer so predisposed to warmly embrace all things new, or to engage in the sort of incisive curiosity that differentiates the exotic from the profound. Moreno Villa's genuine congeniality turned him from a foreigner into a key contemporary. The Spanish poet and painter reinvented himself at the age of fifty, arriving in 1937 as a Spanish Civil War exile. And this wasn't just any poet, but the author of *Garba* who in 1913 had ushered in Spain's "new poetry." But in Mexico he married the widow of Genaro Estrada, his friend and guardian; he had his only child here; and it is here that he is buried, with the Spanish Republican flag over his casket.

Alfonso Reyes* had known Moreno Villa since his early days in Madrid. In 1923, he asked him to take part in a five-minute silence in memory of Mallarmé, which Reyes himself organized at the Madrid Botanical Gardens on the morning of October 14. Later, Reyes asked the attendees—who included Ortega y Gasset, Enrique Díez-Canedo, D'Ors, and Bergamín—for a page about what they'd been thinking during the silent commemoration. Moreno Villa handed in the following response, which sums him up well: "They gave the order of silence, and instinctively I got up, separating from the group a bit. That movement seemed to me to somehow ruin the ceremony a bit, but what ruined it even more was my train of thought. Is this dialogue I'm having with myself a perfect silence? None of my attention was on Mallarmé despite his insistent calls. Instead it was those corporeally present that, in a most domineering way, captured my attention. I wanted to close my eyes, but I laughed. A new heresy was spoiling my part in the ceremony. I let my glance dart around where it would. It fell upon the trees, the paths, and the people. I thought about the psychology of the first, the importance of the second, and the shapes of the third. It's impossible, at this point, to instruct anyone in the psychology of trees; there's no need to ponder the excellence of grand avenues and humble paths if we agree that the virtue of a garden depends upon their breadth and modesty, respectively, as well as the size and expanse of the trees. And as far as the social or public bodies surrounding us, what a topic for insane derision! How many guises for affectation! I turned back to the trees, who get along admirably despite how little space the gardener gives them. They get even by reaching up, catching up to the tallest one, the supreme tree. And if they get along well it's because they have no eyes or ears. Arms, yes; but we all know that it's not arms but intentions that are implacable. I thought, too, about the comfort afforded by cleanliness and security, and finally, about how voluptuous the emerald light was on that day." (Reyes, *Obras completas*, XXV, 1991)

337

The Malagan writer spent his first months in Mexico traveling the country, and he published his impressions in *Cornucopia de México* (1949) and, posthumously, in *Nuevo cornucopia de México* (1976). These are books in which each article—be it about the flavor of a fruit, the outline of a church, or the features of a linguistic expression—fills you with the urge, as Reyes said, to thank Moreno Villa on the spot.

He was a tourist, but a Stendhal-inspired tourist, and whether you're reading his memoirs or his literary criticism, his writing is a breath of fresh air. In both verse and prose, his poetic voice and narrator live an open-minded life, and readers will want to thank their host and author not only for his food for thought but for his after-dinner digestive walk in the park. *Vida en claro* (1944) is an exercise in healthy egotism and—as he predicted—a book that (along with Ramón Gómez de la Serna's 1948 *Automoribundia*) began the yet-to-be-finished establishment of autobiography as a literary genre. *Los autores como actores y otros intereses literarios de acá y de allá* (1951), written in the same vein, contains particularly notable essays on Manuel Machado and Tirso de Molina.

Juan Ramón Jiménez said of Moreno Villa, "I don't know what it is about him, but he's always just what you need." He was truly a Spaniard of two worlds, and he rejected the small-town patriotism—both political and literary—that cloistered, suffocated, and embittered so many Spanish exiles. Moreno Villa never grew up; he was the eternally youthful resident of Madrid's famous Residencia de Estudiantes, where the Generation of '27 writers lived, and he only left when the Spanish Civil War left him no alternative. Even the woman to whom he dedicated the beautiful *Jacinta la pelirroja* (1929) didn't manage to get him out of there. And when he came to Mexico, he brought with him that student attitude, the sense of camaraderie of a man naturally predisposed to seeing literature, fine arts, and criticism as a game among friends, an activity that reconciles community living with the solitary anguish of a Romantic spirit.

Unlike many exiles, the author of *La escultura colonial mexicana* (1941) and *Lo mexicano en las artes plásticas* (1948) came to Mexico more interested in listening than in talking. Very few would have so light-heartedly made a tongue-in-cheek comment such as this: "In the question of tempo we Andalusians were unable to influence Mexicans. I think our rushing flusters them and offends them. It seems aggressive. There's no doubt that rushing drapes whatever is being said in dignity and even majesty. The Andalusian's excessive rapidity turns ordinary men into ne'er-do-wells. No one believes you can think or reflect with such speed."

Octavio Paz* taught us to love his friend Moreno Villa as we would that uncle from overseas who was decisive in our coming-of-age, the man who—morally unfit for sermons or diatribes—gives us just the right book at just the right time, who helps us make sense of things that have yet to happen to us. Paz wrote that only a poet like Moreno Villa—a sensitive man for whom thought and emotion are not in conflict—could have grasped the soul of the people the way he did. It's significant that as late as 1979—the date of his last text on the Malagan poet—Paz used a turn-of-the-century phrase like "soul of the people," in reference to a well-known passage from *Cornucopia de México*. In it, Moreno Villa asks himself, "Didn't you read Mexican history?" and gives his own reply: "To write this book, no. Besides, Mexico's history is still standing. No one has died here, despite the murders and executions. Cuauhtémoc, Cortés, Maximilian, Porfirio Díaz, and the conquistadors: they're all still alive. That's what's so original about Mexico. All of the past is present. The past hasn't passed."

Without those lines, I fear Paz would never have written *The Labyrinth of Solitude*. His penetrating assertion is still true. You could go on forever about Moreno Villa, who coined the term "chirosophy" in order to write about Mexican writers' hands. He also said something very endearing about Mexicans' tendency to use the verbs "mirar" (look at) and "ver" (see) interchangeably. After remarking on a typical usage, "Me quedé viendo a Elena" (i.e. "I stood there seeing Elena," rather than "I stood there looking at" her), he wrote, "I pondered the matter again and again, and after a time I began looking at it . . .'"

Selected Bibliography

Vida en claro. Autobiografía, FCE, Mexico, 1976.

Los autores como actores y otros intereses literarios de acá y de allá, FCE, Mexico, 1984.

Cornucopia de México and *Nueva cornucopia de México*, prologue by Roberto Suárez Argüello, FCE, Mexico, 1985.

MORENO VILLARREAL, JAIME

(Mexico City, 1956)

All of Moreno Villarreal's texts—including aphorisms, essays, poetry, short stories, and songs—allude to the "prehistory" of a writer, a character that might be him or could be an imaginary person. One of his first books was *La estrella imbécil* (1986), one of those early publications that guarantee a writer a comfortable spot in the rear guard, a very happy starting point. For a time, I banally believed in the struggle between Literature and Writing, and I worried that Moreno Villarreal risked losing himself in the latter. But I was lacking in modesty and still lack subtlety, two of Moreno Villareal's virtues (and that's no accident).

La estrella imbécil is a book that gets to the heart of Moreno Villareal, by way of a fake review and invented commemoration of one John F. Woodley, who at the age of 18, in 1908, had written just a few lines in the margins of one of his literature textbooks. "Books and notebooks are personal histories that grow longer each school year. All bored students identify themselves in their class notes by stressing certain words, and writing insolent, delinquent phrases or memorized verses or the initials of their beloved: all things that describe a person's character better than school lessons."

It seems to me that Moreno Villarreal never stopped searching for the distinguishing marks of his literary persona after *La estrella imbécil*, despite the more than twenty years gone by. He writes about skills like typing, stenography, and fingerprinting, and describes the subtle arts of writing student records and free composition, taking dictation, subtitling prints, and summarizing. And although this may be—to some degree—a result of what he learned from Salvador Elizondo's* *Cuaderno de escritura* (1969), Moreno Villareal has been standing on his own two feet for quite some time, busy capturing images and symbols in his memory. A scholar of icons, a man who writes about painting and photography, Moreno Villarreal inhabits a unique world of people and their medals and inscriptions. In *El salón de los espejos encontrados* (1995), for instance, he examines photos of Verlaine, scrutinizes a Pompeian woman asking for silence with a pencil between her lips, and examines the stances and postures of Mallarmé. And even more impressive, he gives an illuminating interpretation of Velázquez's *Aesop*, a truly magisterial reading that puts Moreno Villarreal right up with Carlos Fuentes* among the top Mexican writers on painting, a man whose natural prose is both critically imaginative and blissfully lyrical.

In *Música para diseñar* (1991), another of his miscellanea, Moreno Villarreal takes on rural troubadours, those magnificent primitives that—in Mexico or anyplace else in the world—prove that Homer is a contemporary, an endangered poet. In addition to his keen perceptiveness, Moreno Villarreal has an obsession with the overlap between high and low culture, and thus practices the kind of positive discrimination characteristic of true musical spirits. It's only natural, then, that he'd come out with a book as original as *La leyenda de Edipo el mago* (1998), which includes both popular fable and scholarly essay among its many registers, combined with the dexterity of a true virtuoso.

In *El vendedor de viajes* (2001), Moreno Villarreal turns to more or less traditional short stories. One of them introduces a character who would be the envy of more than one Mexican novelist: a contrite, middle-class, Catholic spinster who finds a unique way to express her freedom without challenging society's conventions. And despite this collection's multiple registers, the book is faithful to Moreno Villarreal's initial project set out in *La estrella imbécil*. Almost all of his characters are subject to some form of vicarious servitude, such as the disabled students who depend on powerful, exemplary teachers like Adhémar, who predicted darkness after the universal failure of electricity, or the miserable—and in the end supernatural—secretary of Henry James.

Finally, *La escalera anaranjada* (1986, 1991, and 2003) is the essay (and story and poem) that Moreno Villarreal dedicated to Edward James, the British surrealist who built Xilitla, a hidden village of twenty-six buildings in San Luis Potosí first seen by Elizondo, who published an account of his trip there in the journal *S.nob*. Xilitla now counts as one of the modern wonders of the world, and Edward James is the perfect incarnation of Moreno Villarreal's obsessions. *La escalera anaranjada* contains fieldwork and oral tradition, eccentric scholarship and despair at the most upsetting ambitions of the avant-garde. Xilitla, where imagination and geography naturally overlap onto the same map, is the place where Moreno Villarreal most fully expresses his freedom, making ancient and modern flow together, and combining the primitive and the sophisticated. These are fusions he's mastered for his readers by being his own disciple.

SELECTED BIBLIOGRAPHY

La línea y el círculo, UAM Iztapalaba, Mexico, 1981.
La estrella imbécil, FCE, Mexico, 1986.
Linealogía, Jordi Boldó y Climent, Mexico, 1988.
Música para diseñar, FCE, Mexico, 1991.
El salón de los espejos encontrados, El Equilibrista, Mexico, 1995.
La leyenda de Edipo el mago, Conaculta, Mexico, 1998.
El vendedor de viajes, Tusquets Editores, Mexico, 2001.
La escalera anaranjada, Alduz, Mexico, 2003.
La doble visión, Conaculta, Mexico, 2005.

MUÑIZ-HUBERMAN, ANGELINA

(Hyères, France, 1936)

Author of an impressive range of works that includes historical fiction, invented memoirs, and poetry, Muñiz-Huberman writes principally about exile—her own personal exile, as the daughter of Spanish Republicans, and that of Spanish Jews. The phenomenon revolves around two pivotal dates in Spanish history: 1492, when the Catholic Monarchs expelled all Jews from the Peninsula, and 1939, when the Second Republic was defeated. This author of *Las raíces y las ramas. Fuentes y derivaciones de la Cábala hispanohebrea* (1993) sees the clandestine Cabalistic legacy as essentially the precursor to an oft-lamented, unrealized Hispanic Enlightenment.

A university professor and lecturer, Muñiz-Huberman has published some of her collected talks in *El siglo del desencanto* (2002), one of the few books of this genre that can actually be read as essay. In its pages, she inevitably notes a connection with the work of María Zambrano, a central figure in both philosophy and exile, and discusses little-known writers (at least in Mexico) including Hermann Cohen and Franz Rosenzweig, as well as modern Jewish classics like Martin Buber, Elias Canetti, Elie Wiesel, and Nelly Sachs.

"If man stands in the center," Muñiz-Huberman says in one of the most distinctive essays in *El siglo del desencanto*, "that means that he's the natural center of God. He is his temporal abode: thus the sense of infinite responsibility or ethical category and thus his defense of life. So Judaism is a religion of life and not one of death, like Christianity. One could almost affirm that God is not external but inherently internal. Edmond Jabès says that one carries the synagogue inside. This explains why Jewish culture is based on the word and on hearing, unlike Greek culture, which is rooted in images and sight. This is also why Jews can speak (and not only speak but argue) with God. It's their only way of communicating: putting the word in the center."

Muñiz-Huberman's work also includes collections of stories such as *Huerto cerrado, huerto sellado* (1985), *Serpientes y escaleras* (1991), *Narrativa relativa* (1992), *Trotsky en Coyoacán* (2000); novels such as *Tierra adentro* (1977), *Dulcinea encantada* (1992), *Castillos en el aire* (pseudo-memoirs, 1995), *Los confidentes* (1997), *El mercader de Tudela* (1998), and *Areúsa en los conciertos* (2001); and poetry: *Villano al viento* (1982), *El libro de Miriam* (1982), *El ojo de la creación* (1991), *La memoria del aire* (1995), and *Conato de extranjería* (1999).

A Jewish Mexican, Muñiz-Huberman is concerned with Jewish irrationality, discussions about the Holocaust that account for the genocide with a total lack of reason or excessive reasoning. The following pearl written by Shelomo Ibn Gabirol—a writer she includes in *La lengua florida: Antología sefaradí* (1989)—is particularly applicable to Muñiz-Huberman herself: "The first step in knowledge is silence; the second, attention; the third, memory; the fourth, effort; the fifth, study or mastery."

SELECTED BIBLIOGRAPHY
El siglo del desencanto, FCE, Mexico, 2002.

MURGUÍA, VERÓNICA
(Mexico City, 1960)

From her captivating first novel *Auliya* (1997) to the short stories in *El ángel de Nicolás* (2003), Murguía has undertaken the difficult task of the commentator. Each of her texts, with varying degrees of success, is a note in the margins of the great book of time, an annotation destined to multiply thanks to her well-wrought prose, always exact if at times perhaps self-restrained.

Auliya is the story of a magical, paralyzed Bedouin girl and her young suitor, who after various rites of passage together undertake a voyage through the desert to the sea. The novel, rightly praised by Carlos Fuentes,* takes on the sensual powers of land and water, physical deformity, psychic beauty, the animal kingdom, and evil spirits. Add to that the author's love of Islamic culture and Berber history, the joy of fiction, the poetic force of images, and *Auliya* becomes both a philosophical tale and fantastical narration.

Murguía's second novel, *El fuego verde* (1999), struck me as too faithful to the sort of conventions that turn Anglo-Saxon epic sagas and medieval imagery into a less-than-credible wonderland more akin to commercial fantasy fiction. But *El ángel de Nicolás* has no readily identifiable formulaic narrative structure, thanks to Murguía's painstakingly fine-tuned perception and her skill at differentiating original sources from their adaptations. The book's opening story, "El idioma del Paraíso," is one of the best Mexican short stories in recent years, a wonderful example of how to take a legend and fictionalize it. Other texts in the collection lack that element of risk that turns a pleasant vignette into a memorable story. But among contemporary Mexican women writers, Murguía is writing some of the most solid prose, a bona fide reinterpretation of the myths and legends of Ancient Greece, the Bible, medieval piety, and Arabic tradition. Today's readers are accustomed to fictionalized monographs that brazenly plunder infinite historical possibilities while offering no real substance. But Murguía is perfecting the difficult art of bringing the ancients back to life, bringing us Marsyas and Apollo, Herod, Salome, and the God that expelled us from Paradise.

SELECTED BIBLIOGRAPHY
El ángel de Nicolás, ERA, Mexico, 2003.
Auliya, prologue by Carlos Fuentes, ERA, Mexico, 2005.

MUTIS, ÁLVARO
(Bogotá, Colombia, 1923)

Fortunately, Mutis is one of those writers who belong to many different literatures; if you look at his work, it's easy to rattle off numerous places that would happily claim him as a favorite son. First, he's a Colombian poet who shares with compatriots Eduardo Carranza, Jorge Zalamea, and Nicolás Gómez Dávila a worldview in which the supernatural is second nature. Second, he's a Spanish-American poet with an Castilian monarchic bent, the kind you thought was an endangered species until writers like him started cropping up throughout Latin America. Third, he's a man who takes inspiration from French memoir writers like Cardinal de Retz, Prince de Ligne, and Chateaubriand. He's also a legitimist, but one who extends gentlemanly bonhomie to those of every political ilk. Mutis is a man who came to Rimbaud by virtue of modernism, and not modernism by virtue of Rimbaud. He's a man of the world: Slavic like Conrad, Byzantine and Russian and Orthodox like Pushkin, and now finally—since 1960 when he published *Diario de Lecumberri*, the account of his time in Lecumberri Penitentiary—he's also Mexican.

An armorial like his would be intimidating if it weren't for the fact that he's also a cult poet and popular novelist. Collections like *Los elementos del desastre* (1953), *Reseña de los hospitales de ultramar* (1958), *Los trabajos perdidos* (1965), and *Caravansary* (1981) have given him cult status; his poems stick with us throughout our lives and—both faithful and inscrutable—crop up at all different sorts of times, whether we're at peace or in turmoil. And he's a popular novelist because the seven novellas now collected in *Empresas y tribulaciones de Maqroll el Gaviero* (1993; *The Adventures and Misadventures of Maqroll*, 2002) have not only earned well-deserved praise and honors but also managed to engrave an utterly sui generis character onto our collective memory.

Maqroll's literary history—or bibliographic biography—is rather peculiar in modern and ancient literature alike. Mutis was a demanding poet with limited themes who wouldn't have minded being called *raté*, and he slowly developed a literary persona—an alter ego—he called "el Gaviero" (the Lookout), who took on a life of his own. This "homunculus" combined Mutis's "verbal splendor and decomposing subjects," which, as Paz* said, defined his poetry. Maqroll, an adventurer and skeptic, was a sort of twentieth-century Marqués de Bradomín (Valle-Inclán's notorious cad) who began cropping up in early Mutis verses and ended up taking over his poetry entirely. In fact, his collected poetic works are called *Suma de Maqroll el Gaviero*.

Whether it was a conscious decision or one imposed by Maqroll himself I don't know, but in the mid-eighties Mutis decided to write the Lookout's saga in a series of novels. One after the other, he released *La nieve del almirante* (1986; *The Snow of the Admiral*, 1992), which toys imaginatively with poetry and prose; *Ilona llega con la lluvia* (1987; *Ilona Comes with the Rain*, 1992), which tells of one of Maqroll's great loves; *La última escala del Tramp Steamer* (1988; *The Tramp Steamer's Last Port of Call*, 1995), the tale of a typical adventure in his life; *Un bel morir* (1989; *Un Bel Morir*, 1992), the premature tale of the hero's death; *Amirbar* (1990; *Amirbar*, 1995), which is my favorite, a sort of erotic novel and Promethean, Caucasian fantasy; *Abdul Bashur, soñador de navíos* (1991; *Abdul Bashur, Dreamer of Ships*, 1995), the story of Maqroll's co-conspirator; and *Tríptico de mar y tierra* (1993; *Triptych on Sea and Land*, 1995), which I haven't read yet, so as to save some Mutis for the future.

It was a privilege to experience, as a reader, the vitality and self-confidence of a great poet who could have easily sat back and rested on his laurels. Each one of Maqroll's new adventures was like an installment, an episode that brought back the childhood pleasure of rushing to the newsstand to pick up the latest edition of a favorite comic book. In fact, some critics have likened the Maqroll saga to *Corto Maltese* or *Tintin*.

At the time, the liberties Mutis took were pivotal for new, younger authors writing in Spanish, and by the same token there are some doubts we should examine. Speaking of Mutis's evolution from poetry to prose, Colombian poet and critic Juan Gustavo Cobo Borda said candidly, "The problem for those who knew and enjoyed Mutis's work is that the novels are saying the same thing, expanding it in prose but without fleshing out the figure of the Lookout, who is incomplete by definition. But perhaps that's a fallacious criticism: the Maqroll's charm resides in the fact that he never presents himself fully."

I myself was initially less than thrilled when his adventures turned into a novelized series, expecting the books to exhibit the sort of narrative consistency you'd take for granted in a professional novelist—which is not necessarily a plus. But I needed to read more widely and have a less solemn take on adventure stories, colonial novels like those of Pierre Loti and Pierre Benoit, and on the sentimental Chateaubriand (*Atala, René*) as well as *The Jungle Book* and *La vorágine* (*The Vortex*). There's no reason that Mutis, like his influences, can't be twee and mawkish, or that he can't be absolute arbiter over his world.

It's interesting that Spanish writer Jon Juaristi says that Mutis's books are not adventure novels but "novels about the concept of adventure." I'm not so sure, because accepting that premise implies that the novels of Conrad (and Blaise Cendrars) aren't adventure stories either, which strikes me as unfair and unconvincing. I think Juaristi is taking Mutis's novels too seriously. Mutis was very familiar with ill-fated twentieth-century adventure writers like André Malraux and Drieu La Rochelle, two sides of the coin of desperation, the former achieving the mundane success of a great writer, the latter committing suicide.

The Lookout is not just a descendent of Colombian botanist José Celestino Mutis or an inheritor of the great eighteenth-century expeditions. His passion for transatlantic voyages, his obsession with the ocean and wide-open spaces comes—as Mutis knows—from reading the poetry of Valery Larbaud and Saint-John Perse, and from seeing circling the world as willful determination. And this determination ends up pairing the Lookout with—of all people—Simón Bolívar, who dies at the end of "El último rostro," in one of the most extraordinary stories I've ever read.

The tale's ambiguous ending stems from Mutis's traditionalism—he himself uses the terms Ghibelline, monarchist, and legitimist, and counts himself among those who more or less see the post-French Revolution world as diabolical. His loyalty to the *Ancien Régime* is not a *boutade*. But it doesn't translate into a literarily conservative credo. As Adolfo Castañón* said, Mutis threw himself into the avant-garde adventure with almost "mystical violence and devotion," and this comes through in his modernist blend of poetry and prose. And Maqroll, another modern, adores the mechanical grandeur of ports, while his sidekick Abdul Bashur is obsessed with the perfect ship.

Guillermo Sheridan* says that Maqroll has suffered as much as he's lived, and that Mutis wrote his adventures as a memoir, a sort of recreation, looking back over his life. So it's a beautiful paradox that Mutis can't, as he's said, imagine Pushkin as an old man walking down the streets of Saint Petersburg, or Federico García Lorca as an exile in Mexico City. Meanwhile Maqroll, the overarching theme of his entire oeuvre, is always already old, living the legendary dissipated life.

SELECTED BIBLIOGRAPHY

La muerte del estratega. Narraciones, prosas y ensayos, FCE, Mexico, 1988 and 2004.

Siete novelas. Empresas y tribuaciones de Maqroll el Gaviero, Alfaguara, Bogota, 1995.

Suma de Maqroll el Gaviero. Poesía reunida, FCE, Mexico, 2002.

Abdul Bashur, soñador de navíos, ed. Claudia Canaparo, Cátedra, Madrid, 2003.

The Adventures and Misadventures of Maqroll: The Snow of the Admiral / Ilona Comes With the Rain / Un Bel Morir / The Tramp Steamer's Last Port of Call / Amirbar / Abdul Bashur, Dreamer of Ships / Triptych on Sea and Land, trans. Edith Grossman, New York Review of Books, 2002.

N

NANDINO, ELÍAS

(Cocula, Jalisco, 1900 – Guadalajara, Jalisco, 1993)

Doctor Nandino lived a long, full life. He was a contemporary and accomplice of the poets at the journal *Contemporáneos*, the doctor who prescribed Antonin Artaud medication in the thirties, and a generous patron of young new writers. As editor of the journal *Estaciones* (1956–1960), he published Carlos Pellicer* and Alí Chumacero* as well as the then-callow Carlos Monsiváis* and José Emilio Pacheco.* And after giving up medicine, he returned to his native Jalisco to foster the next generation of writers, among them the notable Jorge Esquinca. Nandino's poetry has been unfairly compared to that of Xavier Villaurrutia and other friends of his whose work has greater range, but over the decades he developed a very moving clarity, as can be seen by the evolution from *Poemas árboles* (1938), and *Conversación con el mar y otros poemas* (1945–1948) to *Erotismo al rojo blanco* (1983) and *Banquete íntimo* (1993). His longevity allowed him to live through different times, and he was able to come out as a homosexual. Other poets of his generation didn't have that opportunity, and it lent his later poems a refreshing openness. In *Cerca de lo lejos* (1979), perhaps his finest book, we read of an old man's desire without any self-flagellation, as in "Dedicatoria extemporánea": "(Sólo queda del Narciso / que se ahogó: / este anciano delirante / y las ojeras / de la vida que vivió.)" ("All that's left of Narcissus / is that he drowned: / this raving old man / and the tired eyes / of the life he lived.") The genial eyewitness of a century of Mexican literature, Nandino left behind two books of memoirs, *Elías Nandino. Una vida no/velada*, conversations with Enrique Aguilar that he later rejected, and the posthumous *Juntando mis pasos* (2000). Like William Carlos Williams, Doctor Nandino felt the congenial connection between literature and medicine.

SELECTED BIBLIOGRAPHY

Nocturna palabra, FCE, Mexico, 1960.

Cerca de lo lejos. Poesía, 1972–1978, FCE, Mexico, 1979.

Erotismo al rojo vivo, prologue by Carlos Monsiváis, Domés, Mexico, 1983.

Juntando mis pasos, Aldus, Mexico, 2000.

Aguilar, Enrique, *Elías Nandino. Una vida no/velada*, Grijalbo, Mexico, 1988.

NOVO, SALVADOR
(Mexico City, 1904 – 1974)

Who was Salvador Novo? Was he, as Octavio Paz* said, a man with no morals and no ideas who attacked the defenseless and feted the powerful, who wrote in shit and is redeemed only by the aphorisms he wrote attacking himself? Or was he the valiant homosexual that Carlos Monsiváis* admired, the cultural agitator who by defending his right to difference (despite his lack of solidarity) helped others secure their freedom?

One thing all of his critics agree on is that the young Novo was the writer who best encapsulated the modernist literature flourishing in the twenties. He was the most ardent and the most informed of the *Contemporáneos* poets; and although he had no interest in being a literary critic and lacked Xavier Villaurrutia's* sensitivity and Jorge Cuesta's* passion for ideas, Novo was without a doubt *the* modern. Not happy simply to peruse *Nouvelle Revue Française* and *Revista de Occidente*, he read more select publications like *Commerce* and *The Little Review*. His knowledge of vanguard poetry, particularly English-language vanguard, was encyclopedic; he accompanied Paul Morand and John Dos Passos on their travels through Mexico, and he knew Joseph Conrad, Marcel Proust, José Moreno Villa,* H. L. Mencken, Ramon Fernandez, and George Santayana, as he proved in his columns in *El Universal Ilustrado* in 1929 by obsessively reporting their news. Novo didn't necessarily read all of the authors he wrote about; but what is perhaps more important is that through them he was able to keep his finger on the literary pulse of the times and to express its spirit.

In books such as *Ensayos* (1925), *El joven* (1928), *Return ticket* (1928), *Jalisco-Michoacán* (1933), *Continente vacío* (1935), and *En defensa de lo usado* (1938), Novo takes Paul-Morand-style travel writing and makes it his own, as convincing in Guadalajara as it was in Hawaii; he goes from futuristic enthusiasm for the big city to the Léon-Paul-Fargue-style classicism of *Le piéton de París*. And although Novo wasn't considered a canonical writer during his lifetime, never having published that one, definitive, sacrosanct work (think *Pedro Páramo, La región más transparente, La sangre devota*, or *Muerte sin fin*), it must be said that he did possess one virtue that only great writers share: the ability to move seamlessly between the city and the provinces, the high court and the town square, the metropolis of world literature and its backwater. The young writer who came of age (and began to see the fruits of his genius start to rot) with *Nueva grandeza mexicana* (1946) had no qualms about exhibiting, criticizing, and pondering the contrast between his provincial childhood and the city of his adulthood. Novo takes the tribute to the city tradition and makes it his. And his city, truly modern, shows its Creole ancestry, flirts with a tongue-in-cheek Aztec worship, and finds its own unique mestizo style.

The ease with which Novo negotiates the contradictions that paralyzed less sophisticated minds than his can be easily seen in his poetry. In *XX poemas* (1925), *Espejo* (1933), and *Nuevo amor* (1933), as Antonio Castro Leal* says, there is no trace of influence of the "masters" of the day (Enrique González Martínez, Juan Ramón Jiménez), and though he spent his time reading e. e. cummings and H. D., Novo never relied on them, as Villaurrutia did with Jules Supervielle. Although *Nuevo amor* was immediately translated into French, *Poemas proletarios* (1934) found no foreign friends in thirties literature, when it was difficult for a poet to criticize the revolutionary workers' movement in vogue without appealing to ideology and using sarcasm, irony, and ambiguity—which he does to great effect in *Frida*

Kahlo (1934). Neither the Russian Revolution nor the Spanish Civil War had critics as satirical as the Mexican Revolution had in Novo, who despite his satanic reputation was more inclined to try to explain the revolution's heroes in his poetry than to denounce them. "Nuestros heroes / han sido vestidos como marionetas / y machacados / para veneración y recuerdo de la niñez estudiosa." ("Our heroes / have been dressed as marionettes / and crushed in the pages of the books / for the veneration and memory of dedicated children," trans. Rafael Hernández.)

In *Salvador Novo: Lo marginal en el centro* (2000 and 2004), Carlos Monsiváis's most literary and personal work, he shows how Novo used satiric provocation to win the battle in Mexico that his hero Oscar Wilde had lost in the courts of England and aestheticism, managing to tame and even train his enemies by turning them into consumers of his wit. Novo's victory cost him dearly. The man Monsiváis describes as an enemy of lost causes ended up living out a pathetic and perhaps paradoxical old age, given his fear of aging.

In order to make sense of Novo, who courted respectability, it helps to make a detour through the mausoleum he built as headquarters of his own posterity: *La vida en México* (1937–1973), a series of specious tomes ranging from Lázaro Cárdenas's term through the days of Luis Echeverría and edited first by José Emilio Pacheco* (1964–1967) and then by Sergio González Rodríguez* and Antonio Saborit (1996–2000). The collection is the life and times of the institutional regime.

First an anonymous political reporter and then a Goncourt-style diarist, Novo ended up becoming the erudite defender of Mexican despotism, to such a degree that he famously supported the army's occupation of the Ciudad Universitaria in Mexico City in 1968. But historical distance allows for a more nuanced reading of events, and the Novo who began writing articles against Cárdenas in the magazine *Hoy* was neither as reactionary nor as conservative as he's been made out to be. He was indifferent to the political victories of the masses and cruel and spiteful about causes that were not his own, such as the Spanish Republic and its exiles. And, as Monsiváis suggests, he was the sharpest critic of the leftist revolutionary nationalism that evolved into a moral and ideological legacy that still lingers on in the government. Every time we feel exasperated by the authoritarianism of those who revel in their monopoly on popular sentiment, Novo's prose is corrosive against leftist manipulation that can be used by his intellectual heirs, including Monsiváis himself and Guillermo Sheridan.*

Novo, it's fair to say, was neither purely an enemy nor an apologist for the Revolution-cum-government. And while Martín Luis Guzmán*—whose work Novo detested—depicted the revolutionary caudillos with the cold cynicism of a moralist, Novo chronicled the practices of institutionalized power, concentrating on the changing faces of the Republic's presidents, who in *La vida en México* all blend into one.

The risible, provincial worship of General Cárdenas that Novo scorned was politely toned down when it came to the presidents whose admiration he courted, morphing into predestined omniscience and omnipotence. From then on, Novo would have to carry out his human sacrifices in private. Novo became the novelist of presidential ostentation, the writer of those caudillos who he said wrote very well (General and President Manuel Ávila Camacho) or who agreed to show up at the Palacio de Bellas Artes or at a session of the Mexican Academy of the Language (President Miguel Alemán). Novo, once the most cosmopolitan of writers, ended up personifying Valery Larbaud's definition of provincialism: believing that only what was "official" was real.

The man who invented the concept of presidency as "art," Novo imagined a palatial world more perfect than the baroque courts described by Gracián and Saavedra Fajardo. It would be tempting to say that he was the Duke of Saint-Simon of the "institutional revolution," but that's not quite accurate since this chronicler of pretend aristocracy never lived at the palace. Instead he cultivated a series of intermediary spaces and practices—from the National Institute of Fine Arts to the media, avant-garde theaters to cocktail parties, gastronomy to bibliophilia—that acted as civilizing mechanisms. So it's only natural that by the time he died he'd become a television personality who both spouted and supplanted public opinion. Not everything about the mid-century Mexico that Novo seasoned with his own neo-Aztec rococo recipe was deplorable, and those of us who reject it today, considering our current barbaric democracy, would do well to remember that those years were Mexico's cultural golden age, created in large part by the liberal absolutism exemplified by men like Novo (and Carlos Chávez and Jaime Torres Bodet*).

La vida en México seems to have been written to prove that the ghastly country born of the crimes of Pancho Villa (which devastated Novo's family, as they did thousands of others) had hit upon the magic potion that would grant it eternity. The tragedy of these books is that page after page, volume after volume, president after president, Novo uses them to transform the New Regime into the Old Regime. The man who'd been an irritating avant-garde poet was somehow unaware of the black magic of his prose, unconscious of the fact that by invoking modernity again and again, he rendered it obsolescent and made it as grotesque as he himself had become. The official chronicler of Mexico City became a macabre caricature complete with wig and make-up; he and the regime both paid dearly for their fear of growing old.

So: who was Salvador Novo? Monsiváis begged the question when he claimed that sexual heterodoxy was a "limited choice" in a repressive society. Almost every society has in some way repressed homosexuals. Likewise, saying that the way the *Contemporáneos* poets were hounded was "atrocious" implies victimhood not representative of Novo, who was proud and belligerent and a member of the cultural elite on his way up with close ties to the State. The poets and their patrons in the ministries, thanks to their aristocratic mindset, managed sooner rather than later to defeat the homophobic Comité de Salud Pública (Committee of Public Health) that the nationalists orchestrated against them. I prefer to see Novo as a Balzacian social climber who, like Vautrin, saw the glimmering city and decided to conquer it. Astute and cynical, he learned all the tricks, until he had it under his control. Almost a child when the 1910 civil war began, Novo took full advantage of the social mobility afforded by the chaos of the revolutions. And just when they jelled and formed a government, artists and adventurers like Novo, by then ensconced in the heart of the beast, imposed their style.

Novo belonged to the school of immoral moralists who prostrate themselves to the powers that be and their minions. In practical terms, this private religion at times conflicts with public office, and at others just imitates the style and taste of the time. Like Casanova and Jean Cocteau, Novo seemed destined to inhabit the superficial world of appearances. Despite being a gossip, he kept his authorial freedoms to himself (with a handful of exceptions). But it turns out that behind the mask, there really was a face—or at least a shadow, the one that closes *La estatua de sal*, one of twentieth-century Mexican literature's most extraordinary books.

Published posthumously in 1998, *La estatua de sal* had been circulating behind the scenes for almost fifty years. More novel than autobiography, the book is a reply to Octavio Paz's unfair comments about Novo's lack of moral autonomy and intellectual consistency. This work redeems Novo for the hollow, moronic pages of *La vida en México*. In its perfection, it establishes a lasting image for Novo, serving as a prosaic continuation of the most self-reflexive and insightful poems in *Nuevo amor*. Even in the most risqué scenes—such as the one where Novo, paralyzed with desire, lets the proof of his lust slip in front of Pedro Henríquez Ureña—he never gives in to vulgarity.

The opaque beauty of his bravado is astonishing and, despite its brevity, the book depicts both the underbelly of the country devastated by the revolution and the portentous secrets of urban nightlife. Great literature, they say, reveals the underside of reality, painting a deft picture of the times using a different color scheme. *La estatua de sal* is both a moral response and a glorious example of the literature of the grotesque that someone like André Gide, so full of banal theories, would never have been able to write. Novo has been criticized for his amateur Freudianism, as if theories now in vogue somehow better explain his sexuality. The narrator's voice (and suppression of guilt) works devilishly well, as do the references to Wilde and Huysmans, the descriptions of love nests, the blending of the smell of gasoline and that of bodies, and the sentimental education that Novo and Villaurrutia shared. Some will find the book desolate, depressing. I find it edifying in that it's a novel-cum-critique of the world.

Like so many writers, Novo was wrong about the transcendence of his own talent. The last of the old-fashioneds to believe that theater would bring him posterity, he was tormented by the idea of being forgotten. In 1969, he confided to a friend: "I want to make a confession to you, to take off all the masks and bandages in public circulation, to step down from the meringue pedestals on which I've received awards, distinctions, praise, applause, etcetera, and confess my devastating conviction that my life as a writer has been a genuine failure. I don't mean, by that, that I won't go down in or haven't already gone down in the history of Mexican letters as a minor genius of productivity and versatility, of wit, etcetera; what I mean is that I believe, without boasting, that I am naturally gifted and blessed by God with the faculties of imagination, sensitivity, and creative ability which I have not duly taken advantage of by producing that Masterpiece we all dream of and with which every artist tends to justify his fleeting presence in the world" (qtd. in Domínguez Michael, *Tiros en el concierto: Literatura mexicana del siglo V*, 1997).

Even Cyril Connolly, who in *Enemies of Promise* diagnosed the maladies of the modern writer, died bitter that he hadn't managed to write a canonical novel. But after all of his scandal, reputation, or respectability, the poet Novo might have been surprised to know that *La estatua de sal* was his master-piece, unfinished like so many essential works and like the sublunary world that watched, dumbfounded, as Novo passed by.

Selected Bibliography

La vida en México en el periodo presidencial de Lázaro Cárdenas, ed. José Emilio Pacheco, Conaculta, Mexico, 1991.

La vida en México en el periodo presidencial de Manuel Ávila Camacho, ed. José Emilio Pacheco, Conaculta, Mexico, 1994.

La vida en México en el periodo presidencial de Miguel Alemán, ed. José Emilio Pacheco, Conaculta, Mexico, 1994.

La vida en México en el periodo presidencial de Adolfo Ruiz Cortines, vols I and II, ed. Antonio Saborit, Conaculta, Mexico, 1996.

La vida en México en el periodo presidencial de Gustavo Díaz Ordaz, vols I and II, ed. Sergio González Rodríguez, Conaculta, Mexico, 1998.

La vida en México en el periodo presidencial de Luis Echeverria, ed. Sergio González Rodríguez, Conaculta, Mexico, 2000.

Viajes y ensayos, vols I and II, ed. Sergio González Rodríguez, Antonio Saborit, and Mary K. Long, FCE, Mexico, 1999.

La estatua de sal, prologue by Carlos Monsiváis, Conaculta, Mexico, 1998.

The War of the Fatties and Other Stories from Aztec History, trans. Michael Alderson, University of Texas, 1994.

O

O'GORMAN, EDMUNDO
(Mexico City, 1906 – 1995)

Every list of great Mexican books should include Edmundo O'Gorman's *La invención de América* (1958; *The Invention of America*, 1961), a well-polished stone that was first tossed across the water fifty years ago, and has continued to make waves ever since. Eugenia Meyer's 2009 book, *Imprevisibles historias. En torno a la obra y legado de Edmundo O'Gorman,* is testimony to that. The book is a collection of essays and studies O'Gorman wrote, including introductions to Herodotus and Thucydides, his critical editions of some of the great works of colonial historiography (by José de Acosta, Antonio de Solís, Las Casas, Motolinía, Fray Servando Teresa de Mier, etc) and contributions to various symposia and colloquia that showcase his magisterial, unsettling personality. O'Gorman was the type of spirit whose presence is simultaneously comforting and disconcerting—the sort who fights conventionalism, lack of courage, and hackneyed ideas. At the same time, he was quick to polemicize wherever he recognized true intelligence: he took issue, for instance, with Las Casas scholar and revisionist historian Lewis Hanke, rejected Alfonso Reyes's* literary theory as expressed in *El deslinde*, and stood up to Hispanist Marcel Bataillon.

A liberal with no party (as some authoritarians claim true liberals must be), O'Gorman spent most of his intellectual energy (explained sagely in his few scholarly books) fighting the historic mystifications of Mexican liberalism. In "Hidalgo en la historia" (1964), as Roger Bartra* recalled on the publication of *Imprevisibles historias*, O'Gorman fought the myth of Father Hidalgo as the "divine old man," who according to Mexican writer Ignacio Ramírez, should have been seen as the father of all Mexicans (as opposed to the Spaniards or Indians). He mocked Father Hidalgo's supposed "cry of independence," which was in fact invented by another liberal: politician and novelist Don Manuel Payno. And in his last book, *Destierro de sombras* (1986), O'Gorman took on the polemic surrounding the alleged apparition of the Virgin of Guadalupe, and came out supporting anti-apparitionist rigor (often, lest we forget, upheld by Catholics). The pre-Hispanic, to him, was somehow monstrous. And yet each of his demystification endeavors—starting with the most important, his view of America as having been "invented" rather than discovered—in fact intended to do the opposite of what his critics claimed. He had no desire to dispossess Mexican history of its sparkle; rather, he wanted to ground it in the fascinating persistence of myths, legends, and ideas.

O'Gorman was a true "idealist," one of the best of that then-maligned class of philosophers. He may also have been a true Mexican existentialist. Very early on in his career as historian—a career that led him to abandon a successful profession as a lawyer—O'Gorman said (in reference to colonial chronicler Luis González Obregón, whose post he took over at the National General Archives) that we needed to be careful about viewing legend as a source of historical knowledge. Álvaro Matute sees that idea as coming out of Benedetto Croce, one of O'Gorman's inspirations.

And according to his mentor José Gaos,* who never tired of enthusing about his beloved disciple, O'Gorman was a man who showed "the artistic potential of a historian of ideas." That's why, authoritative, brave, and courageous, *La invención de América*—polished, expanded, and evolved over the course of several editions—has been so influential. O'Gorman risked expressing a most unpopular idea, one that's become even more politically incorrect now than it was half a century ago, by affirming that America belonged not only to the Western imagination but to the world of European expansion, a world he saw as having the only desirable—or possible—civilization. It's inevitable (albeit still lamentable) that his "invention" has been used by anti-Westernists and peddled by relativists as the opposite of what O'Gorman was trying to say, turned into the ultimate prescription that sees every reality as some dark form of mystification used to alienate the Other, the victim.

O'Gorman was against both positivism and the obfuscation of Leopold Ranke—who forgot that naturalist historiography is the most pretentious of secondary sources—but he was also against irrationalism, which substitutes truth for the fallacies of scientism.

On reading *Imprevisibles historias* and going back over *México, el trauma de su historia* (1978), I realize that not everything O'Gorman wrote is entirely convincing. His mysterious disdain for the Mexican Revolution—as noted by Enrique Krauze*—concealed the bitter (and conveniently undisclosed) conviction that both the Party of the Revolution and the pre-revolutionary Porfiriato—the vilified, idiosyncratic regime—synthesized the conflicts of liberal Mexico and conservative Mexico. He dispaired (as did Paz in *El laberinto de la soledad*) of the derivative, "extra-logical" nature of nineteenth-century Mexican liberalism, yet exalted that very dependence when harking back to Mexico's early New Spain origins, in his opinion the only origins of value. It seems to me that, siding with and against O'Gorman, *both* the liberal urge to mythologize Mexico and the criollo snobbery expressed by baroque are part of that same universal tendency.

O'Gorman was a nineteenth-century scholar, in the best of ways. By this I mean (quoting Bartra*), "neither totally archaic nor totally modern," an antiquated writer of solid if at times dry prose, and yet he was also a most voracious devourer of myths and the aphorist who wrote, "Ideas die when they become beliefs; beliefs when they become ideas."

SELECTED BIBLIOGRAPHY

México, el trauma de su historia, UNAM, Mexico, 1978.
Destierro de sombras, UNAM, Mexico, 1986.
La invención de América, FCE, Mexico, 2006.
Imprevisibles historias. En torno a la obra y el legado de Edmundo O´Gorman, edición de Eugenia Meyer, FCE, Mexico, 2009.
The Invention of America, no translator listed, Indiana University Press/ Greenwood Press, 1961.

P

PACHECO, JOSÉ EMILIO
(Mexico City, 1939)

Sartre said that hell was other people. Lezama Lima, once he conceded its existence, imagined it to be empty. And Pacheco thinks, "there is no hell. We pay for it all here." As old as Gnostic heresy, this concept serves as a good introduction to the man who signs his articles with the initials JEP, making him unique in contemporary Mexican letters.

La sangre de Medusa y otros cuentos marginales (1990) is a new edition of a collection of JEP's early prose. Pacheco is a man who writes on a wide variety of subjects, as well as a staunch defender of rewriting and active self-editing. Personally, I'm not interested in the argument over whether or not a writer has the right to touch up early texts. You have to differentiate between philological necessity and copyright. But I've looked at some of the first editions Pacheco tweaked, and I can say that the changes he made are small, and beneficial to most of the stories.

"We can change anything but our worldview and our syntax," JEP wrote in the book's introduction. Of course, to say that our worldview can't change is nonsense. Society abounds with individual and collective mutations that never cease to amaze. But for Pacheco himself, it appears to hold true. Indeed, in the time between his early work (1956–1958) and today, there has been no evolution or alteration in his obsessions.

"El triptico del gato," "La sangre de Medusa," and "La noche del inmortal" are a few of these early texts that essentially contain all of Pacheco's ideology: the horrors of history, animal fantasy, nature as sacred, and the everyday apocalypse. Highly original at the time, they are still enjoyable reads and foretell his 1967 *Morirás lejos*, one of the most admirable novels of the second half of the twentieth century.

In *La sangre de Medusa* both the adult and the adolescent live side by side, in pages of dull prose and flash fiction, a genre Pacheco excels at. But what interests me most are the recent texts that so irritate writers of my generation, who see JEP as bête noir dressed as lamb, a man whose laments are melodramatic, facile, and repeated to the point of tedium; intended as calling cards, they're really condolences for the misery and corruption of Mexico, a country that each week he buries anew. Years ago, someone said he flagellates himself every day with a rolled-up newspaper.

You don't have to be an insightful writer to denounce the country's unspeakable decay, and even bad journalists publish articles about it. So what happens to a prophet when the apocalypse comes true on a daily basis? A fulfilled prediction is history, not prophecy. Jeremiah becomes Barnabas.

JEP, like most writers who've achieved fame and fortune, has shown symptoms of loneliness, of lack of self-editing, of the "misunderstood genius" syndrome (or unheeded prophet) that afflicts those who respect few. Among my friends and contemporaries, those who've railed against him tend to be poets who reject civic poetry and glorify cynical (in the philosophical sense of the word) and more hermetic poets like Gerardo Deniz,* whose obscurity makes some young writers froth at the mouth. The two are seen as opposites: in the seventies, JEP was the poster child of understated political poetry that neophytes found easy to imitate. In the nineties, a decade of political dyspepsia and Byzantine aesthetics, they find it easier to try (unsuccessfully) to copy Deniz and pretend that pedantic gibberish is poetry. In truth, Pacheco doesn't deserve our ridicule, nor does Deniz speak the divine language of postmodernity. Both are indispensable authors, and their polarization— spurred on by hard feelings—only serves the infighting.

La sangre de Medusa y otros cuentos marginales is a good point of departure to discuss JEP as a quandary. His authority flows from his rhetoric: he is the writer as moralist. Pacheco took that role from two sources. The first is very modern: Borges's idea of the primacy of reading over writing. The second is the august view of the writer as an intellectual who upholds the values of the Enlightenment (whether Voltairean, Goethean, or Catholic) in the face of political barbarism. Over the course of his career, Pacheco has rejected several roles in the theater of national culture. He is neither public man of letters (à la Jaime Torres Bodet* or Agustín Yáñez*), nor Ivory Tower *artiste* (Salvador Elizondo,* Juan García Ponce*) nor engagé intellectual (José Revueltas,* Octavio Paz*).

Far removed from cultural bureaucracy and political belligerence, JEP followed Alfonso Reyes's* example, but expanded the role so as to encompass a moralist function that the wise older man never exhibited. Invisible but authoritative, enjoying the comforts of the ivory tower with a window overlooking the public plaza (where the faithful await his prophesies), Pacheco proved himself the intellectual who never betrays his humanistic devotion to good causes—as long as they don't cost him ideologically. Unlike his spiritual brother Carlos Monsiváis, who made political mistakes because he was playing politics, JEP managed to remain uncorrupted. There's nothing false about that. In fact, his public stance is so true to heart that it translates into eco-poetry, civic poetry, and a cultural journalism in line with his moral high ground.

But it's wearing thin. When moralizing goes unaccompanied by political commitment, it's simply too safe. When prophecy becomes reality, the poet just turns into a sort of notary, and Pacheco's weary false modesty has made his presence grating. Given that during this time the Mexican elite was becoming highly politicized, regardless of affiliation, Pacheco's heartfelt testimonies simply had less appeal.

Walter Benjamin's phrase about hope being given for the hopeless moved JEP, and he turned it into a personal maxim hard to reconcile with his Gnostic idea of hell on earth. Thus, neither a critic nor a revolutionary or religious prophet, JEP didn't progress beyond whining artist. And he forgets—as all humanitarians do—that the oppressed are sometimes complicit in their own oppression.

Devoid of any politics of spirit, Pacheco takes the easy way out, criticizing the devastation caused by progress, the spent values of nationalism (which no longer dares to go by that name), and the facile academic belief that "dehumanization" is comparable to barbarism while conveniently forgetting that nature itself is by definition the only entirely "inhuman" thing.

And with that I'll turn back to his prose, which is full of animals but short on humans. That's no surprise. JEP writes fables, after all, and his humanized animals serve to express his morality. He just might be the Mexican writer most obsessed with zoomorphism since Dr. Mier. And although this distinguishes him, it also holds him back, keeps anything novel from cropping up in his prose. His creatures depict intellectual oppositions rather than emotional conflicts. Works as successful as *Morirás lejos* and *Batallas en el desierto* (1981; *Battles in the Desert*, 1987) don't have remarkable characters; instead, they're masks for the proverbial antinomies of history and nature, transposed to the persecution of Jews and bogged down by nostalgia for a lost though imperfect childhood.

Fernando Benítez* said that Pacheco surpassed Reyes in talent and culture. I'm sure it's true. What I would add is that Reyes was a great pagan who rejected Christian drama, the very Judeo-Christian dualism that JEP bears like a cross and preaches in his poetry, fiction, and encyclopedic essays. JEP could use some of the festive, outright acceptance of the real world that comes through in Reyes's paganism. And he could stand to lose his discontent with the savage world, since he's never taken the risks of revolutionary agitating, Christian fervor, or Gnostic revulsion. His is a humanitarian rhetoric. But Pacheco, we must not forget, has taught us a lot. And that's why now, talking about him, it's important also to recall his most important lesson: a true writer—like himself—should be judged by his best pages. (*Servidumbre y grandeza de la vida literaria*, 1998)

Pacheco is a writer whose influence can only be compared to that of romantics and modernists of a hundred years ago, people like Juan de Dios Peza and Amado Nervo. *Tarde o temprano*, his collected poetry, has been published on two occasions (1980 and 2000), but its theme is singular. From the first book to the last, from his 1958–1962 collection *Los elementos de la noche* down to *Siglo pasado. Desenlace*, his 1999–2000 collection, he's written about the same thing: the planet's ecological destruction as caused by man. "La honda tierra es la suma de los muertos. Carne unánime / de las generaciones consumidas" ("The deep earth is the sum of the dead. Unanimous flesh / of generations consumed").

I disagree with critics like Jorge Fernández Granados*—who anthologized *La fábula del tiempo* (2005)—who see JEP's poetry as having evolved from testimonial drama of conscience to historical examination to nostalgia for time gone by. For me, I repeat, Cain and Abel are the sole players on Pacheco's stage. What I do agree with Fernández Granados about is that JEP is a talented fabulist, and that some of his best poems are written in this vein. I'd choose the verses written by his heteronym Julián Hernández in "El cancionero apócrifo," as well as those of "El pulpo," "Prosa de la calavera," "A la orilla del Ganges," and "El rey David." These are poems that will go down in history, as Pacheco would want—despite his false modesty and hypocritical humility—and there are enough of them to justify his entire oeuvre.

Until *Irás y no volverás* (1969–1972), JEP's poetry was pleasing, even moving, for its touching clarity and economy; it was a civic poetry almost without antecedents in Mexico, parallel to the experiences of Nicaraguan Ernesto Cardenal or Chilean Enrique Lihn. Gabriel Zaid,* for instance, found *El reposo del fuego (1963–1964)* to be a "dry, chalky, desolate (book) . . . whose function is combative, a fight against the desert and against time, and to a certain degree sacrifice: a preemptive surrender. This battle can also be carried out through silence" (*Obras, 2, Escritos sobre poesía*, 1999). A decade later, Octavio Paz* said that Pacheco was like "an inverse Pangloss, determined to prove to us that we live in the worst of all possible worlds" (*Obras completas, 4. Generaciones y semblanzas*).

Paz's comment was slightly malicious, and unfortunately, over the last few years, JEP's Pangloss bent has been exacerbated by the fulfilled prophesies that both world and national history have granted him. The mimetic austerity so admired by Paz, Zaid, and Guillermo Sucre has been relegated to second place. It's shocking that a man so schooled in both English- and Spanish-language poetry would insist on continuing to write (and edit and rewrite) such primitive verse. His is essentially the voice of a pedagogue, a fact readily ascertainable at the Guadalajara Book Fair, when a line of kids and teenagers stood waiting for him to sign their copies of his opportunely published *Gota de lluvia y otros poemas de José Emilio Pacheco para niños y jóvenes.*

Not altogether different from the poet and the narrator, JEP the translator (in the broad sense of the term) and literary journalist (as he likes to call himself) is, in my opinion, the one who will live on. In both of these facets, Pacheco—who was Juan José Arreola's* amanuenses—is Latin American literature's memoirist. His "approximations" are very free translations, but those that are more "faithful" are no less excellent. He's bequeathed us a treasure trove ranging from Omar Khayyam and ancient Japanese haiku to Goethe and Edgar Lee Masters, from Apollinaire, Rilke, and Marianne Moore to T. S. Eliot, Valery Larbaud, and the North American indigenous poets.

"Poetry belongs to no one: we all make it together" is JEP's tremendous adage. And according to Sucre, it makes sense that the convivial pursuit of poetry corresponds to a man whose poetic temperament is characterized by "paraphrase, collage, variations; his poems constantly recreate the voice or perspective of other poets, chroniclers, artists: his books' and poems' multiple epigraphs reveal a meticulous search for literary effect. Even his versions—'Approximations'—of the most divergent poetic traditions form a considerable, even key, part of his oeuvre" (*La máscara, la transparencia. Ensayos sobre poesía hispanoamericana*, 1985).

Many of us owe a tremendous amount to "Inventario," the weekly column that Pacheco the literary journalist published for almost half a century and that sooner or later will be anthologized as a book. I started reading it in *Proceso* in 1976, and just by way of example, it's unlikely that I'd have decided to become a critic had it not been for that column. It's nearly impossible to itemize the entire list of authors we were introduced to at JEP's invitation, from Mexican masters trapped in limbo, like Martín Luis Guzmán* and Alfonso Reyes, to the great patriarchs of criticism such as Edmund Wilson, Cyril Connolly, and Walter Benjamin, and the inventors of Latin American literature, Francisco Javier Clavijero and Rubén Darío.

It's a motley catalog that also takes in Suetonius, Vladimir Holan, and Walt Whitman, which is no surprise; JEP's passion knows no bounds, and this allows him to link the world's oldest wounds to present-day barbarism. He infected us with his lethal passion for Mexican history and his compulsion to exorcise its demons, with his encyclopedic curiosity for languages and literatures, with his contemporary version of the *Palatine Anthology*. From scholarship to journalism, Pacheco has painted an entire gallery of melancholic and horror-filled paintings, everything from portraits of the parallel lives of tyrants to the singular experience of poets, from the massacre of revolutionary generals at Huitzilac to the horrific death of Jorge Cuesta* and the seldom-visited grave of Luis Cernuda.*

The people and subjects JEP covered as an essayist comprise a literary sensibility that will be associated with the last few decades of the twentieth century, which was so spectacular for Mexican culture. Despite attempting to be a chronicler of disaster, Pacheco will live on as the guarantor of a high literary culture, one representative of a not-too-distant Mexico in which criticism (whether of art, film, or literature) was considered a fine art.

In 1989, after a reading in Madrid at the Residencia de Estudiantes, I dared to ask JEP what he thought about his poetry's apparent impunity, which at the time no one dared to criticize. Maybe I did it out of my generation's need to distance ourselves from our mentors, even the most beloved ones; we all feel compelled to attempt to relive the dispute between ancients and moderns in some small way. But if I criticized Pacheco, I did so convinced of the depth of literary friendship, which he himself taught me from behind his desk: something that is forged entirely outside of writers' circles and literati, and that stems instead from the solitude of reading.

That night in Madrid, Pacheco brushed off my impertinence and we went to dinner. And our conversation went on so long that when we returned to the Residencia de Estudiantes where we were being put up, not a single gate was unlocked at the laudable institution, apparently still unaware of the liberal customs of Spanish nightlife. The only thing we could do was jump the fence. José Emilio Pacheco led the attack on the castle, and for a few unforgettable moments we found ourselves in the best of all possible worlds, contemporaries of every college student in history.

SELECTED BIBLIOGRAPHY

Morirás lejos, Joaquín Mortiz, Mexico, 1967.

La sangre de Medusa y otros cuentos marginales, ERA, Mexico, 1990.

Tarde o temprano (1958–2000), FCE, Mexico, 2000.

La fábula del tiempo. Antología poética, ed. and prologue by Jorge Fernández Granados, ERA, Mexico, 2005.

José Emilio Pacheco: Selected Poems, ed. George McWhirter, New Directions, 1987.

Battles in the Desert, trans. Katherine Silver, New Directions, 1987.
City of Memory and Other Poems, trans. David Lauer and Cynthia Steele, City Lights, 1998.

PARRA, EDUARDO ANTONIO
(León, Guanajuato, 1965)

The hells of Mexico are many, existing simultaneously in multiple times and places. Few writers know them as well as Parra, our best realist. His novel *Nostalgia de la sombra* doesn't interest me as a whodunit—although I recognize the skill with which he pulls the genre's strings—and I object to the final killing, a bloodbath worthy of Hollywood. But Parra turned his paid assassin into a real character in search of his own identity, inhabiting the perhaps implausible zone between mediocrity, misery, and murder. Cigarette after cigarette—and oh, how our hero smokes!—Mendoza the hired gun crisscrosses an empty Monterrey, in need of a photographic memory so he can focus in on the victim and just shoot.

If all novels come from a primordial cave, as Michel Tournier said, then the epicenter of *Nostalgia de la sombra* (2002) resides in the trash dumps that Parra plants magisterially in the heart of his book. That subterranean landscape pays homage to José Revueltas* and bests similar pages written by Ricardo Garibay.* By depicting human beings reduced to the state of animals, Parra expresses the shuddering atrocity of his narrative, chronicling suffering without offering the habitual comforts of sentimentality and sociology.

Parra's stories, as I said when they were first published, strike me as a true rhetorical achievement: the ability to successfully narrate a nightmare. Very unusual in any literature, he came onto the scene a fully formed writer right from his first book (*Los límites de la noche*, 1996), a natural storyteller who doesn't confuse the genre with imitation or periphrasis. He produces in us a childlike urge to beg, "tell it again," which surely is the true sign of literature. Parra's strength stems from his lack of "originality." None of his themes—crime reports, wetbacks, small-town idiocy—is new to the Mexican realist tradition. But the "alarming"—as José Agustín* called it—degree of verisimilitude he achieves reminds us of an elemental truth: form is what governs a story's opening. In *Tierra de nadie* (1999; *No Man's Land*, 2004), Parra returns to subjects that obsessed Revueltas and Juan Rulfo* (as well as less prestigious writers like Francisco Rojas González) and retells them as if they were pure innovation, entirely new hells. Thus we have "El cristo de San Buenaventura" about the scapegoat lynching of a town lunatic, the pathetic romance of drunks in "La vida real," and the humiliation of a prostitute in "Nomás no me quiten lo poquito que traigo." Mexican violence, which we thought was dead after decades of miserabilist literature, was reborn in Parra, whose pen makes new all forms of cruelty. We're talking about one of the most extraordinarily talented writers of Mexican literature. And that's why, when Parra announced his first novel, his readers (like he himself) feared that he'd lose control of his tightly-knit prose in a different narrative form, the novel being digressive by nature. But with *Nostalgia de la sombra*, Parra proved that his hypersensibility, so effective in capturing short bursts in his stories, works equally well on larger scales, as with those expansive road scenes in which what flies by is not the scenery but the character's existence. Parra, like his hired gun, has both long- and short-range weapons in his arsenal. And though his hand might tremble, his writing is more dependent on his eye, squinting to capture every movement off in the shadows.

In 2000, Carlos Monsiváis wrote in *Letras Libres* that the only thing "the ubiquitous, supreme image" of Benito Juárez might possibly lack was, perhaps, an Andy Warhol silkscreen. That statement brought to mind the ominous inauguration of Vicente Fox, who during his induction as President of the Republic was handed a large cross by one of his daughters; the montage led to an immediate outcry by a group of legislators shouting "Juárez, Juárez!," invoking the president known for curtailing the Catholic church's political power. Fox simply repeated them mockingly from the platform, irritated. In the end, it turned out that granting the Catholic Church power was not to be one of Fox's sins—real or imaginary—and the secular state, presided over by the heirs of conservatives of yore, survived unscathed. And today it seems likely that the National Action Party (PAN) will leave executive power in 2012, having made its peace with the ghost of Juárez and his liberal, Jacobin legacy, so advantageously administered by Mexican Revolutionary governments.

But back to Monsiváis. There have been cities, avenues, streets, bridges, and towns named after Juárez. The horrible bust erected in Iztapalapa has become world famous and turned into something of a Mecca for concept art. And since 1972, the Year of Juárez, there have been art exhibits, ballets, movies, and soap operas staged in his honor. The only thing missing is a good contemporary novel. Enter Parra, who was seven years old during the Juarist apotheosis.

Parra is both a professional and a conventional writer. What I mean by that is, since his early stories, he's displayed the kind of narrative talent that seems to come from divine inspiration and yet actually stems from his absolute control over form. This allows him to write, at will, tales that are perfectly self-contained—as per the conventions of twentieth-century realism—be they noir or historical fiction, as in the case of *Juárez: El rostro de piedra* (2008). His models would appear to be Ernest Hemingway, Truman Capote, Raymond Chandler, Cormac McCarthy, José Revueltas,* Juan Rulfo,* and Vicente Leñero. As I've said before, Parra is one of realism's Hard Guys, and it's easy to picture him ensconced in a café, writing by hand in a spiral notebook, fueled by extremely high doses of caffeine, or at home with a keyboard, pounding out the cold realities of life he learned while writing the police blotter in border towns, where his stories percolate. That sort of character was unusual in the years when his short story collections came out (from 1996 to 2010: *Los límites de la noche, Tierra de nadie* [*No Man's Land*, 2004], *Nadie los vio salir, Parábolas del silencio*, now collected in *Cuentos completos*) and thus Parra to a degree restored realism and its conventions, as well as that vile, gory Mexico you'd prefer not to have to experience, except in literature. Parra is the opposite of the Mexican writer caricatured by Roberto Bolaño,* the aesthete who wanders through the city while reading Paul Valéry, oblivious to the ruins and the infamy surrounding him.

A writer with that sort of mettle diving into the waters of a genre as traditional as historical fiction was destined to shine. Parra didn't commit any of the sins of fictionalized biography—a lamentable hybrid that lacks the research-backed rigor and respect for truth of straight biography and yet also lacks, out of laziness and commercialism, the freedom of a real novel. Additionally, historically based fictionalized biographies tend to be

369

the stuff of disillusioned professors on sabbatical: the raw material supplied by history, an inexhaustible breeding ground, meshes with the naïve belief that all you have to do is read novels in order to write one. Thus somehow they pass for art. But in *Juárez: El rostro de piedra*, for example, readers get no "suggested reading" list, intended to validate an author struggling to see his way through the murky waters between history and fiction. Everything Parra ought to have read, he did—from Justo Sierra to Enrique Krauze,* by way of Francisco Bulnes, Ralph Roeder, and Héctor Pérez Martínez. He steeped himself in Juárez's documents, speeches, and letters, which, for the past half century, have been available to the public.

From the outset Parra declined to narrate Juárez's early life, to repeat his infancy, which the national hero himself did in his *Apuntes para mis hijos* (1857), texts that should become part of the historical anthologies of Mexican history. Juárez is also, after all, our Henry Adams. No other Mexican writer has so swaddled his childhood-cum-lost-paradise, turning it into a bucolic idyll free from any doubt or incivility.

Nor does Parra take the Stendhalian route, capitalizing on the Napoleonic side of Juárez's story: a Zapotec Indian from a decent home in Oaxaca, his life as a rewrite of the tale of Julien Sorel's ill-fated rise, though this one with a very happy ending—his marriage to Margarita Maza, a the well-heeled young lady who became, as it's so often been remarked, his source of strength. Their marriage, secular and as bourgeois as a piano in the parlor, compensated for the horror of that earlier "original" couple, Hernán Cortés and La Malinche. The rest of his sentimental education is well known: learning Spanish, preparing for the priesthood, and then entering law—the true liberal religion that made Juárez not only governor of Oaxaca but a lay theologian presiding over the Supreme Court. Then, in 1858, he became President of the Republic after Ignacio Comonfort was forced to resign. The photo that for decades so many Mexicans kept under their pillows, as Julien Sorel did with Napoleon, was of Benito Juárez, a legalistic privateer who clung until death to the power he had risen to without having stolen.

Juárez: El rostro de piedra begins with a rather Hamletian cliché in which the president appears, plagued by insomnia, pacing through the National Palace in the months before his death in 1871. From that vantage point, Parra comes and goes through the key moments of the hero's life, used to weave the plot: incarceration in that very palace during the winter of 1857–58; his days in Veracruz, the carnivalesque city that seems to be the only place Parra's Juárez could sleep, albeit feverishly and with fantasies; the crafting of the Laws of Reform and the rivalries produced by his victories in 1861 and 1867; his time in the dungeons of San Juan de Ulúa (which allows Parra to portray hell in vivid Revueltas* brushstrokes); the execution of Maximilian (and Princess Salm-Salm's indecorous appeal for clemency); and the final battle, in which the conventions Parra adheres to dictate that Juárez must lose his life.

The book's chronology is logical without being linear, and Parra makes good use of the rich cast of characters surrounding Juárez. Thus he manages to discount some of Bulnes's diatribes: Juárez's greatness is measured by the grandeur of his companions, rivals, and enemies, from Lerdo de Tejada, Melchor Ocampo, Santos Degollado, Guillermo Prieto, and Miguel Miramón to people like Porfirio Díaz and even Maximilian himself. It's been ages since anyone in Mexico wrote a historical novel so abounding in unexpected characters, and though Juárez can't surprise us, characters like Ocampo and Prieto are novel fictional creations brimming with narrative possibility.

Juárez: El rostro de piedra corroborates the view that Júarez was the most important Mexican in history. Together with Mohamed, Luther, Cromwell and Odin, he'd have completed Carlyle's "hero" cycle. None of the righteous or the avengers, the generals or the bandoleers of the Mexican Revolution can compare to Juárez in terms of splendor. But novels are the right means of expression for that sort of conviction and I must say that by the time I finished the book I felt almost physically stuffed, defenseless at the omnipresence of Juárez, who from beyond the grave seems to manipulate even writers touching upon him a hundred and fifty years after his death.

My sense of surfeit at the bronze idol is, in part, due to Parra's prose. Vibrant and meaty (and often memorable for its grandiose dramatic flourishes), his writing depends on an omniscient narrator who climbs down from his black, republican carriage to call out to Juárez, addressing him familiarly as Pablo rather than Benito. But the longer it goes on, the more the tribute, ostentation, and nineteenth-century oratory convey an inevitable air of civic commemoration, no matter how Parra tries to humanize his hero by placing him at the center of conveniently equivocal circumstances: called before a transvestite captain in Veracruz, invited by his servant to find some relief with a woman, or humbled by working in a tobacco factory. Parra uses the same noble, renaissance tone as Roeder, whose *Juárez y su México* (1972) he translated into Spanish with Alí Chumacero.* Other dialogues and events seem not like the oversimplification of Victoriano Salado Álvarez in his *Episodios Nacionales Mexicanos* (1902–1906) but more like the historical soap operas that Ernesto Alonso dedicated to Juárez in the sixties.

To read a novel about Juárez is to reread history and burn in the flames of a rhetorical hell. That's inevitable. "Postmodernists" tend to see historical novels as either an opportunity to liberally revise history via transrealism or to judge it, punishing the past and imposing retroactive sentences on it for its horrendous crimes. Parra, though, anachronistically writes from a prior literary moment, and *Juárez: El rostro de piedra* uses—felicitously even—the enlightened tone that Heinrich Mann used in his *Young Henry of Navarre*.

But if historical fiction offers little literary freedom, the margin is even smaller when it comes explicitly to Juárez. Put plainly, Juárez demands the highest form—that of tragedy—while someone like General Santa Anna could only come back to life via a comedy-cum-operetta (which Enrique Serna* understood perfectly, as evidenced by *El seductor de la patria*, 1999), and Maximilian and Carlota are pure romance and Romanticism, just as they're portrayed in Fernando del Paso's *Noticias del imperio* (1987; *News From the Empire*, 2009).

It's hard to imagine how Parra might have avoided tragic grandiloquence. Perhaps by risking the use of the first person, as Martín Luis Guzmán* did in *Memorias de Pancho Villa* (1951), but that was a failed attempt, and he had the advantage of knowing his character. Maybe he could have tried interior monologue when Juárez was on his deathbed, as Hermann Broch did with his oft-imitated Virgil. Or desacralizing Juárez, as only Juchitec painter Francisco Toledo can, plopping him down into a postmodern installation of dubious taste.

Those quandaries made me long—for Juárez's sake—for a less conventional realist (and perhaps a less professional writer, too), so the hero could be freed from himself. But once I finished trawling through the most virulent pages of Bulnes, of Sierra's *Juárez: su obra, su tiempo* (1906), of Roeder's biography, and Pérez Martínez's *Juárez, el impasible* (1934), I realized it would have been illogical for a novel about Juárez to be different from the one Parra wrote. There was, once, an alternative: Austrian playwright Franz Werfel wrote a magnificent play prefaced by Borges called *Juárez y Maximiliano* (1924). In it, Werfel never had Juárez on stage. Instead, he was an absent presence, the conscience of the unlucky emperor. Perhaps *Juárez: El rostro de piedra* does a good job reminding us that the true Juárez is invisible.

SELECTED BIBLIOGRAPHY
Los límites de la noche, ERA, Mexico, 1996.
Tierra de nadie, ERA, Mexico, 1999.
Nadie los vio salir, ERA, Mexico, 2001.
Nostalgia de la sombra, Joaquín Mortiz, Mexico, 2002.
Parábolas del silencio, ERA, Mexico, 2006.
No Man's Land, trans. Christopher Winks, City Lights, 2004.

PASO, FERNANDO DEL
(Mexico City, 1935)

Humor, in the Hippocratic sense of the word, is central to del Paso's most important novel *Palinuro de México* (1978; *Palinuro of Mexico*, 1996). del Paso is an erotic writer, although his is a long way from the eroticism of contemporaries Salvador Elizondo* and García Ponce.* Theirs was both an ordinary and aestheticizing eroticism, derived from Gide's disciples and, prior to them, from the decadents. Unlike them, del Paso—both Rabelaisian and Renaissance—renounces open wounds and sadomasochistic love. Instead he opts for delirium and celebration. For del Paso the flesh, far from being sad, is the sum total of all knowledge: geology, zoology, botany.

In his first novel, *José Trigo* (1966), del Paso prophesied the massacre that took place two years later, in 1968. In *Palinuro de México* he opted not to discuss Tlatelolco but to have the protagonist Palinuro be run over by a tank in the zócalo. For del Paso, although 1968 was certainly not trivial and had haunting consequences, it was also an accident, a risible series of events. And laughter is the other humor without which his eroticism can't be understood. Despite appearances to the contrary, del Paso is not a critical novelist; he devours the world in almost gluttonous fashion.

del Paso's voraciousness might represent the last of the Latin American literary feasts that began with Carpentier and ran rife in the tropics. When we get to del Paso, after Vargas Llosa's *La guerra del fin del mundo* (*The War of the End of the World*) and Fuentes's* *Cristóbal Nonato* (*Christopher Unborn*), New World imagination once again sees its lavish ruins overgrown by jungle. And like Carpentier's *Los pasos perdidos* (*The Lost Steps*), the footprints are growing faint.

So how can we make sense of del Paso's three vast novels? *José Trigo* is Döblin's *Berlin Alexanderplatz* set in Mexico, modernism's last spectral apparition. *Palinuro de México* allows us to devour the world. And with *Noticias del Imperio* we ingest the stuff of history and have a hard time swallowing it all. The verbal delirium of *Palinuro de México* was too much for Charlotte, who, while no doubt strong, was not immortal. *Palinuro de México* is a magnificent Mexican modernist odyssey . . . (*Antología de la narrativa mexicana del siglo XX*, II, 1991)

In 2007, the journal *Nexos* asked a hundred writers what the best novel of the past thirty years had been. *Noticias del imperio* (1987; *News from the Empire*, 2009) won the poll, a fact which doesn't surprise me. It's the most novel-like of Mexican novels, as Agustín Yáñez's* *Al filo del agua* (1947; *The Edge of the Storm*, 1963) had been before it, for decades, according to critic Emmanuel Carballo.* The redundant qualifier conveys the fact that novels such as these meet, apparently, what literary opinion sees as the genre's criteria. *Noticias del imperio* fits our idea of "what a novel should be," now that Proust and Joyce have become canonical, integral to our taste, rather than being seen as authors reserved solely for the initiated.

In addition to a distorted narrative timeline, so characteristic of twentieth-century classics, the book also offers an appealing degree of authority as a historical novel—presumptuously so for some of the few readers who disagree with José Emilio Pacheco's* statement that "there is no nineteenth-century episode that surpasses the tragic intensity of the non-fiction tale of Maximilian and Charlotte."

Playwright Rodolfo Usigli,* as del Paso himself notes at the end of *Noticias del imperio*, was the first to fictionalize this chapter in Mexican history, one so seemingly fictional in reality that only the encounter between Hernán Cortés and Montezuma II measures up to it. Usigli set the precedent with his 1943 play *Corona de sombra*, but del Paso stands up to it admirably. The image readers have of Mexico's "ephemeral emperors"—and to a large degree of President Benito Juárez, their nemesis—is one that's been filtered through del Paso. *Noticias del imperio* is one of the few novels that, in a very nineteenth-century way, actually forms part of readers' historical and political education. And it's my feeling that these virtues make criticisms of the book—such as that of del Paso's systematically monotonous, self-imposed literary devices (the infinite soliloquy, chaotic enumeration)—secondary. And, truth be told, it doesn't seem to have scared off too many readers, as the book is structured such that entire monologues in which Charlotte raves like a loon can be skipped over, while readers forge ahead in the exquisite historical-novel-slash-feuilleton. *Noticias del imperio* also proves that the cult of Clio, using history as fable, requires neither a critical take on history nor the display of historiosophy. All one has to do is compare the novel to ostentatious volume three of del Paso's *Obras completas* (containing his journalism and essays) to see his crushing conventionalism and conformism. It's not the first time a proven cosmopolitan has also turned out to be a narrow-minded nationalist.

Noticias del imperio and *Palinuro de México* chronologically speaking, are two of the Boom's last great novels in which Latin American history becomes a fabulous configuration of the Spanish language, as was true for Alejo Carpentier, José Lezama Lima, and Carlos Fuentes.* But del Paso also has a dual nature, one more pronounced than his mentors and colleagues had: his work is like Rabelais in criollo code, the expression of an insatiable erotic appetite, starved for flesh and world. But it's also baroque or mannerist, exceedingly refined in the decadent sense of the word, as if the result of extreme nervous exhaustion. As I was writing this, I took a look at *El imperio de las voces: Fernando del Paso ante la crítica* (1995), edited by Alejandro Toledo. In the anthology, I discovered that two of the best reviews of *Palinuro de México* were written by contemporary poets, Francisco Cervantes* and Marco Antonio Montes de Oca,* which gives yet another perspective—that of poetic brilliance—on one of the highest summits in Mexican prose.

In 1980, Montes de Oca said, alluding to Palinurus's mythological and medical hypersensibility, "Fernando del Paso's book is one of the most conscientious contributions to Mexican baroque of all times. Of all times? There is no future in *Palinuro de México*. Its richness derives from the perfect omission of the future . . . The story of Palinurus is a pretext that, diverging from its Latin sources, anchors its point of departure in Cyril Connolly's version of the character in the marvelous and perhaps forgotten text *The Unquiet Grave*. Palinurus—helmsman of Aeneas—falls asleep at the rudder, falls overboard, and is dragged to Punto della Spartivento, or Cape Palinurus as it is now called. For del Paso, as for the English poet, a hypochondriac, the myth is symbolic of man, who allows himself to be dragged away by his own dreams, enormous dreams that are dreamed with open eyes and eventually lead to his own death."

SELECTED BIBLIOGRAPHY

Obras I. José Trigo y Palinuro de México, FCE, Mexico, 2004.

Obas II. Noticias del Imperio y Linda 62. Historia de un crimen, FCE, Mexico, 2004.

Obras III. Ensayo y obra periodística, FCE, Mexico, 2004.

Palinuro of Mexico, trans. Elizabeth Plaister, Dalkey Archive Press, 1996.

News from the Empire, trans. Stella T. Clark and Alfonso González, Dalkey Archive Press, 2009.

PAZ, OCTAVIO
(Mexico City, 1914 – 1998)

LIFE

Paz's impact on twentieth-century Mexico is akin to that of Voltaire two centuries earlier. His work will be remembered as one of Latin America's greatest contributions to the world, during a tragic age. His life is comparable to twentieth-century figures like André Gide, José Ortega y Gasset, and T. S. Eliot: committed to utopias and critical of totalitarianism; alternating between silence and uproar; seeing prose as a privileged form, capable of linking Eastern and Western classicism.

A poet of astonishing breadth who used the avant-garde to confront tradition, Paz will be read for as long as the sacrament of reading unites man and book—two revolving signs that defy time and space and make Mayan astrologers, Indian gymnosophers, and Provençal troubadours appear contemporary. In some ways, it is both too soon and too late to discuss his great critical works, masterpieces of modern prose that range from the heterodox surrealism of *El arco y la lira* (1956; *The Bow and the Lyre*, 1973) to the essay *Sor Juana Inés de la Cruz o las trampas de la fe* (1981; *Sor Juana Inés de la Cruz or the Traps of Faith*, 1988), a work that allowed us to reclaim the Mexican poet and spiritual sister of Paz as our own and contested the official history of an entire epoch. But where Paz's critical genius shines brightest is in the hundreds of articles he wrote, fireworks that cast light on the memory of Sartre and Camus, Trotsky and Gandhi, Rivera and Duchamp, as well as all of the poets who've been translated—in the broadest sense of the term— thanks to this greatest Mexican writer of all time.

Anyone familiar with Paz's work will know that I'm not just using my own words here but paraphrasing some of those I recall from Paz's books. Born on Calle Venecia in Mexico City's Colonia Roma in 1914, Octavio Paz Lozano learned to think at the family table, which reeked of gunpowder. His grandfather, Ireneo Paz, was a prominent liberal journalist who passed on his polemical tendencies to his grandson; his father, Octavio Paz Solórzano, a Zapatista lawyer, died young, "stretched on the rack of alcohol" (trans. by Nick Caistor) and defeated by the Mexican Revolution's failure. When he was eighty years old, in 1994, Paz said that the revolution he'd believed in so fervently might have been the tragedy that sealed Mexico's fate, demolishing the place where the idealistic young poet had taught Yucatán peasants to read during the Cárdenas regime.

An intellectual whose doubt was systematic—a way of life—his deferred judgment is both a credit and a source of anguish to men of great genius. And though he might have seemed staunch in public, at times struck down by his own absolutes, his resolve sprung from a daily examining of his own conscience more Socratic than Christian. Paz had an imposing personality and anyone who knew him will recall his changes of opinion, his dialectical and religious fixations, the compulsive questioning that those who knew him adored. His character defects were proportional to his genius, and people tended not to forgive his pride and envy—the very sins we're so indulgent with when it comes to ourselves.

Friends of the world-renowned poet sometimes forget that his success was a direct result of the brave and lonely stands he took, first as a Latin American denouncing the Gulag in the early fifties, surrounded by petty nationalist poets who accused him of not being Mexican, European, or even universal; later when he was threatened by the regime he denounced after the 1968 massacre at Tlatelolco, and finally as a victim of the radical left, who actually burned him in effigy outside the US Embassy after a speech in which he criticized the Sandinistas in 1984.

A poet of the world, Paz died invoking Mexico—his affliction and religion both. On December 17, 1997, in his last public appearance, in a speech that moved both political adversaries and government officials, the wealthy and the erudite, he summoned the "clouds of the Valley of Mexico," eternal and ungraspable. A hundred men and women looked to the sky, and to the poet turned demiurge. For a moment. And then Paz said goodbye, the national poet of a country he said was full of sun and of shadows, hungry for light but covered in blood. Paz was a national poet unlike his Latin American predecessors: a passionate believer in the possibility of a truly democratic republic that had yet to arrive.

He'll be remembered as one of the architects of that democracy that Spaniards and Latin Americans have spent years voting for and awaiting. He was both a precursor and an adversary, fighting the entrenched old regime as well as the Cassandras demanding a proletariat dictatorship. A poet who had engaged in politics since 1929, Paz did of course make his blunders. Impossible not to, for someone who saw morality as a responsibility. The twenty-first century will judge the injustices of a man for whom public virtue was both a daily struggle and a renewed hope. He was an angry man because the times in which he lived called for mindless assessments. Paz, by contrast, discussed everything—and did so in public. With nothing but his intelligence and his honor, he inaugurated a critical tradition that Mexico had previously lacked; and he's not to blame if some of his adversaries were neither intelligent nor honorable. Many others, I believe, will come to see that butting heads with Paz was a beautiful part of one's sentimental education.

Paz was a curious combination of vitriolic hero and fragile poet. At times he forgot he was a Nobel Prize winner and became overcome by bitterness at being spurned. The worst thing we could do is deny him the homage of honest, ordinary criticism. We must therefore read Paz and not abandon him, the way we did Alfonso Reyes,* José Vasconcelos,* Jorge Cuesta,* and José Revueltas.* Otherwise world literature, which has included Paz for the last fifty years, will beat us to it and the poet's life and work will no longer belong to Mexico. And that would be a shame.

Paz was a master of the funeral oration, that venerable form of admiration. He outlived most of the twentieth century's greatest writers, and whether he admired them or abhorred them, he wrote noble, honorable elegies to a great many. And then on December 17, 1997, we saw him—with his wife Marie José—for the last time. For a few moments it was as if the terrible cancer devouring him just disappeared and the wit and sparkle of his younger days was back. But as we were gathered there he learned of the death of his old friend Claude Roy, and he took off his glasses and wept. It was the only time I saw Paz cry. And then he decided to speak about death. "When I learned of the gravity of my illness," he said, "I realized I couldn't take the sublime path of Christianity. I don't believe in transcendence. The idea of extinction calmed me. I'll be that glass of water that I'm drinking. I'll be matter." Faced with our silence, the stoic joked with his wife about her belief in reincarnation. "I've got a heretic at home," he said smiling. And I felt sorrow and joy both, at the enormity of ancient knowledge that I'll never, I'm quite sure, experience again. Tomorrow I won't believe that I was a contemporary of Octavio Paz. (*La sabiduría sin promesa: Vidas y letras del siglo XX*, 2001)

COMPLETE WORKS

A writer's "complete works" are the pinnacle of his oeuvre, compiled only when he's deemed by contemporaries or posterity to merit being read in an established order. Octavio Paz had the good fortune of arranging for the publication of his own *Obras completas*, and he did so at the perfect time since at the age of eighty he was at his critical and artistic prime.

Paz's *Obras completas* can be read in many ways, which I imagine was one of the aims he had in mind when publishing them. The third and fourth volumes, dedicated to Latin American and Mexican literature, made me decide to attempt an alphabetical dictionary of authors and concepts, which serves as proof of the encyclopedic nature of his work. It would be worthwhile to do the same for the other volumes, thereby encompassing the twentieth century's major political players, artists from three continents, writers from other languages and traditions, and the great masters of modern thought. Volume three includes texts whose time span and origin range from the sixties to Nobel speeches in 1990 and culminate in his most recent reflections. Volume four begins with his six perspectives on Mexican poetry and then explores an extensive array of Mexican writers. If we combined the two and ordered them alphabetically, that dictionary would include, among others, Rafael Alberti, Dámaso Alonso, Juan José Arreola,* José Bianco, Rubén Bonifaz Nuño,* Jorge Luis Borges, Luis Cardoza y Aragón,* Camilo José Cela, Luis Cernuda,* Alí Chumacero,* Julio Cortázar, Jorge Cuesta,* Rubén Darío, Gerardo Deniz,* Salvador Díaz Mirón, Salvador Elizondo,* Carlos Fuentes,* Juan García Ponce,* Pere Gimferrer, Ramón Gómez de la Serna, Jorge Guillén, Miguel Hernández, Efraín Huerta,* Vicente Huidobro, Jorge Ibargüengoitia,* Sor Juana Inés de la Cruz, Eduardo Lizalde,* Ramón López Velarde, Gabriela Mistral, Antonio Machado, Marcelino Menéndez Pelayo, Marco Antonio Montes de Oca,* Álvaro Mutis,* Pablo Neruda, Juan Carlos Onetti, Manuel José Othón, José Ortega y Gasset, José Emilio Pacheco,* Carlos Pellicer,* Francisco de Quevedo, José Revueltas,* Alfonso Reyes,* Alejandro Rossi,* Juan Ruiz de Alarcón, Juan Rulfo,* Julio Torri,* Luis G. Urbina, Xavier Villaurrutia,* Emilio Adolfo Westphalen, Agustín Yáñez,* and Gabriel Zaid.*

The list is extensive, but more impressive is the range and plurality of stances and natures that Paz covers, moving seamlessly through different rhetorical times and historical events with breathtakingly vast expertise. He writes about Golden Age poets and contemporary Mexican eccentrics; he captures both Latin American modernism and the Generation of '27; he discusses the failure of Mexican Romanticism and ponders the magnificence of Latin American poetry, which includes him as a central figure. In Paz's encyclopedia, there are lighthouses on both sides of the Atlantic, illuminating their counterparts. The founding of Hispanic tradition and Latin American dissidence have in Paz their discoverer and cartographer both. (1994; *Servidumbre y grandeza de la vida literaria,* 1998)

POLITICS

Octavio Paz is a contemporary classic. And that binary condition—simultaneously traditional and current—intimidates critics. Many are those who balk at the challenge posed by Paz; few have embarked upon any rigorous, detailed, or honest yet uncompromising criticism of his work. This is a poet who established a politics of spirit right from his early days.

Three Mexican political critics did attempt to take on Paz's politics in more or less exhaustive works: Jorge Aguilar Mora,* Enrique González Rojo (junior), and Xavier Rodríguez Ledesma. Aguilar Mora's *La divina pareja: Historia y mito en Octavio Paz* (1978) was a pioneering work that didn't receive the attention it deserved, and the author's challenging theses simply withered away in the face of critical and public indifference. Twenty years later, *La divina pareja* seems to say more about seventies theoretical radicalism than it does about Paz. At times Trotskyite, in parts Nietzschean, with perhaps a bit of Deleuze thrown in, this is the work of a heterodox who holds Paz responsible for the theories that were in vogue in academia at the time and blames him for misreading history. In Aguilar Mora's opinion, Paz blames Marxism for being deterministic and then reproaches Marx for not fulfilling determinist prophesies.

Aguilar Mora is what Maurice Merleau-Ponty called Sartre: an "ultra-Bolshevik." He rejects the intertwining of history and myth he sees in Paz. The way I see it, Aguilar Mora successfully identified an essential element of Paz's thought but drew from it a biased conclusion difficult to share if bubbly "true Marxism" is not what you're dreaming of. Paradoxically, the coupling of history and myth is one of the most eloquent attributes of Paz's politics of spirit. What Aguilar Mora sees as a poor interpretation is, in my opinion, a poetic and majestic reading of history. Ironically, Aguilar Mora—a very original and also somewhat vitriolic essayist—ended up becoming a mythographer himself. *Una muerte sencilla, justa, eterna* (1990), his great tome on the Mexican Revolution, is a book of the dead that exalts the Romantic myth of revolutionary violence. And Aguilar Mora's mythologizing is every bit as rhetorically questionable as Paz's.

But while Aguilar Mora is a lone wolf, poet González Rojo is a heresiarch. During the seventies, he organized a little coterie called EIRA—¡Espartaquismo Integral–Revolución Articulada! (Comprehensive Spartacism–Integrated Revolution!). As one might guess by its moniker, the group attempted to revive Spartacism, awaiting the return of José Revueltas's Leninist theory of the "headless proletariat." Following the Plekhanov model that plots the revolution despite the fact that those blasted historical conditions refuse to cooperate, González Rojo wrote *El rey va desnudo* (1989), a sort of Plato's *Symposium* in which he and his catechumens analyze the "theoretical situation" created by Paz's ideas about the kind of socialism actually being practiced. Magnanimously, the heretic explains to his initiates that Paz is not in fact a Yankee imperialist spy, but simply one of Mexico's first anti-Stalinists, a man who got "lost," not having happened across the true disciples. But it turns out that González Rojo's aims are more human than divine. The professor needed an excuse to expound his theories about IMP (González, a sectarian to the bitter end, loves his acronyms), or the "intellectual mode of production." And Paz was his excuse. González Rojo's doctrine, written in abominable academic prose, is a ragbag of theses combining Trotsky, Bruno Rizzi, Charles Bettelheim, and Rudolf Bahro. This is pure Mexican Marxist heresiology.

In *Cuando se hace cortesano: Octavio Paz y el stalinismo* (1990) the apostate again uses Paz as a pretext to denounce, for the nth time, the intellectual mafias whose ties to the State supposedly have kept independent writers from receiving their proper recognition (from the proletariat, we might guess?). Lacking the heretical bent of his earlier book, here González Rojo espouses the Democratic Revolution Party (PRD) line, since this unusual professor of the meta-Leninist left suddenly discovered that neo-Cárdenas nationalism was the way to integrated revolution.

Xavier Rodríguez Ledesma shares with Aguilar Mora and González Rojo that "ultra-Bolshevism" that consists of problematizing discourses whose squabbles with Marxism can be resolved by taking Paz to task for his heresy. Naturally there are enormous differences between Aguilar Mora's whimsical intelligence, González Rojo's gloomy hermeneutics, and Rodríguez Ledesma's academic neutrality. But all three do appear to believe "true" Marxism exists, awaiting its chance to flourish.

El pensamiento político de Octavio Paz was written by an author of my generation—Rodríguez Ledesma was born in 1960—which might explain why I'm more interested in his take on Paz's criticism of Marxism: it was mine, too. We both attended public universities during the "crisis of Marxism" that seemed to intensify in the years between the Chilean coup (1973) and General Jaruzelski's repression of Polish workers (1981). But what initially seemed like a fever that would break, thereby signaling the patient's return to health, in fact turned out to be a death rattle. It seemed then that the proliferation of Marxist heresies—from Eurocommunism to council communism, Enrico Berlinguer to Rudolf Bahro—would take the place of decrepit Soviet orthodoxy. But with perestroika, the West's recurring dream of Soviet redemption started to fade away, and on January 1, 1992, the Kremlin lowered that hammer and sickle. Having lost their raison d'être, the heresies petered out along with orthodoxy. And thus the Trotskyist dream of a new workers' state—founded on the risible idea that it would be somehow intrinsically superior to capitalism—went up in smoke.

Paz meticulously explained the process by which he distanced himself from Marxism, and Rodríguez Ledesma documented it faithfully. In the early fifties, by denouncing Soviet concentration camps, he made a clean break with Stalinism. Later he relinquished the idea of Stalinism as a terrible cancer on the otherwise healthy body of Marx, Lenin, and Trotsky. And that led him to return to traditional liberalism, which is what Rodríguez Ledesma just can't accept. The sociologist still clings to the hope that heretical Marxism lurks somewhere in the pages of Paz's works. Paz himself was plagued by doubts, moving from Victor Serge and André Breton's utopist hope to the discovery that Marx was a two-faced philosopher: one side libertarian, the other totalitarian. And of course Marxist socialism's susceptibility to despotism became an appalling reality in the Bolsheviks camps. As early as 1844 Proudhon predicted as much in a letter to Marx.

In his attempt to point out Paz's contradictions vis-à-vis Marx—or real socialism—Rodríguez Ledesma forgets what matters most. Paz criticizes Bolshevism not as a historical aberration, but as something easily passed from Marx to Lenin, from Stalin to the international left, thereby establishing a totalitarianism worse that Nazism, since Hitler never bathed in the waters of humanist tradition.

As I was writing this, I came across a passage in Ernest Renan's *The History of the People of Israel* that struck a chord: "All humanitarian dreams are contradictory, for the imagination turns in a narrow circle, and the plans which it traces have, like the lozenge-shaped figures of Oriental mosaics . . . The great idealist Germanism of the Herders and Goethes was to end in an iron realism, which declared that it recognised only action and force. What can be said of modern socialism and of the change in face which it would make if it ever attained executive power." (trans. Joseph Henry Allen and Elizabeth Wormeley Latimer) And this in 1887.

When Paz says that liberalism and socialism should together create a new type of utopia, I don't think he's seeing Marxism as synonymous with socialism. But Rodríguez Ledesma seems to think Marx is the only socialist theorist, forgetting Babeuf, Fourier, Saint-Simon, and Louis Blanc, "utopian" socialists that intolerant Marxists were quick to discredit. Rodríguez Ledesma's systematic documentation, while useful for those rereading Paz as well as initiates, fails as an interpretation. Paz is not an ambivalent or sheepish Marxist. He's a man who shared the communist dream of his day, and then abandoned it in defense of open society.

Rodríguez Ledesma follows Paz's trajectory as a critic methodically, narrating the poet's great polemics diligently and impartially. He notes that Paz was pioneering in his description of Mexican despotism as a "philanthropic ogre," something that even those who slandered him a decade ago now admit. I share Rodríguez Ledesma's impatience with Mexico's revolutionary regime: like the living dead, they awoke from their slumber only when their destruction was already being celebrated. Rodríguez Ledesma appeared hurt by the calm indifference with which Paz awaited the Institutional Revolutionary Party's (PRI) demise. But he sidestepped the fact that Paz's democratism stemmed from the fact that he stopped worshipping the god of revolution, that fraudster who'd conned so many in the twentieth century.

Rodríguez Ledesma is baffled by Paz's long battle with the Mexican left. Always swimming upstream, the poet repeatedly criticized Cuba and the Latin American left, which earned him vitriolic slander and led to his burning in effigy. But as Roger Bartra* said, it was the left who benefited from Paz's aggressive discourse. Counter to those reactions, during my days in the Mexican Communist Party (PCM) I met many upstanding democrats who acted in accordance with their beliefs despite fidelities to Castro or Lenin. And I think Paz overlooked their moral courage. But I must say that in the days following the 1994 neo-Zapatista uprising in Chiapas, when I saw how many "reformists" instantly reverted to their worship of Zapatista guerrillas, I realized that yet again Paz's suspicions were well-founded. If the Zapatista National Liberation Army (EZLN) uprising had spread beyond Las Cañadas

and the country had plunged into civil war, I bet many of those now marching for peace on the streets of Chiapas would be singing the praises of the
revolutionary army.

Regrettably, Rodríguez Ledesma's book doesn't go beyond 1993, so the
1988 elections are the last episode in Paz's political life that he considers. The
sociologist laments Paz not having taken a more belligerent stand against the
contested and highly controversial elections, and I agree. I'd have liked to see
him add his name to those demanding the results be annulled and election
repeated. But Paz, like the PRI, had faith in President Salinas de Gortari, believing that he'd enact true democratic reform and attenuate the illegitimacy
of his election. After mass protests, leftist candidate Cuauhtémoc Cárdenas
finally withdrew, saving the country from bloodshed. And despite colossal
irregularities, I don't think his party has been an obstacle to Mexico's democratization. But once in office, President Salinas de Gortari undertook
economic reform that Paz and much of the public approved of. Then came
1994, the Zapatista rebellion, political assassinations, and the collapse of the
economy. The old PRI regime proved itself incapable of reform, and yet the
same year we had the cleanest elections in Mexican history and the party
took fifty-one percent of the vote.

El pensamiento político de Octavio Paz reproaches Paz for accepting the
snail's pace of democratic transition in Mexico. Born in 1914, Paz is an intellectual whose life ran a parallel course with the Mexican revolutionary regime. His father had ties to the Zapatistas, he himself was a teenager during
Calles's repressive reign (officially 1924–1928, and unofficially until 1935)
and a young and enthusiastic poet during Lázaro Cárdenas's social reforms.
A foreign diplomat in the service of a government applauded by the international left, Paz stepped down as ambassador to India in protest over the
1968 massacre in Tlatelolco, a fact that the Cubans and Soviets overlooked.
Throughout his life he systematically rejected violence against the state. That
deep political conviction may incite impatience or anger, but it's unfair for
a critic to question Paz's intellectual legitimacy based on his own convictions. Rodríguez Ledesma lamented Paz not having been a revolutionary.
He wasn't the first to do so.

When presidential candidate Luis Donaldo Colosio was assassinated, I
found myself having a Bolshevik fantasy: I was to witness the storming of

the Mexican Revolution's own Winter Palace in a few short hours. The next evening, by chance, I went to see Paz to deliver some articles, and made the most of the visit by telling him about my dream—a mixture of both hope and horror. He coldly dismissed my thinking, saying that not only was the PRI's sudden disappearance unlikely but also undesirable. His rejection of my apocalyptic vision—for that's what it was—astonished me. But it also made me understand his conviction that history—when seen as a moral responsibility—can be separated from the whims of violence.

That anecdote sheds light on the disappointment Rodríguez Ledesma shows in Paz in his conclusion. The poet did not share the younger generation's impatience to see the PRI's demise; he viewed the party as a binary power structure that had been legitimized by four generations of Mexicans. His reaction to the state was that of an intellectual reformer who wanted to have a word with the prince, not to dethrone him. After all, the Mexican Revolution had been a sinister attempt at the latter, which was exactly what his critical thinking was founded on.

Paz's modernity defies Rodríguez Ledesma's Marxist intellectual analysis. As Paz saw it, dialectics resided neither in history nor in nature. His politics of spirit were a defense of universal Enlightenment values, the work of a man who didn't give in to the temptation of selling his soul to the devil of secular ideology that had attempted to destroy the open society. (1996; *Servidumbre y grandeza de la vida literaria*, 1998)

Poetry

Paz possesses the kind of genius found in that very rare genus of poet-critics. In the twentieth century, as Julio Cortázar commented, Paul Valéry and T. S. Eliot are the only others to exhibit such a confluence of analytical reflection and poetic oeuvre. Do the two talents ever clash, as Cortázar feared? It would seem not, which makes him very tricky to analyze. Paz's poetics not only probe the history of world poetry but also explain his own poems. The same, by the way, is also true of the authors of "La Jeune Parque" and "The Waste Land."

More than ten years have passed since his death, so Paz now receives diminished attention. He's also the victim of misconceptions inherent to all great writers in their posterity. His political ideas—which seen in retrospect are simply a principled, Socratic chapter in the liberal, social democratic reaction to communism—no longer scandalize. And when the Berlin Wall fell in 1989, proving him right, those who feared that their reputations would be damaged by public association with him and had once claimed to prefer the poet to the critic began their processes of exorcising the divine poet. They concluded that he hadn't been such a great poet after all but had indeed been an insightful observer of history. This type of exoneration is perhaps even more dire and insidious than the former, because it's a crime against the essential unity of his overall oeuvre.

Paz has always been associated with the Romantic tradition that sees poets as visionaries. He was a tremendously contemplative man who spent his life bearing witness—intellectually and religiously—to his time, both rejecting and sanctioning it. For Paz, it's impossible to separate ideas from poetry, just as for Blake—who cannot be divorced from the influence the French Revolution had on him—it's impossible to separate poetry from painting. In Victor Hugo, one can't ignore humanitarian Romanticism, just as the surrealists can't be credibly analyzed without considering the double legacy of Rimbaud and Marx. One might, of course, prefer Paz the poet to Paz the essayist, just as one might with Pound or Breton. But one must not think that without the ideas (a sort of politics of the spirit) expressed in *El arco y la lira* (1955; *The Bow and the Lyre*, 1973) and in much of his literary and political criticism, it's possible to fully *understand* his poetry.

It's not always the case that one needs the essays written by great poets to make sense of their oeuvres. For instance, Luis Cernuda,* whom Paz so admired, wrote *Pensamieto poético de la lírica inglesa* (1958), a somewhat forced, professorial book that fulfils its mission of explaining English lyric poetry but sheds no new light on Cernuda's own verse. But just by reading Pound's *Cantos* or Neruda's *Canto General*, one can surmise the authors' explicitly fascist and communist doctrines; there's no need to digest Pound's didactic teachings or the journalistic declarations Neruda foisted off on the world in his role as great communist poet. Paz's poetry, on the other hand, is so wrapped up in his convincing, captivating philosophical writings that French poet Claude Roy said reading Paz is what it would be like if Hölderlin or Nerval wrote the treatises of Tocqueville or Marx. That may be an overstatement, but it does communicate the sense of bedazzlement

Paz evokes. Those of us who were young in the early eighties approached Paz with the uneasy knowledge that he was not just famous but powerful. And thus the admiration that writers of his generation professed for him was astonishing (and very compelling), given the reigning empire of Marxism at the time and the fact that his politics were divergent from if not hostile to it.

The essential unity of Paz's work can be corroborated in several ways. One is via correspondence: just read a poem written earlier or later—a poet's time, after all, is not the same as a professor's—than one of his essays and the "conjunctions and disjunctions," to borrow the title of one of his books (1991), abound. In other instances, the answers to questions asked in a treatise (i.e. the link between the 1960 edition of *Libertad bajo palabra* and *El arco y la lira*) or in his political, literary, and artistic criticism are to be found in a poem written earlier, or later.

It was in 1942, when taking part in functions honoring the four hundredth anniversary of the birth of Saint John of the Cross (whom he compared to Francisco de Quevedo), that Paz first discussed his "disjunctive" aesthetic. "Poesía de soledad y poesía de comunión" (included in *Las peras del olmo* in 1957) became a sort of dividing tenet, a penetrating binary. And if solitude was embodied by Quevedo, Sor Juana was the source of communion. *Sor Juana Inés de la Cruz o las trampas de la fe* (1982; *Sor Juana Inés de la Cruz or the Traps of Faith*, 1988)—a historical depiction of New Spain's poet-nun—articulated the opposition between a poet's "damned" irreducible individuality and the unavoidable failure of his or her desire for communion with the Church, the Party, and humanity.

Clearly, the associations between a poem and a page of an essay, a verse and an idea, reside on different levels; this is why I speak of correspondence rather than coherence. Paz never attempted to be a systematic thinker nor did he try, like Blake, to be a prophet or to turn his poetry into a personal history of infamy, the way Pound did in his invectives against usury. Paz was a disillusioned Romantic: he dreamed of a lyric religion but was awakened by skepticism, which kept him from expressing any religious enthusiasm or zeal. The magic spell cast by the world was broken by cruelly utopian dreams turned political reality. And then only poetry could enchant the poet.

Paz reached poetic maturity in India, as described by Paul-Henri Giraud in *Vers la transparence* (2002). Two collections of poems written there—

Salamandra and *Ladera Este*—find their correspondence in two books of essays—*Corriente alterna* (1967; *Alternating Current*, 1973) and *Conjunciones y disyunciones* (1974; *Conjunctions and Disjunctions*, 1991). Meanwhile, *Blanco* (1967), his most radical book of poetry, marked the start of a dialogue that began with "Los signos en rotación" (the epilogue to the 1967 edition of *El arco y la lira*) and ended with *Los hijos del limo: del romanticismo a la vanguardia* (1974; *Children of the Mire: Modern Poetry from Romanticism to the Avant-Garde*, 1974), a critique of the century's poetic aesthetics. In theory comprised simply of the talks Paz gave at Harvard, this book serves as a historical preface to *Pasado en claro* (1975) and *Vuelta* (1976), two great poetic memoirs published after his sixtieth birthday.

Towards the end of his life, it's true, the essayist was much more convincing than the poet and although *Árbol adentro* (1987; *A Tree Within*, 1988) contains a handful of his best short poems, his latter-day essayistic vigor is unrivalled by any modern poet. In the last ten years of his life, he wrote incisive prologues to every volume of his *Obras completas* (that of *Itinerario—Itinerary*—is a veritable autobiography) and ended his erotic musings with *La llama doble* (1993; *The Double Flame: Love and Eroticism*, 1996) and his trip to the East with *Vislumbres de la India* (1995; *In Light of India*, 1997). I'm less convinced by his confessional poem, "Carta de creencia" (1987), which completes what he called the "delta of five arms" of his poetry.

Sometimes it takes fifty years for the questions asked in poems to be addressed, as is the case with "Homenaje y profanaciones," the 1949 Quevedo-style poem that was the impetus behind *Reflejos. Réplicas*, which came out in 1997. Quevedo can be seen throughout, in the self-consciousness with which Paz writes: a malevolent, playful, provocative, insufferable self-consciousness. Anthony Stanton sees Paz's Quevedo as a precursor to Baudelaire. And if it's not Quevedo (to name some of those who come and go in Paz's poetry), it's Trotsky, the tragic hero who symbolizes the entire history of communism, so dramatic in Paz's eyes. We see his death rattle, his "quejidos de jabalí" ("moan as of a wild boar," Eliot Weinberger) as he is killed, in an astonishing verse from *Piedra de sol* (from "Sun stone" in *Selected Poems*, 1984).

Paz himself admitted he didn't have an easy time locating his own poetic voice. The first book he published (*Luna silvestre*, 1933) wasn't the first one to receive critical recognition (*Raíz del hombre*, 1937). Nor was it the first book that didn't leave him feeling discouraged (*A la orilla del mundo*, 1942). According to Paz, *Libertad bajo palabra* (1960) was his first true book, and although readers might need the help of Enrico Mario Santí's commentary to make sense of the new titles, subtitles, and revisions the first part of the book underwent, it's clear that his early years were characterized by insecurity. In a letter to Jean Claude Masson, his editor at Pléiade, Paz said he felt the weight of the spiritual indignity oppressing him, a weight that came from his worst pages. He clearly didn't want the bullfighter's plea, for judgment to be passed on his best rather than worst performances.

And that's precisely why, in order to fully read Paz's poetry, it's best to employ two readings: first, following the chronological order of his books as they appeared; then (via *Libertad bajo palabra*'s 1960 and 1968 editions, *Poemas* of 1979, *Obra poética, 1935–1988*, and the last two volumes of his *Obras completas*) reading what he revised, attentive to the fact that he was disputing the sovereignty of his work with his readers. Paz's revisions signaled the way he wanted to be read: the poet and the practitioner of a poetics were there together, a bifurcation that for some may seem excessive or bothersome. But Paz was governed by a tautology: the poet was a critic because he was modern, and modern because he was a critic.

Let's take a look at 1937. That's the year he was ordained intellectual of the century during the Spanish Civil War, the year he met just about everyone, before, during, and after the Anti-Fascist Congress in Valencia: Neruda, André Malraux, Rafael Alberti (whom he already knew), José Bergamín, Paul Éluard. He even met Antonio Machado, who, after the Republic was defeated two years later, crossed the Pyrenees never to return. On his way back to Mexico with his then-wife, future novelist Elena Garro,* he made a stopover in Havana to see Juan Ramón Jiménez. And that same year, *Raíz del hombre* earned him a critical review from Jorge Cuesta,* Paz's mentor and at the time Mexico's main literary critic. Cuesta was not one for passionate praise: he simply recognized Paz as one of many young promising poets.

The richness and profusion of Spanish-language verse that a new poet like Paz was confronted with at the time was astounding, despite the fact that the war in Spain pulled many poets towards militant or *engagé* poetry, despite the fact that Machado stopped writing permanently and Jiménez temporarily. Those were the years of Neruda's *España en el corazón* (1937;

Spain in the Heart, 1993), Xavier Vilaurrutia's *Nostalgia de la muerte* (1938; *Nostalgia for Death*, 1992 published in a single tome with Paz's *Hieroglyphics of Desire*), César Vallejo's *Poemas humanos* (1939), José Gorostiza's *Muerte sin fin* (1938), Cernuda's *Las nubes* (1940), Emilio Prados's *Memoria del olvido* (1940), and Rafael Alberti's *Entre el clavel y la espada* (1941).

Paz called his early poetry "neo-Romantic" (sexualized à la D. H. Lawrence, yet still full of rhetorical verbiage and waffle), which meant simply that it aspired *not* to be pure poetry or *engagé* poetry. Easy to say, harder to carry off. Politically, Paz had to reconcile Revolution and Poetry, taking from one what he gave to the other. This turned out to be quite a Sisyphean task for twentieth-century poets. His attempt to reconcile the two led him to join up with the young Spaniards at the journal *Hora de España*, whom he'd met during his weeks in Spain during the Spanish Civil War. And Paz welcomed those same poets, as Guillermo Sheridan* noted in *Poeta con paisaje* (2004), when they came to Mexico as exiles, founding a journal with them—*El hijo pródigo* (1943–1946), which was both transatlantic and intergenerational.

After his years in the United States and France, in 1949 he published *Libertad bajo palabra*, which was received coldly, so much so that playwright Rodolfo Usigli,* on reviewing it, noted that his friend Paz was "considered a forgotten poet, not one of interest in Mexico." "A book inscribed in time, changing," is how Santí described it, a book of poems akin to Pound's *Cantos*, Cernuda's *La realidad y el deseo*, Jorge Guillén's *Cántico*, that is, a work grounded in the poet's experience, never finished, subject to his creative intemperance.

The 1949 first edition of *Libertad bajo palabra* is easily recognized by two of Paz's most emblematic verses: "Contra el silencio y el bullicio, invento la palabra, libertad que se inventa y me inventa cada día" ("against the silence and the commotion, I invent the Word, freedom that invents itself and invents me every day," trans. Rukeyser in *Early Poems*) and "palabras que son flores que son frutos que son actos" ("words that are flowers that are fruits that are acts," Eliot Weinberger). "Himno entre ruinas" ("Hymn among the ruins") was Paz's first historiosophic poem: Mexico intersects with world history, two tributaries of a poetics of history. The collection also contains less emblematic poems: "Crepúsculo de la ciudad" is an urban poem—he returned to the theme of the city many years later, in "Hablo de la ciudad" ("I speak of the city"), in *Árblo dentro* (1987). The collection also contains his first poetic attempt at dealing with his father's death, in "Elegía interrumpida" and his first poetic portrait, this one of the Marquis de Sade.

Paz's oeuvre is comprised of a series of dialogues that are prolonged, intense, and sometimes cut short. By reading his poetry, one can follow these dialogues from start to finish. This accounts for the fact that so many writers from both sides of the Atlantic—and from different generations—felt addressed by his work. The most important of those dialogues were with surrealism (culminating in *La llama doble*), socialism (in *El ogro filantrópico* and *Itinerario*, between 1978 and 1993), and the Mexican Revolution and Mexicanness (which, from *El laberinto de la soledad* in 1950—*The Labyrinth of Solitude*, 1961—to *Posdata* in 1970, evolved from a historiosophy of political history to an inquiry into the meaning of democracy in Latin America). Finally, his dialogue with India parallels the structuralist upsurge, and all of his writing from that period can be interpreted through that lens, as was his intention in *Claude Levi-Strauss o el nuevo festín de Esopo* (1967). Each of these dialogues oscillates from poetry to essay and from essay to poetry.

Paz lamented the fact that his dialogue with surrealism began late, but perhaps it was better that way. When André Breton visited Mexico in 1937, Paz, it appears, attended only one of his talks, and did so incognito. Breton had been invited to Mexico by renowned Trotskyist painter Diego Rivera (the old head of the Red Army stayed with him and his wife Frida Kahlo), with the aim of having him meet up with Trotsky himself, the bête noir of the all-powerful Stalinist left that the young poet, for better or for worse, belonged to. Plus, Paz saw surrealism as a school or avant-garde approach rather than an epoch-making sensibility that broke with Romanticism. His will to receive a poetic state of being as though it were an ordination lasted until the publication of *Piedra de sol* (1957; *Sunstone*, 1991), translated into French by Benjamin Péret, right-hand man of Breton, who promised—without making good—to write the book's prologue. Breton's reason, or excuse, for not doing so, in the end, was quite hefty praise. In a letter to Gallimard, the publisher, he said that writing a prologue to *Piedra de sol* would be as presumptuous as introducing Mallarmé's "L'après-midi d'un faune."

In 1946, when he was sent to Paris to take up a minor post in the Mexican Embassy, Paz finally met the surrealists and began attending their get-togethers. "More than once, I told myself I'd gotten there twenty years too late. But the embers of the great bonfire that was surrealism still warmed my bones and fired my imagination" (Prologue to *Excursiones/Incursiones, Obras completas 7*, 1994). And thus his poetic world became populated by ghosts and oracles: Nerval, utopian Charles Fourier, Hölderlin, Rimbaud, and the Marquis de Sade—surrealism's greatest character.

What was left of Breton's early crowd met up at the Café Cyrano, far from the stifling quarrels between the existentialists and communists who monopolized French intellectual life. There, Paz befriended Péret (who naturally, given his familiarity with Mexico, became Paz's mediator), André Pieyre de Mandiargues (who called him "the only great, acting surrealist poet in the world"), and Georges Schehadé, the francophone Levant poet. Breton anthologized "Mariposa de obsidiana" ("Obsidian Butterfly"; from *¿Águila o sol?* 1951; *Eagle or Sun?* 1976) in his *Almanach surréaliste du demi-siècle*, a collection of postwar surrealists, and called Paz the Latin American poet who most moved him. Despite Breton's superficial knowledge of Spanish-language poetry, his regard for Paz in later years is quite notable, so much so that when he died in 1966, Spanish poet Guillén (who was close to neither Paz nor the founder of surrealism) said that Paz had been Breton's only Latin American friend.

The Paz of the mid-century was the most surrealist, and when he was admitted to the Bretonian circle, as Jason Wilson notes, he was stylistically loyal, choosing the noble prose poem as genre for his *¿Águila o sol?* It's no coincidence that Péret, in 1957, translated one of his "Trabajos del poeta" presenting the figure—more sleepwalker than dreamer—of the poet tackling (as if from a Leonora Carrington painting) words, which have risen up in rebellion. This collection was also included in phenomenological critic Gaston Bachelard's last book, *La flamme d'une chandelle* (1961; *The Flame of a Candle*, 1988).

Breton famously said in an interview that Mexico was the only surrealist country in the world. He wasn't intending, as has been often claimed, to exalt picturesque Mexican life. The expression—or line of thought, if you prefer— was later developed in "Souvenirs de Méxique" (1939). Breton saw Mexico's surrealism as a combination of age-old sacred life force—a latent, ancient civilization that Lawrence had viewed with morbid fear and fascination a decade earlier—and revolutionary spirit. Thus Mexico, for Breton, was both past and future. A decade later, in Paris, Paz found in Breton what Breton had found in Mexico; if Breton made Mexico surrealist, then Paz crowned the "Mexicanization" of surrealism begun by Péret and Spanish poet Juan Larrea. Just as Breton "surrealized" Mexico after numerous other explicit, implicit, and/or circumstantial antecedents (Eisenstein, Kahlo, Wolfgang Paalen), Paz finished Mexicanizing it, by providing a Mesoamerican poetic-mythological language.

French poet-critic Alain Bosquet concluded in *Verbe et vertige* (1961) that Paz, the creator of "telluric" surrealism, had been able to offer Bretonian surrealism the "neo-Mayan and neo-Aztec" splendors that "French didactic customs" and "Germanic plunges into the subconscious" had not. Note that Bosquet, wisely, spoke of "neo-Mayan and neo-Aztec" almost as neologisms; that is, purely poetic mystifications, rather than claiming any vindication of authenticity Paz could possibly have offered Mesoamerican cosmogony. That can be seen in "Mariposa de obsidiana," where according to Hugo J. Verani the search for otherness in the Aztec presents incongruous images: the oneiric and the reign of erotic communion as a means of re-establishing cosmic balance.

Paz, who arrived late to surrealism, was never an orthodox Breton proselyte, as evidenced by his amicable criticism in *El arco y la lira*. In this, his great treatise on poetics, Paz defends surrealism as the essential spiritual experience of the avant-garde period. Having been forged from Romanticism and enabled the autonomy of inspiration, it fit with his desperate search for a way to make poetry prevail over life. He was certainly never a sectarian. Even while Breton was still alive—and Paz worried about upsetting him—he rejected automatic writing, Freud's scientificist obedience, obviously blasphemous anti-Christianism, and the predilection for the esoteric. In fact, in a 1975 letter to Roger Caillois, Paz said that Breton confused poetry with poetic experience.

It's not his dialogue with surrealism that he's most known for in the fifties, however. No, it's the publication of *El laberinto de la soledad* (1950 and 1959), one of the twentieth century's greatest books—a historico-poetic essay explaining the mythical advent of "the Mexican." The poet, here, coexists with his past, with the 1930s author of "Entre la piedra y la flor," a sort of "Waste Land" shifted to the left, a social poem about the exploitation of Yucatec peasants that came out of his time in the Yucatán as a political militant, right when he was called to participate in the Valencia Anti-Fascist Congress. The young poet of that period—and of his phase as *engagé* author of "Elegía a un compañero muerto en el frente de Aragón"—had a lot more in common with the surrealists than he himself realized when he began frequenting their café after the war.

After Paz's early political poetry, archaeologically preserved via recurrent revisions, came "El cántaro roto" ("The broken water jug"), from *La estación violenta* (1958). This poem provided a less optimistic "vision" of Mexico than *El laberinto de la soledad*, the "novel" that described the Mexican Revolution as a primordial "fiesta" from which sprang "the Mexican," to stand, all things being equal, shoulder to shoulder with the men of the world. In "El cántaro roto," Mexico is equated with its terrifying droughts, and power—as seen in Juan Rulfo's* *Pedro Páramo* (1955)—resides solely in the hands of an absolute *cacique*. For Rulfo, the cacique is a ghost, the father of all men, living and dead; in "El cántaro roto," written the same year, he's an obscene bigwig, an avatar of Gordo of Cempoala, the cacique who aligned himself with the Spaniards on their way to Tenochtitlán, a figure both modern and archaic, lecherous and sterile.

La estación violenta closes with Paz's most famous and oft-recited poem, "Piedra del sol," a poem that—like those of Rimbaud and Neruda—we memorized when we were young, in the hopes of being admitted to the "order" of surrealism, of Paz's "the three-pointed star": love, liberty, and poetry. "Voy por tu cuerpo como por el mundo / tu vientre es una plaza soleada / tus pechos son dos iglesias donde oficia / la sangre sus misterios paralelos" ("I travel your body, like the world / your belly is a plaza full of sun / your breasts two churches where blood performs / its own, parallel rites," trans. Eliot Weinberger). Echoing a comment he'd heard Cyril Connolly make about Pound, José Emilio Pacheco* claimed he had three copies of *Piedra de sol*: one to read, one to reread, and one to be buried with.

The poem is simultaneously strict and free, because Paz wrote it in 584 hendecasyllabic lines to reflect the 584 days of the synodic period of the planet Venus, 584 being the number of days that the ancient Mexicans counted, the sun being both the end of one cycle and the start of another.

But Paz himself—who was adamant in claiming that his most celebrated poem was too Hispanic—warned against a reading that stuck too closely to what Raquel Philips called "the mythical mode" associating "Piedra de sol" with Aztec cosmogony. Nevertheless, Paz almost never stops being a historiosophic poet for whom poetry, as an absolute reality, shows the underside of historical truth: Abel, Agamemnon, Socrates, Robespierre, Trotsky, Lincoln, Madero, and the bombarding of Madrid in the Spanish Civil War all appear in *Piedra de sol* as counterpoints to love. "Todos los siglos son un solo instante / y por todos los siglos de los siglos / cierra el paso al futuro un par de ojos" ("all of the centuries a single moment, and through all the centuries of the centuries / a pair of eyes blocks the way to the future," trans. Eliot Weinberger), states the poet.

Piedra de sol, as Pacheco sees it, is a calamitous love story, akin to Abelard's tale of misfortune with Heloise. Five women—from Melusine to Laura—converge, their essence expressing what Paz sees as the nature of erotic energy. Woman is natural energy, as Guillermo Sucre noted in *La máscara, la transparencia* (1985). Another of Paz's insightful commentators, Saúl Yurkiévich, found that the way to interpret Paz's poetry began with sensual passion, analogy and rhythm, most notable in *Piedra de sol*. Paz, he concluded, did a marvelous job when it came to "positive poetry, that of manifest beauty," which only aggravated the contradiction tormenting him as poet-critic: the better his verses, the more futile he found the language of poetry to be. Alejandra Pizarnik, the Argentine poet, noted that contradiction with admiration in her review of *Salamandra (1958–1961)* (1962), which might be seen as the "hinge" (I use the term to avoid speaking of "transitional books") between the mid-century Paz and the Paz of the sixties.

For many readers, *Salamandra* is their favorite collection by Paz, and it might be mine as well. The book possesses the fire of *Piedra de sol* but stops short of the militancy of the Paz of the sixties. The book's titular poem represents Paz's eroticism via the mythical lizardlike creature that can withstand fire without being burned, an archetype of the sexual encounter and of woman, of passion, and of patience.

Salamandra presents paradoxical conflicts between pure time and the urgency of the moment. Though Paz did not here take the poetic, typographical, or intellectual risks characteristic of *Blanco*, for instance, they were heralded in "Entrada en materia," an anti-establishment, anti-academic poem. It's also in *Salamandra* that Paz stopped being a surrealist poet—to whatever degree he had been—and took on his own unmistakable voices, as Pizarnik noted. This is when he began to win the international literary awards that culminated in the 1990 Nobel Prize.

In "Noche en claro" ("Clear Night"), Paz bid farewell to Breton (who died in 1966) and Péret (who died in 1959) with a memoiristic portrait that began as surrealist poem—"Todo es puerta / basta la leve presión de un pensamiento" ("everything is a door / all one needs is the light push of a thought," trans. Eliot Weinberger)—and ended up a typically Paz-like association between woman and the city: "cara de humo hombre sin cara / el otoño marchaba hacia el centro de París / con seguros pasos de ciego" ("a face of smoke a faceless man / autumn walked toward the center of Paris / with the steady steps of the blind," trans. Eliot Weinberger).

Salamandra was also the book in which Paz made manifest the order of his direct predecessors, with a poem about Luis Cernuda and another about José Juan Tablada, a sort of Mexican Yeats who inspired poets from two centuries, and—more importantly—where he laid out a section called "Homenage y Profanaciones" ("Homage and Desacrations"), that included his never-ending conversation with Quevedo.

Finally, "El mismo tiempo" ("The Same Time") is one of his most revealing poems, including several verses that serve to help decode Paz's historiosophy. After speaking of death and accepting his mortality, Paz makes Mexico City—the Zócalo, specifically—the umbilical cord of the world, and the poet is reprimanded by two Spanish-language thinkers: José Vasconcelos* and José Ortega y Gasset. The Mexican stoically invites him to turn to philosophy as a way of preparing for death; the Spaniard counsels him to think in German and forget the rest. He rebuffs both poltergeists, having rejected transcendental philosophy in favor of the immanentism of poetry: "Yo no escribo para matar el tiempo ni para revivirlo / escribo para que me viva y reviva." ("I do not write to kill time nor do I write to revive it / I write that I may live and be revived," trans. Eliot Weinberger). Along with Baudelaire, Paz assumes that the poet's religion is to seek the eternal in the ephemeral, his "poetics of the instant." It's a poetics that, for Paz, given the torments of History, cannot be solely a verbal riddle, a lyrical mystery. The instant occurs fatefully between "la vida inmortal de la vida y la muerte inmortal de la historia" ("the immortal life of life and the immortal death of history," trans. Eliot Weinberger), as he also says in *Salamandra*.

Had he stopped writing after *La estación violenta* and *Salamandra*, Paz's poetry would have no doubt been considered some of the most vibrant to come out of Latin American heterodox surrealism, and *Piedra de sol* would confer upon him the stature of an author of a great erotic-mythic poem. But it was during his second stay in the Orient that the poet-lover founded his myth, which turned him into a living legend of contemporary literature in India as well as one of the greatest "Orientalist" poets of the century along with Pound, Victor Segalen, and Paul Claudel.

In New Delhi, where Paz was sent as Mexican Ambassador in 1962, he was so drawn to Indian culture that he became not a scholar but something much more difficult: completely at home. I saw the evidence myself a few years after his death, at an Indian university, where I witnessed heated discussions among Hindus about *Vislumbres de la India*. Whether exalted or rejected, he was placed in the best of company, right beside the great nineteenth-century German mythologizer Max Müller, cataloguer of Indian wisdom. Paz's studies took on the obscure Aryan origin of Indians; the incredible and fruitful coexistence between Buddhism and Hinduism; the universality of philosopher Nagarjuna; the role of Islam; monist and dualist controversies in the six schools of traditional philosophy; parallels between art in the Asian subcontinent and medieval Christianity; Indian independence in 1947; his heroes Nehru and Mahatma Gandhi; the sublime, sensual, "baroque," erotic Indian art as seen in Khajarao and Konarak, testimony to the only civilization that created images thoroughly devoted to "terrestrial pleasure." Those philosophers who saw in Buddhism an element of nihilism, a negation of life, he concluded, were either crazy or blind.

Did Paz's Indian poems, as Philips claimed, blend Brahman metaphysics and Paz's own Buddhist temperament, resulting in an amalgam? It's an open question. But by searching "the other shore," finding harmony in opposites and in Tantrism, Paz's India—especially Buddhist India—penetrated far deeper than the surface of his work, producing a mythical mode at least as important as the one left by pre-Hispanic mythology.

Eliot Weinberger sees the dialogue between Mexico and India (the Occident and Orient) as turning into an identity in which the Mayan and the Buddhist might meet (as Orient and Orient). Thus Paz, as he sees it, manages to accomplish one of the avant-garde's great missions: connecting the world. It seems likely that, as Weinberger suggests, he found his Greece in the Orient, as did Pound, whose "ideogrammatic method" Paz approaches in *Blanco*.

In *Blanco* (1966), *Ladera Este (1962–1968)* (1969), and *El mono gramático* (1974; *The Monkey Grammarian*, 1981), Paz's anguish is diminished, turning him into—if Weinberger is right—a "religious poet whose religion is poetry." His theology is based on non-transcendence, on the immanentism of his Buddhist readings. At its core, it's an essentially erotic theology: woman—as lover, wife, muse, goddess, yogini, and the Eternal Feminine, both naughty and complicit—is ever at the center of this erotic splendor, almost entirely unique in modern poetry. In "Blanco," we read: "el fuego te desata y te anuda / Pan Grial Ascua / Muchacha / tú ríes—desnuda / en los jardínes de la llama" ("the fire knots and unlaces you / Bread Grail Coal / Girl / you laugh—naked / in the gardens of the flame," trans. Eliot Weinberger).

Paz said that he never had what it took to convert to Buddhism (Madhyamika, the school he found most philosophically convincing) and preferred to reside—as a Mediterranean and a Christian—in a far-near. In private, an enlightened Romantic, Paz confessed that although Buddhism was Indian culture's great universal legacy, converting was the sort of childishness best avoided by a Westerner. And strictly speaking, his poetry lacked true metaphysical anguish, as has been noted by Elsa Cross*—the Mexican poet most devoted to ashrams.

If Paz had a religious bent, which as an enlightened Romantic he found it difficult to permit himself, it was a tantric one. Tantrism embodied the image of copulation, establishing a perfect interconnection between emptiness and life. As Cross says, Paz understood that both literally and figuratively, "coupling" embodied the two primordial aspects of the beginning of the cosmos: a union of both sex and consciousness, maithuna. Both Buddhist and Hindu Tantrism (i.e. both withholding sperm and ejaculating) fascinated him, as is clear by his treatise on the subject included in *Conjunciones y disyunciones*.

Ladera Este is a kaleidoscope of India. Neither a travelogue (although it contains elements of that) nor an interpretation (he wrote several of those), the book is a series of poems, each memorable in turn, that jump from the days of Babur to the twentieth century, from Himachal Pradesh in the Himalayas to Vrindaban, the city where Krishna fell in love with Radha; it travels the Ganges and the Yamuna. We see, "sanctified" by a Mexican poet, the graves and mausoleums of Amir Khusrow—Afghan founder of Urdu poetry—the Mughal Emperor Humayun, the descendants of the Lodi Dynasty, lingam and yoni, lambs sacrificed to Kali, "dogmatic cows," peepuls, banyans (Paz is the twentieth-century's most arboreal poet), religious bonfires, Westerners—Artemises and demons—left to their fate by Raj in independent India and who, in several of *Ladera Este*'s poems, are the only odd characters, secondary personalities that Weinberger sees as inhabiting Paz's poetry. Also notable in this collection are things Paz picked up from William Carlos Williams and e. e. cummings during his stay in the US during World War II: a certain levity, colloquialisms, vivid imagery, and even a bit of humor (though with Paz it's never much).

John Cage and the victims of Stalin, of the 1968 massacre, and of the Mexican Revolution are all called to appear before India—and before a poet who therein gleaned both wisdom and compassion. And at the center of it all is woman, his greatest form of nourishment.

"Blanco" is the most ambitious and most commented of Paz's Indian poems, although as Weinberger points out, it contains only three Indian words. One is "nim," the tree beneath whose shade Paz married Marie-José Tramini in 1966. Whether or not it's the simplified version of a mandala (scholars disagree on this point), "Blanco" is Paz's great abstract, "modern" poem, his Mallarmé-like challenge. Sucre sees the poem as a direct descendant of Mallarmé's *Un coup de dés jamais n'abolira le hasard* (A roll of the dice will never abolish chance): the page as the space where the poem occurs, the poem as a bas-relief. The verse interrupts itself, breaks down, can be read in multiple fashions: "tu cuerpo son los cuerpos del instante es cuerpo el mundo / pensado soñado encarnado visto tocado desvanecido" ("the bodies of the instant are your body *time world is body* / thought dream incarnated *seen touched dissolved*," trans. Eliot Weinberger). "Blanco," according to Giraud, is an imago mundi, a legible replica of the universe, a poem about conscious enlightenment and about language, in which love is the philosopher's stone.

Paz closed his Indian cycle with a book that was less commented upon but perhaps more prodigious: *El mono gramático*. Prose poem, anti-novel, and essay, *El mono gramático* narrates (and simultaneously deconstructs the narration, as it's created) the road that led him to the ruins of Galta, on the outskirts of Jaipur in Rajistan. First—and here I am combining the readings of his French translator Claude Esteban and of Giraud—he crosses a road crowded with monkeys, *sadhus*, and lepers, amid the filth and misery of India. But beyond this first, purely earthly reading lies another, conceptual one: a room like Eros's cave, a tantric setting officiated by Splendor, born of the sweat of the demiurge Prajapati, a woman shared by ten gods, a woman who becomes the poem.

"The Simian is lost amid his similes," says Paz, and the monkey hidden amid monkeys is Hanuman, son of the wind that sweeps from the Himalayas to the sacred island of Ceylon, hero and demigod of the epic *Ramayana*. Man himself is the monkey grammarian, the "simian imitator," the "Aristotelian animal" who "copies from nature"; he is also the "semantic seed" represented by Hanuman, the "Holy Spirit of India" and Prince of Analogies. At its core, *El mono gramático* is a reflection on the fleeting nature of language, which poetry rises up against: "la fijeza es siempre momentánea" ("Fixity is always momentary," trans. Helen Lane).

Paz renounced his post as ambassador to protest Mexican repression of the student movement and left India abruptly in 1968. He found himself, then, at a crossroads. One road, the poetic one, led to getting lost, scattered. In India he'd written two of the masterpieces of the international avant-garde and experimented with calligrams that were both genius and touching in *Topoemas* (1968), akin to those of Apollinaire and Tablada. His dear friend Charles Tomlinson—with whom he (and two others) wrote *Renga* in 1969, a book by four poets in four languages—warned him that he had to return to syntax. That he mustn't sacrifice himself on the scaffold of the instant. Paz's correspondence with Brazilian concrete poet Haroldo de Campos, published by Manuel Ulacia, explains the dilemma. Believing it to be praise, Campos complimented Paz on his increasing disdain for the "metaphorical, discursive tradition." Paz replied by saying that that *was* his tradition. His 1971 return to Mexico was full of politics and life in the public eye. But it was also a chance, after India had quelled his intellectual character, for him to look back and write *Pasado en claro* (1975) and *Vuelta* (1976).

"Himno entre ruinas" ("Hymn among the ruins"), originally the last poem in the first edition of *Libertad bajo palabra*, is the most representative poem of his memoir cycle; Ramón Xirau sees it as the line between early Paz and mature Paz. In this 1948 poem, for the first time Paz suffers from the "fall in History"—both fatal and untimely—that Pere Gimferrer sees as the mechanism by which Paz engages in what I call "historiosophy": that is, he reflects on the meaning and the aims of History, which he feels both unforgivably condemned to and prophetically attracted to. In "Himno entre ruinas," night falls on the pyramids of Teotihuacán, the city of gods by the Valley of Mexico abandoned years before the Aztec Empire, where boys sit smoking marijuana. Immediately afterwards, Paz depicts an erotic scene: it appears that only woman can save him and after a break, his fall into History takes him even deeper, into the great cities of the twentieth century where humans—"domestic bipeds"—walk.

Modern-day ennui, alienation and totalitarianism, the failure of revolutionary redemption—that "Phoenix's egg" that Paz sought in the Europe of 1945, where he met Kostas Papaioannou, one of his few close friends—faded from Paz's horizon during his time in India. In fact, the banquet of the senses that is *Ladera Este* was crashed by the "Intermitencias del Oeste," brief poems with Western themes (the Gulag, the Mexico City Olympic Games inaugurated just a few days before the October 2, 1968 massacre, the Mexican Revolution). His Indian dream ended right along with the fabulous sixties. As in Jean Paul's prophetic dream, the nightmare was overrun by cadavers.

That's *Vuelta* (which precedes *Pasado en claro* in the order Paz laid out for his poetry), in the three poems—"Vuelta" ("Return"), "A la mitad de esta frase" ("In the middle of this phrase . . ."), and "Petrificada petrificante" ("The petrifying petrified")—dedicated to Mexico City, which Paz returned to and made his main residence, the start and end of each of his trips, his burning obsession. And the one to reintroduce him to the capital could be none other than Ramón López Velarde, one of the four poets to whom he dedicated *Cuadrivio* (1965), his most beautiful book of essays (the other three being Pessoa, Cernuda, and Darío). In spite of everything, he traveled back to what López Velarde called "el edén subvertido que se calla / en la mutilación de la metralla" ("the subverted Eden stilled / among the mutilation of shot and shell," trans. Margaret Sayers Peden), experiencing the famous "reactionary sorrow" brought on by returning to a country transformed—for better and for worse—by the Mexican Revolution. Paz described that Eden as a "latido de tiempo" ("a pulse-beat of time," trans. Eliot Weinberger).

In 1971, the poet returned to Mixcoac, the town where he grew up, by then a neighborhood of Mexico City where his mother still lived. In "Vuelta" we read, "Camino hacia atrás / hacia lo que dejé / o me dejó / Memoria / Inminencia de precipicio" ("I am walking back / to what I left or to what left me / Memory / Edge of the abyss," trans. Eliot Weinberger). Once again, memory propels him through history. He recalls a job he had at the Bank of Mexico when he was young, counting money that was to be incinerated. And the mention of money—like the rest of his generation, Paz is against chrematistics, the science of wealth—takes him to other forms of slavery, like that of the Civic Church governing Mexico, symbolized by "buzzard lawyers," the omnipresent gaggle of litigators in the service of the corrupt regimes of the Revolution.

"A la mitad de la frase" is another example of a very hard fall in history, given that Paz sees being born as falling: the "birthfall," he calls it. The fall is tied to the death of his alcoholic father, a Zapatista attorney hit by a train in 1936, who exemplifies the fall in history of the Revolution itself. "Nuestros oráculos son los discursos del afásico, nuestros profetas son videntes con anteojos" ("Our oracles are aphasic, our prophets seers with glasses," trans. Eliot Weinberger), he says. "Historia, basurero y arcoiris" and later: "lenguaje despedazado" ("History: dump and rainbow"; "mangled language," trans. Eliot Weinberger).

Mexico City, in "Petrificada petrificante," is the ideal place for the poet to act as "gardener of epitaphs." His native city, which he refers to as "Pecho de México," "escalera de los siglos," "desmoronado trono de la ira," "ombligo de la luna" ("chest of Mexico," "stairway of the centuries," "Rage's rotten throne," "Navel of the Moon"), is—like New Delhi—an arid colonial metropolis condemned to be crushed by the dust of history. For Paz, the absent water is synonymous with regeneration: "¿Dónde está el agua otra?" ("Where is the other water?").

"Nocturno de San Ildefonso" ("San Ildefonso nocturne") is a continuation and an expansion of "Vuelta," as *Pasado en claro* is the maximum expression of all of Paz's memoir poems. It stresses the characteristic fall: night comes, and then appears in "México hacia 1931" ("Mexico circa 1931"), in which the young poet makes his way to the old Jesuit school of San Ildefonso that Paz attended. Before he gets to the Zócalo, the great central plaza that is always full of memories, we come upon the characters out of novels Paz read in school: Stendhal's Julien Sorel, Dostoyevsky's Alyosha Karamazov. In *Pasado en claro*, historical and literary heroes blend with the recollection of children's games: Priapos with Captain Nemo, "Abderramán, Pompeyo, Xicotencátl / batallas en el Oxus o en la barda" ("Abd al-Rahman, Pompeii, Xicontencatl, / battles on the Oxus or on top of the wall," trans. Eliot Weinberger). He sees a fig tree whose trunk is cleft, wounded, a premonition of the woman who returns in "Nocturno de San Ildefonso" to stop his fall in History: "Mujer: fuente en la noche / Yo me fío a su fluir sosegado" ("Woman: Fountain in the night / I am bound to her quiet flowing," trans. Eliot Weinberger)

The moral center of this poem resides in the dirty thirties, which Sheridan depicts brilliantly in reference to Paz. That's where we see the poet's poignant self-criticism, which was then adopted by his entire generation—those who at the time believed in the dawn of a new day, post-revolution: "todos hemos sido, en el Gran Teatro del Inmundo; jueces, verdugos, víctimas, testigos / todos / hemos levantado falso testimonio contra los otros / y contra nosotros mismos" ("We have all been, in the great playhouse of the world, judge, executioner, victim, witness / we have all given false testimony against the others and against ourselves," trans. Eliot Weinberger).

"Nocturno de San Ildefonso" metamorphoses into *Pasado en claro*, 628 verses that Peruvian critic José Miguel Oviedo has divided into twelve parts and an epilogue—a true anagnorisis, a process that stems from Paz's poetics: all poems are about poetry. Then History, the perpetual guest, crops up in children's games, presided over in the distance by the venerable prince of adventurers, Paz's liberal grandfather, hero of a thousand battles, Don Ireneo, patriarch of the family house in Mixcoac.

The memoir cycle extends beyond just those two great poems and includes several long poems in *Árbol adentro* (1987; *A Tree Within*, 1988), including "1930: vistas fijas" ("1930: Scenic Views") and "Kostas," Paz's homage to his Greek friend Papaiannou, which along with "Aunque es de noche" ("Although It is Night") serves as the final sketch of his historiosophy. Nevertheless, in *Árbol adentro* memory begins to cede its place to epigrammatic poems. Here, Paz takes liberties and allows the sort of carelessness that, according to Antonio Deltoro,* a younger poet would never have permitted. We also see, in Paz's last book, long poems in which he says goodbye to his city: more than Mexico City per se, it's a leave-taking of modern cities in general. Deltoro sees "Hablo de la ciudad" ("I Speak of the City"), as a "waterfall" akin to the work of Whitman and Álvaro de Campos. Paz also takes on the stoicism of Quevedo, the poet who (along with Neruda, his "most beloved enemy") accompanied him to the end. In "Ejercicio preparatorio" ("Preparatory exercise"), Paz asks to die with "la conciencia del tiempo / apenas lo que dure un parpadeo" ("the consciousness of time / that lasts barely as long as a blink"). That final poem, as Deltoro sees it, has "few evenings, few twilights, and many dawns, increasingly astonishing and welcome."

Historiosophy wasn't some sort of essayistic addendum to Paz's poetry; it was second nature. Sometimes he rebelled against it; other times he accepted it. For Paz, the essay was "poetic illumination," and poetry was critical, as Andrés Sánchez Robayna noted. At the end of "Vuelta," for instance, he makes known that he has no desire to be like Wang-Wei, the eighth-century Chinese hermit poet and one of the many ancient and modern poets Paz translated. He doesn't want, like Wang-Wei, any mountain retreat; he doesn't want to stop being a man committed to his time: "Yo no quiero una ermita intelectual / en San Ángel o Coyoacán" ("But I don't want an intellectual hermitage in San Angel or Coyoacán," trans. Eliot Weinberger). The verse is a bit ironic when seen beside Paz's death in the historic Casa de Alvarado, right in Coyoacán, paid for by the Mexican government so that the poet could live out his last days there. Hermitage or not, the house became the site of a veritable pilgrimage. Friends and admirers (and more than a few adversaries) all crowded in to say goodbye publicly. In the end, Octavio Paz the poet couldn't remain far from what Wang-Wei saw as the "mundo y sus peleas" ("world and its quarrels").

SELECTED BIBLIOGRAPHY
Obras completas, 1–15, FCE, 1994–2003.
Aguilar Mora, Jorge, *La divina pareja. Historia y mito en Octavio Paz*, ERA, 1978.

Giraud, Paul-Henri, *Octavio Paz, Vers la transparence*, Le Monde/PUF, Paris, 2002.

González Rojo, Enrique, *El rey va desnudo. Las ideas políticas de Octavio Paz*, Posada, 1989.

Masson, Jean-Claude, introduction, chronology, and notes for Octavio Paz, *Œuvres*, Gallimard, Paris, 2009.

Phillips, Rachel, *Las estaciones poéticas de Octavio Paz*, trans. Tomás Segovia, FCE, 1976.

Rodríguez Ledesma, Xavier, *El pensamiento político de Octavio Paz*, Plaza y Valdés/UNAM, 1996.

Santí, Enrico Mario, *El acto en las palabras. Estudios y diálogos con Octavio Paz*, FCE,1997.

Santí, Enrico Mario (selections and prologue), *Luz espejeante. Octavio Paz ante la crítica*, ERA, 2009. The cited pieces by Anthony Stanton, Jorge Cuesta, Rodolfo Usigli, Alain Bosquet, Hugo J. Verani, José Emilio Pacheco, Saíl Yurkiévich, Eliot Weinberger, Pere Gimferrer, José Miguel Oviedo, and Antonio Deltoro are collected in this book.

Sheridan, Guillermo, *Poeta con paisaje. Ensayos sobre la vida de Octavio Paz*, ERA, 2004.

Sucre, Guillermo, *La máscara, la transparencia: ensayos sobre poesía hispanoamericana*, FCE, Mexico, 1985.

Manuel Ulacia, *El árbol milenario*, Galaxia Gutenberg/Círculo de lectores, Barcelona, 1999.

Vizcaíno, Fernando, *Biografía política de Octavio Paz o la razón ardiente*, Algazara, Madrid, 1993.

Wilson, Jason, *Octavio Paz: un estudio de su poesía*, Pluma, Bogotá, 1980.

Xirau, Ramón, *Octavio Paz, el sentido de la palabra*, Joaquín Mortiz, Mexico, 1970.

Sun Stone, trans. Muriel Rukeyser, New Directions, 1962.

Selected Poems, trans. Muriel Rukeyser, Indiana University Press, 1963.

Claude Lévi-Strauss: An Introduction, trans. J. S. Bernstein and Maxine Bernstein, Cornell University Press, 1970.

Configurations, various translators, New Directions, 1971.

The Other Mexico: Critique of the Pyramid, trans. Lysander Kemp, Grove Press, 1972.

Alternating Current, trans. Helen Lane, Viking Press, 1973.

The Bow and the Lyre, trans. Ruth L. C. Simms, University of Texas Press, 1973.

Early Poems: 1935-1955, various translators, New Directions, 1973; Indiana University Press, 1974.

Children of the Mire: Poetry from Romanticism to the Avant-Garde, trans. Rachel Phillips, Harvard University Press, 1974.

Conjunctions and Disjunctions, trans. Helen Lane, Viking Press, 1974.

Eagle or Sun?, trans. Eliot Weinberger, New Directions, 1976.

The Siren and the Seashell, and Other Essays on Poets and Poetry, trans. Lysander Kemp and Margaret Seyers Peden, University of Texas Press, 1976.

Marcel Duchamp: Appearance Stripped Bare, trans. Rachel Phillips and Donald Gardner, Viking Press, 1978.

A Draft of Shadows and Other Poems, ed. and trans. Eliot Weinberger, New Directions, 1979 (with translations by Mark Strand and Elizabeth Bishop).

The Monkey Grammarian, trans. Helen Lane, Seaver Books, 1981.

Selected Poems, ed. Eliot Weinberger, various translators, New Directions, 1984.

The Labyrinth of Solitude, trans. Lysander Kemp, Yara Milos, and Rachel Phillips Belash. Grove Press, 1985.

One Earth, Four or Five Worlds: Reflections on Contemporary History, trans. Helen Lane, Harcourt Brace Jovanovich, 1985.

On Poets and Others, trans. Michael Schmidt, Seaver Books, 1986.

Convergences: Selected Essays on Art and Literature, trans. Helen Lane, Harcourt Brace Jovanovich, 1987.

PELLICER, CARLOS

(Villahermosa, Tabasco, 1897 – Mexico City, 1977)

It's often said of Pellicer—one of the pinnacles of Mexican poetry—that he wrote his best work during his extended youth. And while it's true that between 1915 and 1936, he published *Colores en el mar y otros poemas, Piedra de sacrificios, Seis, siete poemas, Oda de junio, Esquemas para una oda tropical,* and *Hora de junio,* we'd do well to remember that his weight was felt (albeit not quite as heavily) beyond the fifties. Even his tiring patriotic and Bolivarian verses—quite unusual at the time, when the Catholic left was a lonely place—contain nuggets of pure gold, hurled from his tempestuous river onto the far shore. And only Pellicer could write an ode such as this to Benito Juárez and come out unscathed: "Eres el presidente vitalicio, a pesar / de tanta noche lúgubre. La República es mar / navegable y secreto si el tiempo te consulta" ("You are the president for life, despite / so many lugubrious nights. The Republic is a sea / navigable and secret if time consults you").

But in addition to his civil obligations as secular hagiographer, Pellicer also—with no apparent turmoil—wrote some of the most beautiful (and solemn) religious poetry in Mexican literature, both in *Práctica de vuelo* (1956) and *Cosillas para el nacimiento* (1978). More Franciscan than Catholic, as José Joaquín Blanco* pointed out, Pellicer was a poet whose Christianity was always fresh, ever renewed. In his "Sonetos a los arcángeles," as lovely to behold as André Derain's barge, Pellicer strips the angels of their baroque lead-footedness and religious certitude, giving them the wings they needed to really fly. Rereading Pellicer makes later Catholic poets like Father Manuel Ponce—who enjoyed a certain prestige twenty years ago—seem superfluous. Put into perspective, Pellicer's work confronts old historic tensions and dares to reconcile the Aztec ruins of Tenochtitlán with the missionaries' Franciscan piety, offering a truce that avoids mention of the Church—a conspicuous absence in this Catholic poet's verses.

As both private collector and public museum curator, Pellicer is more than an archaeologist of Mexicanness. His passion for Mesoamerican antiquities both carries on and renovates the tradition of Sigüenza y Góngora, Francisco Javier Clavijero, and (from his own time) Ángel María Garibay Kintana.* Pellicer is the final link in that chain of Creole humanists who see pre-Cortés civilization as a classic horizon whose influence and brilliance are the mother's milk of Mexican civilization. A disciple of José Vasconcelos,* Pellicer saved the idea of the "cosmic race" from the fire, and put it back in the only non-place it could survive: in resounding poetry of touching, crystalline beauty.

SELECTED BIBLIOGRAPHY
Obras: poesía, FCE, Mexico, 1994.

PITOL, SERGIO
(Puebla, Puebla, 1933)

The Pitol book I find most moving, *El viaje* (2000), in one part tells of an encounter with prose theorist Victor Shklovsky, which to me would be as fantastic as bumping into Napoleon on the corner. Marvels of this sort make rereading Pitol a joy, a comprehensive undertaking that invites readers to recall the countless authors he invokes as guardian angels and daylight devils. A novel full of dreams, *El viaje* gives us Gogol before his repentant death, Chekhov—the perfect artist—and Andrei Bely, the poet of Saint Petersburg. And after the Russians come the Polish, led by Conrad—who before becoming master of the English novel actually was Polish—and Jerzy Andrzejewski at the gates of heaven. We hear Witold Gombrowicz's harangue against pure poetry, meet martyr Bruno Schulz, and can't escape the eccentric Mario Praz's evil eye. The Brits are there too, with the aesthete Ronald Firbank as well as Evelyn Waugh, whose stiff upper lip Pitol learned so much from, and E. M. Forster, whose presence is discrete but essential to understanding Pitol. Irish eccentric Flann O'Brien puts in an appearance. Germans Mann and Kafka go without saying, and the portrait's not complete without the lone figures of Patricia Highsmith and Benito Pérez Galdós, polar opposites overseeing the pageant.

The list of names, especially authors, becomes tedious, it's true, and Pitol himself notes that his enumeration might be a sign of mental lethargy. But readers will concede that not having them would be highly unsettling, akin to unfolding a map on the first day of creation, with no cities, rivers or mountains yet named. There's another, more essential justification, too: Pitol has perfected the art of emulation, and he only measures himself against the best. That unusual demand has turned his exemplary career into a *Bildungsroman* in which his stories, novels, and essays are no more important than the books he has translated, both literally and figuratively.

Of all the masters Pitol weaves into his work, Henry James strikes me as the most apt benchmark, the one who truly stands out. Not only because Pitol is above all else an aesthete or because his legendary years in Europe were so lacking in scandal that his private life is all conjecture, but because of the way he epitomizes the modern novelist. When Pitol speaks about literature—his own and others'—something sends me back to James's prologues, but as soon as I find the book I want in the library, the feeling evaporates and I carry on searching. It's as though Pitol's mastery—infinite and sensual—is like Oscar Wilde's cigarette: an exquisite pleasure that leaves you unsatisfied.

Pitol's Jamesian point of view doesn't fully hit the mark until *El desfile del amor* (1984), when the author realizes—along with the novel's Pedro Balmorán and his collection of old documents on Mexico's nineteenth-century castrati—that a writer's notes, whether travelogues or hurriedly jotted dreams, are not material to be turned into literature but literature itself. And as soon as Pitol lays his cards on the table, making them as visible to his readers as they are to him, he turns chaos into form. That's when his work becomes a work of art, as seen in *Domar a la divina garza* (1988), an outstanding text that's highly impressive in any literature.

Pitol is heir to conservative revolutionaries who turned the novel into a great twentieth-century tradition, as can be seen in *El desfile del amor*. The book plays with the impossibility of historical fiction, taking a time and place (1942, Mexico City), and presenting multiple points of view that reveal each eyewitness to be a liar. His more recent *La vida conyugal* (1991) I found less convincing: a caricature that doesn't achieve the level of farce, the novel reminds me too much of Patricia Highsmith, a bad writer who read too much Nietzsche.

It's not easy to talk about Pitol, because he's one of those authors who offer his poetics alongside his prose. In his case, it's a course in European literature in which he's both teacher and subject, making him hard to disobey. For instance, he kindly—yet firmly—recommends using Bakhtin's poetics of folklore to read his novels, a suggestion many a literature professor has taken literally, thereby almost becoming a Pitol character, as denigrated as the protagonist of *Domar a la divina garza*, Marietta Karapetiz.

In that vein, there's a misunderstanding about Pitol that presents him—either incorrectly or imprecisely—as a revisionist, a man set on upending genres, more Gombrowicz than Thomas Mann. But Pitol often reminds us that his is the battle of an eccentric, not the avant-garde, and there's a yawning gulf between them. In *El mago de Viena*, Pitol explains, "there's a great difference between the work of Tristan Tzara, Filippo Marinetti, and André Breton and that of Gogol, Bruno Schulz, and César Aira. The former are avant-garde; the latter write literature that at the time was novel in its strangeness. The avant-garde is a group, fighting to oust those before them because they see their technique and language as obsolete and believe *their* work—Dadaist, futurist, expressionist, surrealist—to be the only true and valid one. They see taking a step forward as enlightening the literature of their language as well as that outside their borders, purging the canon of those writers they disdain. They rationalize, argue, create theories, sign manifestos, start fights with the literature of the past as well as contemporary literature unlike their own. In general, that's not the case with the eccentrics. They don't hatch plans or strategies and in fact are reluctant to form factions. They're spread out all over the world, almost always without knowing each other. They are, again, a group without a group. They write the way their instinct demands. The canon doesn't bother them and they don't try to change it. Their world is unique, and thus their shape and themes vary. The avant-garde tends to be surly, severe, moralistic; they might proclaim disorder, but at the same time they turn disorder into something programmatic. They love judgments: they're prosecutors; expelling a member from time to time is seen as a triumph. They ban pleasure. By struggling against the past or against a present they reject, their writing is burdened with dreadful humor. Eccentrics' writing, on the other hand, is almost always blessed with humor, even if it's black" (*El mago de Viena* 126).

By reading the passage—whose message is repeated in different guises throughout the book—it becomes obvious that Pitol is not attempting to transform genres; and neither was Gombrowicz—a true modern and a false avant-garde. *El mago de Viena*, which seems to morph from novel to essay, demonstrates to us that Pitol is something different: an audacious, energetic editor of his own texts, which are reviews presented as narrations and memoirs mutated into short stories. Thus biographical notes on Henry James in Venice and Flann O'Brien's morphology are presented first as essays in *La casa de la tribu* (1989) and then also as almost personal tales in *El mago de Viena*; and what passes for essay in *El arte de la fuga* becomes fiction—for want of a better term—in *Cuentos y relatos*, the third volume of *Obras reunidas* (2004).

Right from his first novel *El tañido de una flauta* (1972), Pitol was aware of the fact that he orbited in his own planetary system, as he himself expressed it in *El mago de Viena*: "The writing of my first novel coincided with a universal tendency to discredit fiction, to abhor narration." This positioning must be examined with reference to the literary map that the young Pitol decided not to follow. In a certain sense—perhaps a figurative sense—the Mexican vanguard was comprised of Paz* (the counterculture Paz, the most overlooked one, who published *Corriente alterna* in 1967), and of Juan García Ponce* (to whom Pitol dedicated *Domar a la divina garza*) and Salvador Elizondo* (from whom the author could not be more different). Pitol distanced himself from Mexico's main literary circle both by moving around the world and by writing in a stylistically eccentric way, unsure of his own narrative powers, discovering on his own the sort of classicism appalled by the nouveau roman and all of the "anti-novel" variations that younger Mexicans like Jorge Aguilar Mora* and Héctor Manjarrez* were cultivating. Pitol is one of few Latin American writers who profess to be anti-French, to such a degree that he rarely cites French writers, and when he does chooses a French-born American novelist who wrote in French: Julien Green.

Diplomat first, professor and editor second, between 1961 and 1988 Pitol embarked on an odyssey that took him from Rome, Beijing, and Bristol to Barcelona, Warsaw, and Prague. It wasn't until the mid-eighties, when several of his contemporaries were wearing thin and starting to be viewed as veterans past their prime by the literary circle, that Pitol began publishing his distinctive novels. None is utterly pivotal, the sort that becomes a landmark (like Elizondo's *Farabeuf*), nor is any as ambitious or labyrinthine as García Ponce's *Crónica de la intervención*. But beside Pitol—cosmopolitan novelist, time and space traveler—both of those writers look like *riches amateurs* by comparison.

Pitol's early stories—those prior to *Nocturno de Bujara* (1981)—and his first two novels—*El tañido de una flauta* (1982) and *Juegos florales* (1982)—exhibit the patience of a hunting party. And the writer only misses his mark to the degree that he closes in on his prey. By the time he won the Cervantes Prize in 2006, however, Pitol had gone through a long process of maturation, visible in *Tríptico del carnaval* (1999), *El arte de la fuga* (1996), *El viaje* (2000), and *El mago de Viena* (2005)—the last work being one of Mexico's greatest literary autobiographies. And Pitol, who visits spas in Marienbad and Havana like Gide or Hans Castorp, has also become a poignant observer of the times, both chronicler of the Chinese cultural revolution and witness to the decline and fall of Aldous Huxley.

There are those who pride themselves on Pitol sightings, having bumped into him on the streets of Veracruz, Samarcanda, or Madrid, encounters that have yielded marvelous narrations by Enrique Vila-Matas and Juan Villoro*—who were his disciples until longstanding friendships turned them into something more like brothers than accomplices or characters. Others swear to have spotted him in the halls of the Minerva Building in Plaza Río de Janeiro in Mexico City, where he was searching for the stolen letter he needed to conclude *El desfile de amor*.

Aside from having read him—a worthy source of pride in and of itself—I cannot make those claims. But I can recall a delirious time in my life when the only order (at least of a temporal variety) came at six o'clock in the afternoon, when Pitol and his dog Sancho went for their walk. They'd take Calle Higuera, which joins Plaza de la Conchita to Coyoacán's *zócalo*. Their clockwork routine, of course, reminded me of Kant as mythologized by Thomas De Quincey. And then that calming vision led not only to Thomas Mann's forest but to Virginia Woolf's *Flush*, in which Elizabeth Barrett Browning's dog is narrator, and to *My Dog Tulip*, by J. R. Ackerley. The appearance of Pitol every day revitalized me, the promise of salvation offered by a voyage around the world in eighty literatures.

SELECTED BIBLIOGRAPHY
Obras reunidas, FCE, Mexico, 2004–2005.
   I. *El tañido de una flauta. Juegos florales.*
   II. *El desfile del amor. Domar a la divina garza. La vida conyugal.*
   III. *Cuentos y relatos.*
   IV. *Escritos autobiográficos.*
El mago de Viena, FCE, Mexico, 2005.

PONIATOWSKA, ELENA

(Paris, France, 1932)

"Just as you can't jail Jean-Paul Sartre in France, you can't slander 'Elenita' in Mexico," claimed a biographical sketch published in *Le Monde* on March

13, 2009 to mark the Paris Book Fair, which honored Mexico that year and boasted Poniatowska as one of its stars.[1]

It's a reference to something Charles De Gaulle said, when a minister anxiously inquired about putting a stop to the subversive activities of the existentialist philosopher turned Maoist: Sartre cannot be put in the Bastille. The general was refusing, in 1968, to repeat the mistake made by the Ancien Regime, which had imprisoned Voltaire—the embodiment of the French conscience—and then symbolically paid the price for it. *Le Monde* saw a parallel with Poniatowska—a Polish princess born in Paris in 1932 who became one of Mexico's most influential writers over the course of the next fifty years—because of Mexico's scandalous 2006 presidential elections. Poniatowska wholeheartedly threw her support behind candidate Andrés Manuel López Obrador, and went from being a habitué at rallies to recording TV commercials for him, which led to nasty backbiting. According to *Le Monde*, the left idolized Poniatowska and reacted excessively, treating the spiteful tittle-tattle typical of tough campaigns as if it were sedition. Petitions of solidarity were circulated and, unsurprisingly, the Mexican right was in no condition to fight such a disadvantageous battle: the hullabaloo died down upon publication of a photo of one of the conservatives who had disparaged Poniatowska, caught at a central bookstore buying all her books.

But Poniatowska apparently had considerably thicker skin than most of her outraged admirers, and she plowed on undeterred with the smiling, aristocratic disdain that sets her apart, campaigning with López Obrador till the bitter end, when Calderón was declared president despite election irregularities, appeals, and protests. So: just as Sartre was a symbol of unyielding French ethics, Poniatowska—reigning princess of the Mexican left—was also untouchable. Or so *Le Monde* appeared to conclude.

Her work is exceedingly and invariably linked to life in the limelight, so it would be absurd to read it without considering the unrivaled role that society plays in her books; solitude is something she wishes on no one, not even her most objectionable characters. A society-page correspondent, engaging interviewer, and a young reporter on Mexican (and French) cultural life in the fifties and early sixties, Poniatowska was the writer who made

---

1   Joëlle Stolz, "Elena Poniatowska: « Ici, on est toujours en train d'écrire sur cette réalité qui vous aspire »", *Le Monde*, 13 March 2009.

sense of an entire era with just one book: *La noche de Tlatelolco* (1971; *Massacre in Mexico*, 1975). It was perhaps the most timely Mexican novel to date, not just for its moral and political undertaking but also for the originality (which today seems obvious and academic) of its structure: a collective interview with a despotically, cruelly repressed country desperate for democracy. Later, she took the world of 1968 student demonstrations and added to it the popular and linguistic realism found in her first novel (*Hasta no verte Jesús mío*, 1969; *Here's to You, Jesusa!*, 2001). Next, she had the left descend from heaven to personify civil society (in its "salt of the earth" avatar), whom she pays homage to in *Fuerte es el silencio* (1980). And post-1985 she repeated, with less success, the once-original structure of *La noche de Tlatelolco* in *Nada, nadie: Las voces del temblor* (1988; *Nothing, Nobody: The Voices of the Mexico City Earthquake*, 1995).

But it's Poniatowska's soul and her good heart—both valiant and erratic—that not only rule her but also save her from the hardheadedness of her intellectual Stalinism, as seen in her most recent book *Leonora* (2011), a novel that takes her in another direction completely. Poniatowska's real society, her paradise lost and then fortunately regained, lies not in the "civil society" that worships her and warms her heart. In fact, her old-fashioned social novels such as *El tren pasa primero* (2007) lack verisimilitude: they're "good books" poorly written, works that could douse the artfulness of any novelist, with their methodological Manichaeism that takes the purity of the proletariat for granted.

Nor is hers the world of old, aristocratic families who inevitably bred with the Revolution's new plutocracy. Neither the nouveau riche nor the aristocracy is, for her, anything more than an amuse-bouche, as can be seen in her tender, autobiographical fiction (*La "Flor de Lis"*, 1988) and *Paseo de la Reforma* (1996), a sort of sequel in which the upper classes are exposed to contagious intellectual radicalism.

No, Poniatowska's true milieu is that of the aristocracy of spirit, found in *Leonora* and in much of *Tinísima* (1992; *Tinísima*, 1996), her most ambitious work. She's at her best when discussing the lives of artists, which is why I see *Las siete cabritas* (2000) as central to her oeuvre. It's a book depicting the lives of some of Mexico's greatest eccentrics: Frida Kahlo, Pita Amor, Rosario Castellanos,* Nahui Ollin, María Izquierdo, Elena Garro,* and Nellie

Campobello. To this list we might add Angelina Beloff, the Russian painter and protagonist of *Querido Diego, te abraza Quiela* (1978; *Dear Diego*, 1986) who died in Mexico; Tina Modotti, the militant Italian communist of *Tinísima*; and, of course, the English surrealist Leonora Carrington, born in 1917. So it's in this milieu that I prefer to discuss Poniatowska—writing reports, chronicles, epistolary novels, and fictitious monologues delivered by other women—because this is where we see her act with no condescension, with tenderness and admiration, and at times with the implacable irony of someone who knows herself to be among equals.

Articulating the passion of female artists working twice as hard to attain success despite being predestined to fail in a man's world is Poniatowska's greatest contribution to Mexico's literary tragedy. And it doesn't always take five hundred pages for her to achieve it. A journalist to the end—and from the beginning—she details gruesome cases of failure, like those of Pita Amor and Nahui Ollin, depicts a life deprived of death (as she said of Campobello in *Las siete cabritas*), finds something unholy in Kahlo's postmortem success, and isn't afraid to speak the truth about the tragic tale of Elena Garro. And in hindsight, having reread *Tinísima* in order to write this piece, I no longer think she was wrong to have portrayed Tina Modotti as a sort of automaton. Her sixth sense told her that Tina had no soul.

With Leonora Carrington, Poniatowska faced one of the trickiest chapters of her literary career. First, as she states in the epilogue, she is rewriting the life of a very old friend (nearly a hundred years old) who illustrated two of her own books (*Lilus Kikus* and *Rondas de la niña mala*), a woman with whom—and this is made obvious in *Leonora*—she readily identifies. As in the case of *Tinísima*, Poniatowska either couldn't or wouldn't write an actual biography of Carrington and opted instead for a hybrid genre that I rarely find convincing: fictionalized biography or biographical fiction, which lacks the freedom of a novel and the rigor of a biography. In my opinion (and that of Fabienne Bradu* at the time), when Poniatowska made that decision she both undervalued her own research skills and steered her fiction down a dangerous path.

With Modotti, Poniatowska had to fashion an entire life from scratch, step by step, and she gave it an unparalleled biographical character. To put it in Poniatowska's terms: Tina had no voice, and Elena lent her hers, as is a novelist's privilege. But that couldn't be the case with Carrington, the "enchanting enchantress" (as per Octavio Paz*) already well-known to surrealists as both a painter and writer. The prodigious girlfriend of Max Ernst was anthologized by Breton in his *Anthology of Black Humor* (1940) and had already written fantastic (literally) stories in both English and French: "The Oval Lady," "The House of Fear," and "Little Francis." 1943 saw the first version of *Down Below*, a liminal text that was the product of her surrealist imagination, the "chronicle" of her stay at a Santander asylum where her aristocratic family had her institutionalized. So since Carrington herself had already written—and written brilliantly—the most important, and strangest, chapters of her life, Poniatowska accepted the role of scribe in *Leonora*, respectably condensing the contents of *Down Below*.

Anyone unfamiliar with the life and writing of Carrington will thank Poniatowska for portraying the life she shared with Ernst in Saint-Martin-d'Arlèche, where the couple lived like Adam and Eve until Leonora, personifying surrealism, was locked up in a mental institution. In order to get a sense of the immobilizing vilification she felt as a result of the Cardiazol with which she was treated, of her Edwardian nanny apparitions, the seductive charm of painting, or her chance encounter with (and salvation by) Renato Leduc* in a Madrid dance hall and their subsequent escape via the Mexican Embassy in Portugal, you have only to read the superlative *Down Below*.

But if you want to know more, *Leonora*'s finest achievement is its portrayal of Carrington's 1943 arrival in Mexico, which so naturally blends the painter's gaze with what Poniatowska herself experienced when she first arrived—also in the early forties—and eagerly devoured everything she came across in her newly adopted country. It's not the first time Poniatowska has displayed this transference: she did it with Tina, when she had the Italian photographer discover Mexico in 1922, and via an alter ego in *La "Flor de Lis*," and now again, through her complicity with Carrington. This is the Mexico of the Enlightened Diaspora predicted by D. H. Lawrence and Sergei Eisenstein, the enchanted land where the Mexican Revolution becomes surreal, or is portrayed as the spiritual reserve of the entire planet, as the Bretons and Artauds prophesied, and were seconded by a whole court of cosmopolitan revolutionaries, adventurers, and painters.

In addition to Carrington, her inseparable friends, painter Remedios Varo and photographer Kati Horna, also stand out in this striking, avant-garde fantasy. They—and their families—make the novel an enjoyable read, starting with the wild days of Peggy Guggenheim's clique in New York. Portraying Carrington's passage from Ernst's "modernist" Bohemia to Leduc's nationalist cantinas is one of the novel's triumphs, because Poniatowska excels at acting as fly on the wall between a man and a woman and their artistic lives. She absolutely shines when it comes to depicting the tragicomedy of sullen, symbiotic couples: Frida and Diego (as the result of a feminist century, Rivera is now known as Kahlo's husband); Pita Amor, the crazy lady brought down mid-flight by the death of a child; Tina Modotti who ended up in the arms of Julio Antonio Mella after the death of Commander Carlos; Octavio Paz and Elena Garro; María Izquierdo and Rufino Tamayo; Rosario Castellanos humiliated by philosopher Ricardo Guerra; and Nahui Ollin dragged down by the sinister Dr. Atl. In all of these women, Poniatowska manages to seek out the sparks, captivated by the sight of couples "on fire"; she hones her very perceptive ear and demonstrates, in *Leonora*, that Carrington had the last laugh: she is the great survivor in the war of the sexes, the woman who beat death, literally flying away in the final scene.

But Poniatowska is limited by her journalism, which always ends up interfering with her fiction, distorting the structure with surplus information that has been thoughtfully included to lend readers a hand. This can be seen in *Leonora*, for instance, when she stops to explain who Rimbaud was and what he did: these excessive courtesies are gratuitous in a work of fiction. It's simply not possible to shuffle between journalism and fiction with impunity; each has an order and structure that affect the finished product. And choosing to narrate in the present tense doesn't help; it makes the text less eloquent. Despite how enjoyable *Leonora* is to read, it's more fictionalized than fiction.

In real life—outside the book—mystery continues to surround Carrington, the "impenetrable old lady," as Fernando Savater called her. When she first came to Mexico, she decided what she would and wouldn't say about herself, based on her visions. "She's not a woman, she's a being," said miracle-worker Alejandro Jodorowsky when he met her in 1959. And in *The Hearing Trumpet* (1974), the mystical novel about the Holy Grail that she wrote in the sixties, Carrington foresaw her future, portraying her life at a ripe old age. "If the Old Woman can't go to Lapland, then Lapland must come to the Old Woman."

But let me return to the *Le Monde* piece. It notes that venerated "little Elena," the proud descendent of the first King of Poland, manages never to descend from the heavens but possesses the ability to mediate with celestial beings on our behalf. I wouldn't go quite that far. I'd rather end this sketch by describing her using Henry James's *Princess Casamassima* (1886). Unlike James's princess—who forsakes her houses and servants in order to feel equal to the rebelling proletariat and fit into a world "peopled with a thousand forms of revolutionary passion and devotion"—Poniatowska knows that her charisma stems from what she holds on to, not what she gets rid of. Convictions, James would say, are a naïve source of pleasure, but vital to those—like radical aristocrats—for whom reality "appears" like a revelation.

Poniatowska is—and this partly explains the sway she holds over a good part of Mexico—both by genealogy and by sheer determination, the last in a long line of Mexicans and foreigners—and Mexicans who could only see Mexico through the imperiously naïve, exaggerated lens of the foreign—who made of the whole country an "open city." Those of us who came after her, and found a less picturesque, less fictitious, and more somber country devoid of cultural heroism, sometimes lose our patience with Poniatowska. Maybe she took the flak for the inevitable fall from grace of the Mexico "invented"—as postmodern relativists like to say—by artists, some of them notable women such as Leonora Carrington. But it's important to remember that the Mexico portrayed in *Leonora* was that of the only era in our history when we were at the heart of the modern experience. It's a world that comes to life, as James said of painters—or novelists—when Elena Poniatowska passes "a moist sponge over a 'sunk' piece of painting."

SELECTED BIBLIOGRAPHY

Hasta no verte Jesús mío, ERA, Mexico, 1969.
La noche de Tlatelolco, ERA, Mexico, 1971.
Querido Diego, te abraza Quiela, ERA, Mexico, 1978.
Fuerte es el silencio, ERA, Mexico, 1980.
Lilus Kikus, ERA, Mexico, 1985.

Nada, nadie. Las voces del temblor, ERA, Mexico, 1988.

La "Flor de lis," ERA, Mexico, 1988.

Tinísima, ERA, Mexico, 1992.

Paseo de la Reforma, Plaza y Valdés, Mexico, 1996.

Las siete cabritas, ERA, Mexico, 2000.

El tren pasa primero, Alfaguara, Mexico, 2007.

Rondas de la niña mala, ERA, Mexico, 2008.

Leonora, Seix Barral, Barcelona, 2011.

Massacre in Mexico, trans. Helen Lane, Viking, 1975.

Nothing, Nobody: The Voices of the Mexico City Earthquake, trans. Aurora Camacho de Schmidt and Arthur Schmidt, Temple University Press, 1995.

Tinísima, trans. Katherine Silver, Farrar, Straus and Giroux, 1996.

Here's to You, Jesusa!, trans. Deanna Heikkinen, New York, Farrar, Straus and Giroux, 2001.

Q

QUIJANO, ÁLVARO

(Hermosillo, Sonora, 1955 – Mexico City, 1994)

The greatest virtue of *El libro de Tristán* (1991), Álvaro Quijano's first novel, resides in the fact that it's a parody of exactly that—the first novel we all hope to write and very few of us ever do. Quijano constructs *El libro de Tristán* by exploiting at will all of the commonplaces of a writer's literary and sentimental education. From the storybook choice of title (*The Book of Tristan*) to the series of star-crossed love affairs that culminate in institutionalization and death, Quijano weaves with both skill and humor the story of a self-proclaimed *poète maudit*. Hence the novel's plethora of references as universal as they are literary—*Don Quixote*, Dostoyevsky, *Lost Illusions*, Proust—and toponymic nods readily comprehensible to any Mexico City intellectual. Despite Quijano's attempt to make *El libro de Tristán* a light-hearted, enjoyable novel, there's no doubt that it's also somehow tragic, a novel that assumes all of the risks of having been written instead of that "other," real, dreamed-of novel—the one young writers rarely finish.

SELECTED BIBLIOGRAPHY
El libro de Tristán, Joaquín Mortiz, Mexico, 1991.
Este jardín es una ruina, Trilce Ediciones, Mexico, 1995.

R

REVUELTAS, JOSÉ
(Durango, Durango, 1914 – Mexico City, 1976)

In 1940, José Luis Martínez* wrote, "The trends and driving forces behind pre-1940 Mexican literature have been exhausted, and their time has ended. No new path, no sufficiently provocative movement has taken their place. We've seen no literary personalities of creative force emerge . . ." It was, no doubt, a decisive moment. And the publication of Revueltas's *El luto humano* in 1943, and of Agustín Yáñez's* *Al filo del agua* (*The Edge of the Storm*, 1963) four years later, did not, at the time, seem so momentous. But it was the beginning of a genuine transformation. It wasn't easy to see a few flecks of gold glimmering in the mud of a thoroughly exhausted social and revolutionary narrative. But in Revueltas the Mexican Revolution reached its literary pinnacle, as a chronicle of events and of illusions. Whether major epics or minor ones, the literature that glorified the *Cristeros*, the indigenous, and the proletariat was abandoned—and turned into monuments, anecdotes, pamphlets, and jaculatory prayers. The creative impulse of Martín Luis Guzmán and José Vasconcelos* had been and gone. Mariano Azuela's doggedness had become pitiful. The army of Mexican Revolution writers had sucked the life out of both its history and its rhetoric. At the time, Xavier Villaurrutia's* appeal for a "literature of invention" seemed justified; the literary wasteland Martínez complained of appeared valid. The answer to Villaurrutia's call came in the form of Juan José Arreola.* And the answers to Martínez were Revueltas, Yáñez, and Rulfo.*

Once the blood on the battlefields had dried, once the rebels had passed through the gates of cities fortified by the State, it came time to question the sanctioned mythology and to compare the official consecration to the actual events: politics emerged once more as a form of critique. Revueltas was a writer steeped in two of the thirties' weakest traditions: *Cristero* hagiography and the proletarian novel. Born in Durango—like *Cristero* writer Antonio Estrada—Revueltas had grown up hearing about saints—both those in Heaven above, whose pious existence could be found in catechisms, and those below, the underdogs: soldiers of Christ marching off to the last religious war. That violent, popular breed of Christianity, combined with early communist activism inspired the work of a great novelist.

During his early militancy in the Communist Party of Mexico (PCM) in 1939, awaiting the death of his mother—which would come only a few hours later—Revueltas made the following private confession: "My brother, Jesus Christ, is purer and more sincere. He declared his rebellion, accepted the madness without worrying . . . In the end: I will be as poor. But later, on reading these lines, I'll put on a skeptical smile and mock myself, ashamed to have cried in a public plaza" (Revueltas, *Las evocaciones requeridas* II, 1986).

That statement depicts Revueltas to the core. He was by then working on his first novel, *Los muros de agua* (1941), which chronicled the imprisonment of a group of communists on the Islas Marías but already moved away from social realism. More than didacticism, what it revealed was pathos, a tragic desperation that characterized his entire oeuvre. Dostoyevsky-like despite his ideology, Revueltas saw the world as a penal colony where hope was often both the only salvation and a form of torture. But Revueltas's real transformation came two years later. And if we look at another quotation from 1939, ignoring its predictable political tone, we can see what was essentially a plan of action that outlined Revueltas's split from the prevailing narrative: "We don't know our own people, the people of tears, and we either write colorfully crafted anecdotes, like Rubén Romero, or depict a folkloric, senseless, simply picturesque populace, like López y Fuentes, Ferratis, and other bureaucrats. We have the duty to write that rabid, relentless Mexican novel; we must do it as a contribution to our proletariat and our peasants" (*Las evocaciones*, 1980).

A rejection of the florid, anecdotal prose attributed to José Rubén Romero; a distancing from the naturalist folklore of Jorge Ferratis and Gregorio López y Fuentes; the demand for a "rabid" and "relentless" Mexican novel; the establishment of heartrending hope, first for the oppressed and then for all. *El luto humano* was the first stage of his self-imposed mission. And it was the end of the Mexican Revolution as nationalist decree. It was time for a damning myth, for allegorical recreation, for fiction to reject state idolatry [. . .]

In Revueltas, heaven became hell; rural irrigation, the Flood; Mexican Revolution realism was apocalyptic. Like shipwrecked sailors, campesinos suffering from drought were brought down by water. Their Noah's ark was a ghost ship on which the wolf was human—a werewolf. The history exalted in public spaces by muralists had its opposite in Revueltas's biblical plagues and subterranean aquatic prisons. With *El luto humano*, the possibility of a novel faithful to the official story—or its radical or reactionary variants—faded away. The stuff of myths, history now found the novel to be a horrifying critique of its dreams and accomplishments. The path Revueltas took—despite regular palinodes—was one of no return. It wasn't just that he split politically from the so-called Mexican Revolution ideology. It was that his novels no longer fixed their gaze on the (now macabre) landscape but instead transferred the core of social reality to human consciousness, which he conceived as a torture chamber. (*Antología de la narrativa mexicana del siglo XX*, I, 1989)

On the eve of the millennium, we now know the answer to Revueltas's question in *Los errores*. Yes, in fact, the twentieth century *was* the century of the Moscow trials, of communist against communist. And we owe that conviction to men like Revueltas. Which is why all of us who participated in the drama of communism—young and old, in jail and in books, victims and executioners, kind souls and stooges, honest believers and tortured souls— enjoy hearing about heretics.

In the twenty-first century, the demons that tortured Revueltas will likely lose their haunting, savage quality. They'll become vestiges of a dead language, their diatribes as curious and impassioned as those that pitted Patarenes against Bogomils in the Middle Ages. After communism's demise, which so captivated the twentieth century, can a writer like Revueltas still impact readers? Likely so, given that his odyssey is as old as the history of civilization—the life of a clergyman torn between faith and doubt. Revueltas the communist is one of the richest legends in Mexico's Christian literature.

Octavio Paz* said that Revueltas carried out—in the name of Marxist philosophy—an examination of conscience worthy of Saint Augustine and Pascal. By viewing him as an essentially Christian writer, Paz provided the central core of my interpretation. Revueltas's novels gave Mexican Christianity a spiritual complexity that our Catholic writers were either unable or unwilling to confront.

The ghost of Bukharin presides over Revueltas's fictional universe. A victim of history or a mouthpiece of dialectics, Bukharin is the tragic hero marching out of step in *Los días terrenales* (1949) and *Los errores* (1964). During the Moscow Trials, Buhkarin saw himself as a Dostoyevsky character. And Revueltas's attitude toward the Bolshevik martyr is akin to that of some Christian writers toward Judas Iscariot: rather than the ultimate traitor, he becomes the human—too human—proof that confirms the Passion of Christ and its catastrophic consequences.

For French authors George Bernanos and François Mauriac, talking about God was easy. Not so Revueltas. And that's what led him to search for hidden signs in both the Scriptures and his novels. Exiled communists or tormented Christians, Revueltas's characters meditate on purgatory and calculate their chances for forgiveness. And in *El apando* (1970), the writer finds himself in hell after a pilgrimage through the shadow play of alienation.

Revueltas possessed one of the Christian virtues that Nietzsche was so skeptical about. His work elicited the kind of remorse that is anguish, doubt, and denial all rolled into one. And those who write about him exhibit the same characteristics. Novelist Héctor Manjarrez* ends *Pasaban en silencio nuestros dioses* (1987) with a fictionalized account of Revueltas's burial. In the novel, Manjarrez portrays the militant writer as an insane monk, whose literal death is also the figurative nail in the coffin for the dreams of a generation. Manjarrez teased Revueltas' for his coarse nature. "Eternal agitator, what chaos you unleashed. A bull in a china shop; bet you're happy now . . .

You won't go to heaven, José! You'll stay in that ancestral clay pot. Goodbye, you sinner, infested with every political parasite of the last three quarters of a century . . ."

In *Dialéctica de lo terrenal* (1991), Jaime Ramírez Garrido, an essayist born in 1970, abandons an analysis devoid of pathos when he becomes seduced by an image: "Revueltas with his goatee looks toward the camera, his face and body breaking up the parallel shadows of the bars we can't see in the photograph but know are there by the light coming in from outside, from the other side of the bars, which produce the shadows on Revueltas the prisoner."

Manjarrez and Ramírez Garrido, a generation apart, evoke a contradictory yet imaginative attitude toward Revueltas: libertarian or prisoner, heterodox or bereaved Bohemian. The sensationalism in Revueltas's novels, over and above his role in the universal drama of communism, both attracts and repels readers. In his texts, common criminals and ideological delinquents engage in implausible battles and heated controversies. And although evil is born of a psychological hell, good is never entirely defeated. Revueltas's books are our *Lost Illusions*; his villains the reincarnation of Vautrin; his novel the exploits of moderns.

Berdyaev said that at the Last Judgment Dostoyevsky would be an argument in favor of Russia. Perhaps the same could be said of Revueltas for Mexican realism. Meanwhile, let's remember Revueltas, the rebel cleric who like his brother Jesus Christ suffered for our sins, bearing witness to both leprosy and utopia. (*Tiros en el concierto: Literatura mexicana del siglo V*, 1997)

SELECTED BIBLIOGRAPHY

Obras completas, 3. Los días terrenales, ERA, Mexico, 1979.

Obras competas, 6. Los errores, ERA, Mexico, 1979.

Obras completas, 7. El apando, ERA, Mexico, 1978.

Obras completas, 25 and 26. Las evocaciones requeridas, vols I and II, prologue by José Emilio Pacheco, ed. Philippe Cheron and Andrea Revueltas, ERA, Mexico, 1987.

The Edge of the Storm, trans. Ethel Brinton, University of Texas Press, 1963.

REYES, ALFONSO

(Monterrey, Nuevo León, 1889 – Mexico City, 1959)

When we were kids, Heinrich Schliemann's (1822–1890) adventures were one of the most delightful things to read about. He was the archaeologist who carried out excavations at Hissarlik, proving the complex historical reality of the city of Troy. He'd promised his father that he would complete the mission against all odds, establishing the veracity of the places mentioned by Homer—whose works he carried in his pocket—and uncovering seven superimposed cities at Troy. He also unearthed treasure—not that of Priam, but of a sovereign who'd lived four hundred years before him. And one night he took the liberty of draping the jewels that had belonged to a Trojan woman three thousand years earlier around the neck of his Greek wife.

"The Trojan War was a failure," Reyes wrote in *La crítica en la edad ateniense* (1941). "It's not even possible to say whether it ended in a decisive victory or whether the ruse of the horse was an a posteriori solution that poetry imposed onto reality in order to make sense of it. All we know is that the Greek heroes embarked on a lamentable return, an arduous odyssey, only to find their homes destroyed and their lands overcome by anarchy" (*Obras completas*, XIII, 1961).

Aeneas was a Trojan hero. Reyes, unlike Aeneas, succeeded in founding neither Rome nor Latin culture. A child poet, he delved into the pre-Christian era and converted the barbaric Troy of history into a hallowed Troy of the spirit. His oeuvre is like a walled city, his twenty-five books its fortifications. A magnificent ruin full of multiple treasures as well as dust and baubles, it is essential—replete with splendid secret passageways and hazardous summits. Reading Reyes's books is like reverting to childhood and visiting Teotihuacán or the Acropolis, playing among the stones whose silent enigma is—to paraphrase Edward Gibbon—the living testimony of countless human generations now disappeared.

Reyes knew that literature had slowly destroyed classic heroes. His posthumous book *Los héroes* (1965) is startling in its expository clarity and its refusal to blend myth and literature, the way modern writers do. Jason and Aeneas might have lost their standing as intermediaries between humanity and divinity—the first being made into an ingenue, the second a coward—

but writers were to blame for that. So Reyes turned back the clock, converting Greece into a fantastic voyage to early days—both his own and humanity's. Lucky man. There's no denying that his work is an oasis of "civilization" surrounded by the desert of Mexican reality.

What's his strongest book? All of them, and none of them. Pompous homages to Reyes abound, but the truth is that the *Ateneísta* wrote his books as an escape from the moderns, a refuge from modernism. Anyone searching among the undergrowth of his oeuvre for ideology should save the trip. His classicist ruins aren't ideological. And he doesn't have the divine prerogatives of Tiresias. He was simply a scholar born of the wrong age, nostalgic for Antiquity. He won't be forgotten. But he was no prophet, and a part of us, though we may deny it, needs prophecy.

Reyes is known for his desire to found a Latin tradition. Did he really attempt it? And did the barbarous babble stop him? If we ignore his overly sentimental Virgilian ambassador side, it's doubtful that his classicizing endeavors managed to "civilize" Mexicans. Perhaps he only wrote as a way to act out a hero's role, to become Aeneas, or to recreate a game he used to play with his uncle—explained in *Parentalia*—that consisted of constructing cities of cardboard and populating them with puppets. Reyes's city is a ruin: imposing and absurd, grounds for both archaeology and desolation. His unfinished yet enduring merit—as with any ruins, which are what they are because they no longer are—is that of all relics: being a sanctuary of scholars, children, and poets. And tourists.

A long and complicated polemic has questioned whether Heinrich Schliemann's discovery of the Trojan ruins actually proves the historicity of Homer's poems. Modern experts consider the layer known as "Troy VIIa," dug up by the German archeologist, as the charred remains of a one-horse town. The treasure of Priam might have belonged to anybody. And Reyes's work, like Schliemann's Troy, is a space where history and poetry, science and fantasy, analysis and taste, carry on a heated debate. We ought to read Reyes with the same love that Schliemann felt as he gazed upon Troy. We play before his oeuvre, spellbound among the scattered stones and faded walls of his work. As Heinrich Heine said, it's not until we become ruins ourselves that we understand them. (*Tiros en el concierto: Literatura mexicana del siglo V*, 1997)

Selected Bibliography

Obras completas, XVII. Los héroes. Junta de sombras, FCE, Mexico, 1965.

Obras completas, XIX. Los poemas homéricos. La Ilíada. La afición de Grecia, FCE, Mexico, 1968.

The Position of America and Other Essays, trans. Harriet de Onís, Knopf, 1950.

Anthology, trans. Dick Gerales, ed. José Luis Martínez, FCE, Mexico, 2009.

REYES, JAIME

(Mexico City, 1947 – 1999)

Cholera and poetry are only compatible in a few extraordinary cases. In *Isla de raíz amarga, insomne raíz* (1976), Reyes conveys the unrelenting rage of an academic tribe who feels defeated by history, condemned to saturnine forms of politics and eroticism, sick of crude Mexican authoritarianism, and hurt by the lack of results yielded by their martyrdom: "Porque somos débiles fuimos tolerados" ("Because we are weak, we were tolerated"). Engagé poetry has frequently been a form of snobbery—a fashion that compelled poets to "lend a voice" to those lacking their own, as people used to say in the seventies and eighties. The practice dates back to the days of Lord Byron. The expression implied *recording* the voices of the oppressed, thereby converting the poet into some sort of director of sound, an idea rejected by poets to the left of Reyes—the infrarealists, for example—who saw themselves as the true bards of the lumpenproletariat and denounced "the abject middle-class sport"—as one exegete called it—of "lending a voice" to those who had none.

When the masses managed to find their own voice in the routines of democracy, Reyes's poems were some of the few of that genre to survive. Like a fire-breather on a cruise ship, Reyes is a poet who gargles with gasoline and then spits flames. At its best, *Isla de raíz amarga, insomne raíz* is the ultimate Mexican poem in which loutish conversation manages to come across as both unnerving and scandalous, a farewell to insults that lost their iconoclastic vehemence when tolerance, indifference, and *costumbrismo* began to take hold. Reyes still captures the city in his gaze, and from the dizzying heights of revealed religion, he assumes the role of a muezzin, calling to prayer even as he's torn between a hangover from last night and the inebriation brought on by a dawn of new political realities. The bard stands together with modernism's whore of Babylon. What's new now (thanks to seventies feminism) is that her man, the torturer, is wracked by guilt that he crafts into mournful lament. Reyes really did attempt to hand the dispossessed a microphone. But what he recorded was in fact his own voice, which rings out in every dingy, squalid room lit by a bare light bulb, in which a timeless Bohemian weeps tears of rage over loves lost and impotence at the hands of the powerful.

SELECTED BIBLIOGRAPHY

Isla de raíz amarga, insomne raíz (with *Al vuelo el espejo de un río*), ERA, Mexico, 1977; FCE, Mexico, 1986.

RIVAS, JOSÉ LUIS
(Tuxpan, Veracruz, 1950)

"Life without the sea is incomprehensible," wrote Juan Ramón Jiménez in *Prosas críticas*. "I, at least, cannot comprehend it, and I owe all of my eternities to it; the sea is life without dream, always open; a life without the sea is a closed-off life, closed-off poetry. That's why the poets I call 'open' are more often found on the coast. The inland poet who can't see the sea must 'attain' it through the surrounding things and people, through emanations. It must be materialized in another experience, because perhaps he's heard of it and cannot forget it; and of course he cannot forget it because he cannot recall it. It's an indispensable myth. But the sea can only be thought of as the whole sea, as it can only be evoked as the eternal sea, since, as it can be manipulated by man, it contains its most elemental nature within the realm of the elements, within the sun, or the moon, or the elemental stars."

Jiménez's take helps explain the storybook astonishment that Rivas's poetry, devoted to the sea—and its tributaries—produces. Neither climate change nor ecological degradation has rendered the timeless theme obsolete. And seen from cities of perpetual summer—such as Mexico City, according to Pedro Henríquez Ureña—the sea is still somehow exotic. Or at least that's the case for a poetic country like Mexico that, as French critic Louis

Panabière claimed—in reference to Rivas—suffers from "thalassophobia," a fear of the sea. In the *altiplano*—which Henríquez Ureña saw as propitious for understated, melancholic, flat poetry—it's still considered noble to say that Ramón López Velarde never knew the sea. Such a statement presumes that the great poet, in what must have amounted to an aesthetic decision, deprived himself of the most nourishing lyrical sustenance on earth.

If Jiménez is right and the eternal sea *is* an indispensable myth, then it must be said that Rivas has been its Mexican poet par excellence since the publication of *Tierra nativa* (1982), a cult collection that together with Gorostiza's* *Muerte sin fin* (*Death Without End*) and Paz's* *Piedra de Sol* (*Sunstone*) forms our poetic cornerstone. Guillermo Sheridan* rightly avowed that the anthology proved that "we had before us a poet who charted a unique route on the course of modern Mexican tradition: that of powerful lyricism capable of strengthening the language of the heart via the disciplined study of poetic tradition . . ." As such, *Tierra nativa* marries—splendidly—two elements that tend to be separate and irreconcilable: nostalgia and paraphrase; the poem as a reading of earlier poetry and awe for the land that time forgot. Rivas was a fin-de-siècle man, too, a bard passing down legends. Thus it's no surprise that he loved Derek Walcott's *Omeros* (1990) and translated it into Spanish. For Rivas as well as Walcott, Homer's world is both a genesis and a genealogy.

Rivas's poetry is almost entirely divided between two continents: *Raz de marea* (1993), which includes poems written between 1975 and 1992, and *Ante un cálido norte* (2005), which encompasses those between 1992 and 2002. The latter includes a Shakespeare adaptation (*La violación de Lucrecia*), two chapters of his translation of *Omeros*, *Luz de mar abierto* (1992), *Estuario* (1996), *Río* (1998), and *Por mor del mar* (2002). Not included are two more recent collections, *Un navío un amor* (2004) and *Pájaros* (2005), of which at least the first is magnificent.

Nevertheless, as Rivas's body of work grows, it has also elicited criticisms worth bearing in mind. In 1991 Evodio Escalante noted his doubts about the books following *Tierra nativa*, which rather than reap the benefits conferred by Eliot's "The Waste Land," yielded to a sort of pastoralism—seen as a failure in the trajectory of a "postmodernist" poet who in fact proved himself a "neo-classicist." Alberto Paredes, on the other hand, lamented the "Achilles' heel" of Rivas's beautiful subtle oeuvre, which he saw as the fact that he hadn't again managed to achieve "the human depth and courage of *Tierra nativa*" (Paredes, *Una temporada de poesía*, 2004).

I don't think all of Rivas's books should be seen as poor copies or minor versions of *Tierra nativa*, the flawless paradigm whose perfection would dash the hopes and fate of any poet. I would be less than honest if I said that all of his work moves me equally; but just as untrue would be to claim that *Tierra nativa* is Rivas's be all and end all. Of the many things he's taken from his literary love of Saint-John Perse, perhaps the least obvious and most important is the notion of a poetic continuum: the work as an ever-growing expanse, the poet as navigator ratcheting up journeys across the seven seas. In *Río*, for instance, the voyage back to childhood, to one's first women (mother, sister), is rendered with uniquely meticulous precision and tenderness. *Por mor del mar* is a grave and sententious book, an epic declaration of principles. *Estuario*, in turn, is a collection of images whose majesty is captured via lyric pointillism. "El mundo no acaba aún de urdir la telaraña de su / mano y abre en abanico un atolón cercado de / palmeras" ("The world has yet to hatch the web of its / hand and open in a fan an atoll enclosed by / palms").

Paul Claudel noted that Saint-John Perse "religiously" avoided using the word God. Similarly, Adolfo Castañón,* in an exquisite comment about the Rivas anthologies, referred to a piety he found "radically pagan," the work of an author unfamiliar with Christianity who has proven the existence of "scattered members of another Scripture." That exaltation can be glimpsed here and there throughout Rivas's poetry, as in this verse chosen almost at random: "¡Bebamos otra vez! / Los astros ya comienzan otra ronda también" ("Let us drink again! / The stars, too, are having another round"). But Rivas, despite having come to Saint-John Perse via E. M. Cioran and Octavio Paz, doesn't share their passion for the French Antilles poet as historian sans historiosophy and poet sans tragedy. What Rivas loved was his hymn-like quality; he enlisted only for those endless expeditions that set off in search of childhood-cum-paradise lost. In *Un navío un amor*, the ode moves over to make room for elegy, and again and again we see the face of Helen, in a book analogous to one Elsa Cross* published the same year: *El vino de las cosas: Ditirambos*.

Few Latin American poets of his generation have translated anywhere near the amount of poetry Rivas has. Not only Walcott's *Omeros* but the complete works of Eliot and Rimbaud, Perse's *Eloge* as well as numerous poems by Georges Schehade, Dylan Thomas, Andrew Marvell, Herman Melville, and Tahar Ben Jelloun. Rivas is both himself and a small family of poets, and the line between the original and his version is at times blurry, as though readers were crossing a personal Mediterranean Sea in which Rivas sails from one poet to another, creating a Latin tradition whose hope is founded on the belief that everything dies but *nothing* is vanity. Saint-John Perse, Walcott, and Rivas do, after all, share the same sea. But the voice of Rivas is unmistakable: it's that of an open poet, a man who believes that "un hombre deslumbrado es sólo un niño con suerte" ("a dazzled man is just a boy who got lucky").

SELECTED BIBLIOGRAPHY
Raz de marea (Poesía, 1975–1992), FCE, Mexico, 1993.
Un navío un amor, ERA, Mexico, 2004.
Ante un cálido norte, FCE, Mexico, 2005.

RIVERA GARZA, CRISTINA
(Matamoros, Tamaulipas, 1964)

Cristina Rivera Garza strikes me as something of a twenty-first-century Amparo Dávila. Dávila wrote three books of short stories: *Tiempo destrozado* (1959), *Música concreta* (1964), and *Árboles petrificados* (1977). One of the most beautiful women of her time, she received the Villaurrautia prize in 1977, and in 1985 published the anthology *Muerte en el bosque*. But by the late eighties, when I wrote about her in *Antología de la narrativa mexicana del siglo XX*, she already seemed to belong to a time outside history, a time when sorceresses used their beguiling beauty to cast all sorts of evil spells. Amparo Dávila's stories, many of which are nobly executed, are inscribed within a nineteenth-century fantastical tradition that survived into the twentieth century, helping free Mexican literature from the empire of realism. But Dávila, who started out as a Christian-inspired poet married to painter Pedro Coronel, for a while seemed to have vanished along with the ghosts and petrified trees of her fiction. Then many years later, she was reborn in Cristina Rivera Garza.

Reincarnation is a fairly uncommon phenomenon, even in literature. But Dávila's soul appears to have migrated and been multiplied in the mirrors of Rivera Garza, the writer from Tamaulipas who captured her so well. She published her first book, *La guerra no importa,* in 1991, and her penchant for the fantastical and romantic could already be seen in its pages. In 1999 she came out with *Nadie me verá llorar* (*No One Will See Me Cry,* 2003), a novel that established her as one of Mexico's most unsettling writers. Her second novel, *La cresta de Ilión* (2002), convinced me that she's an absolutely breathtaking prose writer: only a few per decade achieve this stature. And Dávila, it turns out, is *La cresta de Ilión*'s motif. I say "motif" as opposed to "protagonist" because Rivera Garza turns Dávila, her texts, photos on the back cover, and her legend (if we can say she has one) into a sort of force field. The magma of dreams floating under the surface of Dávila's stories has been fully realized by Rivera Garza, one soul transmigrating to another, fully developing all of its complexity as if what was yesterday just a promise today were manifest destiny. *La cresta de Ilión* isn't an homage to Dávila; it's proof that literature can travel through time and only do so (forgive the repetition) *through* literature. Doubles—products of insanity—are often handled naïvely, resorting to ghosts in the mirror, or romantically, by worshiping psychosis. Rivera Garza wisely saw the spirits persecuting her hero as a sort of linguistic potential harkening back to Dávila, a power multiplied to the nth degree. Now, these mathematical multiplications obviously could have referred back to any writer, tradition or perspective. But by choosing to see insanity as a variation (and not a loss) of identity, Rivera Garza turned *La cresta de Ilión* into a fabulous, fantastical tale where the fearsome ancestor (Dávila, or whatever she signifies) is alive, is a sister, a fellow human. And yet the essence of *La cresta de Ilión* goes beyond all that. As the title (which is the largest bone in the pelvis) indicates, and as the reader learns by the end of the novel, Rivera Garza's point is that sex is the cornerstone, something that transcends gender, a mystery borne witness to by our ghosts. *La cresta de Ilión* neither blesses nor curses the mirrors that Borges saw as responsible for the multiplication of our species. Instead it interrogates them. In two or three generations, I wonder if someone will write a piece asking: Who's afraid of Cristina Rivera Garza?

SELECTED BIBLIOGRAPHY
Tiempo destrozado, FCE, Mexico, 1959 and 2003.
Música concreta, FCE, Mexico, 1964 and 2002.
Árboles petrificados, Joaquín Mortoz, Mexico, 1977.
Muerte en el bosque, FCE/SEP, Mexico, 1985.
La cresta de Ilión, Tusquets, Mexico, 2002.
No One Will See Me Cry, trans. Andrew Hurley, Curbstone Press, 2003.

ROSSI, ALEJANDRO

(Florence, Italy, 1932 – Mexico City, 2009)

There are few Latin American writers who one could say became classics the moment they stepped onto the literary scene. Rossi is one. I'm not simply referring to the acclaim that *Manual del distraído* (1978) garnered among the happy few—led by José Bianco—who welcomed the emergence of a new and unique writer whom Octavio Paz* later defined as "the human fruit of a civilization." Instead I'd like to split hairs, to uncover the reason why Rossi's brief oeuvre—which Julio Ortega says reads like an entire library—seemed predisposed to being viewed as a classic, that is, a body of work encompassing precepts, laws, and economics.

Rossi's readers—and oh, has he been blessed with good readers—proposed guidelines (Adolfo Castañón*) and deduced methods (Carlos Pereda and Enrique Krauze*) for approaching his work. This stemmed, first, from Rossi as philosopher—a brilliant student of Gaos at UNAM who studied with Heidegger at Freiburg and Gilbert Ryle at Oxford. The man who established analytical philosophy in Mexican academia, he began a second career as columnist in the mid-seventies. One by one, his texts forged the author of *Manual del distraído*. Rossi's ability to definitively and magisterially discard one occupation and energetically embark on a new adventure in the prime of his life was admirable. And in addition to exhibiting the "Rossi style" that Luis Ignacio Helguera* defined as keen powers of observation, development of detail, ability to reduce things to their logical absurdity, and the "art of concealing lines of argument in the plot and the rhythm of prose," the much-lauded *Manual del distraído* is worthy of still further praise for yet another reason: its felicitous crossover from philosophy to literature. By swapping attributes between the two, the latter gained the rigor of the former, and the treatises Rossi had taught and studied for a quarter of a century were transformed into an imaginative nucleus, the moral pulse of his work. As is the case with George Santayana, another Renaissance man, Rossi's philosophy—not degraded by literature—became the most enduring way of "inculcating habits that are more moral than intellectual: modesty, a playful spirit, inner freedom, an appetite for risk," as he said in the text about Juan de Mairena, the philosopher invented by Antonio Machado, included in *Manual*.

Manual del distraído, which begins his *Obras reunidas* (2005) is—as is by now obvious—a fiendishly well-written book. But it's not just an Azorín-like collection of philosophies or a miniaturist's cameos; no, this is a genuinely "liberal" book written under the adverse conditions of a nation torn between all-powerful presidentialism and the nightmares of a left that was both suffocated and suffocating. The disputes seen throughout *Manual del distraído*, which are also those of *Plural* and *Vuelta*—magazines inconceivable without Rossi—originated in defenses that were not easy to make at the time (such as that of Alexandr Solzhenitsyn), cruel relativizing (as of Salvador Allende and his Unidad Popular party), exposing personal details that offended hundreds of people (including Mexican migration officials) and a prophetic condemnation of revolutionary optimism, which refused to see that "the purges were our Great Lisbon Earthquake."

I'm not trying to divest *Manual del distraído* of its literary aspects—or even of its pure literature—but to emphasize the magnificent professional research and substantiation that sets it apart. The very aspect that astounded Salvador Elizondo* is exactly what allows Rossi to be seen as a classic, the author of a book that will stand the test of time because the sentence that sums it up encompasses a system of values: "Reading a text badly is the easiest thing in the world; not being illiterate is the indispensable condition."

Throughout *Obras reunidas*, Rossi's resolute anti-Romanticism can be seen unfolding, positioning itself against the spellbound and the enlightened, rejecting the legions peddling packaged miracles, the hypocrites convinced of statist solutions. Latin American violence, for Rossi, tended to stem from a moral error he felt was Franciscan in nature: a belief that the virtues of the soul meant that all social organizations would be kind and gentle.

The mathematical proofs afforded by essay, of course, will never be enough. *Un café con Gorrondona* (1999) maximized Rossi's anti-Romanticism, refashioning it as literature and comically embodying the caustic threat of reading badly in fiction. The stories in this collection, written and published over the course of a decade, battle for the soul not only of Rossi but of any writer, as personified by Gorrondona and Leñada, the characters who chose literary vanity as their field of honor. Gorrondona says as much in one of the last texts in *Manual del distraído*: "Writing well is impossible. It implies immortality, being a contemporary of every stage of language, which is the only way to understand it fully. A vain writer is, therefore, an irresponsible artisan, a literary suicide, an ignorant man, a plague we cannot tolerate."

The call for modesty put out to Rossi's characters (and unfortunately, to Rossi himself, as Juan Villoro* said) takes us to the historic events that troubled and overwhelmed his narrator, and comprised the ominous atmosphere of *La fábula de las regiones* (1997). In order to read these six stories, however, first we must reread "Vasto reino de pesadumbre," his essay on *El otoño del patriarca* (*The Autumn of the Patriarch*) in *Manual del distraído*. By entering into conversation with Gabriel García Márquez, Rossi outlines what was good and noble about magic realism, stopping at the precipice and cordoning off its twee pretensions and superficiality.

That essay not only served as a blueprint for Rossi's future stories but also offered a lesson that, twenty-five years later, is still barely understood. In order to move beyond magical realism, we don't need to keep expiating nationalist sins by writing about Nazis but to clear away the mental clutter of feverish imaginations and chaotic enumeration so as to locate the real fissures of our inscrutable nation, as Rossi does in *La fábula de las regiones*. Strolling gloriously and majestically through airports is not what makes one cosmopolitan; it's writing like Rossi and Elizondo, exemplarily focused on divesting Rómulo Gallegos of every superfluous element in his prose to hit upon the moral slant his language concealed. Rossi's *Obras reunidas*, therefore, not only filled a void in Mexican literature but also allowed a whole new generation to benefit from teachings that until then only a select few had enjoyed.

La fábula de las regiones was written in the shadow of Sarmiento's *Facundo* and of a few select episodes in the life of caudillos and Latin American patricians. It's akin to taking a book by Venezuelan Rufino Blanco Fombona (for example) and shaking it out, allowing all of the civic pageantry and painful oratory to flutter away and leave behind just the essentials, getting rid of the nominalist drivel and providing some clues as to which of our myths need to evolve and which to endure. In the text in *Cartas credenciales* that he dedicated to murdered philosophy professor Hugo Margain Charles, Rossi refrains from mentioning—out of both contempt and grace—the name of his presumed murderer. He takes the same moral course of action in *La fábula de las regiones*, which spans from the nineteenth to the twenty-first century and has characters who belong to the "Shameful Sect," the "College of Historians," the "Party of Union," poetic entities created out of a painstakingly detailed (and disparaging) examination of history and its interpretation. His equatorial America, which both is and is not that of Álvaro Mutis,* his "regions," which are and are not the Mexico of the wars of Independence (as Paz said), his fables that invent either the motherland or the shadows (as Castañón said), turn *La fábula de las regiones* into a microcosm that both unites and separates the pampas from the plains (as—last but not least—Julio Ortega said).

History, like old age, Rossi waxes nostalgic, is a past that survives by reinventing itself. In that vein, *La fábula de las regiones* tackles the uselessness of borders; the insolent foolhardiness of utopian redeemers; the (empty) mind of a hit man who'd be more ready for the gallows after a synopsis of national history than torture; murderous mobs and the tireless Argentine paramilitary *mazorca*; the dubiousness of sociological solutions to our problems; governmental co-opting of myths; the involuntary nihilism of petty tyrants; and—modestly—the tender bond between a grandfather and the wife of his grandson.

Alternatives to the empire of magical realism, these stories denounce the aesthetic dictatorship that sees the world as a permanent miracle, a Romantic belief founded in the sort of religiosity Rossi rejected outright. At risk of overanalyzing the world (of Rossi), I think I glimpse overtones of Luchino Visconti in his equatorial decadence.

Born in Florence to a Venezuelan mother and an Italian father, Rossi was a frequent passenger on ocean liners, a Jesuit student in Buenos Aires and a Mexican by choice. His biography, no doubt, qualified him as one of those writers who inhabit the "world literature" Goethe dreamed of, not without a touch of bitterness and melancholy. But visas and passport stamps only partly explain the personality of this man who arrogantly appeared fully realized from day one. Perhaps we could learn more looking to José Ortega y Gasset, his far-off philosophical grandfather, than by searching for parallels in his teacher Gaos.

"Lenguaje y filosofía en Ortega" is the last text in *Cartas credenciales* and the essay that concludes—quite propitiously—Rossi's *Obras reunidas*. To begin with, the essay has the "fullness of meaning" Ortega himself writes with. Reading it, you'd think you were listening to the Spanish philosopher discussing Kant: Rossi possessed a similar ability to synthesize and a familiarity of expression. It's a shame he deprived us of other weighty philosophical meditations. As a philosopher, Rossi was trained in Ortega's respect (and disdain) for the *genus dicendi* of the treatise. Like Gaos and Xavier Zubiri, Rossi was never a spiritual leader in the way that Ortega was in Spain and Paz in Mexico. He did, however, dedicate his life to those saving graces Ortega identified as "a man, a book, a painting, a landscape, an error, a sorrow."

Those were Ortega's paths to secular salvation, the road that led man to "fullness of meaning," which for Rossi was embodied in the defense and erudition of public universities as a professor; research and academic governance; being active in philosophical and literary journals; and his faith in the usefulness of institutions of knowledge that the Mexican government has both created and respected.

I also found in "Lenguaje y filosofía en Ortega" that odd form of reticence that—perhaps because I was steeped in what we used to call the "ideological struggle"—I find exasperating. This isn't the time to talk about Ortega, nor am I the right person to do it. Juan Nuño, Rossi's spiritual brother-in-arms, once discredited Ortega as a "salon philosopher." Taken together with my praise of Rossi, that brings us full circle. But I must say, by way of explication of his essayistic devices, that I was surprised he overlooked Ortega's silence about Nazism, a silence all the more painful in a man who saw himself as one of the great philosophers of his day and had the opportunity to trek—in a miserable procession—through the enormous German cemetery after World War II.

No sooner had I noted this, however, than I came upon a partial explanation that had been formulated a few years earlier, on one of *Manual del
distraído*'s unusually vitriolic pages. Rossi, here, took Ortega to task for his
cheap comparison between Italy and Spain, which allowed him to conclude,
in 1926, that Spanish fascism was an impossibility. "I'm not shocked," Rossi
wrote, "by bad prophets or erroneous predictions. What I do find scandalous is the irrelevance of the premises, the phantasmal methodology . . ."

That comment, the pendular attack and defense of Ortega, not only
serves to exorcise the demons of nationalism and criminal panegyrics to
the fatherland but also epitomizes the Socratic circumlocution Rossi em-
ploys in analyzing his subjects, the way he pretends to assassinate them only
to pardon their lives, condemn them, or praise them to the hilt. I suppose
that's the thinking of a philosopher. And I have no doubt it's the approach
of a classic.

Latin America's image in the world right now is deplorable. On top of the
secular poverty of our democracies we must add the ignorance and disdain
with which not only the United States but also most of Europe look upon
us. With the exception of things involving the noble savage—and his revolutionary counterpart—everything that comes out of Latin America is seen
in Washington as in Rome, in Paris as in Madrid, as a caricaturesque aping
of European ways. An oeuvre like Rossi's refutes that, presenting in essay
and fiction a Latin America that is both liberal and tolerant, republican and
mestizo, regional and cosmopolitan, arguing in favor of that Far West that is
still, despite it all, not the embodiment of that old utopia but the repository
of some of the most illustrious modern traditions.

If we were to chart its place on an imaginary map, Rossi's autobiographical
novel *Edén* (2006) would be located close to Jorge López Paéz's* *El solitario
Atlántico* (1958) and border on Salvador Elizondo's* *Elsinore* (1987). The
former, because Rossi grew up in the literary Mexico of the fifties when the
search for lost childhood (often found in a subverted, provincial Eden) was
a fictional horizon to be reached, as it is in the nominal odyssey of Jorge
López Paéz's novel in which a father leads his child by the hand to see the
sea. But time passed and Rossi spent his days and years on other things: his
philosophical readings and, later, writing magnificent essays and extraordi-

nary tales. At the literary magazines *Plural* and *Vuelta*, Rossi found himself working alongside his contemporaries, writers like Juan García Ponce* and Elizondo himself, and then after a long time, when he was 74 years old, he published *Edén*, the book in which he delineated the size of his province: a wide world, but not—for him—a foreign one, a place where Florence, Caracas, and Buenos Aires are always within reach.

While Elizondo preferred poetic condensation, distilling his prose to the greatest degree possible and turning his entire childhood into a single, stunning dreamlike episode in *Elsinore*, Rossi opted for romance of the almost fairy-tale variety. Alex and Félix, the sibling protagonists of *Edén*, are living out those surreal, supernatural years between childhood and adolescence, and when the tale comes to a close, the *Bildungsroman* begins.

Rossi subtitles the book "Imagined Life," thereby emphasizing the fictional character of this very noble book with a cast that includes a distant, reserved father, a terrible, omnipresent mother, Spanish Republican teachers, a Communist uncle, and discreet Argentine exiles. Of those, Bettina stands out: an unforgettable woman who initiates sex in a scene whose somewhat cinematographic sensuality is one of the book's most marked artistic achievements. In another time, *Edén* would have been seen as an Oedipal novel. I would prefer to view it as per Tomás Segovia,* another of Rossi's contemporaries, as a mediation on incest as one extreme of love.

The impertinent Rossi brothers in *Edén* remind me of the children in *The Turn of the Screw*. It's a somewhat capricious and perhaps unsustainable comparison but that's how a reader's mind works. It's as if Henry James's unfortunate characters, with their suspect intelligence and hypersensitivity to the supernatural world, had been given a second chance and instead of the governess and ghosts they ended up living in the possible paradise described by Rossi: the multiple moves and adventures of an Italo-Venezuelan family, both Creole and European. The horrors of war—Mussolini's world theater repeatedly both yearned for and exorcised—seem to stop at the doors to *Edén*'s heaven, the large winter hotels that not only serve to chart the course of the novel but also act as its metaphor.

I find it intriguing that in both the memoirs Henry James wrote in honor of his brother William, the philosopher, and in *Edén*, visiting wounded soldiers in field hospitals turns out to be an ominous sign that the characters themselves don't fully recognize as the end of their childhood. For James this occurred in Portsmouth Grove at the start of the US Civil War in 1861; for Rossi in Rome, visiting those mutilated in Mussolini's Greek campaign. In both cases the splendor of cosmopolitanism was not to be uprooted and aristocracy was sentenced to die, along with refined civility, seen in the pretense of a stable society whose enigmas (as in the detective novels that characters read in *Edén*) are more suited to a game of chess than to real life.

Nostalgia comes to the fore when Alex fantasizes about General Páez, his great-great-grandfather and the first president of Venezuela, a man "dressed for a ball, with a sword given to him by the King of England," who might just stroll into the dining room of any of the great hotels where the boy's life unfolds. As in the heraldic poetry of Borges, the family ballad marks the end of a cycle—both historical and literary—in which a writer like Rossi would be the last of the Brahmins. *Edén* is a wisely overdue book, a patient recapitulation of not only an imagined life but of the half century of prose written in a Mexico wide open to the world of Latin America.

SELECTED BIBLIOGRAPHY
Obras reunidas, FCE, Mexico, 2005.
Edén, FCE, Mexico, 2006.

RULFO, JUAN
(Sayula, Jalisco, 1917 – Mexico City, 1986)

Who was Juan Rulfo? He starred in one of the most misunderstood and polemical roles of contemporary literature. Was he just lucky, a "donkey who played the flute" as Federico Campbell said, a sort of idiot savant overtaken by a virulent poetic inspiration that left him utterly spent, barren after writing two short masterpieces? Or was he a brilliant modern whose tortured ethics kept him from ever publishing again, knowing that his message had been conveyed so perfectly that any superfluity would have served only to question his posterity? Did Rulfo continue writing novels and short stories after the fifties, only to destroy them, dissatisfied, before his death? Or did he never again compose anything beyond a few hesitant drafts, as a man crushed by fame but essential to the world?

Rulfo was a living classic. Endless biographers traveled to his kingdom only to corroborate that there are no definitive answers to the questions posed by his oeuvre. Reading biographies by Nuria Amat, Reina Roffé, and Alberto Vital, it becomes clear that the Rulfo problem is composed of three closely related yet distinct issues: inspiration, reception, and silence. Regarding the first, Rulfo's pre-*Pedro Páramo* (1955; *Pedro Páramo*, 1967) trajectory aroused a distrust I find irritating, as though his well-known life story were obviously insufficient to explain the genius of his work. Discussions about the creation of *Pedro Páramo* revealed the embarrassing suspicion that in 1954 Rulfo wouldn't have been capable of writing the novel without the help of Antonio Alatorre* and Juan José Arreola* and the work of poet Alí Chumacero,* his editor at the Fondo de Cultura Económica. Although Arreola disavowed the infamous session in which he and Alatorre supposedly solved the problem of the Rulfo text, Chumacero—who in 1955 made public his doubts about the book—did nothing to quash the rumor that he was to Rulfo what Pound was to Eliot.

Research into the *Pedro Páramo* typescript held at the Fondo de Cultura Económica has proven that the version the author handed in was entirely his, and that editors made only superficial copyedits. At this stage, I think no one any longer doubts Rulfo's complete control over his artistic powers, his method whose "unsettling enigma" obsessed his colleague Salvador Elizondo.* But the nagging doubt has caused some of his exegetes—Alberto Vital among them—to go to the other extreme, proposing an impossibly angelic Rulfo, an ethereal Rilkean creature with a chance relationship to literary life, in command of intellectual virtues he lacked and that his work doesn't need. This hypothesis paradoxically turns Rulfo once again into a lucky coincidence, that "donkey who played the flute" described by Campbell, the most intelligent and understanding source out of all Rulfo's friends. Given that his ability even to write *Pedro Páramo* had been questioned, it's only natural that Rulfo himself—as Reina Roffé notes—became obsessed with the myth of his originality, going so far as to assure people—despite biographical and stylistic evidence to the contrary—that he'd never even read Faulkner before publishing *El llano en llamas* (*The Burning Plain*, 1957) in 1953.

I prefer a more "real" Rulfo, one subjected to the pivotal influence of Faulkner as well as the happy accident of having met and read Chilean writer María Luisa Bombal, author of *La amortajada* (1938), which is analogous to his own work in both style and spirit. That Rulfo—a young writer under the wing of good friends like Alatorre and Arreola, a voracious reader who in Guadalajara and Mexico City began drafting his work with millimetric precision—strikes me as more logical and nicer than the Romantic reconstruction that insists on ranking the genius over the man. In my view, Rulfo formed part of the legion of clairvoyant poets, provided you accept that his inspiration came not only from *our* world but also from the world of books where he gorged himself on the likes of Halldór Laxness, Knut Hamsun, and Jean Giono.

Many years later, at the pinnacle of his fame, Rulfo again called into question his own authority. In 1974 at the Universidad Central de Venezuela, he declared whimsically that his prolonged silence was due to the death of his uncle Celerino, who'd been the one to tell him the stories. Absurdly enough, this little *boutade* struck a chord, immediately unleashing the predictable appearance of a host of grammarians who explained that oral tradition was in fact that source of Rulfo's genius. Now, no "Uncle Celerino," whether human or divine, could have dictated anything to Rulfo, a writer who—if you read him well—clearly is not anecdotal. Nevertheless, the whole affair comes to mind because Nuria Amat and Reina Roffé insist on seeing Rulfo as a sort of Bartleby the Scrivener—something Arreola, we should recall, said long before anyone else. The way I see it, Rulfo is like Bartleby in only one way: he preferred not to. That is, he preferred not to keep writing, despite the fact that he turned up every day at the office—of world literature—until his death.

The issue of Rulfo's reception—which Leonardo Martínez Carrizales calls "the construction of public fame" in his book *Juan Rulfo, los caminos de la fama pública* (1998)—appears to have been satisfactorily resolved. It is simply not true that Rulfo has been ignored, and in hindsight it's actually surprising how quickly the radical novelty of his prose triumphed, thanks to the efforts—justly recognized by his biographers—of people like Mariana Frenk, his German translator, and Carlos Fuentes,* who introduced him in France.

At first Rulfo was seen as the coda of old Mexican Revolution realism, whose favorite sons—the campesinos—wailed like lost souls in his prose, proof of the failures and inconsistencies of the post-revolutionary regime. Among the gaffes made in early interpretations of Rulfo, the idea that he was giving a voice to "Indians" is particularly notable. Assuming Rulfo's characters belonged to a collective known as "Indians" illustrates how little academics in Mexico City (not to mention abroad) knew of the indigenous world that all scholars—fifty years later—now take ourselves to be specialists in. Rulfo's people are ranchers of old Spanish stock, as even Nuria Amat— otherwise so prone to Mexicanist clichés in her 2003 book *Juan Rulfo*— notes. Soon it became clear, given how often Rulfo was interviewed, that the skirmishes in his texts were more representative of the 1926–1929 Cristero War than the subsequent failure of agrarian reform.

The sociological folly of trying to identify Rulfo's subjects with specific actors in the Mexican Revolution was compounded by the dichotomy proposed by Emmanuel Carballo* in 1954. Rulfo, he claimed, represented realism, while Arreola—his rival and fellow Jaliscan—embodied the fantastic side of Mexican letters. That opposition, which now seems reductivist and misguided, stems from the taxonomical anguish that seems to afflict critics. And though it might be imprecise to say that *Pedro Páramo* is a fantastical novel, nowadays it's read as the work of a clairvoyant, a mythical fragment that chronicles the events taking place between the world of the living and that of the dead, in which Comala is a sort of limbo or infernal paradise.

None of Rulfo's biographers—who pay too much attention to the overwhelming burden of his international fame—venture to research his international reception. *Pedro Páramo*, unlike other Latin American works, soon stopped being associated with any of our national identities. The novel triumphed the world over, crossing history and languages, given that Pedro Páramo—as Juan García Ponce* stated in 1971—was a Homeric character and, like Ulysses, by being Nobody he became a melting pot of archetypes. The excesses of an interpretation that stripped Rulfo of all uniqueness were mitigated by the belief that his universality resulted from his astonishing ability—comparable only to that of Faulkner—to portray the myth of the patriarch and the destruction of agrarian communities, a wound on this civilizing body that made Rulfo's message legible throughout the world.

Open to interpretation, Rulfo's reception presents a biographical problem that only Reina Roffé, in *Juan Rulfo, las mañas del zorro* (2003), takes into account. Like other famous writers, Rulfo felt persecuted and misunderstood, and these feelings were proportionate to the astronomical proliferation of Rulfology. The author seemed to belittle himself out of hypersensitivity to his lack of literary output. Wounded pride, which other writers dealt with by writing compulsively and publishing incessantly, drowned Rulfo in "living bile," as his protagonist was described.

Reina Roffé gets down to the nitty-gritty, denouncing the self-righteousness and persecution complex that characterized Rulfo's milieu, recalling that "the idea that others harassed him to point out his faults and took delight in tormenting him and not leaving him alone was what bolstered the idea—to some degree a paranoid idea—that there was some sort of conspiracy against Rulfo. Even today there's talk of the existence of a train of conspirators who want to discredit his memory and impede any real assessment of his work, as if there weren't already sufficient criticism. His panegyrists only help propagate the idea of Rulfo as was victim of evil gossip that caused him and his family so much pain, turning him into an anguished, unhappy, increasingly lonely man . . ." (Roffé, *Juan Rulfo, las mañas del zorro*, 2003).

Silence is the third Rulfo problem. Rulfo was one of the most famous victims of what Julien Gracq called "the Rimbaud scandal," an insurmountable modern superstition that views a writer's vote of silence as mystifying and sees the impossibility of his continually producing prose as almost criminal. In other times it wasn't uncommon for men of letters—like courtiers and men of faith—to go and live out their waning days in a monastery or some bucolic idyll. But in this age, so eager to turn creators into degraded publicity machines, people found Rulfo's silence doubly scandalous; after all, Romanticism forced us to choose between elements of that ill-fated triad—silence, insanity, and suicide—that Maurice Blanchot saw as the inevitable fates of writers.

Rulfo was no Rimbaud, a young man who washed his hands of poetry and set out recklessly to earn a living in the desert; nor was he Hölderlin, committed to an asylum and eventually living out his last years under the care of a carpenter; nor was he Salinger, hermetically protected from the rapaciousness of his plebian admirers. No, Rulfo's literary silence was quite mundane, unfolding on a profane stage on which the tortured soul of an ex-writer wandered through airports and conference halls, heedful of the gossip of a clientele perversely demanding of him confirmation of the miracle—and he was equally as demanding of himself.

We'll never know if Rulfo would have traded that bittersweet pilgrimage for a lackluster oeuvre (such as Balzac's hundred novels, as per Jules Renard), an astronomical advance, and good press. But because of his determination—and perhaps against his will—he became the walking bad conscience of a "world literature" made fat on dollars and good causes, and astounded, as Augusto Monterroso[*] said, at the "heroic gesture of a man who, in a world clamoring for his works, respects himself and respects—and perhaps fears—others."

Any of the proposed explanations would justify his silence: insecurity, fierce self-criticism, the dual fear of failure and success, laziness, alcoholism, detoxes. We could choose to believe (deep down it makes no difference) in a Rulfo-Penelope who by day unwove what he'd written at night, or a Rulfo-Sisyphus who rolled the stone of his efforts back down the hill once reaching the top. There is evidence to support both: some people swear to have seen drafts of *La cordillera* and *Días sin floresta*, his two mythical, vanished novels. And there are those who claim that the posthumous *Los cuadernos de Juan Rulfo* (1994) contains all of that and more. But the reality is silence and resignation, and readers of his biographies can draw their own conclusions. I prefer an outlook that combines what Monterroso surmised with what his family said: that Rulfo, regardless of his fantasies and his wavering, essentially remained faithful to his conviction that he'd said what he needed to say in *El Llano en llamas* and *Pedro Páramo*. His agonized silence—regardless of the existential contingencies that brought it on—is a moral lesson to us all.

Of the three biographies, only Roffé's has the proper measure of distance—poised between admiration and distrust—for a biography. Unlike Roffé, who saw Rulfo—like any great writer—as captain of his fame, controlling it like a wily fox, Alberto Vital chose to draw upon significant events that tend toward the hagiographic characterization typical of authorized biographies.

Nuria Amat's book, on the other hand, is alarming in the carelessness she and her publishers exhibit, getting even some of the most pedestrian facts wrong. Amat mixes up tequila and mezcal, misspells Popocatépetl and Ixtaccíhuatl, mentions the "university of Mascarones" when in fact that's the name of UNAM's Faculty of Philosophy and Letters, makes out that the *Contemporáneos* wrote urban novels, and regularly gets names and dates wrong. Along with the crass ignorance of Mexico that Amat displays are a plethora of highbrow assessments, such as equating Rulfo with Kafka, and his mentor Efrén Hernández with Max Brod, and comparing Rulfo to the unfortunate W. G. Sebald based on their shared interest in photography. In an attempt to liken Rulfo to the greatest writers on the planet, Amat exhibits a mawkish reliance on what's already been published about him. Having said that, her attempt to make meaning of Rulfo's psychiatric problems, his stay at the La Floresta asylum, and the effects shock therapy might have had on him is praiseworthy. But that and other events in his life need further documentation before judgments are made.

Rulfo's father was killed—as was Dostoyevsky's—before he reached adulthood. That vital fact led Campbell to surmise that once the writer had narrated and mythologized his death in *Pedro Páramo*, he decided to stop. I tend to concur. But of the events—both legendary and obscure—explained by his biographers, few truly interested me, and given that I'm an assiduous biography reader that's something I found disquieting. Perhaps the answer lies in Vital's *Noticias sobre Juan Rulfo* (2003), an iconography that allows us to pore again and again over those now-famous photos of Rulfo, a poisoned chalice he bequeathed future generations to pique their impatience.

It's impossible not to see Rulfo's photographs as a supreme, metaphysical response to the cry of the century—returning a demand for words with even greater silence. The photographs don't describe or illustrate his work; instead they allow us to hear Rulfo's silence. According to one of his children, he was terrified of the damage his own words—spoken or written—might do him. And thus it was in geography, in the churches scattered across the plains and the self-portraits taken in the mountains, where Rulfo reconciled himself to the experiences of the Cristero War, genesis, and the apocalypse. By leaving behind thousands of negatives, this quasi-secret man opened up his inner world and gave us the rare privilege of glimpsing the landscapes of his clairvoyant soul.

SELECTED BIBLIOGRAPHY

Pedro Páramo, trans. Lysander Kemp, University of Texas Press, 1959.

Obras. El Llano en llamas. Pedro Páramo. Otros textos. El gallo de oro. La fórmula secreta, preface by Jaime García Terrés, FCE, Mexico, 1986.

Pedro Páramo, trans. Margaret Sayers Peden, Northwestern University Press, 1994.

Los cuadernos de Juan Rulfo, ed. Yvette Jiménez de Báez, ERA, Mexico, 1994.

Leonardo Martínez Carrizales, *Juan Rulfo, los caminos de la fama pública*, FCE, Mexico, 1998.

Reina Roffé, *Juan Rulfo, las mañas del zorro*, Espasa-Calpe, Madrid, 2003.

Alberto Vital, *Noticias sobre Juan Rulfo*, Editorial RM, Mexico, 2003.

Juan Ascencio, *Un extraño en la tierra. Vida de Juan Rulfo*, Debate, Mexico, 2007.

Roberto García Bonilla, *Un tiempo suspendido. Cronología de la vida y la obra de Juan Rulfo*, Conaculta, Mexico, 2008.

The Burning Plain and Other Stories, trans. George D. Schade, University of Texas Press, 1953.

S

SABINES, JAIME
(Tuxtla Gutiérrez, Chiapas, 1926 – Mexico City, 1999)

During the last decades of the twentieth century, Sabines was that century's Amado Nervo. But it wasn't just the ease of his sonorous verses, some of which are absolutely beautiful, that made him a national poet—defined by Valery Larbaud as a writer who manages to be adopted by the middle class without being expelled by the republic of letters. The author of *Horal* (1950) and *Tarumba* (1956) was greeted with respect by critics, while legions of sentimental young people devoted to the left after 1968 bought up all the editions of his books and flocked wildly to his readings. But behind Sabines's reputation, his readers endured a sort of family secret, a lesser evil akin to a clandestine affair: his loyalty to the Partido Revolucionario Institucional (PRI). After the 1994 neo-Zapatista uprising, this fact became quite risky since, additionally, the political and military class he belonged to in Chiapas, to whose members he'd dedicated tender, adoring poems, was none other than the target of indigenous protest. When Sabines died his audience had yet to digest that paradox, which is utterly representative of the Mexican Revolution's Ancien Regime.

Selected Bibliography
Otro recuento de poemas, 1950–1991, Joaquín Mortiz, Mexico, 1991.
Pieces of Shadow: Selected Poems of Jaime Sabines, trans. W. S. Merwin, Marsilio Publishers, 1996.

Adam and Eve, trans. Colin Carberry, Exile Editions, 2004.

Weekly Diary: Poems in Prose, trans. Colin Carberry, Exile Editions, 2004.

Tarumba: Poems, trans. Philip Levine, Sarabande, 2007.

SADA, DANIEL

(Mexicali, Baja California, 1953 – Mexico City, 2011)

In every line of every book, for many years now, Sada has proved himself the fiction-man of his generation. Few are as besotted—agonizingly, obstinately—with form as he: a goldsmith for whom each word—and this is unusual in novelists—is worth its weight in the stuff. Which explains why Sada is the author of the most difficult book in Mexican literature, *Porque parece mentira la verdad nunca se sabe* (1998). The sovereignty of language reigns so supreme in this tome that, rather than solicit readers, it almost eschews them. The verisimilitude of Sada's Mexican inferno—the only one we've seen at the turn of the twenty-first century—goes beyond the end and the means, politics and ethics, and rings out in a concert of words subjected to every conceivable denotation, connotation, and declination. Only in appearance is it colloquial; what we have here is the most "artistic" of prose. Sada, like so many great poets, believes octosyllables are the most natural rhythm for Spanish expression, and throughout the novel, he obsessively and eccentrically seeks (and rediscovers) this metric form.

Porque parece mentira la verdad nunca se sabe has been criticized for its length. That reproach, in and of itself, speaks volumes about the demise of fiction-worship in Mexico. To support such an insult—for it's not a critique—you'd have to sustain that the novel could have been written using some other economy of form. And Sada needed his six hundred pages as much as Gertrude Stein needed to go on as long as she did in *The Making of Americans*, as Thomas Wolfe did in *Of Time and the River*, and as Faulkner did in so many of his books, not to mention João Guimarães Rosa, Sada's most beloved inspiration. Length is at the heart of Sada's prose, which assures us that "we're going to move forward in time a bit, as if effectuating an apocryphal journey, but only with the aim of seeing a bird's eye view of the string of events befallen . . ." i.e. the number of words is inversely proportionate to the series of inconsequential events.

Electoral fraud in Remadrín—a godforsaken fictional town in the north-ern state of Capila, in the republic of "Mágico"—might, for readers yearning for magical realism, appear routine. But Sada plays a trick that imprisons us in a reality governed by Beckett-like rigor, where language derails the plot and paralyzes the characters. This is an author who provides no idle chatter for the philistines. It's worth noting that his theme is the pedestrian point-lessness of everyday undertakings. *Porque parece mentira la verdad nunca se sabe* is the *Oblomov* of Mexican literature: an odyssey of immobility, a de-sertology of tedium where every unfeasible aspect of hope has been deferred because "the closest thing to what's real is what should have been."

A novel that would verge on the impossible to translate, *Porque parece mentira la verdad nunca se sabe* recounts the misadventures of a cacique, the trials and tribulations of rivals and henchmen facing repression and death, their fleeting exile to the US, bodies in the trunks of cars, unlucky parents waiting for their disappeared children. And all during the unbearable mo-notony of a journey through the desert during the long, dark, anodyne years of electoral fraud in Mexico. This is a true rhetorical feat for Sada: a political novel with no ideology . . . or politics. The novel is lacking entirely in ulterior motives, be they moral or punitive, realist or mythological. Lunacy seems to summon the words, which moan like ululating old peasants in the Coahuila desert, singing traditional, melancholic "cardenche" songs.

Porque parece mentira la verdad nunca se sabe is as important a novel as Agustín Yáñez's *Al filo del agua* (1947; *The Edge of the Storm*, 1963). And as I note this, I marvel at both the—ungrateful?—oblivion Yáñez has fallen into and the ease with which Sada's astounding linguistic accomplishments will in time be digested. We've forgotten Yáñez's demands because José Re-vueltas* and Juan Rulfo met and exceeded them. And now Sada completes the circle, an author who once again snatches us from the arms of comfort as we head into a new century in which the didactic novel reigns over even the most rigorous minds. Reading this novel reminds us that our lives are a fruitless attempt to escape words, like the flocks of big, ugly birds circling over Remadrín.

I won't deny that on several occasions I was tempted to abandon the book. Or to start skipping paragraphs, pages, chapters. But more than out of re-spect for Sada and his work, more than just to be a responsible critic, it was remorse that kept me going. Each time I found myself growing irritated, each time I found something indecipherable, the pulse of a masterpiece egged me on. I needed to uncover the plot in that palaver like a man hell-bent on staring directly at the sun. And once I was dizzily blinded, the shadows, and shapes and colors, filled the void and meaning shone through.

Even without this masterpiece, Sada's body of work was already extensive. He began with *Lampa vida* (1980) and *Juguete de nadie y otras historias* (1985). *Albedrío* (1990) was his first important book, followed by urban sagas that left behind the northern deserts: *Luces artificales* (2001) and *Ritmo Delta* (2005). Rafael Lemus has written that Sada is not so much "a narrator as a prose. To call him a stylist denigrates him. He's one of the Spanish language's most extreme formalists, the most daring of Mexicans. His prose is invaluable but it's not easy to talk about . . . At the source of all literature was a disjuncture between speech and writing. That dilemma faded away without being resolved and now what prevails is an aseptic, acritical prose. Popular speech is ignored and writers either use a tame, literary style or else ineptly record echoes of the streets, in vain. There is no tension, save for a few authors. Sada's writing is directly connected to that initial problem, weighing up the popular and concealed connotations of every word. He turns to a speculative, Cervantes-style narrator who reflects aloud about the source of each sentence. He fuses *norteño* with academic to create a unique prose as unlike the former as the latter. Intellectual prose, uncommonly conscious. Tense prose, the slowest in our language. Humorous prose, experimenting—thankfully—from a parodic stance. Its greatest merit is constituting a style. Sada is that: a prose, a rhythm, a way of speculating on language. It's enough to read one page to recognize his style. It's so particular that it's not hard to foresee."

With *Porque parece mentira la verdad nunca se sabe*, Sada left me awestruck at the power of his art. He, more than anyone, knows the supreme efficacy of a perfect ending. Frightened off by an army of ghosts, Trinidad and her husband escape Remadrín to find a true home, leaving a note nailed to the door to tell their children—political *desaparecidos*—where they'll await them, certain of their return. While *Pedro Páramo* dramatized a father's fulmination, half a century later Sada recounts the children's never-ending flight, condemned to roam the land as dead as the words that bore them, the same ones that fly over the desert on a mission sure to fail, which is the pursuit of language from start to finish.

The writer with the most unmistakable prose in the Spanish language, Daniel Sada has constantly tested himself over the past decade and, like the true artist he is, emerged all the stronger for it, as his most recent novel *Casi nunca* (2008) proves. After *Porque parece mentira la verdad nunca se sabe*, a novel worthy of the greatest linguistic achievements of José Lezama Lima, Guillermo Cabrera Infante, and João Guimarães Rosa, Sada published a couple of unfocused self-parodies (*Luces artificiales, Ritmo Delta*), then returned to the novella (*La duración de los empeños simples*, 2006) and published two volumes of poetry (*El amor es cobrizo*, 2005, and *Aquí*, 2007) that serve to remind us that his prose is grounded in verse, in poetry.

Casi nunca is both a reflection on life in the provinces and an erotic novel. It's the most classic of Sada's novels, if one can make such a claim, for nothing is more like a Sada novel than another Sada novel. But his unmistakable mark is more than a style, as Rafael Lemus has noted. What's more, in *Casi nunca* he attempted to stem the tide of his prose, to control the flow, refusing to yield to the poetic rapture of his litanies by imposing a more ascetic structure.

The provinces are Sada's great overarching theme, and his novels (not just *Porque parece mentire la verdad nunca se sabe* but also 1988's *Albedrío* and to a lesser degree *Una de dos*, published in 1994) make this clear, as do those of Agustín Yáñez,* Juan Rulfo,* Juan José Arreola,* and Jorge Ibargüengoitia.* Of course Sada writes about the provinces in a way possible only for a writer bridging two centuries, offering a sort of desert baroque, as Roberto Bolaño noted when praising his fellow novelist. What happened over the past quarter of a century is quite interesting: those who were once known as "narrators of the desert," predictably seen as barbarous, became the classics, and their charismatic church attracted many writers hoping to be the new priest. A sort of sociological conception of justice overtook Mexico's literary imagination and following Sada, Jesús Gardea,* Eduardo Antonio Parra,* and Mexico's eccentric houseguest Roberto Bolaño,* the desert of Northern Mexico became the setting for the country's most memorable fiction, winning out over the indigenous south—and its mythology—and Mexico City, so impossible to capture.

I recently set myself the task of comparing *Casi nunca* to the novels of Yáñez, Rulfo, Arreola, and Ibargüengoitia. Like Yáñez, Sada is a lyrical writer, and there's something of the "Song of Songs" in *Casi nunca*. Reading a paragraph of *Al filo del agua* (1947; *The Edge of the Storm*, 1963), followed by one from *Casi nunca* is thought-provoking indeed. One verb tense follows the other like a planet completing its rotation. The events in Yáñez's book take place in the present and those in Sada's have just occurred, but both authors are prophets of the past, authors of another *Rusticatio Mexicana* (the bucolic 1782 Latin poem written by exiled Jesuit Rafael Landívar). Both alternate between vernacular and poetic language. Both have enriched our cultural heritage as well as revolutionized our syntax, testing the limits of word order in sentences and pushing Spanish literary language to the limits of resistance. The good and bad reasons lazily cited for *not* reading Sada are also those that doomed Yáñez: they're both exasperating writers, fastidious and "artificial" in the way that only a baroque soul can be.

Be that as it may, Sada is a reader of Rulfo capable of meeting the demands set by *El llano en llamas* and *Pedro Páramo*. Rulfo created a magical blend of rural expressions, rustic Spanish, and traditional language (though not indigenous, as some misguided critics continue to insist), and Sada realized from the start that because Rulfo's talent for synthesis was absolute, there was no way he could take that road any further that it had already been taken. So he made a decision that estranged him from less demanding readers and he cleared the way for the realm of exceptionalism. Where Rulfo was a master of understatement and strictly measured words, Sada opened the floodgates of language.

Of course, he is not as somber or deep or thoroughly tragic as Rulfo and lacks the lightness and nonchalance of Arreola. If one reads *Casi nunca* side by side with *La feria* (1963), the Arreola novel we tend to avoid most, it becomes clear that what in Arreola is carnivalesque, a vacation, an interruption from the finite order of the world, in Sada is an eternity in hell.

Few prose writers are as oppressive as Sada. His poetry is proof of that: like scarecrows, his poems never move. And thus when compared to Ibargüengoitia, he surpasses him not in humor but in compassion, in the tenderness and expertise with which he writes of the provinces, their narrow-mindedness, the big hell of the small town, and the suffocating atmosphere of the wide-open desert. Cloistered in its vastness, Demetrio Sordo, the hero of *Casi nunca*, flees the remote ranches he administers in order to recapture the boundless universe of the bedroom. While Ibargüengoitia sketches, a carica-turist, Sada, when he engages in humor, is not just funny but takes us back to the innocent world of silent movies. The capers that ensue, for instance as a result of money stolen, hidden, or squandered, are something to see.

And the Catholic world of appearances that is a source of humor in *Casi nunca* might have cured the syphilis that struck down Catholic writer Ramón López Velarde. In Sada's provinces sex is realistic, un-romantic and guilt-free; he demystifies the conservative sexual mores that so tormented López Velarde. Sada doesn't see the provinces as some sort of nascent state of urbanity, and *Casi nunca* gives the discrete, well-documented feel of a his-torical novel taking place during the post–World War II years of industrial-ization in Coahuila, where Demetrio Sordo seeks his insignificant, ordinary destiny. But being historical, the novel is never anachronistic; what interests Sada is unraveling "the essence of man," as Álvaro Mutis* once said—praise that at the time I misinterpreted as pompous but that now, reading his erotic novel, makes perfect sense.

Agronomist Sordo's decision to visit a brothel and his relationship with the prostitute Mireya take up the first half of the book, a genital hymn to Petronius unlike almost anything in Mexican literature, which is more prud-ish than we tend to believe. There are few truly erotic Mexican novels, and those written by the previous generation (e.g., those by Juan García Ponce*) are more like novels of transgression, something alien to Sada. Sada is no sadist. The thousand and one variations on coitus he versifies in *Casi nunca* are instances of joyful freedom, release, and comfort that libertines found in sex—the only natural activity to justify our short stay on earth—without any need for torture, or romance.

Demetrio Sordo abandons Mireya, asleep on a bus, after stuffing a wad of bills into her bust, and like the great writer he is, Sada resists the temptation of having her reappear later in his life. Even that is somehow traditional, and as the brothel is one thing and married life quite another, our hero decides to settle down and submit to the lengthy offensive launched by Renata (his hometown girlfriend) and her mother, which will culminate in securing his hand in marriage.

Casi nunca is a study in both etiquette and sex, which *do* go together although we might forget that. The hooker Mireya and the demure Renata both love and desire equally and the novel's happy ending resides in the triumph of nature, if we can call it that, over society. Sex as both a motor and as anguish will rule the newlyweds' bedroom just as it illuminated the whorehouse room. Renata is the one who decides that sex is sacred, thereby turning a story of the provinces into a libertine novel: sex as the other side of urbanity, the true test of citizenship, that kingdom in the sky that might be hidden behind the neighbors' door.

On leafing through Fuchs's *Illustrated History of Moral Sexuality*, attempting to find something that might sum up the novel's denouement, I came upon a quotation by Austrian baroque monk Abraham a Sancta Clara that prophesied the frigidity later attributed to the bourgeois world: "While once, on regarding the nuptial bed after the wedding night, it looked as if a couple of bears had been fighting, today one can barely see the traces of a sacrificed chicken."

SELECTED BIBLIOGRAPHY

Porque parece mentira la verdad nunca se sabe, Tusquets Editores, Mexico, 1998.
Casi nunca, Anagrama, Barcelona, 2008.
Ese modo que colma, Anagrama, Barcelona, 2010.
Almost Never, trans. Katherine Silver, Graywolf, 2012.

SALAZAR MALLÉN, RUBÉN

(Coatzacoalcos, Veracruz, 1905 – Mexico City, 1986)

Shortly before he died, Salazar Mallén attracted the attention, curiosity, and respect of several young writers. The generations prior to mine were surprised or disgusted at our interest in a writer who some thought dead or retired—the retribution of oblivion. Those of us who got close to him weren't after a literary discovery. We simply heard the call of a dubious legend. And Salazar Mallén postponed his death a few years in order to live out a fantasy and experience the warmth of one last clique. He was a hemiplegic, and men who suffer the misfortune of physical defects often choose between shame and provocation. Salazar Mallén boasted about his twisted body— the spiteful called him "the swastika" for his jutting limbs—and decided to prowl Mexican literature like a lone wolf, turning his nose up at the banquet leftovers and opting to spread his rabid nature.

The man we loved introduced us to a blithering binge that started in the twenties, explained Tina Modotti's complicity in the murder of Cuban communist Julio Antonio Mella, and returned obsessively to the topic of his friend Jorge Cuesta.* On occasion, too, Rubén lost his composure and inappropriately demanded the attentions of women. The ensuing scandals were more than the lusty tragedy of a "dirty old man," as he referred to himself. His feverish passion for an artificial life of booze and whores thunderously conveyed his need to outdo biological discretion and intellectual decorum.

To us, Salazar Mallén evoked a world of cantinas with sawdust floors and urinals by the bar. He tried to unnerve us with barbershop political discussions, and although his ultra-right turns of phrase didn't faze anyone, they embodied the Mexico that was hidden by modernity's clean-up campaigns. Rubén was the alcoholic journalist, the man who knew every brothel, the failed and resentful Mexican, both bitter and vitriolic. His calling card, if he had one, was rejected by power and money, the left and the right. His reputation was that of Evil in its Mexican guise, an incessant irritation, a presence that somehow managed to survive in the desert of a literature crippled by State cultural media, by a recently assumed—and doubly suspicious—open democracy, by protocol and desertions of the cause. Salazar Mallén was rooted there like a weed in the garden of "progress," harmless yet hostile. His story was that of a marginal writer. After the seventies, the term "marginal" still held some political and cultural prestige. And although there was a radical difference between Rubén's marginalization and that being preached by the kids or grandkids of '68, he and his young friends—myself included— agreed not to confuse them. Salazar Mallén put his life on display, having embraced his failure, which was symbolized by poverty and vulgarity. And when the recognition of young writers and institutions was heaped upon him, he didn't apologize, didn't deny the bile-ridden incoherence of his intellectual trajectory, didn't ask for an armchair in academia. He was grateful to be accepted as he was, and that was how he died. José Emilió Pacheco* has noted the last slap in the face of a posterity he didn't want and probably doesn't have: Rubén died the same day as Borges, departing alone, through the back door, far from the bright lights of the century [...]

Within his vast body of work, *Soledad* (1944) restores confidence in his word as a writer. Aquiles Alcázar, the book's protagonist, is a man of strength and weakness, as his name—literally "Achilles Fortress"—suggests. An existential cripple, he's a bureaucrat worthy of Gogol waiting for some workmates in Mexico City's zócalo. Together they are to take a trip to Cuernavaca. It doesn't occur. As he waits, this beast chews his bitterness like cud. *Soledad* is a beautiful and pathetic text, the refuge Salazar Mallén took between his binges, ideological frenzies, and shadowboxing. There he was able to forget the politician and the beggar, the prostitute and the heroin addict. That was when he wrote this melancholic text, the fruit of a lack of love, the memory of lost provinces, the disparaging of a festering city. With *Soledad*, Salazar Mallén freed himself of the most toxic part of himself, stared down into the volcanoes, stopped bearing the cross of hate and set down his pen for a few minutes to wax nostalgic. Just for an instant. It's almost strange that he didn't burn the manuscript when his rage returned.

Salazar Mallén lived in the hell of Mexican culture like a battered, obscene demon chosen from a coven of forgotten writers, brought together to fight each other, their loved ones, the privileged sons of style, those who won. And somewhere far off he's still out there writing his acid comedy and representing the condemned—that cackling, deformed, old bastard. (*Tiros en el concierto: Literatura mexicana del siglo V*, 1997)

SELECTED BIBLIOGRAPHY

La sangre vacía, Oasis, Mexico, 1982.

Soledad, Premiá Editora, Mexico, 1985.

El paraíso podrido, Universidad Autónoma del Estado de Mexico, Toluca, 1987.

Camaradas. Soledad, preface by Christopher Domínguez Michael, Conaculta, Mexico, 2010.

SEGOVIA, FRANCISCO
(Mexico City, 1958)

Son of short story writer Inés Arredondo* and poet Tomás Segovia,* Francisco Segovia sensed early on that he should administer his very rich (and no less asphyxiating) inheritance not like a Romantic writer obsessed with the artist's exceptionality but like a musician happily resigned to being just one more in a family of artisans. Which is why craftsmanship—seen as control over a technique and as well-executed words—is his most notable characteristic. It's better expressed in his essays than in his stories and poems, as if criticism were somehow a more appropriate place to hold an ongoing dialogue with literary families (his own and others), something that defines him.

Without crowing, and with the scruples of an artisan more than the boastfulness of an heir to literary lineage, Segovia has published several books of essays over the last twenty years. Some of them are quite close to my heart. This is only natural, for it's in the work of our own generation that we often find that scrapbook that links our sentimental education to the intellectual one. *Ocho notas* (1984), *Retrato hablado* (1996), *Invitación al mito* (2001), and *Sobre escribir* (2002) all contain outstanding texts that do just that. Some of the more memorable are dedicated to Bulgarian novelist Elias Canetti, Italian writer Cesare Pavese, the epic *Gilgamesh*, general literary history, and the mythological makeup of vampires and other monsters. The book *Jorge Cuesta: la cicatriz en el espejo* also belongs in this category, and it is the longest and most personal of his essays.

It's impossible not to note Cuesta's* refreshing and paradoxical posterity. Although his horrific death made the crime reports—as Gilberto Owen noted in 1942—Cuesta's hundredth anniversary saw a new edition of his complete works—the third in forty years. He's become the crux of an entire academic and bibliographic apparatus that ranges from the sublime to the ridiculous and includes all manner of political, rhetorical, and psychoanalytic studies, as if Cuestaology had become a required visa in the passport of literary knowledge. Trailing behind only Sor Juana's *Primero sueño* and Gorostiza's* *Muerte sin fin*, Cuesta's *Canto a un dios mineral* is on the verge of becoming the most interpreted Mexican poem. This strange poem might be related to Heidegger and the pre-Socratics, although as Segovia himself notes, philosophical readings of Cuesta were nearly all filtered through Ortega y Gasset and José Gorostiza. In truth, we're all responsible for constructing the labyrinth where we place Cuesta, the man nominated time and again as Mexico's first modern, the unexpected classic who bestowed new meaning on Mexican literature.

Segovia opens *Jorge Cuesta: la cicatriz en el espejo* with a recap of the author's adventures in the jungle of pleasure, taking as point of departure Octavio Paz's* exclusion of Cuesta in *Poesía en movimiento* (1966), which he later felt obliged to somewhat dubiously justify. Then he catalogs and expounds the various theses on Cuesta put forth in books by Louis Panabière, Nigel Grant Sylvester, and Alejandro Katz. And, like them or not, these theses all possess the virtue, in my opinion, of addressing the core issues. An academic in the correct sense of the word, Segovia is blessed with the admirable patience required to develop his own arguments, explaining Cuesta's tendency to make us play chicken-and-egg with criticism and creation: the accepted, unresolved tension between Nietzsche's "song" and Valéry's "method"; writing for critique or for the canon. He concludes by proposing that more than living out a destiny, Cuesta lived out a character.

Segovia uses "character" in the Taoist sense, that is, a permanent and preformed condition rather than a fate created or planned in the Judeo-Christian sense, an embodiment chiseled over time, which must by definition be historical. Unlike other exegetes—myself included—who tried to do a balancing act between the tightrope of Cuesta's writing and the void into which he dove personally, Segovia made a categorical choice. For him, there was only one Cuesta, a monist character that included the hermetic poet, the literary critic, and the public moralist; the accursed writer and the sad alchemist; the man of intellectual rigor and the self-mutilating suicide; the sane and the insane. He admits Cuesta's contradictions, but sees them as support for his idea of a monster sent to the world preformed, fated and imperfect in all its harmonious complexity.

Over the last quarter of a century, Cuesta has gone from being "the only Mexican writer with a legend," to becoming counter-proof of a national canon. As both witness and accomplice to that transformation, with some distance I can now affirm that it would have been surprising had he *not* attracted that much posthumous attention, given that he published not one book while living and killed himself after a horrific act of self-mutilation. Morbid curiosity—a wide-open body of work and a mutilated body—probably finds one of its crowning achievements in Segovia's book, which, in that chicken-and-egg, puts criticism before creation.

I said above that *Jorge Cuesta: la cicatriz en el espejo* formed part of the collection of essays Segovia dedicated to vampires and other monsters. That's because for Segovia, Cuesta is—almost explicitly—Doctor Frankenstein's creature, that homunculus who scarred himself by stitching on different pieces of flesh, skin, and humanity. This Frankenstinian Cuesta is a statue—or wax figurine—of stylized classical perfection, a fact that's odder still if you consider that he was almost entirely built out of Romantic materials. The result is disconcerting, alien to the domain of literary history, a writer who—if Segovia is right—could have existed in any part of the post-Nietzschean West.

As we essayists often do, Francisco Segovia ends up confusing the writer with the metaphor he created to describe his oeuvre, merging Cuesta with the critical fiction he himself created. And that Frankenstein displays some of the characteristics that critics have traditionally portrayed as inherent in Cuesta: it's difficult to free his image from the gossip and slander that—despite lack of documentation—plagued him. Segovia's critical intelligence is peppered with the macabre literary folklore surrounding Cuesta. And though Segovia would disagree with my opinion—after all, it contradicts the essence of his philosophy—I think *Jorge Cuesta: la cicatriz en el espejo* shines more for its treatment of his poetry than it does in the overwritten teratological image of Cuesta it portrays.

In the end, the book succeeds due to an intrinsic structure I can't fail to mention: it's a dialogue—neither private nor public—between Segovia and his mother Inés Arredondo, who in 1982 published *Acercamiento a Jorge Cuesta*, one of the first serious studies of the Veracruz poet. After finishing Segovia's book, I reread Arredondo's, which she explicitly dedicated to her children. A quarter of a century later, Segovia is returning that dedication. And although he only cites his mother once, it's still clear (and touching) that the book is a sort of family discussion, a conversation invoking those familial household bugbears, the legacy of a handful of obsessions passed down from generations—which is what makes literature a tradition. It's not that Segovia is contradicting or contesting Arredondo's assertions; instead, he's written a baroque variation on an original theme composed by his mother. Both books, written in very different language, could almost be the same work in a different time. Mother and son looked in the mirror and she reflected for them a certain image of them both—one that sees human reality as a poetics. In the history of literature, there can't be many other cases of a confluence like the one that flowed around Jorge Cuesta, between Inés Arredondo and Francisco Segovia.

SELECTED BIBLIOGRAPHY

Jorge Cuesta: la cicatriz en el espejo, Ediciones Sin Nombre, Mexico, 2004.
Arredondo, Inés, *Acercamiento a Jorge Cuesta*, SEP, Mexico, 1982.

SEGOVIA, TOMÁS

(Valencia, Spain, 1927 – Mexico City, 2011)

In Mexico, Segovia is the great Romantic of the second half of the twentieth century. A strict Romantic, if there is such a thing, like few other Latin American writers of our time. For proof, read his text on Gérard de Nerval, written in 1967, which he reaffirmed by republishing it almost unmodified as the prologue to his translation of Nerval in *Poesía y prosa literaria* more than thirty years later. Now as then, Segovia says, "since Romanticism, not one truly central thing about us has changed." And once the promise of a new society and the convenient idea of a "new man" were postponed or discarded—having been so lightly and earnestly proposed—what was left was Romantic inspiration. For, "despite the astonishingly different appearance of our times, the eyes watching it haven't learned new ways of seeing."

That opinion is hotly contestable, even more so in 2004 than when it first appeared in 1967, precisely because it's truly critical: it gets to the root of the question. And it's interesting and disconcerting to know that it's not the opinion of a traditionalist, but a modern who knows his stuff. He knows his Roman Jakobson, Claude Lévi-Strauss, Jacques Lacan, Michel Foucault, and Jacques Derrida like the back of his hand, having translated them into Spanish. And from—as well as against—their perspectives, Segovia argues that

Romanticism is the insurmountable limit of our time. Whether it's Sartrean, or doctrinaire, or an echo of the emphatic style of the seventies—a Romantic decade it was—Segovia's opinion escapes the relativist thinking and paradoxical ambiguity of those of us who, stuck between the twentieth and twenty-first centuries, still aren't sure whether or not to call ourselves postmodern.

"Nerval's world was absolutely inconceivable from Descartes's world, even from Voltaire's world," Segovia claims. Nevertheless, grand narratives, the ways we project our vision of the world and of life—dialectics, historicism, the Revolution, the unconscious, philosophies of life, and thoughts on temporability including evolution, the idea of progress and communism in the concrete sense—stick around until further notice; strictly speaking, nothing about that is heterogeneous to Nerval's world," he concludes in his essay in *Contracorrientes* (1973).

When someone argues against Romanticism, Segovia claims, it's often in the name of something else that, when it comes down to it, is also Romanticism, and anything that doesn't generate some type of Romanticism is sterile. Even surrealism, taken to be so characteristic of the twentieth century, simply repackaged many of the lost treasures of Romanticism, the moderns' only truly untamed inspiration. Segovia, like Octavio Paz* between 1967's *Corriente alterna* and 1974's *Los hijos del limo*—unsurprisingly the period when the two writers were closest—embodies the sort of neo-Romantic rebellion (in its most profound and least phenomenological iteration) associated with 1968. Through existentialism and structuralism, love as revolutionary knowledge and the mythological jungles of Lévi-Strauss, castigated Romantic insanity and scorned clinical insanity, Freud as a "tragic poet" on a pedestal and the academic empire of Foucault, the "reverse purism" of Breton and his love of Denis de Rougemont's *Love in the Western World*, Segovia has always managed to be witness, commentator, and theoretician. And he's one of the few writers—along with and at times more than Paz, who was more political—who's always had a commanding view, like the Alps, over his time.

But that easy familiarity with great heights doesn't mean that Segovia—like Novalis, Hölderlin, and Kleist—is a visionary poet drunk on Nordic air who sees himself as Caspar David Friedrich's *Wanderer Above the Sea of Fog*, painted in 1818 and reproduced a thousand times since. He's got too much faith in earthly Mediterranean sustenance. Segovia, as seen in *Poética y pro-fética*, sees Romanticists related not to the Middle Ages but to Antiquity—which is a very Hölderlinesque take: Romanticism as Greece.

Since Mexican poetry was dominated for decades by classicists, neo-classicists, and Parnassians (from Enrique González Martínez to the *Contemporáneos*), and since Paz, his closest contemporary, was only partially so, Segovia has been our most convincing Romanticist. Until Paz died, Segovia stood in his shadow, though only because two stars whose orbits cross paths create shadows. And then Segovia became the great Mexican poet. His status as son of Spanish Civil War exiles enabled him, in turn, to take on a certain foreignness that, although convenient for his unique form of vanity, was more imaginary than real.

Segovia, as a writer, is like a mason: he sees writing as a workshop where master artisans meet. And in that sense, he's not Romantic—or at least deviates from the myth (or neurosis) of originality. For him, a poet is not so much an officiator as an artisan who must master meter before venturing beyond its limits. And rather shockingly, meter, he says, was never taught to him as the tool that to a large extent makes a poet. In the various prosodic guides that accompany his poetry—since free verse, he knows, is a largely modern fallacy—Segovia defends the "versed verse" and in fact submits it as the "school" all aspiring poets should attend.

Seen as Romantic and medieval and Greek, Segovia makes sense. His poetic person is "the whole world's relative," as he says in *Anagnórisis*, and as Guillermo Sucre sees him in *La máscara, la transparencia*, his excellent essay on Latin American poetry. That quality, as any reader who picks up *Poesía (1943–1997)* (1998) will see, does not necessarily guarantee variety and at times gives the impression—equally shocking—that Segovia has written the same poem five hundred times, using every possible linguistic combination.

From his earliest verses—somewhere between Gustavo Adolfo Bécquer and Juan Ramón Jiménez—to the books he wrote as a self-proclaimed "old poet," Segovia has consistently remained faithful to worldly sustenance: the day, the light, the seasons (particularly autumn), and especially women as the supreme experience. I find no great downfalls in his work. And with Segovia, rather than the different "color" periods characteristic of painters, what we have are the slightly less perceptible moods of a musician, although I know Segovia sees himself as a disciple of long-lived Murcia painter-poet Ramón Gaya. And for someone who spent several weeks on his *Poesía completa*—certainly not the best way to read a poet—I was very refreshed by his shifting moods in *Noticia natural (1988–1992)* and relaxed lesser poems like "Epistola a Juan Vicente Melo" and the glorious *Sonetos votivos*—some of the most beautiful erotic verses ever written in Spanish.

His monotony, or flatness, is deceptive; in fact, Segovia was constantly ascending, taking us to the peak whence we can see craters and valleys: *Historias y poemas* (1958–1967), *Anagnórisis* (1964–1967), and *Cantata a solas* (1983). After these collections comes not a hasty fall but a meditative, orderly descent, which he himself recognizes. "I was a better poet twenty years ago," he confessed on winning the Juan Rulfo prize. He knows that the goal is not the summit but the return home, the completed journey.

When Segovia started out, he was caught up in the drama of "pure poetry"; now he's almost like Nestor: a great and complete man, made so by the experience of woman and thus deified, as per Romanticist demands. Great writers, true poets, tend to fulfill the prophecies of their own work. In his early days, Segovia augured "completa mi obra será un día / todo un mar rico y cambiante / que en un profundo acorde visto / fundirá todo el pequeño esmero / sobre él flotará mi vida, dischosa como un dios / y como un dios cumplido y sin futuro" ("completed my work will one day be / a whole rich and changing sea / that in one deep chord, seen / will melt all the small troubles / upon it will float my life, lucky as a god / and as a god fulfilled and without future"). And in *Historias y poemas*, we hear the sage speaking in a narrative voice that crops up from time to time in his oeuvre. "I had some children who soon I found sad, some beautiful women who soon I began to avoid, some acquaintances with whom I knew not what to do."

Anagnórisis, a long poem interspersed with a series of shorter poems, is Segovia's most analyzed work and the one that best fits into Mexican poetry, seen as a succession of great, somewhat philosophical poems (Gorostiza's* *Muerte sin fin*, Cuesta's* *Canto a un dios mineral*, Paz's* *Piedra de Sol*, Lizalde's* *Cada cosa es Babel*, Huerta's* *Incurable* . . .). In it, Orfeo and Eurídice are the main characters, but they're not protagonists in the neo-classical sense, as has been claimed. Gabriel Zaid,* for example, sees the poem as "a long Romantic soliloquy ruled by nostalgia, about orphanhood and exile, by a man who was a child, who was king . . . the book did not need the two or three Greek words that instead make us think of a retelling of myths. Although every personal myth is related to all mythology, the true source of *Anagnórisis* lies in experience . . ." (*Obras, 2. Escritos sobre poesía*, 1993).

Segovia's main poetic character is the lover as nomad, and in that sense anagnorisis—defined as the moment when two fictional characters meet and make critical discoveries about one another—is crystal clear. What the lover is searching for is divine equality in incest—that other pole of love—which in 1961 Segovia saw as eroticism's "revolutionary" essence: finding a sister in love to restore—purely—romantic harmony to the world. Segovia's Romanticist militancy has led him to defend heterosexuality at times when it wasn't opportune or politically correct to do so, butting heads with feminism's vindictive simplifications (in *Cuaderno inoportuno*, 1987) and the facile and now traditional association that some homosexual poets established between heterosexuality—which Luis Cernuda* called "conjugal dishwater"—and the bourgeois spirit. If Goethe saw marriage as the only work of art worthy of any mortal, Segovia sees erotic love as being the only transcendent experience still available to today's modern, secular man—and woman.

Cantata a solas is, for several reasons, my favorite Segovia book. First (and this is nothing trivial given that he's a Romanticist), because I read it during a representative phase of my youth—the throes of heartbreak—when I woke up one morning and tore out my hair in desperation, finding my lover of the time gone (the "time" was a living hell). The imprecatory tone of *Cantata a solas* was more than simply consolation; it demanded of "me" a true sacrifice: "Nada te han prometido / De qué te quejas / esta heredad no es tuya / Por qué la tomas y no la dejas / Lo que eres y no eres / Te lo has buscado / Quién tenía que amarte / Quién por haber vivido te debe algo" ("Nothing was promised you / What do you complain of / this legacy is not yours / Why do you take it and not leave it / Whatever you are and are not / You have earned / Who was obliged to love you? / Who for having lived owes you anything?")

Later, the poet of *Cantata a solas* makes a plea to "No disputarle el mundo al formidable invierno / No confundir la casa y la intemperie / No regalar al monte y las arenas / nuestras cuatro paredes / para irnos a vivir en los torrentes / En el lecho sangriento del instante / En el mar para siempre del vagabundeo / Con la pandilla de los sentimientos / Con la tribu de lobos de los elementos / No traicionar los pactos / Y más que nada no creer en el amor del tiempo / Nunca cerrar los ojos en el beso" ("Not challenge the world for formidable winter / Not confuse home and outdoors / Not give the hills and the sands / our four walls / to go and live in the torrents / In the bloody bed of the instant / In the sea that is always roaming / With the gang of sentiments / With the pack of wolves of the elements / Not to betray the pacts / And above all not to believe in the love of all times / Never close your eyes in a kiss").

"Reading a true poem (there are so few) is a tremendous experience," Segovia said in reference to Paz. And reading *Cantata a solas* bears this out. It's an intellectual poem that offers us Nietzsche, Rimbaud, Hegel, Simone Weil, and Heinrich von Kleist, one of his favorite Romantic poets. "De haber querido lo que no he querido / Mi único anhelo exultante escribió von Kleist / Dos días antes del doble suicidio / Es hallar un abismo / lo bastante profundo / Para saltar a él junto a ella / Lo encontró a los dos días / Es cosa de buscar con ganas" ("For having I wanted what I did not want / My only exultant wish von Kleist wrote / Two days before the double suicide / Is to find an abyss / deep enough / For him to jump beside her / He found it in two days / That takes some looking"). And, finally, *Cantata a solas* is a book written at about the same time as *Poética y profética*, and thus the poem resonates with the treatise (and vice versa), creating one of the richest and most stimulating reading experiences I've ever had the luxury and pleasure of encountering.

A profoundly meditated, determined reflection on the academic doctrines that dismantled the teaching of literature in the sixties and seventies, *Poética y profética* (1985) is not the grousing work of a doctrinaire, nor is Segovia a "pyromaniac in slippers," to use J. G. Merquior's phrase, of the sort taking over schools all over the West. The poet Segovia is less informal than he seems, a teacher we'd call an autodidact if the term didn't have such a high-and-mighty air of scornful exceptionalism about it.

Using a forgotten work by Lope de Vega (*El villano en su rincón*) as the basis for his argument in *Prosa y poética*, Segovia both demanded and exercised academic freedom against the literary technocrats who, taking refuge in human sciences and "scientific method," tried to take the literature out of literature. Several years before Harold Bloom (whose work on Shakespeare Segovia translated) published *The Western Canon* and sounded the alarm against the so-called "school of resentment," Segovia stood out as a dissident, at least in the obsequious world of Latin American theory. Those arriving at universities (and graduate programs), he lamented, now lack what used to be called a humanistic education or liberal arts background, a deficiency that turns them into easy prey for quackery, half-truths, and the logophobia of structuralism and post-structuralism.

Segovia, who read Lévi-Strauss—for whom he feels the dangerous empathy that links the Romanticist to the romantic—carefully and passionately, isn't hunting epigones. He examines Roman Jakobson and Louis Hjelmslev directly, alleging that something was wrong from the start with their notion of the poetic function of language. He's not the first to say so, nor does he try to claim he's the village genius who "proves" that the unconscious, natural selection, or the theory of relativity is false. I'm not professionally qualified to thoroughly analyze the insistent, double line of reasoning—as both poet and scholar—that Segovia presents against structuralism. But what I can say is that by confronting Barthes, Segovia convinced me that it's a waste of time— as I already suspected, for reasons my ignorance can't justify—to maintain equivalence between signification and paraphrase, between the most and the least complex. That is, criticism can never equal the work it critiques and to which it owes its existence. It's not often you get to read such a well-mediated and effective declaration against the idea, epitomized by Barthes, that literature is a metalanguage. No, it's not. Literature is a critique of life.

Poética y profética scrutinizes the love of obscurity seen in some post-structuralists, explaining that they're not so much responding to the objectivity required by science as they are to the dogmatic inflexibility of revealed religion and its contingent fanaticism, except that they also close down all that's open and fecund in religious language. Like positivism in its day, logocide—as Merquior called it in *From Prague to Paris: A Critique of Structuralist and Post-Structuralist Thought* (1986)—didn't defeat religion, it just substituted new superstitions in its place. Segovia wasn't the only Mexican writer to dive into the Pandora's box of literary theory, but he was the first to come out with a political-poetic treatise testifying to what a mess it was.

Of the many forms of barbarism in contemporary thought attributable to post-structuralism, *Poética y profética* notes the "vaguely Freudian" mélange of poetry and therapy—the simultaneous veneration and denigration of desire—that characterizes the popular ideas of our times; the vindication of individual sovereignty over psychoanalysis, which pretends that the meaning of life is not to be found where the patient living it lives; and the kind of linguistics that sees the meaning of language as located elsewhere, someplace far off. Segovia, of course, argues for the subject and for a literalness that ties in to his view of the translator as one who is not exactly a reader, since for him "the text begins and ends in itself, it's unusable, totally foreign, uninterpretable, invaluable, unjustifiable."

Segovia's essayistic style isn't brilliant, and he seems to reproduce the obscurity and dryness of many of the texts he critiques. *Poética y profética* is an intentionally vocally arduous and roundabout treatise, a book that doesn't lie to readers and, in a sense, helps them across a wasteland. And that frankness—or rudeness—again justifies a comparison with Paz, which becomes manifest in the many pages of the book on *Claude Lévi-Strauss y el nuevo festín de Esopo* (1965) and structuralist anthropology. Segovia has mastered structuralist thinking and read more and more carefully than Paz, whose little book on Lévi-Strauss, he admits in the first few pages, was written from the notes he took while reading for pleasure, without underlining. But the brilliant reader and his blinding clarity will endure, and Paz's very different Lévi-Strauss—unfairly, perhaps—will be remembered.

Basing his analysis on the case of Kleist, Segovia is convinced that Romanticism is our Greece and that the Romantics' great lyric myth will be, for us, what mythical thought was for the Greeks. That Promethean function appears in veiled form in Segovia's poetry, but in *Poética y profética*, it's forthright. Greek tragedy assumes two laws that man must respect: natural law and positive law. Only Romanticism, Segovia claims, allows us to move toward a possible reconciliation and "go both ways as much as possible" before reaching an erotic outcome. He still believes—as did the Romantic prophets—that the tension between those two laws might explode and in so doing separate the opponents, perhaps overcoming contradictions such as those inherent to Hegelian Marxism and Romanticed surrealism.

In that vein, Segovia, like Paz, puts his faith in the visionary courage—or poetic naïveté—of the erotic myth (i.e., the relationship between the sublimated lovers, akin to Rougemont's sublimation of courtly love) that sees opposition coming to an end either via the orgasm or the child. In fact, one of Segovia's more moving poems justifies the recklessness of being born: "El nacido proviene de grutas inmundas, el aire lo sofoca, y sólo por la espléndidad mirada, tarde, después de los boqueos, se justifica todo nacimiento" ("The newborn comes from filthy caverns, choked by air, and only in the splendid gaze, later, after wailing, is all birth justified"). That scatology can be seen in Paz, too, though his is a more classic (or static) variety, expressed in the poetic instant.

Segovia and Paz (both very Bretonian) believe that only through poetry—and the politics of spirit—can history finally lead, at least figuratively, to harmony. Then the world as we know it will come to an end and poetry will be the news to end all news. Though both are descendents of Nerval's world, Paz and Segovia ended up taking different paths. Attracted by the gravitational pull of politics, Paz became a liberal—or, if you will, a conservative who rejected the smoke and mirrors of prophesy. Segovia, in keeping with his ideas, drifted toward certain iterations of radical humanitarianism, and in his old age—aggravated by the injustices of the world—sometimes loses his cool and puts on the mask of a Hegelian "beautiful soul" much like those he mocked in *Poética y profética*. But even then he's a Romantic, deeming any comparison of "subversive" and "repressive" violence to be illegitimate, which explains his sympathy for rebels, who sometimes use his rationale (with his blessing) in public to lend themselves philosophical credibility. Segovia isn't personally aiming for the love of action that, for Kleist, turned into tragedy (and for Byron turned into heroism, be it hallowed or ridiculed), but he sanctions the possibility of waging war in the name of love—which means that for him it can be both Christian and revolutionary to raise the sword for love.

"Anyone who writes in public," Segovia said in reference to Calderón de la Barca, "is seeking an interlocutor in Greek tragedy, even if they're not thinking about it, or don't even know anything about it." Tragedy is not an event in history but the place where history makes itself visible. That's the revelation, the fount of clarity, that *Poética y profética* is dedicated to, and it's one of the few Spanish-language works of criticism I'd call a must-read, because it asks a crucial question: are we still or have we stopped being Romantics? And this leads to wondering what kind of moderns we've stopped being.

Rereading everything from his first essays, written in the fifties, to *Reco-brar el sentido* (2005), I see that Segovia's enormous significance derives from his always having measured himself against the greatest of the great, poets Juan Ramón Jiménez and Luis Cernuda. "I imagine," he said in 1958, "that seen from within, all centuries must have seemed like centuries of midgets. Not because the eyes seeing them were particularly scornful but simply because the horizon, by contrast, looks to be full of giants from whom the tides of history have washed away the midgets that used to surround them."

In Jiménez (and Ungaretti, and Gilberto Owen, and Pavese) Segovia found an exemplary form of rootlessness, not only historical and existential but also stylistic, alien to the hypocrisy of modern experience, which detests the century's progress while idolizing artistic experimentation. And as for Cernuda, Segovia reproached his immobility: the youngsters in his poems never age, remaining trapped like classical statues, saved from history and old age both. And that's why Segovia has taken such pains to describe a life in time, and to write poems in his old age, like the one that closes *Poesía (1943–1997)*: "El mundo entero ahora es mío / como no lo es de nadie" ("The entire world is now mine / like it is of no one else").

SELECTED BIBLIOGRAPHY

Actitudes, Universidad de Guanajuato, Mexico, 1970.

Contracorrientes, UNAM, Mexico, 1973.

Poética y profética, FCE/El Colegio de México, Mexico, 1985.

Cuaderno inoportuno, FCE, Mexico, 1987.

Poesía (1943–1997), FCE, Madrid, 1998.

Personario, Ediciones Sin Nombre, Mexico, 2001.

Recobrar el sentido, Trotta, Madrid, 2005.

Sonetos votivos, Ediciones Sin Nombre, Mexico, 2005.

El tiempo en los brazos. Cuadernos de notas (1950–1983), Pretextos, Valencia, 2009.

Cartas de un jubilado, Ediciones Sin Nombre, Mexico, 2010.

SELIGSON, ESTHER
(Mexico City, 1941 – 2010)

Seligson's work was inspired by the emulation of great men, the masters to whom she'd given custody of her conscience—both her good conscience and her bad one. From fiction to essay, the most important thing about Seligson's work is her exercising of freedom—that freedom of opinion that students gain over (and against) their teachers. And it's one thing that unites Seligson and E. M. Cioran, of whom she was friend and translator, and Seligson and Cairo poet Edmond Jabès, whom she brought into Spanish, and a select group of writers easy to name but hard to master, as she did via a lifetime of study: Rainer Maria Rilke, Vladimir Jankélèvich, Francisco Tario,* Emmanuel Levinas, Samuel Beckett . . .

With the exception of *La morada en el tiempo* (1981)—a strange, Old Testament sort of novel—Seligson's most representative work has been collected in two anthologies: *A campo traviesa* (2005) and *Toda la luz* (2006). It's a bipartite oeuvre that might actually need to be read as one, for her reviews and essays blend into her fiction. Hers is essentially an intellective sensibility, seen in her evocations, as when she delves into the world of theater—which for her is Polish, from Jerzy Grotowski to Ludwig Margules. She met the latter in his early years while he was teaching at a Jewish school where she, twelve years his junior, was a student.

But her real "school" was that of women: Virginia Woolf and Katherine Mansfield, Marguerite Yourcenar, Clarice Lispector and Elena Garro.* Perhaps the only surprising absence in that formidable cast would be that of Anna Akhmatova, but the great Russian does crop up in the epigraphs of some of her verses in *Rescoldos* (2000). The essence of Seligson's eroticism springs from a view of the feminine as unwaveringly cosmogonic and generative: the androgynous mind that dominates the world, and the bisexual creature that perceives it.

Toda la luz is a collection of the imaginative prose Seligson wrote from the days of *Tras la ventana un árbol* (1969) until well into the nineties. José María Espinasa,* close to Seligson as both critic and editor, said that in the same way people talk of "love poetry," we could talk of her "love narrative." But I beg to differ slightly, more in style than in substance. Seligson is not so much a narrator as a poet who chose prose poetry as her more or less set form of expression. I'm so convinced of it that if I meet his ghost, I'll ask Luis Ignacio Helguera* why Seligson wasn't included in his *Antología del poema en prosa en México* (1993). You could also say that *Otros son los sueños* (1973), *Luz de dos* (1978), *Diálogos con el cuerpo* (1981), *Sed de mar* (1987), and *Isomorfismos* (1991) could by rights be called lyric novels. It's not just their feel and emphasis on prose but the way they play out the greatest theme of lyric novels: the poetic voice that sets off in search of its identity. For Seligson that journey came to an end—if it could ever end—with the incessant interpretation of Scripture.

I'm not entirely convinced by everything Seligson wrote, and in many instances her prose is marred by what in others is a virtue: the enthusiastic celerity of a student who turns everything she touches into scholarship. Often, with Seligson, I find I like what she thinks about more than the way she expresses it. As Vicente Leñero* said, she "well-spent her life thinking and writing," as can be easily and succinctly seen in her *Apuntes sobre E. M. Cioran* (2003), reprinted in *A campo traviesa*. But if Cioran provided her with the dose of bitter cynicism necessary to survive, the philosopher Levinas— another of her mentors—is the one who furnished her overall vision, her perspective. And it was in Jabès—the great monomaniac committed to the Book—where she found the key and the rapture, that decisive claim: "First I thought I was a writer. Then I realized I was a Jew. Then I no longer distinguished the writer in me from the Jew because one and the other are only the torment of an ancient word" (trans. Zygmunt Bauman).

In her poetic prose, Seligson dissolved into different lyric voices that confessed the loss of "something essential, vivid," an absence that ended with her recovery of Judaism, her "home in time"—as per the title of her biblical novel *La morada en el tiempo*. And in *Toda la luz*, she wrote, "She'd rejected the only legacy of her grandparents by renouncing their origins and their tradition, which, annulled, left her at the mercy of desperation and emptiness. The oppressive feeling of belonging to an interminable chain could only be redeemed in the heart of that home still intact outside of time."

SELECTED BIBLIOGRAPHY

A campo traviesa, FCE, Mexico, 2005.
Toda la luz, FCE, Mexico, 2006.

Cicatrices, Páramo, Mexico, 2009.
Negro es tu rostro simiente, FCE, Mexico, 2010.

SERNA, ENRIQUE
(Mexico City, 1959)

Few Mexican historical novels are as faithful to the genre as *Ángeles del abismo* (2004) by Enrique Serna, a writer who took to heart the task of inventing seventeenth-century New Spain. I say "inventing" rather than "reconstructing" because I recognize Serna's profound—almost fussy—understanding, which is the result of putting archives at the service of fiction rather than acting as scholarly scribe or collector of curiosities and documents. What he did was choose a well-known Inquisitorial trial that had been brought to light by Julio Jiménez Rueda and Solange Alberro, the case of the Inquisition versus "the false Teresa de Jesús," a lying lay sister. But he soon ran out of writs and, as he confesses in the colophon, invention soon led to a love story that grew—first flustered and then felicitous—in fictional space and filled historical time.

Not so much a cloak-and-dagger as a sackcloth-and-mask novel, *Ángeles del abismo* is an exciting read that focuses a wide-angle lens on the horizon of viceroyalty, offering a complete picture that includes the theatrical world of open-air *corrales*, with their actresses, their Don Juans, and their light comedies; small-town, ascetic miracle-working that mocks high society; and the day-to-day lives of Indians whose idols are really the core of the novel. This may be Serna's most important book to date, including *Uno soñaba que era rey* (1991), *El miedo a los animales* (1995), *El seductor de la patria* (2001), and his collection of short stories, of the best written by my generation, *Amores de segunda mano* (1991).

It seems to me that Serna's recounting of the adventure of "saint" Criselda Cruz and her Indian apostate lover, Tlacotzin, is an attempt to begin paying an overdue homage to the classics of the serialized *feuilleton* such as General Vicente Riva Palacio's *Martín Garatuza* and *Monja, casada, virgen y mártir* (1868), as well as a means of modernizing a genre that could easily—in the hands of an inept writer or unscrupulous publisher—become obsolete. That modest proposal, backed by solid scholarship and scrupulous academic practices, turned the manuscript into a work that, if my hunch is right, skillfully takes the deep-rooted Manichaeanism out of colonial literature, almost by definition antiquated and quaint from its inception. The trivial or, one could say, passably picaresque episode that leads to Tlacotzin killing his father the shaman is also the moment when the criticism the book makes becomes clear: the spiritual conquest of Mexico is linked to parricide. It's the story of Indian children killing their parents.

A novel's novelty (at risk of pleonasm) stems from the number of beings it adds to reality and the number of characters who leave the pages of the book to inhabit the rooms that tradition reserves for real people. In addition to the Indians who watch the sun go down on their deities from the shores of Lake Mexico-Tenochtitlán, Serna creates a couple of surprising individuals new to Mexican literature. One is the comic Brother Juan, a man obsessed with enemas, who embodies the devil himself in the erotic convent where Fernando Benítez, one of Serna's teachers, studied. The other is the poet, scholar, and windbag don Luis de Sandoval Zapata, whom historiography knew nothing about until he took on a convincing fictional life in *Ángeles del abismo*. He's the linguistic portrait of what might have been a New Spain scholar, and a mirror in which some will see their own reflection.

While following the freely chosen rules of the genre that impose implausibility as a constant, Serna managed to turn *Ángeles del abismo* into a nobly executed novel, written in a language that only relies on seventeenth-century Spanish when it's in the interest of his readers' intelligence, eschewing unnecessary and overly ornate extravagance. The book reads beautifully, doubly so given the rich, evocative contemporary language it uses so sagely, without being out of place. This time, my vote goes to the moderns and not the ancients: old colonialists Don Artemio de Valle-Arizpe,* Julio Jiménez Rueda, and Genaro Estrada would have loved to have written *Ángeles del abismo*.

SELECTED BIBLIOGRAPHY
Amores de segunda mano, Cal y Arena, Mexico, 1994.
El miedo a los animales, Joaquín Mortiz, Mexico, 1995.
Las caricaturas me hacen llorar, Joaquín Mortiz, Mexico, 1996.
El miedo a los animales, Joaquin Mortiz, Mexico, 2003.

Ángeles del abismo, Joaquín Mortiz, Mexico, 2004.
Fruta madura, Planeta, Mexico, 2006.
Giros negros (Crónica), Océano, Mexico, 2008.
La sangre erguida, Planeta, Mexico, 2010.
Fear of Animals, trans. Georgina Jiménez Reynoso, Aflame Books, 2008.

SHERIDAN, GUILLERMO
(Mexico City, 1950)

The fall of the Mexican "empire" at the end of the twentieth century turned out to be quite auspicious for refined artistic creation, political prophecy, and metaphysical contemplation. More than a decade ago, when our particular brand of despotism began to show signs of decay, apocalyptic novels started cropping up on our spiritual horizon and have now come to be a mainstay. Sheridan's *El dedo de oro* (1996) is one of the crowning achievements of that genre.

The call of the fictional apocalypse, that literary urge to predict and act on reality—more as mournful testimony than exorcism—dates back to Carlos Fuentes's* *Cristóbal Nonato* (1987) [*Christopher Unborn* (1989)], and carries on through José Agustín,* Homero Aridjis,* Hugo Hiriart,* Mauricio Molina,* and Pedro Ángel Palou. A cursory critical examination of their novels would reveal the effective use of an outside "detonator"—US invasion, the return of pre-Hispanic men, ecological catastrophe—to bring an end to the implausible survival of Mexico. Sheridan—who doesn't read contemporary Mexican literature and like all good moderns aspires to originality—might be surprised to learn he's written a novel easily placed and historically datable to around the year 2000 A.D. It couldn't be any other way. *El dedo de oro* is a book faithful to the fears and dashed hopes of the generation that came of age in 1968, perhaps the last time the nineteenth-century flag of progress waved over Mexico.

The book has union leader Fidel Velázquez—brilliantly, devastatingly caricatured—and his syndical entourage ruling twenty-first-century Mexico. Of course, casting the most conspicuous of our society's present defects onto the future was no feat of literary imagination. Any one of the surfeit of political analysts-cum-novelists currently devitalizing the genre could have devised the plot—after getting a couple of doctorates in "democratic transition." But that's where Sheridan breaks from the pack of moaning jeremiahs, presenting instead a novel that surpasses its spiritual brothers and renders null and void the profusion of trash literature now in circulation. And it's not only Sheridan's satirical abilities that set him apart, because Fuentes and Hiriart have them, too.

El dedo de oro is one of the most outstanding comical works in Mexican fiction. A few months ago, when Sheridan gave me the very long earlier version of the novel—over 600 pages—I doubted his sense of humor could make me laugh that long. I was wrong. Humor is appreciated in any literature, but even more so in ours, so lacking in funny prose. How did he achieve such linguistic revelry? The key resides in the absolute primacy of language, the radicalism of a novel in which Mexican Spanish is subjected to torture that yields not the usual, colloquial hat-tipping but a parallel reality, different from ours yet authentically bottled at the source, a sophisticated rhetorical exaggeration of every Mexican lingo—high-class and low, full of vocalic omissions and conceptual onomatopoeia, public offenses and private joys, carnivalesque whims and bureaucratic annihilation.

I don't know if laughter is liberating. But Sheridan's decadent portrayal of Fierro Ferráez and his lackeys is a lively and important decoding and transformation of the Spanish of the powerful and the powerless. Adolfo Castañón* sees Sheridan's antihero as a mythical giant of world literature. And although *El dedo de oro* might depress or terrify us—once our laughter subsides—it's not because of the book's dystopic depiction of Mexico but its linguistic genius. If I understand theorist Jean Paulhan, the novel is proof of the "terror in letters," the ability of words to invert order and lead to a painful abyss of isolation.

Sheridan's verbal acrobatics are so impressive that they render almost immaterial my qualms about the narrator, who is sometimes derailed by overconfidence in his own dramatic prowess, describing situations that aren't just implausible but preposterous. But when his creativity flags, the brute force of language appears in time to save the day from fictional weariness.

The most debatable aspect of *El dedo de oro* is Sheridan's view of Mexico. The fact that it's a popular one—based on common sense—makes it no less worthy of examination. Sheridan believes in the proverbial Mexicanness of the tragicomic PRI's (Partido Revolutionario Institutional) despotism, and projects it onto an enormous satirical screen where we see every aspect of our public and social lives mocked.

There's a touch of involuntary *poujadism* (reactionary petit bourgeois attitude) in *El dedo del oro*. Every humorist is a moralist. Sheridan is no exception. His puritanism is betrayed through his systematic, desperate rage against the Mexico he thinks needs to be taught a lesson in ethics—and satire will serve as the teacher. Mexico, he feels, is a nightmare that creeps into the dreams of a creature from another time and place, who lives in a state of honorable abstinence that can be sensed when the book gives in—discreetly but not undetectably—to sentimentalism. But Sheridan is an unusual man, a puritan but not an ideologue, a writer who has faith in the power of language only as way of reacting against the barbarism characteristic of the moribund Mexican empire, which has, in *El dedo de oro*, its Petronius. (*Servidumbre y grandeza de la vida literaria*, 1998)

In some of the texts that have made him one of Mexico's most important satirists, Guillermo Sheridan, born in 1950, boasts that he lived exactly fifty percent of the twentieth century, witnessed five percent of the dawns of the second millennium, and went through two and a half percent of every hundred years since the birth of Christ, which makes him a contemporary of Matisse, Camus, and Stalin. But sharing that sojourn on the planet must be rather thankless for those who form the cadre of his favorite targets: urbanites as well as small-town folk with their everyday barbaric habits and crimes of fashion; UNAM's union and reigning university bureaucracy; the local left who rule by following their own good conscience; the high priestesses of neo-Aztec cults; a good part of the French who live and think like poststructuralists; poets who become revolutionary demonologists; caudillos and the entourages that exalt them; European artists who make pilgrimages to Chiapas to find noble savages amongst the indigenous; and the universal rights of enlightened minorities, in particular students, in whom the campaigns of politicians, labor leaders, sympathetic intellectuals, and drivers all prophetically coalesce.

Sheridan is the current chapter in our history of satire, and he must be read alongside writers like Salvador Novo,* Jorge Ibargüengoitia,* and Carlos Monsiváis.* Novo, the rambling official chronicler of Mexico City, also wrote "Lombardotoledanología" (1937), to which Sheridan owes a lot. That text served as the matrix—part myth, part real—on which much of Sheridan's image of populist leaders and union bosses was based, including labor leader Vicente Lombardo Toledano, union leader Fidel Velázquez (hero of *El dedo de oro*, his only novel), and presidential candidate Andrés Manuel López Obrador. Another of his favorite characters, Subcomandante Marcos, belongs to another clan, that of gushy (but not merciful) guerrillas who broke away not so much from the 1968 student movement as from traditional Cold War polarities.

From Ibargüengoitia, Sheridan learned a few tricks and more than a few obsessions, although not his most essential attribute: the sadness that allows jokes, imprecations, and irony to rid the plot of superfluity and offer straightforward caricature. Ibargüengoitia is a cartoonist; Sheridan, the hypothetical author of a comic book. If he were forced to use the plot of Ibargüengoitia's *Las muertas* (1977; *The Dead Girls*, 1981), a novel whose perfection resides in its fictionalized journalistic simplicity, Sheridan would have written a book describing the plausible horrors of a provincial whorehouse à la *The Decameron*. Finally, Monsiváis, a different kind of puritan, responds to injustice with love for the oppressed, giving a lot of moral stock to those who represent them—or claim to—something Sheridan would be concerned about, moved by his mistrustful skepticism of the human condition.

El encarguito (y otros pendientes) is a collection of Sheridan's texts published in *Letras Libres*—where, as at *Vuelta*, he was the most-read columnist—covering everything from the triumph of Vicente Fox in 2000 to the electrifying and unexpected defeat of López Obrador in 2006, the smoke of September 11 to the French heartland that supported Le Pen during the years that Sheridan—an Anglophile—lived in Paris. The collection attests to the wide-ranging prose styles he's at ease with: pastiche, interpretation, puns, fictional "instructions for use," explicating literal meanings, scholarly quotations, explanatory diagrams. Essentially, he's got the talent of a ventriloquist who speaks, imitates, deforms, and reproduces others' modes, dialects, and languages, for instance using Bernal Díaz del Castillo as a way to illustrate the "new conquest" of Mexico by Peninsular progressives and laying claim— for the left—to the kind of Latin that Alfonso Reyes* only dreamed of.

Rereading Sheridan's columns alongside his essays on Mexican poetry— for example *Cartas de Copilco* (1994) with *Poeta con paisaje: ensayos sobre la vida de Octavio Paz* (2004); *Lugar a dudas* (2004) with *Un corazón adicto: la vida de Ramón López Velarde* (1989, 2002); *Frontera norte y otros extremos* (1988) with *Los Contemporáneos ayer* (1985); *Allá en el campus grande* (1998) with *México en 1932: La polémica nacionalista* (1998)—I find the scrupulous conscientiousness of the literary historian balanced out by the acrimony of the satirist of all things Mexican. Both voices mingle in the writer, as can be seen in the essay "Llueve sobre México," which appears in *Lugar a dudas*. A superb example, this short vignette combines the description of a downpour in Coahuila desert and a sense of nostalgia ("It's always raining in the past") with verses by Xavier Villaurrutia, Carlos Pellicer,* Francisco González León, and Ramón López Velarde, and observations about Kavafis. And in the last paragraph, he says: "The city, today, is something else. Efraín Huerta[*] claims, harshly, that urban rain falls on cadavers. The city's environmental violence increases with the rain. Thousands of cars sit unmoving, spectators of the rain they illuminate with their headlights and try to scare off with their speakers. Suddenly, an incongruent image: a boy of six or seven, wearing a colored wig, does a handstand in front of the car. The water comes up to his elbows. He rights himself and holds out his hands for a tip. The rain pays him in water for his strange trade, making a show of his misery. Then I notice that the clown makeup has run down his face, but also up it, for living upside down: an image that will live on, sadly, in my present."

Unlike H. L. Mencken, whom he sees as essential reading, Sheridan doesn't hate poetry but feeds off of it, presenting himself as the iconoclast who refuses to ply hyperboles in order to replace them with credos that he then tears down and replaces with some new doctrine. But that doesn't mean that Sheridan lacks—just as Swift and Voltaire don't lack—a "non-place," an inverted world that might also be called Mexico, where maybe the city streets are still pedestrian—like those the *Contemporáneos* walked—and the late afternoons are like those Ramón López Velarde watched fall over Calle El Pensativo in San Luis Potosí, where childhood resembles Octavio Paz's* early days in Mixcoac or maybe a bucolic memory of his own youth in Monterrey.

It seems to me that everything that makes Sheridan incisive and bold (and for some unbearable) goes back to Mexican poetry, to what came out of José

Juan Tablada's man-made talent, Efraín Huerta's almost surreal, reckless elegies, Paz's awe at Mayan stones, Manuel Gutiérrez Nájera's contributions, and Renato Leduc's* obscene, melodious moments. Only the most penetrating reader could hit a moving target the way Sheridan does, discerning false from true and quaint from authentic in López Velarde's provinces; just as only someone who's gone back again and again to *Muerte sin fin* could engage in such demanding mental gymnastics. In the end, Sheridan's oeuvre—essays and columns—is both more fascinating and more enduring than that of many of our novelists, who are the writers most often charged with interpreting our world.

In *El encarguito*, readers are offered two paths, seemingly very different. One traverses the poetic world, as Sheridan does in Parisian chronicles in which the Île Saint-Louis serves as a backdrop for poetic citations, following the modernists and the avant-garde. The other path, in texts about intermittent takeovers at the university, obviously delves into politics. But in both, Sheridan uses the same process: he solves a verbal puzzle and simultaneously passes judgment, acting as moralist.

Sheridan's intellectual autobiography, which is relatively easy to work out if you follow the correct order through his texts, takes us through his educational counterpoints—in Catholic Christmas and Protestant Christmas, in John Steinbeck and J. D. Salinger, in pure poetry and *engagé* poetry—to a seemingly Manichean universe where obscurity seems to dominate. But sooner or later we're bathed in the warm glow of a few modest convictions that can be seen, for instance, in the solidarity hinted at by singing in a chorus (a Bach cantata). It's both injustice and Sheridan's hopes as an educator that demonstrate his strict adherence to liberal values. His moral obsession, as he has daringly and indefatigably proven, lies in the defense of public-university education.

Sanctioned government lies, popular new age and old left superstitions, the avant-garde public-cum-electorate, Frida Kahlo mania, inarticulate politicians, fear sublimated into the resurrection of Aztec idols, and the recent trend of running public schools based on the lumpenproletariat's views are just a few of Sheridan's bugbears. *El encarguito* is the book of a puritan who abhors stupidity, fanaticism, corruption, and anything that betrays the affectation and excessive ornamentation of inadequate analysis or action.

The voice Sheridan uses in his chronicles is perhaps his most impressive creation. Both invisible and outrageous, he's Molière's misanthrope Alceste—or at least Paul Bénichou's interpretation of him. He's the idealistic reformer whose rebellion is inadequate to the situation at hand, and this makes him seem aggressive yet thin-skinned, egotistical yet forlorn. Haughtily hostile, it's him against society, to such an overwhelming degree that the misanthrope—given his hypersensitivity—rebels. His is the outlook best suited to pointing out our vices, thereby revealing his passion for virtue.

SELECTED BIBLIOGRAPHY

Los Contemporáneos ayer, FCE, Mexico, 1985.

Frontera norte y otros extremos, FCE, Mexico, 1988.

Cartas de Copilco, Vuelta, Mexico, 1994.

El dedo de oro, Alfaguara, Mexico, 1996.

México en 1932: la polémica nacionalista, FCE, Mexico, 1999.

Lugar a dudas, Tusquets Editores, Mexico, 2000.

Allá en el campus grande, Tusquets Editores, Mexico, 2000.

Un corazón adicto: la vida de Ramón López Velarde y otros ensayos afines, Tusquets Editores, Mexico, 2002.

Poeta con paisaje: ensayos sobre la vida de Octavio Paz, ERA, Mexico, 2004.

El encarguito (y otros pendientes), prefeace by Martín Solares, Universidad de las Américas/Trilce, Mexico, 2006.

Paralelos y meridianos, DGE/El Equilibrista/UNAM, Mexico, 2008.

SOLER FROST, PABLO

(Mexico City, 1965)

When I walked in to the Manuel M. Ponce Palace of Fine Arts in 1984 for Octavio Paz's seventieth birthday celebration, I caught sight of a fluty man a tad younger than myself who looked like he'd just stepped out of Fantin-Latour's portrait of Rimbaud. He was a dandy through and through, his affectations so well executed that they were unforgettable: polite to the point of exasperation and, to top it off, a staunch Catholic. But unlike most of the callow eccentrics inundating literary scenes the world over when they're at an age when all will be forgiven, Soler Frost was already a genuine writer, chosen as the implausible founder of a certain type of new Mexican literature. The novels *Legión* (1992) and *La mano derecha* (1993), short story collections *El sitio de Bagdad y otras aventuras del doctor Greene* (1994) and *El misterio de los tigres* (2002), and curiosities including *Oriente de los insectos mexicanos* (1996) and *Cartas de Tepoztlán* (1997) have defined his style—a catalog of affinities—which has now permeated our entire generation. Soler Frost was the writer who, without a big publicity hullaboo, wrote fiction about the Great War and Byzantium in which Mexico was just a genealogical allusion. But that doesn't mean he ignored Emperor Maximilian and other interests we might refer to as criollo.

Soler Frost's macabre adolescent passion for National Socialism led to a few minor society scandals, then faded over the years and eventually led to *Malebolge* (2001), in which this Catholic who regained his grace undergoes an examination of conscience, denouncing the pagan blight he suffered. Of all the books (and, frankly, there are too many) to come out of what has not-so-comically been called Mexico's "magical Nazism," *Malebolge*—the name of one of the circles of hell—strikes me as the finest. The novel—which received scant critical attention, as tends to be the case with Soler Frost—shines for its pure prose, elegant and convincing without being overconfident. Its Germanophilia incorporates existential realities that other exoticists eschew: a guilt-ridden homoerotic attraction to bodies in combat and rites of initiation, which translate into a worshipping of boyhood camaraderie and titillation at the horrors of history. According to Soler Frost, "Many—Hesse, Mann, Unruh, Jünger—have chronicled this real-life story: two boys, at that critical juncture between childhood and adolescence, love one another; they grow up together, converse under trees, recite poems to each other on desolate streets, argue, try beer and cigarettes. They might be clichés, but they're beautiful clichés. Suddenly one of them, and not the other, begins to feel attracted to women."

Traces of Salvador Elizondo's* *Elsinore* are perhaps too noticeable in *Malebolge*, which unlike his mentor's books is not particularly well constructed: narrative technique is not Soler Frost's forte. But I prefer his blunders—tedious passages—to others' calculated, hollow, commercial bull's-eyes. The difference between a prose artist and someone who writes cult bestsellers, for instance, can easily be seen in *La mano derecha* (the first book in the trilogy in which *Malebolge* is the second). Subtitled a "novel with photographs," *La mano derecha* features travelers who at one point dock in Aden, Yemen, and Soler Frost says that someone named A. R. boards the ship, with no further details. A cult mass-market writer would have written a thirty-page chapter expounding upon Rimbaud and his involvement in slave and arms trafficking after he gave up poetry. Soler Frost just barely touches upon it, resulting in authentic literature; others give us research and bibliography.

With *Cartas de Tepoztlán* it became obvious that after all his exoticism, Soler Frost was having a criollo period. More than a return to origins, this is the voyage of someone anxious to tell his fellow men about his trip, when in fact he never left. *Edén* (2003), the third part of the Jansen trilogy, also takes place in Mexico, in the years between the end of the nineteenth century and the Mexican Revolution. And while *La mano derecha* recounts the fate of one of those Danish adventurers on the Kaiser's German subs, and *Malebolge* is set in Germany's days of National Socialism, *Edén* takes place in the logging camps of Tabasco. The prose in this ode to the tropics is denser than his previous books; its extraordinary verbal cadence is full of humorous touches, as when the atheist B. Traven appears in "New Denmark." This is quite something, given that *Edén* is a Catholic novel, full of saintly indignation against the anti-clerical revolutionary troops in southeastern Mexico. Soler Frost needs to watch out for the intrusion of straitlaced religious sentiment that corrupts style in works of art, and is very common among the converted and born-again.

The author has been seen as a reactionary because he's a traditionalist who opposes modernity. But Jorge Cuesta* disproved that association years ago: being a traditionalist is just an eccentric way of being modern. Which is why Soler Frost can't forget (he sometimes does) that what he takes to be Catholic tradition is actually rather novel, a result of the French Revolution. By hurling their Catholic writers into the pit of public opinion, the revolution turned them not into authors nostalgic for the days of El Cid but into indispensable critics (and accomplices) of the modern adventure.

1767, the historical novel about the expulsion of the Jesuits from the New World, is the final proof of Soler Frost's journey from exoticism to traditionalism, one extreme to the other. Structured like the nineteenth-century novels of Vicente Riva Palacio and Manuel Payno, with an omniscient narrator who's both doctrinaire and dogmatic, *1767* is a devout book aimed at vindicating the suffering of the priests of the Society of Jesus. After being expelled from the Bourbon kingdom, in one of the first totalitarian acts of the modern state, the Jesuits took the seeds of the Mexican Enlightenment with them, resulting in splendid late-blooming flowers such as Clavijero's *Storia antica del Messico* and other notable works. I found myself moved, rather than annoyed, by the way Soler Frost coyly, rather than piously, uses the stories, events, and miracles of the Jesuit tradition, almost always directly quoting their martyrs and scholars.

I am, on the other hand, disappointed by his technique, which takes no personal risks and avoids probing meaningfully into one of the thorniest political and ecclesiastic mysteries of modern history, a complicated mess that a writer with different leanings would have tried to unravel, and should at least include a psychological examination of the crises of consciousness that must have plagued the three Roman pontiffs responsible for banishing the Society. Instead Soler Frost repeated the Jesuit version of the expulsion without subjecting it to any scrutiny, including the insults and caricatures that present Voltaire, Charles III, and all of the Jesuit's other real or imaginary enemies as monkeys and monsters. But I guess we can't ask him to be a Catholic writer *à la française* and have to accept the fact that Soler Frost, after starting down the path of Ernst Jünger and Elizondo, has become his own unique brand of Catholic writer.

Conspicuous Catholicism in *1767* isn't reproachable in and of itself. Nor is communism in José Revueltas* or the reverse consecration of eroticism in Juan García Ponce,* to name other Mexican writers who chose other—rhetorical?—forms of religiosity. What's problematic, however, is the technique in which a naïve narrator—based on Galdos's Gabriel—opts for superficiality as a means of explaining history. Given how unusual a devout novel is in times like these, anyone who doesn't know how sincere a Catholic Soler Frost is would likely assume *1767* to be a postmodern spoof. But it's not. And after the first few rambling chapters, it wins over even skeptics hardened in their stances by what a century ago the Church anathemized as modernism.

Except for my noted reservations, I do think *1767* is convincing, as both a study in piety in a cruel world and the beginning of a saga that will continue in the war of Mexican independence. Along with the clunky sentences that are par for the course with Soler Frost there are also subtle interludes that save him from the dangerous recent tendency to turn controversial issues into oversimplified hagiography. He seems to rediscover, for instance, his love of adventure novels, sometimes to great delight, as when a ship's lieutenant has the panicked realization that a storm has scattered Charles III's secret instruction to banish the Jesuits from the overseas kingdoms. And there are many other episodes, too, in which *1767* seems to savor Mexican Spanish.

This novel, along with *Edén*, is Soler Frost's *Rusticatio mexicana*—that 15-volume Latin poem cataloging Mexico's flora, fauna, and folklore written by exiled Jesuit Rafael Landívar. Worshipping one's homeland and religiosity, of course, is at the heart of all German-inspired Romanticist works: Landívar isn't that different from Oswald Spengler or his titanic disciple, Jünger. And Soler Frost is one of the few writers of my generation who has truly experienced the rigors of an intellectual biography. His is a battlefield where you see prideful warriors (and tin soldiers) hoisting the flags of cruelty that have flown throughout history, Eros fighting Philia and Agape, pennants waving back and forth between self-importance and true vocation. Soler Frost has already walked quite a long path, and it's one of those in Mexican literature that I follow most devotedly.

SELECTED BIBLIOGRAPHY

Legión, Universidad Veracruzana, Xalapa, 1992.

La mano derecha. Novela con fotografías, Joaquín Mortiz, Mexico, 1993.

El sitio de Bagdad y otras aventuras del doctor Greene, Heliópolis, Mexico, 1995.

Oriente de los insectos mexicanos, Aldus, Mexico, 1996.

Cartas de Tepoztlán, ERA, Mexico, 1996.

Malebolge, Tusquets Editores, Mexico, 2001.

El misterio de los tigres, ERA, Mexico, 2002.

Edén, Jus, Mexico, 2003.

1767, Joaquín Mortiz, Mexico, 2004.

Yerba americana, ERA, Mexico, 2008.

T

TARIO, FRANCISCO
(Mexico City, 1911 – Madrid, Spain, 1977)

Years ago, Octavio Paz* told a story that might still be unpublished. Back when he and Elena Garro* were still living together in an apartment in Mexico City, they began hearing extravagant (I remember, he used the word "extravagant") noises coming through the walls. In the next apartment, on an increasingly regular basis, they'd hear blood-curdling laughter, horrific cries, the cackle of nocturnal birds, electric saws, in short, everything you might expect from a séance or sadomasochistic encounter. Alarmed (Octavio said "alarmed"), he and Elena began asking around in their building. In the end, they discovered that their neighbors were using the apartment to record a horror radio show in the wee hours, using all the rudimentary special effects of the time. The mysterious producers of the show were Antonio Peláez and his brother Paco, who became known by the pseudonym Francisco Tario as one of the most admired and arresting Mexican writers of fantastical fiction. In fact, he's the author of a book aptly entitled *La puerta en el muro* (1946). That story is typical of Tario. You'd think his tales were those of Horace Walpole and Charles Nodier, of the great Romantic tradition of the *conte fantastique*, until you discover the trick.

The tale of Tario's rise to fame (albeit mostly posthumous) is a happy one, which began with a few encouraging lines written by José Luis Martínez in

1946. After his death, Esther Seligson* and Alejandro Toledo edited *Entre tus dedos helados y otros cuentos* (1988) and José María Espinasa* recovered three of his unpublished plays and published them in *El caballo asesinado* (1988). Then Mario González Suárez* chose to include Tario in his anthology of twentieth-century Mexican literature, *Paisajes del limbo* (2001), and wrote the prologue to Tario's *Cuentos completos* (2003). *Jardín secreto*, a flawed novel that Tario never saw in print, was published in 1993. While the narrative voice is strong and the prose tight, it also somewhat clumsily exploits every trick in the Gothic and Romantic book, which readers are already familiar with and Tario himself knew by heart. The plot involves incest on a foggy, eerie country estate, a bit of family insanity—conveniently concealed—and even the kind-hearted teacher who can communicate with the dead.

In the forties, when Xavier Villaurrutia was envious of Argentina's Borges and begging for someone like Juan José Arreola to appear on the Mexican literary scene, Tario began writing a series of fantastic tales that, as Seligson sees it, responded to the charm of *Antología de la literatura fantástica* (1940) published by Silvina Ocampo, Adolfo Bioy Casares, and Jorge Luis Borges in Buenos Aires. That alone, the freedom taken by the epigone, makes *La noche* (1943), *Aquí abajo* (1943), *Yo de amores qué sabía* (1950), *Breve diario de un amor perdido* (1951), *Tapioca Inn: mansión para fantasmas* (1953), and *Una violeta de más* (1968) worthwhile. Tario, "our most-trumpeted eccentric, the name that appears first on every list of eccentrics" as Luigi Amara* called him, was a weird and talented reader of fantastic literature who also wrote some of the genre's best stories. And even if *Equinoccio* (1946) had been the only work he'd written, his presence in any history of Mexican letters would be justified. This truly remarkable collection of aphorisms—that I've heard Cioran loved—is an explosion of black humor and hilarious wisdom utterly unlike the solemn literature Tario wrote.

"Huysmans, Lautréamont, Rimbaud: let's play marbles," Tario wrote, and I can just imagine the three big shots of Romantic anguish obeying the sudden demiurge, knuckling down after aggies and tiger marbles, just as I can picture the scene in which Octavio and Elena link hands, on their knees, ears to the wall, trying to make out the macabre sounds of their neighbors.

SELECTED BIBLIOGRAPHY

Equinoccio, Cuadernos del Nigromante, San Miguel Allende, 1989.

Jardín secreto, Joaquín Mortiz, Mexico, 1993.

Cuentos completos, prologue by Mario González Suárez, vols I and II, Lectorum, Mexico, 2003.

TORRES BODET, JAIME

(Mexico City, 1902 – 1974)

Poet and essayist, narrator and civil servant, Torres Bodet is also one of the most eminent and least appreciated writers in Mexico. Emboldened by Salvador Novo,* who said that Torres Bodet, a colleague at the *Contemporáneos* journal, didn't have a real life but only a paper biography, two generations of writers—myself included—carried on with hurtful jibes and confidences that, as José Emilio Pacheco,* one of his defenders, sees it, made him victim of a black legend.

His respectable standing and the republican pageantry of his government appointment made him seem odious to those of us who associated him with the height of the institutionalized revolution. But sooner or later, some of us began to feel remorse, recognizing that the man who'd been José Vasconcelos's* very young secretary was also a great civilizer, architect of twentieth-century Mexican culture, which he served as Secretary of Public Education (1943–1946 and 1958–1964), Chancellor of Mexico, and Ambassador to France.

As Director General of UNESCO from 1948 to 1952, Torres Bodet garnered as much international recognition as he did in Mexico. In *The Defeat of the Mind* (1987), for example, Alain Finkielkraut presents Torres Bodet as the diplomat whose work at UNESCO turned the organization into an Enlightenment guarantee, freeing it of Cold War paralysis and shielding it from the multiculturalism that would eventually corrode it. As Octavio Paz* writes in an essay commemorating him, Torres Bodet would have shone in the courts of Frederick the Great, Catherine the Great, or Charles III. "Torres Bodet," he concludes, "served the Mexican state because he believed that was the way to serve his country. And he served it as few others have. You can count on one hand the Mexicans, this century, who have undertaken as fruitful and beneficent work as he has, in areas as diverse as open education, foreign relations, and high culture" (*Obras completas*, 14. *Miscélanea, II*, 2004).

When reading or rereading *Obras escogidas* (1961) it's important to keep in mind that not all writers feel the call of Romanticism or the revolution, that there are productive scholars, like Torres Bodet, who actively chose order and harmony over the transgression and criticism so exciting to moderns nowadays. In fact, his lyrical novels—from *Margarita de Niebla* (1927) to *Nacimiento de Venus* (1941)—were key to the full realization of Mexican modernity. Torres Bodet's verse, the least read work of the *Contemporáneos* poets, has been seen as diamond-like and perfect, especially that of *Cripta* (1937), an exemplary neo-classical book, both restrained and Parnassian, which really stood out in the first half of the twentieth century.

Torres Bodet, however, wasn't a brilliant writer or an ideas man. The six volumes of his *Memorias* published between 1955 and 1974 should have been essential reading, given his public stature and international experience; instead they turned out to be insipid, predictable, and apprehensive. He's a narrator who's only of interest to literary historians, a poet whose verses languish in anthologies, and his memoirs sit gathering dust in a few old-fashioned bookstores. So maybe the best opportunity to reread and re-evaluate Torres Bodet is via his essays. *Tres inventores de realidad: Stendhal, Dostoievsky y Pérez Galdós* (1955), *Balzac* (1959), *Tolstoi* (1965), and *Tiempo y memoria en la obra de Proust* (1967) are great and much-needed Mexican homages to the nineteenth-century novel.

Torres Bodet's literary and intellectual taste is impeccable, and in the early twentieth century it satisfied even the most discriminating readers: he read Maurice Barrès, Simone Weil, George Santayana, George Simmel, and even Curzio Malaparte, once detested and now being reissued in New York. He was a devotee of Galdós before many, a path later taken by Luis Cernuda* and then by Sergio Pitol,* who—like Torres Bodet—wrote about the childhood illnesses that allowed him, bedridden, to devour Tolstoy.

As a travel writer and museum commentator, in Venice and Florence, Paris and Toledo, Torres Bodet has been snubbed for the touristic superficiality of his texts and for sticking to hackneyed aesthetic conventions. In my estimation, those opinions are neither fair nor true. Torres Bodet both wrote and traveled like a Stendhalian and never pretended to be anything but a humanist dilettante; his pieces are comparable to the travel writing of Henry James and Rubén Darío at the end of the nineteenth century. And his European classicism, the way he was stirred by the Venetian masters and by Velázquez, is no different from André Malraux's Orientalism and primitivism: both are reactions registering genuine scholarly enthusiasm. And unlike Malraux, one thing that tips the scales in Torres Bodet's favor is that he possessed his own "otherness"—that pre-Hispanic world that sat protected in the National Museum of Anthropology, which he himself inaugurated.

Torres Bodet was one of the last writers on the planet who took tribunal eloquence seriously and anthologized his speeches to the court, an act that today seems as odd as Dadaism must have seemed in 1916 Zurich. But Voltaire would have been more interested in those speeches than in the sentimental Romanticist poetry consecrated shortly after. Today, we—rightly— refuse to see humanitarian declamation as literature. That's because now it's just the well-intentioned, prudent, hollow language of philanthropists and ambassadors. Reading speeches is boring. But anyone who takes a look at that section of his *Obras escogidas* just might find a poignant, heroic character, a diplomat fighting not so diplomatically so that culture and education would prevent totalitarianism and warfare from ever again overtaking the soul of the world.

Torres Bodet's suicide on May 13, 1974 is one of the most crushing and inexplicable events in Mexican literary history. At seventy-two years of age, he shot himself in the mouth. Years later, Paz said, "He killed himself as if, having fulfilled all duties to himself and others, he had nothing left to do. He left not one line to say goodbye." And, in shocked irony, Gabriel Zaid* wrote, "Torres Bodet was exemplary to the point of exhaustion. His edifying sermons wore out the presses, courts, and tape recorders. He buried the dark side of his life, and the darkest thing of all: that desire to bury it that might have seemed Apollonian and in fact turned out to be diabolical. He lived for duty, a strange, luminous, sinister passion. Buried alive, in the grave that was his official persona, as he said in his best poems ("Dédalo," "Continuidad"), he turned the best of himself into official culture. He possessed exemplary, but not hypocritical, will, a frightening ability to deny himself that shines in those poems and in the stoic way he died. His trajectory ennobles bureaucracy as the path (along with drugs, alcohol, forbidden pleasures, and insanity) to the absolute and to destruction" (*Obras, 2. Ensayos sobre poesía*, 1993).

Before we forget Torres Bodet again, let's quote one of his last poems: "Viví para los otros, en los otros . . . / Jamás estuve solo con el alba, / ni con el mar, ni con la estrella / ¿Fue biografía siempre mi existencia?" ("I lived for others, in others . . . / Never was I alone at dawn / nor with the sea, nor with the star / Was my life always biography?")

SELECTED BIBLIOGRAPHY
Tiempo de arena, FCE, Mexico, 1955 and 2002.
Obras escogidas: poesía, autobiografía, ensayo, FCE, Mexico, 1961 and 1983.
Narrativa completa, EOSA, Mexico, 1985.
Selected Poems, trans. Sonja Karsen, University of Indiana Press, 1965.
Song of Serene Voices, trans. J.C.R. Green, Aquila/The Phaethon Press, 1982.

TORRI, JULIO
(Saltillo, Coahuila, 1889 – Mexico City, 1970)

"Talent is a question of quantity," according to the famous Jules Renard quotation. But twentieth-century literature seems disinclined to agree. Cyril Connolly would say we reward sparse production. On that front, the reputation of Torri—author of only four books—continues to grow thanks to a reverence for formal restraint and artistic perfection that began around 1880 with Mallarmé. Compared to the oceanic oeuvres like those of placid Alfonso Reyes,* tempestuous José Vasconcelos,* and Martín Luis Guzmán*— who extensively chronicled the Mexican Revolution—Torri's pocket-sized collection is perhaps the most amenable to new readers of the *Ateneístas*. Both *Ensayos y poemas* (1917) and *De fusilamientos* (1940) stand out in academia, thanks to the rhetorical posterity provided by Borges's praise. Torri is the only Mexican writer whose books appear interchangeably in anthologies of poetry, prose poems, and fiction.

A quintessential inhabitant of the Ivory Tower, Torri has lately been pinched and prodded by his critics, but far from being left battered and bruised, this is actually an honor to him. There are those who see him—as if we were arguing over the virility of Mexican literature in 1925—as a sterile creator of "civilized literature." It makes one wonder what they'd choose to see as "uncivilized" literature. Those outmoded Romanticists can't seem to accept the fact that there's room in our canon for both Torri and Nellie Campobello to sit side by side. In *Enemies of Promise* (1938), Cyril Connolly said that a literature's health could be measured by how virulent the war between schools was.

Torri, the Mandarin of Mexico City, lived a legendary life: a scant writer, a soporific professor, a rogue outside the classroom, a bibliophile with *non sanctas* tastes, a self-confessed seducer of plain Janes, a lover of the old Castilian epic, and a devotee of English literature. Countless writers have left moving testimonies of their visits to his grave.

With the publication of *Epistolarios* (1995), Canadian Serge I. Zaitzeff brought fifteen years of research to fruition, thanks to which we now have a couple of literary studies as well as two posthumous books to add to Torri's bibliography: *Diálogo de los libros* (1980) and *El ladrón de ataúdes* (1987). *Epistolarios* begins with the correspondence between Torri and Reyes that had already appeared in *Diálogo de los libros*. I must confess, with a sadness tinged with joy, that while I was concocting this review I discovered Enrique Krauze* had already written it fifteen years ago. I guess that's what you call tradition. Krauze recalled the end of a beautiful friendship, caused by the loss of a book that Torri felt blamed for. The book in question was a second edition of Covarrubias's *Tesoro de la lengua castellana o española* (1611). Zaitzeff includes, as a coup de grâce, a note found at Reyes's house in which courtesy turns to scorn. Reyes claims he doesn't owe Torri any "favors, and he owes me several. I have nothing against him and showed him more benevolence than I would anyone. I suspect I contributed to building his reputation when no one was paying any attention to him. The poor man has been harboring rage against me gratuitously. Perhaps because it bothers him always to be put in my retinue, and he's right about that. When it was my seventieth birthday celebration (1959) and he saw himself as a secondary ornamentation to my joy, he blew up. It's not my fault. I understand, and I forgive him."

Reading their correspondence during the early years of Reyes's exile (1914–1929), all I can say is that Don Alfonso was ungrateful, because Torri took care of all of his Mexican affairs for him—as he had for Pedro Henríquez Ureña. Reyes even went so far as to give him instructions on wrapping packages properly, given the pitiful state in which the parcels he requested had arrived in Madrid. Torri was the *Ateneístas's* concierge during the Mexican Revolution. Reyes repaid him with a few pages of praise, while Vasconcelos got the post of Editor in Chief at the Secretary of Public Education (SEP).

The rest of *Epistolarios* adds little to Torri's biography. A writer who didn't write, and what Spanish writer Azorín would have called a "little philosopher," Torri exemplified the heroic cultural resistance of those in "domestic exile," which culminated in Cvltvra, a publishing house that was preparing a cultural renaissance for the twenties, one that had been planned during the revolution. But once peace was reinstated, Torri hardly lived up to his promise despite no longer having any political obstruction.

His correspondence with Pedro Henríquez Ureña testifies to Pedro's sad posterity: he was vital to his own generation as an intellectual stimulus, but invariably bores contemporary readers, whereas Torri always comes off as a vivacious and acceptably gossipy correspondent. The book also includes important letters exchanged with Rafael Cabrera (1884–1943), translator of Marcel Schwob and by far Torri's most kindred spirit. And it's interesting to note how submissively the feisty Vasconcelos responded to Torri's stylistic edits of his *Estudios indostánicos* and his attacks on the nation's spirituality. During the same time—1917—Vasconcelos never heeded similar suggestions if they came from Reyes, which would seem to suggest that Torri represented no threat or competition to him and his friends. That's why they simultaneously bossed him around and obeyed him.

The book closes with archival material of little literary value: letters from Guzmán, Xavier Icaza, Jesús T. Acevedo, and Enrique González Martínez, among others. There are also courteous messages from French writer Ventura García Calderón and Spaniards Juan Ramón Jiménez, Ramón del Valle-Inclán, José Bergamín, and Ramón Menéndez Pidal. It's sad to note the self-imposed isolation between Latin American writers; reticence, ignorance, and etiquette are what is most notable in the international section of Latin Americans' collected letters.

Epistolarios proves that Torri had artistic sensitivity to both his own generation and up-and-coming writers. Though he hardly traveled outside of Mexico, he was silently enthusiastic about, for instance, the *Contemporáneos* writers. And with regard to his own contemporaries, insecurity about his own work allowed him to see clearly in 1914, when he wrote to Reyes: "Will we be primitives or decadents? In any case, we're close enough to things to be polished, shiny metallic writers of the golden age."

If Torri, like Paul Léauteaud, had kept an impudent, private diary, the story of secular Mexican literature would today be very different. But decorum—blasted decorum—has kept us from experiencing the plenitude of the servitude and grandeur of literary life. (*Servidumbre y grandeza de la vida literaria,* 1998)

SELECTED BIBLIOGRAPHY
Tres libros. Ensayos y poemas. De fusilamientos. Prosas dispersas, FCE, Mexico, 1964.
Diálogo de los libros, ed. Serge I. Zaitzeff, FCE, Mexico, 1980.
El ladrón de ataúdes, prologue by Jaime García Terrés, FCE, Mexico, 1987.
Zaitzeff, Serge, *El arte de Julio Torri,* Oasis, Mexico, 1987.

TOSCANA, DAVID
(Monterrey, Nuevo León, 1961)

A meticulous stylist who's proven himself to be in a constant state of artistic evolution, Toscana nevertheless lacked that one book that would bestow on him his own unique voice, yield a novel that was truly "novel" in Mexican literature. I think *El último lector* (2004; *The Last Reader,* 2009) is that book. After having penned many worthy iterations of a relentless and slightly wearying realism, convinced that the "circus" of his earlier book had gotten as far as it was going to go, Toscana finally found a more personal yet allegorical fictional motif. What I find most interesting about *El último lector* is the way it posits Mexico (or any place like it) as a country with no books, a nation where literature is a manifest eccentricity, a class privilege. And reality—statistically—bears that out; that's what leads to routine (or ritual) pulling of hair among writers and publishers. That being the case, it made perfect sense to create literature out of this public outrage (if it is one), writing a novel about books as obsolescence, vestiges of a shipwreck from another eon.

By inventing Lucio, a librarian at the end of the world (which could be located in virtually any Mexican town) and giving him control over the entire universe, Toscana has written what I hope will be enduring fiction. Given that his library is closed, because no one cares about the books it holds, and considering that the librarian himself has long since been relieved of his official capacities, Lucio assumes the powers of a demiurge: he and he alone chooses life or death, posterity or annihilation, for the books at hand; the fate of every work of world literature in the town of Melquisedec lies with him. At this point in the plot, it would have been easy for Toscana to offer a review of time-honored classics. But he doesn't. Toscana decided to invent not just the plot of his own novel but also the hallowed works his librarian reads, and then saves or condemns; they're exemplary and imaginary books that both are and are not the same ones you and I have read. With *El último lector*, Toscana's near-perfect prose creates a fable that unfolds in northern Mexico, which in the hands of a talented writer is also quite like the metaphysical south of Faulkner and Onetti.

There are, to be sure, other important storylines in the plot, things going on in the biblically baptized town of Melquisedec, but I prefer to concentrate on the difficulties overcome by Toscana, who has successfully woven a very difficult tale to construct, perhaps a variation on the life of *Bartleby the Scrivener*. This is not the story of a scribe who thrives on vicarious servitude but the trajectory of another kind of incurable, a librarian who defends—or not—that which in theory no longer matters: books, expired repositories of knowledge. On Toscana's map, the library is a region condemned by a timeless and proudly illiterate community, a fiction that, at some point in the twentieth century, became an everyday reality.

SELECTED BIBLIOGRAPHY
Santa María del Circo, Plaza y Janés, Mexico, 1998.
Estación Tula, Sudamericana, Mexico, 2001.
El último lector, Mondadori, Mexico, 2004.

Los puentes de Köningsberg, Alfaguara, Mexico, 2009.

Tula Station, trans. Patricia Duncan, Thomas Dunne Books, 2000.

Our Lady of the Circus, trans. Patricia Duncan, Thomas Dunne Books, 2001.

The Last Reader, trans. Asa Zatz, Texas Tech University Press, 2009.

TRUJILLO, JULIO
(Mexico City, 1969)

Trying to reconstruct the (not entirely free) association I made of Trujillo's *Sobrenoche* with my early adolescence is not an easy task. But it's akin to the way I associate Xavier Villaurrutia's literary nocturnes with trips to the "Roller Coaster"—as kids in Mexico City used to call the children's rides at what was then the new amusement park in Chapultapec Park. You see, I read Villaurrutia at an age when going to the haunted house was still fun. And I can recall riding along in what seemed like old mining cars, getting to the part where suddenly cobwebs would fall across your face. Those are the images that sprung up for me while reading *Sobrenoche*. Villaurrutia's *Nostalgia de la muerte* (1938; *Homesick for Death,* 2004*),* after all, is the reason I see the night as a realm populated by half human, half wax beings that as kids we called "insomniacs" (though we might have called them anything): Bogomils or Venusites, beings who paradoxically came to life to haunt his poems.

Those wandering nocturnal beings, deviants forged of fear and literature make me think of the Belgian surrealists' exhibition at the Chapultepec Museum of Modern Art. It was in July 1974, and I know that because I still have the program. Villaurrutia's nocturnes were used as a pedagogical "illustration" of the paintings of James Ensor, and particularly Paul Delvaux and René Magritte—paintings that understandably had a strong impact on me, showing how far poetry, surrealism, the imagination, and "insomniacs" could go. Now, I'm not exactly sure how this relates to Trujillo's poem (which isn't surrealist or anything close) or to my own artistic or critical education. But if I force myself to hazard a guess, I'd say it's because in *Sobrenoche*, as in other Mexican poetic nocturnes, night is depicted as a region to be conquered, a battlefield you flee defeated, a nightmare that has to be lived through as a cruel rite of passage for all insomniacs.

In *Sobrenoche* I see the protagonist as a young hero who burns through the night as well as a lot of booze, and in so doing nets himself a hangover in the wee hours, a dramatic, short-lived sleepless state where hyperesthesia—that excessive and painful physical sensitivity the dictionary talks of—reigns. This poetic accomplishment can be seen as a logical progression, bearing in mind his earlier book of poems, *Esa sangre* (1998), which impressed numerous readers and prompted Guillermo Sheridan* to say that Trujillo was a young classic subject to the freedom and discipline of Mexico's "modern" classics: Villaurrutia, Jorge Cuesta,* and José Gorostiza.*

Sobrenoche is an obsolete expressionist poem, a luminous, imaginary night in the machine room of the twentieth century, which is distinguished—according to theorists—from all other ages by its obsession with the "real." It's also a moral poem (and in that sense goes back to Octavio Paz's* "San Ildefonso Nocturne") that rebels, à la Ezra Pound (who in another Trujillo poem is seen playing tennis), against money-hungry society and its plutocratic world domination. In the end, it can be read as another urban poem, what's left of a "man of the dawn," to allude to Efraín Huerta,* a poet who Trujillo knows well and with whom it's fair to say that he's carrying on a dialogue.

Every poet has a night—a thousand and one nights for a thousand and one different poets. I can think of a few Mexican poetic nights I've traveled recently, while rereading poetry: the dimly lit night of Jaime Reyes's* *Isla de raíz amarga, insomne raíz*, illuminated only by a Soviet lamp (bare bulb); Hiriart's* night that becomes eternal in *Incurable*'s very black morning. Things go bump in the night, shattered night. A gregarious poet, Trujillo fears ending up alone, like Rubén Bonifaz Nuño's* lonely men who "llegan a las fiestas / ávidos de tiernas compañías" ("arrive at the parties / eager for affectionate company") (*Los demonios y los días*, 1956). Trujillo says of the night that its "intrigue is the answer" and that we don't "osemos traducir sus estertores, su robusta / sintaxis" ("dare translate its death rattles, its robust / syntax"), since "[d]e noche somos noche si dejamos / que el abismo tire" ("at night we are the night if we let / the abyss pull").

"Nocturno," a poem included in *El perro de Koudelka* (2003) might have been a harbinger of *Sobrenoche*. Trujillo is a poet who skillfully covered all the time-honored poetic themes: friendship, a life in books, family snap-shots. But now that he's hit upon night as a state of mind and a tribute to Fritz Lang and the anguished cinematic night of the avant-garde, it looks as if he's left behind the belief attributed to Uruguayan poet Eduardo Milán that only in poetry is the world a properly made place.

Selected Bibliography

Esa sangre, Trilce, Mexico, 1998.
Proa, Marsias, Mexico, 2000.
El perro de Koudelka, Trilce, Mexico, 2003.
Sobrenoche, Taller Ditoria, Mexico, 2005.
Bipolar, Pretextos, Valencia, 2008.
Pitecántropo, Almadía, Oaxaca, 2009.
Ex profeso, Taller Ditoria, Mexico, 2010.

U

URIBE, ÁLVARO
(Mexico City, 1953)

From his earliest stories, Uribe—a disciple of Augusto Monterroso*—was so true to form that, sooner or later, he was bound to produce exceptional books. *El taller del tiempo* (2003) is a short novel that will become timeless, thanks to the intelligent way the author dismantles the family saga, one of literature's oldest clichés. The book's grandfather, father, and son form a chosen trinity who serve as a lesson in style—or perhaps it's a lesson in spiritual anatomy, since the transmigration of souls across generations was what Uribe was interested in examining (he'd already begun in his 1999 collection of essays, *La otra mitad*). Uribe was a reader of Roger Martin du Gard, the forgotten Nobel laureate of 1937 and author of *Les Thibault* who wrote hundreds of pages of social and psychological history. In *El taller del tiempo*, Uribe parted from the premise that human genealogy, if we are "absolutely modern"—and we are—must somehow crop up in another dimension of psychological time and historical space. The novelist sees his creations as faces of a polyhedron, and the form of approach to each of them is an exercise in masterful prose. Through the three protagonists, all named Miguel, Uribe presents what the moderns called a "character study," which pictorially depicts the stances of each generation and also doubles as a chronicle of fifty years of Mexican history.

Grandfather Miguel is representative of the efficient civil servants who guaranteed the State their vicarious servitude in exchange for the kind of sophistication that would allow them to wrap their chauvinism up in the clothing of probity and good manners; while in the name of the son we have all the empty promises of social ascent and the pitiful result in alcoholic defeat. Finally, grandson Miguel is sacrificed, with the daily revolutions of 1968 as backdrop; he's the superfluous and desperate heir of a lineage that sold out at a price much too high, a moral defect that only the clan's women—wives and lovers—are able to see. Another writer would have turned this tale into a predictable series of melodramatic vignettes peppered with quips and admonitions. But each character in *El taller del tiempo* has been superbly captured by the hand of this writer, who knows better than most what it means to write a tragedy. What's more, Uribe's Spanish is probably the best of any Mexican novelist writing today.

SELECTED BIBLIOGRAPHY
La linterna de los muertos, FCE, Mexico, 1988.
La lotería de San Jorge, Vuelta, Mexico, 1995.
La otra mitad, Aldus, Mexico, 1999.
Recordatorio de Federico Gamboa, FCE, Mexico, 1999.
Por su nombre, Tusquets, Mexico, 2001.
El taller del tiempo, Tusquets Editores, Mexico, 2003.
La parte ideal, Aldus, Mexico, 2006.
Expediente del atentado, Tusquets, Mexico, 2007.

USIGLI, RODOLFO

(Mexico City, 1905 – 1979)

Hastily, begrudgingly, Mexico celebrated the hundred-year anniversary of Usigli's birth and then, our duty fulfilled, dropped the curtain over the deserted city he roamed in his nightmares. During his centenary, the lack of Usigli plays being staged was conspicuous: better to honor him with silence, apparently, than theater. Trying to uncover the reasons for such disregard, I read several of the comedies and tragedies published between 1963 and 1996 included in his *Teatro completo* (2005).

One thing I realized is that dramaturgy ages faster than almost anything else, and it's important to keep that in mind when judging Usigli. In theater, if you're not Sophocles or Shakespeare, time becomes a bleak measure of things. Even George Bernard Shaw, Usigli's idol, has largely disappeared from our stages. Borges—whom we tend to take as the authority—said that Shaw was the only writer of his time to devote himself to creating heroes rather than delight in the weaknesses of the human condition. Today that seems meaningless.

Both a political statement and an anti-historical representation, *El gesticulador* (1938; *The Impostor*, 2005), the most famous of Usigli's plays, is a snapshot of Mexican revolutionary party authoritarianism in all its splendor. Usigli was the party's faultfinder, and ended up taking refuge—a none-too-comfortable refuge—in the embassies of Beirut and Oslo. But outside of its context (which needs to be honored), this "play for demagogues" is hard going. It's got an elementary plotline featuring an impostor, a failed historian who arranges to pass himself off as a disappeared, heroic, revolutionary general, which turns out to be fatal. But the title is better—or at least it says more—than the play itself, which presents a world that seems oversimplified and prehistoric, a caricature frighteningly similar to the Mexico of the Institutional Revolutionary Party (PRI) seen in Rius's political cartoons.

As José Emilio Pacheco*—one of the playwright's earliest and most convincing defenders—noted, Usigli knew that by rejecting the path of "absurdism" he'd started down, he was losing the opportunity to portray the maze of Mexican power in a light that would soon be referred to as Kafkaesque. In that vein, I fear that *El gesticulador* and its accompanying "Epílogo sobre la hipocresía del mexicano" are only valuable as initial forays into the phenomenon that, mid-century, became a full-fledged obsession with proving one's "Mexicanness." Although *El gesticulador* predated Gabriel Zaid's* portrait of an academic's twisted will to power, Usigli in fact fits in better with Daniel Cosío Villegas,* José Revueltas,* and Octavio Paz:* intelligentsia who, in the forties, lamented the "betrayal" of the Mexican Revolution, whose transcendental social values had been debased, denied, and corrupted by official party demagoguery. In his later years, Usigli came to comprise part of a symbolic council of old writers (along with Martín Luis Guzmán,* Agustín Yáñez,* and Salvador Novo*) who backed the regime after the 1968 student uprisings. Nevertheless, his worst mistake was not that but taking the bait of the supposed "war of generations" and badmouthing young people simply for being young.

I'm not prepared to judge Usigli's comedies and I don't know if they can be condemned for turning realism into *costumbrismo*, a vestige of a bygone world. More important, and of more substance, is to examine Usigli's *tres coronas* (three crowns), his great attempt at staging an interpretation of the history of Mexico. *Corona de sombra* (1943), the play about Emperors Maximilian and Charlotte, is the most successful, which is only natural since the Austrian archduke tinged everything he touched with both charisma and melancholy. Plus, since Antiquity it's been clear that history concedes majesty everywhere it was lacking. President Benito Juárez's absent presence (which Usigli took from Franz Werfel's *Juárez y Maximiliano*) runs through the work as a parallel storyline, as does Charlotte's insanity (which Fernando del Paso* later took from Usigli and used in *Noticias del imperio*). In a way, it seems fair to say that the tolerant, romanticized affection we Mexicans feel for the short-lived emperors began with Usigli.

Corona de fuego (1960) epitomizes the unfortunate risk run by all artists: that the gods of inspiration might one day stop smiling down on them. Satirized in "No te achicopales, Cacama" by Jorge Ibargüengoitia*—Usigli's sharpest student—*Corona de juego* chronicles the conquest in verse form. Usigli, here, achieves the near impossible feat of taking what López de Gomara called the most extraordinary event in the world since God's creation of it, and making it tedious and cumbersome.

If Shaw's *Saint Joan* (1923) was the paradigm, then only in *Corona de luz* (1963) did Usigli come close to lighting his torch in the sun, to paraphrase Alfred de Musset, another discredited playwright. He had on his side a great theme—the Virgin of Guadalupe—and a rich theatrical precursor: the *auto sacramental* or "sacramental act," staged representations of the Eucharist popular in New Spain. And while Usigli's play can of course bring together, quite implausibly, Queen Isabel and Charles V, friars Juan de Zumárraga, Motolinía, Fray Bernardino de Sahagún, Las Casas, Vasco de Quiroga, and Pedro de Gante, he went too far with his holy conciliabulum, who try to deceive the natives by having a Spanish nun supposedly invested with visionary powers pretend to be the Virgin. Usigli tried to reconcile a Shaw-like view of miracles as rationally explainable accidents with an Alarcón-style comedy that showed those who go after the wool being the ones who end up getting fleeced. In the end, the Indians' belittled natural reason is transformed into faith via the miracle of roses. In general, although its modern—even agnostic—sensibility is irksome, as is the reduction of religious phenomena to mere optical illusions, I would venture to say that *Corona de luz* could still be instructive, and astonishing, to twenty-first-century audiences.

A first-generation criollo, Usigli cast doubt upon Juan Ruiz de Alarcón's Mexicanness as a means of affirming his own. Born of an Italian father and Polish mother, Usigli fought for national theater at a time when it was disappearing from the world's stage. He was au fait with the classics as well as commercial playwrights and neo-classics, and saw Brecht as an example of what to avoid. Thus Usigli made a decision that now seems easy to disparage: he wanted to write Mexican tragedies, and to give Mexico—the way Lessing had given Hamburg—a dramaturgy worth not of the Mexican Revolution, but of its critics. "And I failed, in my way," he'd sometimes say.

Usigli would have been offended by Luis de Tavira, one of his most insightful readers and the critic who prefaced volumes four and five of his *Teatro completo*. Tavira compares him not to Shaw, but to Leandro Fernández de Moratín, reformer of Spanish drama in the nineteenth century, which isn't saying much. Usigli called Moratín and his Mexican disciple Manuel Eduardo de Gorostiza "false neo-classics." I think that his own disciples—voluntary and involuntary—have a hard time expressing what they might feel: that master Usigli was a "false modern" and it was his very attempt to be modern that made him seem outdated and unreal.

That nagging sense of false modernity clinging to Usigli's plays is the result of his pedagogical resolve, his (sometimes admirable) view of theater as education, as a tool (very Vasconcelos, this idea) that can be used to educate the masses—beginning with the elites—turning every citizen into a "democratic individual," as he himself said on many occasions. There's a reason why the scandalous debut of *El gesticulador* at the Palacio de Bellas Artes on May 17, 1947 is lodged in the liberal memory of the generation that suffered all the outrages of the Mexican revolution's regime, which came to demand complicity as crude proof of citizenship.

Usigli wrote that "the most apt definition of character, outside of its aggressive connotations, is the one found in French dictionaries still influenced by the eighteenth century: nature of the soul [. . .] [T]here are no great authors who don't have great characters. The great character, the exemplary character is the dramatic poet's opinion come to life—that's what makes him human, and not superhuman; subjective, not objective; profound, not simply moral."

Usigli sets himself up on that one. It's very tempting to turn his words on him and say that over the entire course of his long, dramatic career, the one thing he's lacked is a memorable character. And that absence is even more surprising given his literary virtues: his taste for rolling up his shirtsleeves and getting his hands dirty, his passion for a job well done, his crusade to turn literature into a clean game and a professional trade where improvisation, bohemia, and laziness won't do. In his tragedies and his comedies, prologues and epilogues, prose and free verse, didactic essays and political articles, novels and translations, journals and conversations with other writers, in every genre Usigli practiced, it's hard to find a poorly written page, a negligent paragraph, an unworkable idea.

The re-evaluation of Usigli as more than Mexico's premier dramatist is a work in progress that began with Paz's* prologue to *Poesía en movimiento* (1965). Paz rightly decided to anthologize Usigli as a poet, and as recently as 1991 in "Rodolfo Usigli en el teatro de la memoria" remarked on the close friendship that brought them together in postwar Paris. Since then, Antonio Deltoro* has been one of the few to write about his poetry, along with Pacheco, who compiled and prefaced *Tiempo y memoria en conversación desesperada: Poesía, 1923–1974* (1981). But old suspicion has conspired against seeing Usigli as one of our great poets, doubts ranging from his thankless role as the poor stepchild of the *Contemporáneos* to our apparent difficulty in recognizing a writer's talent in more than one arena. He's a playwright, that's enough fame. And of course his bitterness did nothing to help. According to Pacheco, Paz had to convince him to abandon his long-planned roman à clef about the *Contemporáneos* entitled *Inteligencias estériles* ("sterile minds"), which—who knows?—might be lurking in draft form among his unpublished works.

Usigli's poetry serves to fill a void, the absence of woman, which Paz noted in *Los Contemporáneos* as a "rough, desolate, dry, somber" presence that, as Pacheco sees it, refers to the many women Usigli knew and loved. Without being metaphysical, his poetry avoids the plaintive, crepuscular half tones he hated that are so characteristic of Mexican poets writing of loves lost.

During the months he spent in New Haven in 1936, where he'd gone to study dramatic composition with Xavier Villaurrutia, Usigli—at the time translating as well as living and breathing T. S. Eliot—wrote a whole series about the trifling nature of the male condition, which gets more complicated each day, lurching between Don Juan and his ghosts. Usigli's poetry, specializing in a sort of sorrowful ennui, is both fun and skeptical, talking of both orgasm and abortion, of the banal yet sublime chase and the comically sinister nature of beauty. In the end, he conceded that Shaw was right, concluding in sonnet and free verse, in epigrams and ten-line stanzas, that sex gets better (literary) press than it deserves, and states as much in *Voces: Diario de trabajo (1932–1933)*. Usigli worked on this Stendhalian journal until its publication in 1967, and it's one of the finest (and most unknown) journals in Mexican literature.

In the preface to *Obliteración*, the almost fantastic tale he wrote in 1949—and published in 1973—Usigli said that he's never felt comfortable in Europe, and felt disheartened in his search for what his parents had lost a generation earlier. His own homeland was not so much Mexico as it was Mexico City, which he traversed alone countless times after parties and scandals; it was the place he put down roots as well as a character—more than a setting—in *Ensayo de un crimen* (1944), which is so much more than a detective novel.

Usigli's essays on Mexico were political, in the moral and civic sense Shaw used the word, but they weren't always on target, if indeed they had one. A triple Catholic (as a Mexican, an Italian, and a Pole), Usigli associated his inherited religion with the hypocrisy inherent in public life, and admired what he was as the forthrightness of Protestantism. He had too much indignation and not enough theory. And—and this is serious for a devotee of Shaw—lacking the light-heartedness and joy of a true moralist, although he was ironic and self-deprecating, he saved his humor for his poetry. His diatribes about Mexico, in the end, were biased, the work of a writer who—like Stendhal—didn't mind being ambassador and would have accepted a post as minister had it been offered, convinced that academia had barred the gates to him.

Volume five of *Teatro completo* contains Usigli's texts on the history and teaching of "the history of theater in Mexico." That's a somewhat deceptive title, as many of the essays far exceed the meticulous lectures that the professor took pains to prepare for his students. As Pacheco rightly said, no one in Mexico so thoroughly mastered his field the way Usigli did, and these lectures prove it. They're a brief history of twentieth-century dramatic arts at the time Usigli studied them. All I can reproach him for is his covetousness, which led to not being particularly forthcoming about his sources. But perhaps that's a justifiable fault in someone like him, who felt that only the unoriginal cared about originality, something he felt authentic artists saw as mere adornment. Perhaps originals are only those who go back to the origin. And neither Shakespeare nor Cervantes, he declared, played that Romantic trick. It wasn't Romanticism itself he hated, but its stage machinery—castles and drawbridges and the like. No one had ruined theater as much as Victor Hugo, in Usigli's opinion.

The only Mexican writer to have written a play in French and poetry in English, Usigli—as is obvious reading the essays in volume five of *Teatro completo*—was more widely read than his illustrious compatriots. Perhaps less dense and challenging than Cuesta,* but more interesting than Villaurrutia and free of the stuffy academicism that made Jaime Torres Bodet* asphyxiating.

Expressing admiration is thorny but Usigli was quite comfortable with it, and it paid off. His passion for Shaw had a relatively happy ending (unlike Federico Gamboa, who at the end of the nineteenth century paid a visit to the French naturalists and was rewarded with a bucket of cold water). In *Conversaciones y encuentros* (1974), also included in volume five of *Teatro completo*, Usigli leads readers by the hand through Shaw's house in Ayot Saint Lawrence, where in the spring of 1945, when he was nearly 90 years old, he agreed to two visits. Shaw had been to Mexico before and, as legend has it, while he was there he demanded royalties of a student theater group paying him homage. More a professional stoically fulfilling his role than an old man complacent with his fame, Shaw—oldest son of the new school—bore Usigli's audacity well, and weeks after the visit let him know that he'd read *Crown of Light* (1971), the English translation of *Corona de sombra* that Usigli had left him.

Months earlier, Usigli had visited T. S. Eliot in London. In 1938, Eliot, idiosyncratically, had demanded royalties for Usigli's translation of "The Love Song of J. Alfred Prufrock." The translator responded by saying that in Mexico, those things were labors of love that didn't bring anyone any money. On this second visit, on November 15, 1944, Usigli went by the offices of Faber and Faber at nightfall and it was Eliot himself who opened the door, explaining that due to the bombings all offices needed someone to act as guard at night, and that day it was his turn. The two of them drank beer until four in the morning, discussing theater, death, the unpopularity of poetry, and the Lindbergh kidnapping. A year later, Eliot paid a visit to him at the Piccadilly hotel where he was staying, and Usigli showed him Posada's skeletons. Even if Usigli embellished the story—as we all do when something makes an impression on us—his encounters with Shaw and Eliot (and the forgotten Henri Lenormand and actor Paul Muni, who played both Emile Zola and Benito Juárez) make magisterial chamber theater.

Many people said many things about Usigli. Paz called him Prufrock lost in Mexico City; he also said that, like Paz's own father, he was trapped in a prison of booze. Ibargüengoitia described him arriving at UNAM's Mascarones Center with all of his accessories: cigarette holder, cigarette case, lighter, antacid, cane if it was dry, umbrella if it was wet. Héctor Manjarrez,* with whom he spent time in the seventies, wondered why it was so easy not to express admiration for that "short, skinny, old, wounded, caring, sincere" playwright who worked as ambassador. And Usigli himself recounted being punched by Novo on the stairs of the Palacio de Bellas Artes. These are impressive images, real or figurative, and they've lodged themselves in our memory: stage lights trained on a dramatist who navigated devastating fires—whether bombs in London or the ancient destruction of Mexico-Tenochtitlán—and had a date with Shaw, with Eliot, and with himself.

SELECTED BIBLIOGRAPHY

Teatro completo, vol I–III, FCE, Mexico, 1963.

Teatro completo, vol IV. *Escritos sobre la historia del teatro en México*, ed. Luis de Tavira, FCE, Mexico, 1963.

Teatro completo, vol V. *Escritos sobre la historia del teatro en México*, ed. Luis de Tavira and Alejandro Usigli, FCE, Mexico, 1963.

Diario de trabajo (1932–1933), INBA, Mexico, 1967.

Tiempo y memoria en conversación desesperada. Poesía, 1923–1974, ed. José Emilio Pacheco, UNAM, Mexico, 1981.

Ensayo de un crimen, SEP, Mexico, 1986.

Conversación desesperada, ed. and prologue by Antonio Deltoro, Seix Barral, Mexico, 2000.

Bruce Swansey, *Del fraude al milagro. Visión de la historia en Usigli*, UAM, Mexico, 2010.

Two Plays: Crown of Light and One of These Days, trans. Thomas Bledsoe, Southern Illinois University Press, 1971.

Mexico in the Theater, trans. Wilder P. Scott, University of Mississippi Press, 1978.

The Impostor, trans. Ramón Leyera, Latin American Literary Review Press, 2005.

V

VALADÉS, EDMUNDO
(Guaymas, Sonora, 1915, – Mexico City, 1994)

While he was still alive, no one dared to say that Valadés was what the French call an *écrivain raté*. But he himself admitted it. Once, after a few drinks, he shut up a sycophant by confessing: "I'm perfectly aware that I'm a mediocre writer!" The couple of books Valadés wrote, *La muerte tiene permiso* (1955) and *Las dualidades funestas* (1966), are memorable only to two types of people, polar opposites in cultural terms: literary historians, and everyday run-of-the-mill readers. The first see him as a founder of Mexico's urban violence literature, which began once Juan Rulfo* had concluded the rural trend. The second—those who bought up every copy of successive editions of *La muerte tiene permiso*—love reading an author who makes it easy on them with synthetic colloquialism and an economy of form.

Mediocre writer? Yes, perhaps, if we take mediocrity to be that middle ground that 99% of us, if we're lucky, are condemned to inhabit as writers. I don't know if Valadés will, as Borges might say, beat you and me in the race to oblivion, but nor do I see literary history as an anthology of masterpieces. If it were, at least as far as Mexican literature is concerned, we could close discussion after Guzmán's* *La sombra del caudillo*, Rulfo's *Pedro Páramo* and—in a pinch—Fuentes's* *La muerte de Artemio Cruz* (*The Death of Artemio Cruz*).

Valadés knew that literature was not just the output of a romantic genius. Like so many young writers, he dreamed of measuring up to Proust, his favorite novelist. But he found himself inadequate to the task and, in a sign of genuine intelligence, decided to devote himself to characters who were less brilliant than the Princesse de Guermantes but more numerous and more necessary: readers. And he fought for them.

Through the magazine *El Cuento*—which had two stints: 1939 and 1964–1995—Valadés presented a relatively wide public with the beauty and range of the genre—short stories—that he loved. A true democrat of letters, Valadés gave provincial teenagers, rural schoolteachers, restless housewives, and young writers the joys of Chekhov, Maupassant, Gogol, Pardo Bazán, Joyce, and O. Henry. And when someone writes the history of reading in Mexico, it's going to become clear that the anonymous readers of *El Cuento* were legion, astonishingly so in what's essentially a country that doesn't read. That alone justifies including Valadés—a literary legionnaire—in the annals of Mexican literary life. But, as many people know, he was also a great teacher to both novelists and short story writers. Through workshops and friendships, Valadés taught the trade to many authors who today enjoy fame and fortune. In piano, we venerate those who, while not great performers themselves, produced virtuosos via their instruction. But literature is more unforgiving. Failed, flawed, or infertile writers like Valadés are always judged by their books rather than by their talents.

Let me close with an anecdote. In 1991, I was returning from Tlaxcala, as fate would have it, in the company of both Valadés and a young journalist. We still had a ways to go before reaching Puebla, and the young woman— whether impertinent or just a cretin, I don't know—asked Don Edmundo to "tell her a story," since that was what the old man did for a living. Mortified on her behalf, I decided the best course of action would be to stare out the window. But soon it became clear that Valadés was going to comply. The story he told us, word for word, was Maupassant's "Ball-of-Fat" (*Servidumbre y grandeza de la vida literaria*, 1998)

Selected Bibliography
La muerte tiene permiso, FCE, Mexico, 1959.
Las dualidades funestas, Joaquin Mortiz, Mexico, 1966.
Sólo los sueños y los deseos son inmortales, Palomita, Océano, Mexico, 1986.

VALLE-ARIZPE, ARTEMIO DE

(Saltillo, Coahuila, 1888 – Mexico City, 1961)

Valle-Arizpe used the trappings of the evil History of Man to reinvent our early days: the colonial period. Passionate not so much about religion as he was about liturgy, he had no interest in the flesh, the devil, or even the real world, for that matter. Instead, his literature was born of referents, words designating objects—"cabinet," "candy," "dress"—that, from the moment they are named become phonetic characters, anecdotal characters. By using archaism, the ruins of a semi-dead language, in an exaggerated yet sterile way, he turned authenticity into a joke that consumed his life. Valle-Arizpe was the man who made colonialism routine. His books are still being reprinted, without fanfare but steadily. Who reads them? He wrote for a middle-class readership on the verge of extinction, but there must also be a secret contingency of readers for whom the birth of our nation, far from being an event, is a Romantic invention they can't live without. (*Antología de la narrativa mexicana del siglo XX*, I, 1989)

SELECTED BIBLIOGRAPHY
Obras, vols I–II, FCE, Mexico, 2000.

VALLEJO, FERNANDO

(Medellín, Colombia, 1942)

Unlike other mythological twins, Castor and Pollux—known collectively as the *Dioskouroi*—were quite close and had no rivalry between them, loving each other openly and fondly sharing a whole host of adventures. These fabled siblings remind me of the protagonist brothers in *El desbarrancadero* (2001), the second novel of Mexican-Colombian author Fernando Vallejo, who apparently felt that *La virgen de los sicarios* (1994; *Our Lady of the Assassins*, 2001) wasn't enough and now brings us another tremendous, moving, prodigal novel.

"I'm not a third-person novelist, so I don't know what my characters think," exclaims the narrator of *El desbarrancadero*, the implacable chronicler of the agony faced by his brother who is dying of AIDS. Vallejo, in turn, uses the disease freely—mocking the very concept of metaphor—to describe everything he hates: mothers, families, God and his vicarious Roman Pope, the city of Medellín, corrupt politicos, poor people who kill other poor people. Traveling from the land of embezzlement and lies (Mexico) to the land of murder (Colombia), Vallejo gives us another novel-lampoon that, like *La virgen de los sicarios,* could be read as a nihilist manifesto. But to read Vallejo solely as a Colombian (or Latin American), aggrieved to the point of nausea and derision, is to do him insufficient justice. The whole world is indignant; but only a consummate mastery of the narrative art can turn deprecating bile into violent music. I accept the hyperbolic consequences of what I'm about to say: Vallejo is the Céline of Latin American violence.

When I say "lampoon," I mean a text that's easy to get hold of, passed around secretly, underground, whose aim is to morally or politically lynch people, reputations, parties, or countries. Colombia pains Vallejo; otherwise, he wouldn't lampoon it. And lampoonists are the most desperate of moralists. But Vallejo's pain far exceeds mere routine complaint and national resentment, thanks to his watertight characters. While *Our Lady of the Assassins* showed homoerotic, aestheticized violence, in *El desbarrancadero* the novelist lets himself be pulled along by a rhetorical tide much trickier to negotiate: compassion. I'm using the word in the etymological sense of accompanying someone in his passion, sharing agony through solidarity, black humor, and, in the end, real and symbolic death—the grave from which the novel is narrated. Dario, the dying man, is initiated into homosexuality by his brother, who buys him the services of a boy in Bogotá. And that's when they truly become brothers, not when they began their lives together in a large, Cainite family. Their fateful complicity unites them until the HIV test, when one is condemned to death and the other to write. An ad hoc general practitioner—and enemy of all other doctors—the narrator decides to use veterinary products to medicate his brother, for example giving him a bovine sulphoanimide in an (unsuccessful) attempt to stop his diarrhea. In any other novel, the vignette would have been vulgar, but in Vallejo it becomes a meditation on man's fragile animalism that manages not even to resort to metaphysics. The narrator hates people not because they're black or white, liberal or conservative, Colombian or Mexican, gay or women, drug traffickers or shysters, but because they're human.

El desbarrancadero, like so many great novels, is the chronicle of a family's extinction. And although the beloved father is freed from his existence by a sort of euthanasia, the country and city—Colombia and Medellín—will never be erased from the face of the earth. Weeds never die, though the narrator wishes every atomic bomb China ever wasted on underground tests would be dropped on his country.

Vallejo, who has lived in Mexico since 1971, is a novelist of extreme ideas, one who merits Matthew Arnold's idea of the novelist as supreme critic of life. *El desbarrancadero* seems to stem from the old heretical tradition of the Encratites, who saw reproduction as a diabolical multiplication of Evil. Vallejo's characters, travelers on their own journey to the end of the night, manage to survive their time on earth by harkening back to their happy days, when they lived as individuals. And although Vallejo denounces almost everything, he's not a demagogue, despite the fact that he uses (very well) an entire arsenal of slander. Indignant, yes, foul-mouthed, yes, but this tragicomic writer who chronicles a world of disgrace knows when to stop and offer the antidote to his own venom: "And forgive me for the liberty of speaking on your behalf, for when I smugly said *man*, I ought to have humbly said *I*."

SELECTED BIBLIOGRAPHY
La virgen de los sicarios, Alfaguara, Bogotá, 1994.
El desbarrancadero, Alfaguara, Mexico, 2001.
Our Lady of the Assassins, trans. Paul Hammond, Serpent's Tail, 2001.

VASCONCELOS, JOSÉ
(Oaxaca, Oaxaca, 1882 – Mexico City, 1959)

"History teaches us that barbarism was never capable of producing literature, and nor was decadence," opens Vasconcelos's *La flama* (1959). It's an absurd pronouncement, but it shows where he stood as a theorist of the decadence that he himself embodied and theorized. The barbarity he was referring to was the Mexican Revolution, stressing the religious persecution it unleashed; the decadence in question was that of a nation that never lived up to the Atlanteans, first, or the true Christians of the Cristero Wars, second. From classical paganism to Roman Catholicism, Vasconcelos always preached civilization over barbarism, and the resounding voice in *La flama* is that of father of the bastards, the prophet who tried to legitimize his children both at Olympus and in the baptismal fount. All to no avail. From Athens to the Aguascalientes Convention, Pythagoras to Saint Paul, President Madero to Vasconcelos's own failed run for presidency in 1929, it was all for naught. Which was why the final solution, as the book's title suggests—*La flama* means "the flame"—had to come by fire.

A man who lived through the victories of barbarism, a "civilizer" so often ignored, Vasconcelos bitterly assumed the role of decadent writer. My contemptible old-fashioned prose, he seemed to say, was borne of the ill-fated era in which I lived. A writer who always scorned "Literature," he wrote *La flama* as if to prove that order and style—the *Ateneos'* classicist aspirations—were wasted on a public who, like dogs, could only understand being smacked with a newspaper. Lampoons disguised as op-ed pieces were the remnants of the hellfire verses of the prophets.

La flama was where Vasconcelos first clearly presented his idea—more Gnostic than Christian—of the devil as Lord of the World, monarch of Mexico, the immortal *tlatoani*—or supreme ruler—of the Aztecs, the god of night, Tezcatlipoca, who blinded Mexico with his magic mirror. If the Atlanteans ever existed, they were gone forever. Vasconcelos didn't have to wrack his brains to find the origin of his demonology in the pre-Hispanic world. Like Juan Ginés de Sepúlveda back in the sixteenth century, he saw the war against the Indians as just, given that they were a soulless civilization born of original sin. Fray Juan de Zumárraga was right to have destroyed their idols, and Fray Diego de Landa had good reason to burn their codices. Had they pillaged the Indians *without* teaching them Christian doctrine, he maintained, now *that* would have been barbarous. Las Casas penned the "very brief history of the destruction of the Indies" and Vasconcelos had his own very brief *exaltation* of the destruction of the Indies, in which he condemned Las Casas and Sahagún, calling them dangerous Erasmists and lazy antiquarians. There are no idols behind the altars, Vasconcelos virtually shouted, as the only Indians who'll be saved are those who bowed before the Virgin of Guadalupe when she appeared on the hill in 1531 [. . .]

The overarching theme of Huitzilopochtli—god of war—is easy to make out in Vasconcelos's panorama. It may have been José Juan Tablada, in a curious little novel entitled *La resurrección de los ídolos* (1922), who reintroduced the idea of a deep dark Mexico immune to Christianization, a nation reborn in every crime—real or imaginary—committed by the docile masses before their god. Tablada's text ends with a grotesque vision of the mountains giving birth and the Aztecs rising up from Mictlán to impose their law on modern Mexico. Later, Tablada accused D. H. Lawrence of having stolen his idea to write *The Plumed Serpent*.

In 1929, Vasconcelos still had faith in dualities: on the one hand Huitzilopochtli (personified in revolutionaries Zapata, Huerta, and Calles, for instance); on the other, Quetzalcóatl, the plumed serpent redeemer (represented by Madero and, of course, Vasconcelos himself). But after his failed run for presidency, the devil won for good. In *La flama*, he writes of "Huichiperros" instead of Huichilobos (the Spanish for Huitzilopochtli)—"perros" meaning "dogs" rather than "wolves" ("lobos")—so as not to offend the wolves, who—the author explains—at least are not cowards. And Huichiperros lives and barks within every Mexican: from lowlife thugs to the Supreme Chief of the Revolution, all were Cristero killers, torturers, rapists.

Having initially been the great theorist of the Mexican Revolution, the man who posited it as a universal act of redemption, Vasconcelos became its most virulent detractor. But seeing the universe as an apocalyptic place ruled by Huichiperros wasn't something that happened overnight, come 1929. The battle between civilization and barbarity raged through his work from the start. And when history lurched irremediably towards barbarity, Vasconcelos was consistent with his values and, like other disillusioned twentieth-century intellectuals, renounced 1789, when the revolutionary proletariat flaunted good sense like a whore before Notre Dame. As he'd suspected ever since the 1914 Aguascalientes Convention, all the revolution did was drastically accelerate barbarism: only "wretched souls could worship the Revolution, which equates to venerating corruption" [. . .]

Once he'd abandoned the Platonic myth of Atlantis and its Pythagorean overtones, Vasconcelos assumed the more placid, moderate duality of Catholicism. But in time, his fear of Marxism and liberalism ended up throwing the system out of whack, as the darkness of the Antichrist lurked throughout the land, thus requiring a return to monism for the Final Solution: apocatastasis. Vasconcelos's trip around the world of Reason didn't end, as he thought it did, with Our Father, but with the Manichean nausea of Creation. Theologically speaking, the prophet stopped being a Christian.

I wrote this little divertimento as a way of illustrating the end of Vasconcelos's rocky road to heresy. His life was the story of Mexican heterodoxy, his turbulent path full of grandeur, pathos, and idiocy. From his view of a "cosmic race" to nuclear inferno, from Atlantis to apocatastasis, Vasconcelos always aspired to measure up to both the Greek classics and the church elders. That's why I see him as the North star of Mexican classicism—a galaxy he presided over with lonely, mercurial sovereignty—the splenetic monarch who set Creation alight with one breath of fire, a philosopher prince who destroyed Mexican tradition every time he seemed to complete it. Vasconcelos, it's been said, was both a giant and a dwarf. A poor devil and the actual Devil. The spiritual leader who redeemed the Mexican Revolution, only to deny it three times. The great educational reformer, Teacher of America who dreamed of every child having an intimate encounter with books, applauded the autos-da-fé of Hitler and Franco. The prophet of the "cosmic race," the only non-racist racial utopia conceived of at that time, ended his days endorsing every diabolical persecution there was. The democratic candidate defeated in 1929 died expecting favors from the same wretched authoritarianism that had let him down from the start. The only thing that didn't change was his love of Antonieta Rivas Mercado, whom he'd saved from hell, watching over her time in purgatory. Vasconcelos, our redeemer, concluded his oeuvre with an ode to the H-bomb. At this point, I'm unsure as to whether his "fire" was allegorical or literal. I have to pause, distraught, to mention this ode, "La B-H" (1950), a defamation of all humanity, the cruelest rhetorical revenge any intellectual has ever sought on his fellow man. A great writer but a petty theologian, he went too far in his search that Primal Energy that had always fascinated him. Vasconcelos punished us with fire, incinerating the cosmic race that was never created despite his call, disowning us all, the bastard children who denied him as Father. His prophetic curse will hound us to the end of history. (*Tiros en el concierto: Literatura mexicana del siglo V*, 1997)

SELECTED BIBLIOGRAPHY

Memorias, vol I, Ulises criollo. La tormenta, FCE, Mexico, 1982.

Memorias, vol II, El desastre. El proconsulado, FCE, Mexico, 1983.

La otra raza cósmica, ed. and trans. Heriberto Yépez, Almadía, Oaxaca, 2010.

A Mexican Ulysses: An Autobiography, trans. and abridged by W. Rex Crawford, Greenwood Publishing Group, 1963.

The Cosmic Race: A Bilingual Edition, trans. Didier T. Jaén, Johns Hopkins, 1979 and 1987.

VICENS, JOSEFINA

(Villahermosa, Tabasco, 1911 – Mexico City, 1988)

El libro vacío (1958; *The Empty Book*, 1992), disparaged when it first came out, has increased notably in estimation over the years. The book's theme, like its prose, is very straightforward. It's an office worker's notebook, in which he writes about his desire to write a novel that he'll never write, and which will theoretically be written in another notebook set aside for just that purpose, which is and will ever remain blank—the "empty book" of the title. Vicens's style is as meticulous as it is basic: nothing peripheral derails her fundamental accessibility. The life of her protagonist José García is that of thousands of anonymous men and women [. . .] Yet on a higher plane, Vicens encapsulates the spirit of the times. Of all the novels written by her generation, none compares to *El libro vacío* in terms of how profoundly it probes the essence of what it means to be modern. An all-encompassing synthesis, the book invokes an empty city devoid of any of the attraction of community, a place that engenders empty souls, shells of human beings. In their own way, contemporaries Rubén Salazar Mallen,* Rodolfo Usigli,* and Rafael Bernal all knew this. But each of them looked to the mirror of otherness as a way of rendering meaninglessness. Lonely men, bureaucrats, killers, and cops are all characters who have faith in the certainty of action. José García, on the other hand, places no faith in anything aside from the act of writing, that pleasureless urge. (*Antología de la narrativa mexicana del siglo XX*, I, 1989)

SELECTED BIBLIOGRAPHY
El libro vacío. Los años falsos, FCE, Mexico, 2006.
The False Years, trans. Peter Earle, Latin American Literary Review Press, 1989.
The Empty Book, trans. David Lauer, University of Texas Press, 1992.

VILLEGAS, PALOMA
(Mexico City, 1951)

Almost a decade after *La luz oblicua* (1995), Paloma Villegas published her second novel *Agosto y fuga* (2004), which, like the first, is a well-crafted story that unfolds in the terrain where political passions and personal dramas overlap, a realm cultivated by authors of the sixties and seventies. But while *La luz oblicua* dealt with the aftermath of 1968—twenty years later—*Agosto y fuga* sets itself an even greater challenge: chronicling the Mexico of 1994 via a group of political militants working for Cuauhtémoc Cárdenas's second presidential campaign and reveling in the euphoria college students felt at the January 1 Zapatista uprising. I call it a greater challenge because a decade is not the same as twenty years, and *Agosto y fuga* could easily have suffered from the scant historical distance separating us from that *annus horribilis* whose daunting convolutedness Villegas so skillfully captures.

Having set a precedent for careful dissection with *La luz oblicua*'s sentimental and political autopsy of the early seventies, Villegas shocked me with her tender, agreeable depiction of characters in *Agosto y fuga*—good middle-class kids busy constructing civil society, seemingly cosseted by the novelist and threatened only by imponderable erotic and amorous mishaps. Villegas's world is a small one (the same as mine, as chance would have it: Coyoacán), and hers is a conservative novel in the same way that, say, Edith Wharton is conservative. The only difference I see between the way Wharton manages to preserve the ecosystem of 1900s New York high society and the way Villegas recounts the lives of politically committed denizens of Coyoacán is chronological. In both cases the novelists depict immobile worlds whose relationship to political history (in Villegas) or to a cosmopolitanism as esteemed as it is erotically dysfunctional (in Wharton) is merely incidental.

Nothing will change their ways (e.g., their ambiguous relationships to "the help," so typically bourgeois) or destroy their view of themselves as a self-sufficient, morally upstanding social caste, an elite accustomed to witnessing historical transformations that never meet their utopian expectations. Disappointment and desperation, thus, not only form part of the narrative structure but of their generation's routine. But I like Edith Wharton, and I compare her to Villegas not just for the apparent paradox of radical characters being depicted as conservative but for a whole host of technical virtues: the restrained narrative thread, agile prose, the way she treats her readers, and her ability to capture strong female characters and their physical movement. Disconsolate Nora, traipsing on foot across a Mexico City on the cusp of becoming forever unnavigable, is a fine requiem.

Novels like *Agosto y fuga* need time to steep awhile before revealing their true nature. Most turn out to be *costumbrista* works that date quickly, and then die; a few prove themselves to be well-painted family portraits with broad color schemes that take on new nuances with the patina of time. In just two novels, Villegas has said more about the life of a generation—her own— than many who write for a lifetime without her patience and discretion and in particular her anguished realization of the fact that artists can only assign a handful of fictional characters the task of making sense of their existence.

SELECTED BIBLIOGRAPHY
La luz oblicua, ERA, Mexico, 1995.
Agosto y fuga, ERA, Mexico, 2004.

VILLORO, JUAN
(Mexico City, 1956)

Villoro's career is the chronicle of an anomaly, one that over the years has become increasingly unsettling. He's sharp and intelligent, but he lacks a truly great work to honor what is indubitably his love of literature. I don't know if *El testigo* (2004) is a masterpiece or not, but it's an excellent book that fits his literary trajectory, a trajectory that may have been hindered by his being prematurely feted as the epitome of our literary promise.

While his short story collections *La noche navegable* (1980) and *Albercas* (1985) were nightmarish continuations of the trivial, adolescent world of *Gazapo*, his first novel *El disparo de Argón* (1991) possessed Nabakovian virtues that simply magnified our disappointment with *Materia dispuesta* (1996), a deplorable *Bildungsroman* that did a terrible job of recounting the intersecting lives of a father and son between the earthquakes of 1957 and 1985. The confirmation of his talents in a third book of stories—*La casa pierde* (1999)—couldn't mitigate the by-then almost routine feeling that Villoro wasn't living up to expectations. *Efectos personales* (2000) didn't have the dazzling depictions of writers like Thomas Bernhard and Valle-Inclán, and was nothing like the stimulating prologue he wrote to Lichtenberg's *Aforismos* (*The Waste Book*, 2001); his novels lacked the magnificent observations of his nonfiction, such as his vignette on sportswriter Ángel Fernández and his recounting of the Zapatista convention in *Los once de la tribu* (1995). But when called on to replace Salvador Novo* and Carlos Monsiváis,* who had chronicled Mexican life with such sensitivity that they captured all of its societal complexities and audaciously transcribed it, he refused. Villoro remained faithful to his honorable temperament, incompatible with ideological confrontations and fields mined with moral outrage.

El testigo is one of those works that give meaning to a life in literature. It's the last piece of the puzzle that allows us to see the whole writer, a vital contemporary we feel the urge to converse with, knowing that his conversation ensures our survival. *El testigo* is both exciting and surprising, for in it Villoro has boldly decided to attempt The Great Mexican Novel in a way that hasn't been seen since Carlos Fuentes,* Fernando del Paso,* Juan García Ponce,* and Jorge Aguilar Mora.* Nowadays, Mexican fiction tends to be split into two types: the kind that perverts the Latin American cosmopolitan tradition with an often-commercial exoticism, and the kind that—out of fear or judiciousness—refuses to try to turn fiction into a way to explain Mexico, a country that rejoices now more than ever in its monopoly on mystic teratology. But Villoro, using the earliest known myth—Ulysses returning from Ithaca after twenty years—dares to present a nineteenth-century fictional image of Mexico, that is, a mosaic that includes the city and the country, the rich and the poor, usufructuaries of cultural power and patrons of the arts, inconsequential authors and criminals—in short, the clash between old and modern.

Trained in the best Balzacian school that sees fiction as exposing society's underside, Villoro chose Mexico in the year 2000—the end of the long reign of the Institutional Revolutionary Party (PRI)—as the country his hero would return to. And his "hero" is an academic—a fraud—specializing in López Velarde, failed candidate for the post of national poet. Julio Valdivieso, Villoro's Ulysses, finds himself in a country that's become a sort of postmodern soap opera in which he plays a minor role: chance witness to the filming of a TV miniseries about the Cristero War whose vindictive political connotations clash with the views of the ultra-Catholic Ramón López Velarde. The location, conveniently, is Los Cominos hacienda, where the protagonist grew up and where he'll pretend he's Pedro Páramo in a pick-up.

A carefully crafted novel that aspires to replace Fuentes's* *La región más transparente* (*Where the Air is Clear*) in its educational imaginary, *El testigo* is a critique of the national melodrama that our society has become, and it ends up being quite a high-budget production itself. While Villoro's visuals required expensive rural locations reminiscent of those captured by cinematographers Gabriel Figueroa and Robert Rodríguez, his Mexico City is a more nostalgic backdrop than it is retro—an aquatic Aztec garden where, predictably, the go-getters come to die, victims of coke and violence (perpetrated by drug cartels and cops in equal parts). Julio Valdivieso himself, in the end, will become a chance witness to this violence. In my opinion, that final episode is a sort of pathetic fallacy that's out of sync with the novel and expresses the terror that we intellectuals feel on finding ourselves frenetically entangled in the kind of horror that seems to demand accomplices rather than witnesses. In this sense, Villoro exemplifies something Salman Rushdie said shortly before his fatwa was issued: "Realism can break a writer's heart."

The literary heart of *El testigo* resides in the attempt of some rich San Luis Potosí farmers—and their leader, the memorable Father Monteverde—to canonize López Velarde. And within the fictional sacristy, I sense the benevolent spirit of two of Villoro's most important contemporaries: Roberto Bolaño* and Enrique Vila-Matas. It's impossible not to read "Saint" Ramón López Velarde without sensing Bolaño's parodic viewpoint or Vila-Matas's idea of the writer as protagonist of a universal novel about (redundantly) world literature. I can't blame Villoro: if I wrote novels, I'd find it impossible to write without feeling the pair of them flitting around behind me.

But by choosing not to capitalize on the plotline provided by that group of Mexico City laymen who band together to fight the religious appropriation of López Velarde that Julio Valdivieso barely registers, Villoro tackles the anguish of one's influences: combating ecclesiastical rogues would have been something the savage detectives took on. But the similarity between Villoro and Bolaño is both logical and well-founded: both undertook their literary educations in 1970s Mexico City, where "infrarealists" abounded. In *El testigo* Villoro portrays them; in *The Savage Detectives* Bolaño turns them into an art form.

Mexican literature is beset with miniaturists, poets awed by the underside of the dining-room table. But Villoro is the only one to actually make sense of the anodyne, the disposable, the fleeting, that magic of everyday domestic paraphernalia, and he does so via his own special syntax, which culminates in *El testigo*. A reverence for idiosyncratic banality, so characteristic of his phrasing, paradoxically made me appreciate *El testigo* more for its surprising—and very beautiful—poetic accomplishments (the result of an almost geological immersion in Rulfo and López Velarde) than for its Balzacian quality. Let me pose, as an example, the prosodic cadence with which he associates a well, coins, and water during those final chapters in which Julio Valdivieso meets his own destiny while probing into that of López Velarde.

Villoro ends *El testigo* with the same response Octavio Paz* gave Borges when the Argentine asked him what chia water, mentioned in López Velarde's *La suave patria*, tasted like: "It tastes like the earth." I was at first touched by that ending, after having read—pages earlier—that the protagonist was going to take a loan and move to the country. But in a process that says more about me than it does about the author, hours later I began to feel disappointed, even personally outraged at how easily I'd been duped. It was the oldest of tricks: the solution provided by good, country people, by a Mother Earth I find hard to swallow, one that allows intellectuals to see the burning plain as a metaphor for the redemption of a nation whose savage modernity both pains and repulses them. The triathlete Julio Valdivieso, having gone the distance and passed the tests—erotic, nostalgic, and intellectual—Villoro subjected him to, finds a warrior's rest with a peasant woman, hypostasis of the nation whose bed the author literally drives him to.

In Guillermo Fadanelli's* *Lodo*, we have the opposite itinerary—a trip through the Mexican provinces that, unlike *El testigo*, ends not in reconciliation but in murder, a Revueltas*-style prison rather than Velarde-esque chia water. Like Villoro's Julio Valdivieso, Fadanelli's hero Benito Torrentera is an academic, a member of that layer of degenerate urban society that Russian populists referred to as the "intellectual proletariat." But while *Lodo's* protagonist goes through a comic metamorphosis in which he changes from superfluous man to common criminal, *El testigo* presents a sort of *Narodnik*, a scholar who is saved (or condemned) by returning to the "simple" life, which is how intellectuals see agrarian communities, repositories of self-hatred that torment them.

With all due respect to the distance realism posits between an author and the ideas expressed by his characters, I'm not sure how aware Villoro is of having written a painfully nationalist novel, which I think shows more than a few similarities with the Mexico that's artificially enriched by remittances and drug money. It betrays a profound and controversial nostalgia for rural society—the enlightened, Catholic, *ranchera* version, a savage idyll just clamoring for the most resolute, petty bourgeois world. These are things that we can and should ask of a realist novelist who writes as masterfully as Villoro.

El testigo explains certain aspects of Villoro's literary personality that, in my opinion, the realities of life in the public eye had turned into ambiguous, even slightly questionable characteristics—the combination of impenetrable decorum and gregarious enthusiasm so typical of old-school Mexicans, a superstitious respect for peasants (whether Cristeros or Zapatistas), and an affiliation with certain leftist political causes motivated more by middle-class decency than ideological fervor. *El testigo* is an outstanding novel for what it testifies to—the almost chthonic persistence of nationalism in a literature desperate to be not universal but exotic. From his take on rock 'n' roll as a civilizing force to his easy familiarity with German literature, from cultural journalism as democratic militancy to Barcelona's frenetic publishing world, Villoro has finally caught up to the shadow of his promise. *El testigo* forces us—once more—to revisit the myth of origins, the historic vitality of dead Mexicans that so awed José Moreno Villa,* a ghost story we cannot and must not forget.

In his journals—which were not so much personal as semi-private, semi-public texts—André Gide said of the artist that "rather than recounting his life as he has lived it, he must live his life as he will recount it" (*Journals, 1889–1913*, trans. Justin O'Brien). Villoro quotes him in *De eso se trata* (2008). I found it odd to see a reference to Gide in a book of Juan Villoro's criticism, but my shock subsided as I came to realize that, as writers, they both share the qualities of a long-distance runner: a certain hard-headedness, a spirit of sacrifice, a desire to be true to and yet outlive the age in which they live. For Villoro, even a collection of literary essays follows narrative strategies, for instance. *De eso se trata* ("That's what it's all about") takes its title from the Tomás Segovia* translation of Hamlet's monologue, which culminates not with "That is the question" or "Thus the dilemma" but with a hilarious, off-handed, sonorous "De eso se trata," and a few pages later, having rolled up his sleeves, Villoro turns the phrase into the promise of a story.

Villoro uses an anecdote to illustrate the age-old theme—recently reexamined by Steiner—of teacher and student in their Socratic exchange. And with the controlled velocity that some would call "rhythm," he leads us to WLH 203 at Yale, where Harold Bloom is discussing Shakespeare, the only sign of the snow outside appearing in his lightly ruffled hair. The narrator segues from Bloom's fear of being left behind, of "falling on his back and being unable to get up, like Humpty Dumpty," to the amulet that makes the entire book possible: a notebook that a co-ed gave Villoro, and in which he takes his Shakespeare notes at Yale. This happens during the critical, historical moment of Mexico's *annus horribilis*, 1994, and thus we get to hear his testimony as well as watch him sketch a Strindberg-like portrait of his mother. And so it was that before coming to the end of page twenty-one, I found myself already inhabiting the strange world—simultaneously so familiar and so outlandish—that only our most lucid contemporaries are able to evoke.

Those first few pages on Shakespeare and Cervantes set the tone for a book whose aim brings me great joy, especially considering that "what it's all about" is texts I'd mostly read in the past decade. It's not often that this sort of collection—a peccadillo that as essayists we're sometimes obliged to commit—manages to replicate, wholesale, what we learned in school, in parts. And although if push came to shove, Villoro would swear he's a short-story writer, I consider him one of our best critics. *De eso se trata*, his second book of essays, confirms it. It's more unrestrained (though less elaborate) than *Efectos personales* (2000), a book memorable for many reasons, including its portraits of Valle-Inclán, Arthur Schnitzler, and Carlos Fuentes* with Goya, as well as a heroic feat only Villoro could pull off: discussing Julie Andrews from "The Sound of Music" in an essay on Thomas Bernhard.

The eighteenth century is where Villoro is most comfortable—from wigs to long locks—and in *De eso se trata*, this period belongs to Casanova, who bids farewell by night but leaves the light in his window on, where it shines into the future. Villoro's subjects all somehow seem like *Sturm und Drang* protagonists of a rock opera: they're young (sometimes absurdly young) and yet perfectly suited in their roles as classics. Villoro's Goethe (so human, so implausible) is as good as Alfonso Reyes's* Goethe. Perhaps Villoro is so adept in the eighteenth century because he began "writing" as a translator, when in 1989 he translated (and prefaced) German writer G. C. Lichtenberg's aphorisms. And in fact, Lichtenberg's adventures in the New World are the subject of one of the chapters in *De eso se trata*.

Villoro found in Lichtenberg a model for his own literary style. Whether you like his short stories and novels or not, they're all underpinned by a sense for balance he took from Lichtenberg, which posits wit and reason side by side and then obeys feelings after reason has disqualified them. As Lichtenberg would have it, what he does is consider the spirit from its satellite body or the body with its satellite spirit.

Had he not been so steeped in the eighteenth century, I doubt Villoro would have risked an undertaking like *El testigo* (2004), a populist, Romanticist novel. His confidence comes from a combination of skepticism and illusion, and has a stylistic corollary, seen in his felicitous phrasing, sentences that are simultaneously synthetic and idiosyncratic, and sprinkled throughout Villoro's work. Venetian librettist Lorenzo da Ponte, for instance, was plagued by "debilitating deadlines for versification," which—hypothetically—led to him recruiting Casanova to collaborate on *Don Giovanni*.

But at the core of *De eso se trata* is Ernest Hemingway. The author of *For Whom the Bell Tolls* has no better reader in Spanish than Villoro, who learned a lot from the undervalued American master who—like Onetti, another of his penates—insisted on carrying on, regardless of anyone else. Villoro found in Hemingway's moral and political convictions—or in the way they paled beside his style and vanity—a distinctive fragility, a quality somehow characteristic of the twentieth century. Thus Villoro created a sort of style manual comprised of paradoxes: the search for heroism became dangerous literary publicity, as when Hemingway was injured in the war in 1918; in the avant-garde presided over by Gertrude Stein and Ezra Pound, Hemingway became the most journalistic writer and his horrific, lovely little war—the Spanish Civil War—both established and destroyed him. No less admirable is the funeral song for the fleetingness of fame and the eternity of myth that is Villoro's reading of *The Old Man and the Sea*, one of the few books I read as a teenager and still remember almost in its entirety, so unforgettable was it.

Villoro feels a sense of camaraderie for those who go abroad, and he's taken with the wanderings of Malcolm Lowry and D. H. Lawrence in Mexico, high-risk tourism in our "infernal paradise." More akin to Octavio Paz* and Carlos Fuentes* than to the writers of his generation in this sense, Villoro directly inherited the will to see Mexico (to love it, to endure it, I suppose) with the liberating, dreamy eyes of Anglo-Saxon writers (and Breton), acting as stranger in his own strange land. Rather than avoiding archetypes, he takes them seriously and takes them to their logical conclusions, which as far as I'm concerned, are only two: irony or sentimentality.

In that sense, *De eso se trata* helped me reread *El testigo* and find that— following on from a text in *Efectos personales*—it both develops and exhausts the notion of the "theme park," making it unwieldy for a writer who flirts with Mexico's exceptionalism, cultivating and deploring it in equal measure. The book's so-called "extraterritorial itineraries" (Roger Bartra* and his savages, Venezuelan Ibsen Martínez's play about Humboldt in Latin America, the Tijuana of Luis Humberto Crosthwaite, César Aira's vision of German landscape painter Rugendas) seem to show that paradoxically associating Mexico with Disneyland is a tedious, lost cause that brings the adventures of the Lowrys and D. H. Lawrences of the world to an end.

Villoro is a loyal disciple and never misses an opportunity to talk about his mentors, whether they be Alejandro Rossi* and Sergio Pitol,* Juan José Saer and Ricardo Piglia, or Roberto Bolaño* and César Aira. He's a team player who finds relays the healthiest form of competition and the best way to win at literature. That's why his reading of Adolfo Bioy Casares's book *Borges*

(2006) is in a sense the memoir of a collective reading that dozens of Latin Americans have been carrying out. A reading that will confirm, as Villoro himself suggests, that after Laurel and Hardy, and Lennon and McCartney, all that's left is Borges and Bioy. The art of quotation—a consideration debased by bad professors—is one of Villoro's essayistic fortes, and he profits from a sense of timing that means that he quotes often and well, whether it be Heinrich Heine pondering Casanova, Lionel Trilling pontificating on Chekhov, or Yeats waxing lyrical about himself. Or Barry Gifford, who when "asked about the obvious influence of Jack Kerouac's *On the Road* on his novel *Wild at Heart*, responded that all road novels originally came from *Don Quixote.*" That's what it's all about.

SELECTED BIBLIOGRAPHY

La noche navegable, Joaquón Mortiz, Mexico, 1980.
Albercas, Joaquín Mortiz, Mexico, 1985.
Los once de la tribu, Aguilar, Mexico, 1995.
Materia dispuesta, Alfaguara, Mexico, 1996.
La casa pierde, Alfaguara, Mexico, 1998.
Efectos personales, ERA, Mexico, 2000.
El testigo, Anagrama, Barcelona, 2004.
El disparo de Argón, Anagrama, Barcelona, 2005.
De eso se trata. Ensayos literarios, Anagrama, Barcelona, 2008.

VOLKOW, VERÓNICA

(Mexico City, 1955)

Anyone who knows anything about the Mexican literary scene knows that Volkow is one of Leon Trotsky's Mexican great-granddaughters. And despite her discretion about it, I don't think bringing up her illustrious origins is either inane or anecdotal when reading her poetry, which she began writing before her twentieth birthday. Between *La Sibila de Cumas* (1974) and *La noche viuda* (2004), Volkow has amassed a legacy I'd call more Mexican-ist than Mexican, and I don't mean that pejoratively. The sort of pictures (or imaginary fragments) of Mexico (the part of Mexico that's one big archeological ruin) summoned up by Sergei Eisenstein, André Breton, and Victor Serge also make a sort of final appearance in Volkow's poetry. That's the sort of "Mexican air" circulating through her verses: it's no coincidence that reading her made me also decide to reread French surrealist Benjamin Péret's *Aire mexicain* (1952).

It's no secret that Volkow was raised in a world of exiled European and Russian artists and revolutionaries, the twentieth-century avant-garde that taught her to see Mexico as Other, a sort of critical rite of passage. It's no surprise that she felt comfortable practicing the same analytical distance from Mexico that Octavio Paz* did, over and over.

Volkow's perspective is very Russian, very distant, and rarely—though not never—a folksy snapshot or a touristic jingle. Her poems on Mesoamericans, those "religiones primeras / de oscura / precisión y miedo" (*primal religions / of dark / precision and fear*), as she calls them in *Oro del viento* (2003) tend to be more convincing than other texts written by poets with comparable sensibilities. As with Paz when he saw himself as the son of the Zapatista lawyer he was, Volkow worries about the scar that separates the lost, pre-Hispanic Arcadia from its descendants, sometimes silent witnesses and other times noisy ones, now residing in the trash dump of progress. In "El valle de Zapata," Volkow depicts Mexican peasants as if it were the first time she'd seen them, showing no familiarity and also no tedium, as was also the case in some of Eisenstein's work (and words) and certain early drawings by Vlady, Serge's painter son.

When discussing poetry that couldn't be more different from her own— that of Elizabeth Bishop, whom she's translated—Volkow portrays herself as part of the uncertainty of a new world, one who must be translated to make sense of. She did the same in *Diario de Sudáfrica* (1988), which recounts the agony of apartheid and introduced us to now-famous authors such as Nadine Gordimer and J. M. Coetzee.

Volkow's most recent book, *La noche viuda*, is not poetry but prose, and it impressed me less. José María Espinasa,* the critic who best interprets her, called the book "poet's stories" and liked them. Precisely because they are "poet's stories," however, I did not. But it must be said that rarely in contemporary Mexican literature has a woman honored a dead lover so insistently and so unerringly as Volkow does in *La noche viuda*.

In books such as *El inicio* (1983), *Los caminos* (1989), and *Arcanos* (1996), as Espinasa notes, Volkow successfully became part of the Mexican tradition of abstract poetry, of cold eroticism, of crystal passion. And with its inevitably Bretonian overtones, *Arcanos* is her most complex and risky work, in which she says, memorably, "Hambre de lo que mira / tiene el fuego" ("Hunger for what it sees / has the fire").

SELECTED BIBLIOGRAPHY
Oro del viento, ERA, Mexico, 2003.
La noche viuda, FCE, Mexico, 2004.

VOLPI, JORGE
(Mexico City, 1968)

Few Mexican writers have induced the raptures Volpi has; likewise, few have suffered such venomous, misguided attacks. Thus, before discussing *En busca de Klingsor* (1999; *In Search of Klingsor*, 2002), it makes sense to give a brief history of Volpi and his group. Success is a kind of failure, it's been said. There are several factors involved in building a literary empire, from intelligent behavior to the industrial fabrication of talent. In 1996, Volpi and his friends (Ricardo Chávez Castañeda, Vicente Herrasti,* Ignacio Padilla, Pedro Ángel Palou, and Eloy Urroz) published the "Crack Manifesto," calling themselves the Crack generation, a fraternity of novelists who, according to publicity, were destined to be the turn-of-the-century parting of the seas for Mexican literature. Three years later, with *En busca de Klingsor*, Volpi won the Premio Bilbioteca Breve, a reinstated prize whose prestige dated back to the Latin American Boom generation. With this award came literary agents, translation contracts, international tours, and, later, a posting in the Mexican diplomatic service. Among young authors (and a fair few old ones) this was viewed with envy and bile in predictable measures. After all, this new leader of a literary movement, the man admired, had realized what many dreamed of. Volpi's political skills (and generosity) allowed him to be inserted into the market en masse along with his Crack buddies, who also obtained Spanish publishing contracts and were translated into several languages thanks to the publication "bundles" that multinational publishing monopolies now employ.

The Crack generation, like Chilean Alberto Fuget's McOndo movement before it, aroused the interest of run-of-the-mill society comprised of editors, agents, and complacent readers, who in Spain and the re-colonized cities of Latin America tend to believe that publishers' present-day output (generally fiction) is actually literature. Amenable—to varying degrees—to that context, the Crack novels form a heteroclitic band of uneven (and some abominable) tales that fly the banner of false cosmopolitanism. It's literature written by Latin Americans who decided to abandon—as if this in and of itself were novel or radical—old national themes and present themselves as contemporaries not of all men but of the superstars of world literature. These new authors ably navigate the archives of the recently defunct twentieth century, ordering up its precepts à la carte: alienation, emptiness, the eternal return of the apocalypse, the death of ideologies, and other contemporary mythologies. Frankly, I find it as questionable in Mexican writers as it is in Michel Houellebecq.

It's no coincidence that the spread, history, and consequences of Nazism have been at the center of the efforts of Volpi, Ignacio Padilla, and Spanish writer Juana Salabert (another Premio Biblioteca Breve winner). After all, it's an exceedingly malleable topic, one that substitutes the old tales of intrigue with the presentation of Absolute Evil, arousing the horror of all mankind and a morbid curiosity in even its most ardent enemies. Padilla's *Amphytrion* (2000; *Shadow Without A Name*, 2004) is exemplary in several senses: it's a well manufactured collection of narrative snapshots born of the renewed interest (thanks to the Italian Claudio Magris and other writers) in the Austro-Hungarian Empire and its role in creating the Weimar Republic and Nazism. But in *Amphytrion* the historical tragedy occurs outside the text, a mere didactic, bookish reference. It's an irritatingly superficial novel that only serves to invite readers to delve into its sources—from Joseph Roth to Hannah Arendt.

The problem with the Crack writers stems from their pretentious nonsense, often emanating from Padilla, who is actually a good stylist but will tell anyone willing to listen that before the Crack, who constituted a "liberation" akin to that of poet Rubén Darío a hundred years ago, cosmopolitanism in Mexico was purely coincidental. My view of literature is precisely the opposite: I believe in the variety and influence of a cosmopolitan tradition, which led to great Mexican literature from Alfonso Reyes,* Jorge Cuesta,* José Revueltas,* and Octavio Paz* to Salvador Elizondo,* Sergio Pitol,* and Alejandro Rossi.* And I find it hard to believe that he's been able to overlook literary magazines *Vuelta* and *Plural,* founts of that kind of literary wealth in the thirties.

Cosmopolitanism is a spiritual outlook that can't be measured by the number of topographical references and historical contexts that are unconnected to the author's nationality. Padilla himself is more a frequent flier than a cosmopolitan writer, and novels such as *Amphytrion* form part of another trend—exoticism—that always disconcerts Europeans when it comes out of Mexico or Buenos Aires, as if readers on the other side of the Atlantic were unaware that it's the same movement they themselves invented back in the day. It's as respectable (and as questionable) for Padilla to write about the Great War as it was for Hungarian László Passuth (1900–1979) to write about the Conquest in *Tlaloc Weeps for Mexico.* Borges was cosmopolitan; Manuel Mujica Lainez is an exoticist lost in a German candy shop, though that didn't keep him from writing a novel as commendable as *Bomarzo.*

The preposterous idea that there was now some sort of "new" Mexican novel, simply because in it there was no mention of Mexico or Mexicans, was feted by the generally obtuse Madrid journalists making the rounds at cultural centers Casa de América and Círculo de Lectores. And when Padilla's *Espiral de artillería* (2003) came out, one Spanish commentator went so far as to extol him with the honor of being a "European writer born in Mexico," an honor which implies that being European is a guarantee of loftiness, nonsense that obliges me to repeat what Mexican critic Jorge Cuesta* noted in 1932: "Spanish literature from Mexico has been seen in Spain as an outcast. This judgment has not been misguided, as it restores Mexican literature to the tradition of heresy, which is the only possible Mexican tradition [. . .]. All classicism is a transmigrating tradition. In the Spanish thinking that came to Mexico from Spain, it wasn't Spain but universalism that emigrated, a universalism Spain was unable to retain, as it allowed it to emigrate intellectually" (*Obras: Ensayos y crítica,* II. 2004).

Peninsular ignorance about Latin American literary universalism, which writers like Padilla have made the most of, makes it necessary for me to incur the triteness of a brief history of exoticism and how it was that it came to take hold in Mexico in the forties—if not earlier—when the fantasy of utopia decided to turn its civilizing, Latinized gaze on barbarous Europe. To bring an end to the Crack's supposed originality once and for all, let me supply an irritating enumeration. One of the first short stories Juan José Arreola* ever wrote was called "Gunther Stapenhorst" and took place in Germany. That was in 1946. In 1972, one of the greatest writers of the Spanish language, Hugo Hiriart,* wrote *Galaor*, a novel of chivalry, which he followed up by inventing an entire civilization in *Cuadernos de Gofa* (1981) and undertaking something similar in *El agua grande* (2002). Others who delved into extraterritoriality include Héctor Manjarrez* (*Lapsus*, 1972), Emiliano González (*Los sueños de la Bella Durmiente*, 1973), María Luisa Puga (*Las posibilidades del odio*, 1978), Jordi García Bergua* (*Karpus Minthej*, 1981), José María Pérez Gay (*La difícil costumbre de estar lejos*, 1984), Carlos Fuentes* (*Valiente mundo nuevo*, 1991), Alejandro Rossi (*El cielo de Sotero*, 1987), Alberto Ruy Sánchez (*Los nombres del aire*, 1987), Pedro F. Miret* (*Insomnes en Tahití*, 1989), and a long etcetera that includes several stories by Pitol, Álvaro Uribe,* Alain-Paul Mallard, Javier García-Galiano and Enrique Serna,* in which Mexicans, happily, make no appearance whatsoever.

Talking about London's counterculture, the South American wars of independence and their caudillos, nineteenth-century fin-de-siècle fantasies, Arab eroticism, and life in Africa, cosmopolitanism (or Mexicanophobia, if you prefer) has been one of two or three traditions in Mexican literature. If we're generous, we might concede that at first the Crack writers were usufructuaries of a legacy, writers who allowed—with some swaggering—the press to sell them as the perfect remedy to indigestion-causing *mole poblano*. And a modicum of honesty requires that we recognize Pablo Soler Frost* (1965), indifferent to publicity at the time, as the one who first began the exoticism trend of the current literary generation with novels set in Byzantium and in German submarines.

But the Spanish prizes awarded to Volpi and Padilla unleashed the wicked tongues of nationalism and envy, enemies we must always close ranks on, come what may. There's not much that can be said about the tireless mouthpieces of nationalist claptrap who accused the Crack writers of being traitors to the nation and, in an act of faith worthy of President Díaz Ordaz—the man in power during the 1968 massacre at Tlatelolco—divested them of their Mexican nationality. They simply persist in meriting the textual beating Jorge Cuesta gave Ermilo Abreu Gómez* about his jingoism, a corrective no one would mind applying. Envy, on the other hand, is a more interesting moral phenomenon to analyze, and to do so I suggest reading (backwards) *La generación de los enterradores* (2000 and 2002), by Chávez Castañeda and Celso Santajuliana. This two-volume "handbook" explains how to achieve success à la Volpi, who, the authors claim, has achieved a sort of living posterity, while the rest of his industrious peers languish as an obligatory peloton of cyclists (I have to believe that this metaphor comes from Pierre Bourdieu scholars) who go all out against the struggles of a life in publishing, which is apparently the only conceivable outlet for literature. These dimwits actually went so far as to obtain Volpi's elementary-school qualifications in order to explicate the origins of his literary career (more than oeuvre), which strikes them as titanic.

I've never read anyone—including friends and enemies of Volpi and Padilla—who envies their prose, style, or ideas the way I envy José Lezama Lima, André Gide, and Edmund Wilson. What they envy is their success, particularly in a time when people want to be writers in order to win prizes and live the life of Riley, just as twenty-five years ago the form of urbanity considered most desirable was different—and much more humble. Back then, people aspired to die as *poètes maudits* in hovels or live in the poetic triumph of some Central American revolution.

The Crack is an archetypal commercial publishing phenomenon, but that doesn't mean it won't leave a few worthy novels, and I'm sure some of Volpi's will be among them. Susana Fortes, a member of the jury that selected *En busca de Klingsor*, was the first to include the novel in the nouveau riche family presided over by Umberto Eco's *The Name of the Rose* (1980). Without Borges (an enemy of the novel) and his faux scholarship, it would have been hard—as Eco knew—to turn theological intrigue and scientific paradigms into narrative literature. At once learned and vernacular, refined and popular, this type of narration revitalized the novel, apparently ever on the verge of exhaustion. It also unhinged the novel's frequently tense relationship with the market.

Eco's formula—which he himself devalued in subsequent novels—suffered the degradation we can expect when high art is popularized. It's not that prior to 1980 there were no exciting novels of ideas, it's just that they didn't feel the need to make systematic use of the techniques of the thriller in order

535

to seduce readers. On the one hand, Thomas Mann had no fear of "boring" his thousands upon thousands of faithful devotees, and on the other the lone Ernst Jünger of *Heliopolis* (1949) wrote for a handful of initiates. By contrast, the type of novel Eco made popular must pay its respects to both Stephen King and the deceased Sebald simultaneously, must appeal both to the customer looking for a book for the beach and the academic eager for curricula, aiming for the kind of legitimacy that Valery Larbaud sought a century ago, the kind conferred by national readerships and the aristocratic elite who preside (or ought to) over world literature. Authors of this type of literature suffer anguish proportionate only to their financial and media recompense, obliged as they are to meld ever-pressing metaphysical concerns with the well-oiled machinery of intrigue. It also explains why those books so often end up on the silver screen: their truths are easily translated into images.

A full-time man of letters, Volpi was destined for an undertaking like *En busca de Klingsor*, a novel about German science racing unsuccessfully against the clock to develop the atomic bomb. The attempt on Hitler's life on July 20, 1944 provides the novel's backbone. Volpi chose a thrilling topic and researched and presented it convincingly, thanks to his brilliant skill at synthesis. And, a product of his time, his familiarity with the cinematic rhetoric of thrillers is almost inborn. *En busca de Klingsor* follows the genre's conventions like a novel of intrigue. The axial relationship between Lieutenant Bacon and the mathematician Links—a dialectics of victor and vanquished on which the narration relies—during the months following the Nazis' defeat in 1945, reflects many of the plot's complex exigencies.

The main problems with *En busca de Klingsor* are canonical, that is, related to the genre popularized by Eco that Guillermo Cabrera Infante dubbed "science fusion." I'm irked at how diligently—for the convenient edification of his readers—Volpi follows the established concessions of the genre: the intellectual prestige prompted by relating his novel to a myth of origins, the commercial idiocy of providing a love interest. Inevitably didactic, *En busca de Klingsor* bares all when Faust-like, German Links recounts the plot of Wagner's *Parsifal* to pragmatic American Bacon as a way to dramatize the clichéd relationship between Nazism and Wagner's opera.

Volpi has been fascinated by the misfortunes of tragic geniuses since his first novel, *A pesar del oscuro silencio* (1991), devoted to Jorge Cuesta. And like a gallery of Faustian works, *En busca de Klingsor* showcases the talent of a fine painter. I found myself able to see and smell, more than hear, his cast of European physicists who, in Germany and the United States, turned the theological dilemmas pondered by early Christian scholars Origen and Titus Flavius Clemens into questions of patristic practicality, that is, making apocatastasis a reality of contemporary physics: Could God allow the destruction of his creation? Does he intuit it, desire it, is he indifferent to it? How did Prometheus become an agent of free will? Volpi's determined interrogation of Einstein, Johannes Stark, Werner Heisenberg, and Erwin Schrödinger displays an analytical precision reminiscent of that of Héctor A. Murena and Pedro Salinas fifty years ago, a quality I thought had disappeared from the Spanish language.

El fin de la locura is an unofficial continuation of *En busca de Klingor*, continuing Volpi's master plan of writing twentieth-century fictional sociology. And he undertakes it with the didactic impulse characteristic of a professorial spirit. That Volpi *is* one doesn't bother me—it's a decision like any other. You can easily detect the pedagogue all set to lecture his apparently docile student-readers. His aim in *El fin de la locura* is risky, and Peruvian writer Alfredo Bryce Echenique already set the Latin-American-in-Paris precedent. What Volpi does is place a failed Mexican intellectual in Paris, a buffoon who basically fell out of the sky in May 1968, and became—*deus ex machina*—a jester in the courts of Lacan, Barthes, and Foucault. His caricatures of the *maîtres à penser* of French structuralism are splendid, assumed with the distance of a Latin American writer who aspires neither to hagiography nor condemnation. Volpi portrays the theorists with the critical detachment of an entomologist captivated by the maelstrom of '68 that hurled them to public fame and cultural power, by the utter political irresponsibility of the time, and by their undoubted genius.

No less impressive are the risks he takes by having his Doctor Aníbal Quevedo psychoanalyze Fidel Castro, in a hilarious Cuban episode that takes to the extreme the pathetic story of revolutionary tourists who went (and still go) to Cuba in search of paradise. Thus for several chapters, Volpi successfully puts his research skills and his essayist's concerns at the service of fiction.

After Roland Barthes dies in 1980, Aníbal returns to Mexico and begins living out the *non sanctas* relations between Mexican intellectuals and politicians. Like Barthes himself, Volpi decided to present this final stage in

Aníbal Quevedo's life via a series of newspaper clippings, diary entries, interviews, therapy sessions, and bank statements aimed at helping the reader solve the puzzle of the protagonist's ventures. The result is bittersweet. It's hard to tell: is the novel intended for Parisians or denizens of Coyoacán? Honestly, I don't think Volpi actually cares where his readers are, which is a true sign of maturity. The success of *En busca de Klingsor* earned him some freedom that he's capitalized on, settling scores with the Mexico that both praises and envies him. But the Mexican portion of *El fin de la locura* is flawed. I don't mind the fact that it probably verges on the incomprehensible for Volpi's international readership. But what does concern me is the fact that his criticisms are timorous and superficial when it comes to investigating the complex combination of tolerance and authoritarianism, legitimacy and influence-peddling, erudition and decadence that characterized the relationship between intellectuals and politicians during the zenith and twilight of the Institutional Revolutionary Party (PRI).

The novel's verisimilitude is perhaps best proven by the fact that a number of habitually astute readers assumed Dr. Aníbal Quevedo really existed, and attempted to find out more about what turned out to be his fictitious bibliography. However, against the interests of fictional truth, Volpi calculated his own status as a rising star on the cultural scene and stopped short. It's easy to caricature Jacques Lacan compared to the political risks involved in, say, taking on Carlos Monsiváis* or any other of our cultural caudillos. Aníbal Quevedo, a bizarre Mexican who speaks in infinitives, lacks sufficient complexity to embody what Professor Mark Lilla refers to as intellectuals' "tyrannophilia."

El fin de la locura's basic flaw is one of degree. Volpi should have given his character more picaresque substance. As it is, he loses all psychological intensity when he returns to Mexico, becoming simply documentary proof. Some reviewers have seen him as a credible, realistic character, from the barricades in Paris in May '68 to his relationship with ex-president Salinas de Gotari. If that were the case, the novel would be absurd. The hesitation resides in Volpi's professorial ambiguity, his own ambivalence when faced with a choice between artistic will and political calculations, the ends and the means. What we have here is a tragicomic novel that doesn't quite make good on its initial intent—recounting the improbable adventures of his own Alonso Quijano—also known as Don Quixote—facing the revolutionary faculties of the Sorbonne, and unable to transform the world or his life.

El fin de la locura is the story of two paths that never meet. As a chronicle of Parisian insanity and the frivolity of the great French thinkers, and a caricature of the gauche divine, it hits the target. But as an explanation of how post-revolutionary Mexico self-servingly orchestrated its own "treason of the intellectuals"—and how Mexican intellectuals survived—it falls far short of the mark, more notable for what it doesn't dare say than what it does. And that's unforgiveable in a writer like Volpi, called on to rationally explain intellectuals' silence and their admonitions.

My position on Jorge Volpi's literary career is ambivalent, as are my feelings about his novels. I'm bewildered at the contradiction between his artistic will and the political means he uses to pursue his aims, internalized in almost all of his novels. But I have plenty of personal and intellectual reasons to admire him. I was vehemently critical of several of his first novels. And—unlike many of the writers I've dealt with—he responded with neither sneering nor insults. Instead he showed the noble interests of man who accepts not so much bad reviews, which are always circumstantial, but the vital need for critics. The deep literary conviction allowed us to become friends, without precluding our frank and often-uncomfortable exchanges. Which is how I also learned to love him, as well as to believe in his unflagging work ethic and his vocation.

Selected Bibliography

En busca de Klingsor, Seix Barral, Barcelona, 1999.

El fin de la locura, Seix Barral, Barcelona, 2003.

No será la tierra, Alfaguara, Madrid, 2006.

Mentiras contagiosas, Páginas de Espuma, Madrid, 2008.

El jardín devastado, Alfaguara, Madrid, 2008.

Oscuro bosque oscuro, Almadía, Oaxaca, 2009.

El insomnio de Bolívar. Cuatro consideraciones intempestivas sobre América Latina en el siglo XXI, Debate, Madrid, 2009.

In Search of Klingsor, trans. Kristina Cordero, Simon and Schuster, 2002.

Season of Ash, trans. Alfred MacAdam, Open Letter, 2009.

X

XIRAU, RAMÓN
(Barcelona, Spain, 1924)

Son of Spanish philosopher Joaquín Xirau y Palau (1895–1946) and father of Mexican poet Joaquín Xirau Icaza (1950–1976), Xirau is not only an academic, essayist, and Catalan poet, but also a teacher of several generations of philosophers in his post at UNAM, and of writers in the less formal setting of the Centro Mexicano de Escritores. Xirau also taught a select audience via *Diálogos*, the warmly commemorated cultural magazine he edited from 1965 to 1986. In the book *Ramón Xirau: en los jardines del tiempo* (2006), José María Espinasa*—one of the critics most inspired by Xirau's teaching—briefly and perceptively examines the personality of a teacher associated with "the personal intuition, I wouldn't quite call it reasoning, that one doesn't think alone but in company."

Other critics, Adolfo Castañón* among them, have described Xirau's pedagogical style, noting how when he speaks, "his person disappears, and the eyes of his voice—the eyes of an Athenian owl who can see in the darkest night—create a realm where three voices seem to converse, that of the text being analyzed—let's say one of the last Platonic dialogues, *Parmenides*, for instance—that of the analyst (a man who seems to have read and reread many libraries without having sacrificed the view of his heart) and that of the students and listeners [...] By modulating his voice and his glance, he's able to go from one point of view to the next. He's quick and unequivocal, but clear and firm. One would say he not only converses with the texts; he feels the silence in their margins as much as the varying degrees of interest and vigilance of his interlocutor" (Castañón, prologue to *Entre la poesía y el conocimiento*, 2001).

Xirau attests to the evolution of the *Contemporáneos* and Octavio Paz* in *Tres poetas de la soledad: Gorostiza, Villaurrutia y Paz* (1955), which as José Emilio Pacheco* recalls was the book that first presented modern Mexican poetry in terms of a "great tradition." Since then, his influence on the reception of contemporary Spanish-language poetry has been key, as is easily evidenced in *Entre la poesía y el conocimiento: Antología de ensayos críticos sobre poetas y poesía iberoamiercanos* (2001), which is something of a history of poetry viewed through a religious filter. Inspired by personalism—that Catholic form of "existentialism"—Xirau covers everything from Saint John of the Cross to modernism, including Juan Ramón Jiménez, César Vallejo, and José Lezama Lima. In essays and interpretations, he examines the tradition and the avant-garde from a stance Espinasa sees as falling somewhere between Paz's position in *Los hijos del limo* (1974) and that of Guillermo Sucre in *La máscara, la transparencia* (1975 and 1985).

A Catholic who reflects on the convergence of poetry and philosophy, Xirau is an essayist akin to Emmanuel Mounier and Teilhard de Cardin, which makes him a sort of primeval critic concerned with both the religiosity of the poet and the poetry of mysticism. Juliana González, a colleague of many years at UNAM, has said as much, adding that Xirau is concerned with "the cognoscitive ability of poetry, which reveals not so much human truth as divine: poetry's ability to approach the sacred, to discover the world (inside and outside) as sacred, to be eminent testimony of religious experience."

Many things have been said about Xirau, and they're all true: That his readings of Sor Juana's "First Dream" and of Paz—he was the first to write an entire book on him: *Octavio Paz, el sentido de la palabra* (1970)—are strictly canonical. That in his work, as Espinasa notes, God and the divine are not simply concepts but a tradition, a history. That he's an unrivaled figure as a Spanish exile in Mexico, where he arrived as a teenager and where his intellectual life has been inextricably rooted for the past fifty years. That perhaps his best prose is to be found in the epigraphs and commentaries in *Ars brevis* (1985), where via fragments he expresses himself with clarity, rigor, and charisma, whether speaking of the Polish church, eastern horizons, or Chapultapec Park. That his Mediterranean poems are so silent they sound like the work of Catalan composer Federico Mompou, so mystically joyous they could have been written by French composer Olivier Messiaen. And that, for those of us born around the same time as his *Introducción a la historia de la filosofía* (1964) came out, Xirau is like an Elgin marble, solid and imperturbable, something that's always been with us.

SELECTED BIBLIOGRAPHY

Entre la poesía y el conocimiento. Antología de ensayos críticos sobre poetas y poesía iberoamericanos, prologue by Adolfo Castañón, ed. Adolfo Castañón and Josúe Ramírez, FCE, Mexico, 2001.

González, Juliana, et al., *Presencia de Ramón Xirau*, UNAM, Mexico, 1986.

Espinasa, José María, *Ramón Xirau: en los jardines del tiempo*, illustrated by Manuel Pujol Baladas, Jus Mexico, 2006.

Y

YÁÑEZ, AGUSTÍN

(Guadalajara, Jalisco, 1904 – Mexico City, 1980)

Yáñez's appearance on the literary scene was indubitably brilliant, as well as different, for various reasons. Ten years older than José Revueltas* and classified by John Brushwood as part of the 1924 generation of novelists that included Miguel Ángel Asturias and Alejo Carpentier, Yáñez was a late bloomer. He started off at the magazine *Bandera de Provincias* (1905–1935), which at one point attempted to follow the path of the journal *Contemporáneos*, but it wasn't until 1947, when he published *Al filo del agua* (*The Edge of the Storm*, 1963), that his reputation reached its peak. And began its fall. *Al filo del agua* was seen for many years as "the most novel" of Mexican novels. And as recently as 1977 Emmanuel Carballo* endorsed that view.

Yáñez overburdens his novel with the stylistic triumphs of secular fiction: unexpected changes of scene, indeterminate time and place, extensive use of stream of consciousness, and a profound awareness of the textual framework of the novel. This last feature was one of his obsessions, as he made clear when he said, "Musical prose is somewhat instinctive for me. When I write I try to give the words, sentences, periods a certain euphonic quality made up of verbal rhythm and melody. I believe that prose should express these qualities, which are always seen in great writers even if they are not constitutive of their nature. I remember that in Guadalajara I often recited passages from *La Celestina*, and from Azorín [. . .] The supposedly baroque quality of my style is debatable and unacceptable as a general qualifier. I see the baroque as superfluous, sumptuary ornamental abundance [. . .] What I am concerned with is turning around a word, searching for the term most adequate to the suggestion, even the syntactic collocation that will make the expression most effective. What I mean is that my zeal, my scrupulous approach to the struggle with the word reveals my ambition to suppress all that is vacuous or false and keep only elements of authentic expression. My Precept can be condensed into two terms: discipline in search of precision" (Carballo, *Protagonistas de la literatura mexicana*, 1986).

Never before had a Mexican novelist declared himself in possession of a precept explaining his stance vis-à-vis the text. So while Revueltas was seen as creator of an apocalypse, Yáñez—a systematic soul—aspired to cosmogony. Revueltas's *El luto humano* is a sort of terminus, the end of the line, while *Al filo del agua* is the cornerstone of a spiritual topography of Mexico. Yáñez announced that he was aspiring to create "a synthesis of our history. What's more: to the idea of History as eternal return."

But both Revueltas and Yáñez saw the Mexican Revolution as a consummate, historically discernible event—whether apocalyptic or foundational—that had concluded and was subject to mythical reworkings. For both authors, only the novel as critique of the past could unravel the origins of our present. Products of their time, Revueltas and Yáñez were brimming with ontological anxiety, full of doubts and questions about Mexican identity and its eventual metamorphosis.

Al filo del agua is the compound novel of a small town on the eve of the Mexican Revolution, a paradise that becomes corrupted and begins to awaken its passions. A conservative, Yáñez couldn't decree an expulsion from Eden, and his entire oeuvre is the examination of the supposed dawn of a new day. He substituted landscapes for atmosphere and customs for character. But after *Al filo del agua* and its remarkably ambitious form, subsequent works such as *La creación* (1959), *La tierra pródiga* (1960), *Las tierras flacas* (1962; *The Lean Lands*, 1968), and *Las vueltas del tiempo* (1973) gradually suffocated, finally killing off the literary author's literary corpus: careful creation turned into complacent deadweight, the rich prose of his litanies became incomprehensible sermons. A modern novelist, he used fragmented time as a tactic in every text. But this all-inclusive strategy eventually turned Yáñez's breath—something he found vital—into asthmatic wheezing.

A nationalist, Yáñez wanted to create "a Mexican art of fiction writing." What he got was a paradox. By destroying—and he did destroy—the possibility of the provinces as picturesque setting, by penetrating them in modern novels, he also rid them of their holism. His successors rejected from the start the idea of trawling the nation like cartographers anxious to designate its human and natural dimensions. But it was only thanks to Yáñez that they knew each part of the whole was influential and universal. (*Antología de la narrativa mexicana del siglo XX*, I, 1989)

SELECTED BIBLIOGRAPHY

Obras, Narrativa, vols 1–5, ed. Alfonso Rangel Guerra, El Colegio Nacional, Mexico, 1998–2001.

Imágenes y evocaciones, prologue by Jaime Olveda, Alfaguara/El Colegio de Jalisco, Mexico, 2003.

The Edge of the Storm, trans. Ethel Brinton, University of Texas Press, 1963.

The Lean Lands, trans. Ethel Brinton, University of Texas Press, 1968.

YÉPEZ, HERIBERTO

(Tijuana, Baja California, 1974)[2]

Heriberto Yépez is one of the most active and protean writers of his generation. He is noted for the radicalism (feigned or real) of his poetry, novels, and essays. He carries something of an aura (or a halo) as a pioneer blogger, installation artist, psychotherapist, ethnopoet, and novelist who breaks the boundaries of genre. As a professor of Critical Theory, he has been uniquely focused on deciphering the spectacle of our times (or of our space, as he would have it). And while the border between Mexico and the United States may be the primary focus of his meditations, as *El imperio de la neomemoria* (2007; *The Empire of Neomemory*) makes clear, from up in Tijuana Yépez is watching us.

2 Translated by Lorna Scott Fox. Originally published in *Literature and Arts of the Americas*, Issue 80, Vol. 43, No. 1, 2010, 41–45.

To his capacity for hard work and shrewd sense of opportunity, Yépez adds a habit of self-purification, denouncing with liturgical regularity the wickedness of a distant Babylon: Mexico City, whose literary cliques fabricate as many distortions and corruptions as television does, or political power. Affecting an insular purity, Yépez is quick to impugn the morality of some of his colleagues by firing off volleys of indignant articles, open letters, and emails; outbursts that seek, in imitation of Charles Olson, his favorite writer, to condense the meaning of the world onto a postcard. But Yépez the sniper would not be very interesting, if he weren't the author of an oeuvre that is both sizable and significant.

Perhaps the best introduction to this oeuvre for new readers would be *Tijuanologías* (2006), a two-part essay that stands out for its terse efficacy of style—unusual for a writer whose prose tends to be cumbersome. Part intellectual chronicle, part veiled autobiography, *Tijuanologías* lacks the author's habitual theoretical jargon. But this doesn't imply a deviation from his central obsession with the frontier as the supreme observatory of postmodernity, the infernal paradise of hybridity founded by the invasion of Flores Magón's followers in 1911, the treasure cave that awaits behind the door of every cantina and brothel. This short book testifies to the continuity of a genre that is, as José Gaos* has noted, typically Hispano-American: the essay of national interrogation. In *Contra la tele-visión* (2008; Against Tele-Vision), Yépez claims that Mexican thought, from Octavio Paz* to Carlos Monsiváis* via Jorge Portilla, is only really interesting as psycho-history. This is the tradition to which Yépez, too, belongs.

And in his remarkable case, the nation is Tijuana: a place that Yépez, both a destroyer and a maker of myths, strips of the folksiness and other misapprehensions produced by the cheap intellectual tourism many of us have been guilty of—indulging in occasional *flâneries* along Avenida Revolución, that eighties version of Amsterdam's red-light district for boorish metropolitans. After leading us, Virgil-like, through the real dens and dives of his land, Yépez pours scorn on tourists, creatures equipped with barely an elementary spark of appreciation; and scolds Monsiváis, José Agustín,* and Juan Villoro* for having imagined that this was multiculturalism. No, says Yépez, the poet and etymologist: Tijuana is way beyond that. It is the original Waste Land, a cosmic scrapyard, a link (and by no means the weakest) in the chain of serial production.

Yépez dislikes Chicanos, and his Tijuana is Chicanophobic. He sees no need to correct the image of the *pachuco* presented in Paz's *Labyrinth of Solitude*, however hostile he is to this writer on other fronts. To a Tijuana man (painted by Yépez as a supreme ironist), the Chicano for all his metamorphoses has not managed to rise above the pathos so accurately identified by Paz. And yet this pathos is brandished by many Chicanos as a positive trait, with an identity-building, mythopoetic reach. In the light of *Tijuanologías*, his polished but never complacent vision of the frontier city, I'd now expect Yépez to find the nerve to write a *Critique of Chicano Reason*, the book for which he is surely predestined.

Yépez is a nationalist, then, but I'm not sure how "postnational" his nationalism may be. His take on Tijuana—politically correct and theoretically à la page when saluting it as the apostolic seat of mutation, hybridity, remixes, and remakes—sets up a paradoxically rigid border between that city and the North American empire. Tijuana is made to seem unassimilable, as in his recent novel, *Al otro lado* (2008; To the Other Side). It emerges as profoundly immune to Americanization, the nightmare against which books like *El imperio de la neomemoria* have been written for practically two hundred years. Resisting assimilation, Tijuana fans the author's nationalism to ever more vehement heights—or so it seems from here, in the collaborationist *altiplano*. Yépez reminds us that the empire's first and oldest enemy was Mexico, leading to the theft of half her territory in 1847. At best, argues Yépez, the United States is quixotic and Mexico sanchoesque. He fantasizes about a Mexican resistance within the US, dreaming of an unlikely wetback with a bomb.

I prefer in him the poet to the novelist: the poet who traveled from the miseries of the artist as a young dog, in early poems that were at once melomaniacal and humble, toward the vivid excitement reflected by a handful of poems in *El órgano de la risa* (2008; The Organ of Laughter). In "Vida del Diábolo" (Life of the Diabolo), "Epístola del Manco" (The Amputee's Epistle), and the pair of "autobiographies" that follow, Yépez suggests his own persona better than in any of the novels. But still he insists, being a man of our time, that prose fiction is the higher form of expression. From *El matasellos* (2004; The Postmark), a harmless rhetorical frolic, to *Al otro lado*, I find nothing but the didactic reiteration of a universe that contracts when subjected to the narrative rules reluctantly accepted by Yépez.

547

In *A.B.U.R.T.O.* (2005), the thinly imagined story of the man who killed presidential candidate Luis Donaldo Colosio in Tijuana, Yépez proves unable to generate the artistic power necessary to recreate the inner drama of a mind both trite and demonic, like that of his supposed solitary gunman. The novel winds up as a caricature, an uncritical repository of all the journalistic, ideological, and esoteric clichés that accumulated during the *annus horribilis* of 1994. And if we're going to dream, then I'd rather Mario Aburto's ordeal were related some day by a new Norman Mailer, not a new Philip K. Dick.

Al otro lado is more subdued, far from the addictive irascibility of the apocalyptic mode, closer to the sobriety of *41 clósets* (2005), a gay love story well served by its barely-contained lyricism. *Al otro lado* is set in a washed-out city devoid of Tijuana's landmarks. It tells the story of El Tiburón, the Shark, a drug addict as well as a kind of mutant, who tries to get across the border. Our antihero does not reach his goal, since he is made to disintegrate, literally, in the air. Other characters in the novel are insubstantial: their only purpose is to set up the elementary narrative conditions for the protagonist to disappear in a puff of smoke, like a signal to warn us of the criminal, post-proletarian horror of life in the "waste land." Yépez does well to infantilize certain details, as when he grants sentience to cars and cell phones, and gives a moving account of the dog who dies, horribly burned by the desert sun, following its master. But the absence of conceptual play and the dilution of autobiographical content makes this novel far less dramatic than *Tijuanologías*, the essay that inspired his most brilliant insights— chiefly the conception of the frontier as an "embezzled ontology," the blind spot of the grand narrative of capitalism as he perceives it.

El imperio de la neomemoria constitutes a departure. In this streamlined biography of Charles Olson (1910–70), Yépez approaches his subject's letters, poems, and essays (especially *Call Me Ishmael*, the complex, bitter study of Melville published in 1947) as a kind of Sumerian tablet through which it might be possible to decode the United States. This is the real spur, one feels, to the writing of this convoluted jumble of a book. Yépez remains faithful to Adorno in believing that theoretical obscurity, farfetched terminology, and uninhibited neologism decorate a thought, while shielding it from the objections of logic. The best of Yépez is certainly not to be found in the blather that consumes whole pages of *El imperio de la neomemoria*.

548

The book's central thesis is that the North American empire—like its great creation, television, and the other screens TV has spawned—is omnipresent and omniscient. A culture industry yoked to a military-industrial complex, it requisitions space by disguising it as historical time, and sets up control mechanisms that have reified humanity more and more, with ominous consequences. There's nothing here that can't be got by sitting through *The Matrix*, or, for greater depth, by studying the Frankfurt School and its critical theory. *El imperio de la neomemoria* abounds in intelligence and sensitivity, but such qualities are overshadowed by typical Frankfurtian table-thumping. Convinced that liberal democracy is really a sly refinement of totalitarianism, this line declares, with Yépez, that "Hollywood is nothing but post-Nazi propaganda," or that "the reordering of memory is fascist."

If I didn't think that the real subject of *El imperio de la neomemoria* is Olson, I wouldn't see much difference between this book and the repetitive apocalyptic fantasies emanating from US academics. By identifying himself with Olson, by reading and rereading him, Yépez brings about the detachment of figure from background, in a perceptual operation that can be traced back to the very first work of his that I read, *Ensayos para un desconcierto y alguna crítica ficción* (2001; Essays in Disarray and Some Critical Fictions). This is the book with the memorable (and necessarily succinct) history of aphorisms in Mexico; the one where he claims that our own pre-Socratics were the Guatemalan writers Luis Cardoza y Aragón* and Augusto Monterroso.*

I also like the way in which Yépez, who sometimes writes in English, examines another literary galaxy: that comprising the poets of the San Francisco Renaissance, the cloudy minds of Black Mountain College, and the antics of the penultimate avant-garde, including, but only as propagandistic outriders, the Beats. In contrast to the unreserved gushing with which the preceding generation of Tijuanans fell for this batch of writers, gurus, and patriarchal performance artists, he regards them coolly as his classical horizon: that explains not only the fecundity of his reading of Olson, but also the nonchalance with which he depicts the titanic clash between Jerome Rothenberg and María Sabina, or the last days of Allen Ginsberg. Yépez believes—and here we glimpse his shamanic side—in the curative, hypnotic, and sacred properties of language. He is not the first poet to believe in this, nor will he be the last. The frontiersman revels in the company of translators and mediums.

Olson, for Yépez, is an enemy as well as a master, and this adds an extra layer of density to *El imperio de la neomemoria*. With the help of psychoanalytic and anti-Oedipal concepts, the author exposes his subject as an ideologue of the empire, a bard celebrating plunders and abuses; while this seems reprehensible to Yépez, it has escaped the notice of the naïve countercultural left in the US. Olson's voyage to Mexico, in 1951, provides a neat opportunity to round off the account of a poet obsessed with outdoing Pound but incapable of grasping Mayan wisdom, such as, in Yépez's example, quincunx theory. If the Beats are, here, the Ancient Greeks, the Indians, nomadic or imperial, stand in for telamones, and this returns us by way of a further paradox to José Vasconcelos.* Without subscribing to "indigenism" as such—the literature currently produced under that name, by Subcomandante Marcos perhaps, must surely strike him as base *octography*, vulgar outpourings—Yépez takes refuge in romantic nostalgia for the originary otherness the West has lost. Here lie the secrets of the Great Pyramid, good Sancho.

Yépez is against Enlightenment, an anti-liberal. He is also a Marxist in the only sense in which it is still possible to be one, in my view: by replacing Marx with Guy Debord, and casting the imperium of the spectacle in the role of classic capitalism. Or traveling, courtesy of Freud, from Marxism to Buddhism in the tracks of Erich Fromm, that great simpleton who is never mentioned on anyone's résumé these days. Like the reactionary old aristo, Joseph de Maistre, Yépez considers the unity of Western civilization illusory. In fact, we dwell in an "oasis of the gibbet," a "last imaginary scaffold" where the technological guillotine chops off not our heads but our souls. "Neomemory" is just the latest avatar of the alienation discovered long ago by the young Marx. Consumed on a planetary level, it equates with the "*phoco*" that drugs the would-be traveler in *Al otro lado*.

As one who entertains a number of the superstitions Heriberto Yépez denounces, I can only take off my hat to his scholarly passion, and bow to the exalted state in which he moves. He cuts a singular figure, considering that Mexican literature is notoriously uninterested in ideas. I don't mind adding that I myself am fascinated by the Frankfurt crew, in that I think they may be half right—and half is enough to drive anybody crazy.

Selected Bibliography

Ensayos para un desconcierto y alguna crítica ficción, Fondo Literario de Baja
  California, Mexico, 2001.

El matasellos, Sudamericana, Argentina, 2004.

41 clósets, Conaculta, Mexico, 2005.

A.B.U.R.T.O., Sudamericana, Argentina, 2005.

Tijuanologías, Umbral, Mexico, 2006.

El imperio de la neomemoria, Almadía, Mexico, 2007.

Al otro lado, Planeta, Mexico, 2008.

Contra la tele-visión, Tumbona, Mexico, 2008.

El órgano de la risa y otros diábolos, Conaculta, Mexico, 2008.

Babellebab: Non-Poetry on the End of Translation, Duration Press, 2003.

Here Is Tijuana!, with Fiamma Montezemolo and Rene Peralta, Black Dog,
  2006.

WARS. THREESOMES. DRAFTS. & MOTHERS, Factory School, 2007.

Z

ZAID, GABRIEL

(Monterrey, Nuevo León, 1934)

One day, someone will write the history of Mexican literature we so need, the one we dream of. And when they do, we'll have some perspective; posterity will prove that we in the twentieth century failed in our calculations and compilations of oeuvres and dates. But there will be realms charted by critics like Zaid that remain: true geographies of literary imagination. *Tres poetas católicos*, a compendium of thirty years of curiosity, maps the routes, passages, and morasses of Mexican Catholic literature, of which we're piously ignorant.

Zaid, starting with a preliminary text entitled "Muerte y resurrección de la cultura católica," confronts the kingdom of that cannibalistic, two-headed monster: Jacobinism and clericalism. The former—victor of the Reformation and executioner during the Cristero War—confined Catholic culture to its polar opposites: procession and seminary. The latter, defeated and humiliated, hid behind the miter and was regularly involved in clandestine, shady deals or in new forms of millenarianism such as liberation theology. The consequences were dire: rather than an anatomy of Mexican spirituality, what we had was teratology. Mexico, a Catholic country founded on *paraenesis*—that religious agreement between the preachers and the converted—had no official Catholic culture.

That dramatic sham inevitably seeped into our literary history. With the little-known exceptions of Antonio Estrada (1927–1968) and Jesús Goytortúa (1910–1969), the Christian novel chose a martyr's justification over artistic dignity. Thus it was that a Communist, José Revueltas,* was our great Christian novelist. And Catholic intellectuals (that beautiful anomaly, the accidental lovechild of the French Revolution and Romanticism) had to choose between imagination and scandal, between being like the discreet brothers Alfonso and Gabriel Méndez Plancarte, or being like old José Vasconcelos,* who was more Catholic than Christian in his later litanies. Others, like Antonio Caso—father of Ángel María Garibay Kintana*—and Antonio Gómez Robledo, opted for prudence, voluntarily positing themselves as secondary to the great chorus of pagans, Masons, and Jacobins led by the revolutionary Martín Luis Guzmán,* Socratic Alfonso Reyes,* and the metaphysics of the *Contemporáneos*.

Catholic poets were granted a bit more room to maneuver. The Catholicism of Ramón López Velarde and Carlos Pellicer* was *tolerated*, apparently seen as inoffensive. In the case of the former, people condescended to his provincial reactionary sadness, and the latter was celebrated for the naïve Franciscan joy he found in landscapes. But Zaid put an emphatic end to that withering tolerance. Piecing together the puzzle of the National Catholic Party—that uncomfortable and later crushed ally of President Francisco I. Madero, Zaid comes up with the official bard of the Mexican Revolution, López Velarde, and presents him as the Catholic intellectual that modern Mexico longed for. Analyzing the relationship between the poet and his friend Eduardo J. Correa (as have Jean Meyer* and Guillermo Sheridan*), Zaid presents intellectual life during the revolution in a different light.

Tres poetas católicos then moves on to Pellicer. I'm not going to reiterate Zaid's most feted critical qualities, such as his ability to teach prosaic spirits like mine how poetry works. But his readings will make me go back to Pellicer's poetry with far greater understanding. And in addition to discussing Pellicer's "*azules que se caen de morados*" (blues so purple they fall), Zaid recalls a crucial event recounted by Juan Ramón Jiménez that's been ignored by literary history: the indirect link between the Latin American modernist poetry and Pope Pius's Encyclical *Pascendi* in September 1907, in which he condemned "modernism" as heresy.

When Pius IX condemned the modern world in *Syllabus* (1864), Catholic intellectuals, especially in France, rebelled. Impressed by German metaphysics, by Ernest Renan's bible criticism, by reading of Eastern Catholic traditions, open to modern science and its implications for Catholic dogmas, modernist theologians like Alfred Loisy, Eduard Le Roy, and Oratorian Lucien Laberthonière put themselves on the line, coming out in favor of the *aggiornamento* of the Church. Perhaps Teilhard de Chardin was the last of this line, and the Second Vatican Council was a partial, posthumous victory for Catholics condemned at the turn of the century.

The influence of Catholic modernism in Mexico was decisive. It fueled— as much if not more than dogmatic positivism—the Christian heterodoxy of Amado Nervo and José Juan Tablada when they were young. It fired Reyes's and Guzmán's skepticism, Vasconcelos's insatiable religious anxieties, Madero's spiritism, Caso's spiritualism, López Velarde's (proto-) Christian democracy, and—as Zaid notes—Pellicer's Christian optimism, which clearly had Franciscan overtones but was even more modernist in its Catholic lyricism. My sole point of contention is regarding Reyes, whose flagrant paganism I don't believe was tempered one bit—as Zaid seems to claim in one of his appendices—by Christian occasional poetry.

The third Catholic poet he analyzes is Manuel Ponce (1913–1994), whom Zaid himself introduced to our profane literary society in the late seventies. He uses Ponce, author of the unforgettable *Ciclo de vírgenes* (1940)—one of the few Mexican Catholic poems to amaze nonbelievers—to close a book that demonstrates the role Catholicism played in revolutionary politics (López Velarde), modernist poetry (Pellicer), and the pulpit. And it seems that the "three" Catholic poets could have been four, five, six, or more if we restored Father Alfredo R. Plascencia and proposed Concha Urquiza—whom Zaid calls our own Simone Weil—along with Francisco Alday, the group at the magazine *Trento* (1943–1968) edited by Ponce, and younger poets like Javier Sicilia.

Tres poetas católicos is essential for the literary resurrection of our Catholic culture. There's still a long road ahead but the starting point has been established by Zaid, who portrays himself as a reactionary, a *mocho*, one who sustains his Catholic beliefs when in urbane society, and a believer who calls himself lay when confronted by Catholicism. I must say that Zaid is an odd sort of Catholic critic: Cardinal Newmann and the first Blanco White would have found fellowship with a modernist like him who, at the end of the twentieth century, has censured both what he calls "unproductive progress" and academia.

Tres poetas católicos is a paradigm for literary criticism as open thinking, a celebration of the joys of research, an occasion for questions more than answers, an invitation to read poetry not unlike Zaid's prose, in talking about the Christian beginnings of Pellicer, whose soul shone a light on the vulnerable vault of heaven as well as the inexplicable joys of the world below. Zaid, a scholar specializing in an endangered and wounded field, has—more than his three chosen poets—exemplified what it means to be a modern Catholic. (*Servidumbre y grandeza de la vida literaria*, 1998)

As the years go by, when reading, rereading, or even just leafing through old issues of the journals *Plural* and *Vuelta*, it's impossible not to reflect on the richly nuanced scope of the group that was behind them. The sway Octavio Paz* held in world literature, the political animosity surrounding the magazines and some people's desire to see them quickly forgotten, coupled with the conceit of their main players have kept us from fully taking stock of what was a collective experience in the history of Latin American letters. But as important as Paz to the magazines' intellectual infrastructure were Alejandro Rossi,* Gabriel Zaid, and, later, Enrique Krauze.* These three writers are key when it comes to understanding Paz's political perspectives and intellectual certainties, which held sway over Mexican culture.

Zaid was an eccentric at *Plural* and *Vuelta*—the only Catholic in a group of agnostics and skeptics. Juan García Ponce* and Salvador Elizondo* were presented as feuding brothers, descendents of the same progenitors: Bataille's aesthetics of transgression and deviant Western literature. Poet Tomás Segovia* could be read as an heir to Juan Ramón Jiménez and the Generation of '27, but Rossi's stories and essays branch off from the tree of Borges, Bioy Casares, and José Bianco. Meanwhile, although Zaid's joyous poetry is so transparent it can be traced, his role as critic (of poetry, the publishing industry and political power) was an intellectually complicated arrangement that began to burgeon in articles published in the seventies in *La Cultura en México*, *Diálogos*, and *Cuadernos del Viento*. Zaid, who later authored two critical anthologies (*Omnibus de poesía mexicana* in 1970 and *Asamblea de poetas jóvenes de México* in 1980), wrote memorable and polemical interpretations of poets Alfonso Reyes,* Carlos Pellicer, José Carlos Becerra,* Luis Cernuda,* Marco Antonio Montes de Oca,* and José Emilio Pacheco,* as well as essays analyzing the literary mob and investigating the role of anthologies. Then through his column "La cinta de Moebius" in *Plural*, Zaid became one of the sharpest critics of the Institutional Revolutionary Party (PRI) regime, which at the time was obsessed with getting back into the good graces of intellectuals, having lost their legitimacy after the Tlatelolco massacre of 1968 and then again with the Corpus Christi student massacre of 1971.

In order to unravel Zaid's critical perspective, we have to dig deeper than his militant Catholicism, which progressively became more public, culminating in *Tres poetas católicos*. Zaid presented himself as a literary critic strangely free of—at least in appearance—essentialism, a sort of practical moralist who could easily have been seen as a Protestant spirit. And then, in an intellectual milieu where theological brawls between every possible Marxist school broke out with stultifying regularity, Zaid decided to examine—in *Leer poesía* (1972) and *Cómo leer en bicicleta* (1975)—the material conditions in which literary life and literature itself were produced. It seemed outrageous at the time. He wasn't advancing a method or founding any sociology of reception but pruning literature of all the metaphysical and ideological twaddle surrounding it, in order to display the way poetry functions as a "machine for singing," as per his celebrated 1967 book *La máquina de cantar*.

But even more surprising, Zaid's criticism was not only *not* academic, it was actually an attack on academia, on the theories and practices of academic knowledge. Zaid went from revealing the mechanisms of "inspiration" to radically (and in the end, excessively) critiquing the university as a body that creates and usufructs cultural hegemony. And it was only then, in books like *El progreso improductivo* (1979) and *De los libros al poder* (1988) that the moral nature of his criticism could fully be discerned. Literary criticism devoid of euphuism—that precious ornateness and self-conscious sophistication—was just the first step in his crusade to free public life of the superstition of "unproductive progress" that universities offer society as a panacea.

Zaid's technique turned out to be the same whether he was analyzing poetry anthologies or Central American revolutions: dismantling reality, stripping it down to its constituent parts and divesting it of the artistic, metaphysical, ideological, or humanitarian prestige it enjoyed as a totality, then subjecting it to the light of common sense and—frequently—*reductio ad absurdum*. But while his literary criticism had limited reach given that he wasn't advancing principles (if he were, he'd be another Emerson or a Chernyshevsky), his political criticism turned out to be both devastating and spot-on, given the moral scale of the fraud he was denouncing. By analyzing the Sandinista government and the Salvadoran guerrillas with the same blueprint Silvio Zavala used in *Los intereses particulares en la Conquista de la Nueva España* (1991), Zaid found a new application for some of the political elite's theories, and it worked surprisingly well as journalism. The result was essentially a moral proof: using Marxism-Leninism, Jesuitism, and nationalism, the guerrillas were in effect inventing popular will in order to usurp it. After the Sandinistas' 1990 electoral defeat and the Chapultepec Peace Accords between the Salvadoran guerrillas and the government, even Joaquín Villalobos (the guerrilla leader involved in the assassination of poet Roque Dalton and Zaid's prime target in these memorable texts) had to admit that democracy was the only political space where the elite's ambitions could be derailed. Paz had criticized totalitarianism for ideological reasons; Zaid gave a more pragmatic reasoning for his moral reservations. Unlike Paz, Rossi, and Krauze, Zaid is more a democrat than a liberal. He's not interested in comprehensive political traditions but ideal civic communities.

Zaid's method has some obvious limitations: in some of his criticisms of the publishing industry and cultural hegemony the type of critique he's trying to subject reality to simply doesn't work. In other cases, Zaid just seems representative of that character of yore, the intellectual who hates intellectuals. It's no coincidence that one of his first (and most famous) poems is dedicated "to the Larousse dictionary": for this new-style Catholic humanist, the world shouldn't be an encyclopedia but a pocket dictionary whose definitions are not always entirely convincing.

Kindness, balance, gentleness, and generosity were the virtues of the perfect man according to Renaissance humanism. For a Catholic humanist like Erasmus to emerge from that spiritual framework, Christianity had to submit to the godliness of all human endeavors. The young Zaid who wrote his inaugural text, "La ciudad y los poetas," for his fellow Monterrey denizens in 1963 was akin to the early Catholic humanist, prolonging the take on literature that Reyes had abandoned in his pagan phase. That's why it's logical (albeit counterproductive and a tad obnoxious) that the older Zaid should try to save Reyes from limbo via the Catholicisim of his religious poetry.

This early Zaid addressing the city is a Catholic humanist conversing with the Philistines, convinced that no one should be excluded from reading the Scriptures or having communion with the poetry, which Zaid associates— with the methodological modesty of Santayana—with the origins of religion. Throughout his career, Zaid followed that path faithfully, and that allowed him to set up camp with the laity, to take the humanities out of academia's ivory tower. This explains both the breadth and the restrictions that he sought and imposed. It also explains his false modesty (which Chamfort saw as the most decent sort of falsehood), publishing in massive academic journals and refusing to transcend the limits of the written word. After all, action brings pain, and the futility of knowledge is burdensome enough without adding to it futility of the world.

In the sixties, that Christian humanist mission found a world where certain Renaissance principles were at odds with harsh, new religious wars. In Latin America, the climate of the Second Vatican Council—which had in Zaid one of its most incisive cultural theorists—turned ecclesiastic reformers into guerrilla priests. Zaid's fierce criticism of universities in Mexico, Nicaragua, and El Salvador stemmed from his Erasmianism: he saw the early Scholastics who became Lutherans, Calvinists, Zwinglians as fervent prophets who divided what ought to have been indivisible—namely, Catholicism.

Zaid isn't interested in condemning the modern world, and in that sense Paz was wrong to have called him a traditionalist. Zaid possesses a sort of evangelical optimism—as did Pellicer and Father Manuel Ponce, who were more emblematic poets for him than López Velarde was. And that optimism recognizes the reactionary spirit of all millenarianism, whether leftist or rightist. On the other hand, Zaid sees the utopian construction of the city of God as a daily task rooted in the permanent redesign of the humanity of laws, *Legum humanitas* that in the twenty-first century can only be expressed via the conservative anarchism that supports things like self-sufficient agrarian communities and sees cultural consumption as what separates barbarism from civilization.

Like all complex thought—particularly that which sees itself as simple—Zaid's thinking is a drama that has no dramatic solution. By not proposing a system he betrays a profound need for utopia, and by offering practical solutions to complex problems, Zaid might be right, but he remains utopian. His small-scale projects aspire to an immense social engineering project that's not—in appearance, at least—of this world. Faced with the problem of free will that separated Rome from the Reformation, Erasmus left both parties dissatisfied: he offered neither a theology nor a dogmatic solution. But in the aftermath of religious wars, the Erasmian vocation of showing how grace and free will gladly conspired in the ordinary divinity of the human was worth more than treatises, atrocities, and ruses. Zaid spoke neither from the pulpit nor from any political platform but from literature—the only place in the modern world that could guarantee his freedom. His is a utilitarian conception of literature, one that sees inspiration and common sense as having joined forces theologically to create one of those rare oeuvres where the dignity of his intelligence redeems an age of its infamies.

SELECTED BIBLIOGRAPHY

Obras, El Colegio Nacional, Mexico, 1995–2004.

1. *Poesía. Reloj de sol.*
2. *Ensayos sobre poesía.*
3. *Crítica del mundo cultural.*
4. *El progreso improductivo.*

Tres poetas católicos, Océano, Mexico, 1997.

So Many Books: Reading and Publishing in the Age of Abundance, trans. Natasha Wimmer, Paul Dry Books, 2003.

The Secret of Fame, trans. Natasha Wimmer, Paul Dry Books, 2008.

TRANSLATOR'S NOTE

This project would have verged on the impossible were it not for the steadfast support of Christopher Domínguez Michael, as well as his eagerness to answer hundreds of questions via email, telephone, and in person for nearly two years. I am profoundly thankful to him for his generosity and friendship, forged during this time, as well as for the opportunity I had to spend time with him, both in Canada and Coyoacán. As a result of our myriad discussions, several entries have been either expanded or condensed, so as to provide needed background for non-Spanish speaking (and at times, non Mexico City-residing) readers, or to omit information that might be more peripheral to an English-speaking readership. I am also deeply grateful for the three weeks I spent at the Banff International Literary Translation Centre in 2010, where Christopher and I first met, and for the faculty and co-participants in that program, which was undoubtedly the most uninterrupted, intense translational experience of my life.

In translating the *Critical Dictionary of Mexican Literature (1955–2010)*, I acquired vast stores of knowledge about not only Mexican literature and literary history, but also about international cultural history. Christopher Domínguez Michael quotes liberally from critics, historians and other authors writing in Spanish and a number of other languages so a note on translations may be of use.

Whenever possible, for quotations from texts with published English translations, I have used those and credited the translator. If the texts are literary, the book and translator are listed in the Selected Bibliography following each entry. Translations of scholarly texts written in Spanish are mine unless otherwise noted in the text, and although I have done no translations from any language other than Spanish for this project, occasionally I had to translate from Spanish a quotation originally made in a third language.

For quoted poetry, the translation is fairly literal, as it is intended to give readers access to the thematic content of the poem, rather than to serve as an artistic contribution to the field. Poems with published English translations are noted in parenthesis and/or in the Selected Bibliography.

Spanish book titles followed by English titles in parenthesis (in their first citation only) have been published in translation and are listed in the Selected Bibliography. Finally, the Selected Bibliography often includes English translations of books not discussed in the original entry or included in the Spanish portion of the Selected Bibliography; this is intended as a service to English-speaking readers who may wish to know which additional works by a given author have already been translated.

LISA M. DILLMAN, 2011

Christopher Domínguez Michael was born in Mexico City in 1962. He is a literary critic, historian of ideas, and novelist. He's a contributor to such prestigious periodicals as *Vuelta, Letras Libres,* and the literary supplement of the newspaper *Reforma.* His biography *Vida de Fray Servando* was awarded the Xavier Villaurrutia Prize in 2004, and one of his books on literary criticism (*La sabiduría sin promesa*) was awarded the international prize of the Art Circle of Santiago de Chile in 2009.

Lisa M. Dillman translates from the Spanish and Catalan and teaches at Emory University in Atlanta. Her recent translations include Eslava Galán's *The Mule* and Juan Filloy's *Op Oloop.* She's currently translating novels by Sabina Berman and Yuri Herrera.

PETROS ABATZOGLOU, *What Does Mrs. Freeman Want?*
MICHAL AJVAZ, *The Golden Age.*
The Other City.
PIERRE ALBERT-BIROT, *Grabinoulor.*
YUZ ALESHKOVSKY, *Kangaroo.*
FELIPE ALFAU, *Chromos.*
Locos.
JOÃO ALMINO, *The Book of Emotions.*
IVAN ÂNGELO, *The Celebration.*
The Tower of Glass.
DAVID ANTIN, *Talking.*
ANTÓNIO LOBO ANTUNES,
Knowledge of Hell.
The Splendor of Portugal.
ALAIN ARIAS-MISSON, *Theatre of Incest.*
IFTIKHAR ARIF AND WAQAS KHWAJA, EDS.,
Modern Poetry of Pakistan.
JOHN ASHBERY AND JAMES SCHUYLER,
A Nest of Ninnies.
ROBERT ASHLEY, *Perfect Lives.*
GABRIELA AVIGUR-ROTEM, *Heatwave and Crazy Birds.*
HEIMRAD BÄCKER, *transcript.*
DJUNA BARNES, *Ladies Almanack.*
Ryder.
JOHN BARTH, *LETTERS.*
Sabbatical.
DONALD BARTHELME, *The King.*
Paradise.
SVETISLAV BASARA, *Chinese Letter.*
RENÉ BELLETTO, *Dying.*
MARK BINELLI, *Sacco and Vanzetti Must Die!*
ANDREI BITOV, *Pushkin House.*
ANDREJ BLATNIK, *You Do Understand.*
LOUIS PAUL BOON, *Chapel Road.*
My Little War.
Summer in Termuren.
ROGER BOYLAN, *Killoyle.*
IGNÁCIO DE LOYOLA BRANDÃO,
Anonymous Celebrity.
The Good-Bye Angel.
Teeth under the Sun.
Zero.
BONNIE BREMSER,
Troia: Mexican Memoirs.
CHRISTINE BROOKE-ROSE, *Amalgamemnon.*
BRIGID BROPHY, *In Transit.*
MEREDITH BROSNAN, *Mr. Dynamite.*
GERALD L. BRUNS, *Modern Poetry and the Idea of Language.*
EVGENY BUNIMOVICH AND J. KATES, EDS.,
Contemporary Russian Poetry: An Anthology.
GABRIELLE BURTON, *Heartbreak Hotel.*
MICHEL BUTOR, *Degrees.*
Mobile.
Portrait of the Artist as a Young Ape.
G. CABRERA INFANTE, *Infante's Inferno.*
Three Trapped Tigers.
JULIETA CAMPOS,
The Fear of Losing Eurydice.
ANNE CARSON, *Eros the Bittersweet.*
ORLY CASTEL-BLOOM, *Dolly City.*
CAMILO JOSÉ CELA, *Christ versus Arizona.*
The Family of Pascual Duarte.
The Hive.
LOUIS-FERDINAND CÉLINE, *Castle to Castle.*
Conversations with Professor Y.
London Bridge.

Normance.
North.
Rigadoon.
HUGO CHARTERIS, *The Tide Is Right.*
JEROME CHARYN, *The Tar Baby.*
ERIC CHEVILLARD, *Demolishing Nisard.*
MARC CHOLODENKO, *Mordechai Schamz.*
JOSHUA COHEN, *Witz.*
EMILY HOLMES COLEMAN, *The Shutter of Snow.*
ROBERT COOVER, *A Night at the Movies.*
STANLEY CRAWFORD, *Log of the S.S. The Mrs Unguentine.*
Some Instructions to My Wife.
ROBERT CREELEY, *Collected Prose.*
RENÉ CREVEL, *Putting My Foot in It.*
RALPH CUSACK, *Cadenza.*
SUSAN DAITCH, *L.C.*
Storytown.
NICHOLAS DELBANCO,
The Count of Concord.
Sherbrookes.
NIGEL DENNIS, *Cards of Identity.*
PETER DIMOCK, *A Short Rhetoric for Leaving the Family.*
ARIEL DORFMAN, *Konfidenz.*
COLEMAN DOWELL,
The Houses of Children.
Island People.
Too Much Flesh and Jabez.
ARKADII DRAGOMOSHCHENKO, *Dust.*
RIKKI DUCORNET, *The Complete Butcher's Tales.*
The Fountains of Neptune.
The Jade Cabinet.
The One Marvelous Thing.
Phosphor in Dreamland.
The Stain.
The Word "Desire."
WILLIAM EASTLAKE, *The Bamboo Bed.*
Castle Keep.
Lyric of the Circle Heart.
JEAN ECHENOZ, *Chopin's Move.*
STANLEY ELKIN, *A Bad Man.*
Boswell: A Modern Comedy.
Criers and Kibitzers, Kibitzers and Criers.
The Dick Gibson Show.
The Franchiser.
George Mills.
The Living End.
The MacGuffin.
The Magic Kingdom.
Mrs. Ted Bliss.
The Rabbi of Lud.
Van Gogh's Room at Arles.
FRANÇOIS EMMANUEL, *Invitation to a Voyage.*
ANNIE ERNAUX, *Cleaned Out.*
LAUREN FAIRBANKS, *Muzzle Thyself.*
Sister Carrie.
LESLIE A. FIEDLER, *Love and Death in the American Novel.*
JUAN FILLOY, *Op Oloop.*
GUSTAVE FLAUBERT, *Bouvard and Pécuchet.*
KASS FLEISHER, *Talking out of School.*
FORD MADOX FORD,
The March of Literature.
JON FOSSE, *Aliss at the Fire.*
Melancholy.
MAX FRISCH, *I'm Not Stiller.*

Man in the Holocene.
CARLOS FUENTES, *Christopher Unborn.*
   Distant Relations.
   Terra Nostra.
   Where the Air Is Clear.
WILLIAM GADDIS, *J R.*
   The Recognitions.
JANICE GALLOWAY, *Foreign Parts.*
   The Trick Is to Keep Breathing.
WILLIAM H. GASS, *Cartesian Sonata*
   and Other Novellas.
   Finding a Form.
   A Temple of Texts.
   The Tunnel.
   Willie Masters' Lonesome Wife.
GÉRARD GAVARRY, *Hoppla! 1 2 3.*
   Making a Novel.
ETIENNE GILSON,
   The Arts of the Beautiful.
   Forms and Substances in the Arts.
C. S. GISCOMBE, *Giscome Road.*
   Here.
   Prairie Style.
DOUGLAS GLOVER, *Bad News of the Heart.*
   The Enamoured Knight.
WITOLD GOMBROWICZ,
   A Kind of Testament.
KAREN ELIZABETH GORDON,
   The Red Shoes.
GEORGI GOSPODINOV, *Natural Novel.*
JUAN GOYTISOLO, *Count Julian.*
   Exiled from Almost Everywhere.
   Juan the Landless.
   Makbara.
   Marks of Identity.
PATRICK GRAINVILLE, *The Cave of Heaven.*
HENRY GREEN, *Back.*
   Blindness.
   Concluding.
   Doting.
   Nothing.
JACK GREEN, *Fire the Bastards!*
JIŘÍ GRUŠA, *The Questionnaire.*
GABRIEL GUDDING,
   Rhode Island Notebook.
MELA HARTWIG, *Am I a Redundant*
   Human Being?
JOHN HAWKES, *The Passion Artist.*
   Whistlejacket.
ALEKSANDAR HEMON, ED.,
   Best European Fiction.
AIDAN HIGGINS, *A Bestiary.*
   Balcony of Europe.
   Bornholm Night-Ferry.
   Darkling Plain: Texts for the Air.
   Flotsam and Jetsam.
   Langrishe, Go Down.
   Scenes from a Receding Past.
   Windy Arbours.
KEIZO HINO, *Isle of Dreams.*
KAZUSHI HOSAKA, *Plainsong.*
ALDOUS HUXLEY, *Antic Hay.*
   Crome Yellow.
   Point Counter Point.
   Those Barren Leaves.
   Time Must Have a Stop.
NAOYUKI II, *The Shadow of a Blue Cat.*
MIKHAIL IOSSEL AND JEFF PARKER, EDS.,
   Amerika: Russian Writers View the
   United States.
DRAGO JANČAR, *The Galley Slave.*
GERT JONKE, *The Distant Sound.*

Geometric Regional Novel.
   Homage to Czerny.
   The System of Vienna.
JACQUES JOUET, *Mountain R.*
   Savage.
   Upstaged.
CHARLES JULIET, *Conversations with*
   Samuel Beckett and Bram van
   Velde.
MIEKO KANAI, *The Word Book.*
YORAM KANIUK, *Life on Sandpaper.*
HUGH KENNER, *The Counterfeiters.*
   Flaubert, Joyce and Beckett:
   The Stoic Comedians.
   Joyce's Voices.
DANILO KIŠ, *Garden, Ashes.*
   A Tomb for Boris Davidovich.
ANITA KONKKA, *A Fool's Paradise.*
GEORGE KONRÁD, *The City Builder.*
TADEUSZ KONWICKI, *A Minor Apocalypse.*
   The Polish Complex.
MENIS KOUMANDAREAS, *Koula.*
ELAINE KRAF, *The Princess of 72nd Street.*
JIM KRUSOE, *Iceland.*
EWA KURYLUK, *Century 21.*
EMILIO LASCANO TEGUI, *On Elegance*
   While Sleeping.
ERIC LAURRENT, *Do Not Touch.*
HERVÉ LE TELLIER, *The Sextine Chapel.*
   A Thousand Pearls (for a Thousand
   Pennies)
VIOLETTE LEDUC, *La Bâtarde.*
EDOUARD LEVÉ, *Autoportrait.*
   Suicide.
SUZANNE JILL LEVINE, *The Subversive*
   Scribe: Translating Latin
   American Fiction.
DEBORAH LEVY, *Billy and Girl.*
   Pillow Talk in Europe and Other
   Places.
JOSÉ LEZAMA LIMA, *Paradiso.*
ROSA LIKSOM, *Dark Paradise.*
OSMAN LINS, *Avalovara.*
   The Queen of the Prisons of Greece.
ALF MAC LOCHLAINN,
   The Corpus in the Library.
   Out of Focus.
RON LOEWINSOHN, *Magnetic Field(s).*
MINA LOY, *Stories and Essays of Mina Loy.*
BRIAN LYNCH, *The Winner of Sorrow.*
D. KEITH MANO, *Take Five.*
MICHELINE AHARONIAN MARCOM,
   The Mirror in the Well.
BEN MARCUS,
   The Age of Wire and String.
WALLACE MARKFIELD,
   Teitlebaum's Window.
   To an Early Grave.
DAVID MARKSON, *Reader's Block.*
   Springer's Progress.
   Wittgenstein's Mistress.
CAROLE MASO, *AVA.*
LADISLAV MATEJKA AND KRYSTYNA
   POMORSKA, EDS.,
   Readings in Russian Poetics:
   Formalist and Structuralist Views.
HARRY MATHEWS,
   The Case of the Persevering Maltese:
   Collected Essays.
   Cigarettes.
   The Conversions.
   The Human Country: New and

Collected Stories.
The Journalist.
My Life in CIA.
Singular Pleasures.
The Sinking of the Odradek
    Stadium.
Tlooth.
20 Lines a Day.
JOSEPH McELROY,
    Night Soul and Other Stories.
THOMAS McGONIGLE,
    Going to Patchogue.
ROBERT L. McLAUGHLIN, ED., Innovations:
    An Anthology of
    Modern & Contemporary Fiction.
ABDELWAHAB MEDDEB, Talismano.
GERHARD MEIER, Isle of the Dead.
HERMAN MELVILLE, The Confidence-Man.
AMANDA MICHALOPOULOU, I'd Like.
STEVEN MILLHAUSER,
    The Barnum Museum.
    In the Penny Arcade.
RALPH J. MILLS, JR.,
    Essays on Poetry.
MOMUS, The Book of Jokes.
CHRISTINE MONTALBETTI, Western.
OLIVE MOORE, Spleen.
NICHOLAS MOSLEY, Accident.
    Assassins.
    Catastrophe Practice.
    Children of Darkness and Light.
    Experience and Religion.
    God's Hazard.
    The Hesperides Tree.
    Hopeful Monsters.
    Imago Bird.
    Impossible Object.
    Inventing God.
    Judith.
    Look at the Dark.
    Natalie Natalia.
    Paradoxes of Peace.
    Serpent.
    Time at War.
    The Uses of Slime Mould:
        Essays of Four Decades.
WARREN MOTTE,
    Fables of the Novel: French Fiction
        since 1990.
    Fiction Now: The French Novel in
        the 21st Century.
    Oulipo: A Primer of Potential
        Literature.
GERALD MURNANE, Barley Patch.
YVES NAVARRE, Our Share of Time.
    Sweet Tooth.
DOROTHY NELSON, In Night's City.
    Tar and Feathers.
ESHKOL NEVO, Homesick.
WILFRIDO D. NOLLEDO, But for the Lovers.
FLANN O'BRIEN,
    At Swim-Two-Birds.
    At War.
    The Best of Myles.
    The Dalkey Archive.
    Further Cuttings.
    The Hard Life.
    The Poor Mouth.
    The Third Policeman.
CLAUDE OLLIER, The Mise-en-Scène.
    Wert and the Life Without End.
PATRIK OUŘEDNÍK, Europeana.

The Opportune Moment, 1855.
BORIS PAHOR, Necropolis.
FERNANDO DEL PASO,
    News from the Empire.
    Palinuro of Mexico.
ROBERT PINGET, The Inquisitory.
    Mahu or The Material.
    Trio.
A. G. PORTA, The No World Concerto.
MANUEL PUIG,
    Betrayed by Rita Hayworth.
    The Buenos Aires Affair.
    Heartbreak Tango.
RAYMOND QUENEAU, The Last Days.
    Odile.
    Pierrot Mon Ami.
    Saint Glinglin.
ANN QUIN, Berg.
    Passages.
    Three.
    Tripticks.
ISHMAEL REED,
    The Free-Lance Pallbearers.
    The Last Days of Louisiana Red.
    Ishmael Reed: The Plays.
    Juice!
    Reckless Eyeballing.
    The Terrible Threes.
    The Terrible Twos.
    Yellow Back Radio Broke-Down.
JOÃO UBALDO RIBEIRO, House of the
    Fortunate Buddhas.
JEAN RICARDOU, Place Names.
RAINER MARIA RILKE, The Notebooks of
    Malte Laurids Brigge.
JULIÁN RÍOS, The House of Ulysses.
    Larva: A Midsummer Night's Babel.
    Poundemonium.
    Procession of Shadows.
AUGUSTO ROA BASTOS, I the Supreme.
DANIÈL ROBBERECHTS,
    Arriving in Avignon.
JEAN ROLIN, The Explosion of the
    Radiator Hose.
OLIVIER ROLIN, Hotel Crystal.
ALIX CLEO ROUBAUD, Alix's Journal.
JACQUES ROUBAUD, The Form of a
    City Changes Faster, Alas, Than
    the Human Heart.
    The Great Fire of London.
    Hortense in Exile.
    Hortense Is Abducted.
    The Loop.
    Mathématique:
    The Plurality of Worlds of Lewis.
    The Princess Hoppy.
    Some Thing Black.
LEON S. ROUDIEZ, French Fiction Revisited.
RAYMOND ROUSSEL, Impressions of Africa.
VEDRANA RUDAN, Night.
STIG SÆTERBAKKEN, Siamese.
LYDIE SALVAYRE, The Company of Ghosts.
    Everyday Life.
    The Lecture.
    Portrait of the Writer as a
        Domesticated Animal.
    The Power of Flies.
LUIS RAFAEL SÁNCHEZ,
    Macho Camacho's Beat.
SEVERO SARDUY, Cobra & Maitreya.
NATHALIE SARRAUTE,
    Do You Hear Them?

FOR A FULL LIST OF PUBLICATIONS, VISIT:
www.dalkeyarchive.com

Martereau.
The Planetarium.
ARNO SCHMIDT, *Collected Novellas.*
Collected Stories.
Nobodaddy's Children.
Two Novels.
ASAF SCHURR, *Motti.*
CHRISTINE SCHUTT, *Nightwork.*
GAIL SCOTT, *My Paris.*
DAMION SEARLS, *What We Were Doing*
and Where We Were Going.
JUNE AKERS SEESE,
Is This What Other Women Feel Too?
What Waiting Really Means.
BERNARD SHARE, *Inish.*
Transit.
AURELIE SHEEHAN,
Jack Kerouac Is Pregnant.
VIKTOR SHKLOVSKY, *Bowstring.*
Knight's Move.
A Sentimental Journey:
Memoirs 1917–1922.
Energy of Delusion: A Book on Plot.
Literature and Cinematography.
Theory of Prose.
Third Factory.
Zoo, or Letters Not about Love.
CLAUDE SIMON, *The Invitation.*
PIERRE SINIAC, *The Collaborators.*
KJERSTI A. SKOMSVOLD, *The Faster I Walk,*
the Smaller I Am.
JOSEF ŠKVORECKÝ, *The Engineer of*
Human Souls.
GILBERT SORRENTINO,
Aberration of Starlight.
Blue Pastoral.
Crystal Vision.
Imaginative Qualities of Actual
Things.
Mulligan Stew.
Pack of Lies.
Red the Fiend.
The Sky Changes.
Something Said.
Splendide-Hôtel.
Steelwork.
Under the Shadow.
W. M. SPACKMAN,
The Complete Fiction.
ANDRZEJ STASIUK, *Dukla.*
Fado.
GERTRUDE STEIN,
Lucy Church Amiably.
The Making of Americans.
A Novel of Thank You.
LARS SVENDSEN, *A Philosophy of Evil.*
PIOTR SZEWC, *Annihilation.*
GONÇALO M. TAVARES, *Jerusalem.*
Joseph Walser's Machine.
Learning to Pray in the Age of
Technique.
LUCIAN DAN TEODOROVICI,
Our Circus Presents . . .
NIKANOR TERATOLOGEN, *Assisted Living.*
STEFAN THEMERSON, *Hobson's Island.*
The Mystery of the Sardine.
Tom Harris.
JOHN TOOMEY, *Sleepwalker.*
JEAN-PHILIPPE TOUSSAINT,
The Bathroom.
Camera.
Monsieur.

Running Away.
Self-Portrait Abroad.
Television.
The Truth about Marie.
DUMITRU TSEPENEAG,
Hotel Europa.
The Necessary Marriage.
Pigeon Post.
Vain Art of the Fugue.
ESTHER TUSQUETS, *Stranded.*
DUBRAVKA UGRESIC,
Lend Me Your Character.
Thank You for Not Reading.
MATI UNT, *Brecht at Night.*
Diary of a Blood Donor.
Things in the Night.
ÁLVARO URIBE AND OLIVIA SEARS, EDS.,
Best of Contemporary Mexican
Fiction.
ELOY URROZ, *Friction.*
The Obstacles.
LUISA VALENZUELA, *Dark Desires and*
the Others.
He Who Searches.
MARJA-LIISA VARTIO,
The Parson's Widow.
PAUL VERHAEGHEN, *Omega Minor.*
AGLAJA VETERANYI, *Why the Child Is*
Cooking in the Polenta.
BORIS VIAN, *Heartsnatcher.*
LLORENÇ VILLALONGA, *The Dolls' Room.*
ORNELA VORPSI, *The Country Where No*
One Ever Dies.
AUSTRYN WAINHOUSE, *Hedyphagetica.*
PAUL WEST,
Words for a Deaf Daughter & Gala.
CURTIS WHITE,
America's Magic Mountain.
The Idea of Home.
Memories of My Father Watching TV.
Monstrous Possibility: An Invitation
to Literary Politics.
Requiem.
DIANE WILLIAMS, *Excitability:*
Selected Stories.
Romancer Erector.
DOUGLAS WOOLF, *Wall to Wall.*
Ya! & John-Juan.
JAY WRIGHT, *Polynomials and Pollen.*
The Presentable Art of Reading
Absence.
PHILIP WYLIE, *Generation of Vipers.*
MARGUERITE YOUNG, *Angel in the Forest.*
Miss MacIntosh, My Darling.
REYOUNG, *Unbabbling.*
VLADO ŽABOT, *The Succubus.*
ZORAN ŽIVKOVIĆ, *Hidden Camera.*
LOUIS ZUKOFSKY, *Collected Fiction.*
VITOMIL ZUPAN, *Minuet for Guitar.*
SCOTT ZWIREN, *God Head.*
